# Salon culture in Japan
## making art, 1750–1900

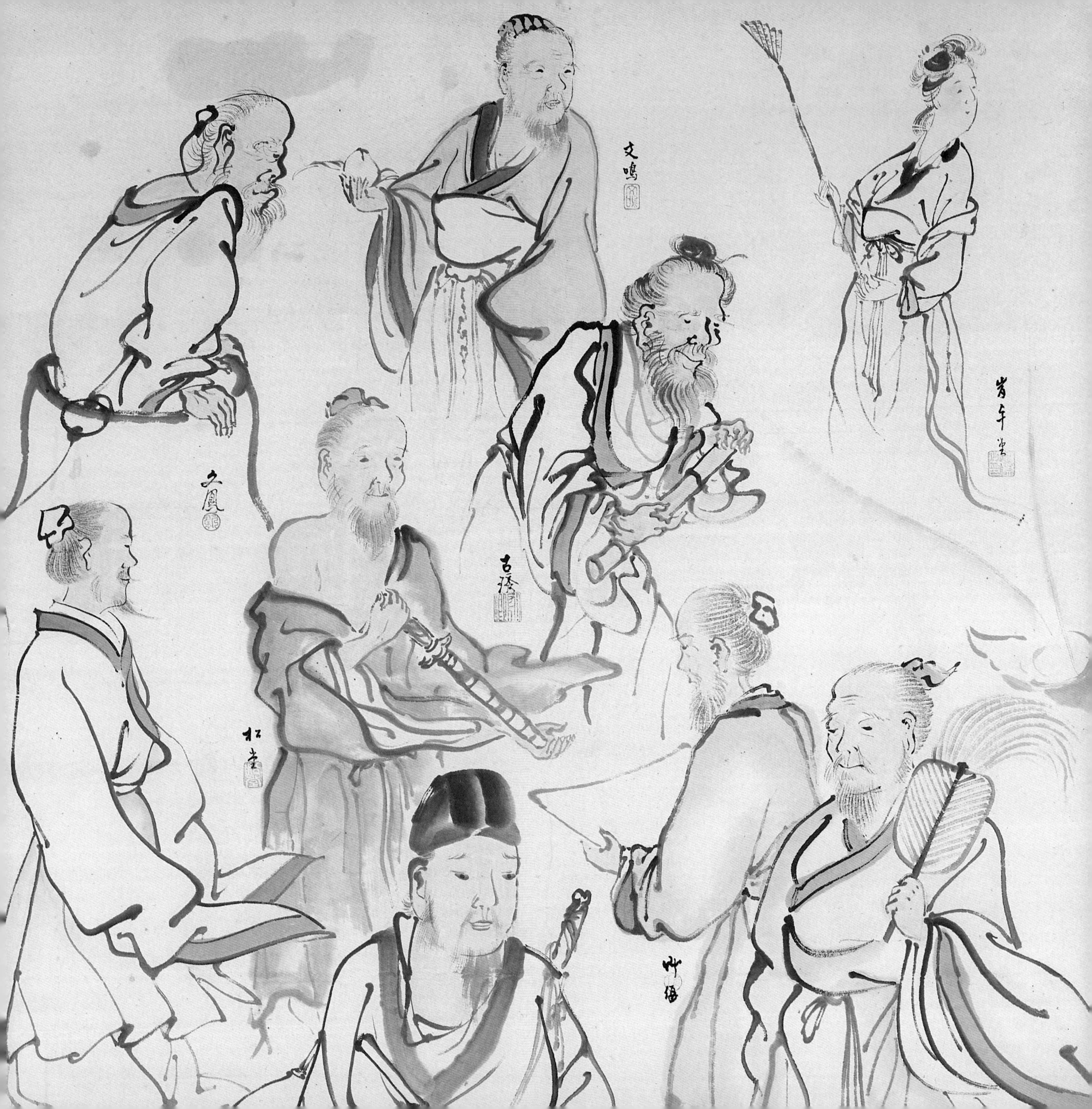

Edited by Akiko Yano

# Salon culture in Japan
## making art, 1750–1900

Akama Ryō
Akeo Keizō
Paul Berry
Rosina Buckland
Timothy T. Clark
C. Andrew Gerstle
Sophie Gong
Alfred Haft
Hirai Yoshinobu
Scott Johnson
Nakatani Nobuo
Ellis Tinios
Akiko Yano

The British
Museum

Published to accompany a special display in the
Mitsubishi Corporation Japanese Galleries at
the British Museum from April 2024 to March 2025.

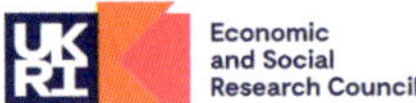

This book is an outcome of the collaborative
research project, *Creative Collaborations: Salons
and Networks in Kyoto and Osaka 1780–1880*, led
by Ritsumeikan University and the British Museum.
The project was supported by UK Research and
Innovation through the Economic and Social
Science Research Council, and by the Japan
Society for the Promotion of Science through
an international joint research programme
[ES/W011956/1].

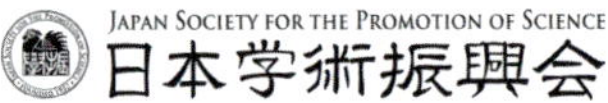

This work was supported by JSPS International
Joint Research Programme (JRP-LEAD with UKRI)
[JPJSJRP 20211708].

First published in the United Kingdom in 2024
by The British Museum Press

A division of The British Museum Company Ltd
The British Museum
Great Russell Street
London WC1B 3DG
britishmuseum.org/publishing

*Salon culture in Japan: making art, 1750–1900*
© 2024 The Trustees of the British Museum

A catalogue record for this book is available from
the British Library.

ISBN 978-0-7141-2496-4



Designed by James Alexander / Jade Design
Colour reproduction by Altaimage
Printed in Belgium by Graphius

Images © 2024 The Trustees of the British
Museum, courtesy of the British Museum's
Department of Photography and Imaging, unless
otherwise stated on page 253.

Further information about the British Museum and
its collection can be found at britishmuseum.org.

Front cover
Detail of fig. 0.10: *Parrots on a Grape Vine*, early
1800s. British Museum, London, 2021,3013.842.

Back cover
Detail of fig. 4.17: *Gathering at the Orchid Pavilion*,
1815. British Museum, London, 1982,0520,0.2.

Frontispiece
Detail of fig. 4.11: *Chinese Immortals*, c. 1805–13.
British Museum, London, 2002,0906,0.2.

The papers used in this book are natural,
renewable and recyclable and the manufacturing
processes are expected to conform to the
regulations of the country of origin.

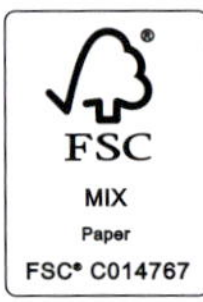

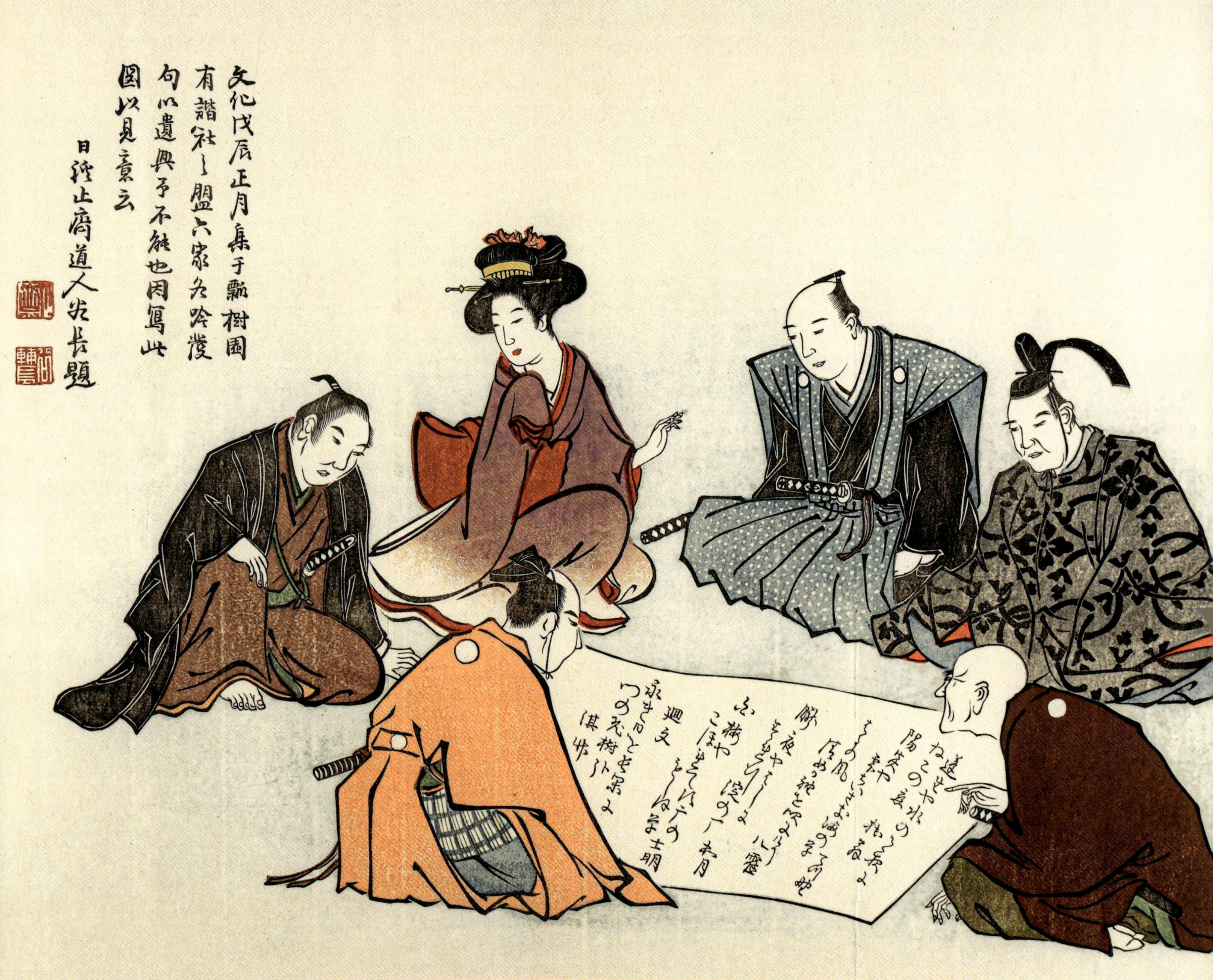

# Director's foreword
## *Mark Jones*

In late Edo-period Japan (1603–1868) the arts were not solely the realm of professionals. During this time, Japan was ruled by the Tokugawa government, which adopted a seclusion policy eschewing international relations and focusing on domestic affairs. This meant that the arts were at the centre of social life. It became customary for amateurs to make art for pleasure, often as a life-long pursuit. It was common for ordinary individuals, both men and women from all walks of life, to form groups, large and small, of like-minded amateurs, often under a teacher. Significantly, those who joined such circles would adopt a pen or art name. Professionals mixed with amateurs, as well as among themselves, to create both individual and collective works. In this book, this kind of collaboration is termed 'salon culture'. The work shown opposite, *Six Poets* by Tanida Sukenaga, encapsulates the phenomenon: one woman and five men sit for a poetry gathering.

The British Museum's Japanese collections reveal the material evidence of people's participation in a wide range of cultural activities – particularly in the fields of painting, calligraphy and poetry – and they include a large number of collaborative works made by poets and artists, both professional and amateur. It is a great pleasure to be able to publish these exquisite works, many for the first time, in the context of salon culture in the eighteenth and nineteenth centuries. This book is one outcome of the three-year international research project with Ritsumeikan University in Kyoto, 'Creative Collaborations: Salons and Networks in Kyoto and Osaka 1780–1880', funded by a major research grant from UK Research and Innovation through the Economic and Social Research Council and the Japan Society for the Promotion of Science (2022–5). The publication coincides with a special display in the Museum's Mitsubishi Corporation Japanese Galleries. Our warm thanks go to Mitsubishi Corporation for their generous long-term support, to UKRI/ESRC and JSPS and to the scholars of the research project, who have kindly shared their expertise.

Participation in the arts is still a resonant subject in today's world. We hope that this book and the display, both of which explore such a fascinating social and cultural phenomenon, will stimulate creativity and communication through the arts among readers and visitors to the Museum from across the globe.

Tanida Sukenaga (artist) and six poets, *Six Poets* (imitating the theme of 'Six Immortal Poets') (detail), 1808. Surimono, colour woodblock. 36.1 × 46 cm. British Museum, London, 1987,0729,0.2.

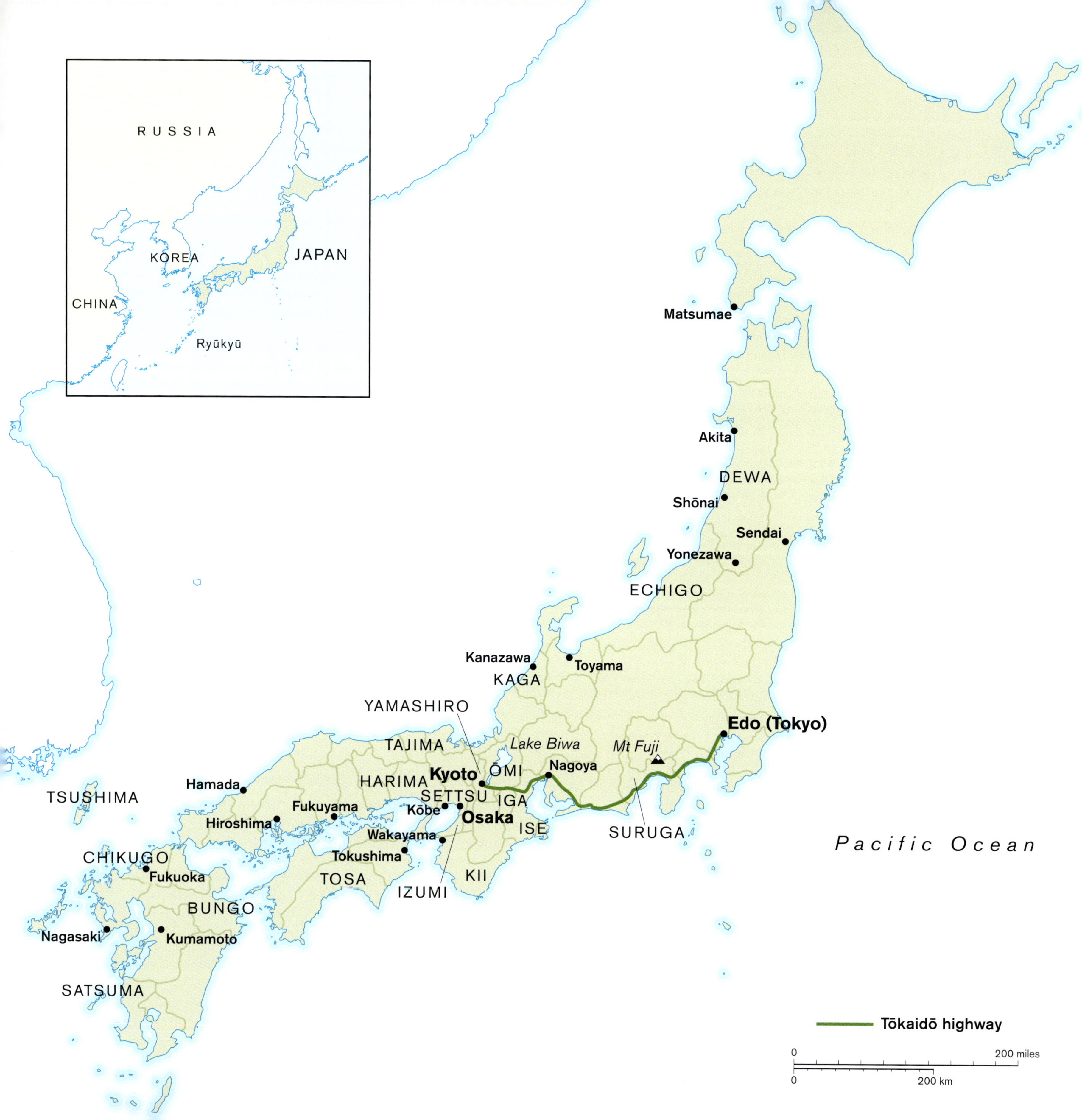

RUSSIA
CHINA
KOREA
JAPAN
Ryūkyū
Matsumae
Akita
DEWA
Shōnai
Sendai
Yonezawa
ECHIGO
Kanazawa
Toyama
KAGA
YAMASHIRO
TAJIMA
Lake Biwa
Mt Fuji
Edo (Tokyo)
Kyoto
ŌMI
Nagoya
HARIMA
SETTSU
IGA
SURUGA
Hamada
Fukuyama
Kōbe
Osaka
ISE
Hiroshima
Wakayama
TSUSHIMA
Tokushima
KII
CHIKUGO
Fukuoka
TOSA
IZUMI
BUNGO
Nagasaki
Kumamoto
SATSUMA
Pacific Ocean
Tōkaidō highway
0                    200 miles
0                    200 km

# Introduction: an age of salons
### *Akiko Yano*

The Japanese language does not have a single word that corresponds with 'salon' – instead, there are several different words for cultural circles. The term 'salon' is usually applied to intellectual gatherings in the West, held by a host (often a woman) to exchange and discuss ideas on a range of topics, from the artistic and literary to the philosophical and political. But what are salons in the Japanese context? In eighteenth- and nineteenth-century Japan (during the early modern period), there were many types of groups, large and small, formal and informal, that were frequently centred around a teacher in areas including painting, calligraphy, tea ceremony, performing arts, music, academic studies and Japanese and Chinese poetry, or around a connoisseur of cuisine[1] or a consortium of horticulture enthusiasts. This book uses the term 'salon culture' broadly to refer to this phenomenon in which participants, both women and men, shared a space to interact, and to practise and study artistic or other hobby activities as involved practitioners, not as passive onlookers. Fortunately, these gatherings, whether one-off or recurring, often produced 'records' that have survived and which take the form of paintings, woodblock-printed books and prints (see p. 6). A number of treasured artworks in the British Museum's Japanese collections are highlighted here for the first time from the perspective of 'salon culture' in Kyoto and Osaka.

This book covers the period from about 1750 to 1900, roughly the last 120 years of the Edo period (1603–1868), when the Tokugawa shogunal government ruled Japan, and the first thirty years of the Meiji era (1868–1912), when, after the fall of the Tokugawa, the emperor was restored as the head of the modern Japanese political system. It was clearly an era of great socio-political and economic change in Japan. But even though the impact of Western customs and values in Japan gradually increased at the elite level after the Meiji Restoration in 1868, there was still considerable continuity in cultural practices.

It is significant that under the Tokugawa regime culture was meant to be kept separate from politics, although there were sporadic occasions of censorship of visual and literary representations (see pp. 92–4). Whereas politics was the preserve of the samurai class, participation in culture was open to everyone. Due to the government's policy of seclusion from the wider world during the Edo period, engaging in cultural activities became popular in all parts of the Japanese archipelago. This helped to secure a long period of political and social stability. Interest in – and information from – the outside world was maintained primarily through the long tradition of engaging with Chinese culture. Large quantities of Chinese books, visual artworks and other goods were regularly imported via Nagasaki and served as significant stimuli in the material and intellectual arts generally (see chapter 4). The importation of Dutch (and other European) books from the 1720s onwards, though on a much smaller scale, had a considerable impact on culture and science in late eighteenth- and nineteenth-century Japan. In addition to the trade with China and the Netherlands, there were interactions through the Tsushima domain (in present-day Nagasaki prefecture) with Korean officials, who sent several diplomatic envoys to the Tokugawa shoguns. There was also contact with the Ryūkyū kingdom via the Satsuma domain (in present-day Kagoshima prefecture) and with the Ainu via the Matsumae domain on the present-day island of Hokkaido (see map, p. 8).

## Salon membership

Who were members of salons? This question is difficult to answer in detail because most participants were ordinary people whose pseudonyms – pen names for literary works and art names (*gō*) for visual or performing arts – are

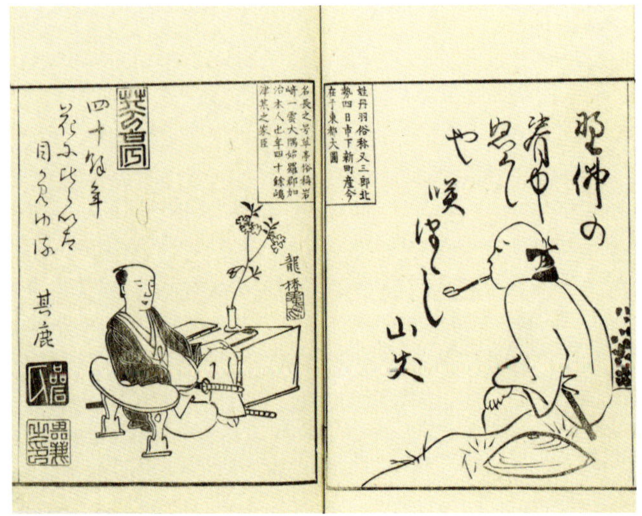
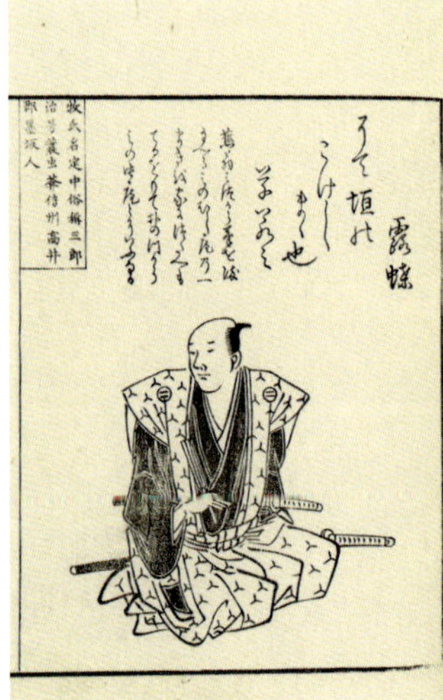

listed in the records of the activities of these respective salons, but whose biographies are today largely unknown. These pseudonyms often appear, for example, on *surimono* (literally 'printed thing', privately issued and circulated woodblock prints with poems and pictures). But usually little is understood beyond which town, village or area these individuals came from. It is important to note that people in the Edo period and even into the Meiji era would use a variety of names over a lifetime: names as an infant and as an adult; formal and everyday names; a business name; a name related to social status or rank; and, most significantly here, pen and art names for cultural activities that could be chosen and changed, generally at will. Whether as a professional or as an amateur, almost everyone who took part in cultural circles had a pseudonym, the use of which seems to have made it easier for participants of different social status or rank to mingle within the space of the salons (see p. 49).

Despite these hurdles, there are some good biographical sources from the late Edo period. For instance, in the field of *haiku* (*haikai*) poetry, there is a five-volume Osaka publication, *Who's Who from Myriad Houses* (*Banka jinmei roku*, 1813) (fig. 0.1). About 400 people, professional and amateur, who composed haiku are recorded from all across Japan. Every poet is accorded a portrait, a haiku with their pen name and, in the cartouche on each page, brief biographical information, such as their other names, place of origin, occupation, address and occasionally useful notes, such as the other arts in which they excelled. A wide range of people – aristocrats, samurai, merchants, farmers, artists, scholars and priests as well as professional poets – feature in this fascinating directory.



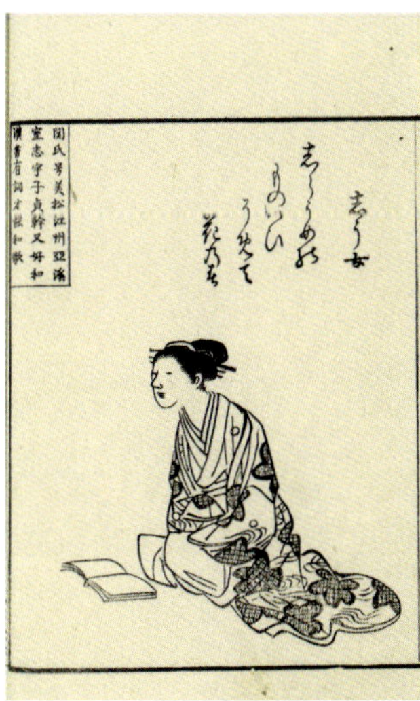
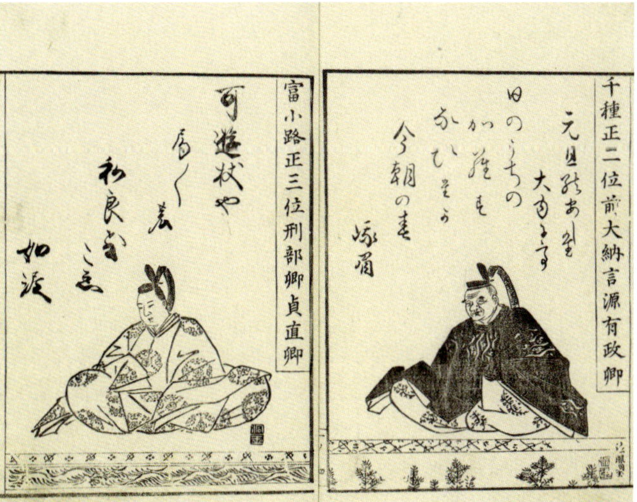

## Sites of gatherings

The specific locations of these salon activities are in many cases yet to be identified. Sometimes existing records reveal, for example, a certain haiku gathering took place at a certain local temple or at a particular venue, such as a restaurant. In the case of collaborative paintings, which are discussed below, the site and the context of the gathering are seldom known. In one rare instance of around 1810, seven artists co-created a painting of autumn flowers in response to a commission by a high-ranking samurai official of the Hamada domain (in present-day Shimane prefecture). The artists were invited to a private room of a restaurant in the Maruyama district of Kyoto where the Hamada official entertained them, and they reciprocated by producing paintings on the spot.[2] Kyoto's Maruyama district on the eastern fringes of the city centre was renowned for its concentration of large restaurants with private rooms for hire, as seen in the Sa'ami restaurant illustrated here in a fan painting (fig. 0.2). These venues were also used for art exhibitions called 'calligraphy and painting gatherings' (*shoga-kai*), or 'display gatherings' (*tengan / tenran-kai*), which showed the artists' latest work to the public (see fig. 4.23). They were often accompanied by extemporaneous painting and calligraphy demonstrations by participants.[3]



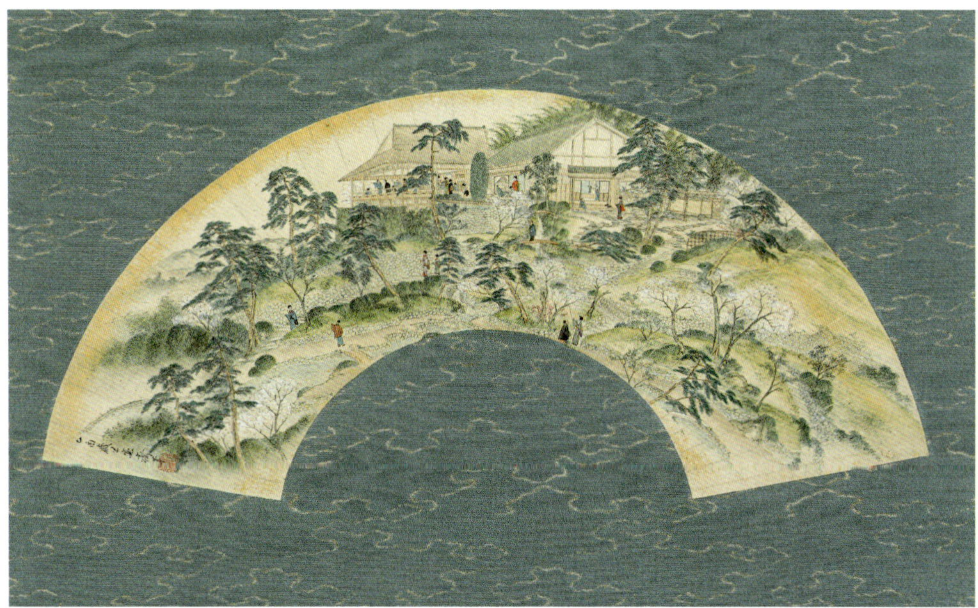

**0.2** *and detail opposite*
Mori Kansai, *Sa'ami Restaurant in Kyoto Higashiyama*, 1885. Fan painting mounted as hanging scroll, ink, colour and gold on silk. 53.9 cm (max. width). British Museum, London, 2002,0311,0.1.

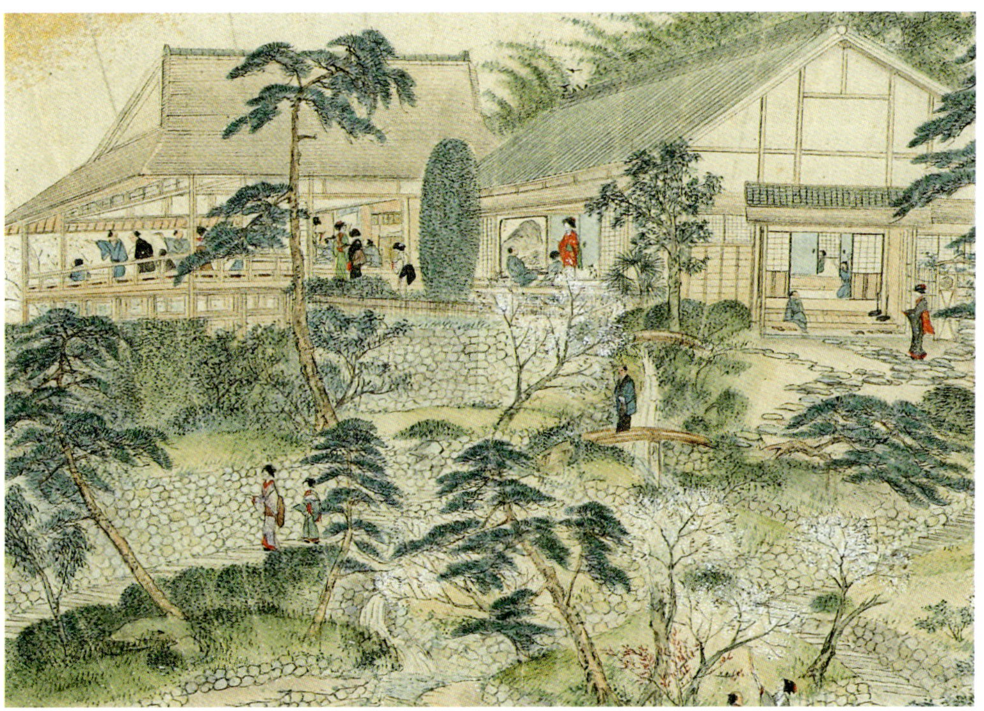

## The beginning of salon culture

For Japanese elites – members of the imperial court, aristocracy, shogunate and major religious institutions – the appreciation and practice of the arts were essential elements of their lives. Elite cultural circles had existed for centuries before the establishment of the Tokugawa shogunate in 1603. The steady spread of education among lower-level samurai and commoners from the seventeenth century onwards led to a rapid increase in the number of people involved in cultural and artistic activities.

Salon culture of the late eighteenth to nineteenth centuries appears to have been inclusive. Ordinary people took lessons from professionals. In the famous Confucian academy for merchants in Osaka, Kaitokudō (see also pp. 62, 64), the seating arrangement in the classroom was open even if noble attendees entered to listen to a lecture, and students were allowed to excuse themselves from a class without permission whenever business matters required attention.[4]

The roots of cultural salons and the enthusiasm for taking lessons in the arts can be traced back in Kyoto to the late seventeenth century. *Great Compilation of Kyoto's Finest Silk Fabrics* (*Kyō habutae daizen*; '*habutae*' could also mean stylish surcoats made from such material) was a popular series of multivolume Kyoto gazetteers published from the 1680s to the 1830s. Editions always contain a chapter called 'Various Teachers and Various Arts' (*shoshi shogei*), which was a directory of arts professionals. The arts in volume 3 of the 1784 edition, for instance, number more than fifty, including not just typical examples – poetry, music, painting, calligraphy, tea ceremony and so on – but also medical matters, mathematics, court rituals, astronomy, divination, board games and the connoisseurship of swords.[5] This directory was a guide for those seeking professional instruction, providing the names and addresses of literally hundreds of teachers.



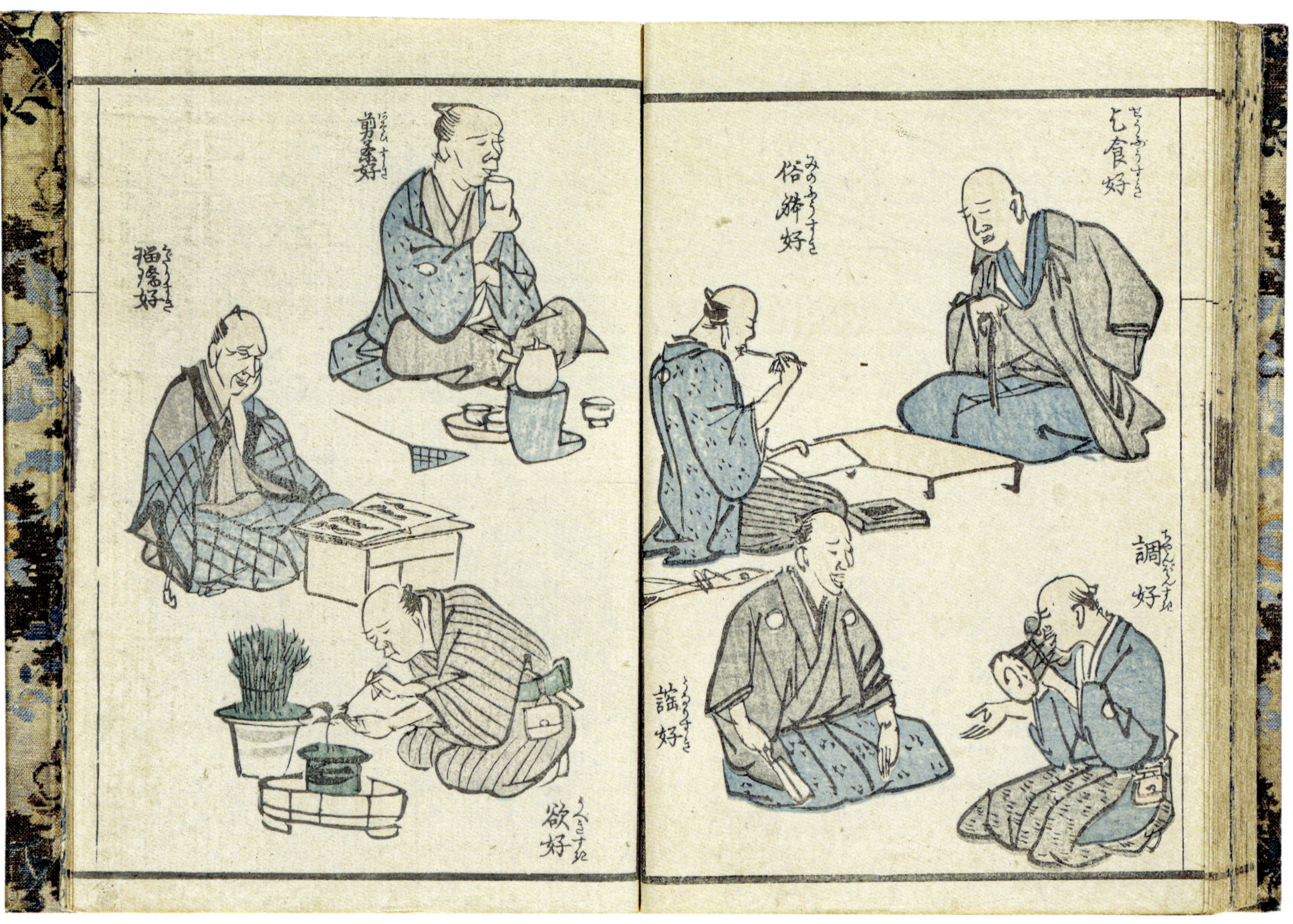

In Osaka the enthusiasm for art lessons can also be traced to the late seventeenth century. Wealthy male merchants who took lessons in several arts – tea and nō drama seem to have been popular choices – were commonly targets of satire and admonition, mocked for trying to emulate the sophistication of nobles. One trope is that such passion for the arts could lead even those from exceptionally wealthy families to bankrupt their business.[6] In Chikamatsu Monzaemon's play *The Courier for Hell* (*Meido no hikyaku*, 1711) the young hero Chūbei, who grew up on a farm, is introduced as a dashing young courier (*hikyaku*) in Osaka, described as adept in tea ceremony, haiku poetry, and *go* and *sugoroku* board games.[7] The number and range of people who practised the arts as a serious hobby continued to grow. Some delightful pictures of various types of hobby enthusiast are found in an illustrated book, *Rough Sketches of One Hundred Objects* (*Soga hyakubutsu*, 1832), by Ōishi Matora (1792–1833) that features Osaka genre scenes (fig. 0.3). Although the author's view reflected in the image appears to be somewhat critical and set to caricature these passionate amateur practitioners, this example nonetheless captures how deeply cultural engagement had become ingrained in the lives of commoners in Osaka, and indeed in the major cities of the period.

### Salon culture collections from Kyoto and Osaka at the British Museum

The British Museum has a rich collection of visual materials that are the direct products of collaborative artistic activities. The foundations of the Museum's Japanese painting collection were laid mainly by two individuals, William Anderson (1842–1900) and Arthur Morrison (1863–1945). Although their collecting approaches differed, they shared a common objective: the attempt to amass pieces that represented the entire history of Japanese painting up until their own times. Each collected substantial numbers of works by late eighteenth- to nineteenth-century artists in Kyoto and Osaka. Some of the painters were even their contemporaries. Following in the footsteps of Anderson and Morrison, more recent generations of curators at the Museum, notably Lawrence Smith and Timothy T. Clark (the author of chapter 2), further strengthened the holdings from Kyoto and Osaka, with a continued focus on collecting artworks in the Maruyama-Shijō school lineages.[8]

There are several collaborative paintings by Kyoto and Osaka artists. In one hanging scroll (see fig. 4.11) each of the eleven artists contributed at least one image of a Chinese sage. (One artist must have drawn two figures because there are twelve sages.) This type of joint painting was known at the time as a 'combined work' (*gassaku*) or 'collective painting' (*yoriai-gaki*), and most date from the nineteenth century. About half of the artists represented in this painting of Chinese sages had been pupils of one of the most influential Kyoto artists, Maruyama Ōkyo (1733–1795). Ōkyo is credited with reinventing the mainstream Kyoto artistic style through his technical excellence, which is characterised by a union of tradition and innovation often encapsulated by the phrase 'sketching from life' (*shasei*) (see pp. 87–92). Even in depictions of traditional subject matters, Ōkyo, with his meticulous approach and close observation of nature, produced a radically original vision that is further refined to elegance (fig. 0.4). He attracted an enormous range of patrons, from imperial aristocrats to townspeople.

Go Shun (1752–1811) is another key Kyoto artist. He initially studied haiku and painting with the celebrated poet-painter Yosa Buson (1716–1784). In this example (fig. 0.5), Go Shun (then known as Matsumura Gekkei) created a fan painting illustrating a branch of white plum blossoms and copied his master Buson's haiku to accompany it. Later he would learn and incorporate Ōkyo's new painting style. Go Shun and his pupils lived close to Shijō (Fourth Avenue) in Kyoto's city centre, which led to the name 'Shijō school'. Ōkyo's base was also along Fourth Avenue, and so, given the geographical and stylistic proximity of the two masters, today their pupils and the following generations of artists are often collectively termed the 'Maruyama-Shijō school'. Although some may argue that each had separate lineages, the appellation Maruyama-Shijō is generally adopted in the present book. The influence of the Maruyama-Shijō style reached neighbouring Osaka and then spread to cities such as Nagoya, Edo and beyond. The artists who worked on the hanging scroll in fig. 4.11 are normally included in the range of the Maruyama-Shijō school. As salon culture matured, interactions among individuals practising different styles and artistic genres appear to have become commonplace, which makes it difficult to define the precise parameters of the Maruyama-Shijō school.

There were several other important artistic schools in Kyoto and Osaka. One was the literati (*bunjin*) school. Japanese literati were steeped in Chinese art and literature and pursued an idealised notion of the lifestyle of the classical Chinese scholar-artist (see chapter 4). A painting by the Confucian scholar Nukina Kaioku (1778–1863), renowned for his painting and calligraphy, represents the peaceful setting of a Chinese scholars' retreat in a grove facing a stream (fig. 0.6). Compared with Maruyama-Shijō paintings, those by literati artists may be described as more self-expressive. Although each lineage was distinct, at the individual level artists in fact engaged with others outside

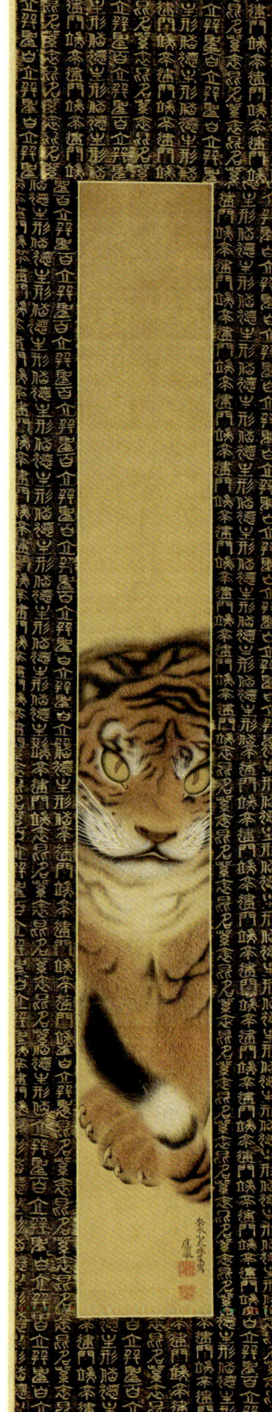

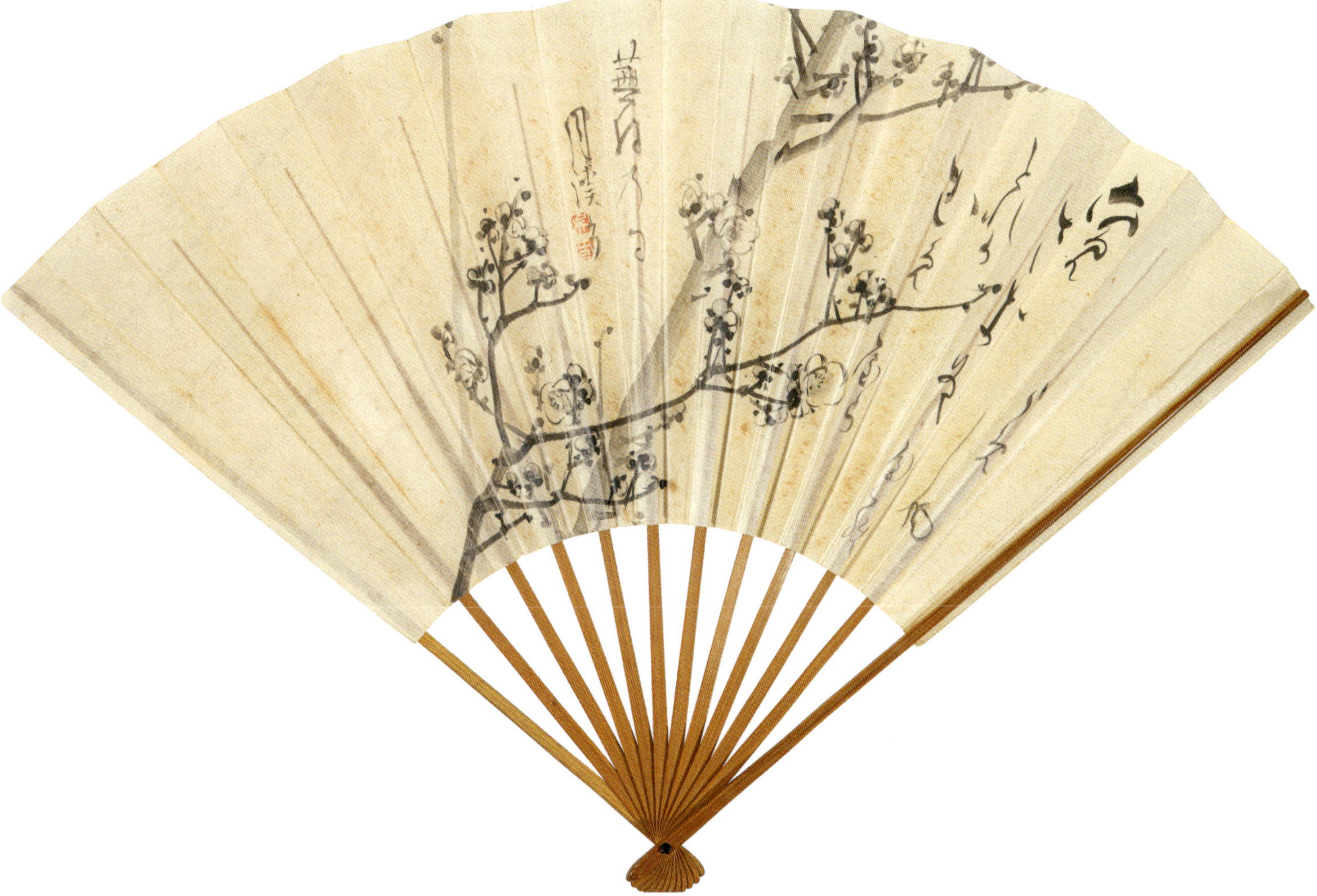

**0.4**
Maruyama Ōkyo, *Seated Tiger*, 1775. Hanging scroll, ink and colour on silk. 128.7 × 14.9 cm. British Museum, London, 1977,0404,0.2. Ex-Coll.: Nakamura (Kariganeya) Hanbei.

**0.5**
Go Shun, *White Plum Blossoms*, c. 1789–1801. Fan painting, ink on paper. 18.1 × 45 cm. British Museum, London, 2006,0222,0.2. Ex-coll.: Ozu family, Matsuzaka, Ise province.

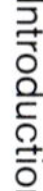


17

of their affiliated schools. The increasing inter-action among artists irrespective of school is a particular phenomenon of the nineteenth century, with artists in Kyoto and Osaka at the forefront in this dynamic cross-fertilisation of ideas – not only painters but also practitioners in fields such as literature, calligraphy and particularly poetry. This notwithstanding, artworks by a single artist were by far the most common form of painting. In the present book, therefore, efforts are made to examine both collaborative and single author works by Kyoto and Osaka artists, literati artists included, in order to explore this intricately con-nected, complex and dynamic art world.

## Paintings

The collaborative works in the British Museum are mainly paintings, prints and illustrated books. *Turtles* (fig. 0.7) is a hanging scroll by ten Osaka artists. The turtle at the top, with a long bundle of seaweed extending from the back of its shell like a tail, holds its head up proudly with its legs firmly planted on the ground. It is accompanied by the signature of Mori Shūhō (1738–1823), which reads: 'Shūhō of *hōgen* rank, brushed at the age of 78 years' (*hōgen*, or 'Eye of the Law', was an honorary title bestowed by the imperial court). Shūhō's artistic lineage came to be known as the Mori school, after the artist's family name. Two other Mori-school artists participated in this work: Tetsuzan (1775–1841), Shūhō's son (see figs 3.24, 4.4), and Yūsen (1780–1851), the son of Shūhō's younger brother Sosen (1747–1821), who became Shūhō's adopted son.

Other contributing artists to *Turtles* are, interestingly, not members of the Mori school or family members, although based in Osaka.

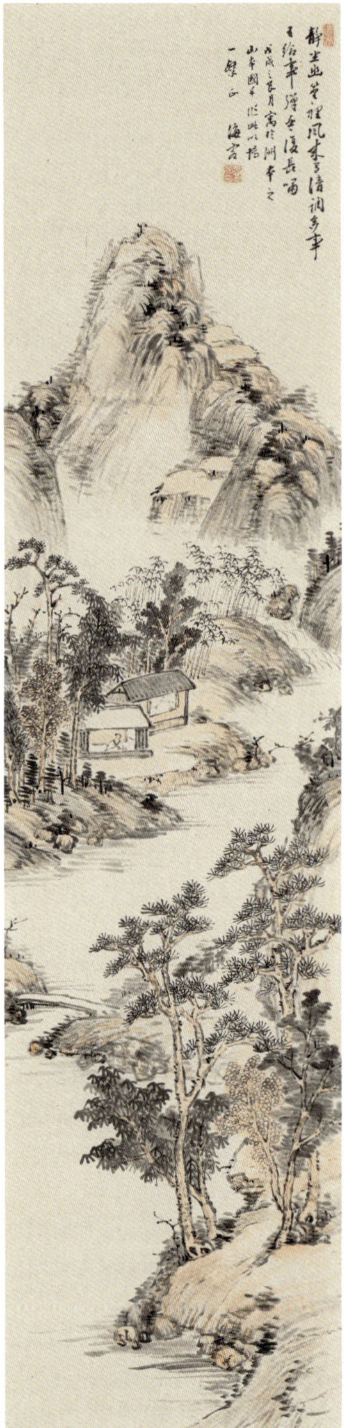

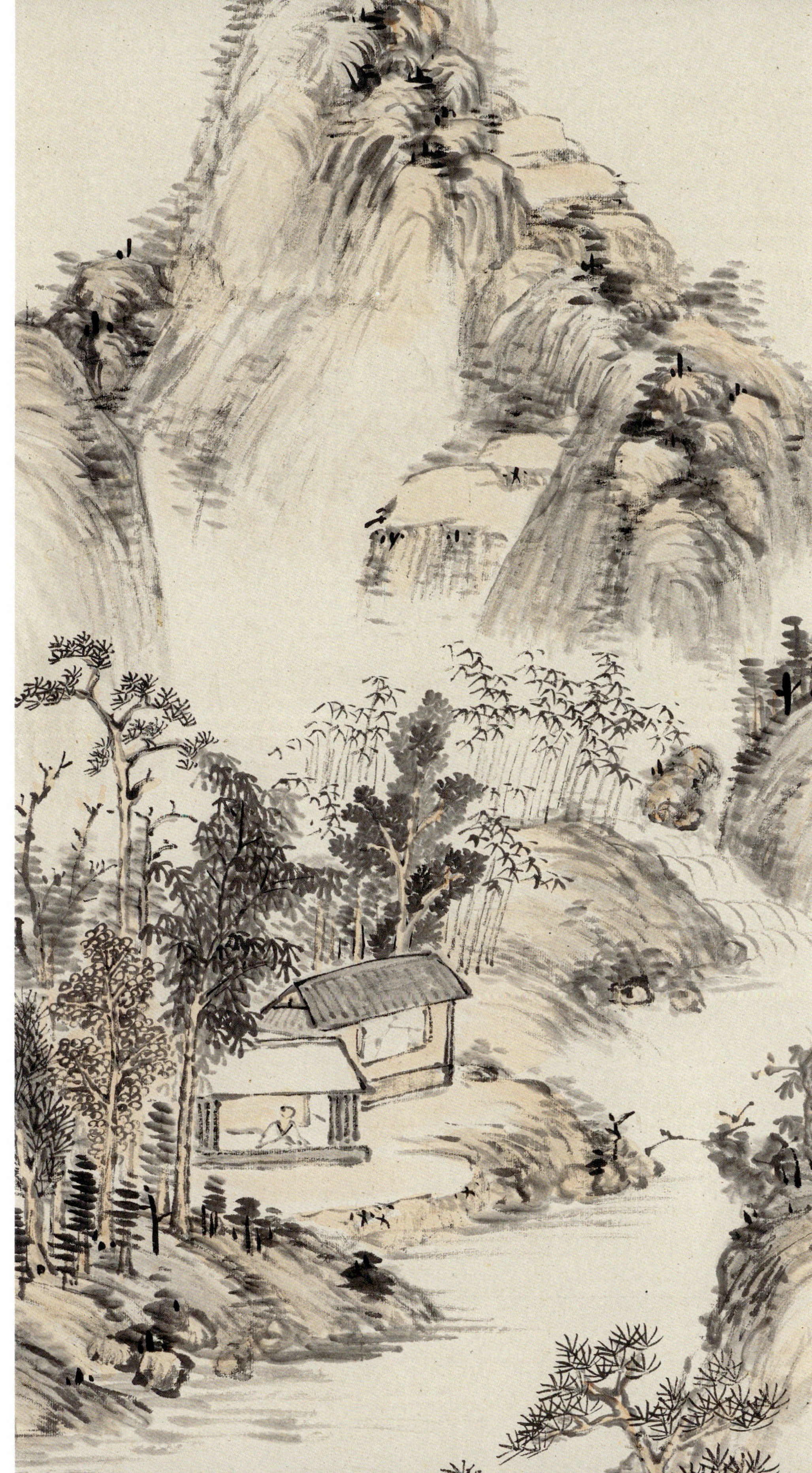

**0.6** *and detail right*
Nukina Kaioku, *Scholar's Huts
by a River*, 1838. Hanging scroll,
ink and light colour on paper.
206 × 49 cm. British Museum,
London, 1968,1014,0.1. Purchase
funded by the Brooke Sewell
Bequest.

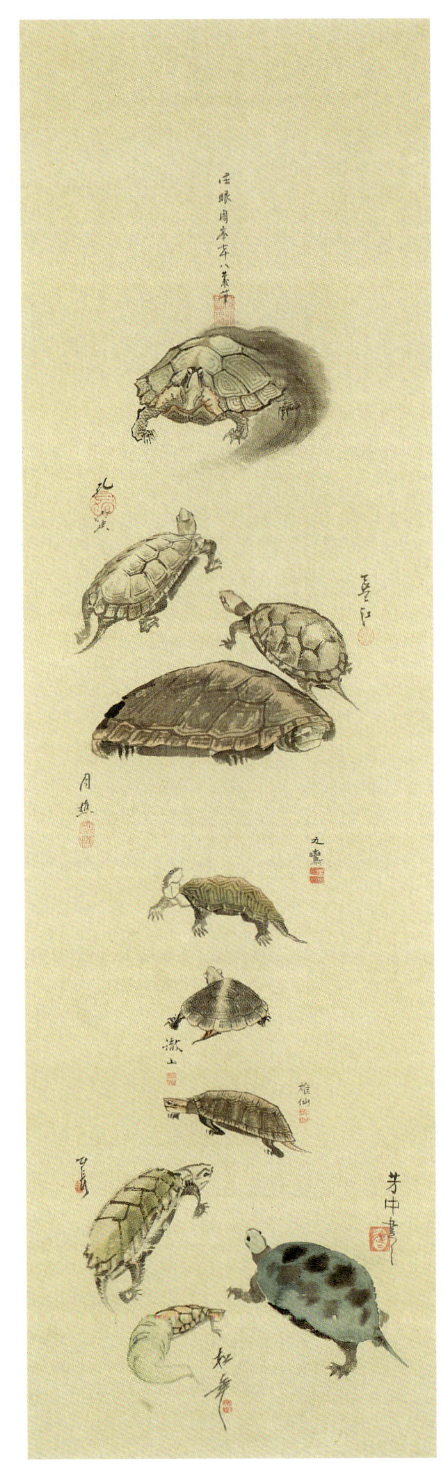
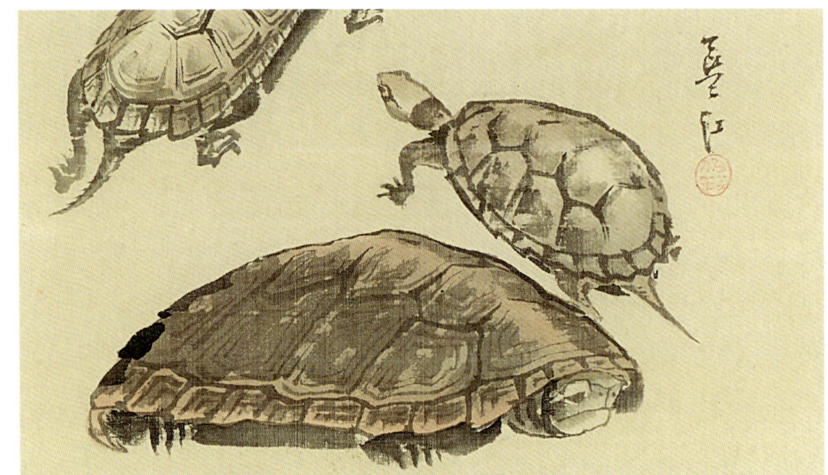
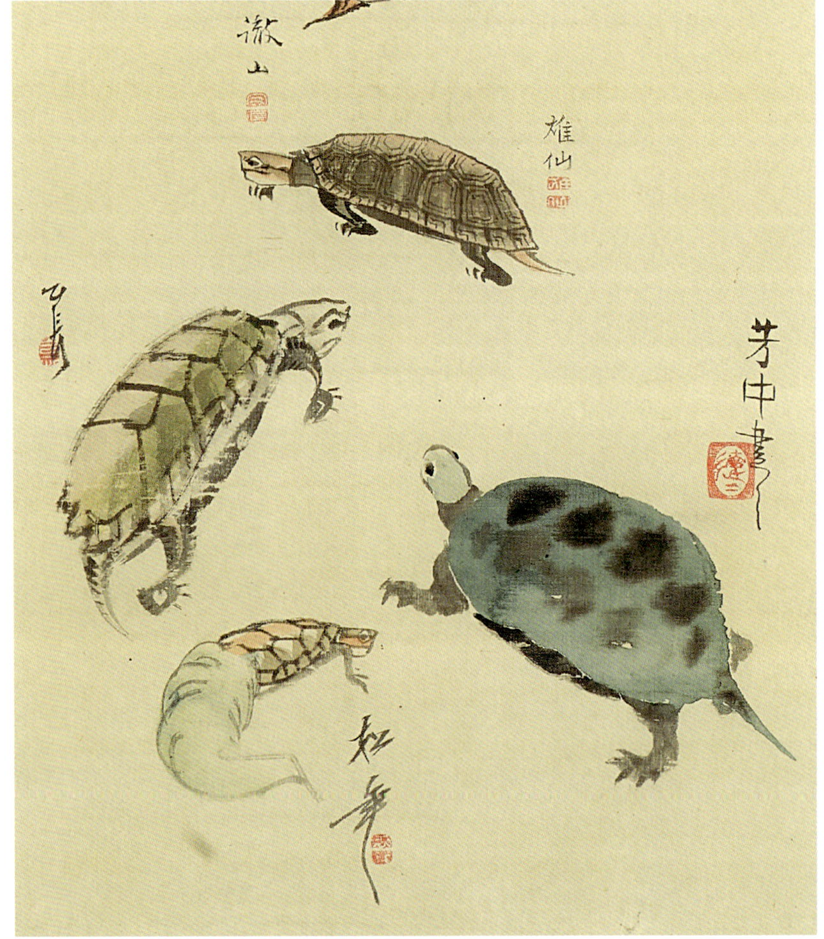

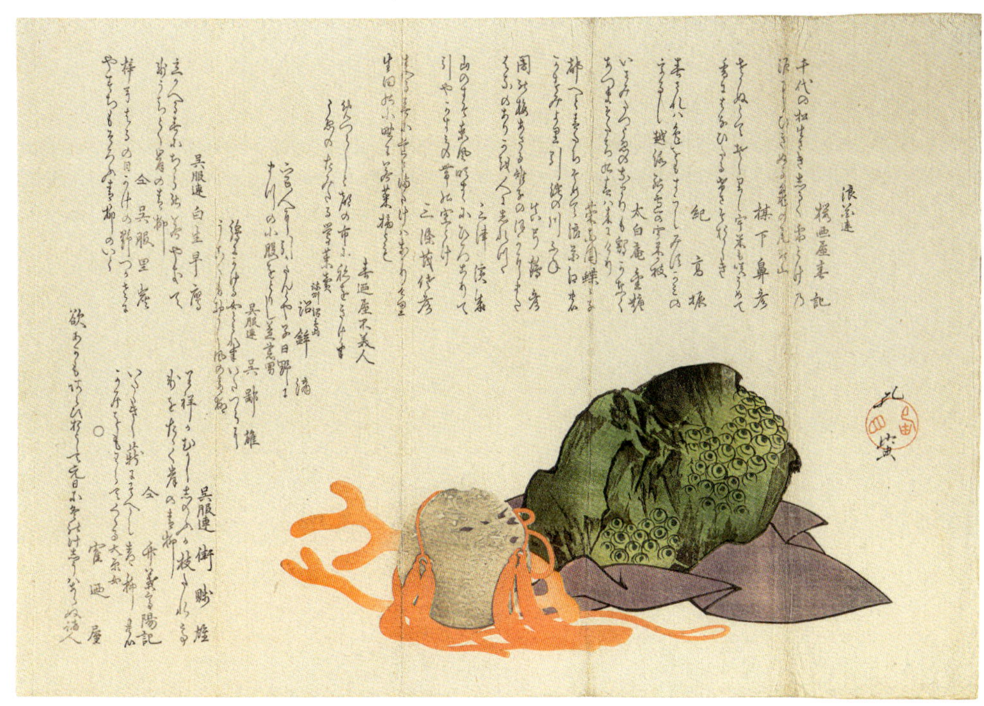

After Shūhō the artists are (in order from second from the top): Nagayama Kōin (1765–1849), a Shijō-school artist who was also a poet of 'crazy verse' (*kyōka*) (fig. 0.8); Nakai Rankō (1766–1830), an artist who studied eclectic styles (fig. 0.9); Murata Gesshō (active *c.* 1800–10s),[9] whose turtle shyly hides its head under its shell (see fig. 0.7, detail top); and Fuji Kyūran (active 1810s–20s), a literati painter who formed friendships with scholars of Chinese studies, such as the eminent merchant-scholar-painter Kimura Kenkadō (1736–1802) (see figs 4.33–4.34). After the two turtles by Tetsuzan and Yūsen are three more (see fig. 0.7, detail bottom). The turtle shown walking, third from the bottom, is by Ueda Kōchō (1788–1850), who studied under Go Shun before becoming a pupil of Nakai Rankō and eventually establishing his own school in Osaka. The turtle with the distinctive green-and-black-patterned shell, painted with watery ink and colour, is by Nakamura Hōchū (d. 1819). The technique of puddling still-wet pigments, known as 'dripping in' (*tarashikomi*), seen here is usually associated with the Rinpa school (Hōchū was a late associate) (see fig. 3.7).[10] Originally from Kyoto, Hōchū was active in haiku circles (see fig. 5.32); he travelled to Edo and finally settled in Osaka. His characteristic style is unassumingly skilful, evoking a warm and humorous quality. Finally, the small turtle with a long, thick tail at the bottom

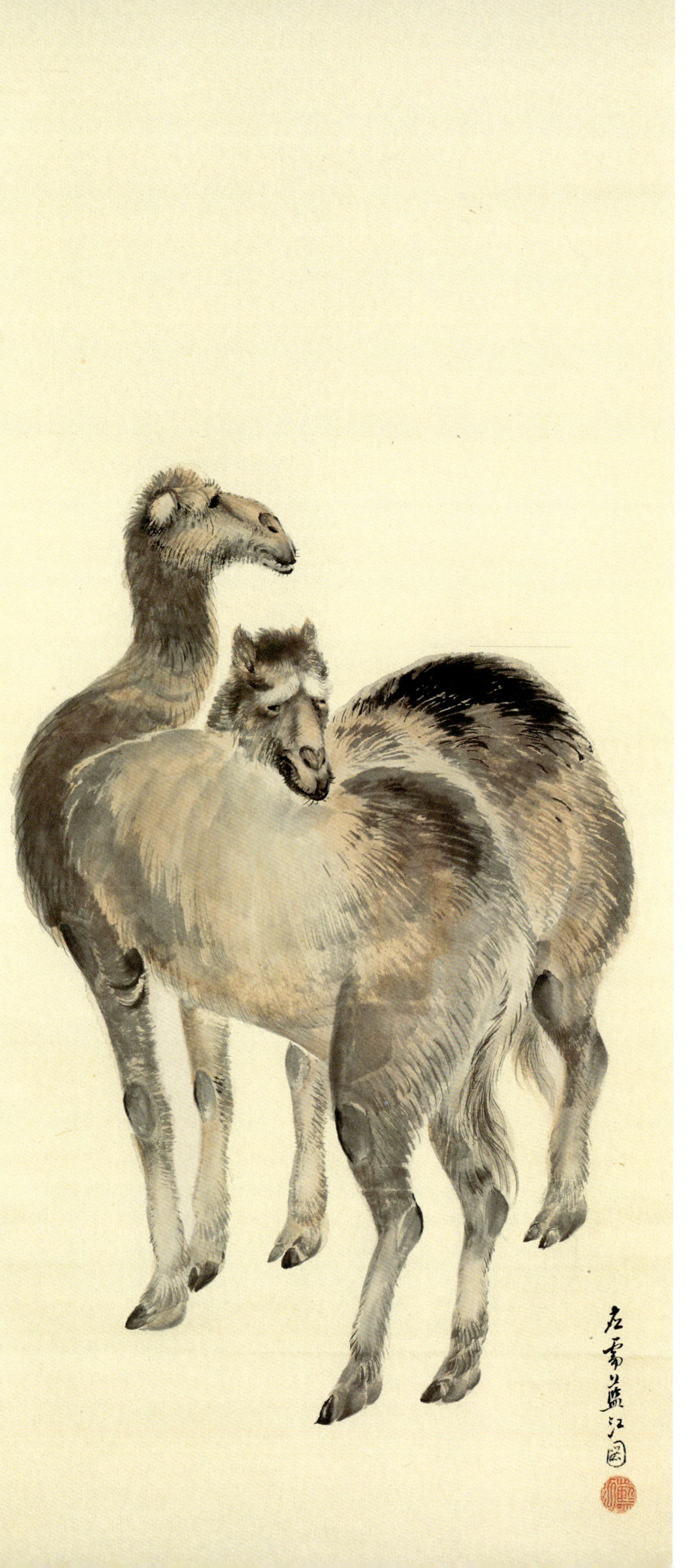



**0.9**
Nakai Rankō, *A Pair of Camels*, *c*. 1800–30. Hanging scroll, ink and colour on paper. 128.5 × 54 cm. British Museum, London, 1881,1210,0.2307. Ex-coll.: William Anderson.

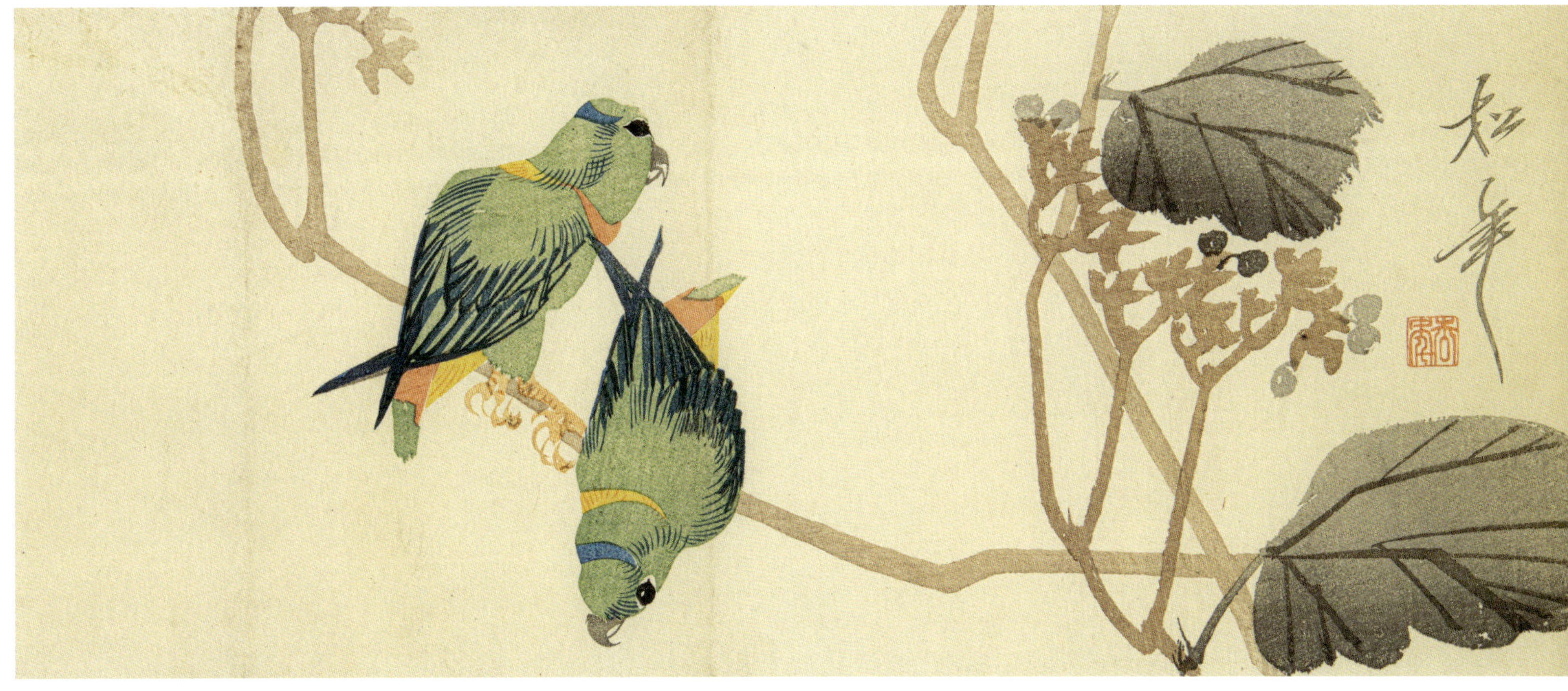



**0.10**

Yamanaka Shōnen, *Parrots on a Grape Vine*, early 1800s. Surimono (fragment), colour woodblock. 19.3 × 51.8 cm. British Museum, London, 2021,3013.842. Purchase made possible by the JTI Japanese Acquisition Fund. Ex-coll.: Dr Scott Johnson.

is by Yamanaka Shōnen (d. *c.* 1819). He is mainly known for his surimono, which testify to his exceptional sensibility as a graphic designer (fig. 0.10).

The context for the *Turtles* painting is unclear. It might have been made for a celebratory occasion for Shūhō, considering the auspicious associations with turtles. In fact, this simple-looking hanging scroll involves many artists from diverse schools or groups and moves beyond conventional artistic styles and media. Untangling the connections between these individuals is a challenging task, as in reality these interactions were more complex than cultural studies might have us believe. The painting nonetheless offers a fascinating window into the phenomenon of creative cooperation. Collaborative paintings on a set theme, such as *Turtles,* were popular throughout the nineteenth century and even into the early twentieth. Other examples are *Fish and Shellfish* (fig. 0.11),[11] *Rabbits* (fig. 0.12),[12] *Wish-Granting Jewels* (fig. 0.13) and *Puppies Have Buddha Nature: A Collaborative Work* (*Kushi busshō gassaku*) (fig. 0.14).[13] These paintings are often more spontaneously brushed than works by a single artist, and generally appear light-hearted and approachable.

Similarly the *Collaborative Work of the Twelve Months by Renowned Kyoto Artists* (*Heian sho-meika jūni-tsuki gassaku*) (fig. 0.15) features twelve Kyoto artists from different lineages: from the traditional and prestigious Tosa and Kanō schools,



23

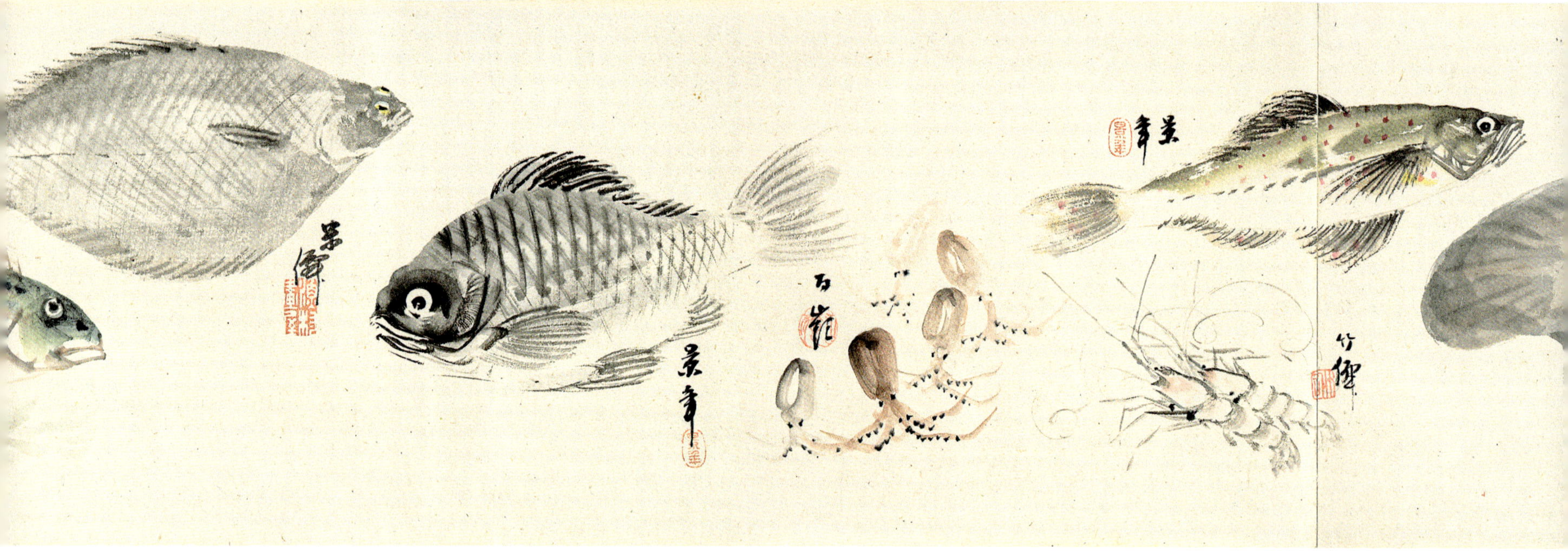

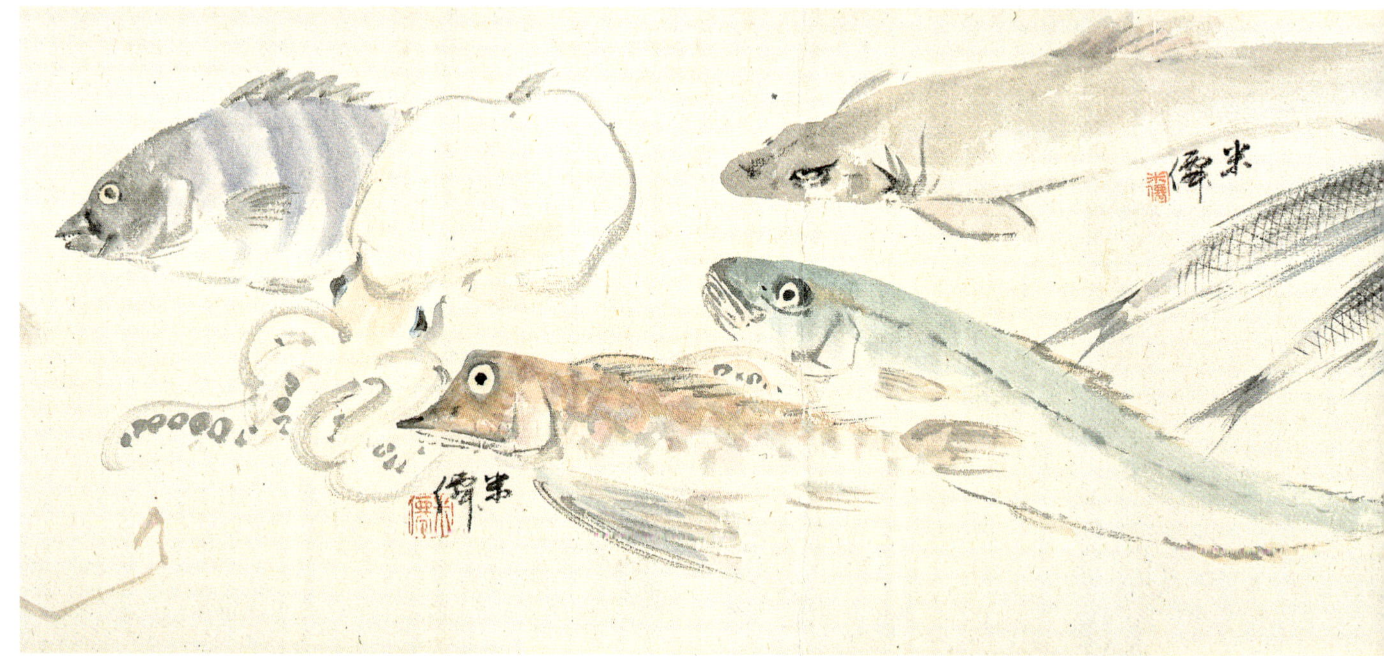

**0.11**
Hishida Nittō, Imao Keinen,
Izawa Kyūkō, Kubota Beisen,
Mokusen, Nishida Chikusen,
Ōyabu Kodō, Rankei, Sakurai
Hyakurei, Suzuki Hyakunen,
Suzuki Hyakurui and Suzuki
Shōnen, *Fish and Shellfish*,
*c.* 1870–3. Handscroll, ink
and colour on paper. 32 ×
679.1 cm. British Museum,
London, 1991,0701,0.1.

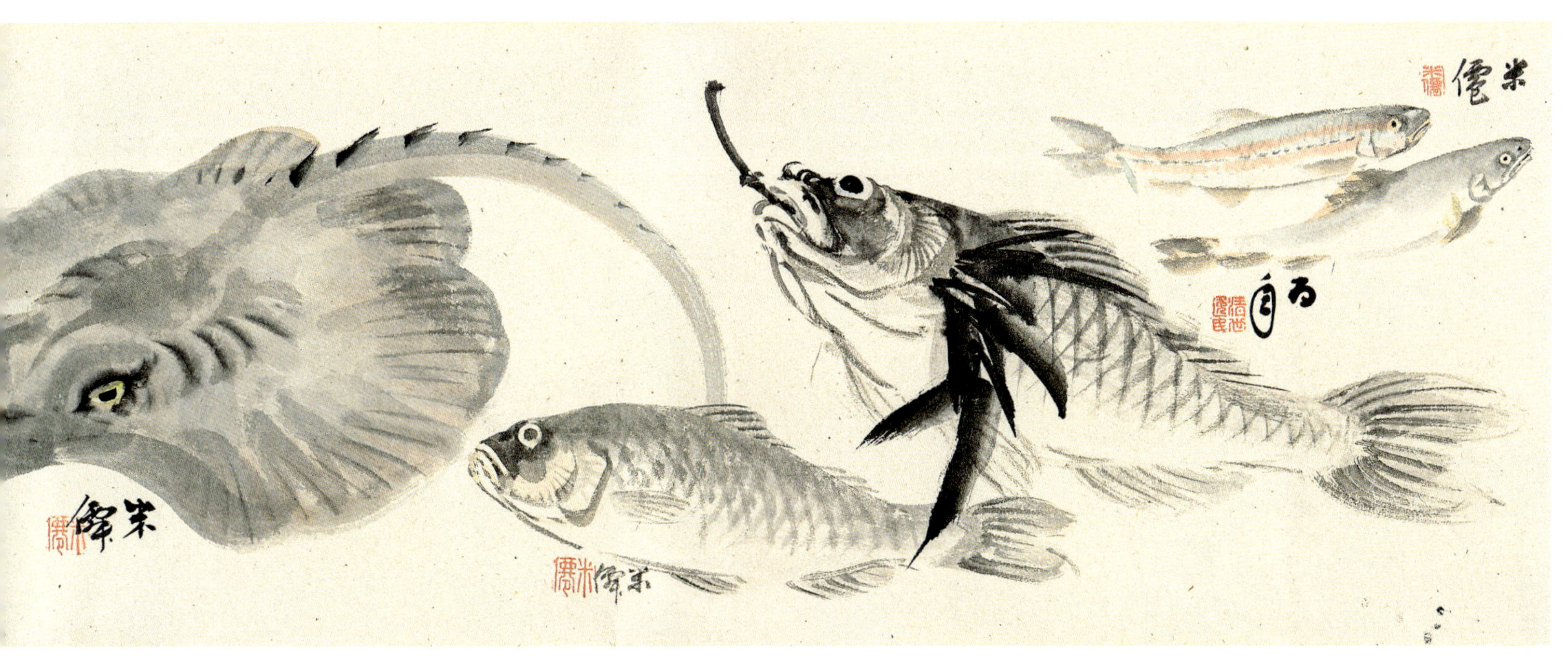

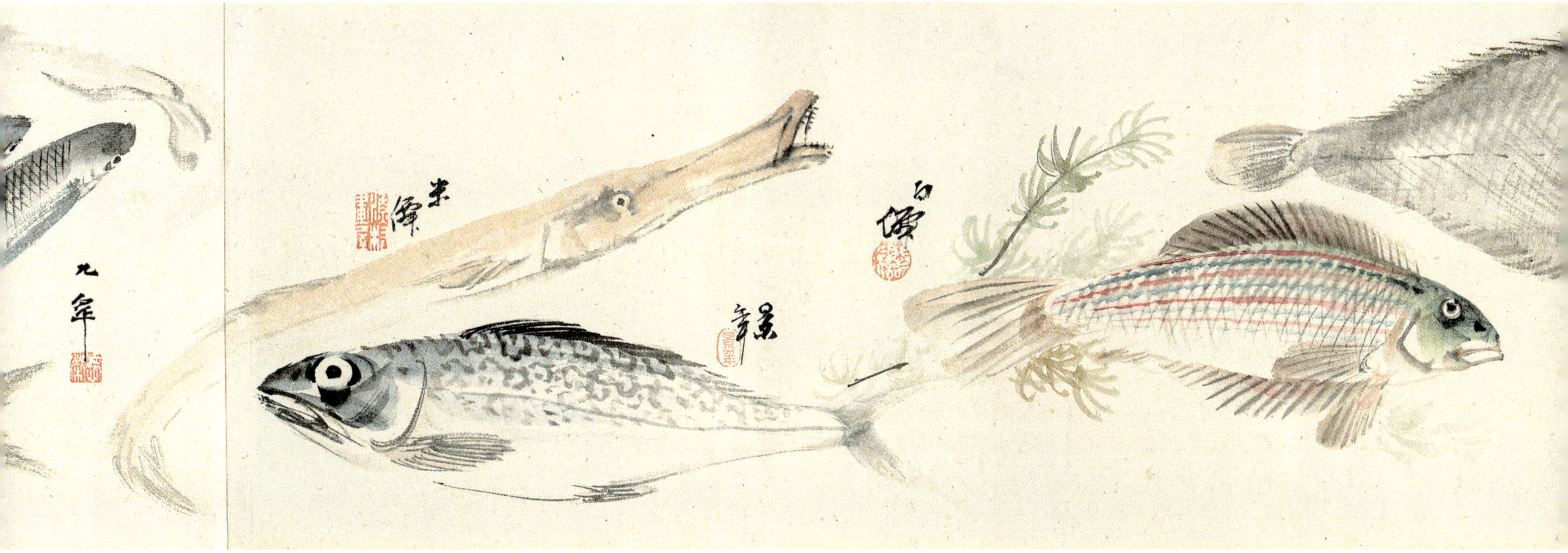

as well as from newer schools such as the Shijō and Kishi.[14] The techniques used for each element of the composition, which brings together seasonal Kyoto motifs, span from monochrome ink to richly coloured representations. This might indicate that the work was created over a period of time with contributions added one by one, rather than all on one occasion. If this were the case, then there was likely an agent who circulated among the artists. One possible reason behind this elaborate work was perhaps the commemoration of the seventh death anniversary of the artist Matsumura Keibun (1779–1843; see figs 2.22, 5.21), the younger half-brother of Go Shun and a second-generation master of the Shijō school.[15] The great popularity of Keibun's works resulted in the circulation of many forgeries; in some cases Keibun's own pupils apparently produced fakes in their teacher's style. Five of the Shijō artists – Isono Kadō (active *c.* 1840s), Mori Gishō (1802–1873), Tomita Kōei (active *c.* 1840s), Yagi Kihō (1806–1876) and Yokoyama Seiki (1793–1865) – all of whom are represented in this painting, had in fact pledged some two years after Keibun's death never to generate such forgeries.[16]

Collaboration could sometimes overcome the boundaries of language and nationality. In 1881 the grandsons of the British monarch Queen Victoria, Prince Albert Victor (1864–1892) and Prince George (1865–1936), visited Japan. The two princes were entertained in Kyoto with a performance of impromptu painting by Japanese artists, including Kubota Beisen (1852–1906) (see fig. 0.11), a newly appointed professor at the Kyoto Prefectural School of Painting (Kyōto-fu Gagakkō). Beisen first did a painting on the spot, and then the royal guests were encouraged to take up the brush and to make dots, dashes and other shapes on prepared paper.[17] Prince George made





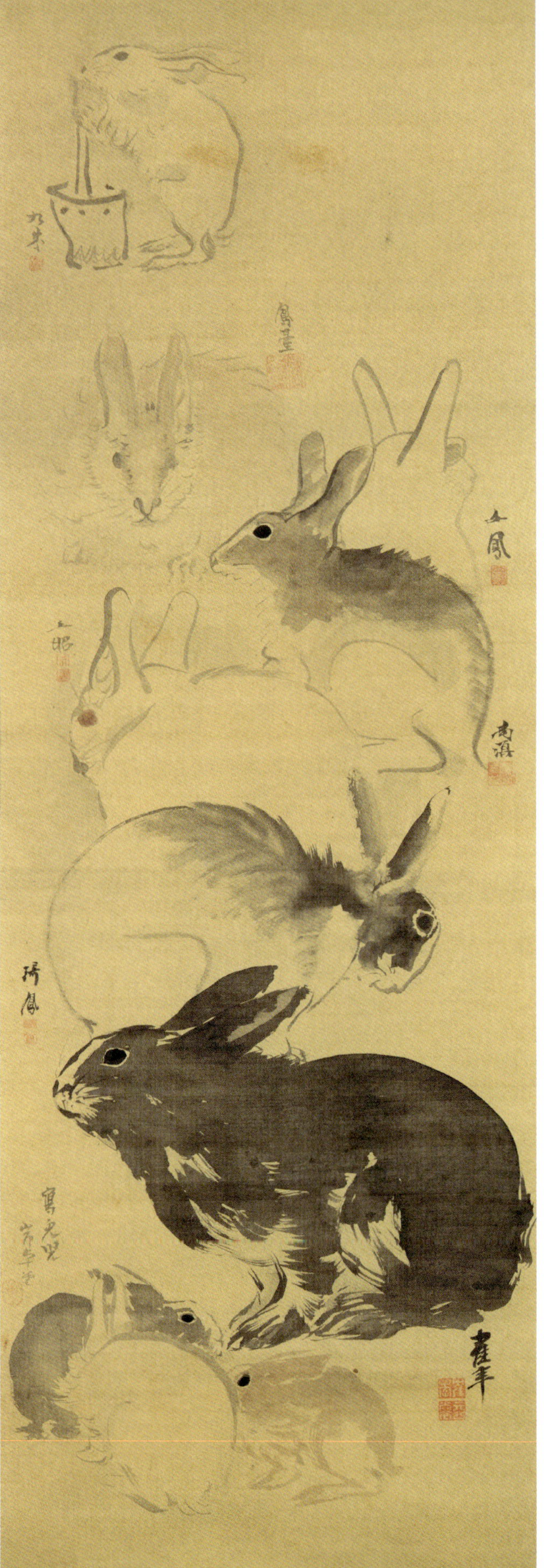

**0.12**

Akamatsu Kakunen, Bunshō, Gan Tai, Hōdai, Kawamura Bunpō, Kawamura Kihō, Masuda Kyūboku and Nanmei, *Rabbits*, before 1821. Hanging scroll, ink and light colour on silk. 186.5 × 47.9 cm. British Museum, London, 2019,3038.1. Gift of Israel Goldman in honour of Timothy T. Clark.

**0.13**

64 artists including Tomioka Tessai and Ueda Kōchū, *Wish-Granting Jewels*, 1905. Pair of hanging scrolls, ink and light colour on silk. 203 × 72 cm. British Museum, London, 2018,3037.1.1–2. Purchase made possible by the JTI Japanese Acquisition Fund.

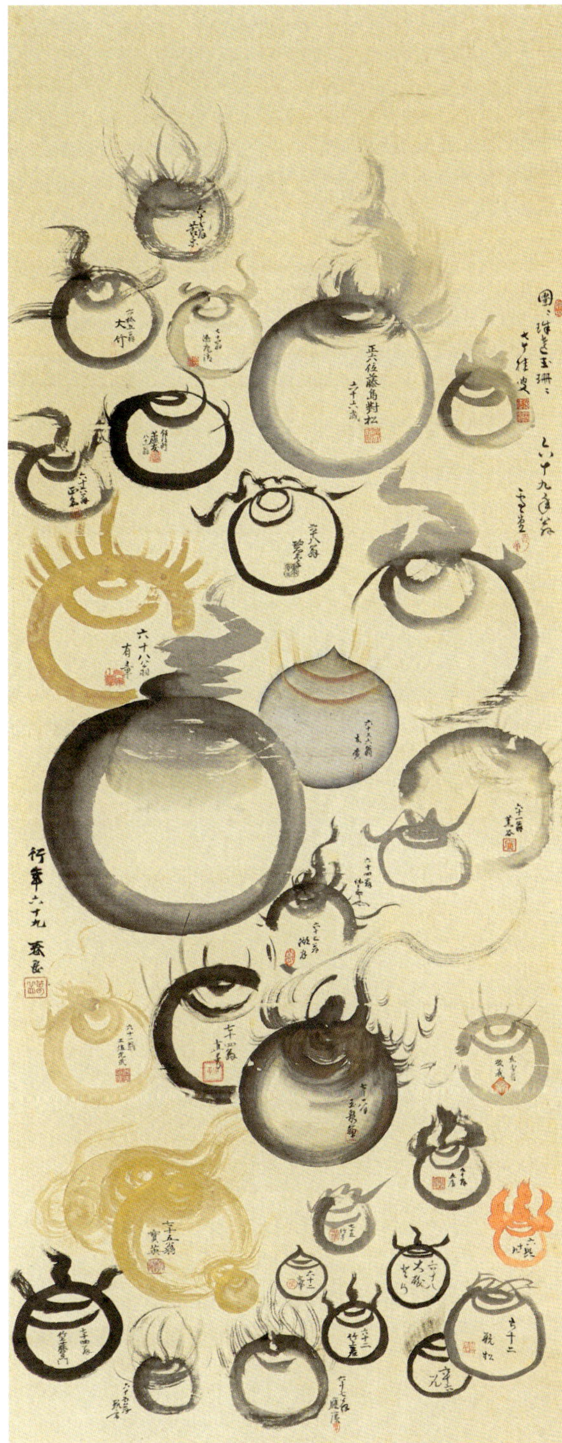

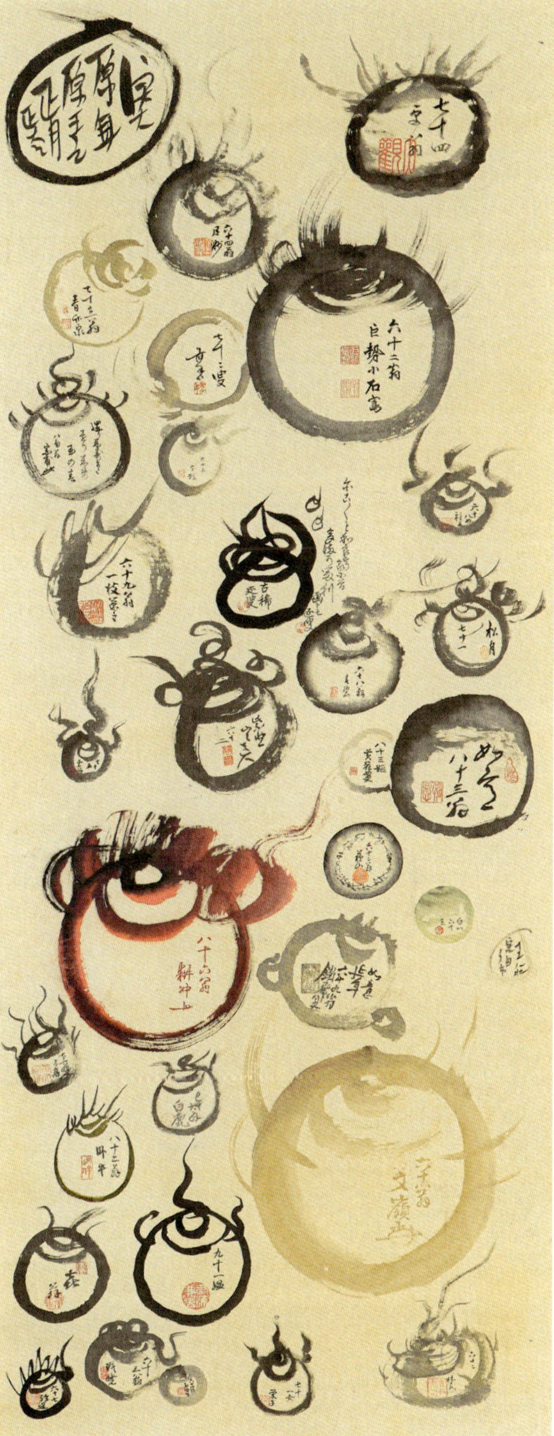

several simple ink spots on the paper. Responding to this amicable visual banter, Beisen swiftly took his brush and added short strokes around each dot to create an image of dancing fireflies (fig. 0.16).

One of the most prestigious painting projects that involved the working together of professional artists from diverse schools was the interior decoration of the imperial palace in Kyoto, which was destroyed in the Great Fire of 1788 and rebuilt in 1790. This project was funded by the Tokugawa government, and the imperial court selected the artists following a rigorous investigation into their background and practice.[18] It is not surprising that members of establishment schools such as Tosa and Kanō were chosen. Significant, however, is that many other artists from Kyoto and Osaka were also included after their artistic lineages had been verified. For instance, Maruyama Ōkyo and his pupils and Mori Shūhō seized this opportunity to participate. The interior decoration of the imperial palace was a large-scale collective project, but the nature of this formal artistic cooperation was very different from the examples discussed in this book, which were more friendly and spontaneous, and more likely to have been based on personal connections.

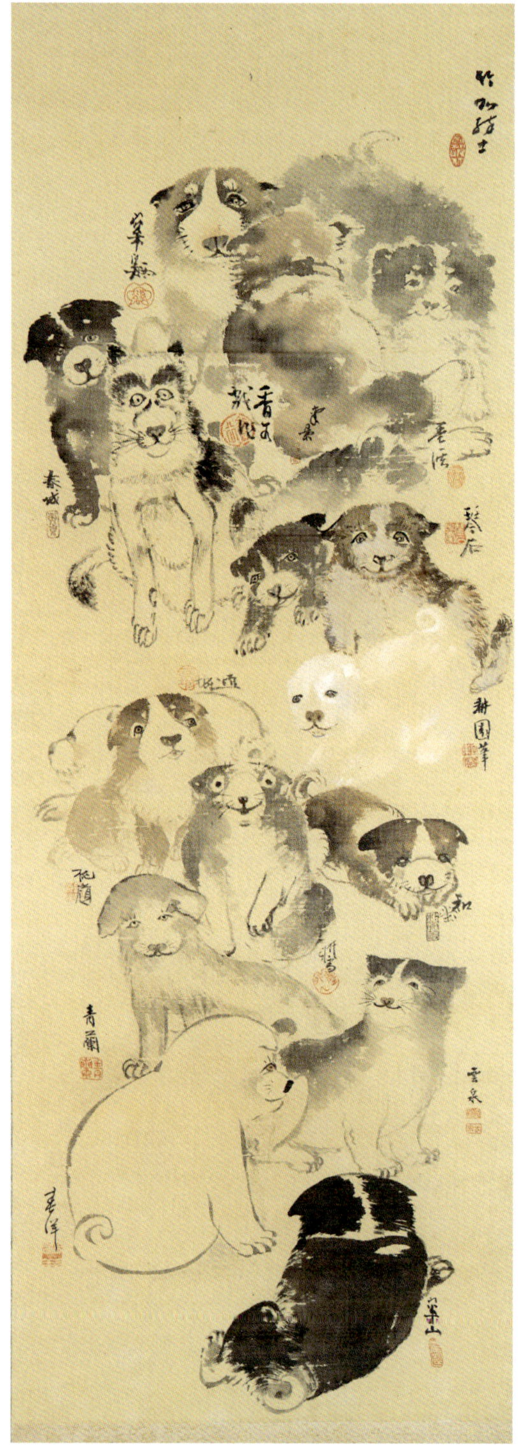



Salon culture in Japan

**0.14**

Fukada Chokujō, Himejima Chikugai, Kawabe Seiran, Kawasaki Bokkei, Koyama Unsen, Mori Kinseki, Murata Kōkoku, Nagamatsu Shun'yō, Nakagawa Wadō, Niwayama Kōen, Nobuchika Shunjō, Sakata Kōsetsu, Shōzan, Ueda Tōrei, Wakabayashi Shōkei and one unidentified artist, *Puppies Have Buddha Nature: A Collaborative Work* (*Kushi busshō gassaku*), 1910. Hanging scroll, ink and light colour on silk. 101 × 36 cm. British Museum, London, 2018,3029.1. Gift of Israel Goldman in memory of Florence Williams Goldman.

**0.15**

Gan Tai, Isono Kadō, Kanō Eigaku, Kishi Renzan, Mori Gishō, Nakajima Raishō, Shūsui, Takemura Bunmin, Tomita Kōei, Tosa Mitsuzane, Yagi Kihō and Yokoyama Seiki, *Collaborative Work of the Twelve Months by Renowned Kyoto Artists* (*Heian sho-meika jūni-tsuki gassaku*), 1849. Hanging scroll, ink and colour on silk. 229 × 78 cm. British Museum, London, 2019,3016.1. Purchase made possible by the JTI Japanese Acquisition Fund.

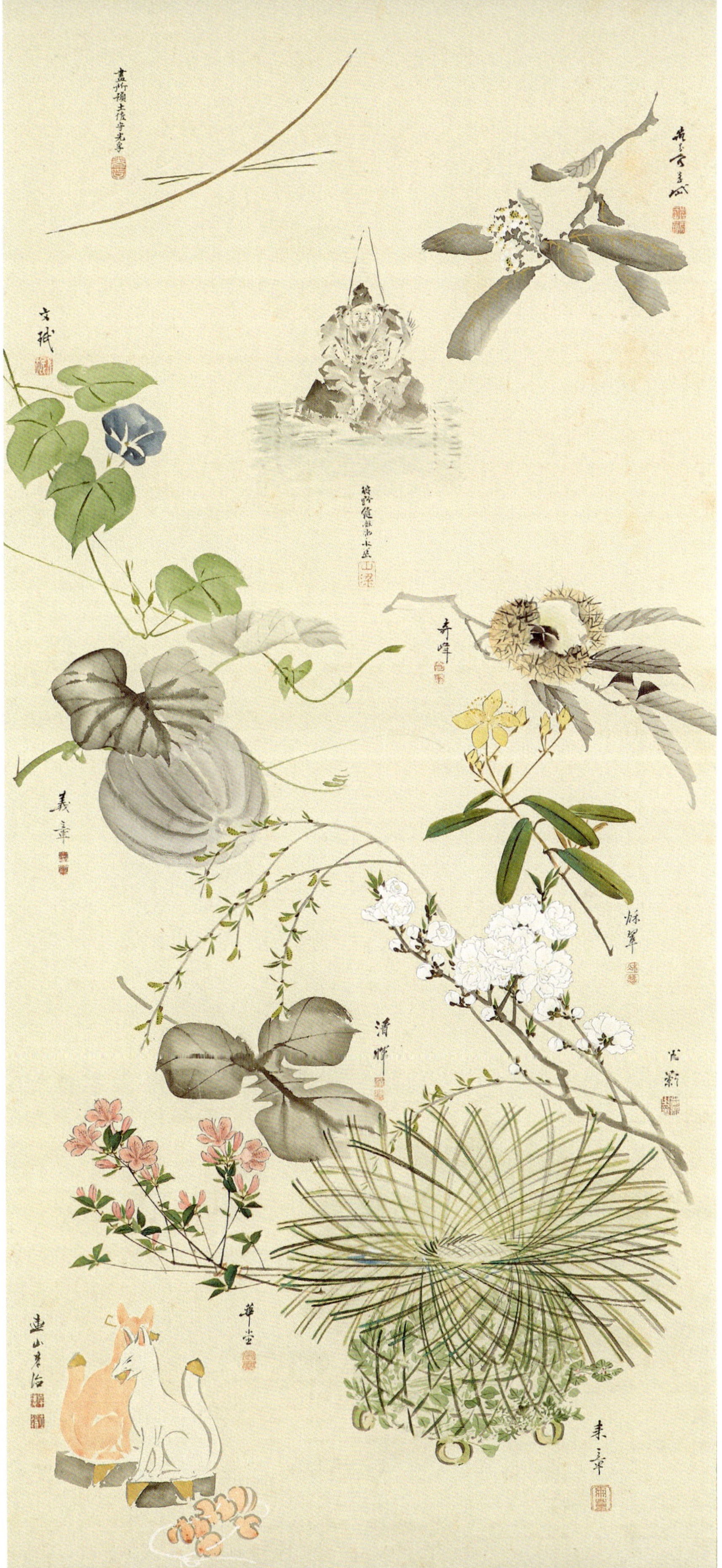

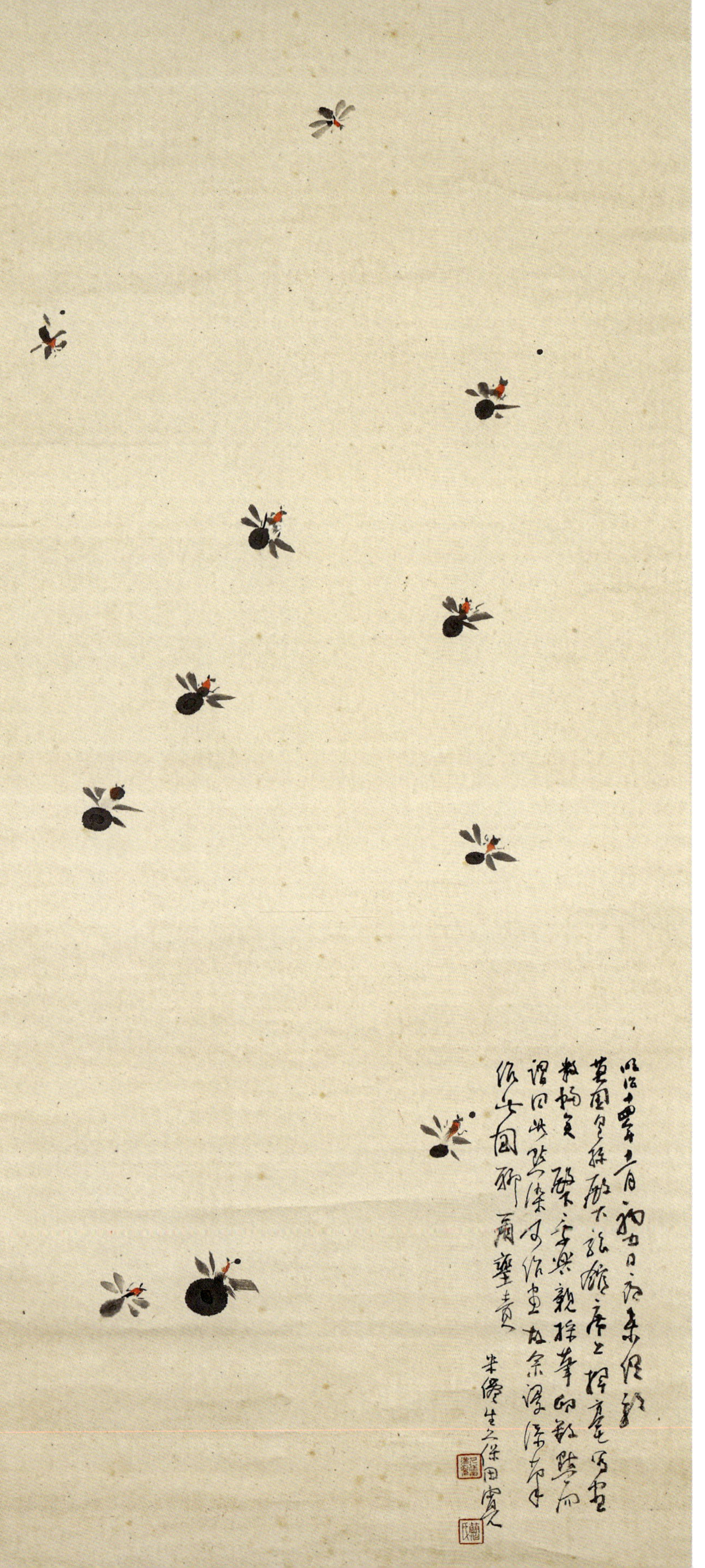

**0.16**
Kubota Beisen and Prince George (the future King George V), *Fireflies*, 1881. Hanging scroll, ink and colour on paper. 193 × 76 cm. British Museum, London, 2011,3032.1. Purchase funded by the Brooke Sewell Bequest.

## Surimono

Close collaborations among artists across various schools in Kyoto and Osaka are also seen in the type of prints mentioned above known as surimono (see also chapter 5). A diptych of large surimono with nearly 200 haiku poems and images of seven sparrows by seven artists (fig. 0.17) suggests a major project among friends and acquaintances. The featured poets are from Osaka, Kyoto, Edo and other towns, mainly in western Japan. The contribution of poems from more distant locations was most likely done via the postal system. The poets include the courtier Tominokōji Sadanao (1761–1837; see fig. 0.1), whose pen name is Jodei ('Muddy'), the 86-year-old silk-thread merchant and haiku enthusiast Teramura Hyakuchi (1748–1836) ('One Hundred Ponds'), several professional haiku instructors and Kitagawa Baika ('Prince of Plum Blossoms'), a doctor at the temple Nishi-Hongan-ji in Kyoto. Pen names were often of the individual's choosing, although in more formally organised poetry circles one character of the teacher's pen name might commonly be adopted by their pupils to emphasise group identity. The spirit of playfulness in pen names is evident.

On the right sheet of the diptych is a cluster of five sparrows depicted by five artists from Kyoto: the second-generation masters of the Shijō school, Matsumura Keibun and Okamoto Toyohiko (1773–1845), and their pupils Tanaka Nikka (d. 1845; see fig. 0.26) and Yokoyama Seiki (1793–1865; see fig. 0.15), as well as Baika's son Saigyo, who was skilled at both haiku and painting. The other two sparrows on the left sheet are by the Kanō-school painter brothers Eigaku (1790–1867) (see fig. 5.4) and Eitai (d. 1842), the latter

**0.17**
Kanō Eigaku, Kanō Eitai, Kitagawa Saigyo, Matsumura Keibun, Okamoto Toyohiko, Tanaka Nikka, Yokoyama Seiki (artists) and 190 poets, *Sparrows*, 1835, from *Album of Surimono with Haiku Poems for the Four Seasons* (*Shiki hokku surimono-jō*), *c.* 1829–42. Diptych surimono, colour woodblock. 39.4 × 56.7 cm (each). British Museum, London, 2017,3075.1.104–5. Purchase funded by the Theresia Gerda Buch Bequest in memory of her parents, Rudolf and Julie Buch.

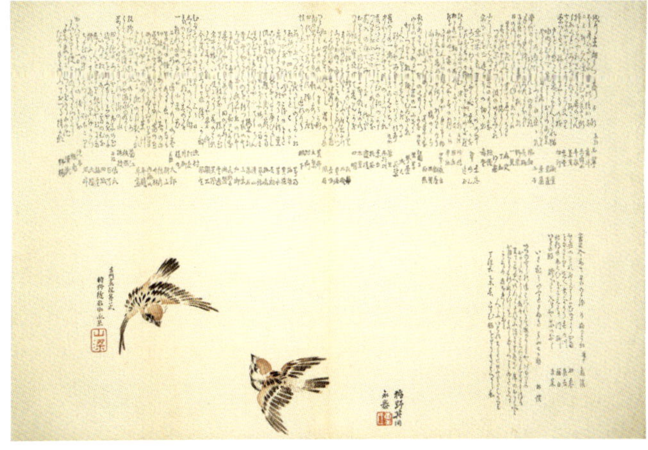
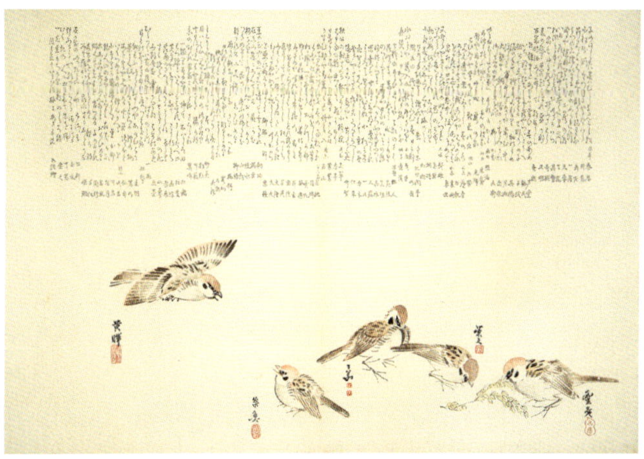

of whom was Baika's son-in-law. In fact, it is Baika who was given the very last position in the sequence of poems, which is usually allocated for the organiser of the surimono or the most important person in a group. This suggests that Baika's personal connections were likely the organising motivation behind this project. Baika humorously laments his old age in his text.

## Poetry anthologies

Alongside paintings and surimono, illustrated books were an essential product of and vehicle for salon activities. Publishing a book is by its very nature collaborative, mobilising authors, contributors, illustrators, block-cutters, printers and publishers.

The haiku anthology *Album of the Crane's Cry* (*Kakusei-jō*, 1828) (fig. 0.18, see fig. 2.32) was edited by the poet and retired Kyoto publisher Kikuya Tahei (b. 1756), who appears under his pen name Suishitsu Kisei ('Drunkard Room, Jolly Me'). This publication was issued by Kikuya Hikohei (active 1820s), the next generation head of the Kikuya, who specialised in haiku books, in particular those that followed the style of the famous seventeenth-century poet Matsuo Bashō (1644–1694) (see p. 85). According to a Kikuya advertisement at the back of the book, the shop also dealt in various kinds of paper for surimono and calligraphy. This haiku anthology contains compositions by some 260 poets and pictures by over twenty artists, many from the

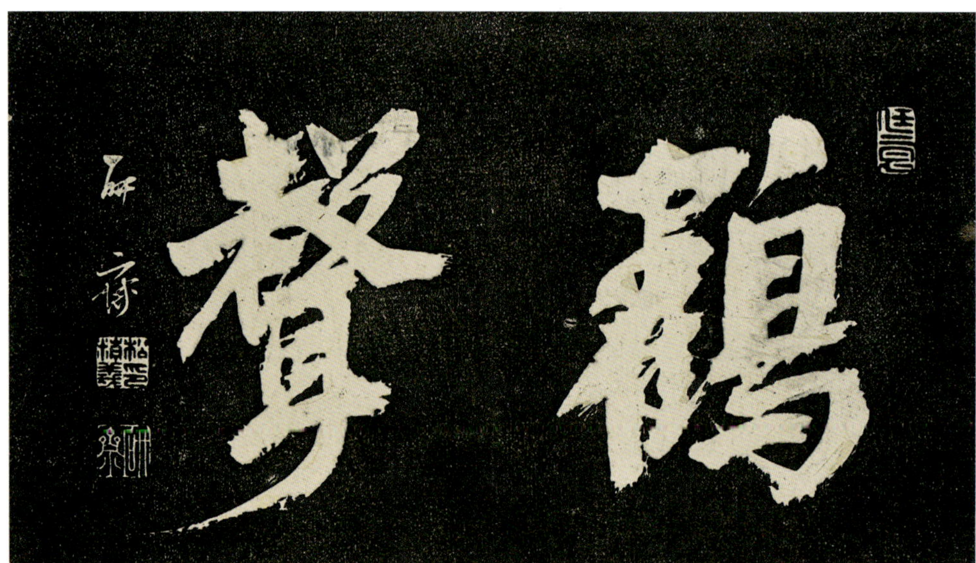

0.18 *left and opposite*
19 artists, including Azuma Tōyō, Kawamura Kihō, Oda Kaisen, Okamoto Toyohiko, Maruyama Ōzui, Matsumura Keibun, Murata Kagen, Nishimura Nantei, Tanaka Nikka and Yokoyama Seiki, and about 260 poets, *Album of the Crane's Cry* (*Kakusei-jō*), 1828. Album, colour woodblock. 24.8 × 18.7 cm (cover). British Museum, London, 1979,0305,0.297. Ex-coll.: Jack Hillier.

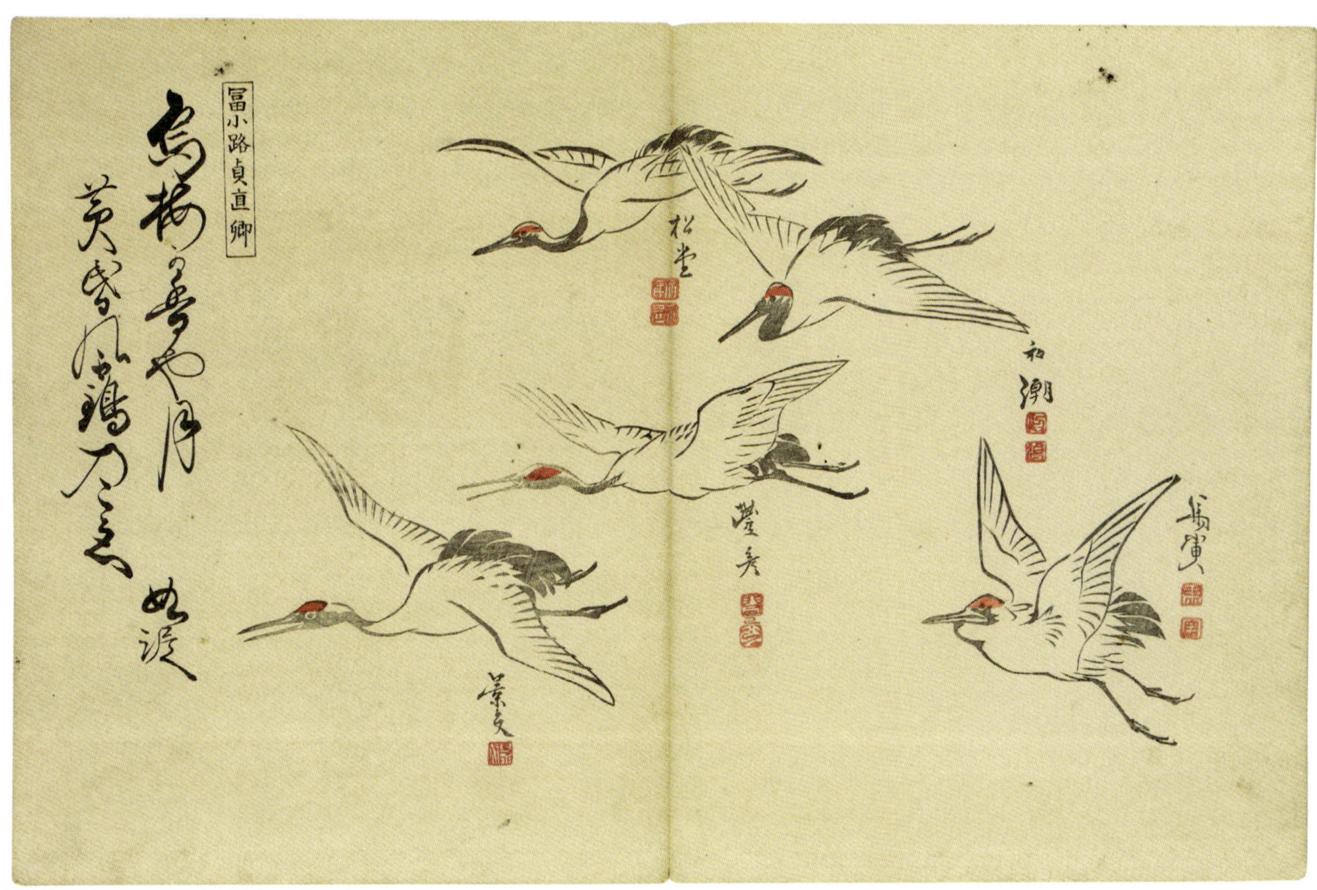

Maruyama-Shijō school. Some images are by the poets themselves, some by figures unidentified today. An opening haiku is supplied by the Kyoto courtier Jodei mentioned earlier.

Japanese poets of Chinese-style verses also formed poetry groups. *Admiring the Fragrance of Spring* (*Shōshunpō*, postscript dated 1777) (fig. 0.19) is an anthology of Chinese-style poems with accompanying illustrations. The book is printed in the dramatic white-on-black printing technique called 'surface rubbing' (*shōmen-zuri*) or 'stone printing' (*ishi-zuri*), which evokes the Chinese ink-rubbing technique for copying texts from ancient stone stelas and was strongly associated with classical Chinese scholarly and visual culture. The postscript states that the initial occasion for composing the poems was an outing to view cherry blossoms by a few members of the Chinese poetry circle Shōrakan in Kyoto, including the group leader Iwagaki Ryūkei (1741–1808). It was later expanded to include poems from other members and accompanying

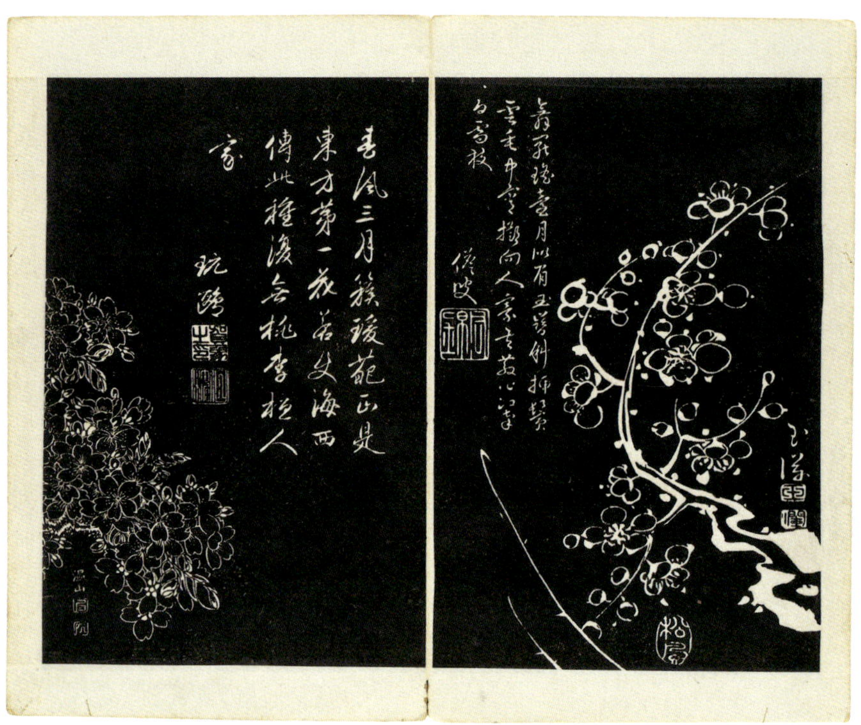

**0.19**
Emi Nagatoshi (editor), 26 artists, including Ike no Gyokuran, Ike no Taiga, Itō Jakuchū, Maruyama Ōkyo, Murakami Tōshū, Ōshima Raikin and Kakutei, and 26 poets, *Admiring the Fragrance of Spring (Shōshunpō)*, 1 vol., postscript dated 1777. Album, woodblock. 25 × 16.5 cm (cover). British Museum, London, 1979,0305,0.131. Ex-coll.: Jack Hillier.

**0.20**
Ike no Gyokuran, *Waterscape with Willows and a Boat*, from an album of 24 paintings and calligraphy on fans, mid-1700s. Fan painting, ink and light colour on paper. 30.5 × 56 cm (cover). British Museum, London, 1981,0702,0.2. Purchase funded by the Brooke Sewell Bequest.

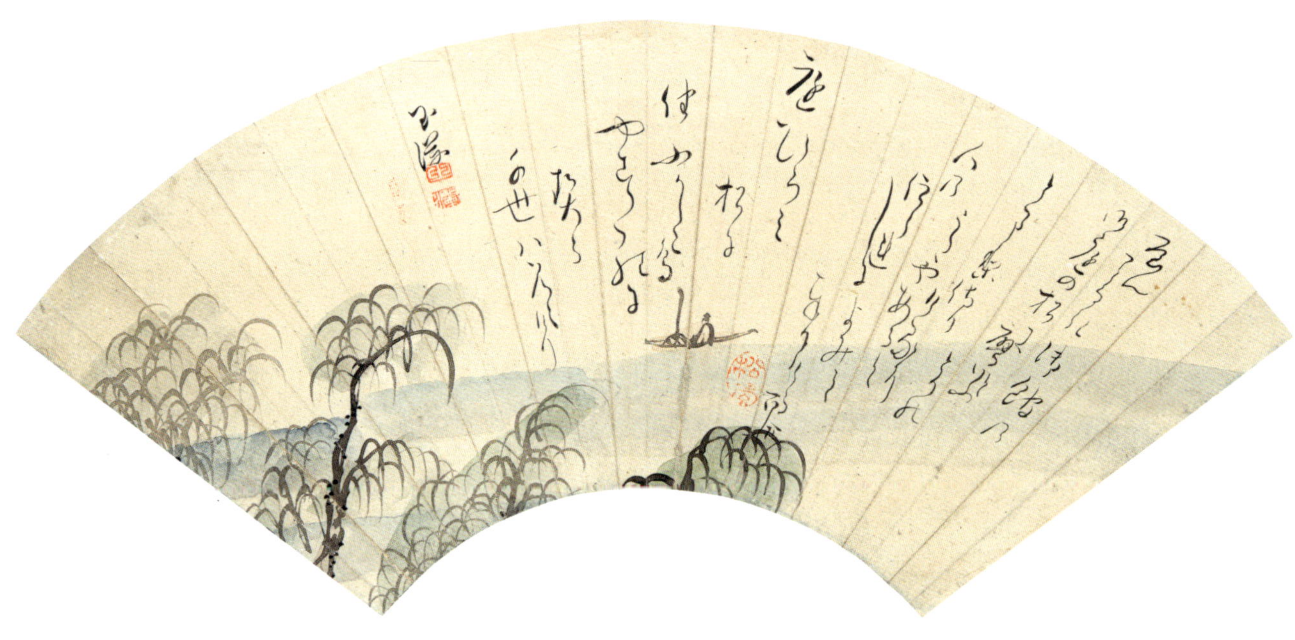

illustrations from artists.[19] The images were done by some of Kyoto's most sought-after artists, such as the literati couple Ike no Taiga (1723–1776)[20] (see figs 0.28–0.29) and his wife Gyokuran (1727–1784) (fig. 0.20); the vegetable-wholesaler-turned-artist Itō Jakuchū (1716–1800); Maruyama Ōkyo; and the female literati artist Ōshima Raikin (active late eighteenth century). Neither picture nor verse is subordinate, and the balance between the two elements suggests an amiable collaborative design process between poets and artists. The book is thought to have been initially a private publication, which was subsequently released as a commercial title in 1782.[21]

### Other illustrated books: hobbies, commercial collaborations and painting manuals

Many cultural salons were gatherings of fellow enthusiasts centred around particular 'hobby arts' (*yūgei*). Some traditional hobbies had a formal structure and organisation, others were more informal and relaxed. An example of the latter is the art of making miniature landscape arrangements in a basin (*senkeiban*). The scenes were created around a rock, to which was added greenery, a miniature house and small figurines; this activity was enjoyed alone and with friends. Suminoe Buzen (1734–1806) was a reputable Osaka artist and a central figure in this art of miniature landscapes, which was very popular in the city in the early nineteenth century. Before becoming an artist, Buzen had been a boatman. He excelled at intricate miniature work and was also known for his incised metalwork designs. The publication *Designs for Miniature Landscapes in a Basin* (*Senkeiban zushiki*, 1826) (fig. 0.21) was the second to bring together Buzen's miniature landscape designs (the first was *Senkeiban* of 1808); it was issued posthumously and privately by Buzen's son Aizan (dates unknown). The second publication was a commercial collaboration between six Kyoto and Osaka publishers, an indication of the prevalence of the art of miniature landscape at this time. The main publisher, Imazuya Tatsusaburō in Osaka, was himself an enthusiast of the art, and several artists, scholars and poets contributed either images or inscriptions, in some of which they explicitly refer to Buzen as their 'friend'.[22] Such hobbies, it is evident, had social and cultural significance.

Commercially planned publications were also often highly collaborative efforts. The publisher likely had the greatest influence on the selection of authors and artists from a strategic business point of view. *Illustrated Guide to the Famous Places along the East Coast Road* (*Tōkaidō meisho zue*, 1797) (fig. 0.22), a six-volume illustrated gazetteer authored by Akisato Ritō (active *c.* 1770s–1820s),



Introduction

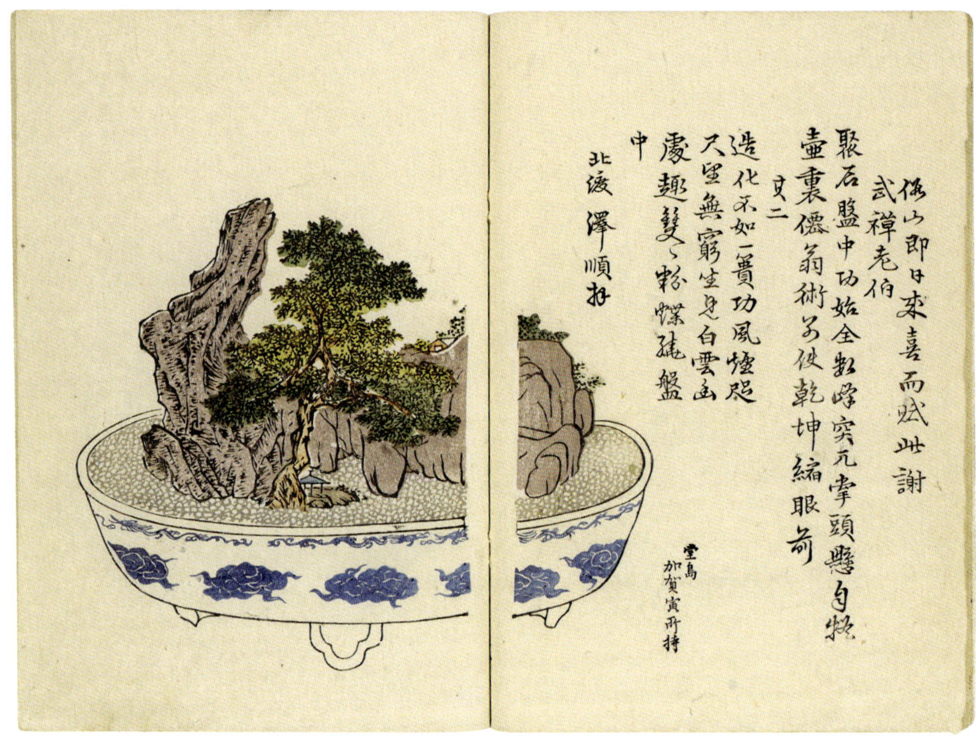

**0.21**
Suminoe Aizan and Suminoe Buzen, *Designs for Miniature Landscapes in a Basin* (S*enkeiban zushiki*), 2 vols, 1826. Illustrated book, colour woodblock. 26 × 18.6 cm (cover). British Museum, London, 1939,0524,0.63.1–2.

**0.22**
Akisato Ritō (author) and over 20 artists, *Illustrated Guide to the Famous Places along the East Coast Road* (*Tōkaidō meisho zue*), 6 vols, 1797. Illustrated book, woodblock. 26 × 18.5 cm (cover). British Museum, London, 1979,0305,0.178.1–6. Ex-coll.: Jack Hillier.

*Below left*  Tosa Mitsusada (artist), 'Scene of an imperial court ritual on New Year's Day (*ko-chōhai*)', from vol. 1
*Below right*  Yamaguchi Soken (artist), 'Street scene in Kyoto', from vol. 1
*Opposite left*  Takehara Shunsensai (artist), 'Ferry boat from Kuwana, Ise', from vol. 2
*Opposite right*  Kitao Masayoshi (artist), 'View of Nihonbashi with Mount Fuji', from vol. 6

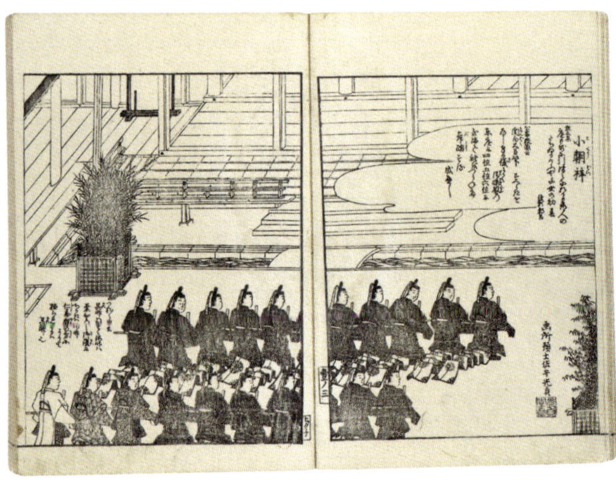

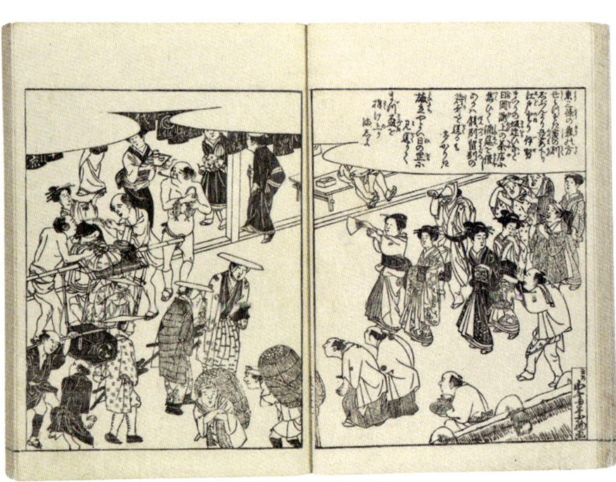

was an ambitious attempt to organise the contributions of over twenty artists from Osaka, Kyoto and Edo as well as from a few towns along the Tōkaidō highway. According to the notes to the reader at the beginning of the book, the plan from the outset was to create a collaborative work by artists from each location. Although the majority of the illustrations are by one Osaka artist, Takehara Shunsensai (active *c*. 1790s–1800s), the remaining artists represent the whole spectrum of styles of the era.[23] It was an ambitious project involving as many as eleven publishers, including distributors from Osaka, Kyoto and Edo.

*Journey to the East: Colourful Tales from Various Provinces* ([*Shokoku kidan*] *Tōyūki*) (fig. 0.23) recounts the travels of the Kyoto doctor and author Tachibana Nankei (1753–1805) through Japan's northern provinces. Initially the text was available only in manuscript copies and circulated among a limited readership. Since it details the customs, climate, legends and curious episodes concerning the northern provinces, publishers in Kyoto and Osaka saw it as a potential commercial success and co-published it with illustrations by Maruyama-Shijō artists, who made the images based on Nankei's description.[24] One of Ōkyo's greatest pupils, Nagasawa Rosetsu (1754–1799), who rarely contributed to such collaborative ventures, is found among them. Rosetsu was the son of a samurai and according to contemporary anecdotes, he had an aloof character. His clever sense of design and sharp brushstrokes are evident in his contribution.

The scale of the publishing industry during this period was considerable. Kyoto, Osaka and Edo were the centres of commercial publishing, with smaller hubs such as Nagoya. Illustrated painting manuals and picture albums were an established genre (see pp. 122–3). The seventeenth-century Chinese publication *Mustard Seed Garden Painting Manual* (C: *Jieziyuan huazhuan*) and its Japanese translation *Kaishien gaden* were models for this genre. From the

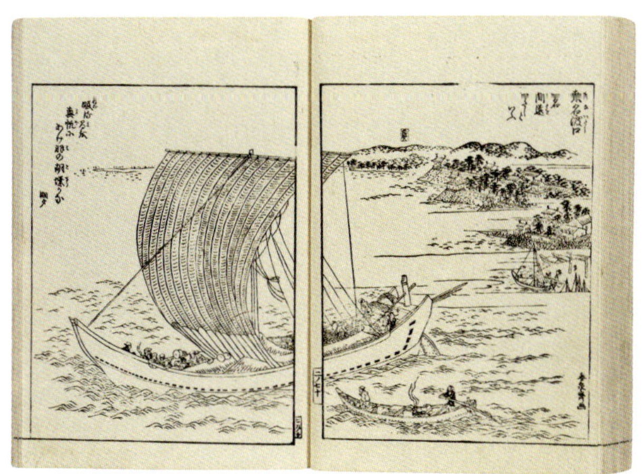

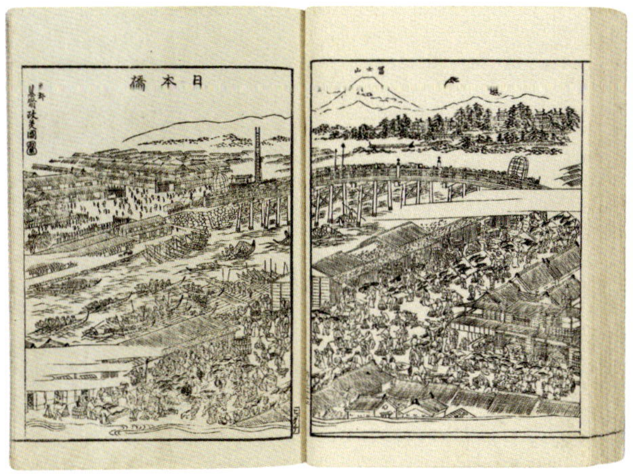



Introduction

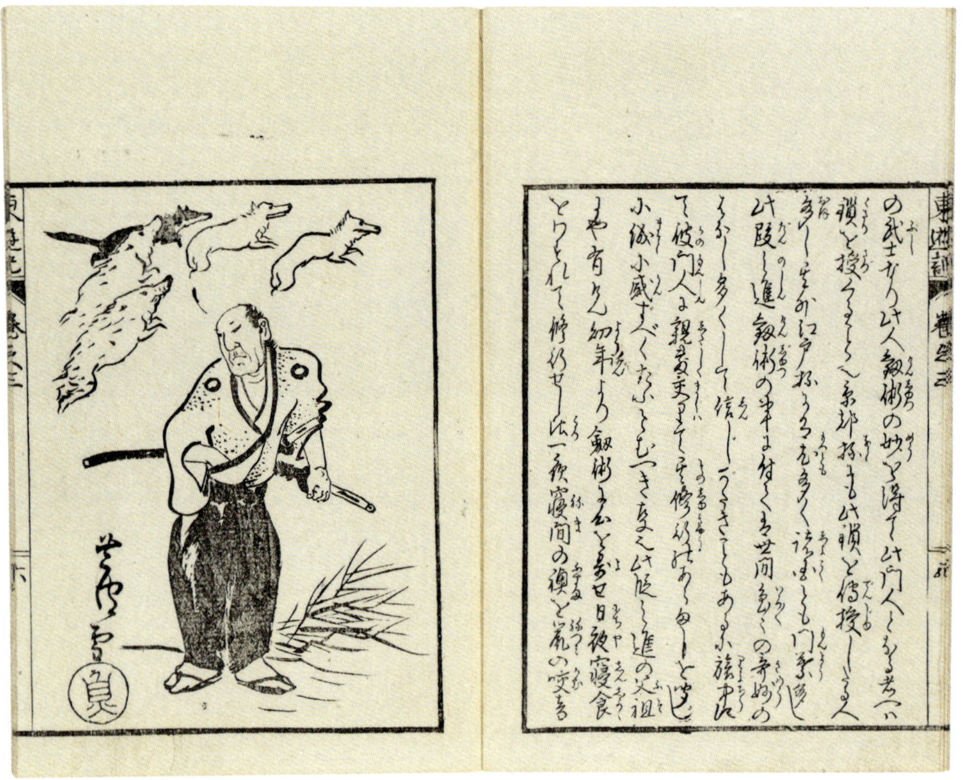

**0.23**
Nagasawa Rosetsu (artist), 'The swordsman Masaki Dan'noshin of Ōgaki, Mino', from vol. 3 of Tachibana Nankei (author) and 12 artists, *Journey to the East: Colourful Tales from Various Provinces* ([*Shokoku kidan*] *Tōyūki*), 6 vols, 1795. Illustrated book, woodblock. 24 × 16 cm (cover). British Museum, London, 1979,0305,0.175.1–6. Ex-coll.: Jack Hillier.

early eighteenth century, anthologies with compositions by historical master painters from China and Japan also gained in popularity. The increase in the number of 'teach yourself' painting manuals in the nineteenth century reflects the prevalence of amateur painting. Commercial publishers and some samurai government institutions produced these types of books. One example is the manual *Teach Yourself Chinese Painting* (*Kanga hitori-geiko*, 1807) by the Osaka-based artist Miyamoto Kunzan (d. 1827) (fig. 0.24). The publisher was Shabenkan, the herbology academy of the Kii domain (in present-day Wakayama and southern Mie prefectures).

Numerous picture albums aimed to deliver purely aesthetic pleasure rather than practical painting instruction, although these could equally have been used as sources for paintings. *Suiseki's Picture Album, Part II* (*Suiseki gafu, nihen*, 1820) (fig. 0.25, see fig. 2.40) by Satō Suiseki (Gyodai, active 1806–40) of Osaka, for instance, presents delightful designs based on birds, flowers and animals in daily domestic settings rendered through his masterful brushwork. Printed in delicate colours, the painterly quality of the images would have given much visual delight in addition to offering inspiration to take up a brush.

Picture albums were sometimes compilations by pupils celebrating or commemorating their master's career. *Kyūhōdō's Picture Album* (*Kyūhōdō gafu*, 1856) (fig. 0.26) is a collection of painting designs by Tanaka Nikka (Kyūhōdō was his atelier name), a well-respected Shijō-school artist whose name appears in three editions of *Record of People in Heian* [*Kyoto*] (*Heian jinbutsu shi*). The album was compiled by his student Ikeda Kyūka (1809–1881), who was originally a medical doctor in Kanazawa in Kaga province in northern Japan (in present-day Ishikawa prefecture). He went on to study painting under Nikka. For Kyūka, painting remained a hobby, but his talents exceeded the level of most amateurs (fig. 0.27). Three of Kyūka's fellow students helped with the compilation and commissioning of the woodblock cutting for the book's text and images, and Kyūka asked a friend in Kanazawa to write a preface. It was Kyūka's private publication, meaning that he owned the set of printing woodblocks. The preface notes that it was originally Nikka's idea to publish a picture album, but as it did not materialise during his lifetime, Kyūka issued it posthumously in memory of his teacher's delicate and elegant painting style.

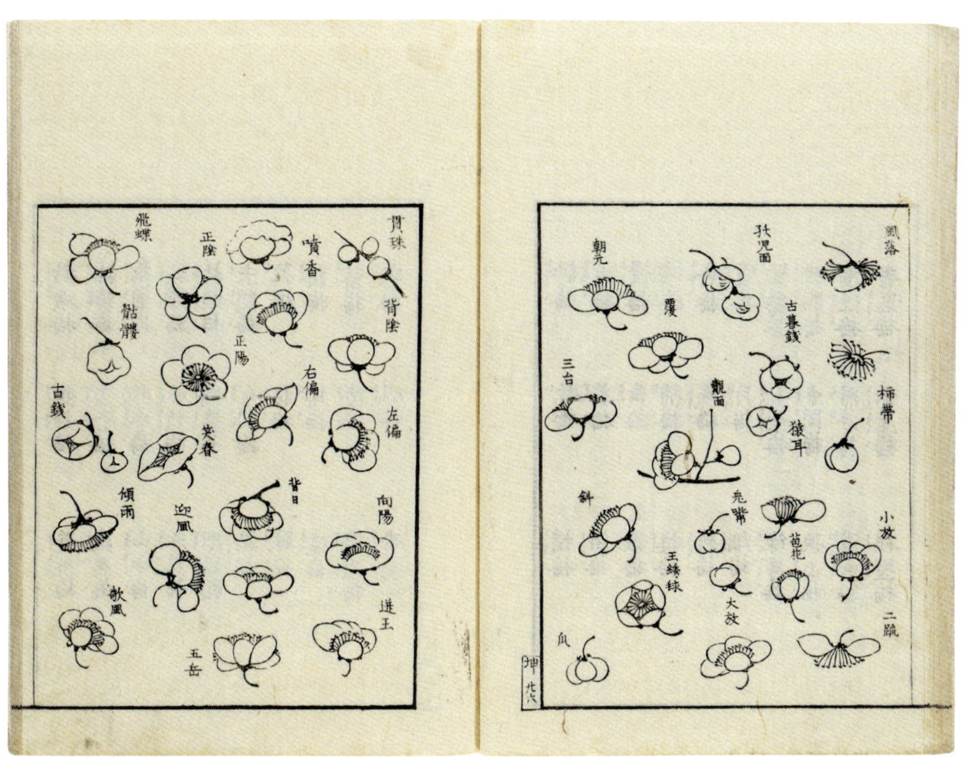

**0.24**
Miyamoto Kunzan, *Teach Yourself Chinese Painting* (*Kanga hitori-geiko*), 2 vols, 1807. Illustrated book, woodblock. 25 × 17 cm (cover). British Museum, London, 1979,0305,0.214.1–2. Ex-coll.: Jack Hillier.



Introduction

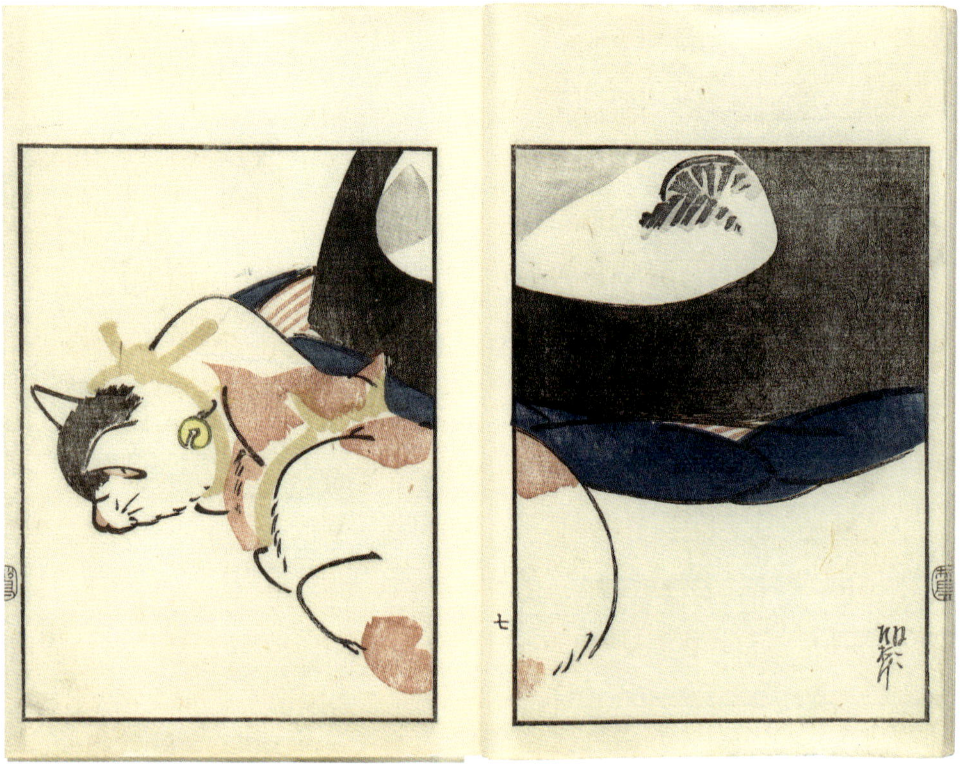

**0.25**
Satō Suiseki (Gyodai),
*Suiseki's Picture Album,
Part II* (*Suiseki gafu, nihen*),
1 vol., 1820. Illustrated book,
colour woodblock. 25.7 ×
17.7 cm (cover). British Museum,
London, 1979,0305,0.268.
Ex-coll.: Jack Hillier.

## Literati, amateurs and eccentrics

To understand society's general endorsement of and mass participation in cultural activities, it might be instructive to consider three distinct but related concepts in the practice of the arts: literati (*bunjin*), amateurs (*shirōto*) and eccentrics (*kijin*).

Many Edo-period Japanese intellectuals and artists aspired to follow the model of the elite Chinese scholar-artist. Chinese literati (C: *wenren*) were imagined as retired high-ranking officials leading reclusive lives and immersing themselves in literature and the arts, not for commercial gain but for self-cultivation. Those who shared this vision in Japan can broadly be categorised as bunjin. They could be professional scholars, poets, artists or alternatively amateurs. Although it is not easy to come to a comprehensive definition of a literatus, in essence the ultimate ideal was to practise art for art's sake, notwithstanding the fact that professionals had to earn money by teaching the skills and knowledge they had acquired and/or selling their art (see chapter 4).



Salon culture in Japan

**0.26**
Tanaka Nikka, *Kyūhōdō's Picture Album* (*Kyūhōdō gafu*), 2 vols, 1856. Album, colour woodblock. 30 × 19.6 cm (cover). British Museum, London, 1979,0305,0.363.1–2. Ex-coll.: Jack Hillier.

**0.27**
Ikeda Kyūka (artist) and 83 poets, *Pufferfish and Rockfish*, 1852. Surimono, colour woodblock. 38 × 51.5 cm. British Museum, London, 2021,3013.205. Purchase made possible by the JTI Japanese Acquisition Fund. Ex-coll.: Dr Scott Johnson.


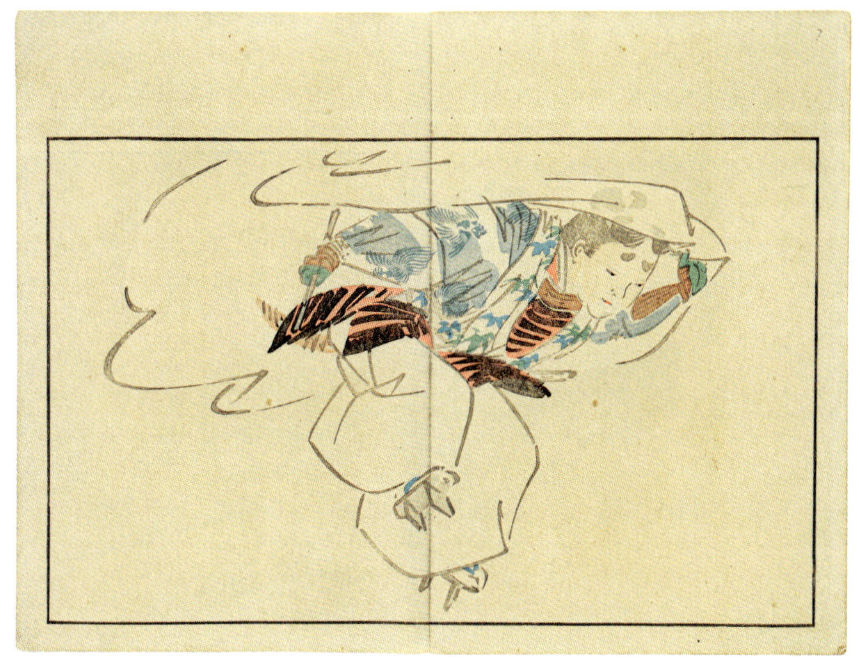

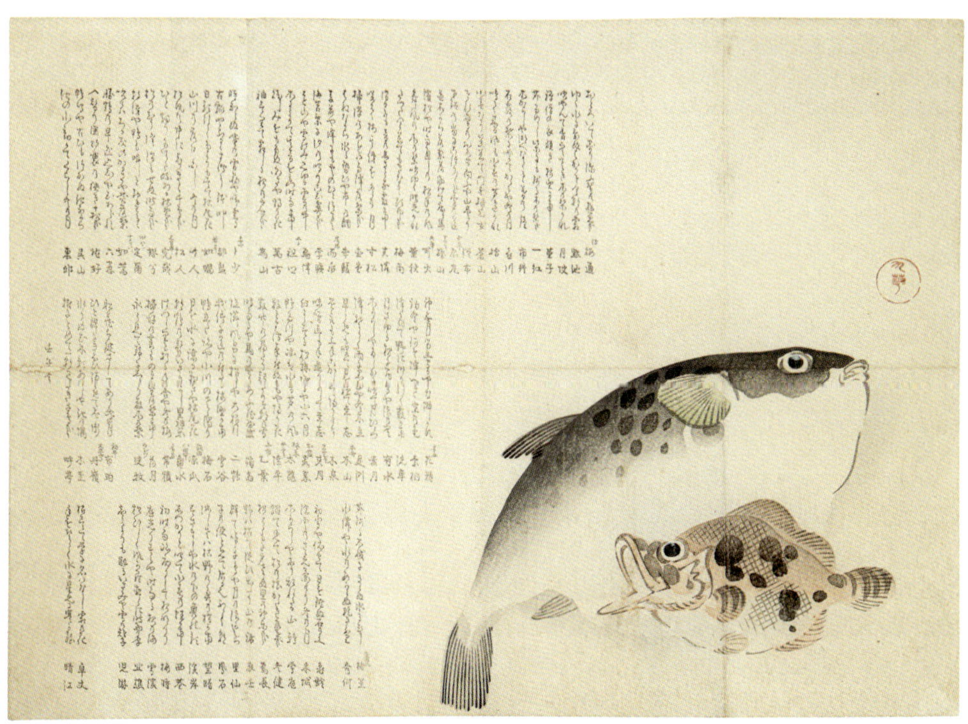

The literati model was a positive incentive for those who took up arts and literature as their hobby. They were shirōto (amateurs) in the sense that they did not make their living from practising their hobbies. In reality, some amateur practitioners were as good and serious as professionals (see pp. 64–8). For example, the shirōto Kimura Kenkadō in Osaka was one of the most respected bunjin in Japan (see fig. 4.34). His reputation as a scholar was even known in Korea through his interactions with officials of the Korean embassy delegations (see p. 204). Kenkadō, a wealthy merchant who owned a sake brewery, was a collector of rare books and artefacts, a keen practitioner of art and literature, and an antiquarian with scholarly pursuits in the natural sciences; his lifestyle was admired by many as that of an exemplary literatus.

Whatever the motivation – be it vocational, personal interest, educational or for social advancement – large numbers of people engaged with one or another form of the arts in the Edo period. When someone devoted oneself too much to the arts, whether as a professional or as an amateur, that person was regarded socially as an eccentric. Ike no Taiga, one of Kyoto's most respected bunjin in painting (fig. 0.28) and calligraphy, was one such figure, deemed eccentric because, according to legend, he focused exclusively on his art. He is said to have been free from desire for fame, prestige or wealth and from jealousy or pretension.[25] Similarly, Yanagisawa Kien (1703–1758), a high-ranking samurai official of the Yamato Kōriyama domain (in present-day Nara prefecture), was seen as eccentric because he mastered over a dozen different arts, most notably painting, and because he took delight in meeting anyone who had a particular talent, however trivial and ephemeral. Kien would invite them to stay as guests in his home for extended periods, almost to the point of his financial ruin.[26]

Importantly, the term 'kijin' was not pejorative. A popular Kyoto publication, *Biographies of Modern Eccentrics* (*Kinsei kijin den*, prefaces dated 1788 and 1790) (fig. 0.29), recounts stories about many eccentrics in the Edo period, including Taiga and Kien. The book ran to many editions. The preface author, the Buddhist monk Jishū (Rikunyo, 1734–1801), explained the meaning of kijin: 'There are "*ki*" individuals (*ki naru hito*) among Confucian scholars, Zen monks, samurai, medical doctors, poets, calligraphers, painters and other various artists. In short, all these people are covered by "ki" (eccentricity), and it is difficult for others to tell what this person really is. Hence, they can only be described as kijin.'[27] In Japan at this time, the idealism of bunjin, the passion of shirōto and the excessiveness of kijin were not only accepted but also perceived positively in the realm of artistic engagement and cultural participation.

**0.28**
Ike no Taiga, *Rocky Landscape*,
from an album of 24 paintings
and calligraphy on fans, mid-
1700s. Fan painting, ink and light
colour on paper, pasted on gold
leaf and mica-covered paper.
30.5 × 56 cm (cover). British
Museum, London, 1981,0702,0.2.
Purchase funded by the
Brooke Sewell Bequest.

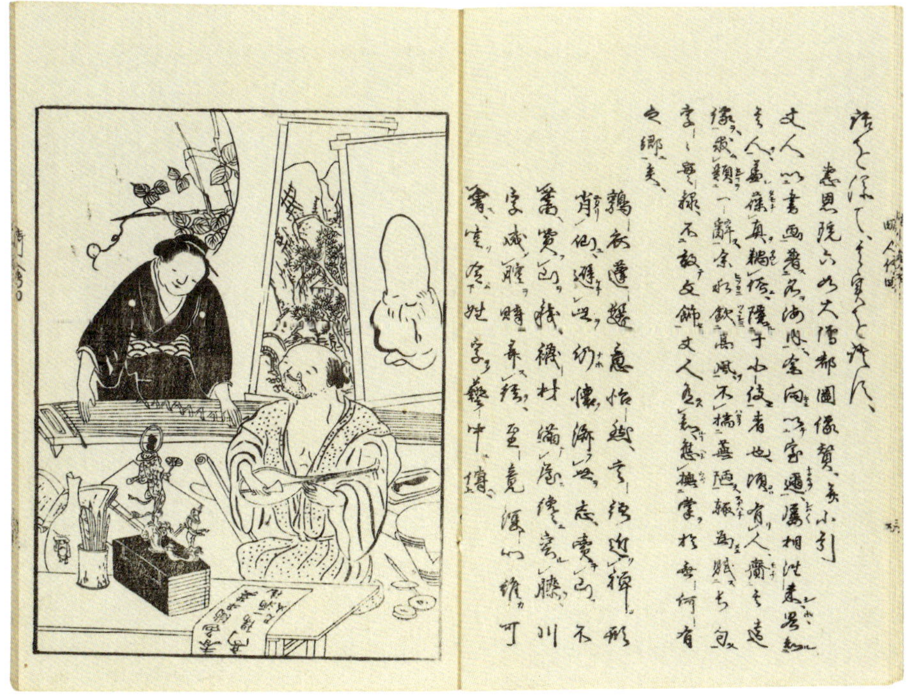

**0.29**
'Ike no Taiga and his wife
Gyokuran', from vol. 4 of
Mikuma Katen (artist) and Ban
Kōkei (author), *Biographies of
Modern Eccentrics* (*Kinsei kijin
den*), 5 vols, prefaces dated
1788 and 1790. Illustrated book,
woodblock. 25 × 17 cm (cover).
British Museum, London,
1979,0305,0.166.A.1–5. Ex-coll.:
Jack Hillier.



43

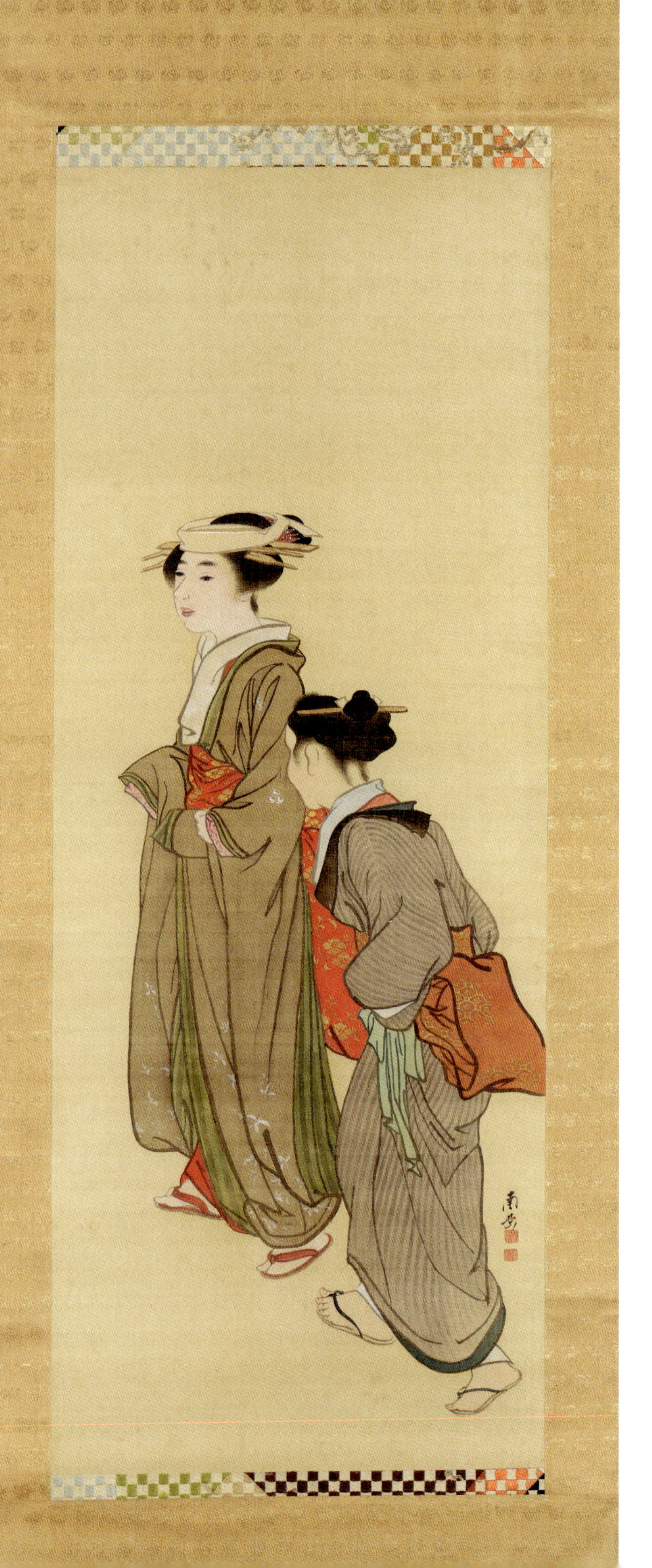

**0.30**
Watanabe Nangaku, *Beauty
and Her Maidservant
Walking Outdoors*, c. 1800.
Hanging scroll, ink, colour
and gold on silk. 204 × 62 cm.
British Museum, London,
1982,0701,0.10. Gift of Dr
and Mrs Michael Harari.

## The movement of artists, artworks and information

Those who became professional artists and those who pursued hobbies did not necessarily remain in their neighbourhoods. Domestic travel under the Tokugawa government was restricted to a degree, but it was allowed with the proper permits. Professional poets and artists who had pupils outside the cities would visit them. These pupils were often well off and able to accommodate their teachers for a prolonged visit. During their stay, the master could instruct locals and interact with fellow professionals and amateurs.

One of Ōkyo's most talented pupils was Watanabe Nangaku (1767–1813). Nangaku was known for painting figures, such as the two women depicted in the hanging scroll *Beauty and Her Maidservant Walking Outdoors* (fig. 0.30). He spent an extended period of time in Edo, probably through the connections he formed with haiku poets while in Kyoto, their networks linking the two cities (see fig. 5.31). Nangaku's sojourn in Edo was particularly significant because he transmitted Ōkyo's style to eastern Japan. Ōkyo's paintings garnered the highest praise from both aristocratic and bourgeois clients in Kyoto. The new Maruyama-school style seems to have suited some Edo artists. During Nangaku's almost three-year stay in Edo around 1802–4, he had several pupils, some of whom became prominent Maruyama-school-style artists. Suzuki Nanrei (1775–1844) and Ōnishi Chinnen (1792–1851), the latter being a very young artist at the time, were the most talented. Nanrei painted a handscroll of famous Japanese places in typically Maruyama-Shijō-style light brushwork (fig. 0.31), whereas Chinnen in his later career painted a delightful image of doves and morning glory in skilfully swift brushstrokes (fig. 0.32). Nangaku was active in haiku circles and interacted with major Edo haiku poets. The sharp-tongued Osaka author Ueda Akinari (1734–1809) (see p. 221) made satirical comments about Nangaku's journey to Edo and his extensive connections with Edo poets, hinting that they were for financial gain and flattery.[28]

Amateur poets also travelled within Japan, not ostensibly for poetry but usually for business. Participating in haiku groups was a means to meet like-minded people during a business trip. One such individual was the businessman Yamatoya Zen'emon (pen name Ōemaru, 1722–1805), who managed a hikyaku (courier) service based in Osaka that linked eastern and western Japan.[29] Hikyaku services were essential not only for daily business but also for the formation of nationwide networks of haiku, kyōka and other poetry genres, as verse composition began to increase in popularity. It is likely, for example, that contributions to a haiku poetry anthology to be published in Kyoto from a geographically distant location would have been delivered by couriers (fig. 0.33).

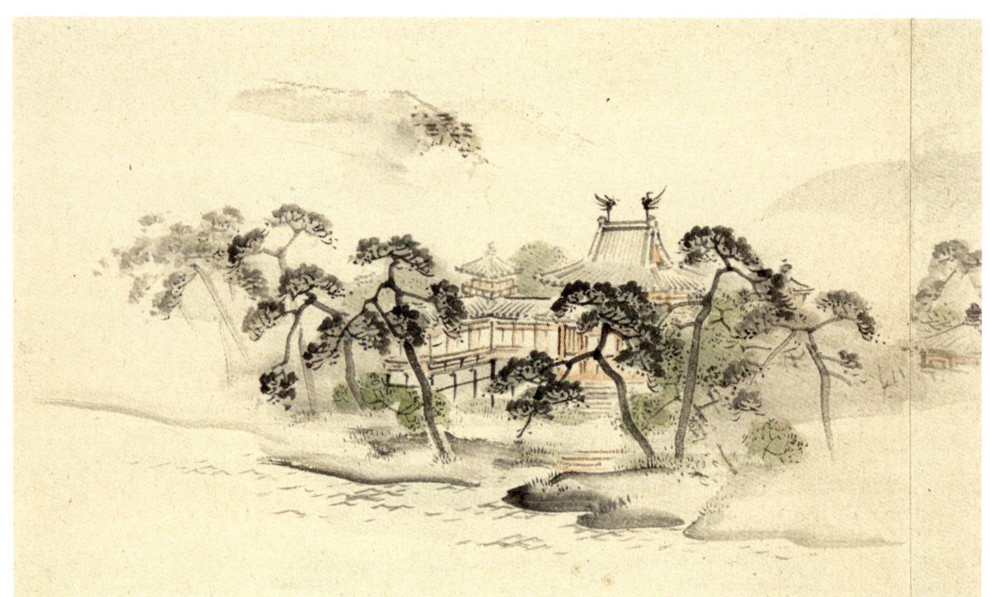



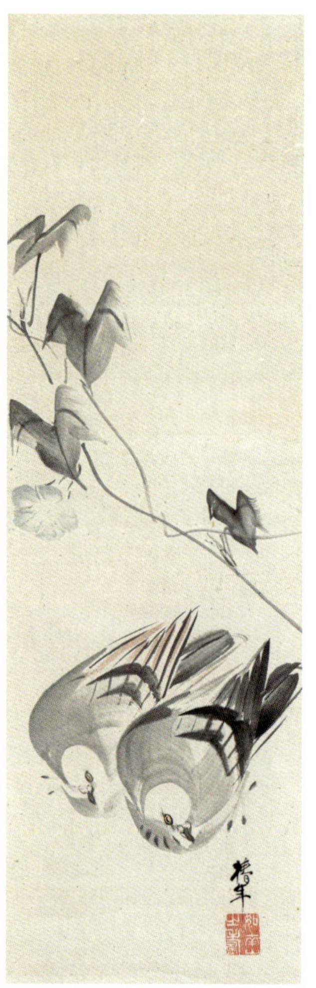



People, information, goods and artworks therefore travelled overland and along the domestic sea trade routes, most notably the westward maritime trade route. These linked with Osaka and stretched as far as Hokkaido via the northern coasts, with stops at ports along the way (see p. 76). One striking object representative of this trade activity is an armour surcoat (*jinbaori*) made from painted paper, wool and silk (fig. 0.34). The painting of a dragon emerging from rough water was composed by Gan Sei (1827–1867), the third son of Gan Tai (1785–1865; see figs 4.6, 4.28) and a grandson of Gan Ku (see figs 3.20–3.21), in Kyoto. The inscriptions on the reverse side of the lapels reveal the name of the owner of this garment: a certain samurai Satō Yoshinori in the Shōnai domain (in present-day Yamagata prefecture). The great distance between Kyoto and Shōnai suggests that the commission was possible through the commercial sea trade routes. This is not an isolated instance of artworks by Kyoto and Osaka artists connecting with northern domains. The reputations of the artists in the cities were disseminated around Japan via commerce, a strong driving force for cultural interactions and diverse personal ties fostered by means of salon culture networks.

To explore the fascinating and complex nature of salon culture from around 1750 to 1900, the chapters of this book focus on five broad themes: the three key cities of Kyoto, Osaka and Edo and their role in the phenomenon (chapter 1); everyday life during this period and how it is revealed in art

**0.33**
An image of an Edo-period
courier (hikyaku), from
*Who's Who from Myriad
Houses* (*Banka jinmei roku*),
vol. 5, 1813. Illustrated book,
woodblock. 26 × 19 cm (cover).
British Museum, London,
1991,1112,0.75.5. Ex-coll.:
Dr Scott Johnson.

The poem by Hira reads:
*asakaze to / akekawaru ma o /
tsuyu no tama*
jewel dew drops / between
dawn / and morning breeze

**0.34**
Gan Sei, armour surcoat
(*jinbaori*) with a painted dragon
design (reverse), 1847–67. Ink,
light colour and gold on paper,
silk and wool. 91 cm (height).
British Museum, London,
2017,3028.1. Purchase made
possible by the JTI Japanese
Acquisition Fund.

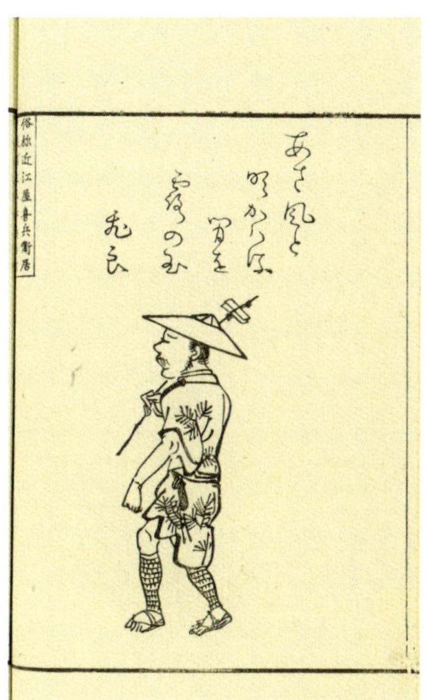

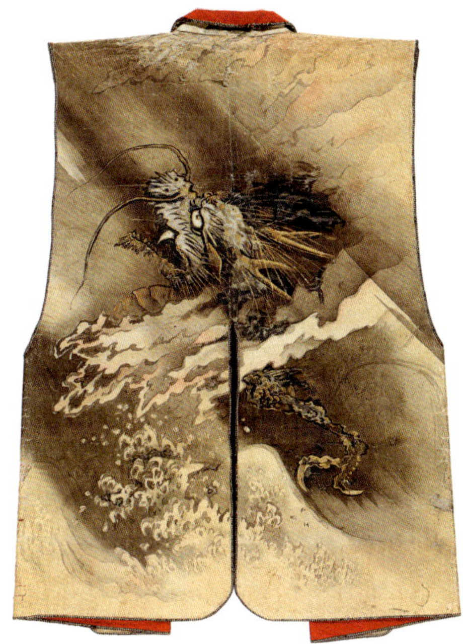

(chapter 2); artists' depictions of nature (chapter 3); the influence of China in Japan (chapter 4); and the interplay of poetry and image in artistic works (chapter 5). A series of short vignettes focuses on specific topics that illuminate salon culture – from specific figures such as Kenkadō (see pp. 204–6), to the practice of adopting pen and art names (see pp. 48–9), to the legacy of salon culture in modern times (see pp. 80–1). Together they reveal surprising connections and intimate stories as well as showcasing exceptional works of art.

An engagement with culture resulted in relationships between individuals whose paths otherwise may not have crossed. Local and national networks formed an infrastructure that supported the development of lively art scenes and subsequently art and literary production in Edo-period Japan. The phenomenon of mass participation in cultural salons began at this time, peaking in the nineteenth century and linking people from different walks of life. It continued into the twentieth century, changing and modifying some aspects while retaining others, and even today remains to a considerable extent a core element of Japanese society, adapting to diverse trends: artistic, social, technological, philosophical and political.[30] The products of these cultural salons, as this book explores, offer us windows into the past through which we can witness communal enjoyment, friendship, creativity and a zest for life – all through the pursuit of the arts.

# 'Art names': an escape from social status
## C. Andrew Gerstle

To understand early modern Japan, it is crucial to consider the social status system (*mibun seido*). The separation of samurai as a distinct status above other groups was established in the late sixteenth century under the government of Toyotomi Hideyoshi (1537–1598) before the advent of the Tokugawa shogunate in 1603. The Tokugawa instituted the rule that households had to register their members at a temple according to the status of the family head.

Following Chinese precedents, the status system was hierarchical.[31] In China, scholar-bureaucrats were at the top; in Japan it was samurai. The emperor and Kyoto courtiers were notionally above the status system, although in practice they were restricted to their traditional residences in Kyoto. Samurai, as a rule, resided in castle towns. Beneath samurai came farmers on the land, then, in towns and cities, artisans and merchants. Shinto priests, Buddhist monks and physicians were in a separate category. Below all these were performers, sex workers and certain occupations considered to be unclean. Individuals were generally expected to remain within their birth status. Each status group was further subdivided into ranks.

The view that the 'samurai, farmer, artisan, merchant' (*shi-nō-kō-shō*) hierarchy was rigid and constrictive has been challenged in recent years, however. Studies have proposed that while samurai status was firmly on top, below that there was in fact no particular distinction of rank among farmers, artisans and merchants.[32] But although historians have now come to see the system as more fluid, the consensus is still that it was highly discriminatory and constrained individuals no matter what their station in life.

The Tokugawa system depended on this putative social status hierarchy for its legitimacy; only samurai could collect taxes and rule. The system did not go unchallenged. In 1789 Nakai Chikuzan (1730–1804), a commoner who became head of the Kaitokudō, an academy of Chinese studies in Osaka founded in 1724 (see below and pp. 62, 64), presented Matsudaira Sadanobu (1758–1829), *de facto* ruler of the Tokugawa government (1787–93), with the radical idea to abandon the privileged position of the samurai as part of an extensive package of proposals for reform. Sadanobu did not accept Nakai's proposals.

After the fall of the Tokugawa and the restoration of Meiji imperial rule in 1868, the samurai's privileged status was dissolved almost immediately.

What was life like on the ground in early modern Japan's highly stratified society? The historian David Howell argues that the status system – with its fundamental unit being the 'household' – was originally exploited by the Tokugawa government to marshal resources for the authorities. By the late eighteenth century the system had become generally accepted by the population.[33] As long as an individual followed the outward signs prescribed for their station, for instance, appropriate dress, the system seems to have been quite relaxed in everyday life. In legal matters, however, distinctions could be strictly enforced, as seen in the government's arbitrary confiscation in 1790 of some of the possessions of the Osaka scholar and artist Kimura Kenkadō (see pp. 42, 127, 204–6). Kenkadō had a famous private collection of objects and a library, which were bolstered by his numerous contacts in China and Korea, as well as Japanese contemporaries from all around the country. Low-status individuals, including kabuki actors, enjoyed relative freedom. But at times of government clampdown, as during the Tenpō reforms (1841–3) (see p. 67), they could be and were punished indiscriminately. Two top kabuki actors – Ichikawa Danjūrō VII (1791–1859) from Edo and Nakamura Tomijūrō II (1786–1855) from Osaka – were banished to set an example to performers not to live extravagantly above their low station. In this case each of the two stars simply moved to the other's city and ironically, despite the government's intentions, became even more successful.

Within this complex hierarchical system, scholarship and the arts came to be a kind of utopia, a 'virtual space' outside the status world. As described by the scholar Maeda Tsutomu, this was enhanced by institutions like private academies for Chinese studies, such as the Kaitokudō, which developed the fundamental precepts that everyone participated as equals and could interact without regard to wealth or status.[34] In the arts, there are two common principles throughout East Asia that support artistic practice. The first is the belief that the seeds of poetry and art come from within the heart, and that all of us have the ability to create art – a very different idea

**0.35**

Anonymous artist, *Twelve Named Amateur Poets*, c. 1850. Surimono (fragment), colour woodblock. 19.5 × 48.9 cm. British Museum, London, 2021,3013.840. Purchase made possible by the JTI Japanese Acquisition Fund. Ex-coll.: Dr Scott Johnson.

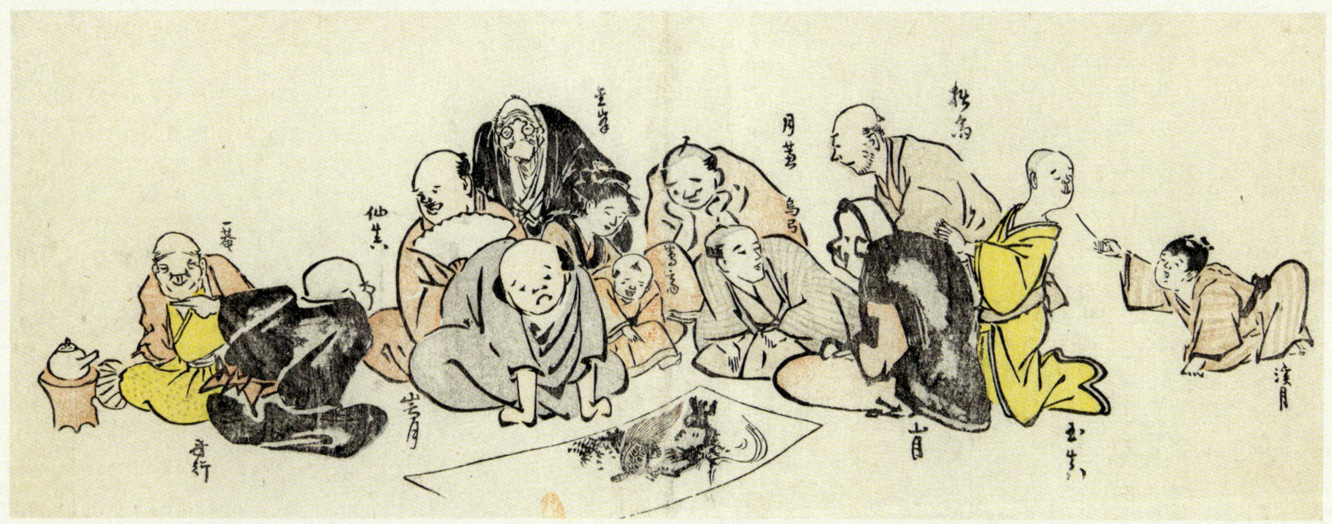

from the Western tradition of the muse that inspires the poet-artist as an especially gifted individual. The second is the prominent concept of the literatus (J: bunjin). Fundamental to this idea, which originated in China as *wenren*, is the importance of artistic activity regardless of one's station or vocation. An extension of this is the encouragement of amateur (shirōto) aesthetic pursuits more broadly. The historian Moriya Takeshi has shown how extensive engagement with the arts was in Japan from the late seventeenth century onwards, ranging from poetry and painting, to tea and flower arranging, to dance and theatrical chanting, as well as medicine.[35]

Traditionally, since the twelfth century, artists and writers would take a pen or art name (gō) when pursuing their vocation full time. From the seventeenth century onwards, this custom spread more widely, permitting individuals to take part as an 'artist-performer' within a cultural circle, whether a professional or an amateur. In some traditional arts, such as the tea ceremony, individuals were granted an 'art' name by the master, or *iemoto* (literally 'family head'), of the school. An art name offered an escape from one's societal status – an alternate identity – allowing individuals to interact notionally without reference to status. Individuals active in different cultural circles could have several art names, while a professional painter, for example, could also have a pen name for 'amateur' activities such as haiku or *jōruri* (*bunraku*) puppet theatre chanting. The historian Owaki Hidekazu has emphasised the fluidity in practice of 'official' names and status, pointing out that commoners serving samurai households could temporarily take a surname and the trappings of status, such as carrying a sword.[36] The term for this during the era was 'one person, two names' (*ichinin ryōmei*).

For most, then, the pursuit of an art, be it as an amateur (fig. 0.35) or as a professional, was not merely a pastime but also provided access into cultural circles that linked to networks throughout Japan. This framework of egalitarian alternative identity therefore presented many opportunities for enhanced social interaction. It also encouraged an individual to pursue their chosen art with vigour, to proudly take their turn composing a poem, performing music or brushing a painting, even as an amateur. In this way, 'hobby arts' (*yūgei*) came to form an essential feature of life under the Tokugawa system and into modern times. This fostered a strong societal framework that supported the production of paintings, prints, illustrated books and the theatre arts.

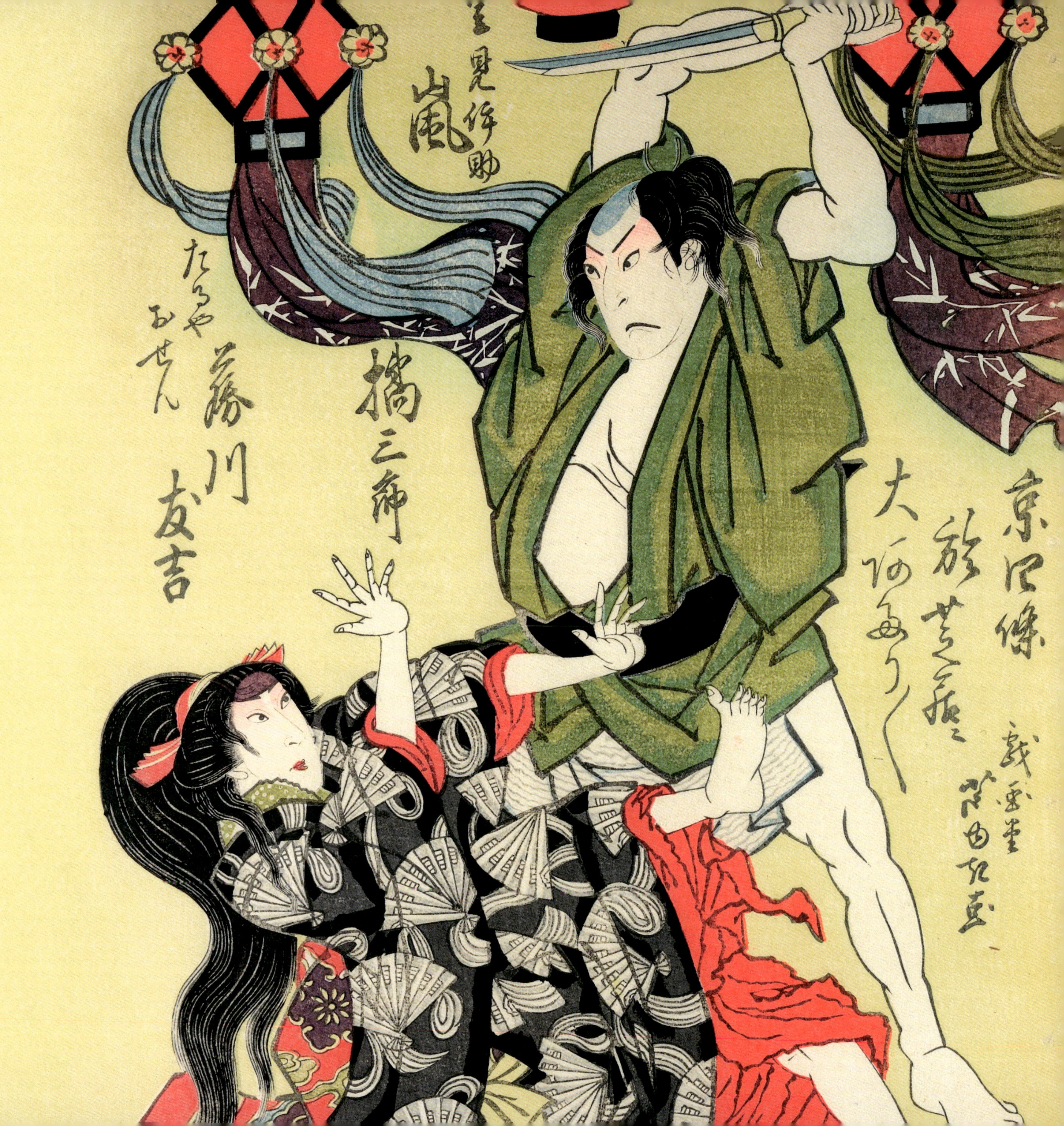
嵐伴助
橋三師
勝川　友吉
京口條
大河内

*C. Andrew Gerstle*

# 1 Cities and the performing arts

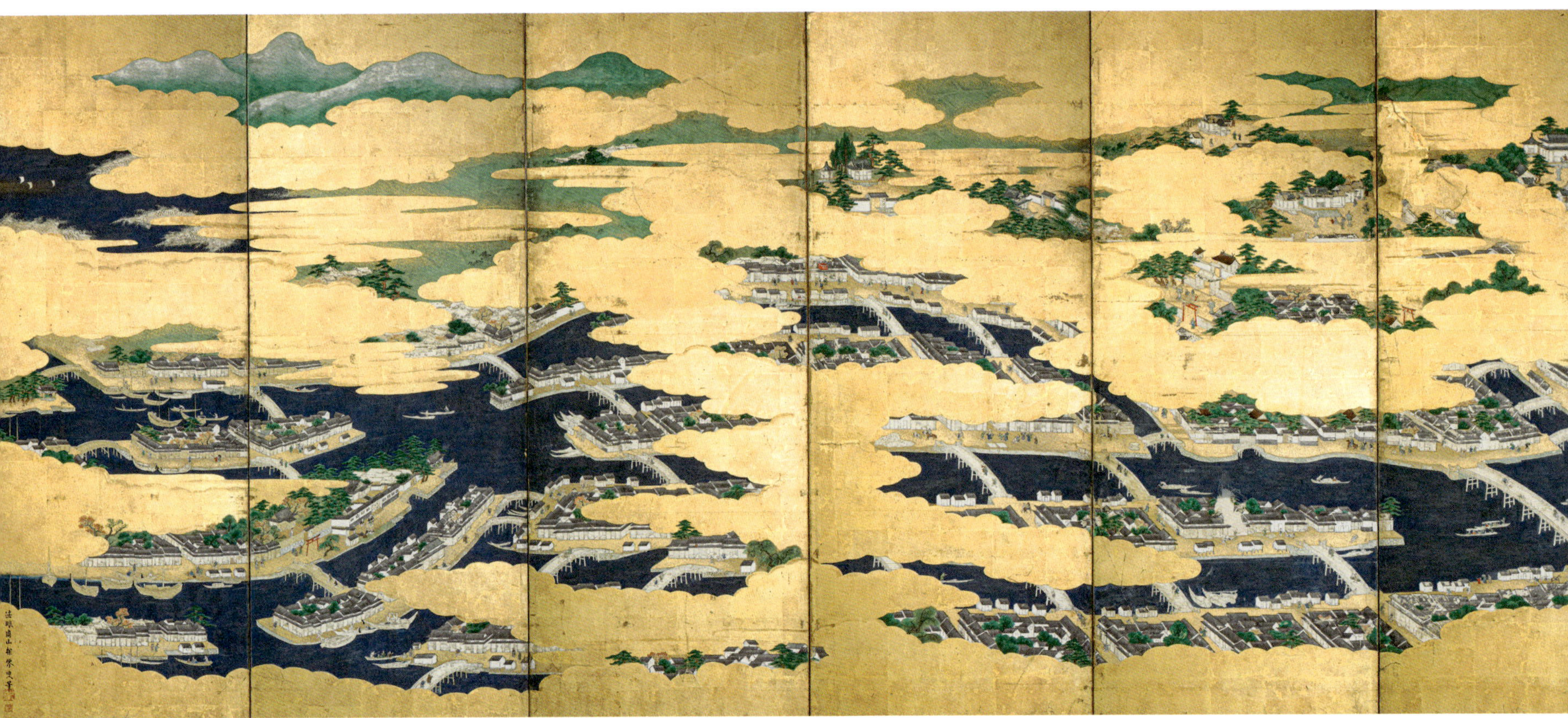



**Previous page**
Gigadō Ashiyuki, *Arashi Kitsusaburō II as Satomi Isuke* (right) *and Fujikawa Tomokichi II as the Cooper's Daughter O-Sen* (left), in the play *Masterpiece: Murder at Dawn* (*Meisaku kiriko no akebono*) from a performance in Kyoto, from an album of 104 sheets, 1826. Colour woodblock. 37 × 25.8 cm (each). British Museum, London, 1983,0523,0.1.19.

**1.1**
Yoshimura Shūzan, *Panorama of Osaka*, c. 1750. Six-panel folding screen, ink, colour and gold leaf on paper. 174.8 × 363.2 cm. British Museum, London, 2001,0627,0.1. Purchase funded by the Brooke Sewell Bequest.

Early modern Japan was relatively closed off from the outside world until the 1850s. While objects of cultural production (such as Chinese and Dutch books and goods) and a small number of individuals (mostly Chinese, Dutch and Korean) regularly entered Japan, until 1866 its people could not legally return if they left the country. This policy might have led Japanese culture to stagnate, but the arts in fact flourished during this period. The variety, quality and quantity of paintings, print art, theatre and literature created at this time is remarkable. The impact of Japanese arts on the wider world, when exported in vast amounts to the West from the late nineteenth century – the cultural movement known as Japonisme – was also considerable.[1]

There were two principal reasons for this creative vitality. The first was the formation during the seventeenth century of a vibrant national economy with interaction and competition among regions, especially among the three main cities of Kyoto, Osaka and Edo. Coastal ships going in and out of Osaka circulated all around the archipelago. Each of the three cities developed distinctive characteristics (figs 1.1–1.3). The second was the active

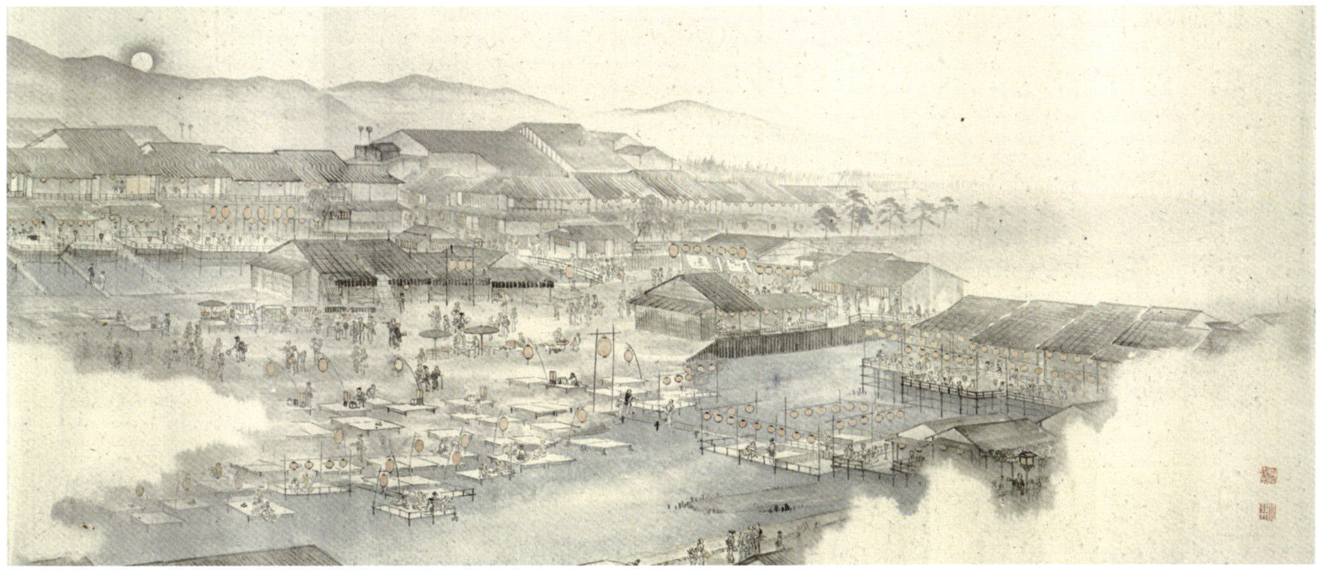

**1.2**
Maruyama Ōkyo, *Kamo Riverbed at the Fourth Avenue* (*Shijō-gawara*), from *Sixteen Views of Kyoto*, 1773. Handscroll, ink and colour on paper. 31.7 × 59.2 cm. British Museum, London, 1967,1016,0.1.

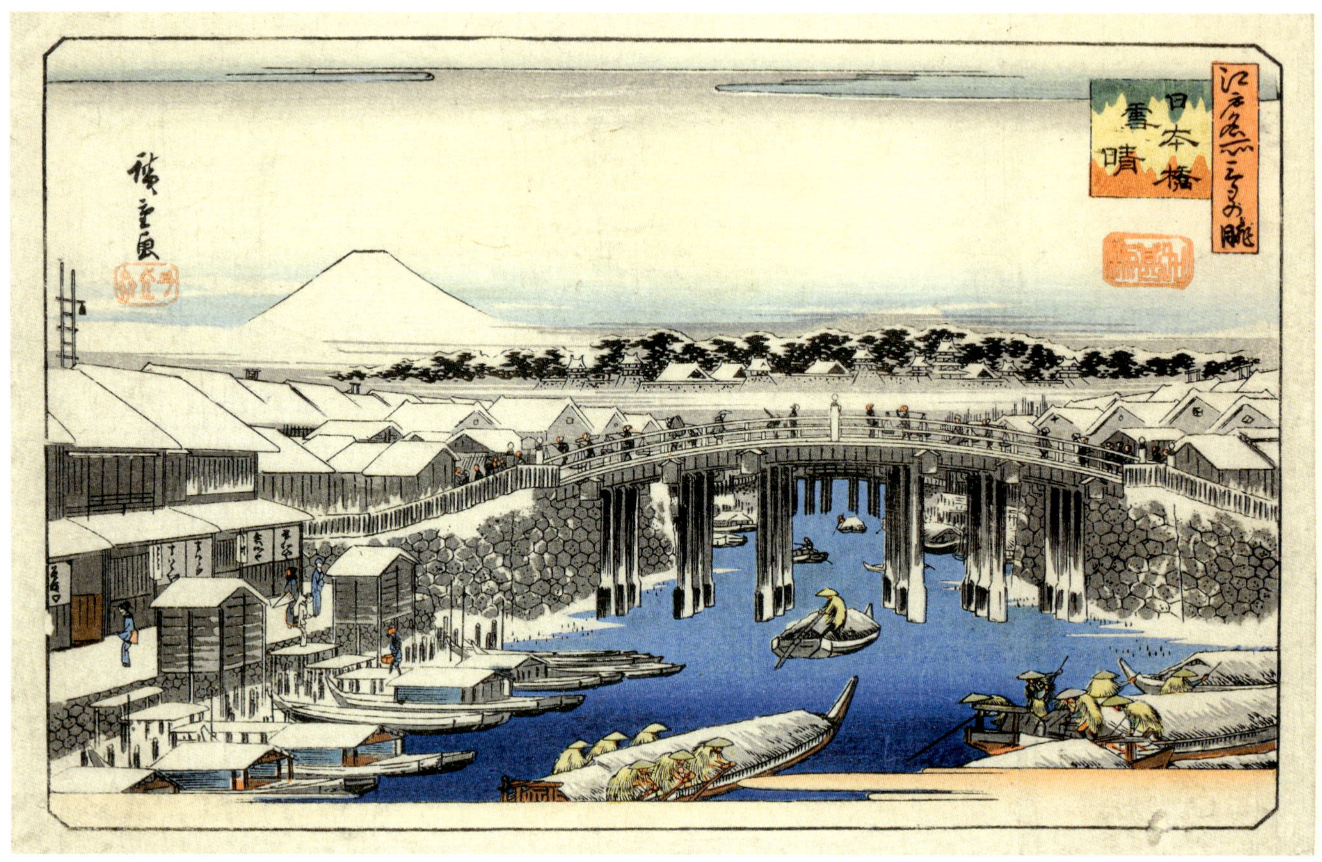

encouragement of participation in the arts (*yūgei*), traditionally an essential practice for the upper classes, which was promoted afresh by the Tokugawa military government and which spread widely in general society as literacy rates rose from the mid-eighteenth century onwards. Practising an art usually meant assuming an alternate identity under a pen or art name (*gō*) when joining a group under a master, and involved a collaborative 'salon culture'.

**1.3**
Utagawa Hiroshige, *Clearing Weather after Snow at Nihonbashi* (*Nihonbashi yuki-bare*), *c.* 1840s. Colour woodblock. 25.3 × 36.8 cm. British Museum, London, 1948,0410,0.49. Gift of Henry Bergen.

## A tale of three cities: Kyoto, Osaka and Edo

Around 1800, Japan's three major cities, all under direct Tokugawa government control, ranked as important world urban centres in terms of population, with Edo at about a million inhabitants and Osaka and Kyoto each at around 350,000 to 400,000. Major castle towns such as Nagoya, Kanazawa, Kumamoto, Sendai, Hiroshima and Fukuoka were smaller but still urban in terms of their population density. Wheeled vehicles were generally forbidden – a policy imposed by the shogunate to limit opportunities for rebellion – but travel between cities was well organised, with an infrastructure of post stations and inns, and well-developed mail and courier services. Literacy levels were high, even by western European standards, and itinerant lending libraries (*kashi-hon'ya*) reached all corners of the country. Furthermore, the alternate attendance system (*sankin kōtai*) of requiring feudal lords and their extensive retinues to spend alternating periods of time in their Edo residence and at their home castle meant that remote areas also interacted with Edo and other sites along the way, as many samurai journeyed back and forth along highways such as the East Coast Road (Tōkaidō) between Kyoto and Edo.

The fourth city directly under Tokugawa government control was Nagasaki, the port at the far west of the island of Kyushu in south-western Japan (fig. 1.4). A town of about 40,000 to 50,000 people, officially Nagasaki was the sole international gateway for ships and trade until the 1850s, and home to a substantial Chinese and much smaller Dutch merchant community (fig. 1.5). Nagasaki was therefore the key venue for those seeking interaction with the outside world, be it China or the Netherlands. It was particularly significant for the visual and literary arts, and Japanese artists were able to meet Chinese people in person there and learn about new continental trends. Increasingly, from the second half of the eighteenth century, Nagasaki was also a centre for 'Dutch' (that is, European) studies (*rangaku*).

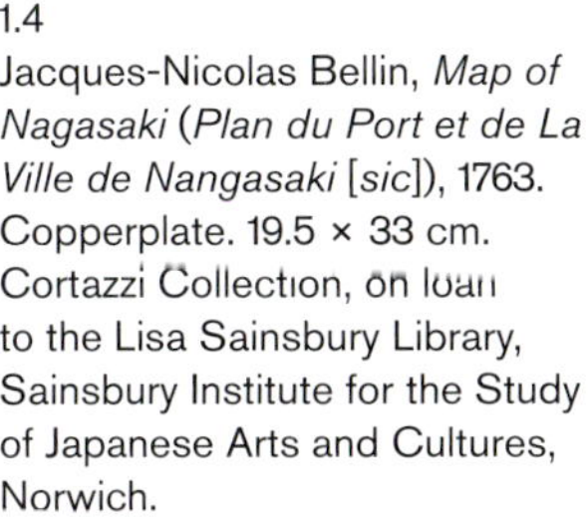

1.4
Jacques-Nicolas Bellin, *Map of Nagasaki* (*Plan du Port et de La Ville de Nangasaki* [*sic*]), 1763. Copperplate. 19.5 × 33 cm. Cortazzi Collection, on loan to the Lisa Sainsbury Library, Sainsbury Institute for the Study of Japanese Arts and Cultures, Norwich.

This French map shows the deep port leading to the small artificial island Dejima, residence of the Dutch traders. To the north is the much larger Chinese community, host to both long-term residents and short-term traders. Military installations are shown on both sides of the bay.

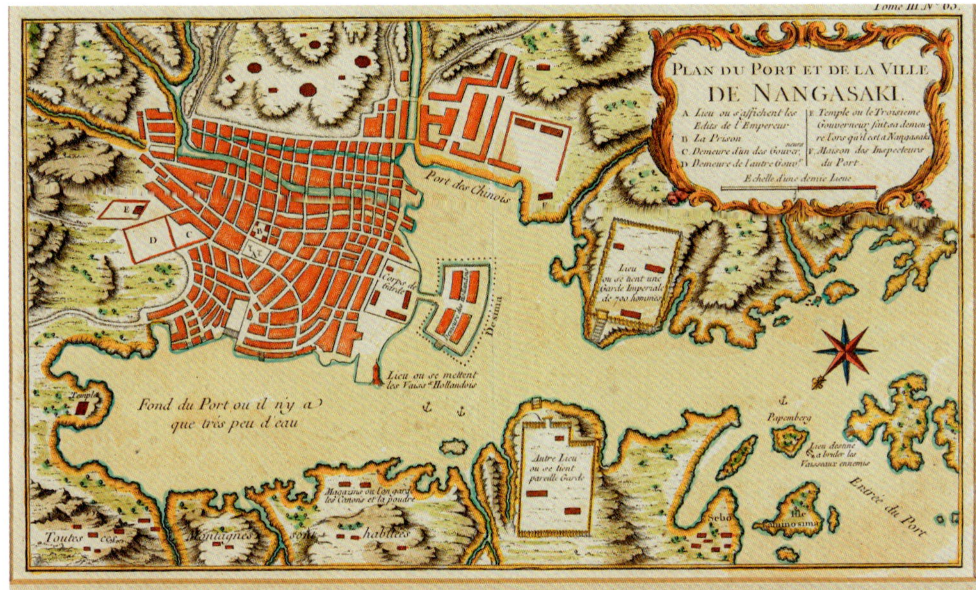

There was – and still is – a clear sense among Japanese people that the three major cities are different. Each had distinctive key traits. Kyoto was an inland city surrounded by mountains, an ancient capital that was home to the emperor and the imperial palace, the residences of courtier families and large communities of artisans, and a traditional centre for artists (fig. 1.6). At the time, it was considered 'feminine' in contrast to 'masculine' Edo, and few samurai lived there. There were many small businesses, but it was not a centre of commerce or financial services. Instead it was the location of the headquarters of many Buddhist sects and extensive temple complexes. Nijō Castle was the base for the Tokugawa military.

By contrast, Osaka was a major port and centre of national trade with a network of canals and rivers (fig. 1.7). It was the country's financial centre and home to rice and commodities markets. Osaka had a commercial culture with an atmosphere of self-reliance and respect for merit, and it was the primary

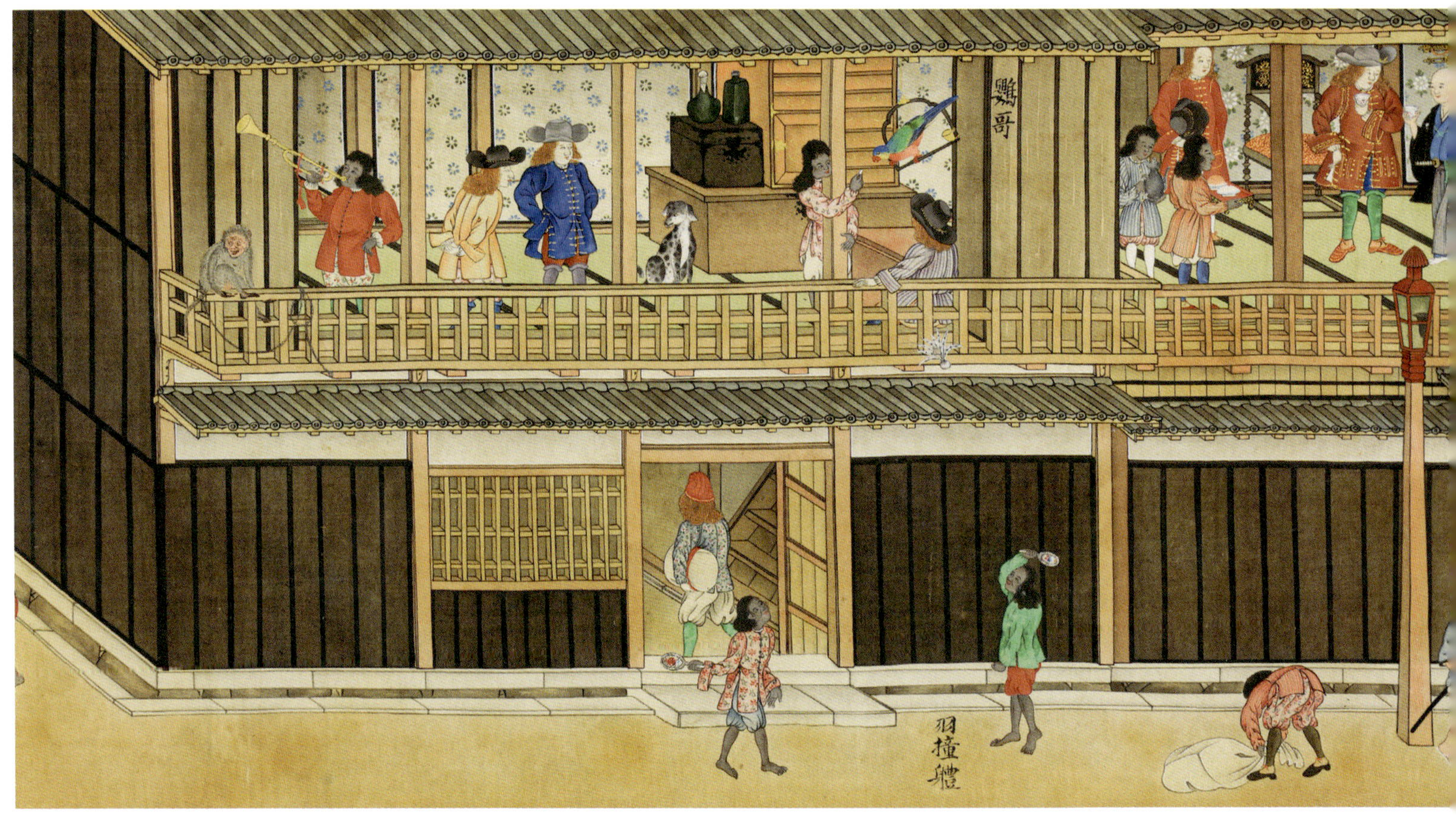

moneylender to samurai lords. Samurai composed only about 1.5 per cent of the city's population and there were no courtiers. Osaka Castle was the site of Tokugawa military hegemony over the city.

Edo, in eastern Japan, was also a port city and the Tokugawa political capital; more than half of the population was samurai (fig. 1.8). The vast Edo Castle – the site of today's imperial palace – dominated the cityscape, and samurai properties comprised 60 per cent of the city. In Edo rank, ritual and status were pre-eminently important. Originally formed from an immigrant population from other regions, the city had a rough, brash image. With the large number of samurai, it was considered a consumer rather than producer culture.

All three cities came to be major publishing centres, with Kyoto flourishing initially, then Osaka and finally Edo from the second half of the eighteenth century. Edo is distinctive for its vast quantities of visual works – such as *ukiyo-e* ('pictures of the floating world') prints (see pp. 98–9), illustrated books and

**1.5**
After Watanabe Shūseki, *Scenes of Life in the Dutch Factory in Nagasaki* (detail), late 1700s. Handscroll, ink and colour on silk. 33 × 406 cm. British Museum, London, 1944,1014,0.22. Purchase funded by Marjorie Coldwell Fund.

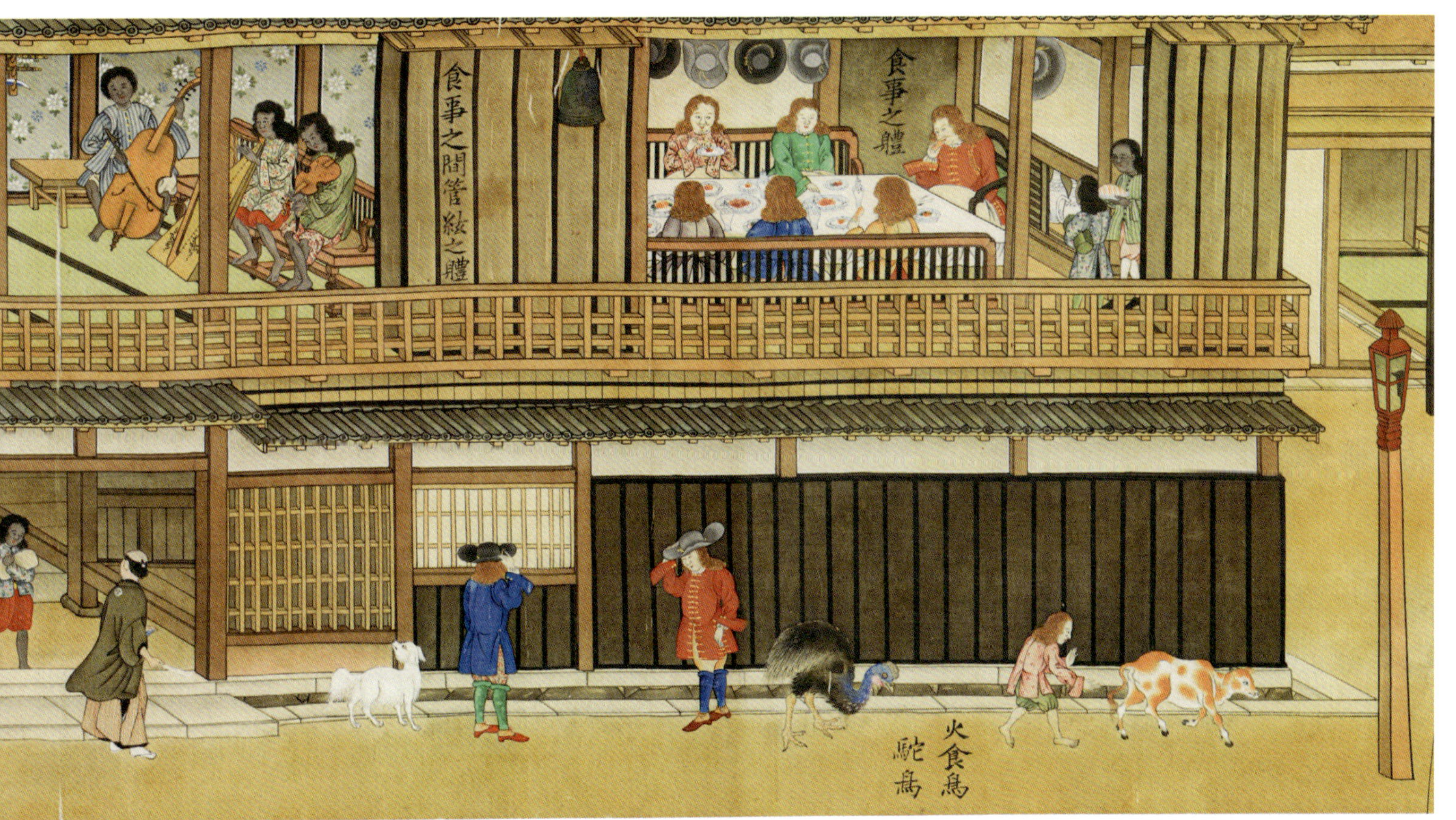

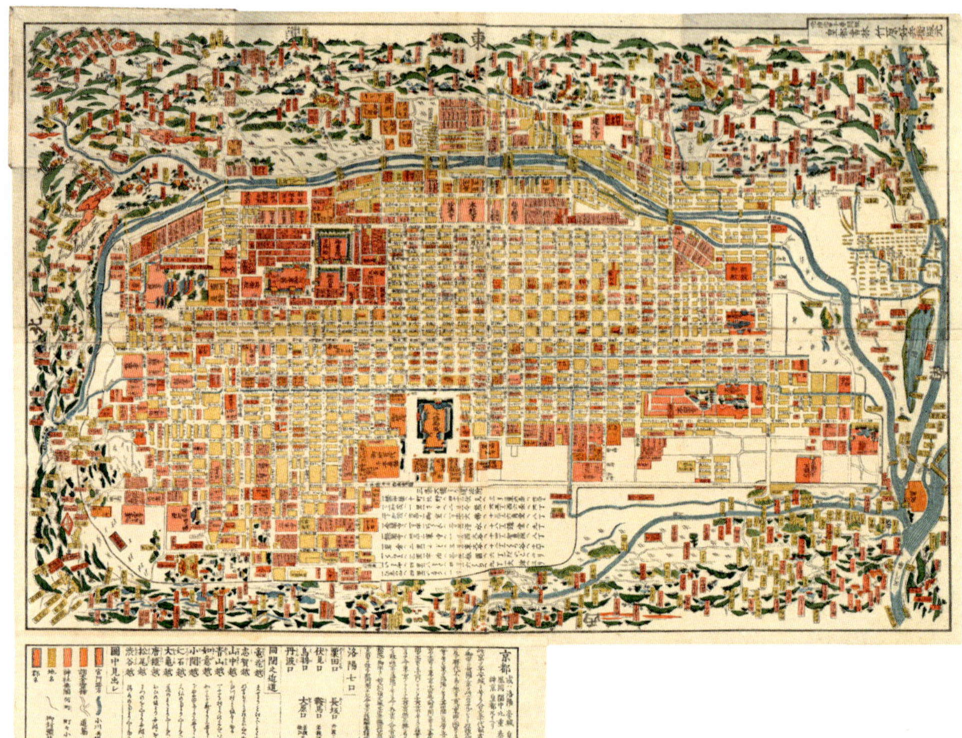

**1.6**
Takehara Kōbē, *Detailed Map of Kyoto and its Suburbs* (*Rakuchū rakugai machimachi shōmyō: taisei Kyō saiken ezu*), 1864. Colour woodblock. 60 × 90 cm with 10 × 50 cm extension. University of British Columbia Library, Vancouver.

Laid out with north to the left, this map shows imperial and courtier residences in dark red; Tokugawa Nijō Castle and samurai residences in orange; and religious sites in light red. The Kamo River, running north–south, is at the top. Kyoto is shown surrounded by mountains with many religious institutions.

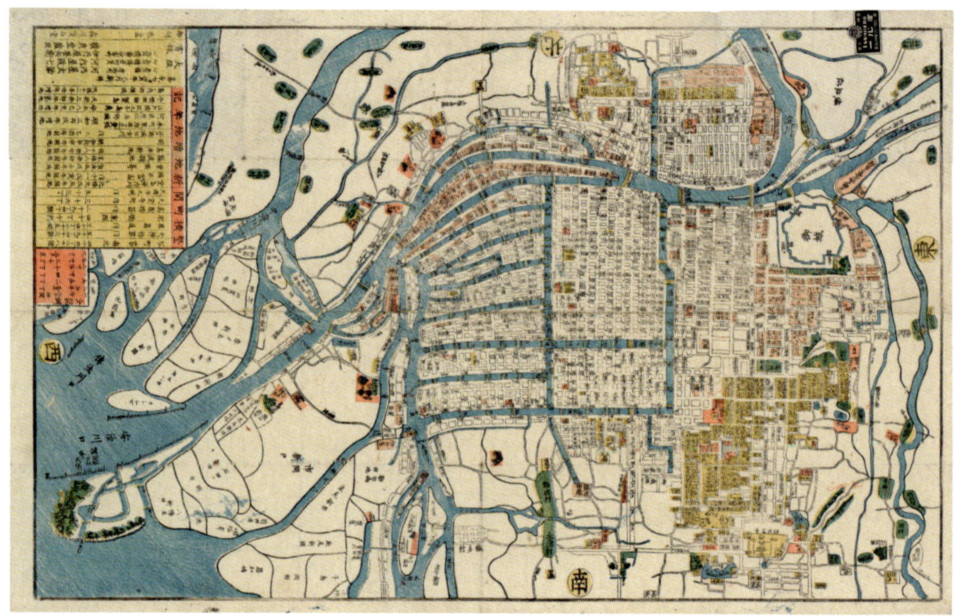

**1.7**
Morikawa Hōbyakudō, *Scaled Plan of Osaka, Revised in Ka'ei Era* ([*Ka'ei kaisei*] *Bunken Ōsaka zu*), 1854. Colour woodblock. 40.4 × 65 cm. University of British Columbia Library, Vancouver.

Osaka has many rivers and canals. Its castle is located at the confluence of rivers at the top-right of this map. Dōjima, home to the *daimyō* warehouses, is shown in a light red crescent shape at top-centre. The theatre district is along Dōtonbori, the horizontal canal at bottom. The temple district is at bottom-right in yellow.

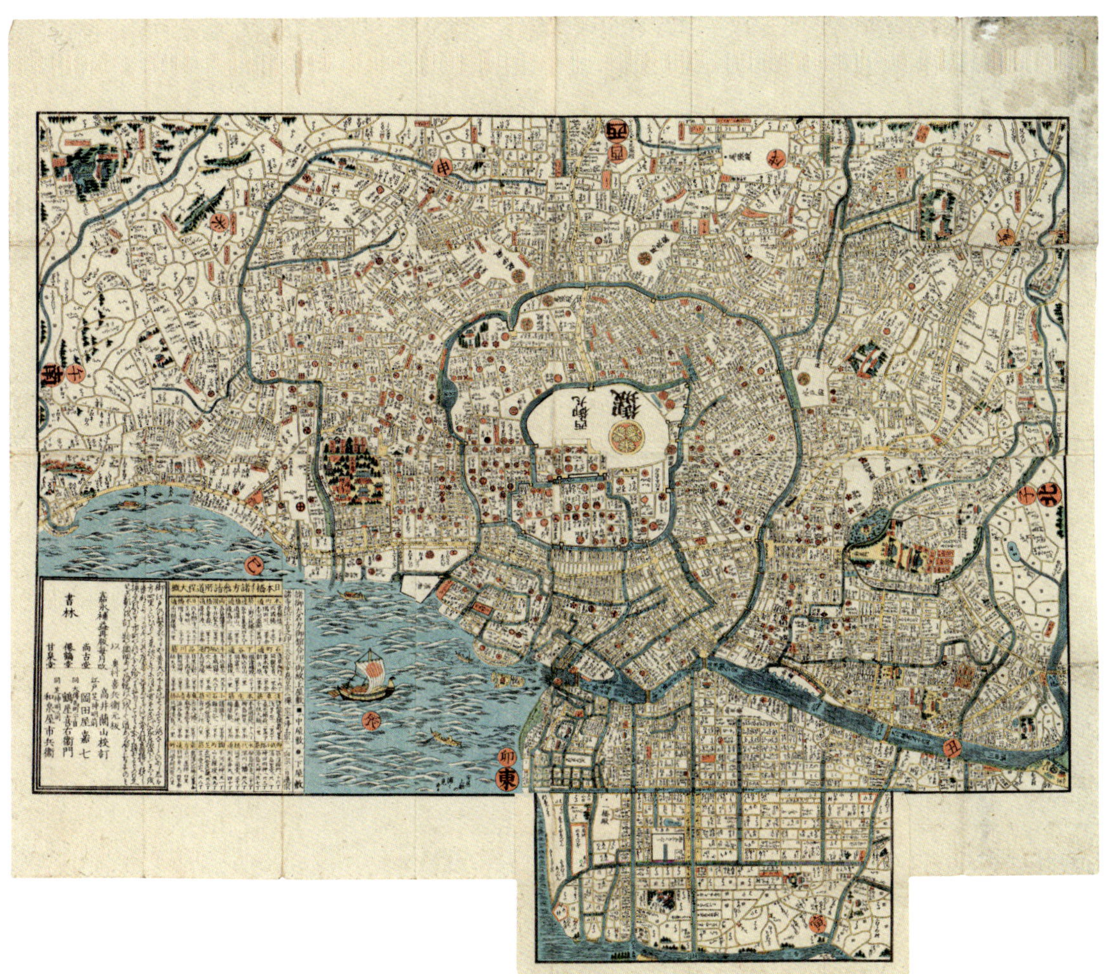

**1.8**
Okumura Kihē (artist), Takai
Ranzan (editor), *Plan of
Peaceful Edo* (*Taihō on-Edo
ezu*), 1848. Colour woodblock.
55.7 × 86 cm. University of
British Columbia Library,
Vancouver.

Laid out with north to the right,
this map shows Edo Castle
and the samurai residences
at centre with moats radiating
outwards. Nihonbashi is east
of the castle. The Yoshiwara
pleasure quarter and the theatre
district are at bottom-right near
the Sumida River.

graphic fiction – compared with Kyoto and Osaka, where illustrated books were issued but traditionally focused more on text than image. Edo predominated in the release of large-format colour kabuki actor prints, while Kyoto and Osaka led in the biannual production of detailed actor critique books that covered performances in all three cities, as well as discussions of the plays and acting skills (fig. 1.9). Publishers in Osaka distributed texts for kabuki and jōruri (bunraku) puppet plays, even for performances originating in Edo.

A contemporaneous perspective on the three cities exhibits a sharp, critical consciousness of the differences among them. *Valuable Notes on Playwriting* ([*Sakusha shikihō*] *Kezairoku*, 1801), a guide for kabuki playwrights, contrasts the types of plays staged in the three cities:

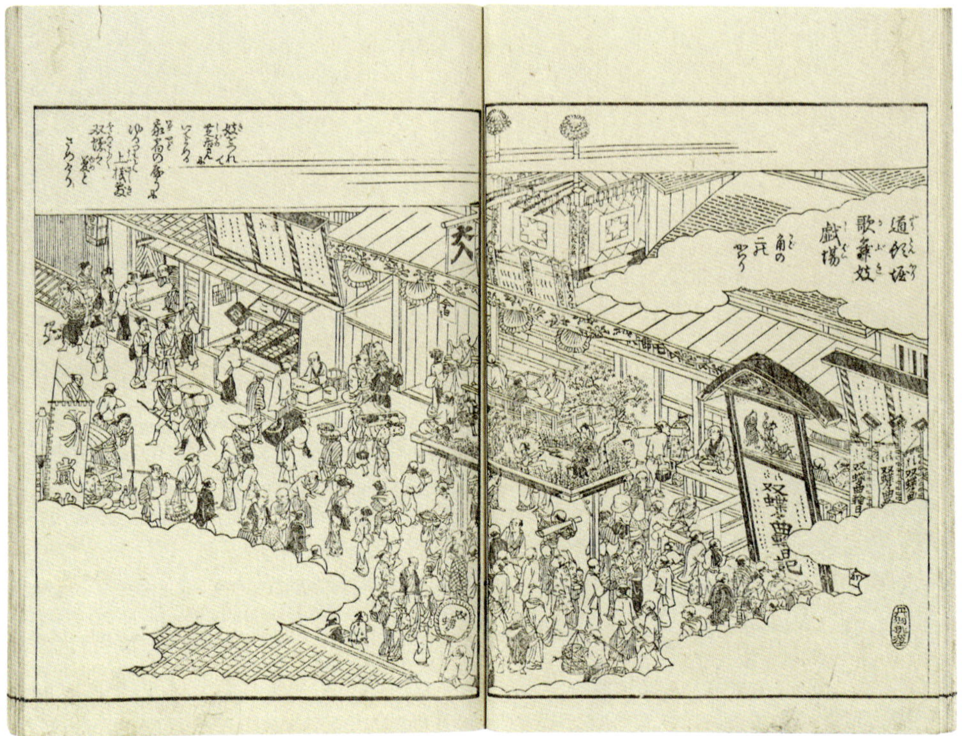

**1.9**
Niwa Tōkei (artist), 'Kado Theatre in Dōtonbori', from vol. 5 of Akisato Ritō (author) and 7 artists, *Illustrated Guide to Famous Places in Settsu Province* (*Settsu meisho zue*), 12 vols, 1798. Illustrated book, woodblock. 25.6 × 17.9 cm (cover). British Museum, London, 2002,0815,0.2.1–12. Purchase funded by the Brooke Sewell Bequest.

The people of Kyoto are gentle and in conformity with their nature, about 60 per cent of their plots have always been about love affairs. On the whole, these plays are extremely calm and lacking in vigour. They carry the aura of a beautiful woman, and if we were to liken them to a part of the human body, it would be the skin.

Edoites are rough and in conformity with their nature, 70 per cent of their plots have been grand *daimyō* [samurai lord]-house period plays, rough and carefree. They are rigidly constructed and masculine in their appeal. They carry the aura of the samurai and can be likened to bones (fig. 1.10).

Osaka people care about reason and consistency, and in conformity with their nature, 80 per cent of their plots have been logically constructed. Because their plots are often tortuous, overly complex, they can be boring. They carry the aura of the gallant dandy and can be likened to flesh (fig. 1.11)[2]

The author goes on to state that playwrights mix aspects of the styles of each city, but nevertheless each still retains its essential characteristics.

Hirose Kyokusō (1807–1863), a scholar originally from Bungo province in northern Kyushu, spent periods in Kyoto, Osaka and Edo. He also characterised the three cities in his collection of essays *Notes from the 'Hall of Nine Katsura Trees among the Grass' (Kyūkei-sōdō zuihitsu)*, composed most likely in the 1850s:

> Kyoto people are tender; Osakans are greedy; Edoites are proud. Most Kyotoites are proud; Osakans tend to be intense; Edoites tend to be impulsive. Kyotoites revere their land; the meaning of this is that both Edo and Osaka are considered to be rustic. From Kyoto's perspective, nowhere can match the capital as a place to live.
>
> Osaka folk revere wealth; the meaning of this is that though the courtiers [*kuge*] have the highest status and a stipend, they are poor and curry favour with us businessmen. Osakans consider there is nothing more important than wealth in this world.
>
> Whereas Edo people revere rank and status – the daimyō lords are poor these days – they don't consider poverty shameful. Edoites aim to advance up the ranks and gain recognition, even if it means borrowing money to do it. This is how the people differ in the three cities.
>
> Countryfolk should definitely visit the three cities. If they don't see Kyoto, they won't realise our long, unbroken imperial tradition is more valuable than that of any other country of the world. If they don't see Osaka with its many industrial goods and shipping facilities, they won't realise how we are wealthier than other countries in the world. If they don't visit Edo with its huge population where the grand daimyō lords of the land assemble, they won't realise that our country flourishes like no other.[3]

Kyokusō's perspective in considering how the three cities together are greater than the sum of the parts and how they represent Japan as a nation of the world is unusual for this time, as Japanese people could not travel abroad. Domestic travel was common in the Edo period, however, and individuals like Kyokusō often spent long periods in other areas of the country. Originally from northern Kyushu, he opened a private Confucian academy in Osaka in 1836 at the age of 29. Then, in 1843, he moved the academy to Edo, returning to Osaka in 1846.

Kyoto and Edo were similar cities in that both the court nobles and the Tokugawa military government considered the cherishing of tradition and ritual essential. Osaka received little if any assistance from the government, however, and needed to be self-reliant. A famous example is the grand Yodoya family business, headed by a wealthy merchant of the same name. In the seventeenth century it built a bridge in Osaka that, although later rebuilt in the twentieth century, still bears the name Yodoya-bashi. In 1706 the Yodoya business was confiscated by the government on the pretext that the head of the family was living in extravagance beyond his station as a merchant. Another significant example is the Kaitokudō academy, founded in 1724 by Osaka businessmen (see pp. 13, 64). It was granted a Tokugawa charter two years later that gave it the right to comment on governmental matters.[4] The academy aimed, initially at least, to argue that economics and commerce were essential for the nation. Its name 'Kaitokudō' was provocative, meaning 'Academy for Holding Virtue in One's Pocket': within Confucian thought, 'virtue' (*toku*) was seen as a necessary attribute for rulers, and only samurai were expected to possess it.

Cultural traditions differed across the three cities too. The role of the iemoto (family head) – the ultimate authority over arts such as nō theatre or tea ceremony (*chanoyu*, using matcha powdered tea) – was an essential aspect of Japanese traditional arts. In Osaka, where puppet theatre and the Chinese-style tea ceremony (*sencha*, using steeped tea) flourished, the role of the family head was not as influential as in Kyoto or Edo. Literati (bunjin) such as Ueda



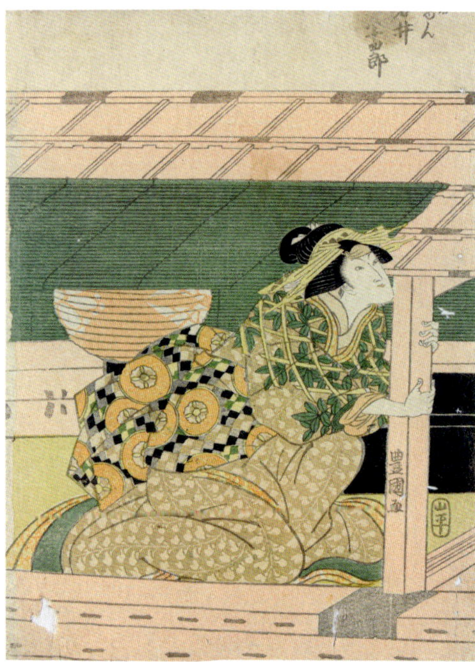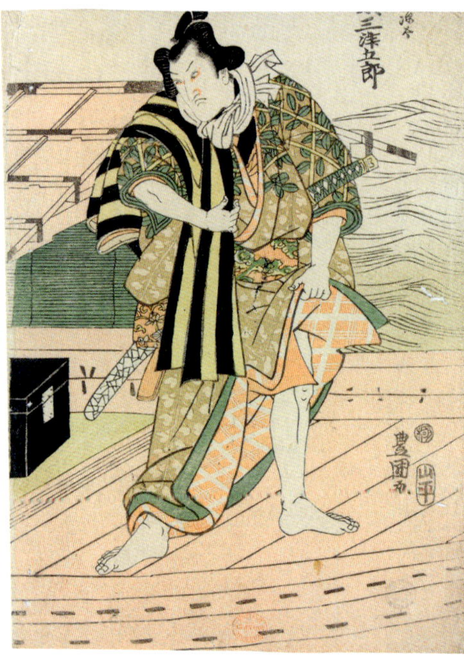

**1.10**
Utagawa Toyokuni I, *Bandō Mitsugorō III as Shirafuji Genta* (right) *and Iwai Hanshirō V as Oshun* (left), in the play *Winning Sumo: Scandal Rumours Blossoming* (*Kachi-zumō ukina no hanabure*), performed at the Ichimura-za in the third month, 1810. Diptych, colour woodblock. 35.7 × 25.9 cm (left); 35.5 × 26.1 cm (right). British Museum, London, 1915,0823,0.872.1-2.

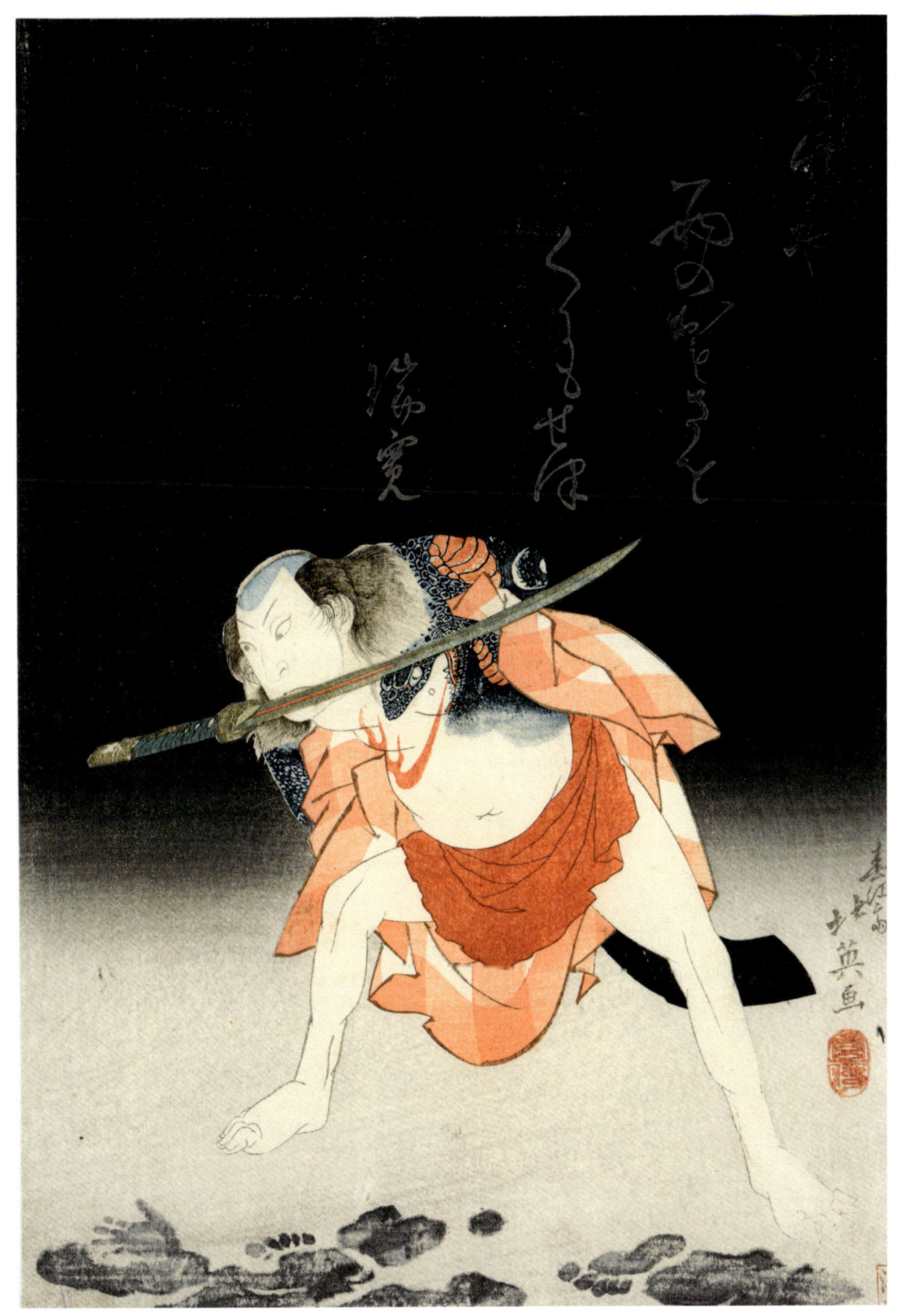

**1.11**
Hokuei, *Arashi Rikan II as Danshichi Kurobei*, in the play *Summer Festival: Mirror of Osaka* (*Natsu-matsuri Naniwa kagami*), 1832. Colour woodblock. 37.5 × 25.4 cm. British Museum, London, 2023,3014.2. Purchase made possible by the JTI Japanese Acquisition Fund. Ex-coll.: John Adams.

Akinari stressed the role of nonprofessional sencha tea practitioners as an ideal of bunjin culture.[5] Puppet theatre did not adopt the iemoto system, following instead a strict code of individual merit.[6]

## Hobby arts and passionate amateurs

In the eighteenth century, literati aimed to be creatively independent, eschewing official patronage or commercial ambition and instead cultivating a free spirit to produce art as much as possible for oneself and friends. An offshoot of this practice, particularly among commoners in Kyoto and Osaka, was the notion of 'amateur' (shirōto) cultural activities as positive and important, not just as hobbies or pastimes but as serious lifelong, passionate pursuits. This seems to have worked well in Osaka and Kyoto, where the average townsperson was expected to run, or work in, a household business as their primary responsibility.[7] One of the most celebrated figures who fits both the literatus and amateur roles is Yamagata Bantō (1748–1821), who ran a successful finance business in Osaka and later wrote treatises on philosophy after studying at the Kaitokudō.

Osaka has a strong tradition of encouraging amateur participation in the arts. In painting, three individuals dominated the production of self-teaching guides to traditional (and hitherto secret) Kanō-school painting techniques in the first half of the eighteenth century. The first was the 1721 *Net of Paintings* (*Gasen*) by Hayashi Moriatsu (1679–1721); next was Tachibana Morikuni (1679–1748), who published nine multivolume painting manuals detailing Kanō-school techniques; the third was Ōoka Shunboku (1680–1763) (see fig. 5.30), who issued seven multivolume guides to painting.[8] These books offered access to the secrets of professional painters in the public realm, opening up new worlds for aspiring artists, both professional and amateur. Such an egalitarian ethic was fundamental to the non-samurai commoner culture of the time.

Learning to perform as an amateur has been, and remains, customary for fans of Japanese theatrical arts. Connoisseurs of nō drama learn both chanting (*utai*) and dance (*shimai*); kabuki fans learn dance (*odori*); and puppet theatre patrons learn chanting (*gidayū* or jōruri) and *shamisen* (a three-stringed banjo-like instrument, struck with a plectrum). As early as the seventeenth century jōruri amateurs requested access from professional performers to the hitherto secret musical notation for voice. This stimulated the publication of playbooks (*shōhon*) with complete authentic notation. Amateur jōruri chanting increased dramatically from the second half of the eighteenth century, initially in Osaka and Kyoto and then throughout the country. The Osaka merchant and comic artist Nichōsai was known to be multitalented, with a cutting edge to his works. He was especially proficient as an amateur jōruri chanter, and a detail from one of his handscrolls shows his witty take on the forty-seven *rōnin* vendetta story depicted in the serious jōruri play *Treasury of Loyal Retainers* (*Kanadehon chūshingura*, first performed in 1748) (fig. 1.12).

Three books on amateur performers document the popularity of jōruri chanting. *Performing for the Gods: Amateur Jōruri Critiques* (*Kishin shirōto jōruri hyōbanki*, 1786) is a remarkable record attesting to the high quality of amateur performances. Audiences paid to attend, and the proceeds went to support the hosting temple or shrine. The following quotation from the preface to this critique alludes to the famous preface of the imperial anthology *Collection of Ancient and Modern Japanese Poems* (*Kokin wakashū* or *Kokinshū*, 905), arguing that the performance of jōruri chanting has the power to move one's heart:

> Amateur jōruri takes as its seed, from the outset, the aim of 'consoling the heart' (*nagusami*) and thereby presents a challenge to the many professional performers. A geisha, wooed with gifts, and the purest priest, when holding a shamisen, can manage it well and will surely sometimes also want to chant. Without even sending a missive, one can entice a woman, and excite the passion of a blind performer (*goze*), as well as calm the fierce spirit of a warrior.[9]

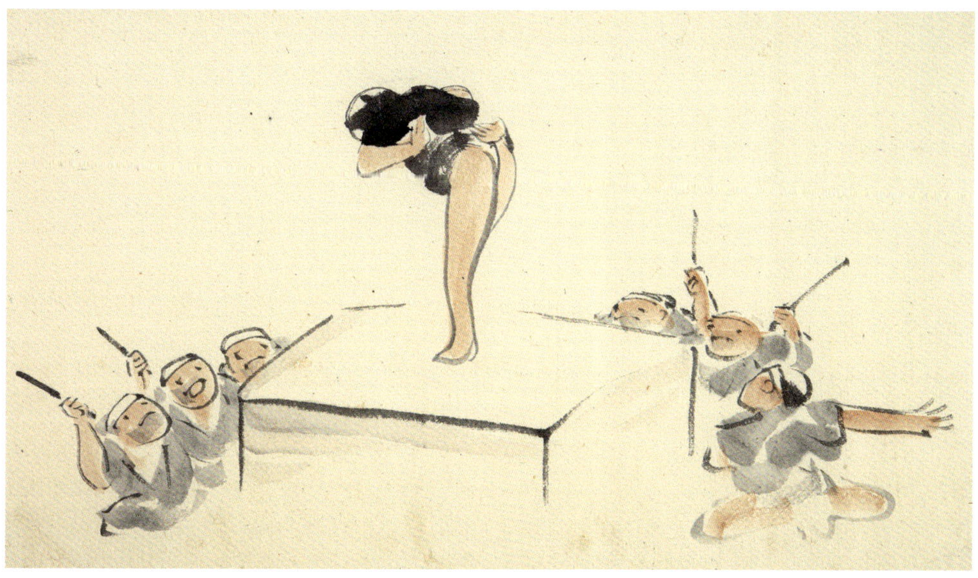

**1.12**
Nichōsai, *Picture Scroll of Scenes from the Treasury of Loyal Retainers* (*Chūshingura emaki*) (detail), *c.* 1800. Handscroll, ink and light colour on paper. 32 × 781.6 cm. British Museum, London, 1982,0701,0.7. Gift of Dr and Mrs Michael Harari.

This passage makes it clear that the ethic being promoted is the pride of the amateur: the performances are offerings to the gods and door receipts go to the shrines, not to the performers. The critique evaluates top amateur chanters as better even than professionals. Each individual is listed within their club.

In contrast, *Nose Clippers* (*Hanakenuki*, 1797), another lively treatise on amateur jōruri chanting, jokingly suggests that there are too many amateurs ('pouring out of the ground like ants')[10] and argues that individuals are too eager to perform publicly before being ready. The thrust of *Nose Clippers* is that chanting is a serious art in which moral teachings are elucidated through tales easily understood by all. A decade later, *Box of Secrets about Jōruri Training* (*Jōruri keiko himitsu-bako*, 1808) describes the popularity of jōruri chanting among men and women in all three major cities, and far into the countryside beyond.[11]

Several 'sumo-style' playbills (*mitate banzuke*), which rank amateur jōruri performers in order of their skill, attest not only to the extent of these activities but also to their social and networking aspects, usually noting the person's address. Another text, *Map of Kyoto Amateur Jōruri Performers and Rankings*, documents the popularity of amateur jōruri (fig. 1.13).[12] The inscription at the top left describes this world of performance as 'Kintarō Island'. In Kyoto and Osaka, 'Kintarō' was slang for someone obsessed with practising jōruri chanting, or indeed any cultural art, be it literary, musical or otherwise. Decades later, another playbill, 'Sumo-Style Rankings: Parlour-Room Amateur Jōruri Performers in Kyoto' (*Miyako shirōto jōruri zashiki sumō mitate kurabe*, 1846), listed more than 300 individuals under their performance names with their neighbourhood addresses.[13] A third such playbill, 'Osaka Parlour-Room Amateur Jōruri and Shamisen Performers: Ranked Sumo-Style' (*Naniwa shirōto jōruri shamisen zashiki sumō*, 1865), records amateur jōruri performers in Osaka, ranking more than 500 of them and noting the neighbourhoods in which they live.[14]

A fascinating example of the extent of amateur jōruri activity, which is still alive today and nationally recognised as an 'Intangible Folk Cultural Property' (*mukei minzoku bunkazai*) by the Osaka prefectural government, is the tradition found in the town of Nose at the northern edge of modern Osaka prefecture. Here, starting in the early decades of the 1800s, amateur jōruri chanting and shamisen playing became widespread among men, to the point that everyone was expected to participate.[15] Jōruri chanting was so popular among women as well that they developed an independent stream of commercial performances of chanting and shamisen, without puppets. 'Women's' jōruri became so popular in the 1830s that an appreciation of their performances was even published, like those for kabuki actors. *Critique of Young Women's Jōruri and Actors in the*

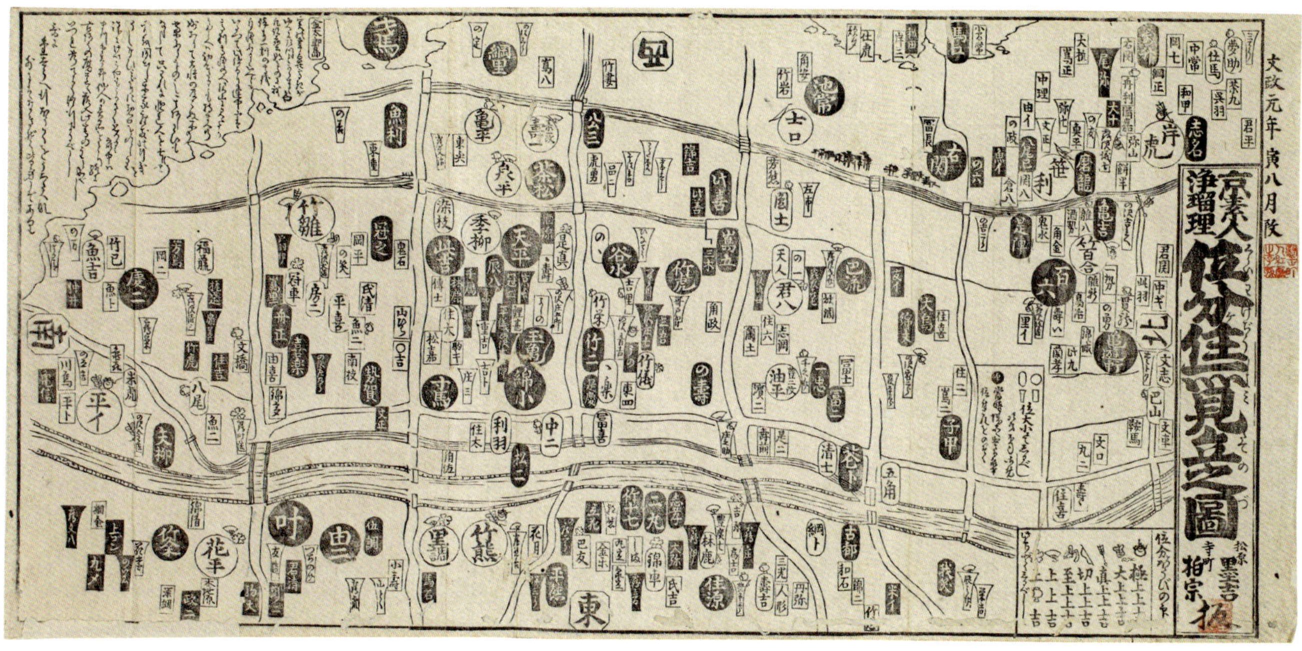

**1.13**

*Map of Kyoto Amateur Jōruri Performers and Rankings ([Kyō shirōto jōruri] Kurai-wake jūsho mitate no zu)*, 1818. Woodblock. 34.8 × 71 cm. National Institute of Japanese Literature, Tokyo.

*Three Cities* (*Santo yakusha musume jōruri gei shina-sadame*, 1837),[16] for instance, lists each female performer with a male kabuki actor from Edo, Osaka or Kyoto. The preface notes that women's jōruri was particularly successful in Edo.

The government's Tenpō reforms of the early 1840s, which aimed to restore government finances, included many austerity edicts. Women performers were banned, but only for a few years. Their performances continued, peaking in the early twentieth century. Teaching jōruri was one way for women to earn an independent living. The profession was common enough for Tamenaga Shunsui (1790–1844), author of the romantic novel *Spring Colours and the Plum Calendar* (*Shunshoku ume-goyomi*, 1832–3), to have one of the two female lead characters, Ochō, live independently as a jōruri performer and teacher.

Amateur recitals were sometimes advertised via surimono, elegant privately published prints that combined text and image. The example here lists an amateur programme of chanters and shamisen players, all members of the Omuro group (Omuro-ren) (fig. 1.14). Omuro is an area of north Kyoto, near the temple Ninna-ji. Five chanters' names (Takeuma, Takeki, Fusaji, Sankōsai, Sanba) and one shamisen player's name (Tsuchinosuke) on the surimono are seen in the 1846 'Sumo-Style Rankings' mentioned above. One individual, Noroku, from the 1818 map of performers (see fig. 1.13) also appears on this

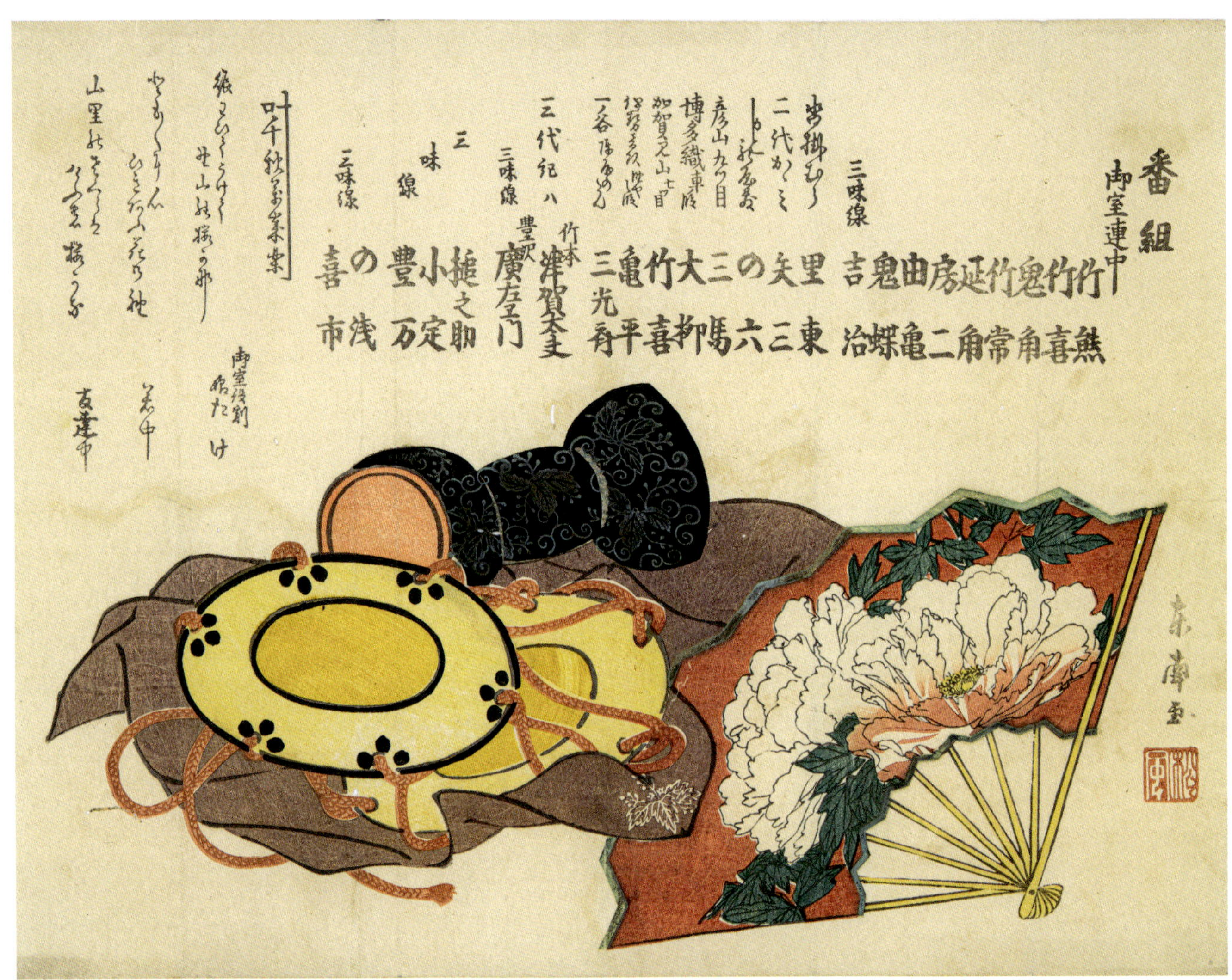

1.14
Umekawa Tōnan (artist) and 3 poets, *Amateur Jōruri Performance Programme with Design of Drum and Fan*, c. 1855–60. Surimono, colour woodblock. 37.0 × 50 cm. British Museum, London, 2021,3013.462. Purchase made possible by the JTI Japanese Acquisition Fund. Ex-coll.: Dr Scott Johnson.

surimono, which demonstrates that multiple records of amateur performances survive in different media.

This tradition continued strongly into the modern period. Amateur performers, under a teacher, belonged to groups (*ren*) that linked individuals into networks around their city and beyond. In the 1890s, we see the birth of modern printed coterie magazines catering to amateur performers: in Tokyo it was *Gidayū zasshi* (from 1893), in Osaka *Jōruri zasshi* (from 1899) and in Kyoto *Jōruri sekai* (from the early twentieth century). Each of these titles lasted until the advent of the Second World War, with *Jōruri zasshi* in circulation until the very end of the war.

## Kabuki fan clubs

Fans of kabuki in Kyoto and Osaka supported their favourite actors by joining a fan club, designing actor prints or contributing poems to prints. Osaka's well-organised fan clubs performed their rituals in the theatre at key moments in the annual calendar and when welcoming the return of actors from tours to Edo.[17] A colour woodblock print depicts a member of the Sakura fan club dressed in costume on the kabuki stage, leading the group's chants to welcome the actor Seki Sanjūrō II (1786–1839) home to Osaka in 1826 following a long tour to Edo (fig. 1.15). A portrait print dated to 1823 shows a fan named Rojū, who was known to be a master at wielding the wooden clappers for the Sasase fan club's ritual chants in support of their favourite stars (fig. 1.16). Rojū was also active in haiku circles and known to be proficient on the transverse harp (*koto*).[18]

There was extensive amateur activity in ukiyo-e production in Osaka. The print scholars Peter Ujlaki and John Fiorillo have counted more than 300 individuals who created Osaka actor prints. Of these, only five or six at most were professional in the sense of making a living from their art. Osaka-Kyoto

**1.15**
Gigadō Ashiyuki, *Sakura Fan Club Welcoming Seki Sanjūrō to Osaka from Edo*, 1826. Colour woodblock. 37.7 × 25.8 cm. British Museum, London, 2014,3039.18. Purchase funded by the Theresia Gerda Buch Bequest in memory of her parents, Rudolf and Julie Buch. Ex-coll.: Okada Isajirō; Dr C. Andrew Gerstle.

**1.16**
Utagawa Kunihiro, *Rojū Leading Clapping Ritual of the Sasase Kabuki Fan Club for the Beginning of the Season Performance*, 1823. Colour woodblock with metallic pigment. 37.9 × 25.7 cm. British Museum, London, 2014,3039.17. Purchase funded by the Theresia Gerda Buch Bequest in memory of her parents, Rudolf and Julie Buch. Ex-coll.: Okada Isajirō; Dr C. Andrew Gerstle.

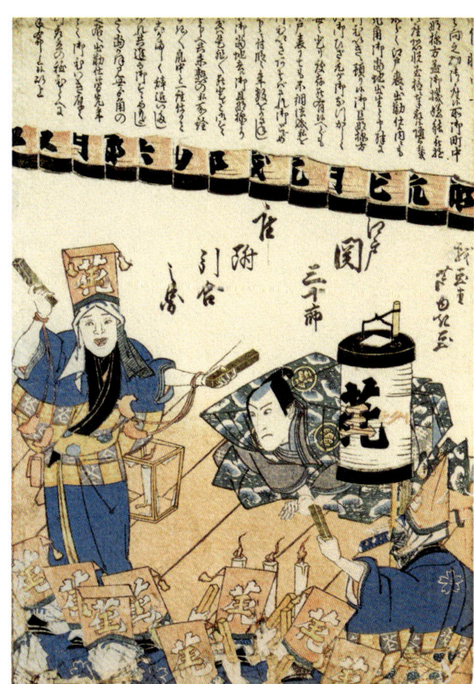

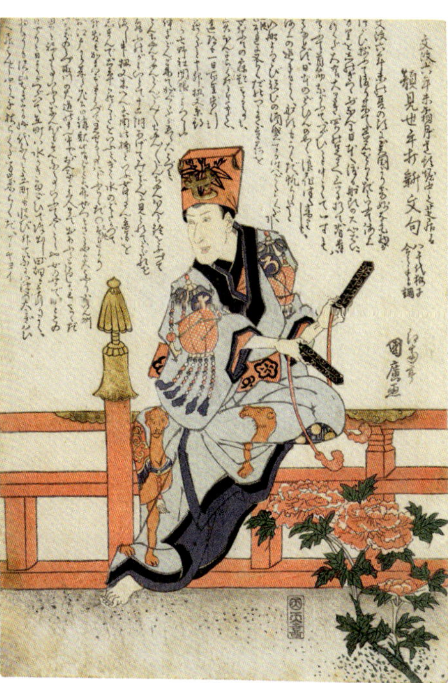

actor prints were mostly produced by passionate fans: the longest active was Hokushū (active 1802–30), thought to be a lumber merchant,[19] but for many other artists we have only a few surviving designs. This situation contrasts sharply with Edo, where actor prints were dominated by professional studios/schools such as the Katsukawa and the Utagawa, and individual artists were each responsible for hundreds, sometimes thousands, of designs.

A striking 1820 example of an actor portrait with a 'crazy verse' (kyōka) poem praises the Osaka actor Nakamura Utaemon III (1778–1838), who plays the role of the warrior hero Katō Masakiyo in flamboyant, bold Edo-style make-up. The design is by Hokushū and the poem by one Usokusai ('Likely a Liar') Fuminari, a member of the kyōka poetry circle of Akatsuki Kanenari (1793–1861): 'Kiyomasa is the moon / Shining over the world / Eyes bright and piercing, / His art strikes our hearts. Usokusai Fuminari.' Utaemon is the star whose acting 'shines' unparalleled (fig. 1.17). The historical warrior Katō Kiyomasa (1562–1611) in the print was an Osaka hero who, after initially siding with the Tokugawa, later tried to save the Toyotomi clan from being destroyed by Tokugawa Ieyasu (1543–1616).

Poems by Akatsuki Kanenari and his kyōka poetry group are also included in a diptych giving support to Bandō Mitsugorō III on his arrival in 1821 for a tour in Osaka, along with two other Osaka actors returning home (fig. 1.18). The artist is Jukōdō Yoshikuni (active 1813–32), another amateur actor print designer and amateur jōruri chanter who led his own 'Jukōdō-sha' haiku poetry group. This kind of amateur participation was essential to Osaka-Kyoto kabuki. The text conveys the lively atmosphere of engagement by fans in Osaka kabuki culture:

> Master Yoshikuni earnestly asked me (Kanenari) to contribute something. I found it hard to refuse, and so composed this with a feeble hand while drunk:

> Casting his light
> Like the morning sun
> Rising over the tide of Naniwa Bay,
> Mitsugorō summons smiles
> On all the mountains
> Across the land.

Kanenari is being modest when he refers to his 'feeble hand' and drunkenness: he was deeply involved in kabuki and edited an important book devoted to the actor Arashi Kichisaburō II (Arashi Rikan I, 1769–1821).[20]

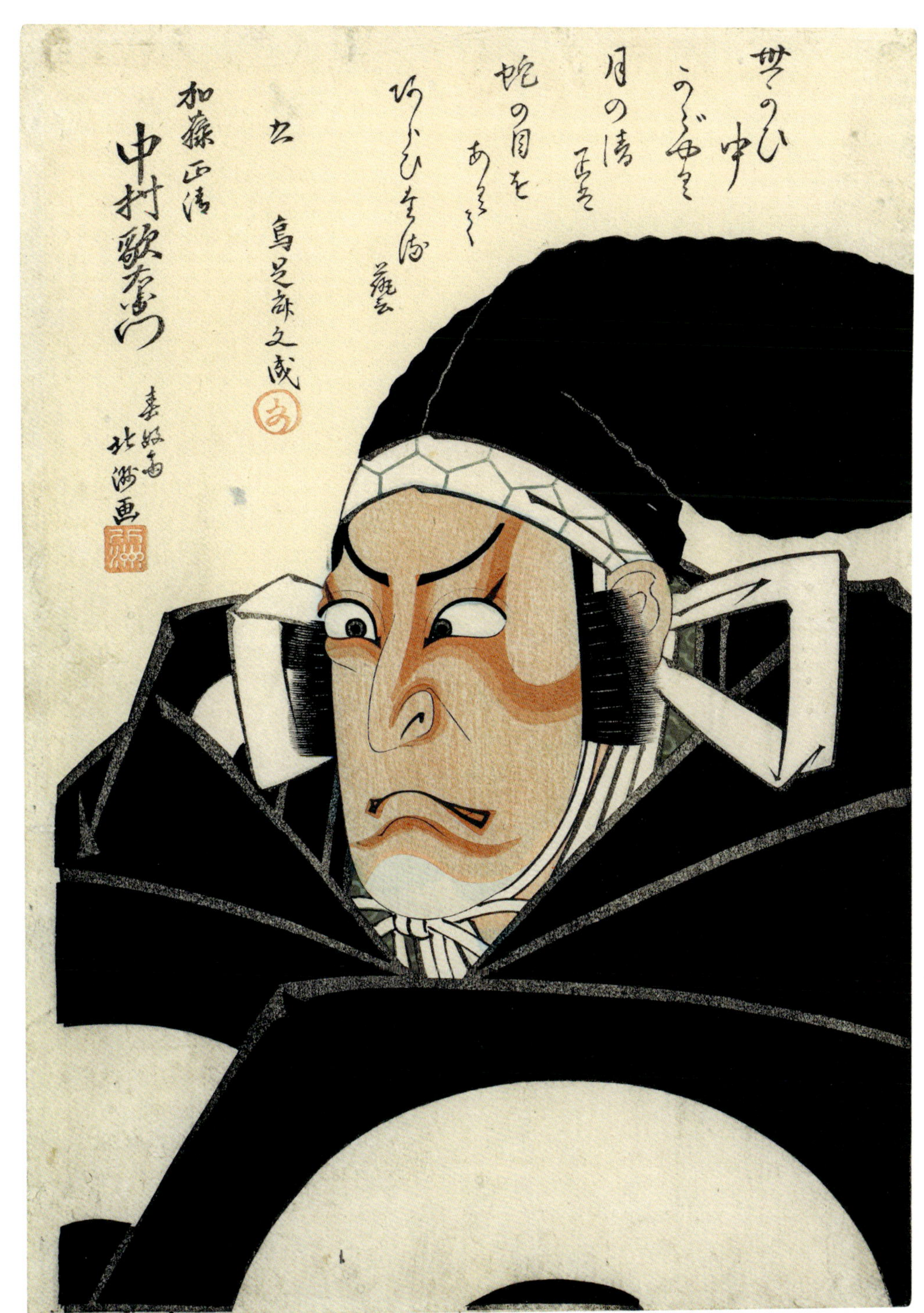

**1.17**
Shunkōsai Hokushū,
*Nakamura Utaemon III as
Katō Masakiyo*, 1820. Colour
woodblock. 39.2 × 27.3 cm.
British Museum, London,
2003,0821,0.1. Purchase
funded by the Brooke
Sewell Bequest.

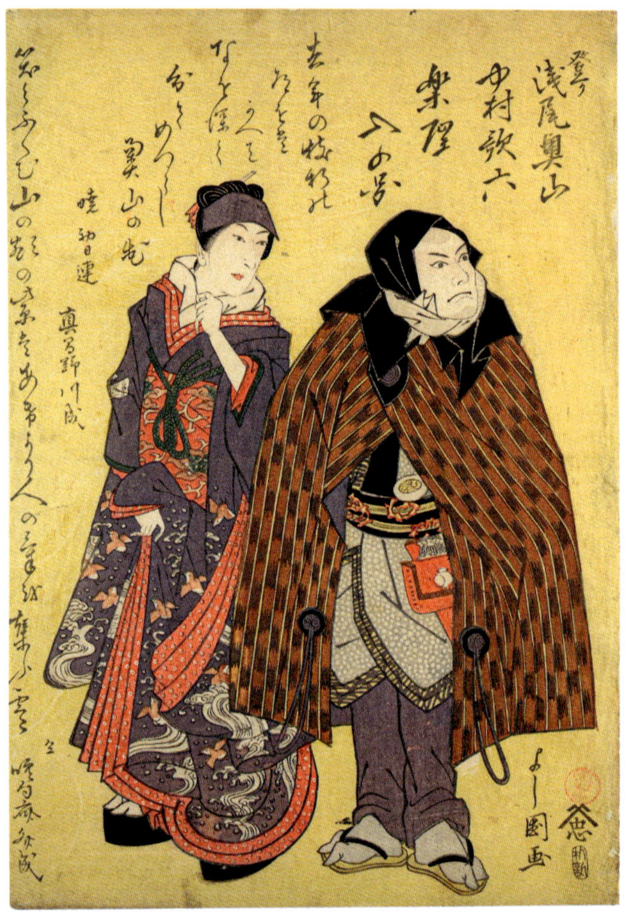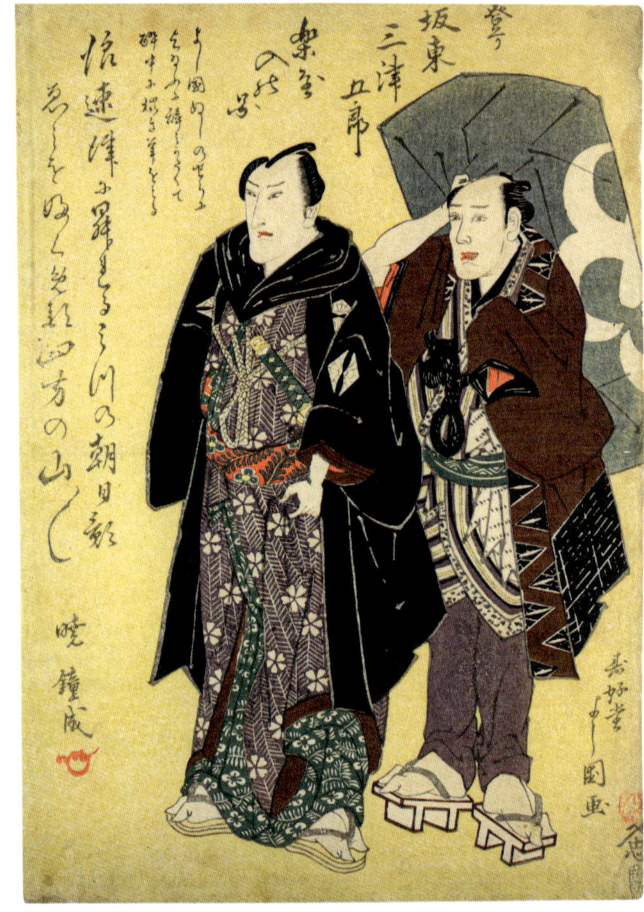

The cult of the amateur was extensive across many fields, and performance was just one of the many hobby arts that individuals pursued. Haiku poetry was a key link in the cultural network system that crisscrossed Japan. Virtually anyone who socialised outside their immediate neighbourhood – men and women alike – needed a pen name and to be able to turn a seventeen-syllable haiku verse on any occasion. Surimono were records of participation in such group events, either by attending a gathering in person or sending a poem by courier (see chapter 5).

Surimono were equally a convenient and elegant means for performers to interact with patrons and to advertise themselves. The first sheet of a handsome diptych of surimono prints promotes a professional jōruri chanter's succession in 1827 to the name Toyotake Konotayū (d. *c.* 1837) (fig. 1.19). The artist is Murata Kagen (or Yoshikoto, d. 1849), a poet and scholar of Japanese

**1.18**
Jukōdō Yoshikuni (artist) and Akatsuki no Kanenari (poet), *Bandō Mitsugorō III* (right, with attendant) and *Asao Okuyama II and Nakamura Karoku I* (left) *Arriving in Osaka from Edo*, 1821. Diptych, colour woodblock. 37.3 × 25.5 cm (left); 37.3 × 25.9 cm (right). British Museum, London, 2003,0822,0.1. Purchase funded by the Brooke Sewell Bequest.

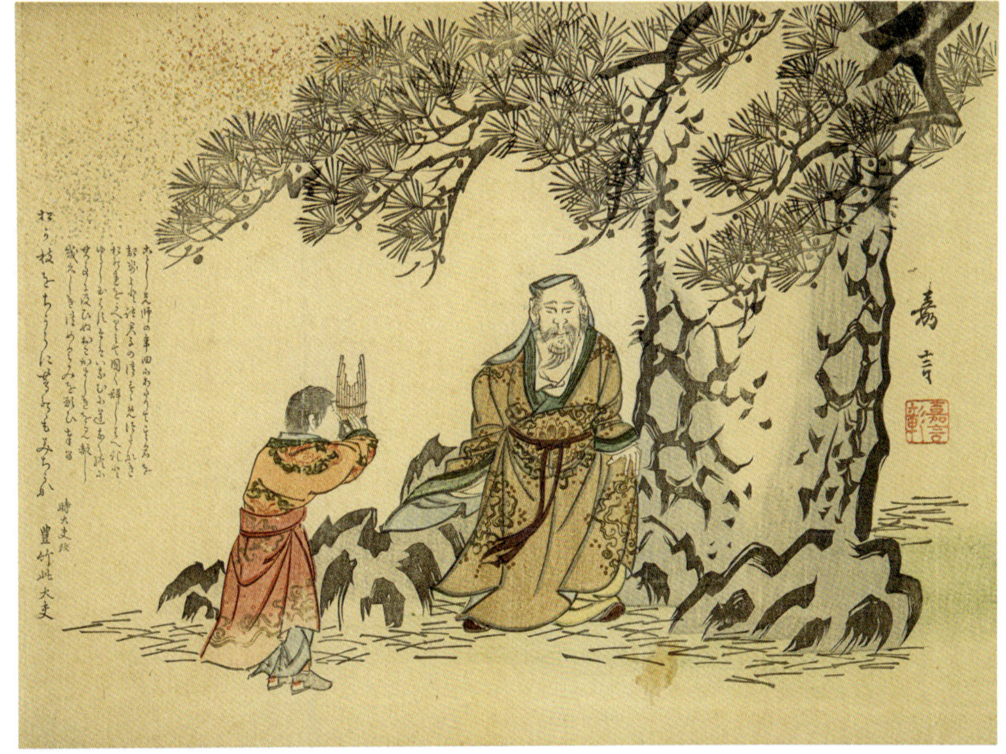

literature. The image, a literati theme, illustrates a Chinese sage listening to a youth playing a pipe organ (*shō*). The figure here is most likely Tao Hongjing (J: Tō Kōkei, 456–536), a Daoist master who liked listening to the shō under a pine tree. The forty-five individuals represented on the surimono is considerable. Most are Konotayū's jōruri colleagues, chanters and shamisen players, but there are also several others, mostly unknown except for their pen names. The penultimate three announce their native places – Dōjima (the business district of Osaka); Izumi province (south of Osaka); Yamato province (the Nara area) – and the final individual is Hassenbō III (Ishii Oku'u, 1755–1830), known as an Osaka haiku poet.

Surimono prints often evidence extensive networking that shows individuals interacting across status groups and native regions. Such interactions were crucial for performers who relied on patrons for their livelihood. One surimono, dated summer 1819, commemorates a moon-viewing party at the temple Nakō-ji in Amagasaki (between Osaka and Kobe) (fig. 1.20). It features actors whose poems begin the text of the print, top right, designating them as invited guests: Asao Kuzaemon I (Kigan, 1758–1824), Arashi Koroku IV

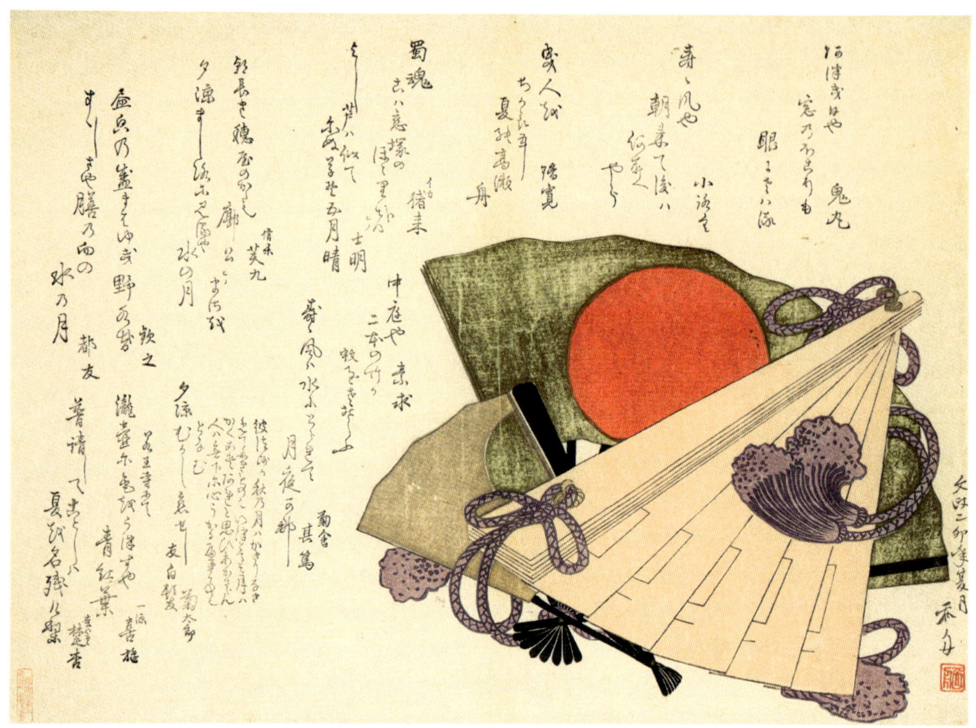

**1.20**
Ōhara Donshū (artist) and 14 poets, *Three Folding Fans*, 1819. Surimono, colour woodblock. 37.7 × 51 cm. British Museum, London, 2018,3007.8. Purchase funded by the Theresia Gerda Buch Bequest in memory of her parents, Rudolf and Julie Buch.

(1783–1826) and Arashi Kichisaburō II. The three actors were performing in Kyoto at the Kita Theatre in the fifth month, 1819. Other participants include the Kyoto publisher Kikuya Kitoku (son of Kisei) and poets from various places: Iga, Hino and Shigaraki in Ōmi, Osaka and Kyoto. Kikuya was well known for issuing haiku collections.

This surimono tradition continued into the twentieth century, at least until the 1940s. A surimono dating to April 1941 celebrates the name-taking of the bunraku chanter Takemoto Hamatayū V (Tsudayū IV, 1916–1987) that month (fig. 1.21a–b). With a picture of an auspicious rising sun, a pine tree and plum blossoms signed by the Osaka artist Suga Tatehiko (1878–1963), it is a huge print (45 × 60 cm) with more than 250 haiku poems by bunraku performers and patrons from all over Japan, and has poems by Shirai Matsujirō (1877–1951), Ōtani Takejirō (1877–1969) and Shirai Shintarō (1897–1969), three executives of the entertainment company Shochiku, which managed bunraku. Tsudayū was conscripted into the army in 1937 and served in China. He was discharged in September 1940; this surimono was issued with the aim of relaunching his career.[21] This is one of the last in the theatre-related surimono tradition that began in the middle of the eighteenth century.

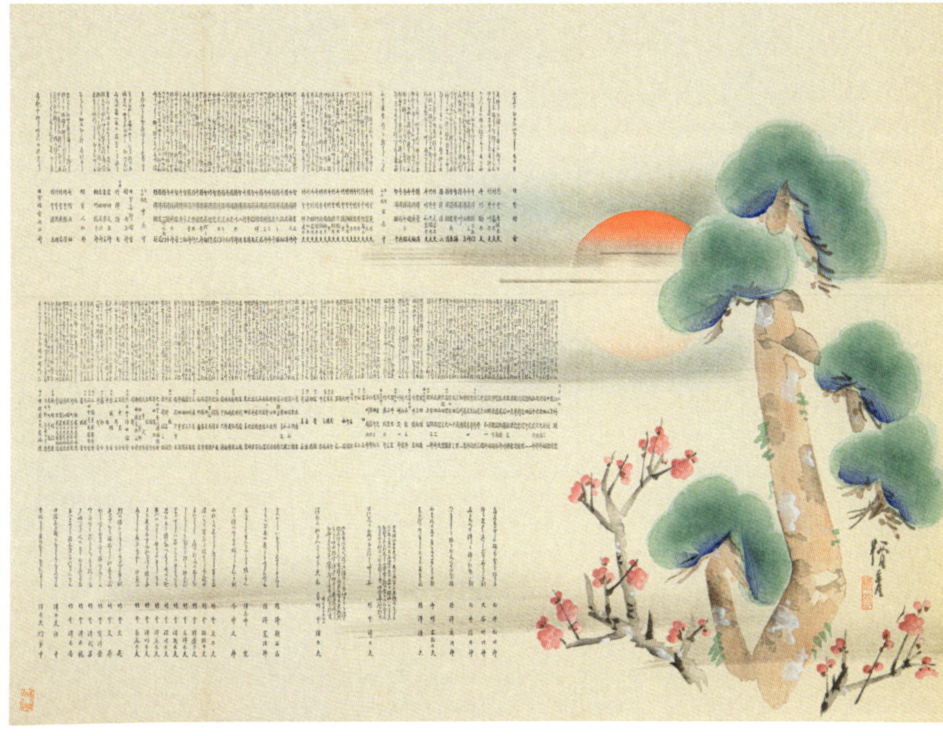

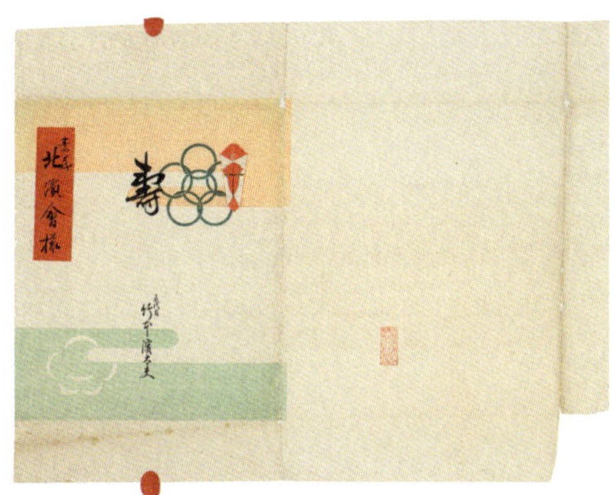

**1.21a–b**
Suga Tatehiko (artist) and 249
poets, *Rising Sun, Pine and
Plum, Celebrating the Name-
Taking Ceremony for Takemoto
Hamatayū V (Tsūdayū IV),
and accompanying wrapping
paper for the surimono*, 1941.
Surimono, colour woodblock.
45 × 58.8 cm. British Museum,
London, 2021,3013.1517.1–2.
Purchase made possible by the
JTI Japanese Acquisition Fund.
Ex-coll.: Dr Scott Johnson.

The tremendous creativity that produced the many Japanese eighteenth- and nineteenth-century artworks found today in Western collections – such as the British Museum – was underpinned by the wide interest and participation in the musical, literary and visual arts by professionals and amateurs in the cities, towns and villages across Japan. We witness in this era a moment when the arts were at the core of civil society, an essential means for communication and interaction. Competition and collaboration were key in this world where poetry and the arts were deeply embedded in everyday social life, offering participants access into what we might term a virtual utopia, where everyone could be an artist regardless of their status or rank. This phenomenon continued into the twentieth century, not in the modern school system but in neighbourhoods. It was only with the widespread destruction and upheaval of the Second World War that we see its dissolution. Salon cultural networks in the late Edo period stretched across the land, fostering a sense of national consciousness among the many regions with their distinct dialects that subsequently helped Japan to successfully maintain its independence and to modernise after the forced opening of the country in the second half of the nineteenth century.

# Domain warehouses (*kurayashiki*) and Osaka urban literati

*Akeo Keizō*

*Kurayashiki*, or domain warehouses, played a significant role in the creative and cultural circles of early modern Japan. They provided a venue – a kind of salon – to nurture relationships that transcended social status and wealth, bringing new dimensions to cultural life in Osaka. The Kaga-domain warehouse established in the late sixteenth century under the regime of Toyotomi Hideyoshi is believed to have been the first such building in the city. But the construction of large numbers of warehouses only began after the reconstruction of Osaka Castle in 1619 under the Tokugawa government and with the relocation of the daimyō residences formerly around Fushimi Castle in southern Kyoto to Osaka the following year. These warehouses stored commercial products, most importantly rice – the main commodity when calculating revenue – and they were concentrated in the city's trading hub Nakanoshima (fig. 1.23). The development of the westward maritime trade route up the northern coasts to Hokkaido by the entrepreneurial merchant Kawamura Zuiken (1618–1699) contributed greatly to the expansion of kurayashiki building, which turned Osaka into the 'kitchen of the world'.

At its peak, it is said that there were nearly 600 warehouses in Osaka: daimyō, the imperial and noble families, major temples and shrines, high-ranking shogunal vassals and feudal retainers all owned them. During the 1830s and 1840s there were 124 warehouses in the city run by daimyō alone, with the vast majority nestled around Nakanoshima. The author Ihara Saikaku (1642–1693) described this vibrant mercantile setting during the 1680s:

> At the Kitahama rice market, located in the foremost port in Japan, a future contract of rice for 50,000 *kan*[22] can be negotiated in two hours … Looking west from Naniwa Bridge, with a hundred fine views; thousands of warehouses stand side by side with neatly arranged roof tiles on top, and their white walls shine like snow at dawn. Piles of rice sacks stacked high in the triangular shape of cedars; it is as if mountains were moving. When carried on horseback, the land beneath the road seems to roar and shake like ground thunder …[23]

Saikaku's use of imagery – from 'moving mountains' to the weight of the rice making roads 'shake' – creates a vivid sense of the scale and lucrative nature of the rice trade at this time. The main commodity was clearly rice, but other speciality products from each of the domains were also traded, including bonito flakes from Tosa (present-day Kōchi prefecture), tatami mats from Fukuyama (in present-day Hiroshima prefecture), sugar from Satsuma (in present-day Kagoshima prefecture) and indigo from Tokushima (in present-day Tokushima prefecture). Warehouse managers, or *kuramoto*, were responsible for procuring goods that could not be supplied within the domain, and during times of famine stored goods could be used for relief. Kurayashiki had other functions too: for daimyō from the south-western domains, Osaka's warehouses also served as lodgings during their travels to and from their official residences in Edo. In the event of emergency, these facilities could also serve as a military base. While domain warehouses in Edo had a political role in negotiations with the shogunate, in Osaka their role was primarily financial.

Domains appointed officials known as 'caretakers' (*rusu-i*) who were responsible for the warehouses. They also dealt with transactions. Gradually it became customary for specialist merchants to run the warehouses as kuramoto. Other experienced merchants were appointed as accounting managers (*kakeya*), who handled the money received from sales. Both types of merchant managers – kuramoto and kakeya – were allowed to charge transaction fees. Some were promoted to the samurai class and paid a stipend in rice for their services. Merchants entered into regular commerce with the warehouses, through which specialist products of the western domains, as well as Chinese products and medicines imported via Nagasaki and the Ryūkyū kingdom, were distributed around the country.

The relationship between these warehouses and salon culture is demonstrated by the activities of two merchant literati. The first was Kimura Kenkadō (see pp. 42, 127, 204–6), who had close ties with both the Satsuma and Tosa domains. He was born into a family that had been engaged in the sake-brewing industry for generations at Kita-Horie in Osaka.[24] Described as both a literatus and a painter in *Record of Fellow Osakans* (*Naniwa kyōyū roku*, 1775),

**1.23**
Niwa Tōkei (artist), 'Men carrying rice sacks into a domain warehouse', from vol. 4 of Akisato Ritō (author) and 7 artists, *Illustrated Guide to Famous Places in Settsu Province* (*Settsu meisho zue*), 12 vols, 1798. Illustrated book, woodblock. 25.6 × 17.9 cm (cover). British Museum, London, 2002,0815,0.2.1–12. Purchase funded by the Brooke Sewell Bequest.

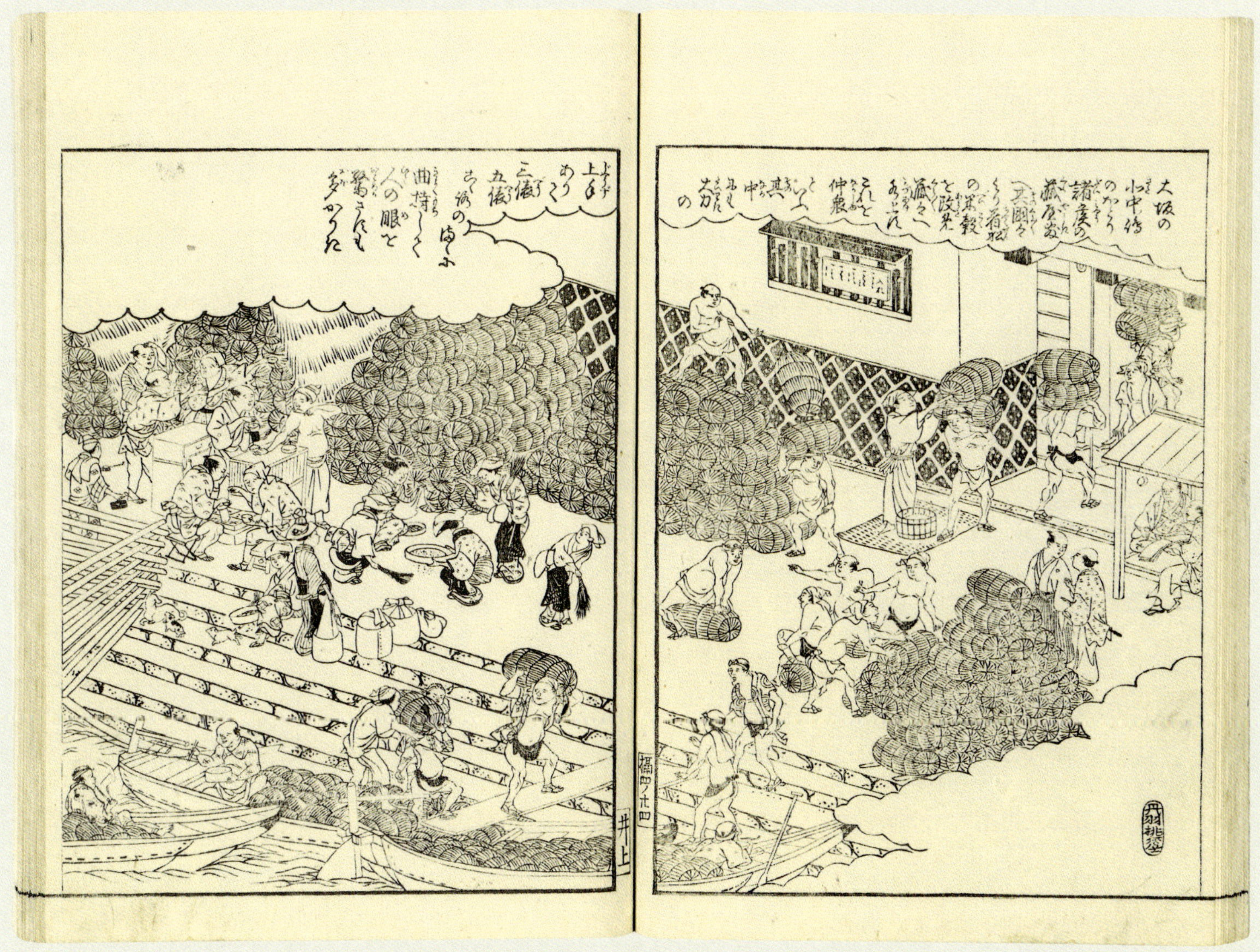

Kenkadō had assembled an encyclopaedic collection of objects that was celebrated throughout the country and attracted numerous visitors. *Kenkadō's Diary* (*Kenkadō nikki,* 1779–1802, with the years 1781, 1792 and 1795 missing) offers a glimpse into Kenkadō's varied social interactions; his vast social network is said to have resulted in as many as 40,000 visits to his home, all of which are recorded in the diary.[25] It is interesting to note that Kenkadō not only went to the warehouses of the Satsuma and Tosa domains near his house, but he was even granted audiences with the daimyō of Satsuma. He was also recognised for his close association with Mashiyama Sessai (1754–1819), the daimyō of the Ise-Nagashima domain (in present-day Mie prefecture) (see also p. 134), who was appointed by the government as one of the officials overseeing Osaka Castle. Rai Shunsui (1746–1816), a poet and close friend, described Kenkadō as 'a person known for his wide range of interests. He is skilled in diverse arts, ranging from painting, calligraphy and seal carving to machine mechanisms, and many other intellectual hobbies. People admire most his paintings and his knowledge of specialist local products.'[26] Shunsui also remarked that Kenkadō had an incredible bibliographic memory for imported books – for example, the ability to distinguish different editions – and was able to answer any question in detail. It is likely that most of the foreign books and goods in Kenkadō's collection were acquired through his trips to the kurayashiki, evidence of the connection between the arts and mercantile trade.

A second significant figure is the rice dealer Komeya Hikobei, also known as Okada Beisanjin (1744–1820), who was a self-taught painter and Confucian scholar. After being granted samurai status around 1790, Beisanjin was appointed as an official under the manager of the Ise-Tsu domain (also in present-day Mie prefecture) warehouse of the Tōdō family. In the 1790 edition of *Record of Fellow Osakans*, he is introduced, just like Kenkadō earlier in 1775, in the sections on literati and painters. In Japanese, bunjin (literatus) is sometimes written with characters that mean 'person who has been heard of'. Both Kenkadō and Beisanjin are described as such in the *Record*.

Kenkadō and Beisanjin were urban literati unique in Japanese history through their links to Osaka kurayashiki, which played a key role in the cultural life of the city and now offer invaluable insights into the lives of cultivated individuals.

# Creative networks in late Edo-period Kyoto and Osaka
*Akama Ryō*

Kyoto's Great Fire of 1788 reduced much of the city to ashes. It was the worst fire in the capital's history, resulting in the destruction of the imperial palace and Nijō Castle. The disaster accelerated the shift of Japan's cultural centre from Kyoto to Edo in the east, a process that had already begun before the conflagration. One positive outcome of this eastwards movement was the spread of sophisticated cultural activities from Kyoto and the surrounding area, including Osaka, to Edo and other cities and rural villages. Although Kyoto's cultural influence may have been diminished, its absolute status as a major cultural hub never waned.

Stimulated by the Kyōhō reforms, a series of economic and cultural policies of the 1720s, policymakers of every domain in Japan encouraged the development of their own unique industries. This not only promoted commercial activity, but it also led to more extreme income disparities in the cities, towns and farming villages. This resulted in the rise of affluent sectors in villages of large landowners and great farming families who had extensive operations. Products from around the country were distributed by merchants of the 'three cities' (Kyoto, Osaka and Edo) (see chapter 1). The establishment of a commercial economy between urban and rural spheres also invigorated cultural interactions. It became common for prosperous individuals in the countryside to avidly seek out the trappings of urban culture. They frequently spent a considerable amount of their wealth on cultural activities to secure social respect and status, and this included the patronage of urban cultural figures. Kyoto was home to a concentration of 'family heads' (iemoto) of various traditional art 'schools' that had branches around the country, and this hierarchal system of culture topped by family heads was the model for many new arts.

The Uematsu family at the Hara post station along the East Coast Road (Tōkaidō) in Suruga (in present-day Shizuoka prefecture) is among the best-known examples of rural patrons. Thanks to the family's convenient location for travellers, a number of important cultural figures from eastern and western Japan passed through the town. They were offered free lodging and often left behind their works – paintings and calligraphy as payment in kind and as gifts. The haiku poet Matsuo Bashō (see p. 85) was one such

early visitor, and others, including the literati painter Ike no Taiga (see p. 42) and the Confucian scholar and Chinese-style poet Rai San'yō (1781–1832), would have been unable to sustain their creative lives without the support of patrons outside the cities. In the Kyoto and Osaka region, the Inatsuka family in Ikeda and the Nakanishi family in Suita, both in present-day Osaka prefecture, are further instances of influential patrons; their respective family lineages continue even today. Patrons who supported these artists also formed local cultural groups, which linked with larger gatherings ('salons') in major cities. Nationwide networks blossomed as a result.

The extent of these networks is revealed in the *Record of People in Heian [Kyoto]* (*Heian jinbutsu-shi*), a guidebook for Kyoto cultural figures (fig. 1.24). This title was originally published in 1768 and revised editions were regularly issued until the final (ninth) edition in 1867. The first edition states that the book 'records the names and addresses of Kyoto's scholars and persons of culture' and that it was 'for the convenience of those who come from outside Kyoto to study, including study for pleasure'.[27] In short, it is a list of teachers, with the names of 101 scholars, 24 calligraphers, 16 painters, 5 seal carvers, 4 fortune-tellers and 3 physiognomists. The main subjects to be studied in Kyoto were academia, calligraphy and painting. Kyoto's publishing industry understood people's needs well and produced guidebooks for those coming to the capital: the earliest title in what became the popular genre of 'illustrations of famous places' (*meisho zue*) is the *Illustrated Guide to Famous Places in the Capital [Kyoto]* (*Miyako meisho zue*, 1780) (see fig. 2.30).

The largest academic field at this time was Confucian studies. Scholars in this discipline also tended to form poetry groups to sharpen their Chinese compositional skills: for example, the Yūran-sha led by Uno Meika (1698–1745) and Ryū Sōro (1714–1792), and the Sanpaku-sha led by Minagawa Kien (1735–1807), Shibano Ritsuzan (1736–1807) and Akamatsu Sōshū (1721–1801). *Record of People in Heian [Kyoto]* can, in one sense, be seen as a representation of networks of numerous circles in literature, painting and calligraphy in Kyoto. Minagawa Kien, an impressive self-taught scholar, opened a private academy

**1.24**
Rōkanshi (editor), *Record of People in Heian* [*Kyoto*] (*Heian jinbutsu-shi*), 1768. Book, woodblock. The C.V. Starr East Asian Library, University of California, Berkeley.

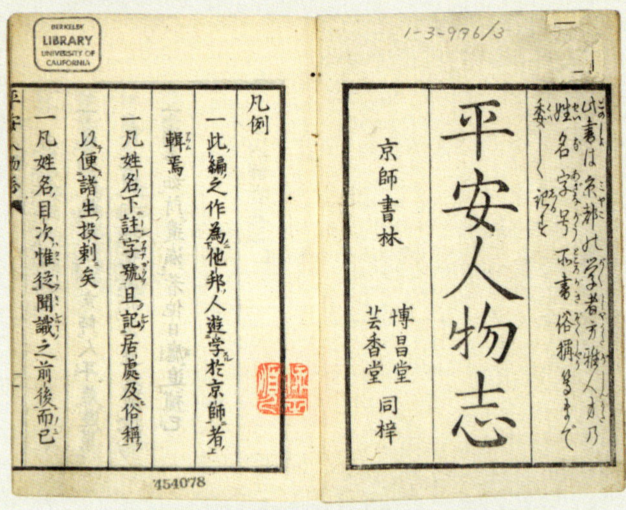

official Confucian academy in the Akita domain (in present-day Akita prefecture) in the 1780s and 1790s. He then moved to Fukuroi-chō in Kyoto, close to Gion, Kyoto's most famous pleasure district (see figs 2.25–2.26), where he nurtured poets of Chinese verse (*kanshi*), such as Umetsuji Shunshō (1776–1857) and Nakajima Sōin (1779–1855), both significant Kyoto poets of the next generation. The Osaka author Ueda Akinari also lived in Fukuroi-chō at one point in his life; Sōin lived in Nijō Shinchi in Kyoto. Rai San'yō's famous residence, named Sanshi-suimei-sho ('Site of Purple Mountains and Clear Water'), was close to the Sanbongi pleasure quarter in central Kyoto. That a number of literati lived near Kyoto's various pleasure quarters may be explained by the fact that in order to sustain their lives as cultural figures, they needed to be near pleasure quarters as such areas attracted a diverse cross section of individuals.

After the 1820s private academies and domain schools were set up throughout Japan. In addition, interest in scholarship such as Dutch studies (rangaku), National/Nativist studies (*kokugaku*), and military strategy – rather than just Confucian studies – shifted the academic centre from Kyoto to Osaka, notably to the Kaitokudō (est. 1724) (see pp. 62, 64) and the Tekijuku (a school for Dutch studies and medicine) led by Ogata Kōan (1810–1863). In the same period, scholarship steeped in literati artistic practice lost its dynamism, and Kyoto gradually slipped from its prime position as a centre for cultural creation. In the field of medical studies, however, Shingū Ryōtei (1787–1854) from Tango province (in present-day Kyoto prefecture) started his practice in Kyoto in 1819 after studying European medicine in Edo. In 1839, a year after the establishment of Tekijuku in Osaka, he founded a medical school called Junsei Shoin (fig. 1.25) in Kyoto's Higashiyama ('Eastern Mountain') district. The school was also known as a venue for lively cultural activities.

Several of the private academies in Kyoto and Osaka opened in the late Edo period endure today as part of universities. The Medical School of Osaka University has its direct ancestry in the Tekijuku. The educator Fukuzawa Yukichi (1835–1901), a student at the Tekijuku, established Keiō Gijuku University in Tokyo. The Kaitokudō was absorbed into Osaka University and the Kyoto Prefectural

named Kōdōkan. Its records document that there were as many as 3,000 students from the Kyoto and Osaka region and western Japan, as well as from provinces on the northern coasts that were connected by domestic maritime trade. This suggests that the cultural sphere of Kyoto and Osaka was distinct from that of Edo. In Osaka the Chinese poetry circle Konton-sha (est. 1764) headed by Katayama Hokkai (1723–1790) dominated the literary scene. It originally evolved out of the notional 'salon' formed around Kimura Kenkadō (see pp. 42, 127, 204–6), which was the largest literati salon. Anyone interested in the arts and sciences interacted with Kenkadō regardless of their official status and vocation. Rai Shunsui, Shinozaki Santō (founder of the academy Baika-sha in Osaka) and Kan Chazan (founder of the private academy Renjuku in Fukuyama) were members of this significant group.

Viewed from another perspective, academic studies provided a space for social interaction, and the nature of 'study' tended to move away from the serious academic pursuit of the classics towards a more 'self-indulgent' focus on the arts. The Confucian scholar Murase Kōtei (1746–1818), for instance, was a contemporary of Minagawa Kien and in his early years as a scholar he worked hard to establish an

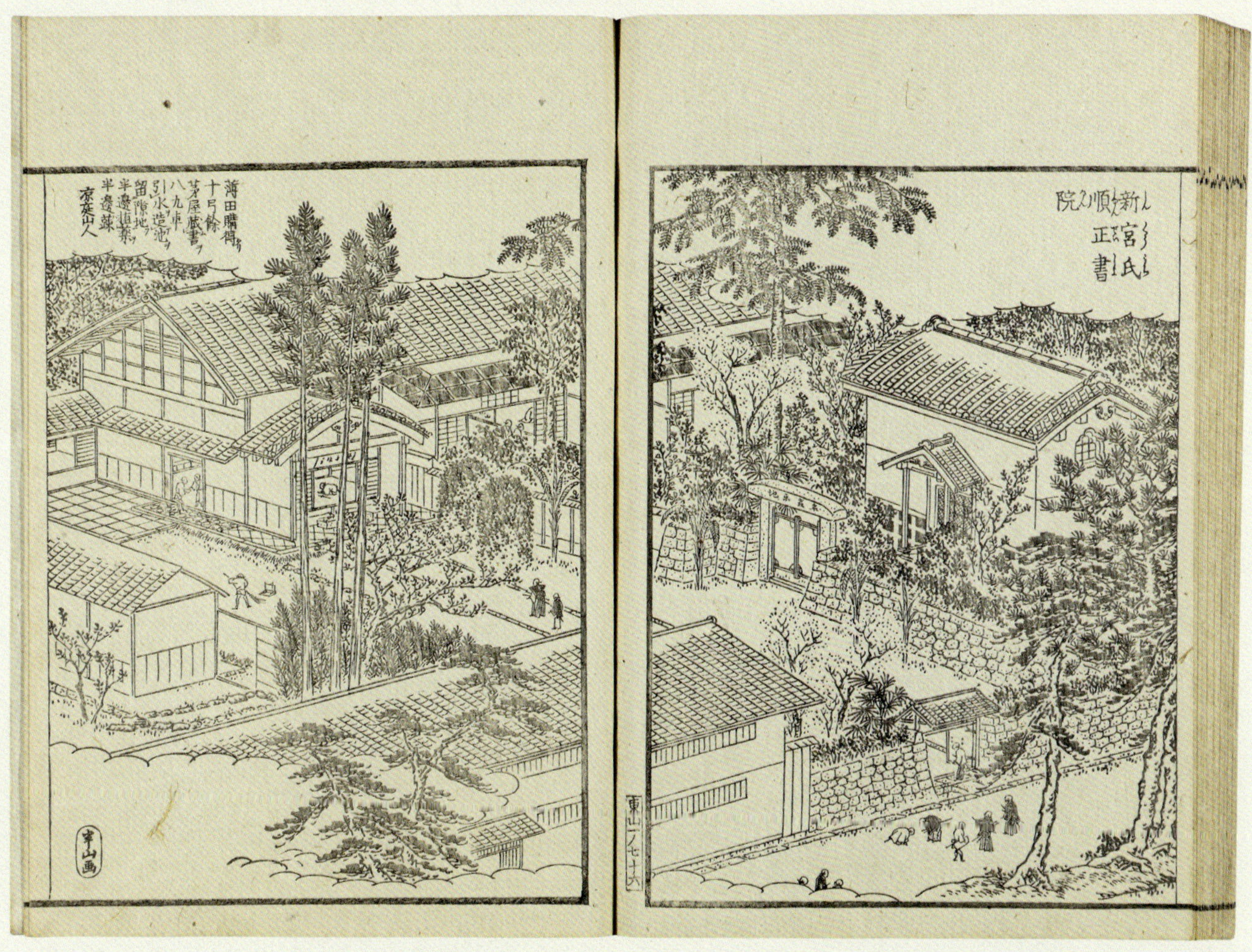

University of Medicine has its origins in Junsei Shoin. The foundation of Kansai University in Osaka was built upon the Hakuen Shoin for Confucian studies started in Osaka by Fujisawa Tōgai (1794–1864). And finally, Ritsumeikan University in Kyoto was originally a private academy (Ritsumeikan) opened in 1869 by Saionji Kinmochi (1849–1940), a courtier before the Meiji Restoration and subsequently a politician and prime minister. These are testaments to the long-lasting impact of academic and cultural networks of the late eighteenth and early nineteenth centuries, demonstrating how interest in both scholarship and the arts was a catalyst for social interaction across regions and status. Cultural salons in fact continued to flourish until well into the twentieth century, and even today in the twenty-first century they remain an important means through which the Japanese socialise and interact.

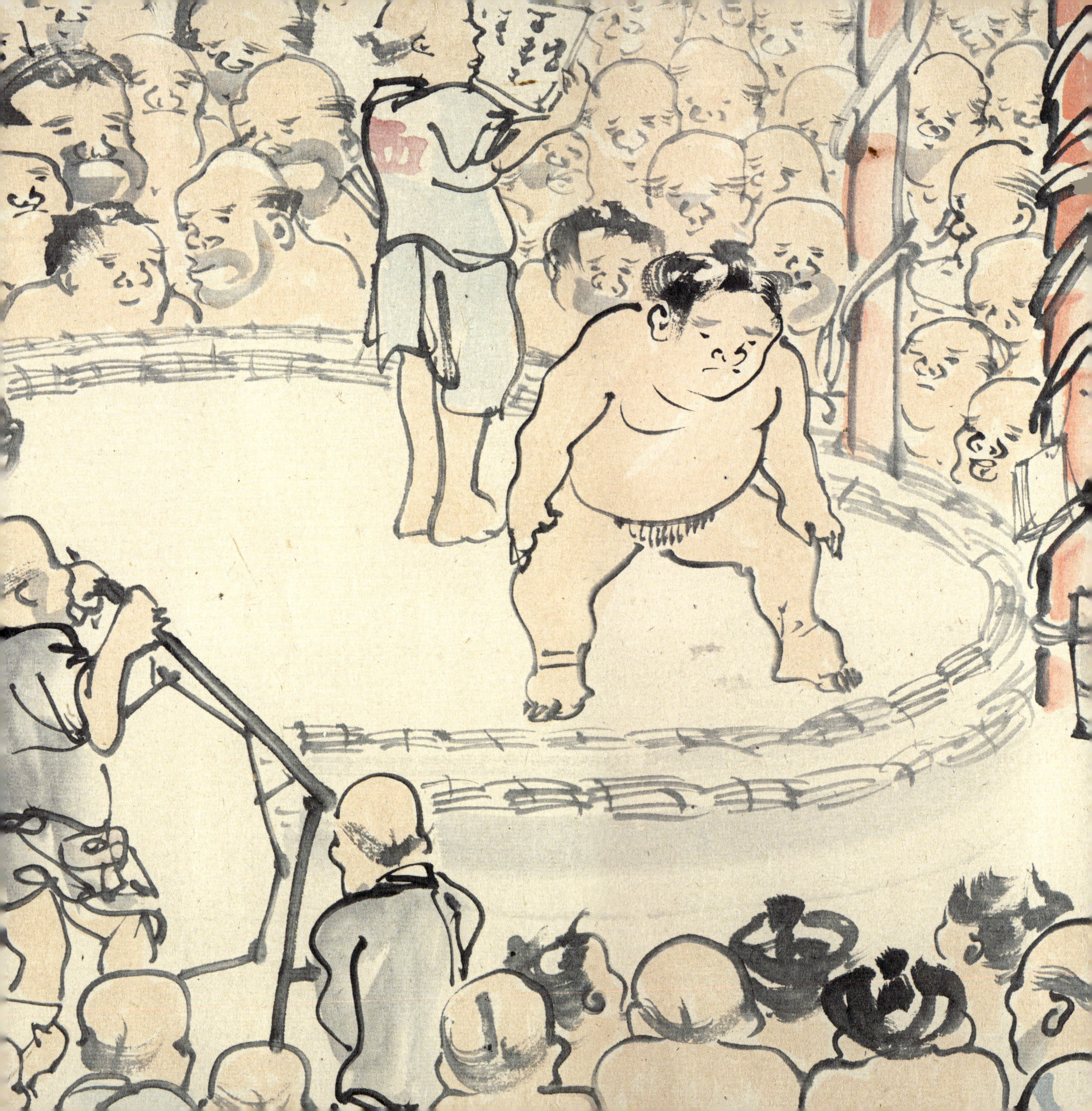

*Timothy T. Clark*

# 2 Painting everyday life

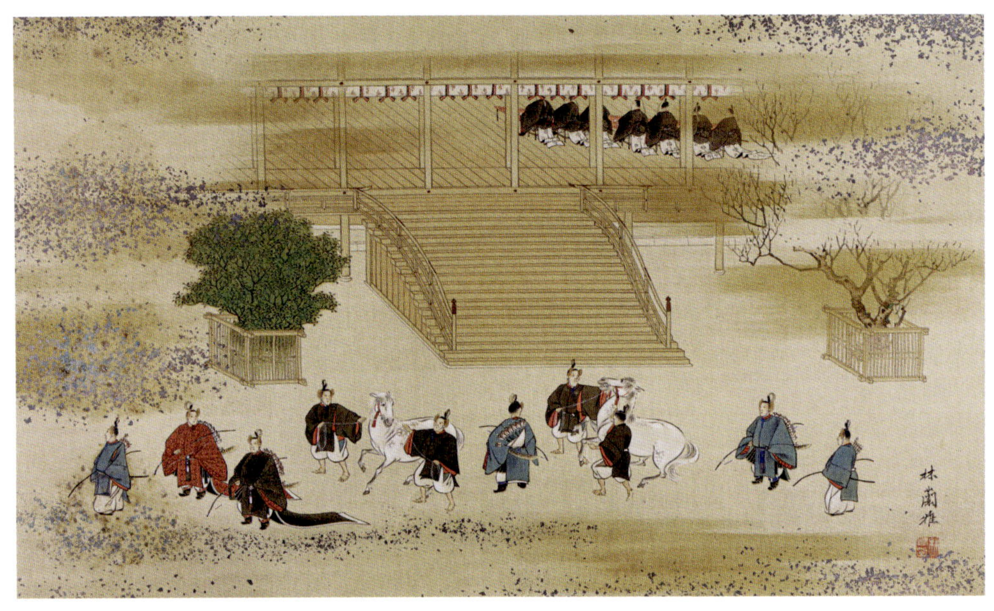



**2.1**
Hayashi Ranga, *Court Nobles
at the Imperial Palace in
Kyoto*, *c.* 1840–69. Hanging
scroll, ink, colour, gold, and
silver leaf on silk. 59.3 × 87 cm.
British Museum, London,
1881,1210,0.236. Ex-coll.:
William Anderson.

**2.2**
Nishiyama Kan'ei, *Picture Scroll
of Scenes in Osaka* (detail),
*c.* 1854–68. Handscroll, ink and
colour on paper. 31.5 × 427.4 cm.
British Museum, London,
1902,0606,0.28. Bequest of
Sir Augustus Wollaston Franks.

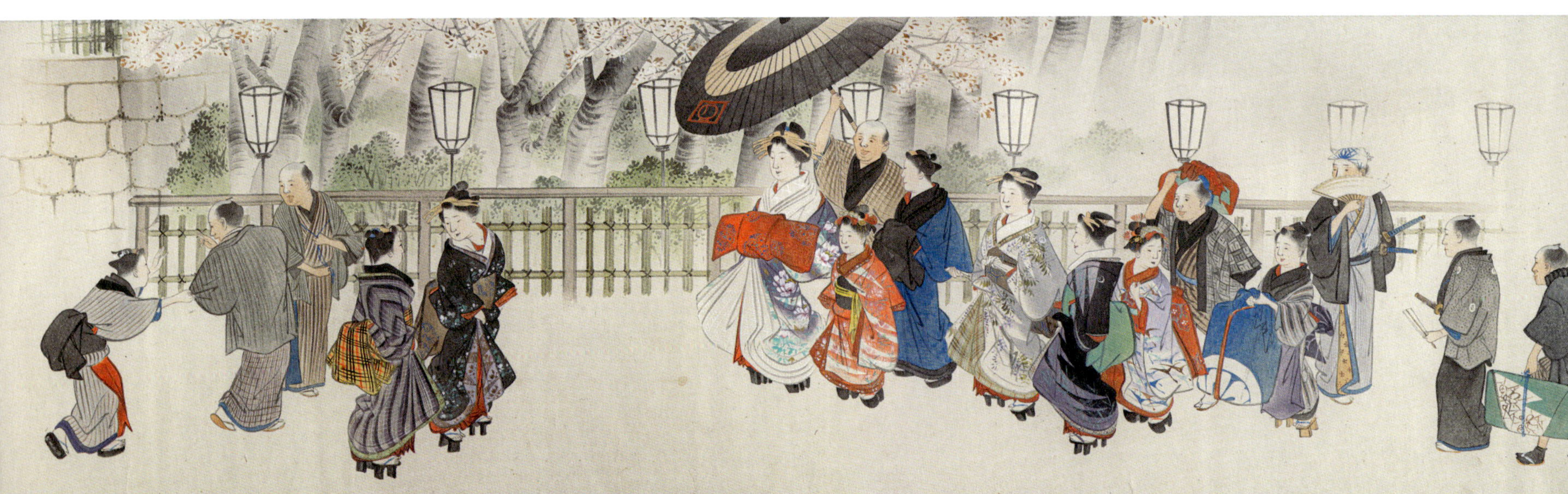

In the period between about 1750 and 1870, depictions of all kinds of contemporary life and experience came to enliven major new strands of art in Kyoto and Osaka, and beyond. The focus in this chapter is on cityscape, city life and still life, and on the activities of people in the here and now. Early modern Japan was an increasingly complex and stratified society, particularly in its major cities. 'Everyday life' was therefore very different for a Kyoto courtier in comparison to, say, an Osaka courtesan, albeit that ritual display played a key role in the lives of both. One annual New Year observance of the court in Kyoto was for white horses to be presented to the emperor, while a splendid spring event for a high-ranking courtesan of the Osaka Shinmachi quarter was parading with attendants to admire blossoming cherry trees illuminated by lanterns at night (figs 2.1–2.2). Haiku sensibility encouraged close personal engagement with the world: how to capture in fragile words and pictures an individual's intense receptivity to experiences of nature and life (fig. 2.3), while also paying tribute to the proud poetic tradition of Matsuo Bashō and other great exponents of the art form. At the same time, the Tokugawa shogunate declared large swathes of public subject matter – anything that criticised the ruling classes or otherwise critiqued contemporary events – off-limits. What was the range of what could and could not be depicted, and in what tenor?

There was a steadily growing appetite among what can broadly be termed middle-class audiences to enjoy genial images of everyday life, in both painted and printed formats (fig. 2.4). Since the late seventeenth century, 'pictures of the floating world' (ukiyo-e) had famously burgeoned in Edo (fig. 2.5). How did the new art of contemporary scenes differ in western Japan, the Kamigata (today's Kansai) region of Kyoto and Osaka in the late eighteenth and early nineteenth centuries? New art styles steadily evolved to reflect such subjects back to the people who lived them. Mechanisms of production and consumption – ateliers, exhibitions, art books, who's-who listings, dealers – flourished to support and foster what was now recognisably a modern 'art world'.

The full plethora of painters and 'schools' active in this vibrant secular art world is likely only ever to be the purview of specialists. Hundreds of professional or semi-professional artists, and thousands of amateur ones, regularly participated – a measure of the strong cultural significance of pictorial arts.

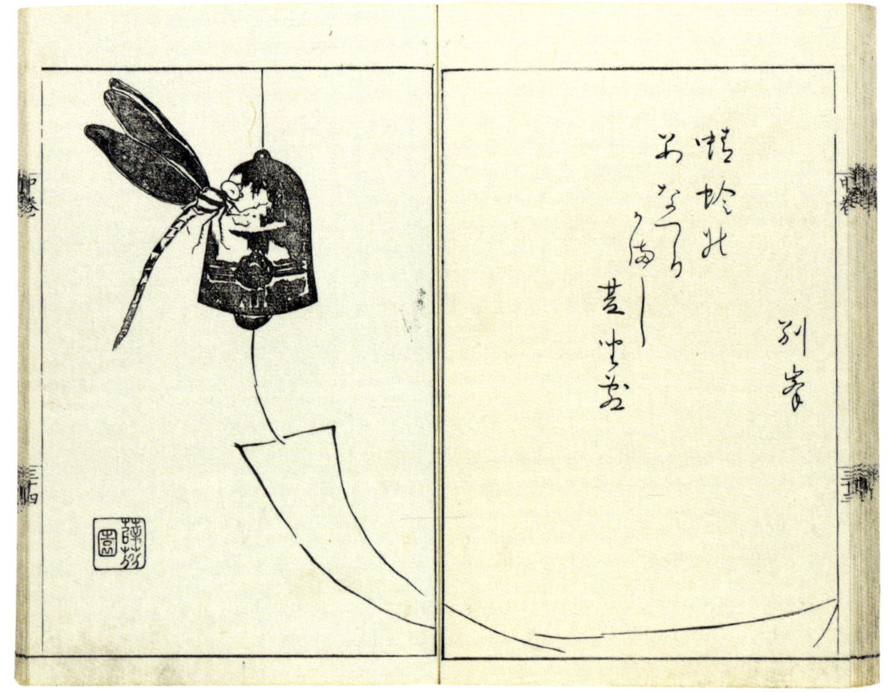

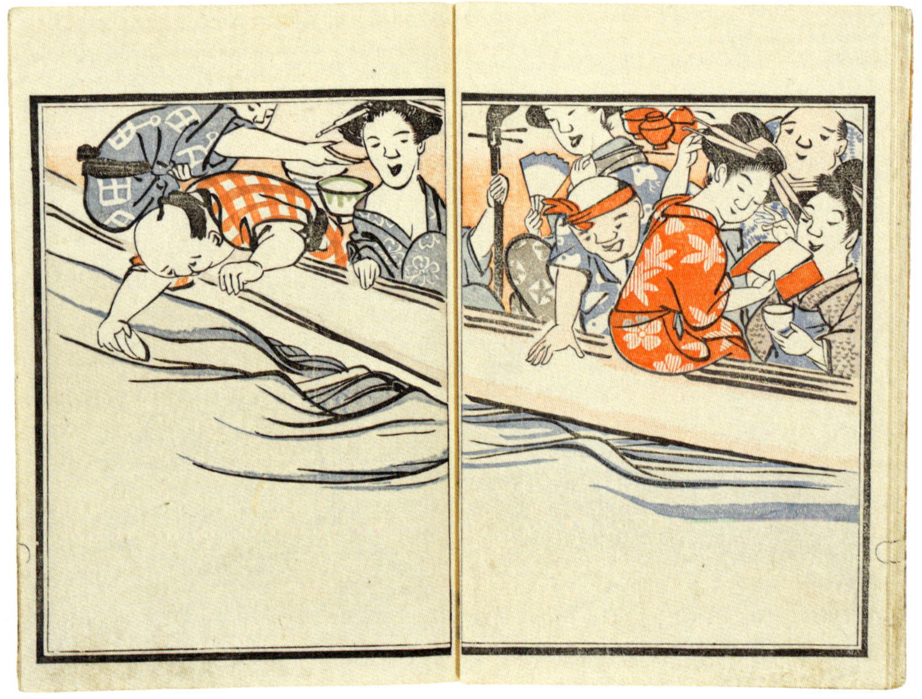

**2.3**
Naitō Tōho (artist), 'Dragonfly and wind chime', from vol. 2 of Katō Kyōtai (editor), *Koya Library* (*Koya bunko*), 3 vols, 1768. Illustrated book, woodblock. 26 × 17 cm (cover). British Museum, London, 1979,0305,0.115.1–3. Ex-coll.: Jack Hillier.

The poem by Beppō reads:
*kagerō no / anatsuri-gamashi / natsu zashiki*
the dragonfly / wants to hover / at the summer party

**2.4**
'Boating party', from vol. 2 of Saitō Shūho, *Mr Aoi's Chronicle of Charm* (*Kishi enpu*), 3 vols, 1803. Illustrated book, colour woodblock. 25.7 × 18.2 cm (cover). British Museum, London, 1952,1108,0.11.1–3. Ex-coll.: Hayashi Tadamasa.

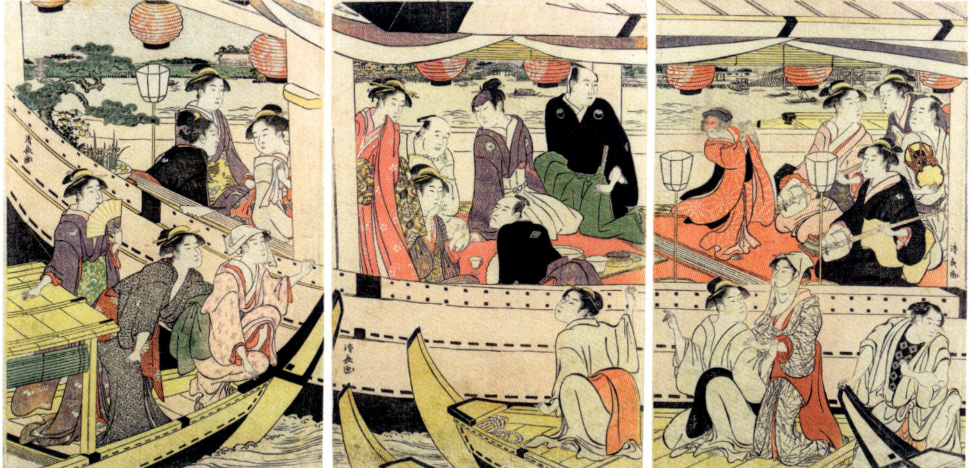

**2.5**
Torii Kiyonaga, *Scene of Pleasure Boats on the Sumida River*, mid-1780s. Triptych print, colour woodblock. *c.* 39 × 25 cm (each sheet). British Museum, London, 1927,0613,0.20.1–3. Gift of Robert N. Shaw.

Since the late fifteenth century, the Kanō school had painted for the military ruling class, temples and shrines; the Tosa school more for the Kyoto aristocracy and latterly for samurai lords who aspired to aristocratic culture. In the period under consideration, the Kanō school grew revamped local lineages in Kyoto and Osaka. Otherwise, Ukiyo-e, Sumiyoshi, Zen, Rinpa, Literati (*bunjin-ga*, 'scholar painting'), Nagasaki, Maruyama, Shijō and Yamato-e Revival are just some of the main new painting schools that modern art history has identified as having positioned themselves alongside the traditional ones over the course of the seventeenth to nineteenth centuries. This is even before we begin to enumerate important familial lineages of painters such as Kishi (Gan), Hara (Gen), Mochizuki, Mori, (Tani) Bunchō and so on. From the 1790s there was also increasing exposure and competition in public exhibitions (see fig. 4.23). Little wonder that publishers regularly printed who's-who volumes of practitioners in many cultural fields, notably painting, with addresses so that people could petition a teacher or commission a work.

## Painting life versus painting ideas

Arguably, all the schools listed above engaged in some way with everyday life as a subject, to a greater or lesser extent. This book focuses on the two broad new streams of bunjin-ga (see chapter 4) and the Maruyama-Shijō school. (Strictly speaking, 'Maruyama-Shijō' is a neologism coined in the early twentieth century to refer to the interlinked schools of Maruyama Ōkyo and Matsumura Gekkei (Go Shun) (fig. 2.6), with the latter's studio located near

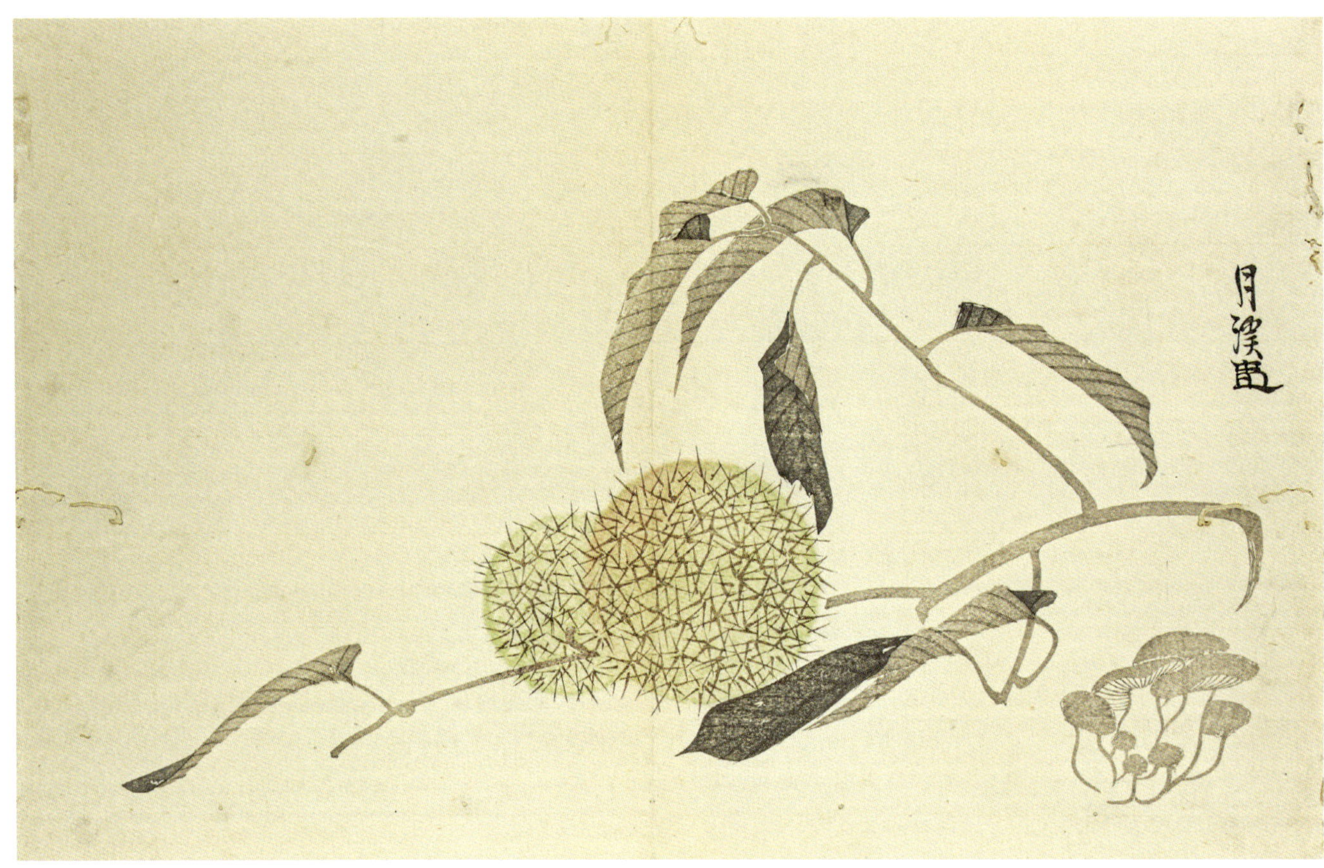

Shijō avenue in Kyoto.) Everyday life was much more likely to be a subject for Maruyama-Shijō artists; indeed, it became a defining characteristic of their work. A much simpler perspective that cuts across the complex matrix of artists and schools, one that would have been familiar to people at the time, is to contrast the ambition to 'paint life' (*shasei*) with the preference to 'paint ideas' (*sha'i*). It was theoretically possible to combine both ambitions, of course, but the following oppositional pairings can usefully be applied to analyse the innovative art of the time: appearance/essence, nature/concept, concrete/abstract, contemporary/historical and even Japan/China. Broadly speaking, Maruyama-Shijō artists tended towards shasei, while literati painters cultivated sha'i. Many artists successfully used a variety of styles, however, in response to different contexts of patronage.

The concept and practice of 'copying from life' (another possible translation of shasei) was firmly established among certain key artists of the Edo period, including such luminaries as Kanō Tan'yū (1602–1674), Ogata Kōrin

**2.6**
Go Shun (Matsumura Gekkei),
*Chestnuts and Mushrooms*,
from *Roots of the Heart* (*Kokoro
no nezashi*), 1 vol., 1793. Album,
colour woodblock. 27.8 ×
21.1 cm (cover). British Museum,
London, 1979,0305,0.169.
Ex-coll.: Jack Hillier.

(1658–1716), Maruyama Ōkyo (1733–1795) and Utagawa Hiroshige (1797–1858) (fig. 2.7). Their brush sketches in ink outline, sometimes with simple additions of colour, give an indication of having been done impromptu 'in nature' – rather like a European artist of the day would have used pencil and watercolour in a sketchbook. But when it comes to how artists developed their sketches to create finished works, cultural practice diverged. Filling the picture plane in a naturalistic way, opening a window directly onto the natural world as a post-Renaissance European painter might seek to do, was rarely the ambition of artists in early modern Japan. Rather, vivid and lifelike details

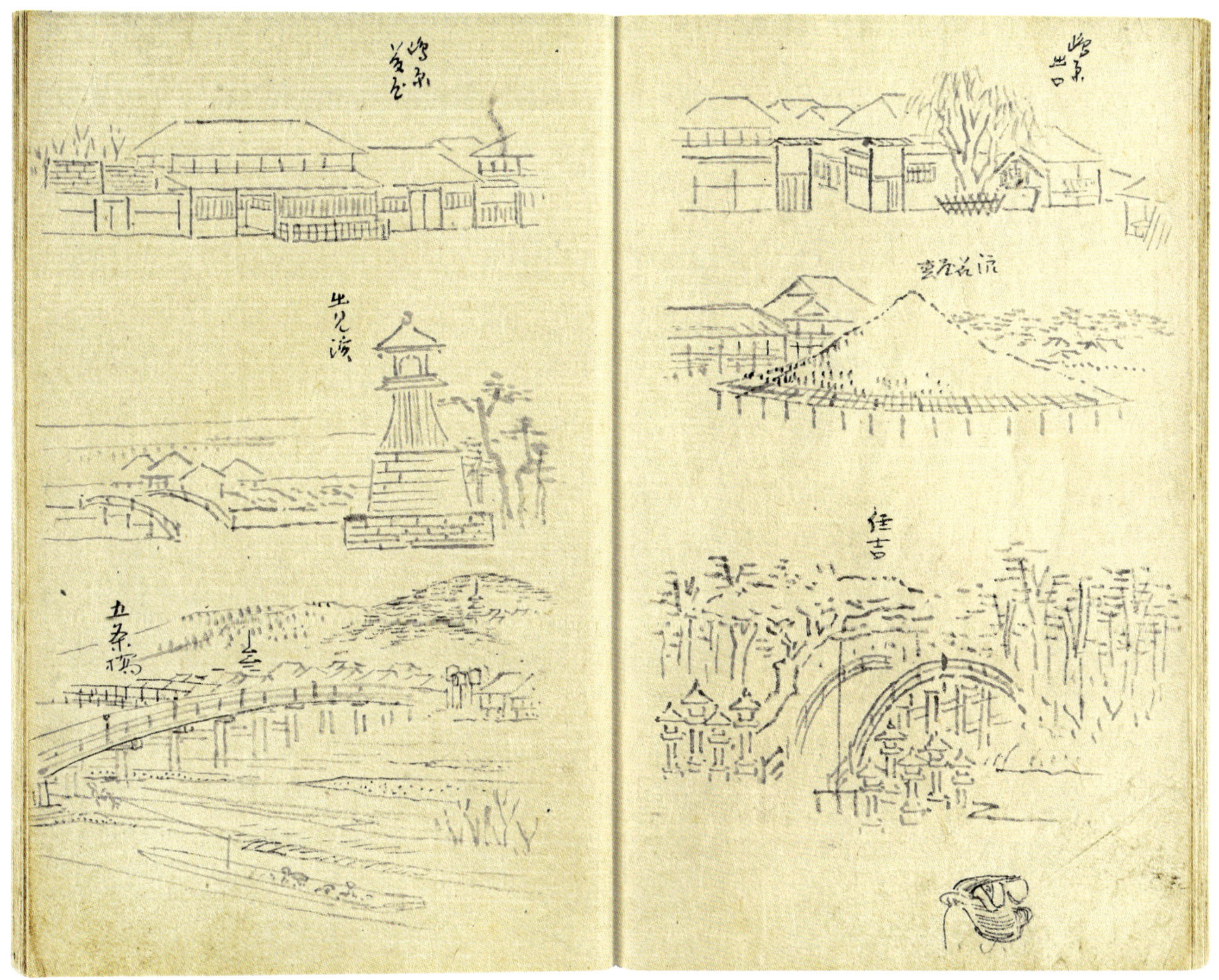

were invariably incorporated into a composition that, overall, had decorative, non-naturalistic flair, and was appropriate to the artefact being made. (Grand painted screens, with six or eight folding panels, were of course both furniture and artwork.) In his ground-breaking study of Shijō-style art, *The Uninhibited Brush* (1974), Jack Hillier famously juxtaposed paintings of trees by Ōkyo and the English landscapist John Constable (1776–1837) (figs 2.8–2.9):[1] 'naturalism' in art is not universal; rather it appears at particular times and in particular places and is dependent on experience and technique.

For example, Ōkyo and his followers became associated with a particular brush technique known as *tsuketate*, sometimes translated as 'boneless' or 'contourless' painting, described as a way of 'expressing shadow and



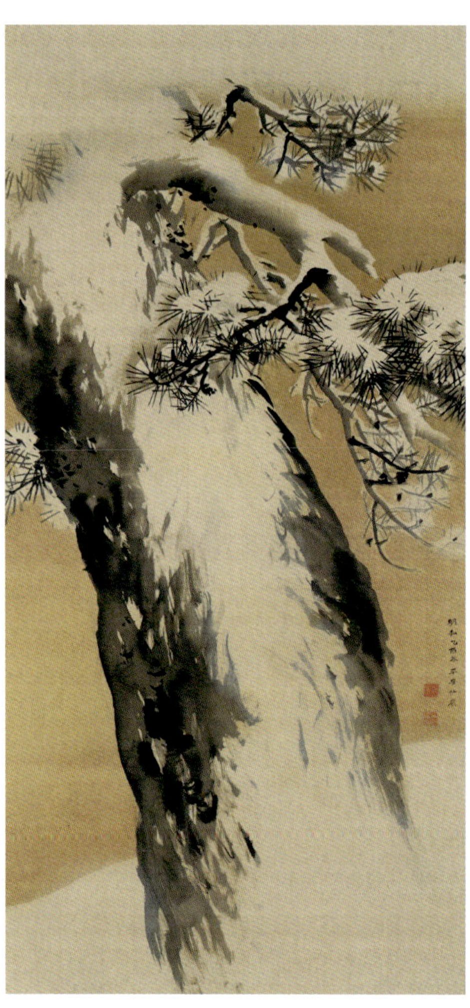

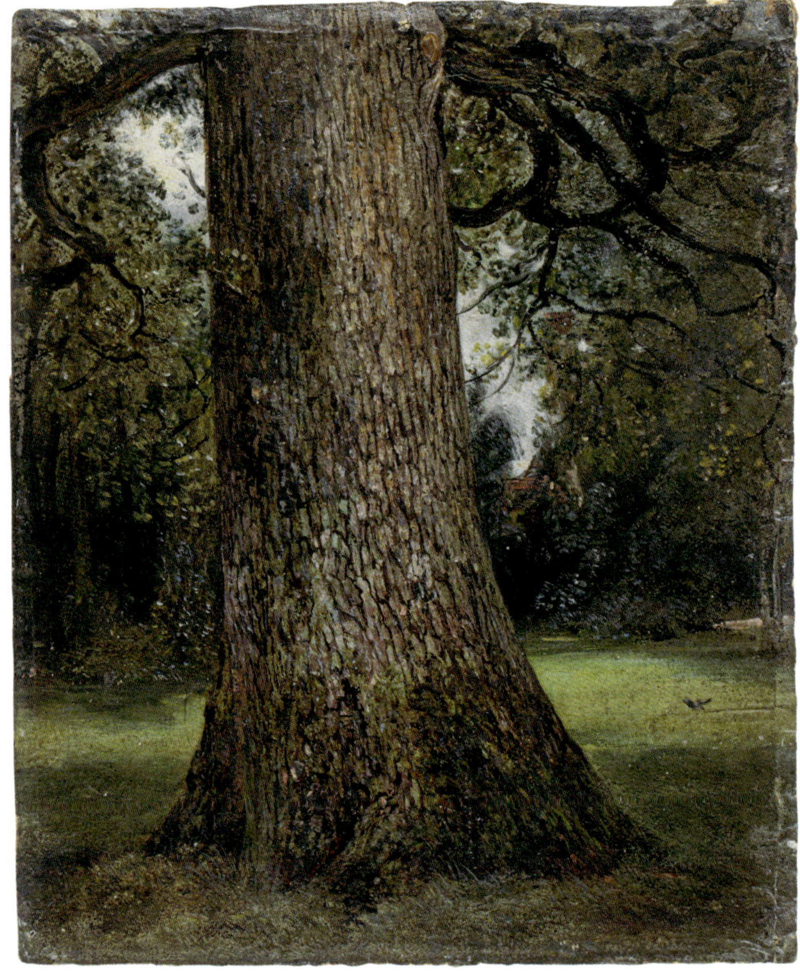

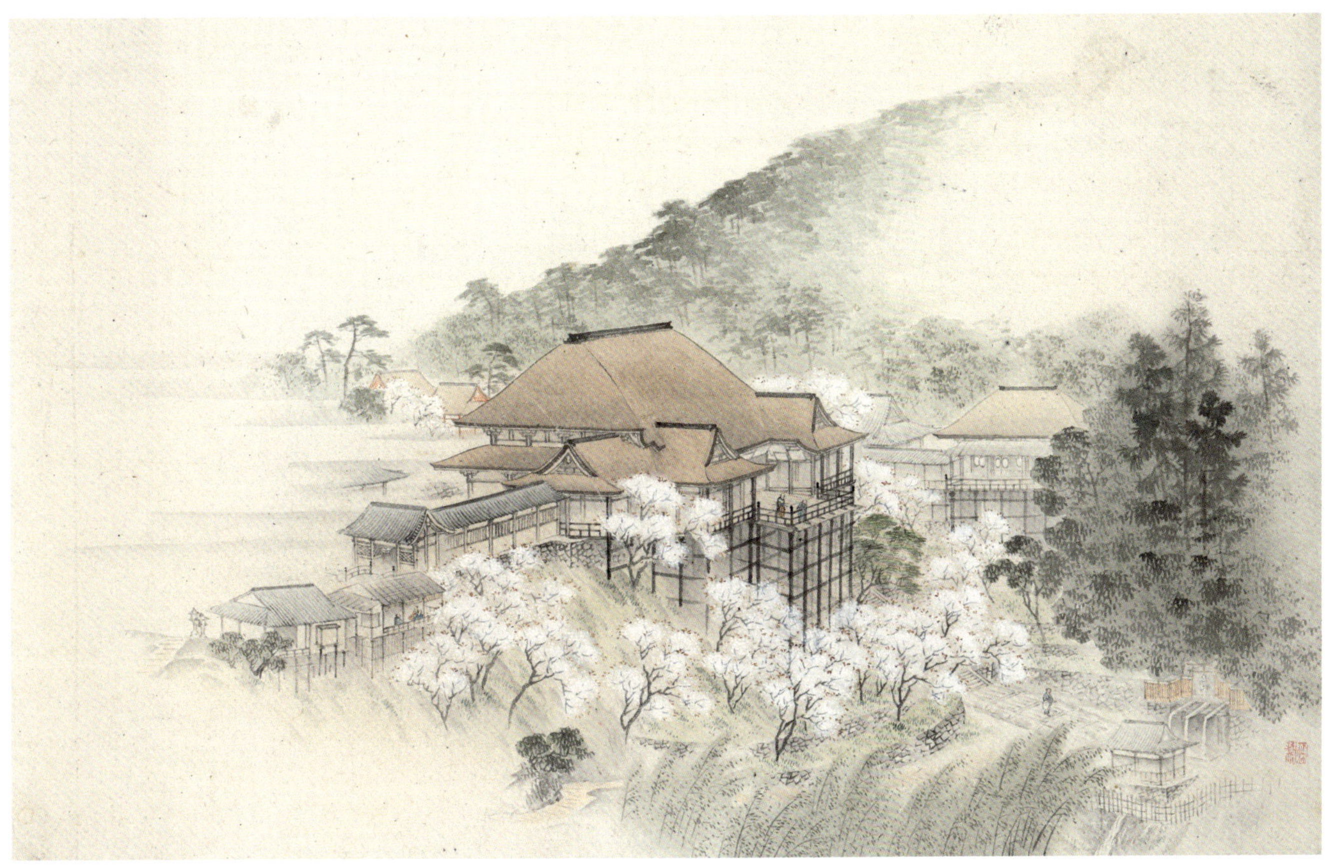

2.10

Maruyama Ōkyo, *Kiyomizu-dera Temple* (*Kiyomizu*), from *Sixteen Views of Kyoto*, 1773. Handscroll, ink and colour on paper. 31.7 × 43.8 cm. British Museum, London, 1967,1016,0.1.

three-dimensionality without outlines by painting the subject in a single stroke using the long edges of the hairs of the brush'.[2] In *Pine Tree in the Snow* (fig. 2.8) tsuketate is employed for the snow-covered branches of the tree. Another innovation that spread widely from Ōkyo's example into general art practice was to create a sense of deep spatial recession in a composition (see fig. 3.19) Ōkyo first learned this technique in his twenties, when he was hired to paint 'perspective pictures' (*megane-e*) that were used in portable peep-show devices, initially imported from Europe. This style became the basis for his intricate 1773 painted handscroll of cityscapes, *Sixteen Views of Kyoto* (fig. 2.10), as well as for the extended series of printed illustrated gazetteers (meisho zue) (see fig. 2.30 and p. 77) by a range of other artists that featured Kyoto, Osaka and many other cities and regions of Japan, and were published from 1780 through to the middle of the nineteenth century.

In a mature, large-scale work by Ōkyo and pupils, the screen painting *Tigers Crossing a River* (see fig. 3.18), there are novel elements that in the

Japanese context would have appeared strikingly 'realistic' – the closely observed matted wet fur of the mother's breast or the way the river seems to flow out towards us from deep inside the composition. Yet the main impact of the gold-leaf covered screen, which would have lit up a gloomy interior, is surely decorative.[3] Ōkyo brilliantly synthesised innovative technique with a new take on such traditional subjects.

## Censorship: what artists could not show

Life and behaviour in Edo society was strictly controlled in attempts to conform with the 'ideal' model established by the military government at the beginning of the seventeenth century, symbolised by a social stratification into the (descending) hierarchy of 'samurai, farmer, artisan, merchant' (see p. 48). In the material realm, people were limited in what they could wear, build and consume by detailed sumptuary laws, according to status. In visual and textual realms, books and other publicly printed works were censored for their content before publication. There was a blanket ban on commenting on contemporary events of consequence and the affairs of the ruling classes – in striking contrast with, say, the ferociously satirical prints of Thomas Rowlandson (1756–1827) and James Gillray (1756–1815) in Great Britain at the time. Unlike Europe, which constantly memorialised its rulers with public portraits and coins, the person of the emperor was never depicted in Japan (fig. 2.1, in which the presence of the emperor is implied inside the building and the nobles are shown outside), and the shogun only very rarely so. Popular writers and artists did find oblique means to comment on current political affairs in ephemeral genres of illustrated fiction, such as 'yellow backs' (*kibyōshi*) – sometimes characterised as 'comic books for adults' – and in kabuki theatre by transposing plotlines to the distant past. Insects and animals were on occasion co-opted to poke gently satirical fun at rulers, as in *Insects Parodying the Procession of a Samurai Lord* by the Osaka artist Nishiyama Hōen (1804–1867) (fig. 2.11). Unsigned (and unauthorised) scandal sheets called 'tile prints' (*kawaraban*), generally crudely produced in woodblock and sometimes illustrated, did in fact circulate widely. But there was always the real risk of suppression and punishment.

In 1788 much of central Kyoto, including the imperial palace, was destroyed by fire. No painted representations of this cataclysmic disaster have survived (if they were ever made).[4] In 1864, as the samurai system of government was collapsing, again there was large-scale destruction in Kyoto, the outcome of civil war fought in the streets of the capital. Finally, at this late

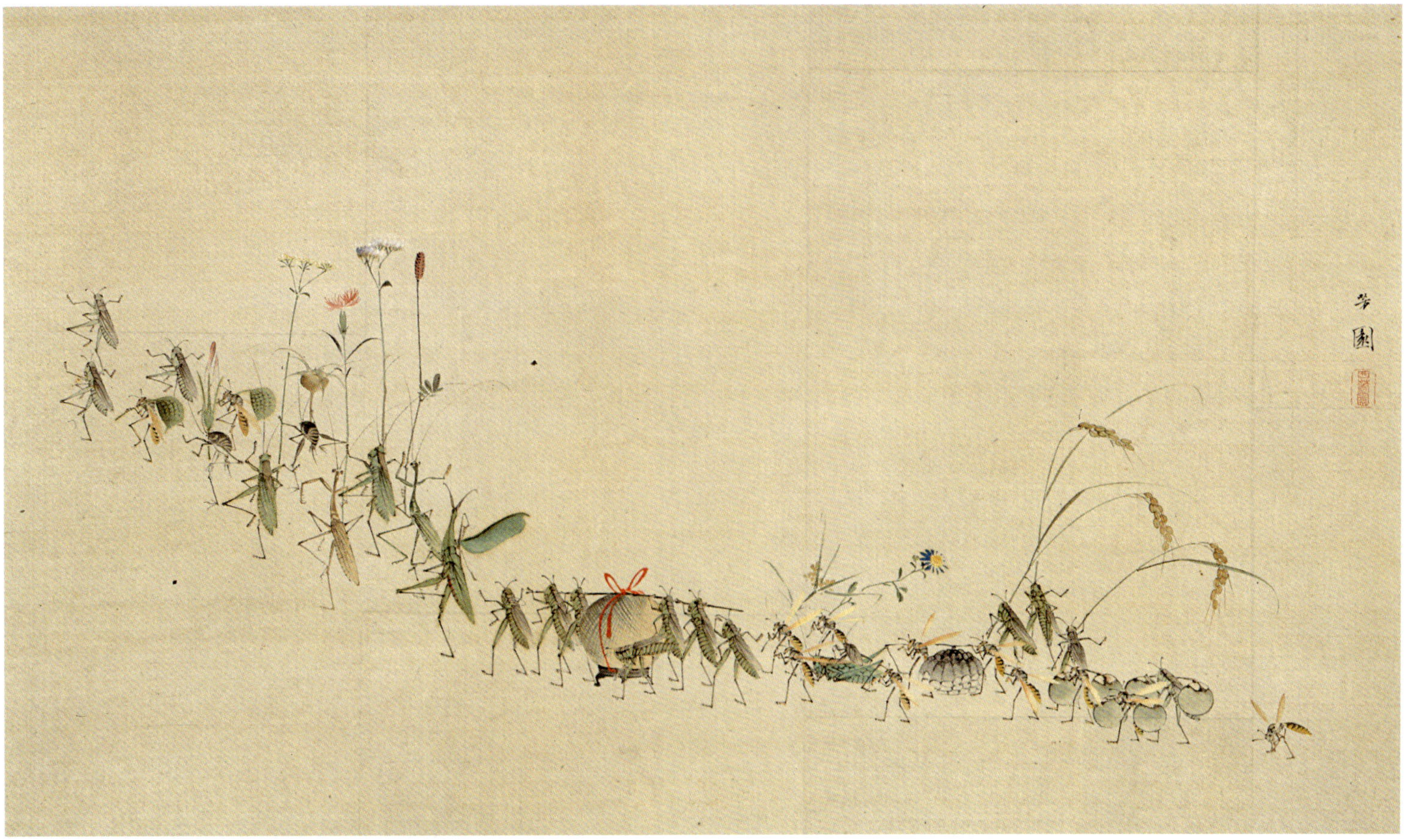

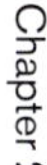



**2.11**

Nishiyama Hōen, *Insects Parodying the Procession of a Samurai Lord*, before 1851. Hanging scroll, ink and colour on silk. 49.2 × 86.1 cm. British Museum, London, 1881,1210,0.2264. Ex-coll.: William Anderson.

date, there is a pair of painted handscrolls contemporary to the events by the Shijō artist Maekawa Gorei (1805–1876), *Civil War in Kyoto* (fig. 2.12). In Osaka in 1837 there was a major popular rebellion protesting economic hardship led by Ōshio Heihachirō (1793–1837), formerly a senior samurai administrator in the city. Scenes of the uprising, from Ōshio's career in the city magistrate's office until his suicide when the rebellion failed, are recorded in four unique hand-painted volumes now preserved at the Osaka Museum of History (fig. 2.13), although this may be a manuscript drawn sometime after the happenings portrayed. In contrast to Europe during this epoch, which was constantly riven by religious and revolutionary wars, Japan was relatively at peace for the two and a half centuries of the Edo period. Yet there were occasional popular uprisings, as well as frequent fires, earthquakes, floods and other disasters, which by samurai government decree could not legally be depicted and distributed in pictures. Images of non-controversial current events, such as the spectacle of a visit of a camel to Osaka in 1823 were, however, permitted, as exemplified by a large surimono by Tanaka Kōu (active 1820s–50s) (fig. 2.14), which comically contrasts the ungainly form of the beast with the elegantly dressed figure of a spectator, likely a courtesan.

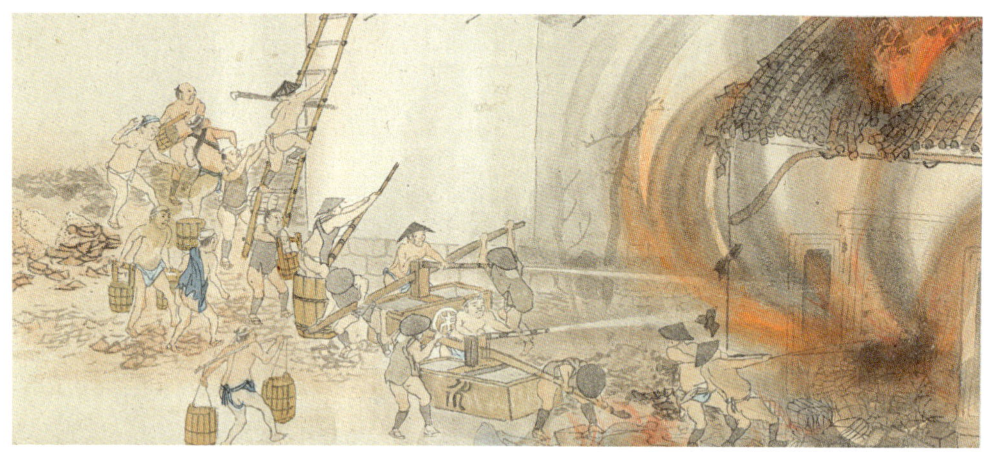

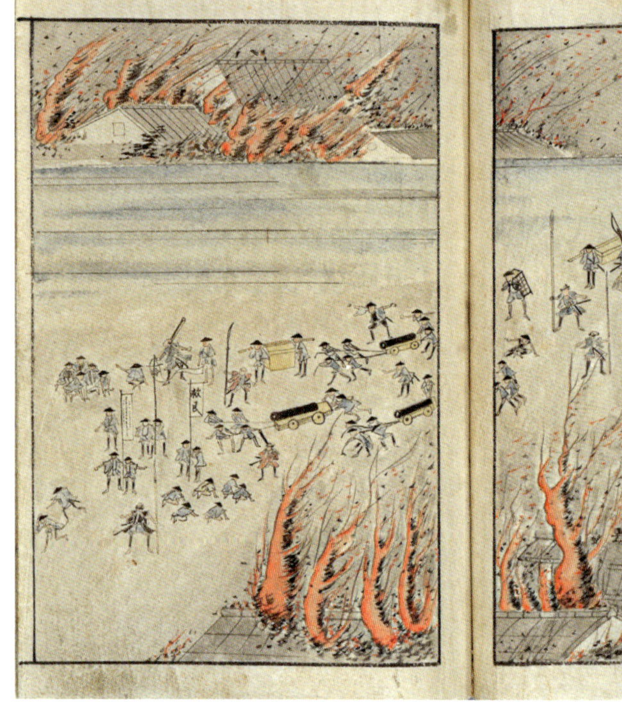

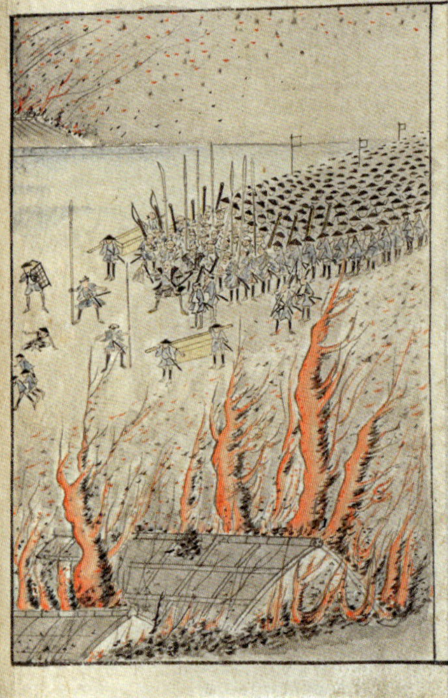



**2.12**
Maekawa Gorei, *Civil War in Kyoto* (*Kōshi heisen zu*, detail), 1864. Vol. 1 of a pair of handscrolls, ink and colour on paper. 26.9 × 1076.6 cm (each). Harvard Art Museums/Arthur M. Sackler Museum, Cambridge, 1985.758.1. Bequest of the Hofer Collection of the Arts of Asia.

**2.13**
Artist unknown, *Collected Records of the Rebellion of Ōshio Heihachirō* (*Deshio hikishio kanzoku monshūki*), 4 vols, 1800s. Illustrated book, ink and colour on paper. 24.2 × 17 cm (cover). Osaka Museum of History.

## Emotional range

A key early painting commission for the ambitious young Ōkyo was what became the set of three handscrolls *Seven Disasters and Seven Happinesses* (*Shichinan shichifuku*, 1765–8) (figs 2.15–2.16).[5] His patron Yūjō (1723–1773), abbot of the aristocratic temple Enman-in at Ōtsu, sought powerful imagery that would illustrate the fundamental Buddhist concept of karma (cause and effect); demonstrating to people that their actions and intentions determine what happens to them. Ōkyo's three handscrolls were divided into scenes of 'heavenly disasters' (such as the flood in fig. 2.15), 'human disasters' and '[human] happinesses' (such as the banquet scene in fig 2.16). He devised an innovative style of appropriate clarity and, when required, gravity, and the frequency with which the work was studied and copied by later artists indicates its canonical status. 'Those who see the pictures break into sweats, their hair stands on end, and even though they are not cold, they start to shake,'[6] wrote Oku Bunmei (1773–1813), Ōkyo's pupil and early biographer.

In the generations that followed Ōkyo, and notwithstanding their study of his *Seven Disasters and Seven Happinesses*, few artists seemed to have had the

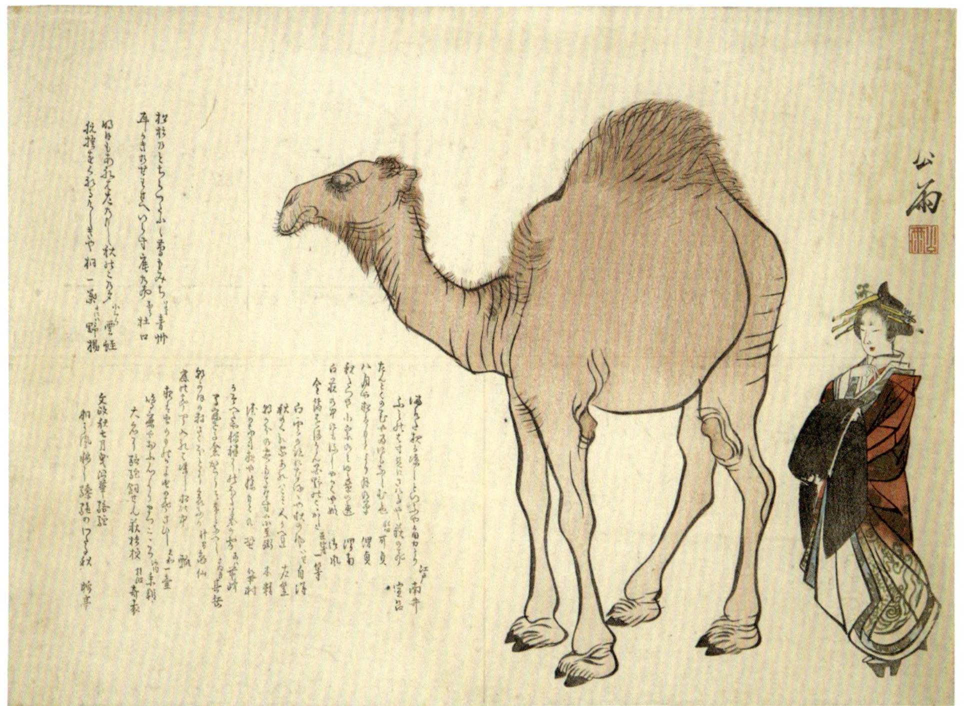

**2.14**
Tanaka Kōu (artist) and 23 poets, *Camel and Courtesan*, 1823. Surimono, colour woodblock. 38.2 × 51.8 cm. British Museum, London, 2021,3013.08 Purchase made possible by the JTI Japanese Acquisition Fund. Ex-coll.: Dr Scott Johnson.

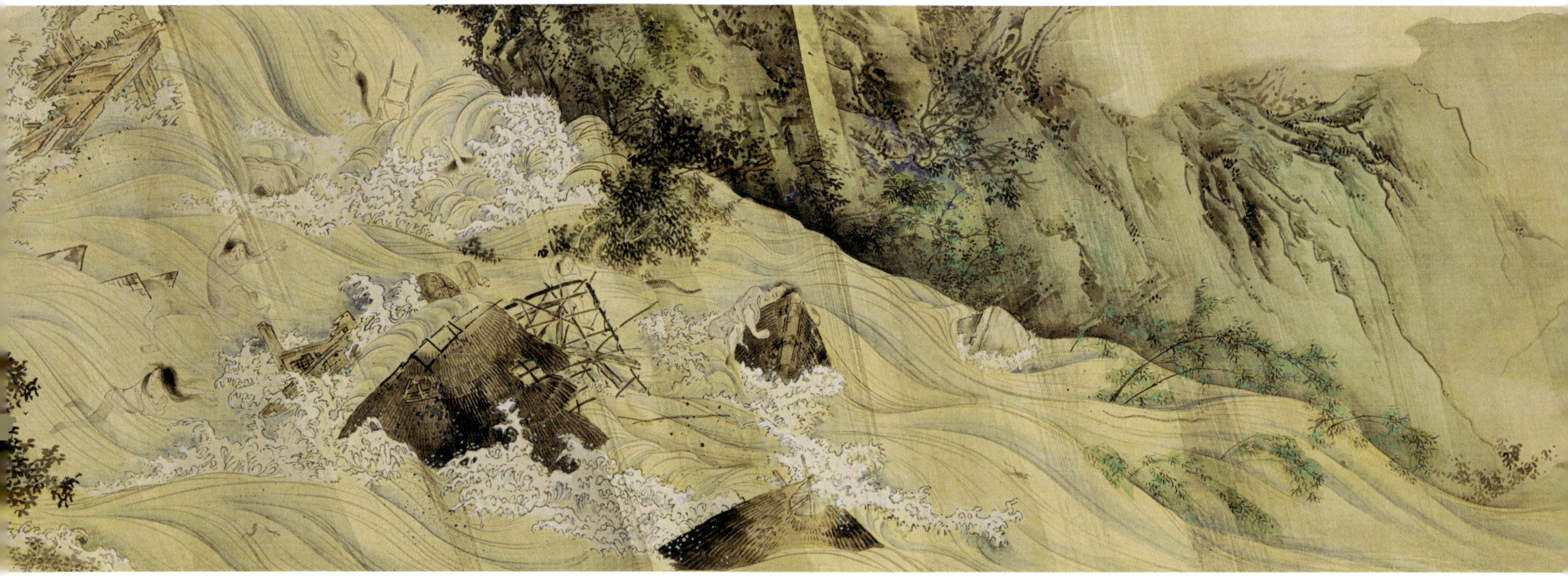

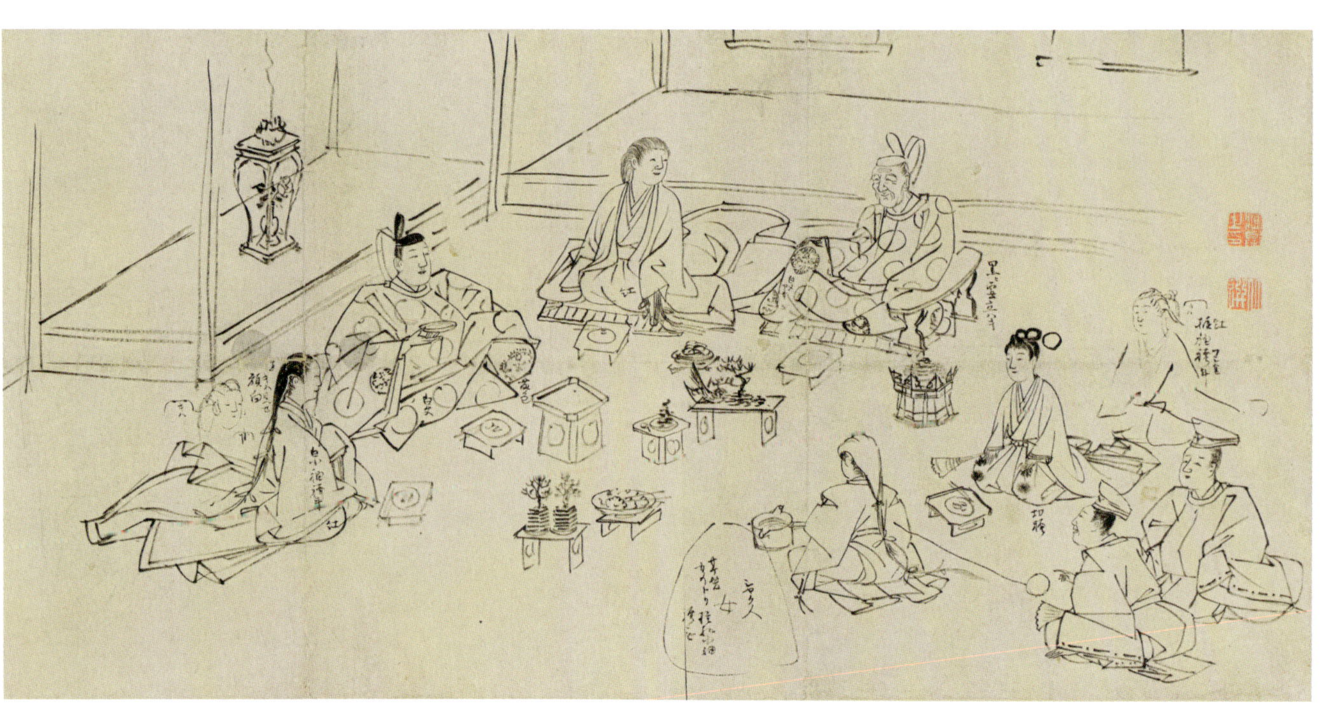

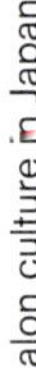
Salon culture in Japan

inclination – or perhaps the occasion – to create figural works with such serious, life-and-death subject matter. One notable exception, once again grounded in Buddhist beliefs in cause and effect, albeit from a more popular milieu, was the book *Leave Sorrows and Joys to the Brush* (*Kafuku ninpitsu*, 1809) illustrated by the Kyoto artist Kawamura Kihō (1778–1852). Developing further the forceful, inflected and expressive brushwork of his teacher and adoptive father Kawamura Bunpō (1779–1821) (see figs 2.34–2.35, 2.37) and commissioned by Kyoto art publisher Yoshidaya Shinbei (Bunchōdō), Kihō devised fifteen vivid scenes of unfiltered daily life, informed by the popular divination system of *sanzesō* (literally 'physiognomies of the three worlds [past, present, future]'). The pictures starkly juxtapose, as in Ōkyo's handscrolls of some forty years earlier, the trials and the rewards of life. In a humble farming kitchen, an angry and likely drunken man raises a pestle and his fist as his wife begs him not to get violent, even as their baby plays alongside (fig. 2.17). No text guides us in how to interpret the scene and this was a fundamental part of the Ōkyo revolution: to endow pictures with the veracity to speak for themselves.

In the first four decades of the nineteenth century, the democratisation of art is represented by the kaleidoscope of bravura artist picture manuals (*gafu*) that began to appear (see pp. 122–3), fostered by publishers such as Yoshidaya. A key early trend-setting publication was *Yamato jinbutsu gafu*, its title evoking something like *Picture Album of the People of* [*Our Native*] *Japan* (as opposed to China). The first part (in three volumes) was published in 1800 by Kyoto's



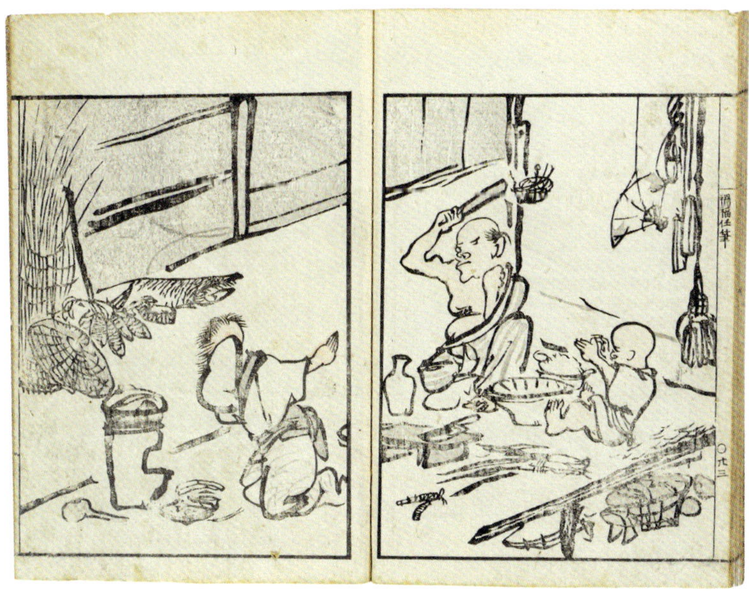

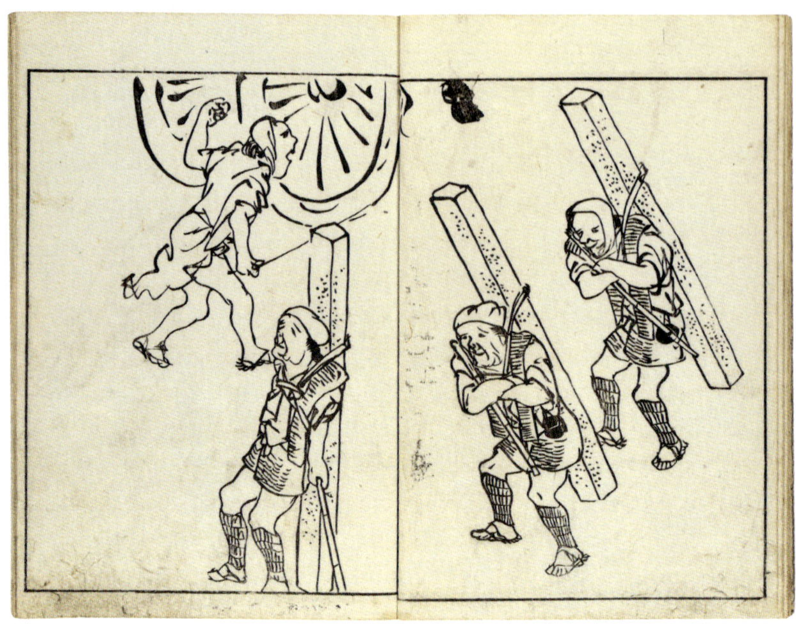
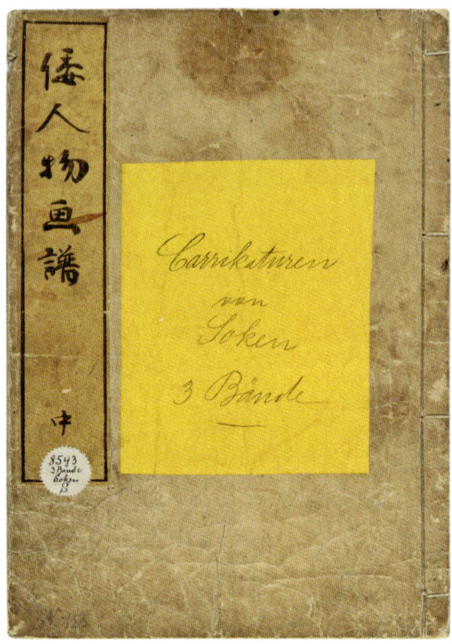

Hishiya Magobei and the arresting black-and-white images are by Yamaguchi Soken (1759–1818), a key Ōkyo pupil. An image such as 'Porters (*Se-oi*)' elicits both empathy with the elderly workmen struggling to carry stone posts on their backs and admiration for Soken's bold compositional flair, the spokes of a cart's wheels echoing the precarious angles of the stone posts (fig. 2.18). A former owner of one copy of the book pasted onto the cover of volume two a label hand-written in German that reads 'Caricatures' (fig. 2.19).

## Painting modern life

'Pictures of the floating world' (ukiyo-e) were celebrated as a famous product of – and appropriate souvenir from – Edo, the eastern capital that was the seat of power of the shoguns. A popular art form predominantly produced as affordable colour woodblock prints, ukiyo-e were permitted, even encouraged, to focus on the commercial pleasures of the city, the many entertainment districts predicated on widespread sex work and the wildly successful kabuki theatre. This was therefore a figure-dominated art form, whose tone was unfailingly upbeat and glamorous – in the eighteenth century, at least. The style is considered to have reached its apogee with Torii Kiyonaga (1752–1815), whose prints are populated by implausibly tall figures arranged in elegant



**2.18**
'Porters (*Se-oi*)', from vol. 1 of Yamaguchi Soken, *Picture Album of the People of Japan* (*Yamato jinbutsu gafu*), 3 vols, 1800. Illustrated book, woodblock. 26 × 18.2 cm (cover). British Museum, London, 1979,0305,0.184.1–3. Ex-coll.: Jack Hillier.

**2.19**
'Caricatures by Soken, 3 Volumes' (*Carrikaturen von Soken, 3 Bände*). Label pasted onto the cover of Yamaguchi Soken, *Picture Album of the People of Japan* (*Yamato jinbutsu gafu*), vol. 2, 1800. Illustrated book, woodblock. 26 × 18.2 cm (cover). British Museum, London, 1979,0305,0.184.2. Ex-coll.: Jack Hillier.

groupings (see fig. 2.5). Not everyone approved of modern life being represented by sex workers and 'river beggars' (the discriminatory term for kabuki actors). The conservative statesman Matsudaira Sadanobu, shogunal Senior Councillor and *de facto* ruler from 1787 to 1793, even tried to foster a non-erotic school and style of contemporary figure art.[7] Ukiyo-e continued to flourish, nonetheless, establishing significant local offshoots in Kyoto and Osaka (see figs 2.25–2.26) sustained by the culture of the pleasure quarters and theatres in those cities, albeit not on the same vast scale as in Edo.

The figure styles of literati and Maruyama-Shijō artists in Kyoto and Osaka developed in deliberately non-idealised directions that contrasted strongly with ukiyo-e in Edo. Indeed, a naivete of style was cultivated that was valued for its authenticity and truth, particularly among literati artists such as Ike no Taiga, Yosa Buson and their followers (fig. 2.20). In the 1790s Buson's pupil Go Shun strove to combine this naive style with the more professionally slick idiom of Ōkyo and pupils. The resulting figure style developed a certain squatness markedly removed from elegance. In a mature Go Shun painting such as *The Red Cliff* (fig. 2.21), even Chinese protagonists are given these characteristics, which are then inherited by Go Shun pupils such as his younger

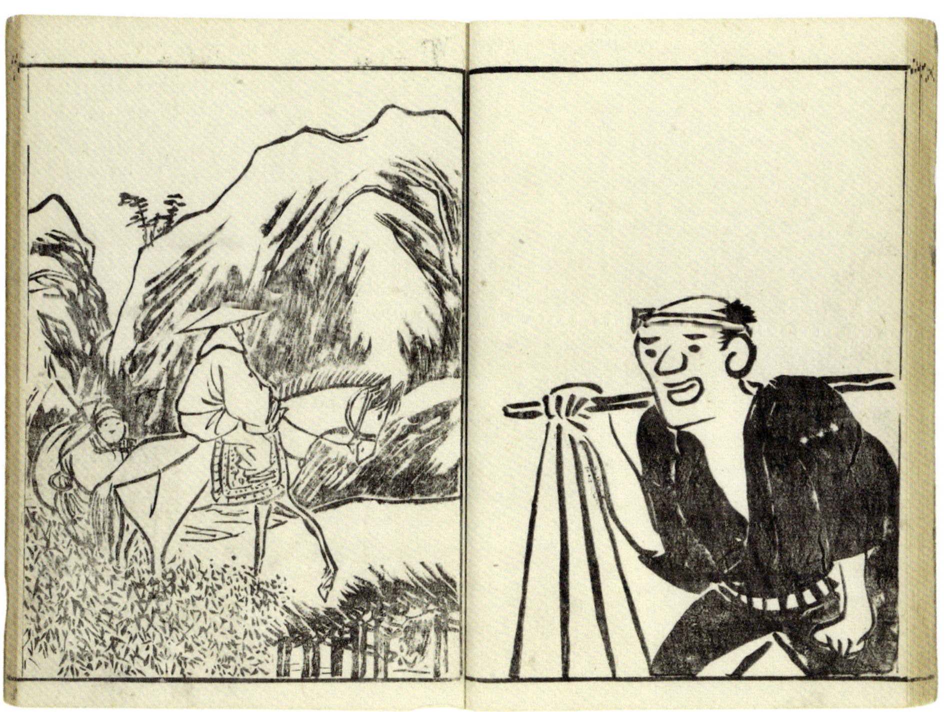

**2.20**
'Delivery man' (right) and 'Travellers in mountains' (left), in Ki Baitei, *Kyūrō's Picture Album* (*Kyūrō gafu*), 1 vol., 1797. Illustrated book, woodblock. 26.1 × 18.6 cm (cover). British Museum, London, 1979,0305,0.183. Ex-coll.: Jack Hillier.

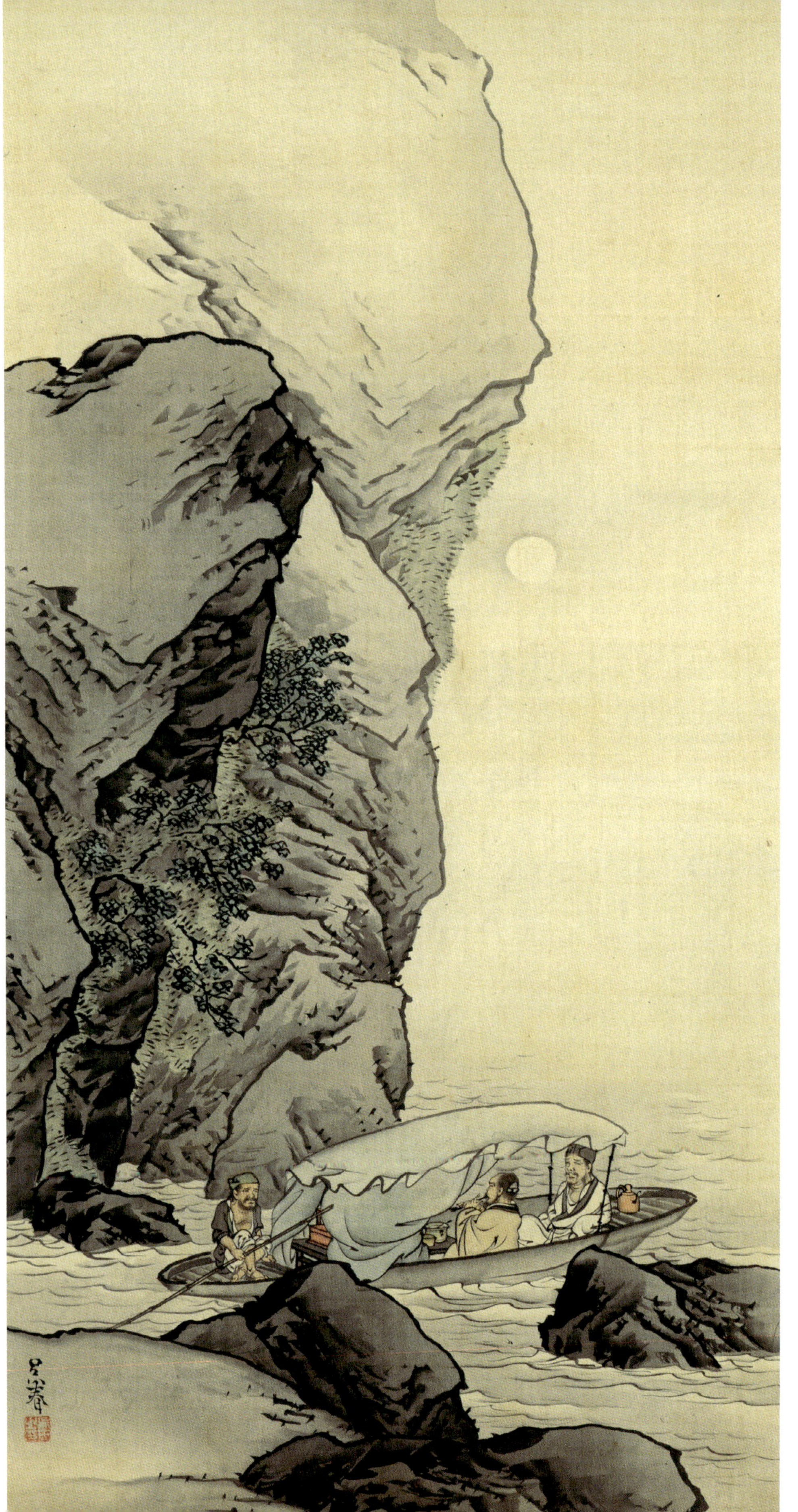



**2.21**
Go Shun, *The Red Cliff*, *c.* 1800.
Hanging scroll, ink and colour
on silk. 101.3 × 50.2 cm. British
Museum, London, 2000,1128,0.1.

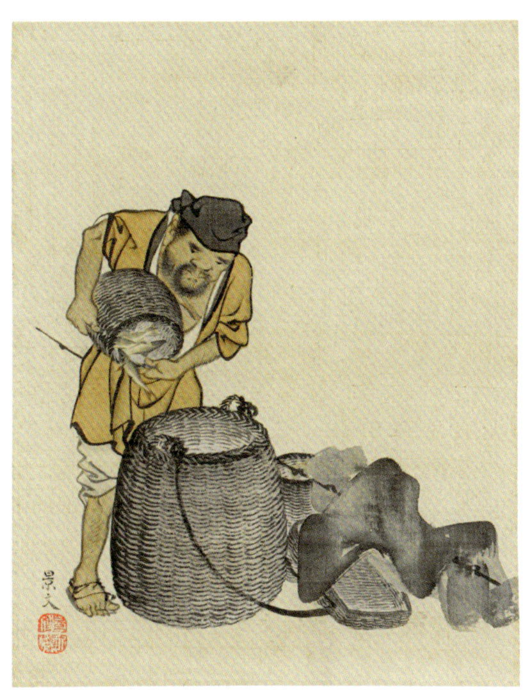

**2.22**
Matsumura Keibun, *Fisherman*, c. 1800. Hanging scroll, ink and colour on silk. 29 × 21.9 cm. British Museum, London, 1881,1210,0.2267. Ex-coll.: William Anderson.

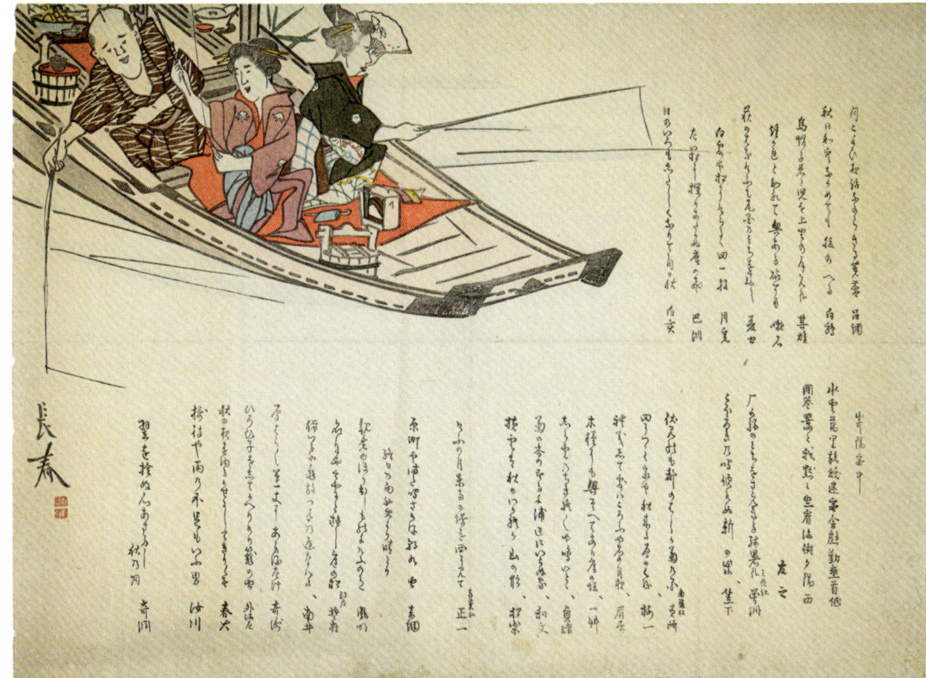

**2.23**
Nakamura Chōshun, *Boating Party*, early 1800s. Surimono, colour woodblock. 38.2 × 51.9 cm. British Museum, London, 2021,3013.56. Purchase made possible by the JTI Japanese Acquisition Fund. Ex-coll.: Dr Scott Johnson.

half-brother Matsumura Keibun (fig. 2.22), a major figure in the second generation of the Shijō school. Squat figures come to populate the works of many subsequent Kyoto and particularly Osaka artists, an extreme example being Satō Suiseki (Gyodai) of Osaka. Undoubtedly such works would have been savoured in their original cultural milieu for their 'true-to-life' qualities.

An instructive comparison can be made among three pictures of people enjoying boating (figs 2.23–2.24, see fig. 2.6). Nakamura Chōshun's (active early nineteenth century) large surimono of the early 1800s (fig. 2.23) includes, at top left, a vignette of a fishing party with refreshments shown from above at an arresting angle and with daring cropping – leaving plenty of space to accommodate the couple of dozen haiku poems printed below. The relaxed, genial style of the figures emphasises the informality and fun of the occasion. Contrast this with the frieze-like formality of the earlier Kiyonaga triptych print of the 1780s from Edo (see fig. 2.5) in which spectators on smaller boats gather to gawk at the celebrity kabuki actors who party on the pleasure barge across the back of the composition. Ōnishi Chinnen was a key artist in the Edo offshoot of the Maruyama-Shijō school, and his book illustration of 1834 features travellers brought briefly together as they cross what is likely the Sumida River at Mimeguri (fig. 2.24). The printed outlines of the figures and

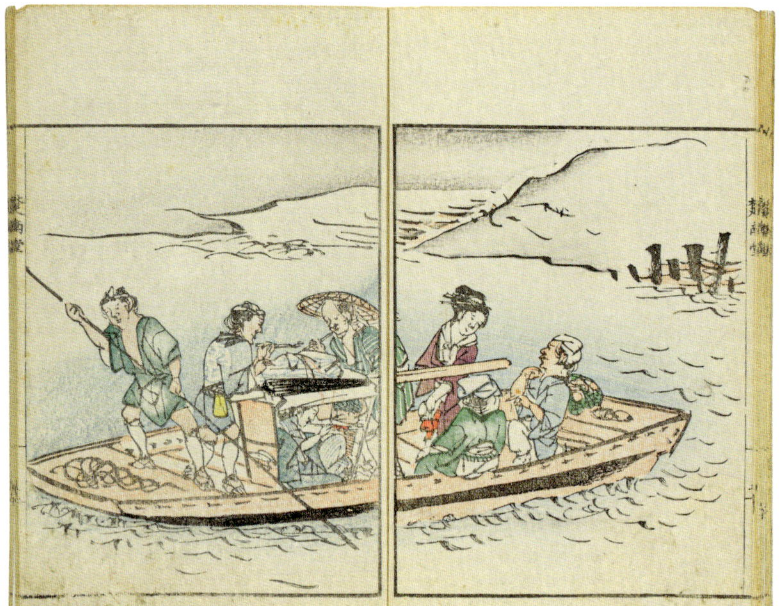



**2.24**
'Ferryboat', in Ōnishi Chinnen, *Sonan's Picture Album* (*Sonan gafu*), 1 vol., 1834. Illustrated book, colour woodblock. 26.9 × 18.3 cm (cover). British Museum, London, 1979,0305,0.325. Ex-coll.: Jack Hillier.

their garments reproduce a brush style that is quirky and flavoursome – quite different, for example, from the idiom of Hiroshige, his famous contemporary working in the same city. Shijō art invariably showcases its own informality.

## Pictures of beautiful people

*Bijin-ga*, pictures of beautiful women and attractive young men, were a well-established genre in Japan since the second half of the seventeenth century. For wealthier clients these were typically elaborate paintings of a richly dressed, alluring single figure – a courtesan or a youth, perhaps a trainee kabuki actor – on a silk or paper hanging scroll. Pictorial evidence suggests such scrolls were hung in the display alcove of a party room in the entertainment districts, alternatively in the study of a man who might himself be a patron of the person depicted. Sometimes the painting would even be inscribed with the actual calligraphy of the sitter.

Other professional entertainers were celebrated in addition to female and male sex workers, and such is the case in the charming hanging scroll *Kyoto Geisha* of around 1800 by Yamaguchi Soken (fig. 2.25). The young entertainer, carrying her trademark shamisen and ivory plectrum, leans forward seemingly to engage with someone outside of the picture. The inscription is a

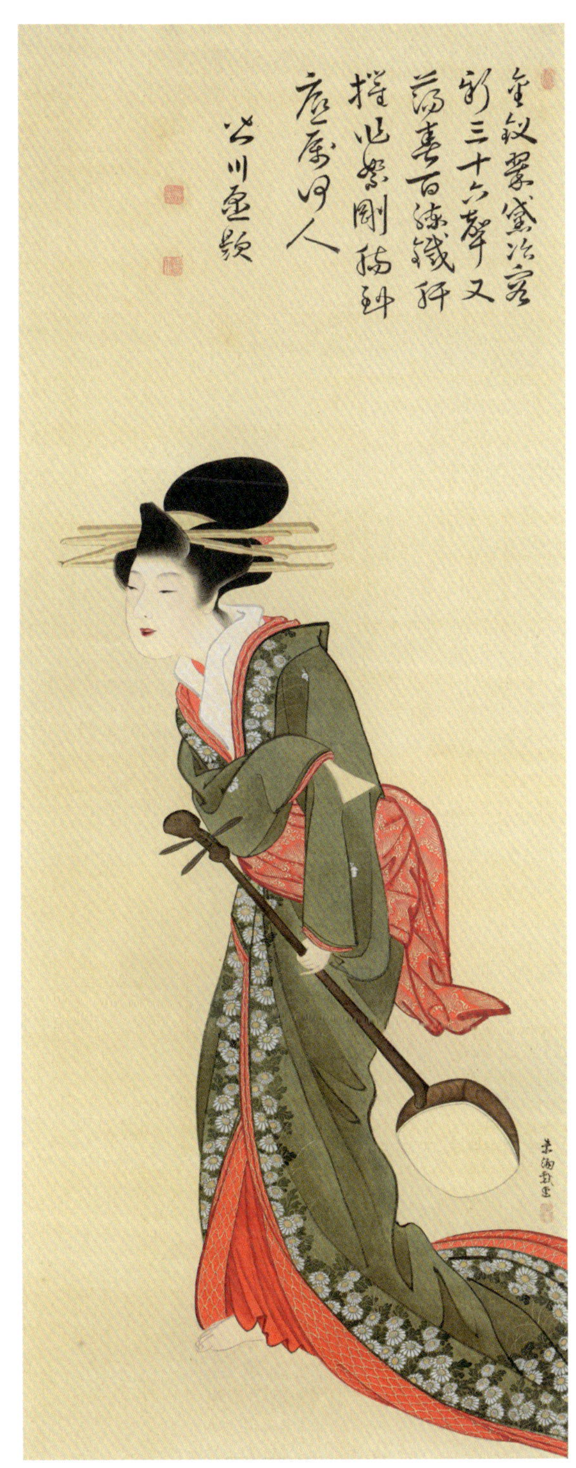

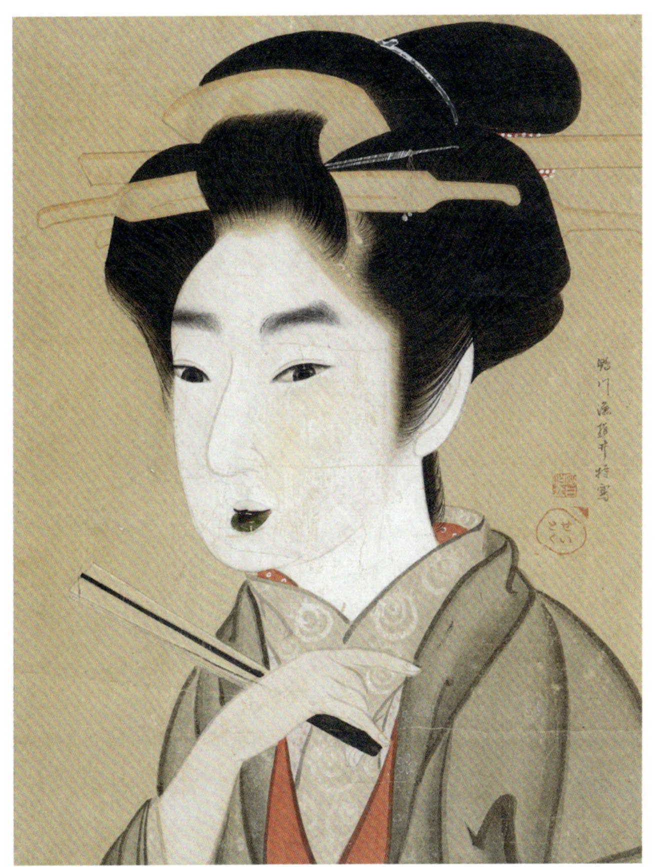

**2.25** *left*
Yamaguchi Soken (artist) and
Minagawa Kien (calligrapher),
*Kyoto Geisha*, *c.* 1800  Hanging
scroll, ink and colour on
silk. 106.8 × 40.6 cm. British
Museum, London, 2006,0222,0.1.
Purchase funded by the Brooke
Sewell Bequest. Ex-coll.: Ozu
family, Matsuzaka, Ise.

**2.26** *above*
Gion Seitoku, *Kyoto Apprentice
Geisha*, *c.* 1800–10. Hanging
scroll, ink and colour on paper.
55.8 × 41.3 cm. British Museum,
London, 2020,3020.1. Gift of
Rowena Kinsman.

Chinese-style poem by the Kyoto Confucian scholar and *bon viveur* Minagawa Kien (see pp. 79–81), which evokes both the voluptuous allure of the painting and the captivating musical performance by the young entertainer.[8] An arresting head-and-shoulders portrait by their contemporary Gion Seitoku ('Seitoku of Gion' [Gion being the entertainment quarter], *c.* 1755–after 1827) likely shows a trainee geisha (called a *maiko* in Kyoto), who wears the iridescent beetle-wing lipstick frequently used by Kyoto and Osaka women (fig. 2.26). Her piercing gaze insistently communicates with us across the centuries.

During the eighteenth century, more paintings in Kyoto, Osaka and Edo came to feature wealthy women who were not associated with the entertainment quarters (unless they are relatives of brothel or restaurant owners; it can be difficult to determine their identity). Such is the case with *Woman and Maid* (fig. 2.27), a rare surviving work by Yamamoto Shurei (1751–1790), one of Ōkyo's ten leading pupils who died young, predeceasing his teacher. The maid is holding a beautiful porcelain cup with a blue-and-white design of a moonlit Chinese landscape and a poem inscribed above. It looks to contain incense sticks and charcoal, which were perhaps used to scent clothes. Luxurious painting materials and techniques have been deployed – brilliant azurite blue for the standing woman's robe and pressed gold-leaf dragon roundels against vibrant orange on her stiff silk sash – celebrating the material wealth (sumptuary laws notwithstanding) of the Kyoto merchant families into which Shurei was born. From two generations later dates *Young Woman and a Dog* (fig. 2.28) by Mihata Jōryū (active *c.* 1830–44), which showcases the fashionable élan of a young woman dressed just so. She looks directly at us, even as she modestly averts her head, apparently oblivious to the pet dog that paws at the trailing skirts of her robe. The dog's scarlet ruff has been artfully selected to match her stiff brocade sash. Jōryū of Kyoto was a pupil of Toyohiko and therefore a third-generation Shijō school artist. It is recorded that he also lived in Osaka for a period, and he is sometimes classified together with ukiyo-e artists active in the Kansai region.


## City as subject

Alongside its contemporary prosperity, Kyoto was also a repository of rich cultural traditions stretching back to 794 CE, when it was first designated as imperial capital (see p. 56). In the late sixteenth and early seventeenth centuries the city even boasted a certain cosmopolitan atmosphere, and Portuguese and Spanish visitors were occasionally to be glimpsed in the streets. In the top



**2.27**
Yamamoto Shurei, *Woman and Maid*, *c.* late 1700s. Hanging scroll, ink, colour, gold and gold leaf on silk. 109.8 × 47.2 cm. British Museum, London, 1982,1004,0.1.

**2.28**
Mihata Jōryū, *Young Woman and a Dog*, *c.* 1830–44. Hanging scroll, ink and colour on silk. 102 × 36.8 cm. British Museum, London, 1986,1112,0.1. Purchase funded by the Brooke Sewell Bequest.

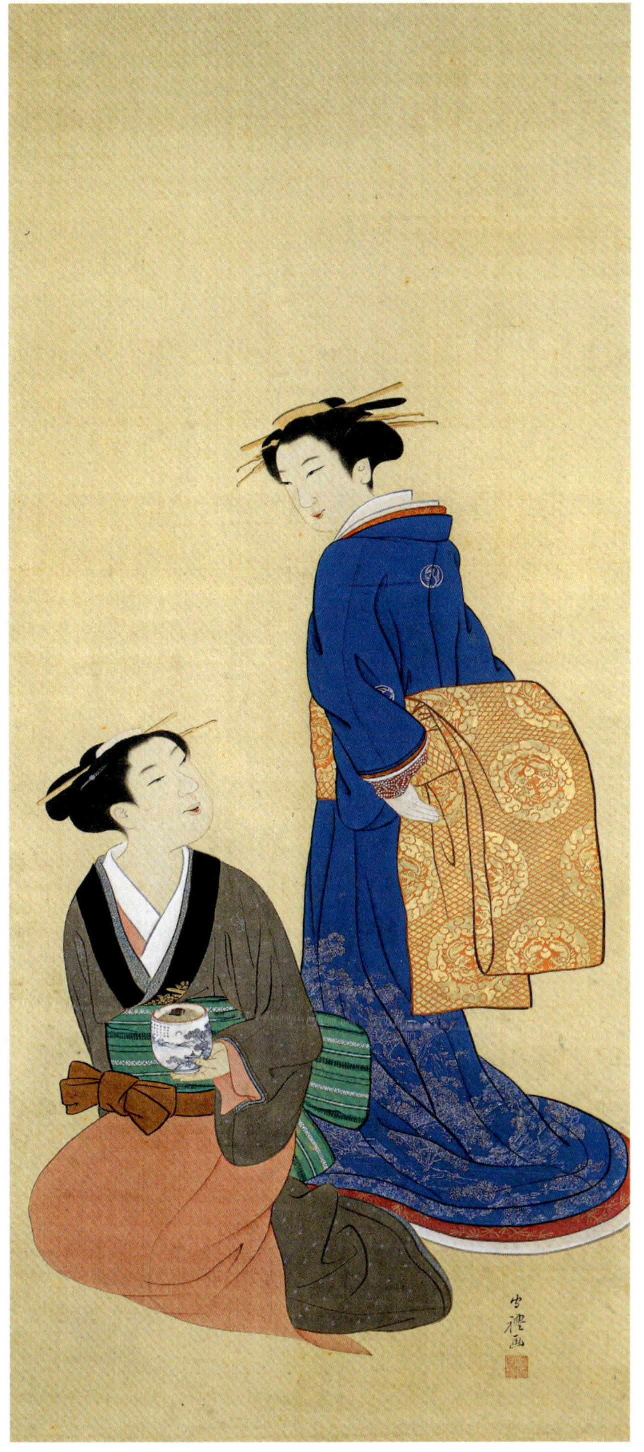

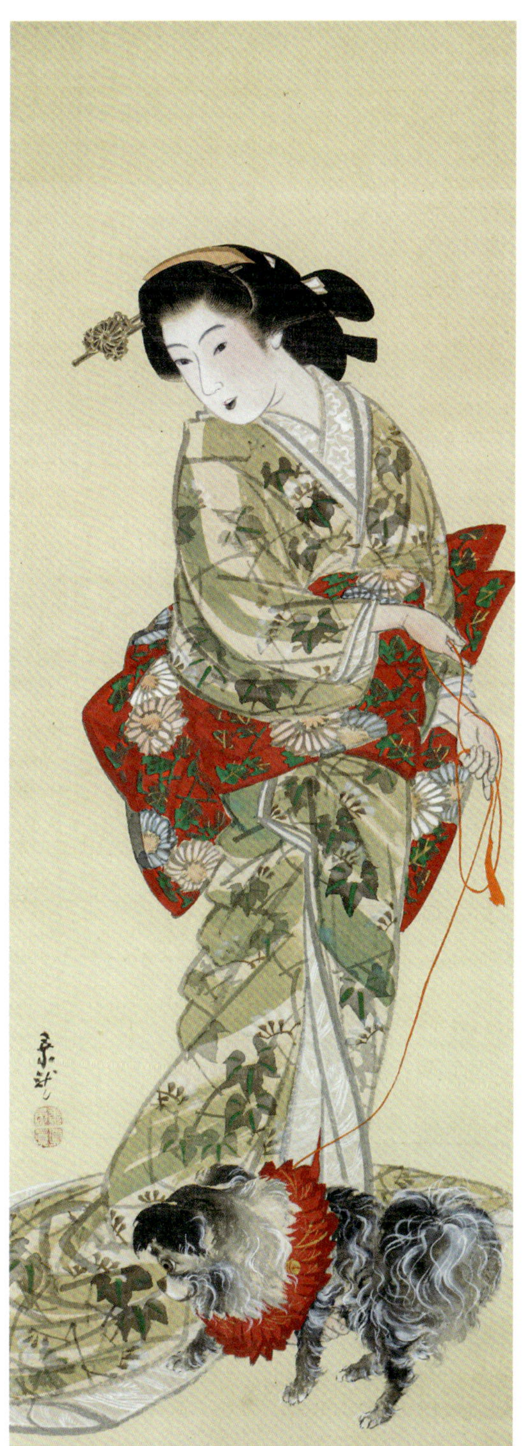

right corner of the screen painting *Scenes of Kyoto* (fig. 2.29) of about 1596–1615, for example, three southern Europeans in balloon pants are accompanied by a Southeast Asian servant holding a parasol. The main scene extending across the two leftmost panels features a lively circle dance in matching costumes (*fūryū-odori*), performed in the courtyard of a mansion for an aristocratic audience. This genre of 'scenes in and out of the capital' (*rakuchū rakugai*), presenting imagined aerial panoramas of Kyoto, was supremely class-conscious. There is the overriding sense that the wealth and prosperity of the capital is literally being spread out for the inspection of its rulers.

As the Edo period progressed, wealth steadily migrated away from the samurai rulers towards the merchant and artisan classes, even though political power was never ceded. The rise of Maruyama-Shijō art surely reflected this economic transformation, and by the late eighteenth century, pictorially, the viewer was brought right inside the world of consumption and pleasure-seeking of the urban bourgeoisie. With the expansion of domestic travel – and provided authorisation could be secured – Kyoto became the prime tourist destination of choice, then as now, for those seeking the authentic roots of 'Japanese' culture. The many temples and shrines, not to mention the hidden-but-august imperial palace, vied with restaurants and shopping to attract the visitor. Kyoto actively marketed its living traditions and they were featured extensively in its visual arts in pictures of famous places and seasonal popular events. It is no coincidence that the first major publication in the genre of meisho zue was an ten-volume gazetteer of Kyoto, *Illustrated Guide to Famous Places in the Capital* [*Kyoto*] (*Miyako meisho zue*) (fig. 2.30) – first published in 1780 and with sequels and spin-offs continuing to appear for the rest of the eighteenth century. The genre would go on to cover much of Japan by the mid-nineteenth century.

Every summer, when the waters of the Kamo River that flowed through central Kyoto dwindled, a thriving temporary entertainment district was constructed on the dried-out riverbed where it was crossed by Shijō (Fourth Avenue). Temporary stages erected here had been one of the prime locations for performances of early kabuki at the beginning of the seventeenth century. A scene in the painted handscroll of 1773 by Ōkyo (see fig. 1.2) shows in intricate detail how wooden platforms were built out over the water, connected to the riverbank or to sandbanks by pontoons. Each night, these platforms, festooned with lanterns, became pop-up, al fresco party rooms, where revellers could 'enjoy the evening cool' (*yūsuzumi*). The large building at the back in the centre of Ōkyo's composition is the city's main permanent kabuki theatre.

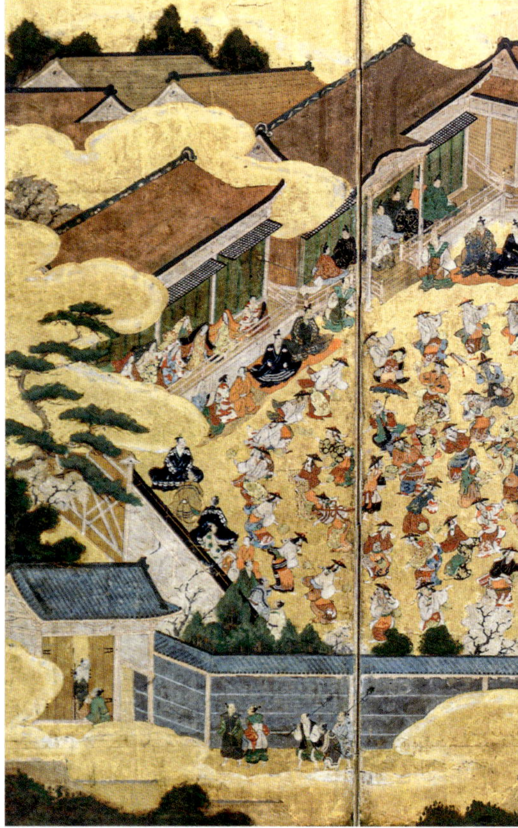

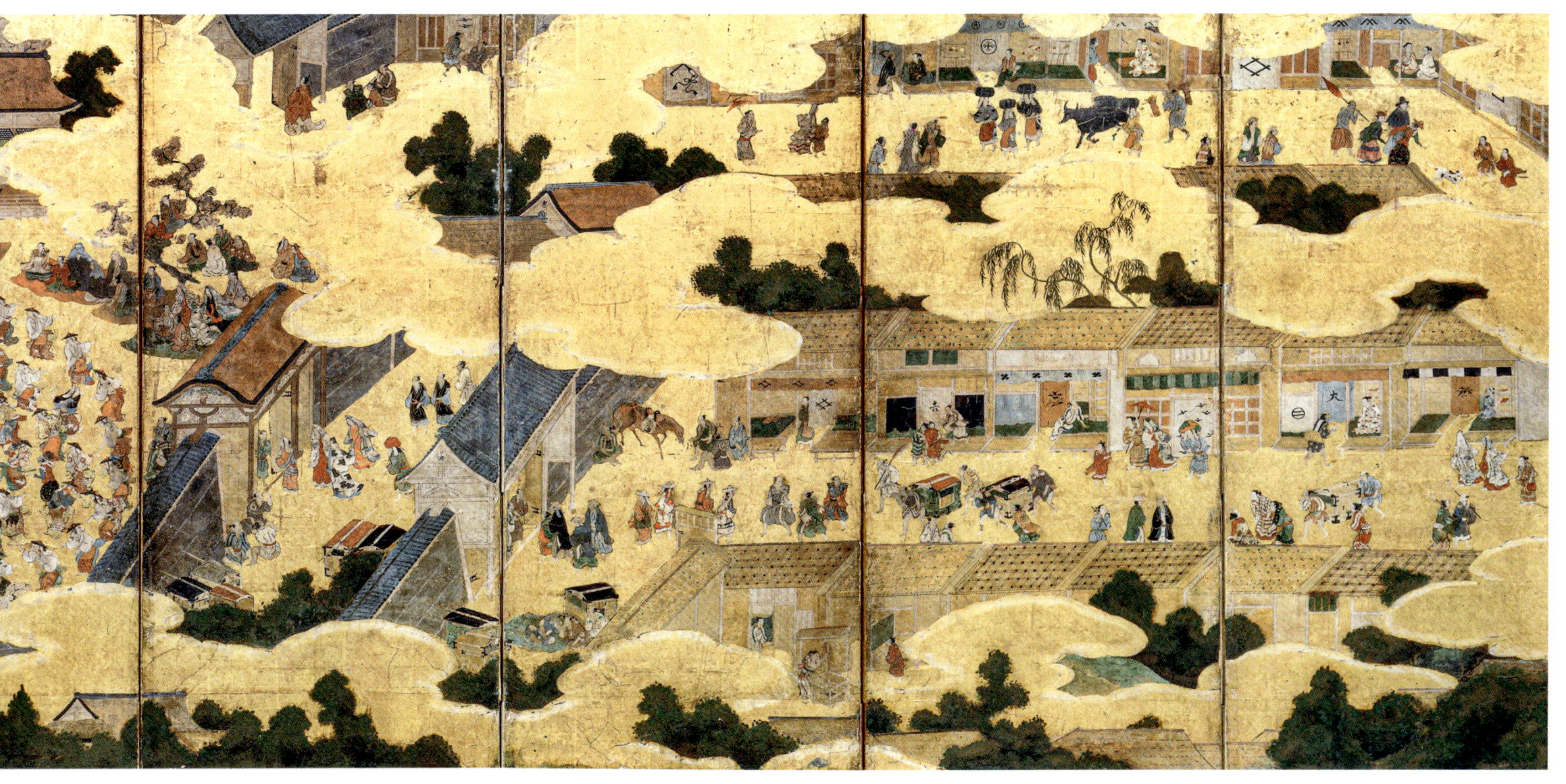

**2.29**
Kanō school, *Scenes of Kyoto*,
*c.* 1596–1615. Six-panel folding
screen, ink, colour, gold and
gold leaf on paper, 103.3 ×
261 cm. British Museum,
London, 1961,0408,0.3.

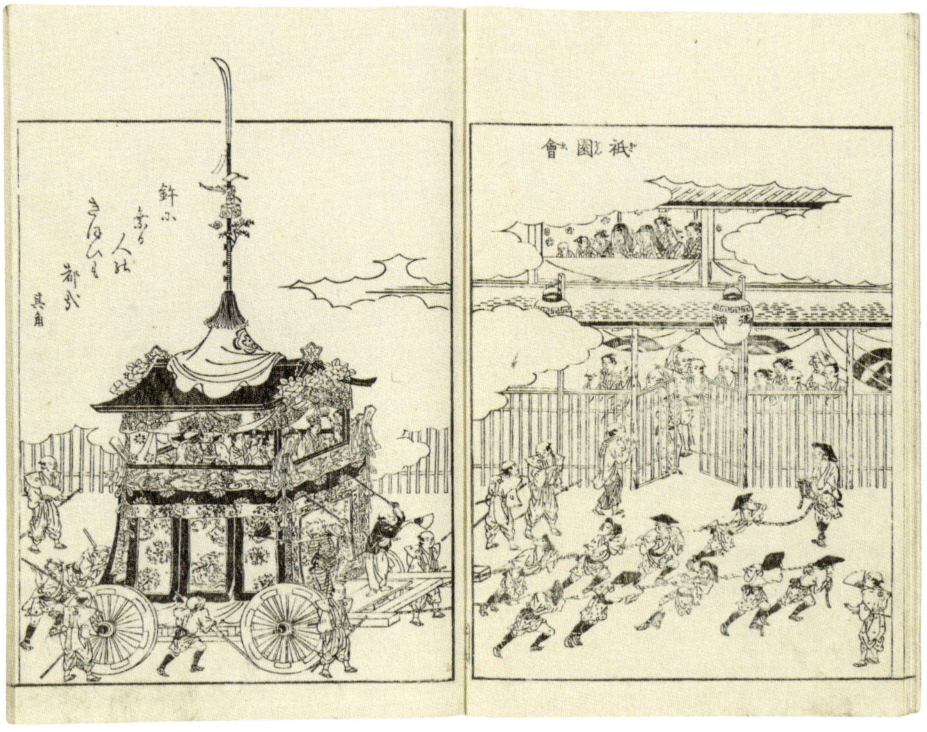



**2.30**
'Gion festival [*Gion-e*]', from vol. 2 of Takehara Shunchōsai (artist) and Akisato Ritō (author), *Illustrated Guide to Famous Places in the Capital* [*Kyoto*] (*Miyako meisho zue*), 6 vols, 1786 (later edition). Illustrated book, woodblock. 27 × 18.5 cm (cover). British Museum, London, 2002,0815,0.1.1–6. Purchase funded by the Brooke Sewell Bequest.

As with the other fifteen scenes depicted in the Ōkyo handscroll, the dry riverbed at Shijō (*Shijō-gawara*) had become one of Kyoto's 'famous places' (*meisho*) – perhaps the most famous place. In later Edo period pictorial arts it became metonymical of summer fun. Returning to *Picture Album of the People of Japan*, Soken's innovative illustrated book of 1800, Ōkyo's cinematic 'panorama shot' of the whole district in 1773 has been replaced with a 'medium shot' of a party of men being entertained by geisha on one of the river platforms (fig. 2.31). Even though the style is quite abbreviated and the scene generic, Soken nevertheless includes in the background a particular signifier for Shijō – the turret of a temporary performance space. Milling crowds in silhouette remind us that it is getting dark. A similar trope is used in a colour-printed illustration of 1828 from the *Album of the Crane's Cry* (*Kakusei-jō*) by the Kyoto artist Tanaka Nikka (fig. 2.32, see fig. 0.18). Nikka's diagonal festoons of hanging lanterns create additional complexity within the composition, giving the sensation that the viewer is actually going into the picture to join the party. The perspective has radically shifted from proprietarily surveying all of Kyoto's riches in the early 1600s (see fig. 2.29) to fully participating in its amusements in the late 1700s and early 1800s.

The mid-summer Gion Festival, originally a celebration of deliverance from plague in ancient times, had by the Edo period become a competitive showcase for the affluence of the merchant neighbourhoods of downtown Kyoto (see fig. 2.30). Large elaborately decorated 'floats' were reassembled each year and pulled through the streets, some even incorporating a platform for musicians. Such a float is shown in a scene from an expansive set of four painted handscrolls, *Kyoto in the Four Seasons* (fig. 2.33), by Okamoto Toyohiko, a key second-generation Shijō artist. By this period, in the early nineteenth century, the annual ritual observances of the court (*nenjū gyōji*) had been progressively usurped by public revelries throughout the year that all could enjoy. While Toyohiko likely first sketched out a rough composition in charcoal, essentially this handscroll shows off the flashy, rapid brushwork in ink and light colour – the 'uninhibited brush'[9] – that this leading Kyoto painter could apparently mobilise so effortlessly. Notice particularly the bravura wet-on-wet ink strokes he used to suggest the shingles on the roof of the festival float.

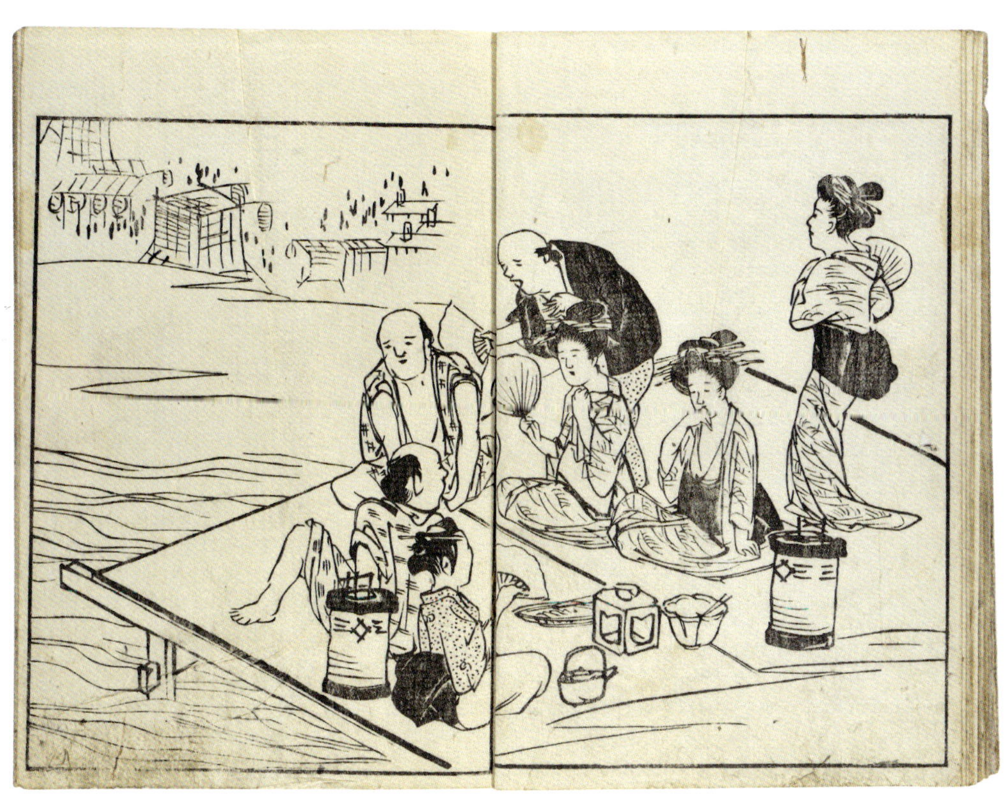

**2.31**
'Enjoying the evening cool [*nōryō*] at Shijō', from vol. 2 of Yamaguchi Soken, *Picture Album of the People of Japan* (*Yamato jinbutsu gafu*), 3 vols, 1800. Illustrated book, woodblock. 26 × 18.2 cm (cover). British Museum, London, 1979,0305,0.184.1–3. Ex-coll.: Jack Hillier.

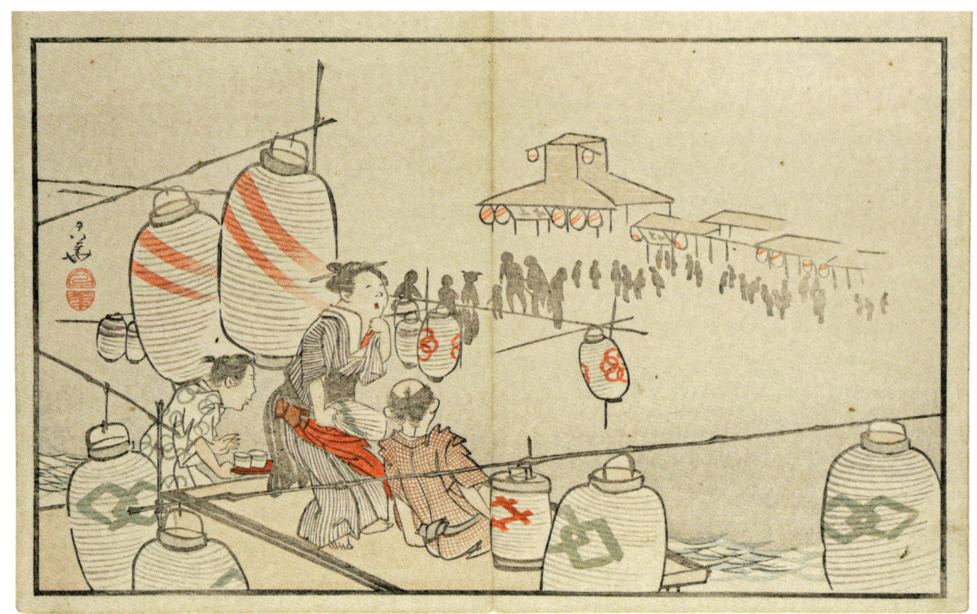

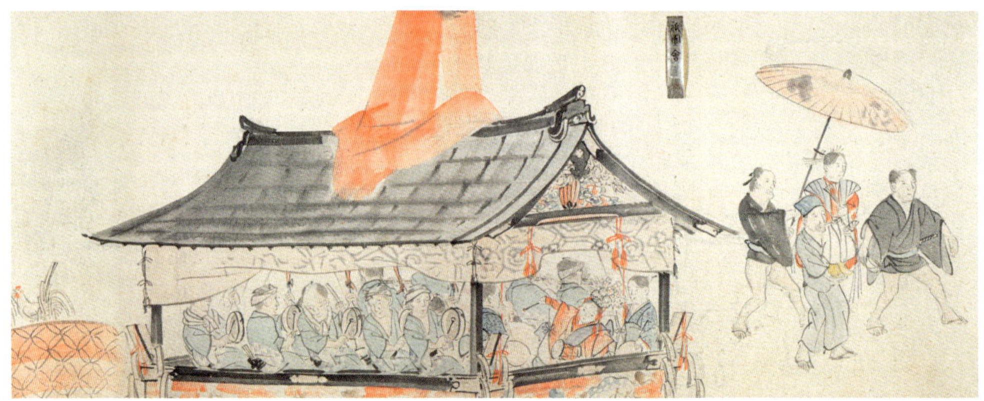



**2.32**
Tanaka Nikka, 'Enjoying the
evening cool [*nōryō*] at Shijō',
in *Album of the Crane's Cry*
(*Kakusei-jō*), 1 vol., 1828. Album,
colour woodblock. 24.8 ×
18.7 cm (cover). British Museum,
London, 1979,0305,0.297.
Ex-coll.: Jack Hillier.

**2.33**
Okamoto Toyohiko, *Gion
Festival*, from *Kyoto in the Four
Seasons* (detail), early 1800s.
From a set of four handscrolls,
ink and colour on paper. 28.5 ×
950 cm (each). British Museum,
London, 1984,0607,0.1.

Painterly depictions of Kyoto festival processions became a forte of the artist Kawamura Bunpō, a theme also regularly found in his book illustrations and fan paintings (fig. 2.34). A pair of handscrolls, with calligraphic preface by the famous author Ueda Akinari, contrasts the solemn ritual elements of the events with the increasingly tipsy antics of straggling procession members (fig. 2.35a–b). Bunpō developed a personal manner of painting unkempt types with pronounced five o'clock shadows. This surely reflects the empathetic geniality of the artist towards his fellow Kyotoites. There is little evidence to suggest who such works – here a pair of handscrolls in a custom-made storage box inscribed by the artist – were painted for. A major patron of the shrine? A visiting dignitary from Edo? An instructive comparison can be made with a printed large haiku surimono by Ōkyo's leading pupil Watanabe Nangaku, which has a design of the red-wigged, masked performers under decorated parasols that are still seen today in the Yasurai festival of the Imamiya shrine in north-western Kyoto (compare fig. 2.36 with fig. 2.35). At present it is unknown which of the Bunpō or Nangaku works is earlier. But there clearly seems to be a period style at work, a pictorial fashion of the time, whereby animated festival participants are depicted with similarly wriggling outlines and abbreviated facial features.

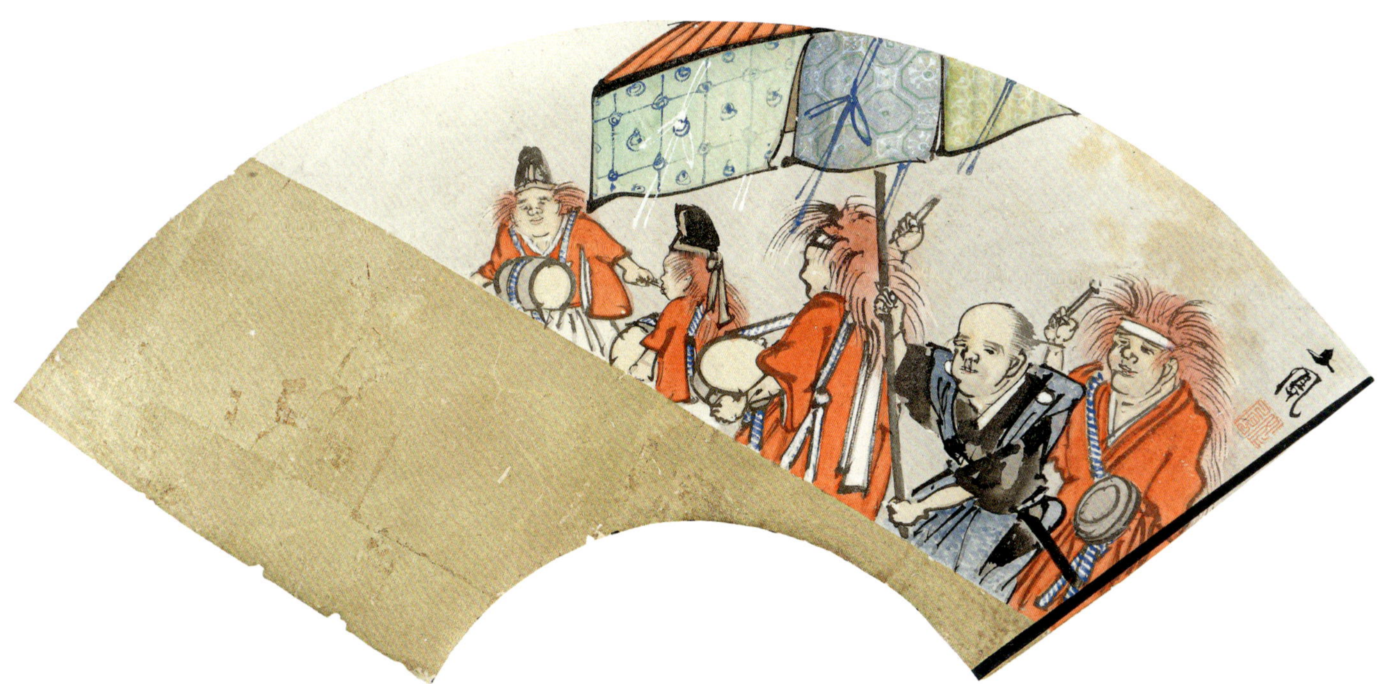

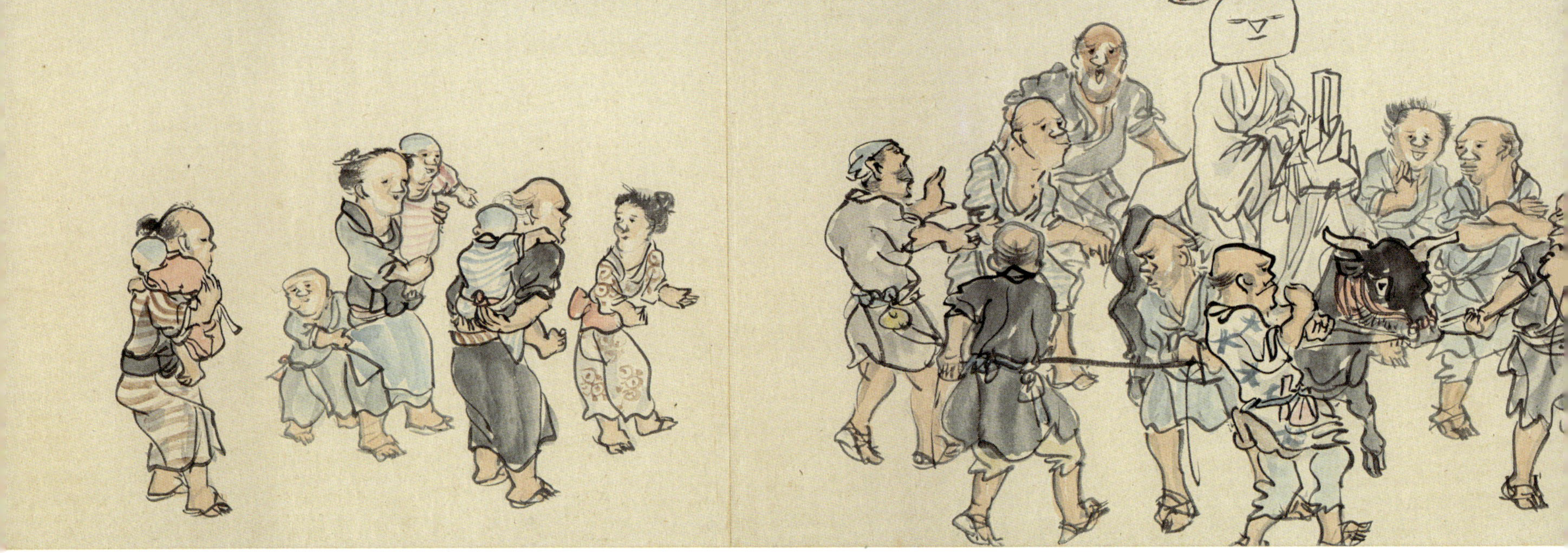

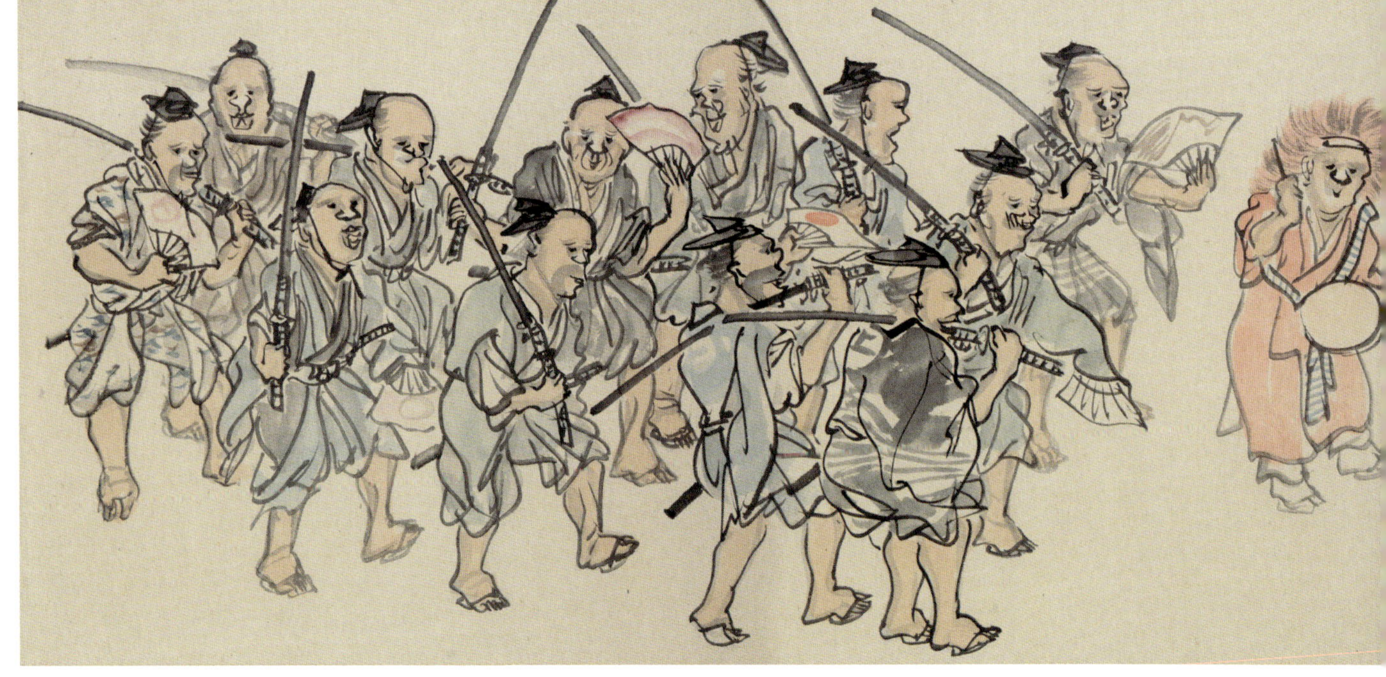

**2.35a–b**
Kawamura Bunpō (artist)
and Ueda Akinari (preface
calligrapher), *Ox Festival at
Uzumasa, Kyoto* and *Yasurai
Festival at Imamiya Shrine,
Kyoto* (details), *c.* 1800. Pair
of handscrolls, ink and colour
on paper. 29.2 × 610 cm; 29.2
× 613.5 cm. British Museum,
London, 1998,1109,0.1. Ex-coll.:
Dr Scott Johnson.

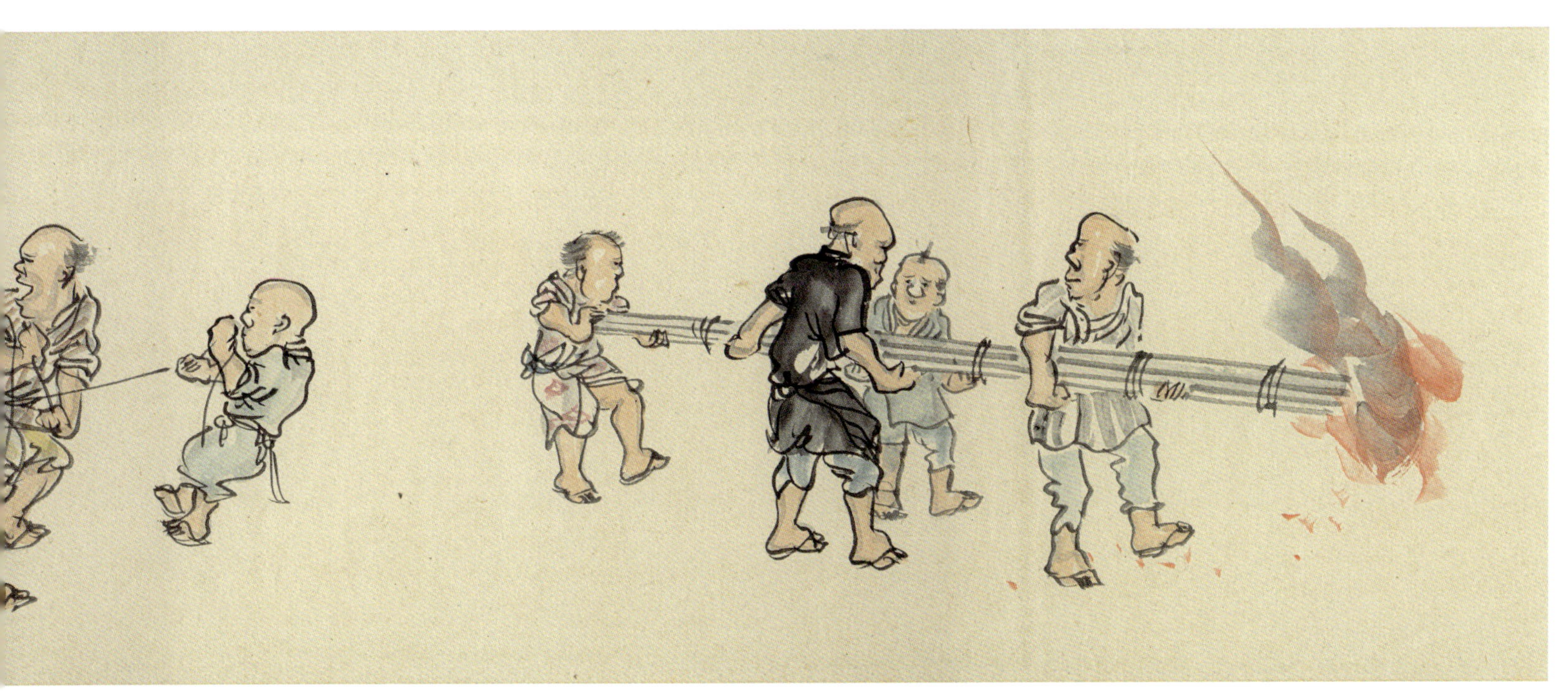

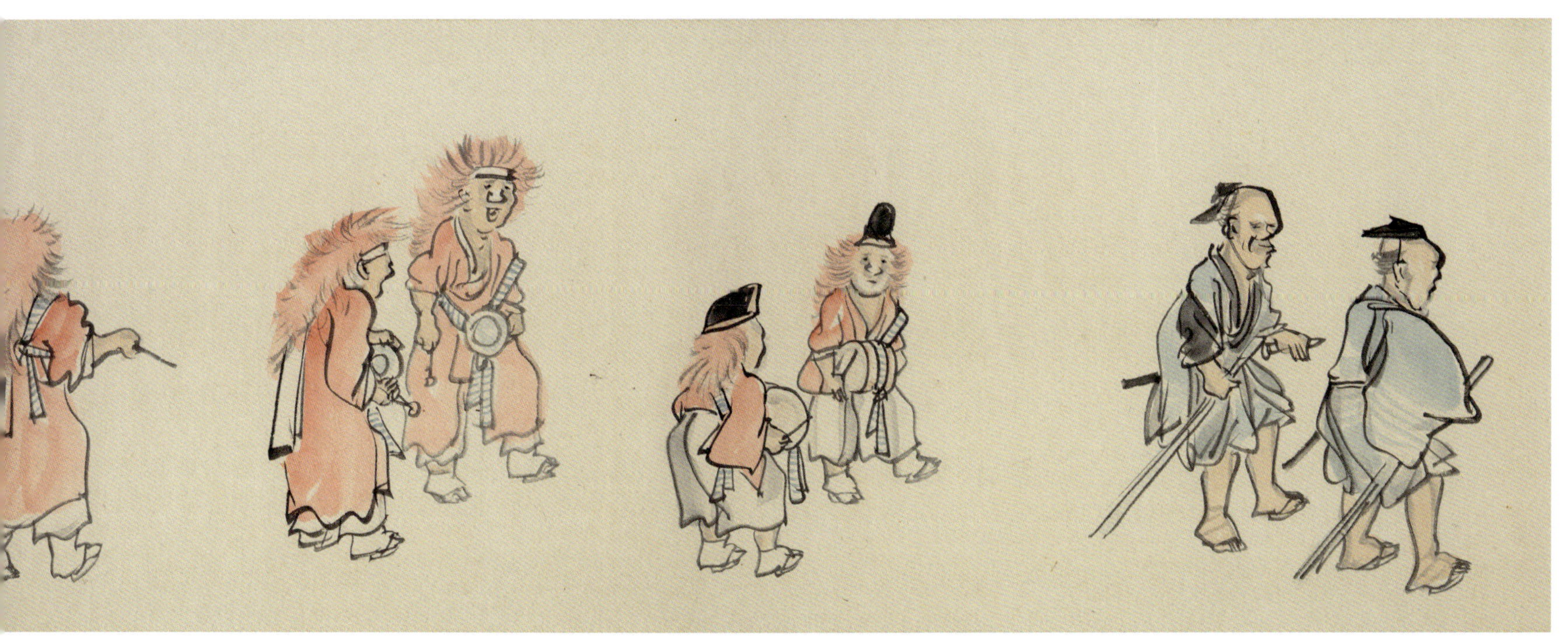

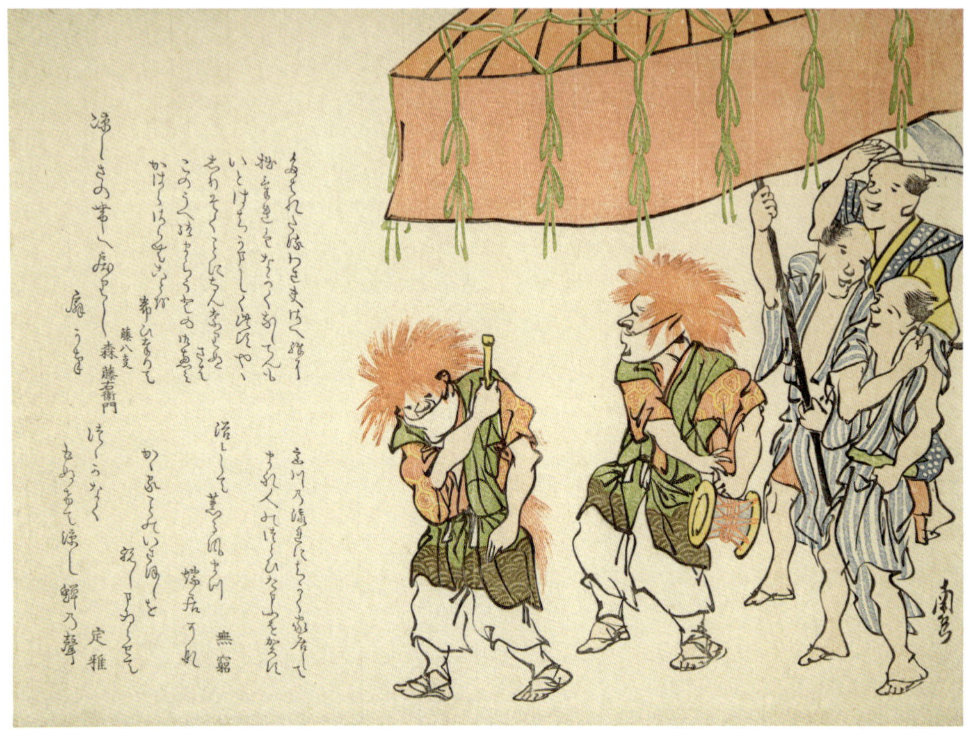

**2.36**
Watanabe Nangaku (artist) and three poets, *Yasurai Festival at Imamiya Shrine, Kyoto*, c. 1800. Surimono, colour woodblock. 39.2 × 52.1 cm. British Museum, London, 2021,3013,179. Purchase made possible by the JTI Japanese Acquisition Fund. Ex-coll.: Dr Scott Johnson.

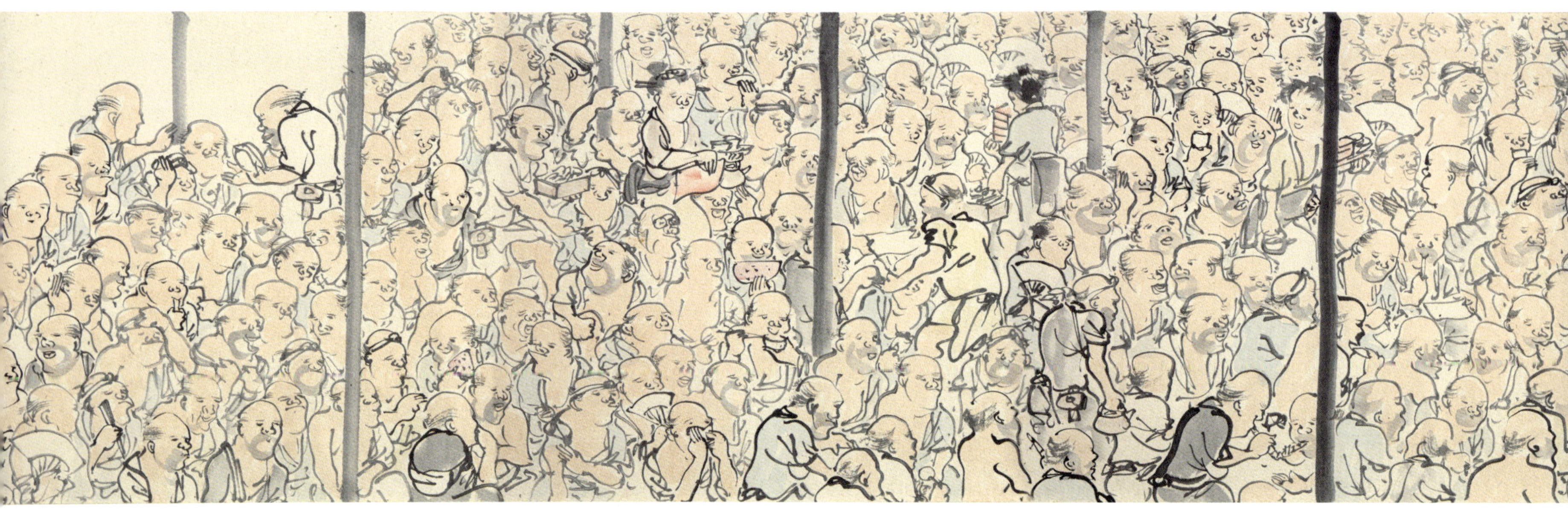

Bunpō's delight in the painting of crowds reaches a crescendo in a long handscroll (over 18 metres) showing the excitement before and during a major public sumo wrestling tournament that was staged around 1805 in a temporary tent-like stadium alongside the Kamo River in the Higashiyama district of Kyoto (fig. 2.37). Apart from a few serving women, the patient spectators crowded into the arena are exclusively male and patently of the same type as the festival participants already described (see fig. 2.35a–b). As was the case with Soken's *Kyoto Geisha* painting (see fig. 2.25), title characters have been inscribed by the Confucian scholar Minagawa Kien, and there is also a Chinese-style calligraphic preface by the Kyoto doctor Murakami Hikotoshi (dates unknown) and a Chinese-style postscript by the Confucian scholar Seita Ryūsen (1746–1808). As we triangulate further the social positions and accomplishments of those who inscribed Shijō paintings, the cultural matrix for art of this kind will come better into focus.

Chō Gesshō (1765–1832) was an idiosyncratic stylist, the son of a painting mounter from Hikone, who trained with Go Shun in Kyoto before making a life and career as a literati-style artist in Nagoya, finally painting for the Owari Tokugawa samurai lords. His book illustration 'Sumo wrestlers' (fig. 2.38) from 1817 injects high tension into the positions and attitudes of the figures (where all was pre-match calm in Bunpō's painting, fig. 2.37). As one wrestler is just about to be pushed out of the ring, so Gesshō bulks his composition radically to the left. The contortions of the umpire, seen from

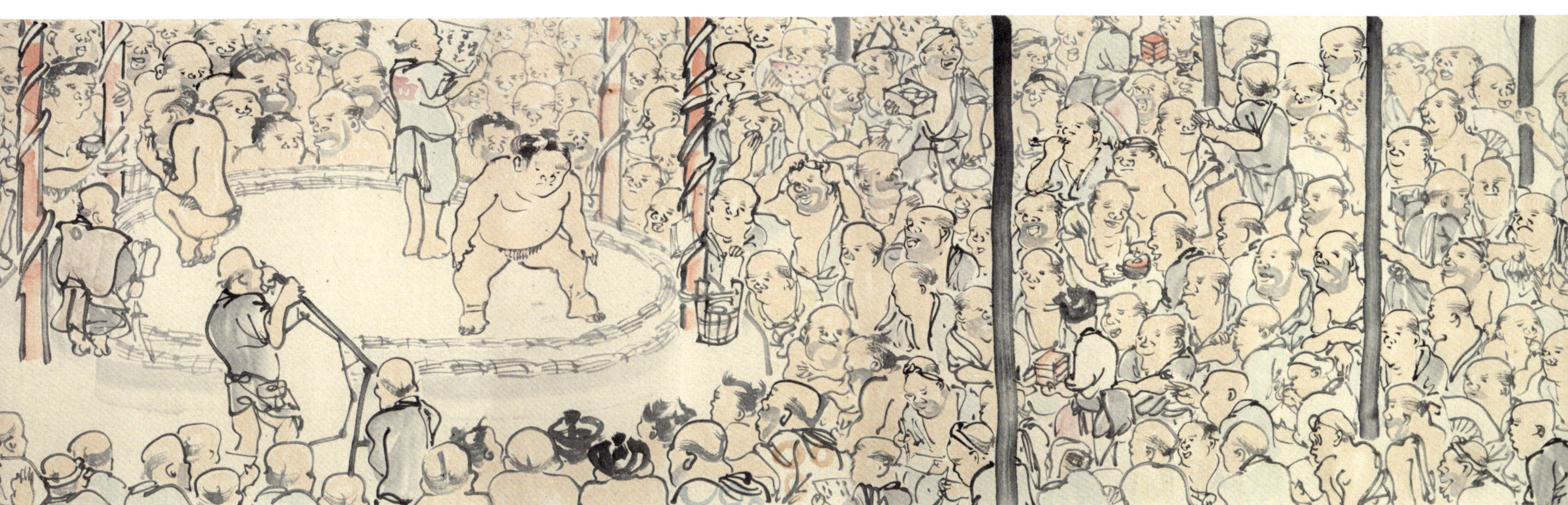

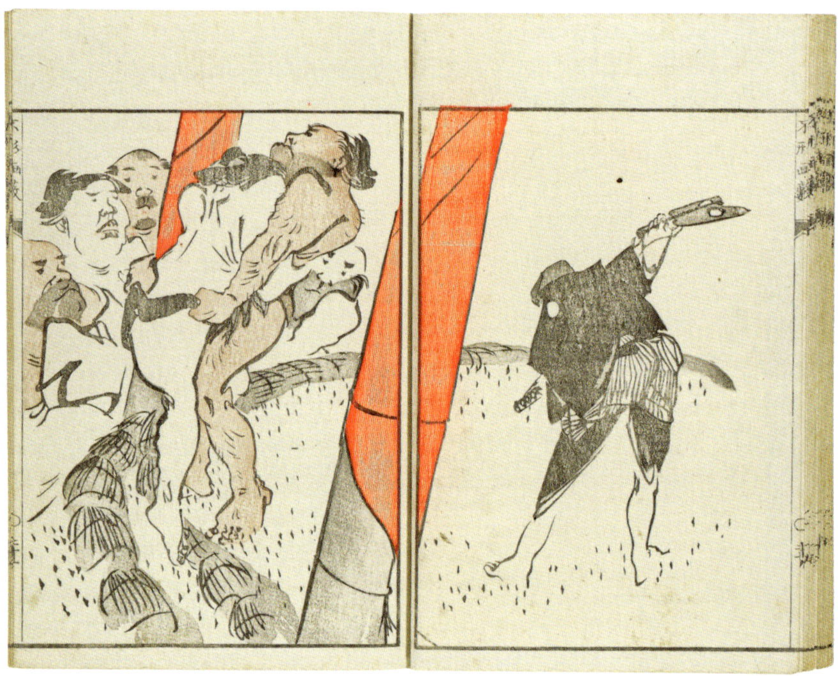



behind, are satisfyingly performative. Gesshō's mixed training in the slick Shijō and expressive literati styles leavens the unique appeal of his art, and this is one of his greatest printed designs.

## Living still lifes

Already in the late seventeenth century, during the lifetime of the great haiku poet Bashō, the genre of 'haiku paintings' (*haiga*) flourished.[10] The image, lightly done in an abbreviated style, might illustrate directly the content of the poem, or evoke tangentially an equivalent or related experience. From the mid-eighteenth century haiga images began to appear in woodblock-printed illustrated books (see fig. 2.3). Such book illustrations were one of the key precursors that led, in due course, to the evolution of single-sheet prints combining image and poetry (haiku, kyōka or Chinese-style), now known simply as 'printed things' (surimono). (Another important precursor, of course, was the hanging scroll painting directly inscribed with a poem, see p. 215.) In Kyoto and Osaka the most impressive surimono were made in the 'full large presentation sheet' (*ōbōsho zenshiban*, about 40 × 53 cm) size. This grand format was sometimes used in Edo as well but was much more common in the two western cities.

*Peonies* (fig. 2.39), a large surimono of around 1829 with a design by the Osaka artist Nagayama Kōin, was made two generations after a beautiful haiku poem by Buson from 1783:

| | |
|---|---|
| *hironiwa no* | a peony |
| *botan ya ama no* | in the open garden |
| *ippō ni* | a corner of heaven[11] |

The two dozen or so poems printed around the flowers in the surimono are 31-syllable kyōka, not 17-syllable haiku. Furthermore, the peonies are apparently cut rather than still growing in the garden. Yet the vivid intensity with which the blossoms are presented, based on close observation of nature,

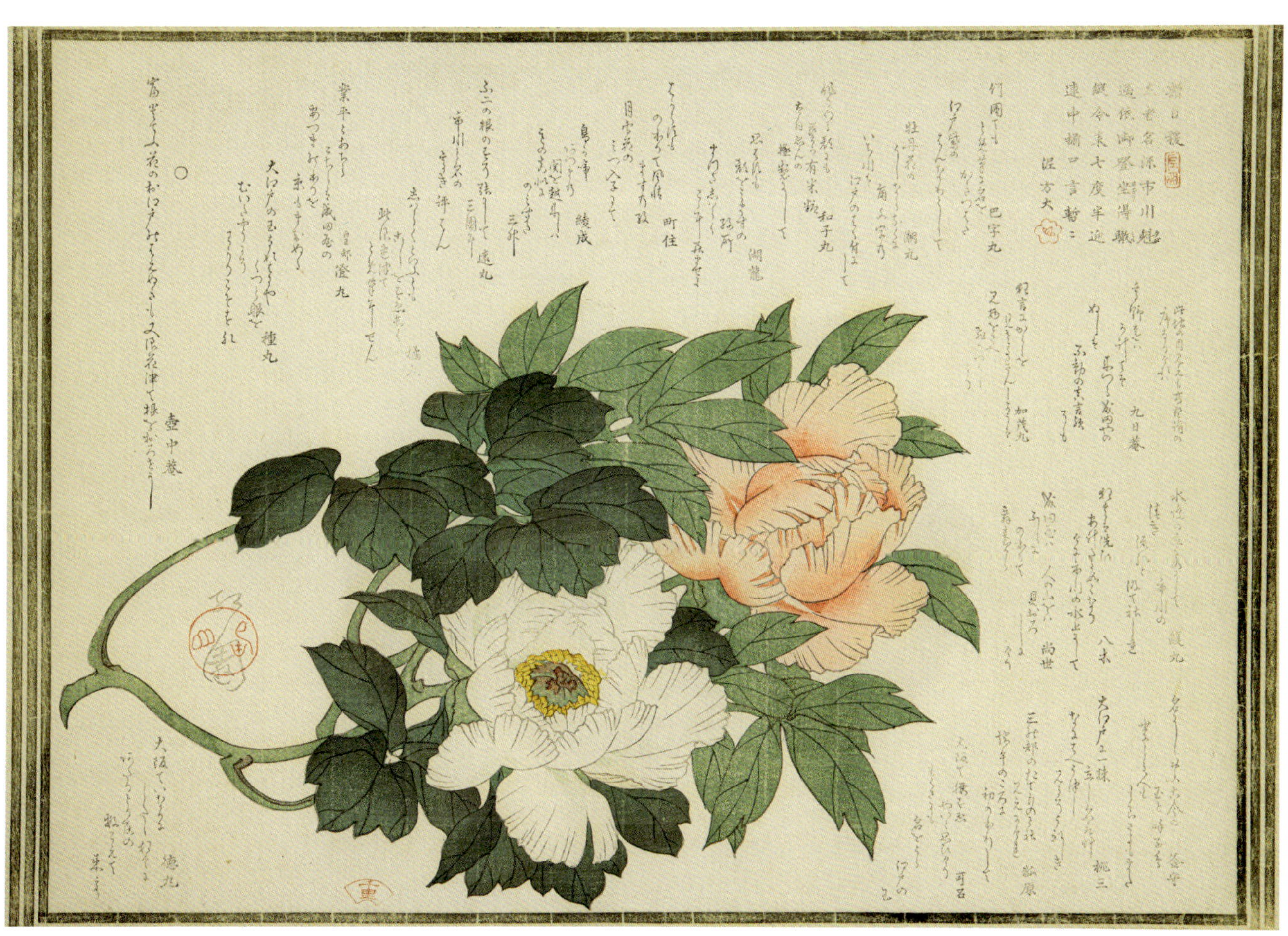

**2.39**
Nagayama Kōin (artist) and 22 poets, *Peonies*, *c.* 1829. Surimono, colour woodblock. 39 × 54.9 cm. British Museum, London, 2021,3013.340. Purchase made possible by the JTI Japanese Acquisition Fund. Ex-coll.: Dr Scott Johnson.

chimes well with Buson's earlier poem. Western art would classify the subject as 'still life' (*nature morte*, that is, 'dead nature'), but so bursting with life force are most of the examples in Japan that they could be termed 'living still life' (*nature morte vivante*).[12]

'Living still life' also found its way into book illustration. The squat figure style of the Osaka artist Suiseki (Gyodai) in his *Suiseki's Picture Album* (*Suiseki gafu*) of 1814 has already been discussed. The sequel to this picture book, *Suiseki's Picture Album, Part II* (*Suiseki gafu, nihen*) of 1820 boasts a bravura, idiosyncratic style that far surpasses the first volume. In 'Potted plants' the viewer encounters, down at ground level, spiky, characterful portraits of (right to left): 'wild ginger' (*saishin, Asarum sieboldii*), 'bishop's hat' (*ikarisō, Epimedium grandiflorum*) and 'Japanese woodland poppy' (*yamabukisō, Hylomecon japonica*) (fig. 2.40). The wooden printing blocks for the coloured plant pots have been deliberately abraded so as to leave horizontal white textural striations in reserve. Some of the plants are outlined, others are not. Suiseki explores new potentials for colour woodblock printing even as he showcases his sensitive, angular style (see fig. 0.25).

As with Dutch still-life painting of the seventeenth century, there is the sense that many still-life surimono prints made in Japan at this time celebrate

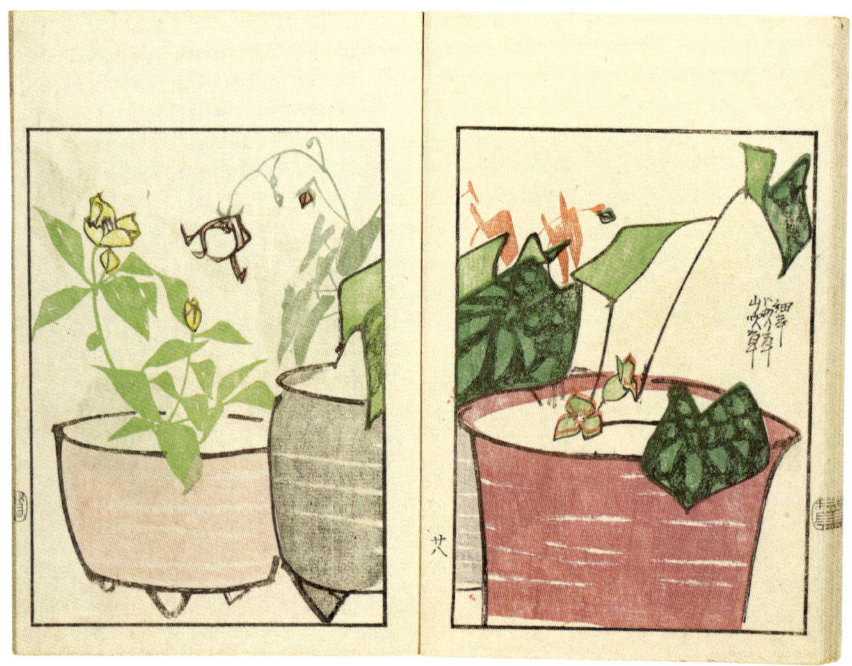

2.40
'Potted plants', in Satō Suiseki (Gyodai), *Suiseki's Picture Album, Part II* (*Suiseki gafu, nihen*), 1 vol., 1820. Illustrated book, colour woodblock. 25.7 × 17.7 cm (cover). British Museum, London, 1979,0305,0.268. Ex-coll.: Jack Hillier.

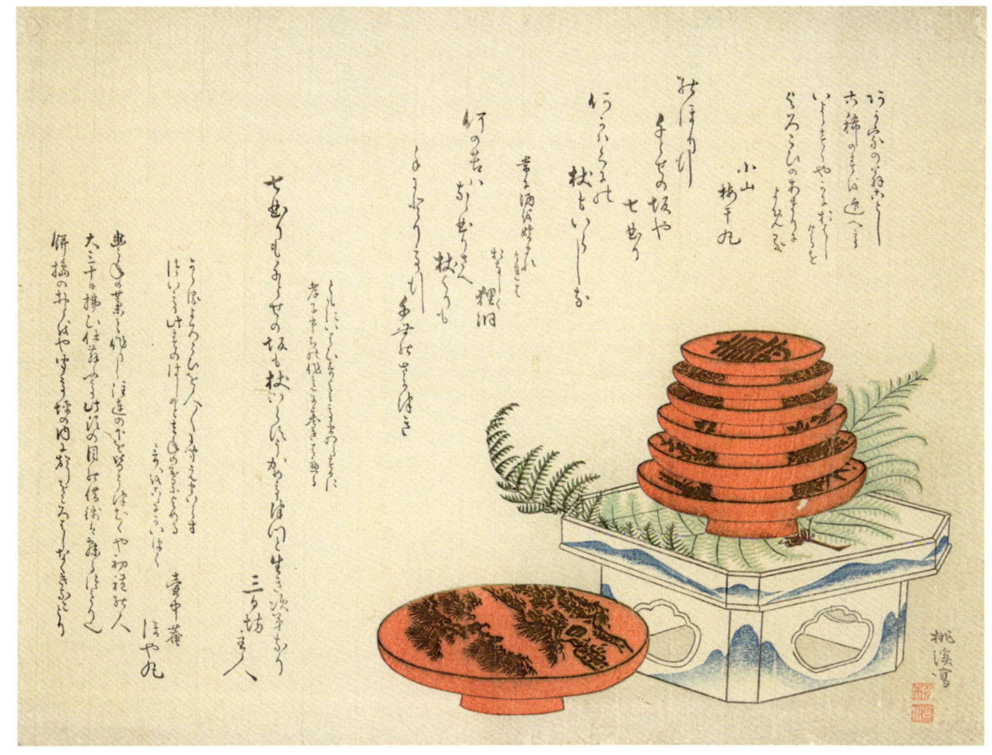

**2.41**
Niwa Tōkei (artist) and four poets, *Stacked Sake Cups on a Stand*, early 1800s. Surimono, colour woodblock. 42.2 × 55.2 cm. British Museum, London, 2021,3013.419. Purchase made possible by the JTI Japanese Acquisition Fund. Ex-coll.: Dr Scott Johnson.

an 'embarrassment of riches'.[13] Yet the generally limited space available alongside the poems encouraged a certain synecdoche in the selection of motifs. *Stacked Sake Cups on a Stand* (early nineteenth century) (fig. 2.41) by the Osaka artist Niwa Tōkei (1760–1822), graced with four kyōka poems and explanatory inscriptions, commemorates a seventieth birthday. The shallow sake cups look to be luxuriously crafted in red lacquer with auspicious motifs in gold (here actually printed in powdered brass) of pine, plum and dwarf bamboo and so on, the top one prominently emblazoned with the character 'long life'. Resting on fresh fern leaves, the whole ensemble is presented on an octagonal stand of fresh wood, decorated with blue mountains. The relatively modest vignette of the stacked cups therefore evokes in the mind of the viewer a much more extensive formal gathering for an important life event.

'A hot [summer] day' (*atsuki hi ya*) is the theme for an exquisite large haiku surimono featuring a leopard lily (*hiōgi, belamcanda chinensis/iris domestica*) and hanging bamboo blind (fig. 2.42) designed by the artist Ōhara Donshū (1792–1857), who was primarily active in Kyoto. Two of the six poets are described as 'from Heian [Kyoto]' and 'from Ōmi', so the print was perhaps produced in Hino, Ōmi province, commemorating a summer gathering of poets. Flowering plant, blind and poems are all finely balanced, with the extending leaf seeming to point to the verses. Haiku sensibility has completely infused the design, the abbreviated motifs signifying cultivated distractions that help the poets to endure the stifling heat of mid-summer in the Kansai region.

## The reception of Shijō art

*Lilies and Bamboo Blind* (fig. 2.42) carries in its bottom right corner the tiny collector's seal of Henri Vever (1854–1942), the leading Parisian Art Nouveau jeweller and fabled connoisseur of Japanese pictorial art. Vever was foremost a collector of ukiyo-e prints, but his appreciation also extended to Shijō books and surimono prints. Nevertheless, the suave ukiyo-e style of Edo, exemplified by the work of Kiyonaga (see fig. 2.5), held overwhelming sway among European artists and art connoisseurs in the late nineteenth century. Pioneering biographies of the Edo artists Kitagawa Utamaro (d. 1806) and Katsushika Hokusai (1760–1849) were penned by the French critic Edmond de Goncourt (1822–1896) in the early 1890s.

Judged against the canonical standards of idealised academic figure drawing promoted by the Académie des beaux-arts and its associated Salon exhibitions in Paris, the unheroic, often schematic, figure style of Shijō art of Kyoto and Osaka must have presented a challenge of classification. (Perhaps this is why one German-speaking collector described it as 'caricature'; see fig. 2.19 and p. 98.) It would take the revolutions of post-Impressionism and Expressionism in Western art for such schematic figure drawing to be championed.

So how should Shijō art be evaluated now? Hillier's idea of 'the uninhibited brush' points to its stylistic freedom, and audiences can also celebrate its upbeat engagement with life, often shown from the ordinary person's perspective.

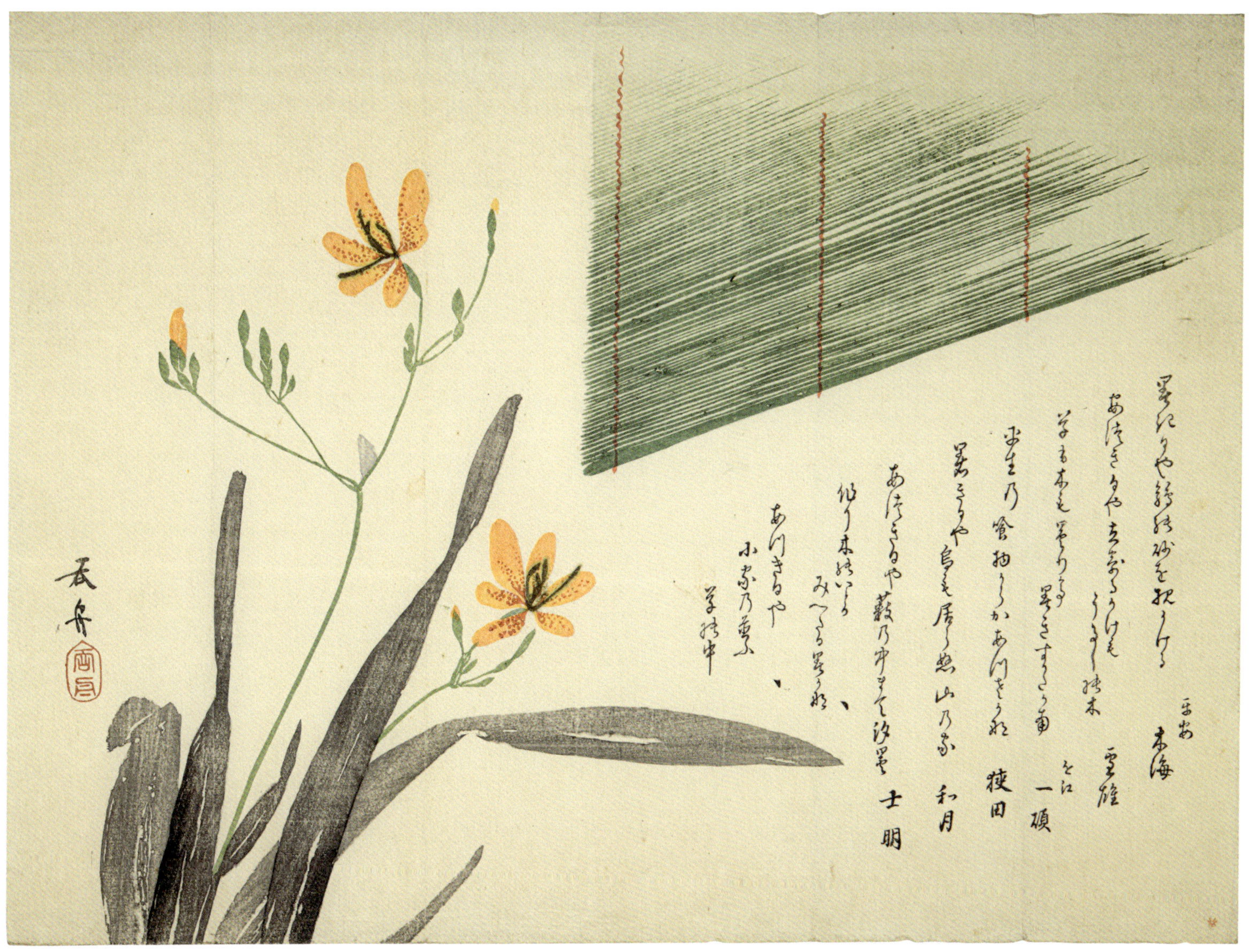

**2.42**
Ōhara Donshū (artist) and six poets,
*Lilies and Bamboo Blind*, mid-
1800s. Surimono, colour woodblock.
38.7 × 51.1 cm. British Museum,
London, 2021,3013.11. Purchase
made possible by the JTI Japanese
Acquisition Fund. Ex-coll.: Henri
Vever; Dr Richard Lane; Dr Scott
Johnson.

# Printed manuals and the popularisation of art
## *Ellis Tinios*

By the middle of the seventeenth century, commercial publishing based entirely on printing from cut woodblocks was well established in Japan. The industry grew and prospered, with major production centres in Edo, Kyoto and Osaka, and lesser ones in Nagoya, Wakayama and elsewhere. The technology employed produced print facsimiles of the texts and images inscribed by calligraphers and artists on sheets prepared for the block-cutters. This mode of production allowed for the seamless interplay of text and image on every page. Publishers exploited this potential to issue a vast array of richly illustrated books that included gazetteers, poetry anthologies, works of fiction and a wide range of instruction manuals. The latter ranged from cookbooks to copybooks (*e-dehon*).

From the 1720s, Japanese publishers, inspired by printed copybooks imported from China, regularly commissioned similar works from Japanese artists to supply a growing constituency of amateur artists (see fig. 4.24). Simultaneously, over the course of the eighteenth century, some artists gained fame for the individuality of their vision rather than their adherence to the stylistic parameters of a particular school. The wider distribution of their work through the medium of print enhanced their celebrity.

The suffix *gafu* (C: *huapu*), meaning 'collection of paintings', figured in the titles of copybooks imported from China. It was first used in conjunction with the names of Japanese artists in the second half of the eighteenth century. These copybooks provided examples of the artists' brushwork for aspiring amateurs to learn from. The emphasis in these books was on images – they did not contain extended texts on the theory or practice of painting. Some were posthumous tributes to a departed master compiled by devoted followers (see fig. 0.26). Most, however, presented



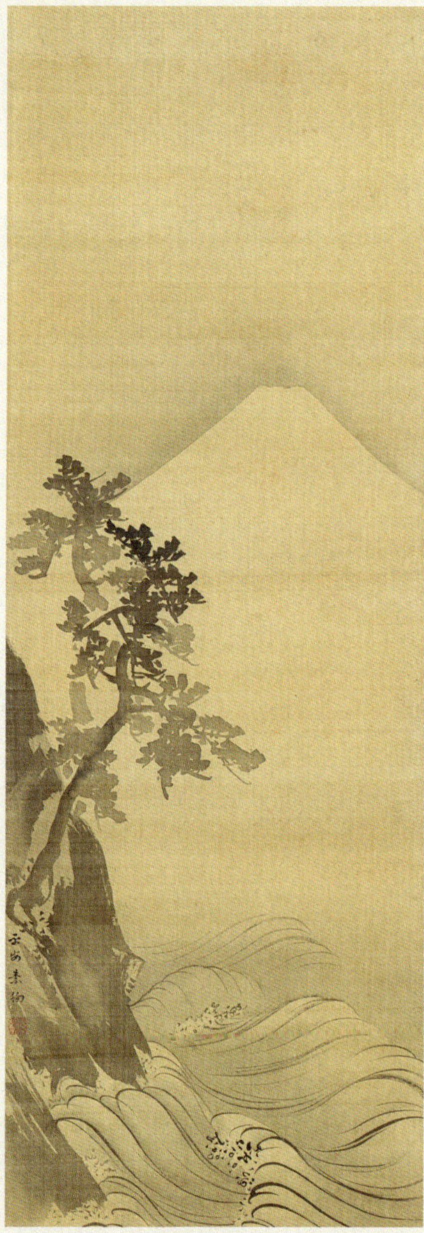

**2.43**
Yamaguchi Soken, *Picture of a Coastline* (*Kaihin no zu*), 1785–1818. Hanging scroll, ink and light colour on silk. 100.9 × 34.4 cm. British Museum, London, 2018,3008.1. Purchase made possible by the JTI Japanese Acquisition Fund. Ex-coll.: Dr Ellis Tinios.

the brushwork of living painters. Their message was that models worthy of emulation existed in contemporary Japan, not just in a distant past in faraway China.

A significant phenomenon in publishing in Kyoto and Osaka in the first four decades of the nineteenth century was the production and marketing of gafu by artists of the Maruyama-Shijō school. In those years, two leading Kyoto publishers, Yoshidaya Shinbei (Bunchōdō) and Hishiya Magobei, significant figures in the cultural life of the city, dominated the commissioning, publication and distribution of these books. The artists they engaged included Yamaguchi Soken, Kawamura Bunpō, Nishimura Nantei (1755–1834), Kawamura Kihō and Ueda Kōchō (1788–1850).

The preferred format of these artists was the painted hanging scroll (fig. 2.43). If such a composition were reduced for reproduction in a copybook, the viewer would not be able to appreciate each painter's characteristic brushwork. Therefore, spacious vertical compositions, such as a scene of Mount Fuji from the coast by Soken, were cropped and reconfigured by the artist to fill the horizontal double-page spread that was the preferred image field in copybooks (fig. 2.44). This meant that every brushstroke in the printed book was easily read and understood. In their publicity, publishers repeatedly stressed the liveliness of the brushwork encountered in the gafu they were offering to the public and emphasised their utility as copybooks. Their key selling point was that such books allowed you to learn to paint in a fine style without the expense of engaging a teacher.

The content of these gafu was, for the most part, the subjects beloved of Chinese literati painters: idealised Chinese landscapes, close-ups of flowers and birds, and figure studies. The latter were restricted to sages, scholars and their boy attendants, male peasants and fishermen. (Women rarely figured in this world.) Their dress and hairstyles were those of the Ming period (1368–1644).

Soken broke with these conventions, extending the content of gafu to encompass men, women and children from all stations in Japanese society engaged in familiar, often mundane, activities in his three-volume *Picture Album of People of Japan* (*Yamato jinbutsu gafu*, 1800) (see figs 2.18–2.19, 2.31). The immense popularity of this title

led to the publication of a second part, also in three volumes, in 1804. Other artists quickly took up the genre. Nishimura Nantei created the three-volume *Collection of Paintings by Nantei* (*Nantei gafu*, 1803), which offers rollicking glimpses of life in Kyoto. Kawamura Kihō uniquely ventured to portray the sorrows as well as the joys of life in his single-volume *Leave Sorrows and Joys to the Brush* (*Kafuku ninpitsu*, 1808) (see fig. 2.17). Somewhat later, Ōnishi Chinnen launched the first (and only) volume of his *Customs of the East (Edo)* (*Azuma no teburi*, 1829), which, uniquely, was devoted to daily life in Edo.

While advertised by publishers as utilitarian copybooks, gafu could also be viewed for pleasure. They were consumed by aspiring artists and art lovers alike. These volumes reflect the popularisation and commercialisation of the practice of painting and art appreciation in early modern Japan.

**2.44**
Yamaguchi Soken, *Soken's Album of Landscape Pictures (Soken sansui gafu)*, 2 vols, 1818. Illustrated book, woodblock. 26 × 18 cm (cover).

British Museum, London, 1979,0305,0.520.1–2. Ex-coll.: Jack Hillier.

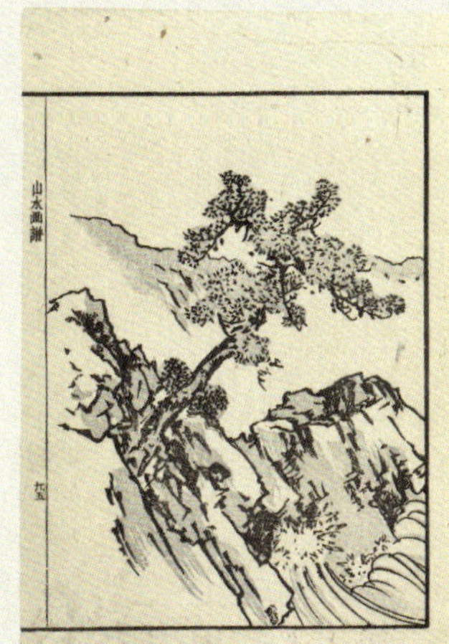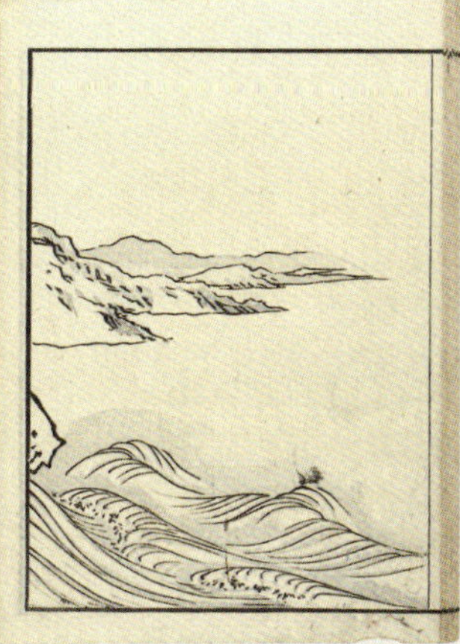

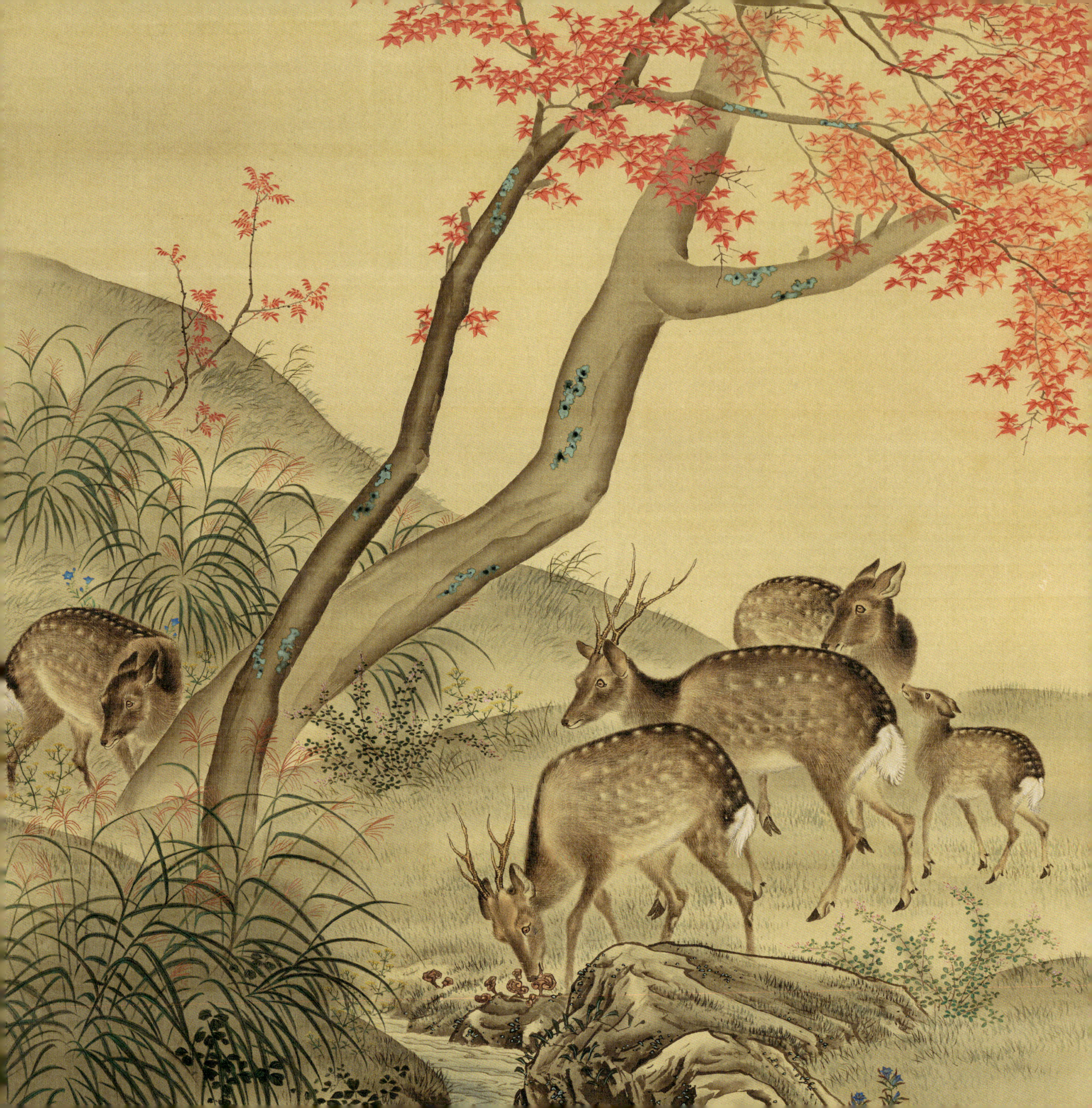

*Alfred Haft*

# 3   Capturing nature

The pioneering Kyoto artist Maruyama Ōkyo conveyed a vision of nature that held his contemporaries spellbound and shaped how generations of Japanese artists would study and depict the natural world.[1] He did not, though, win universal acclaim. His gentleness and refinement, his understated brushwork and appreciation for the world around him, vexed some in Kyoto who also belittled his sound business sense, work ethic and frugality, and considered his art to signal the decline of painting. One local rival, Soga Shōhaku (1730–1781), remarked, 'If it's paintings you want, talk to me. If you're looking for diagrams, find Maruyama Mondo', dismissively referring to Ōkyo by his given name rather than his art name.[2] Ōkyo, however, knew his own worth and stayed his course, as calm and collected as many of the subjects that he painted. By the 1830s, with his students prospering, his style a source of inspiration in ever-expanding cultural circles and the world of art unquestionably not at an end, even Tanomura Chikuden (1777–1835), a leading thinker and practitioner of the literati (bunjin) tradition, could praise his talents and importance.[3]

Nature signified many things during the Edo period, depending on how one made a living.[4] It also went by many names, serving a complex set of functions as both a tangible and a cultural resource.[5] Beyond the assorted significations and terms, elements of contemporary philosophy and religion suggested that all celestial and terrestrial bodies and beings constitute a whole, and merit equal attention and compassion.[6] Ōkyo and his students lived during an era of scholarly interest in the natural world, inspired by neo-Confucian thought, but they also received the patronage of the Buddhist clergy.[7] A combination of Confucian and Buddhist ideas, infused with the poetic seasonality of haikai (haiku) (see p. 213), seems to have guided the Maruyama-Shijō approach to portraying nature and contributed to the style's compelling allure. Ōkyo and his followers altered the meaning of nature for the cultivated men and women who formed Kyoto-Osaka salon culture and helped to give their enthusiastic participation in the arts a new direction. This chapter considers what 'nature' meant during this time, as a tangible resource, a cultural resource and as an artistic resource developed by Ōkyo, his school and related schools in the region.



**Previous page**
Detail of fig. 3.24

## Nature as a tangible resource

The natural world supported the needs of industry, scholarly collecting and hobbyists. Osaka's manufacturing and shipping magnates almost certainly would have counted nature, in the first instance, as a tangible resource, for every day the riches of the mountains and seas passed through the city's ports en route to markets around Japan (see also pp. 56, 76).[8] Osaka served as a market hub for provinces throughout western and northern Honshu as well as Kyushu. Sake, soy sauce, lumber, tatami facing and rice comprised around 80 per cent of the city's overall outbound cargo.[9]

The five-volume *Illustrated Guide to Notable Products of Japan's Mountains and Seas* (*Nippon sankai meisan zue*, 1799) reveals the assortment of industries that flourished in Osaka's sphere of influence (fig. 3.1). The Osaka scholar, cultural host and sake brewer Kimura Kenkadō wrote the preface and may have sponsored or at least supported the publication. Perhaps for that reason the entire first volume is devoted to sake brewing. It traces the industry's history from the mythical age of the gods to contemporary Itami, a town located across the Yodo River west of Osaka, where, the reader is told,

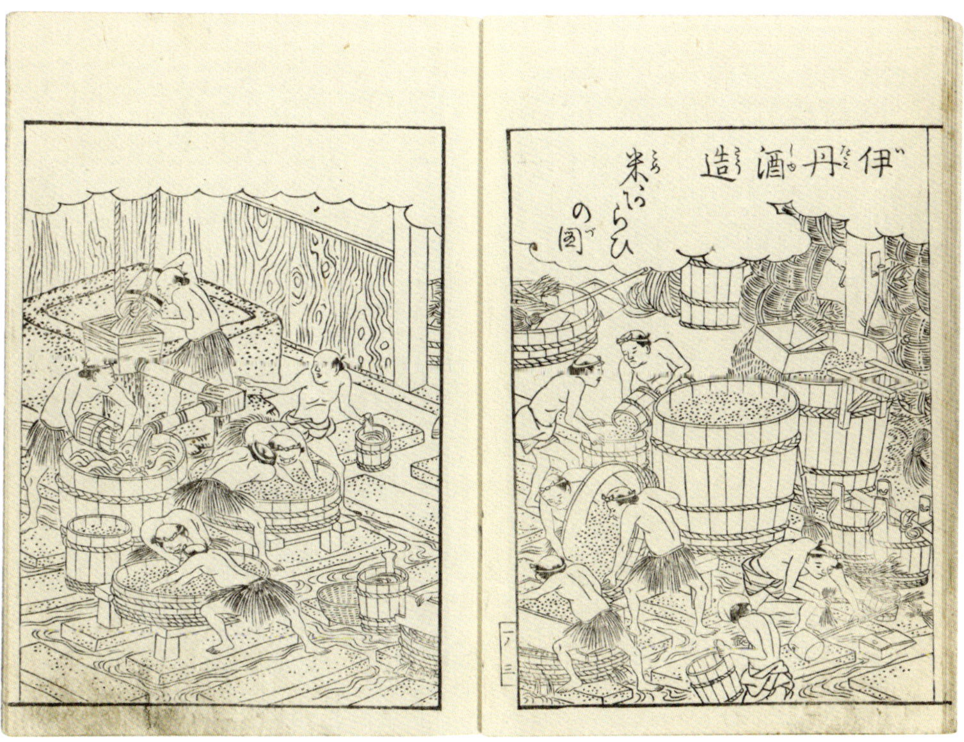


**3.1**
'Sake-Making in Itami', from vol. 1 of Shitomi Kangetsu (artist) and Kimura Kenkadō (preface), *Illustrated Guide to Notable Products of Japan's Mountains and Seas* (*Nippon sankai meisan zue*), 5 vols, 1799. Illustrated book, woodblock. 26.5 × 18.5 cm (cover). British Museum, London, 1914,0528,0.5.1–5. Gift of A. Moseley.

they make the 'purest, most excellent sake in Japan'.[10] This book encapsulates the complex, nature-dependent commercial system that underwrote the salons of western Japan. *Notable Products* is an informative book and the illustrations by Shitomi Kangetsu (1747–1797) – depicting people labouring in all kinds of industries, the equipment they used to accomplish their tasks and the product of their efforts – make it engaging to study. Like others in his position, Kenkadō took up the study of nature as a cultivated pastime. Through his many contacts, he amassed a collection of minerals, rare plants and animal specimens, which he catalogued and displayed for discussion with others.[11] Among the many contemporary intellectuals who attended the social events he hosted was Ono Ranzan (1729–1810), perhaps the foremost botanist of the day, whose interests ranged from zoology to pharmaceutical botany.

In urban centres across Edo-period Japan, fledgling zoos sprang up, opening the natural world to samurai and commoners of all ranks. A day touring the shrines and temples of southern Osaka might include a stop at the Peacock Teahouse (*kujaku chaya*), where visitors could view displays of exotic birds, among them peacocks and rare pheasants. The Peacock Teahouse

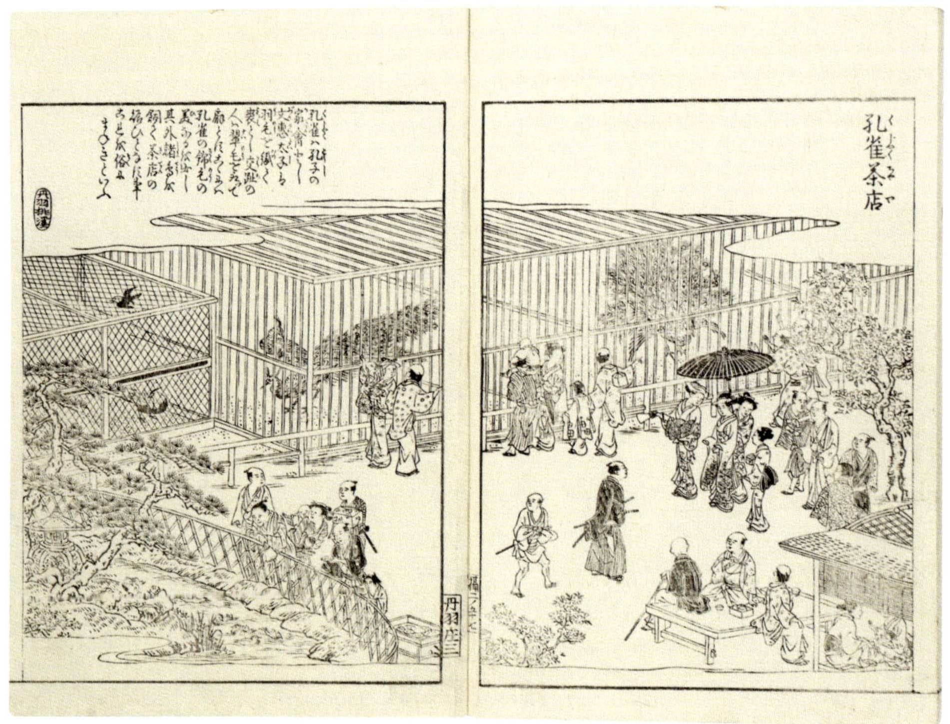

**3.2**
Niwa Tōkei (artist), 'Peacock Teahouse (*kujaku chaya*)', from vol. 2 of Akisato Ritō (author) and seven artists, *Illustrated Guide to Famous Places in Settsu Province (Settsu meisho zue)*, 12 vols, 1798. Illustrated book, woodblock. 25.7 × 18.1 cm (cover). British Museum, London, 2002,0815,0.2.1–12. Purchase funded by the Brooke Sewell Bequest.

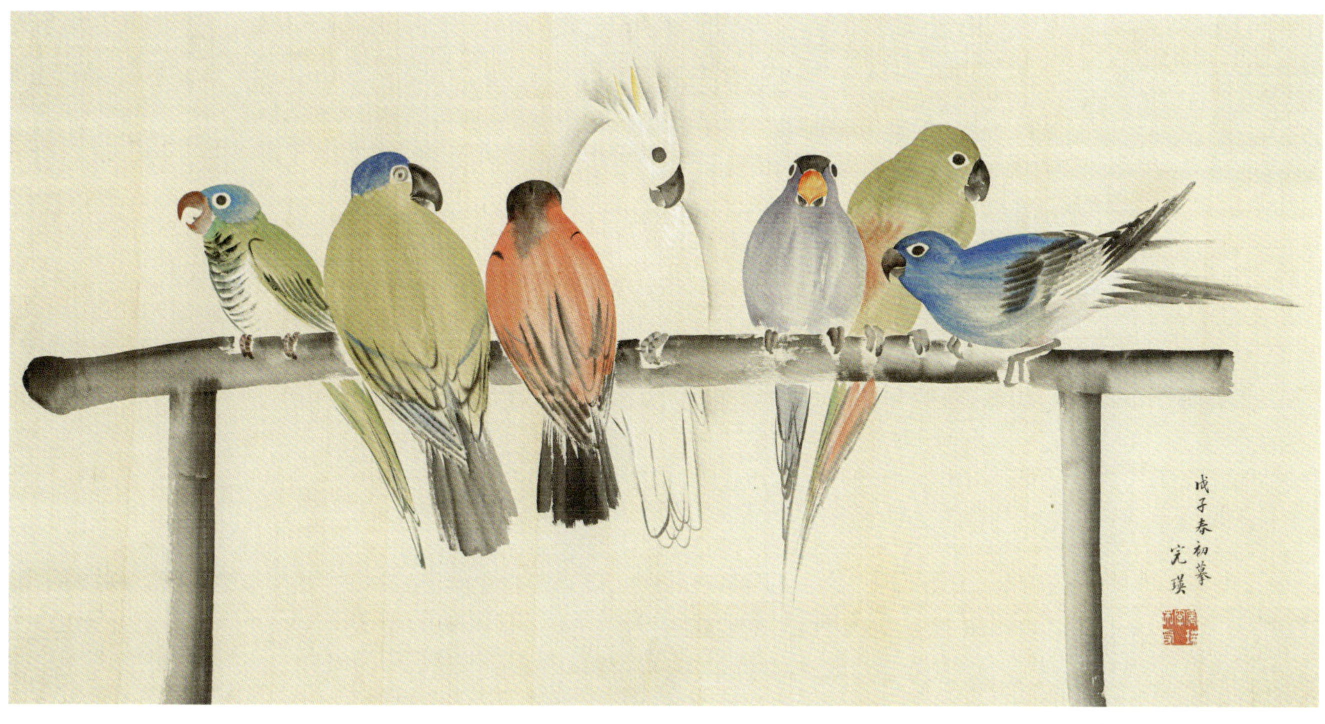



**3.3**
Nishiyama Kan'ei, *Six Parrots and a Cockatoo*, 1888. Hanging scroll, ink and colour on silk. 49.7 × 91.1 cm. British Museum, London, 1987,1006,0.1.

seems to have been a favourite with children (fig. 3.2). By using nature as a 'draw' to bring in business, novelty teahouses like this gave urbanites a hint of living worlds beyond their crowded streets and must have carried special interest at a moment when foreign travel was prohibited. They had parallels in the private menageries kept by the elite. Sometime before 1795, for example, Ōkyo produced a painting, known through a copy by Nishiyama Kan'ei, an advocate of the master's style in Osaka, depicting six parrots and a white cockatoo resting on a lacquered perch, as though kept in a private residence (fig. 3.3). Each parrot presents a range of jewelled tones and assumes a different pose. Kan'ei painted the birds in controlled ink washes, surrounding the cockatoo with a light grey aura to differentiate it and lend it a sense of volume. In that detail he may have diverged from Ōkyo's original, which probably used finely painted white lines to articulate the cockatoo's feathers.[12] Kan'ei trained under his father Nishiyama Hōen (see fig. 2.11), studied neo-Confucianism at a private academy in Osaka and later served the Akashi domain in Harima province (in present-day Hyōgo prefecture).

Enthusiasm for the study and collecting of plants and other natural specimens led to a boom in gardening and the publication of horticultural guides. Perhaps best representing the phenomenon is the mania for morning-glory plants that periodically swept Japan (1810s–20s, 1840s–50s, 1890s–early 1900s) and the publications that supported them.[13] A hanging scroll by Nagasawa Rosetsu, one of Ōkyo's leading students, hints at the flower's spreading appeal (fig. 3.4). Working in his characteristically precise yet liberated style, Rosetsu depicts a morning-glory vine in its natural condition, stretching in several directions at once, a picture of growth and health. A single opened flower suggests that the time is early morning. Directly below, an adult sparrow keeps a lookout for sluggish insects, while its two young call for a meal. The scene has the affectionate observational quality of a haiku poem.

Morning-glory enthusiasts cultivated endless varieties, along with personal connections through social clubs and appreciation societies. Reference books supported their ambitions. At the outset of the first craze of the 1810s, *Depictions of Varieties of Morning Glory (Kengo hinrui zukō, 1814)* introduced forty species of the flower (fig. 3.5). Beautiful full-colour pictures accompany detailed descriptions of leaves, blossoms and hues. Traditional Chinese botanical sources seem to have recorded only a handful of morning-glory species, but the preface to this book rallies enthusiasts by suggesting that an even greater number of species than those illustrated is likely to be cultivated in years to come. The book's artist, Niwa Tōkei (see fig. 2.41), trained under Shitomi Kangetsu and pursued his career in Osaka, where he apparently enjoyed a friendship with Kimura Kenkadō.


## Nature as a cultural resource

Nature's role in Japanese culture reflected the long-term confluence of native interests and contacts with China. A watershed moment arrived with the first imperially commissioned poetry anthology, *Collection of Ancient and Modern Japanese Poems (Kokin wakashū or Kokinshū, 905)*. Among other innovations, the anthology's first six books are arranged thematically according to the cycle of the four seasons. The preface locates the root of poetry in nature, likening the emergence of a poem to the sprouting of leaves and comparing the impulse to create poems to the singing of birds and chirping of frogs.

The *Kokinshū* established a preference for nature as filtered through centuries of cultural interpretation, a concept recently termed 'secondary nature'.[14] Legacies of this courtly standard include Edo-period pictures in which plants of the four seasons appear to grow simultaneously in an idealised garden. For example, relatively early in his career, during the late 1760s and early 1770s, Ōkyo produced a pair of hanging scrolls depicting an array of seasonal

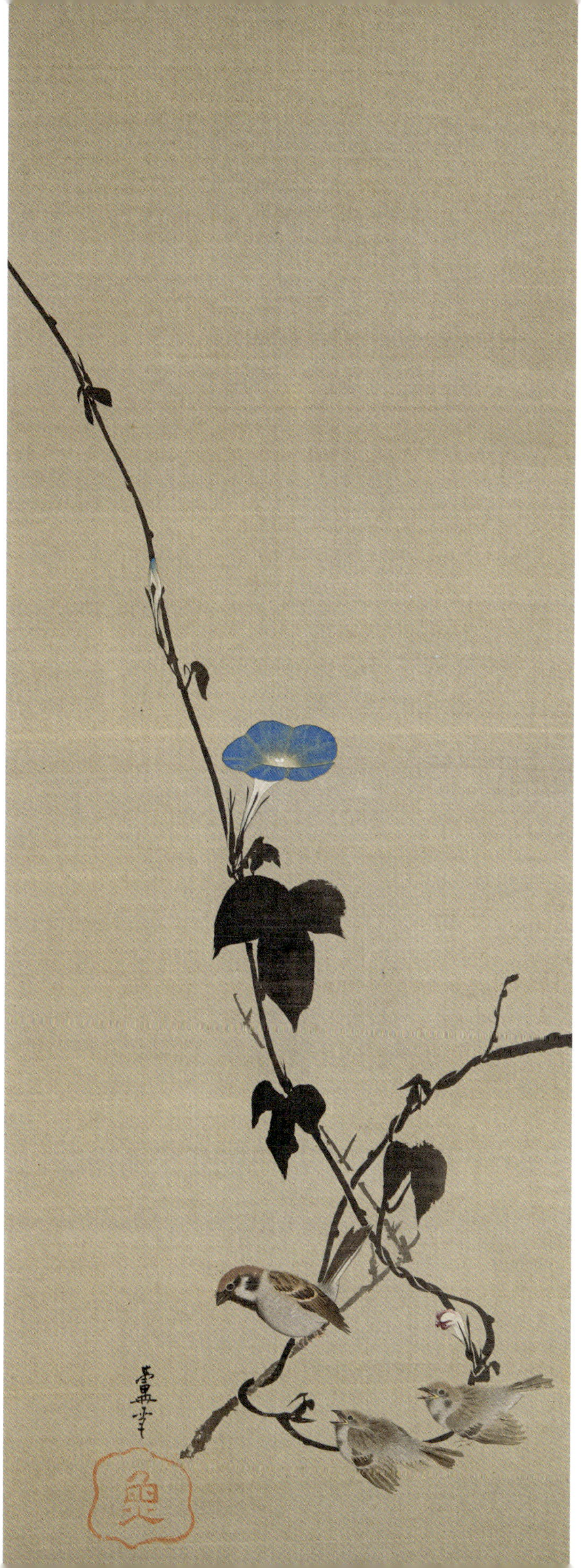

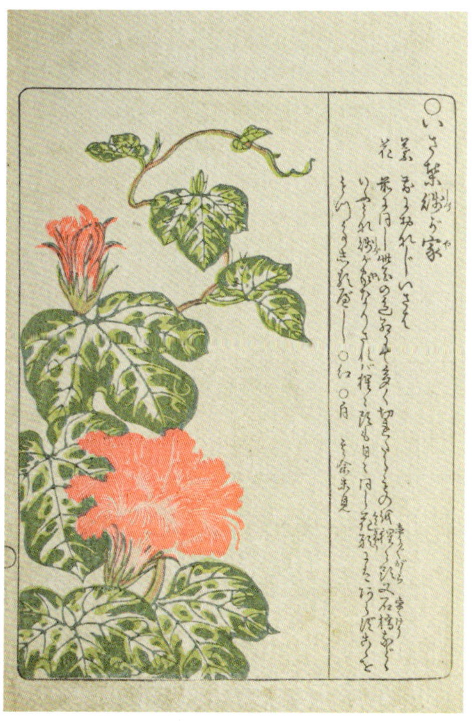

**3.4**
Nagasawa Rosetsu, *Sparrows
and Morning Glories*, late 1700s.
Hanging scroll, ink and colour
on silk. 99.1 × 35.5 cm. British
Museum, London, 1950,1111,0.7.
Gift of James Martin White.

**3.5**
Niwa Tōkei (artist) and Minegishi
Ryūfu (author), *Depictions
of Varieties of Morning Glory*
(*Kengo hinrui zukō*), 1 vol.,
1814. Illustrated book, colour
woodblock. 22 × 15 cm (cover).
British Museum, London,
1979,0305,0.251. Ex-coll.:
Jack Hillier.

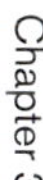



131

plants (fig. 3.6), probably inspired by Ming- or Qing-period Chinese bird-and-flower paintings, which began to reach Japan in significant numbers around the 1720s through the port of Nagasaki. At right in Ōkyo's diptych, the branch of a flowering peach tree winds above a cluster of giant peonies, with perhaps two violets sprouting at the base. Further enlivening the scene are two red-billed blue magpies, posed as though courting. At left, cotton roses blossom alongside chrysanthemums and nearly hidden bellflowers, with a slender stalk of bamboo reaching upward. Completing this scene are two black-naped orioles, again possibly engaged in a courting ritual.[15] Around thirty years later, the Osaka artist Nakamura Hōchū handled the theme differently in a pair of six-panel screens (fig. 3.7) that recall the work of the Kyoto Rinpa school, a line of seventeenth-century artists culminating with Ogata Kōrin. The signature Rinpa painting technique is 'dripping in' (tarashikomi), where the artist introduces small drops of pigment into painted areas that are still wet, creating pools of ink and colour almost infinitely varied in gradation and texture. Maruyama-Shijō artists would also adopt the technique, but Hōchū seems to have used it with special enthusiasm, as seen in this pair of screens showing around forty-five species of seasonal plants arranged to produce a visually engaging composition rather than a temporal sequence.[16] Different as they are, Ōkyo's diptych and Hōchū's screens both treat nature as a cultural delight and could easily have been offered for delectation in an elite salon setting.

To portray what might be called 'Chinese nature', artists in western Japan used two main techniques: colourful, heavy pigments and monochrome ink. Pictures in colour tended to be finely detailed and aspired towards realism, like the diptych by Ōkyo. Adhering perhaps even closer to its Chinese sources is a minutely crafted painting by Kakurin (Kakutei II; active 1770s–90s) depicting an adult male silver pheasant and a tree peony with enormous blossoms (fig. 3.8). Kakurin trained under the Nagasaki-born Ōbaku Zen monk-painter Kakutei (Kaigan Jōkō, 1722–1786) (see p. 165). His name literally means 'Crane Grove', a term usually referring to the sacred sala trees that turned white with grief at the moment of the Buddha's death. It is an unusual name for an artist, and suggests that he, like his teacher, may have been a Buddhist cleric. He was active in Osaka, but few of his works survive. This painting signals his mastery of the Nagasaki-school style, with delicate shading in the petals and leaves and the exotic bird's breast feathers. The inscription is a Chinese four-character quatrain by Dokuan Sōjō (active late eighteenth century), sixth abbot of Seigen-an, a sub-temple of Daitoku-ji in Kyoto:

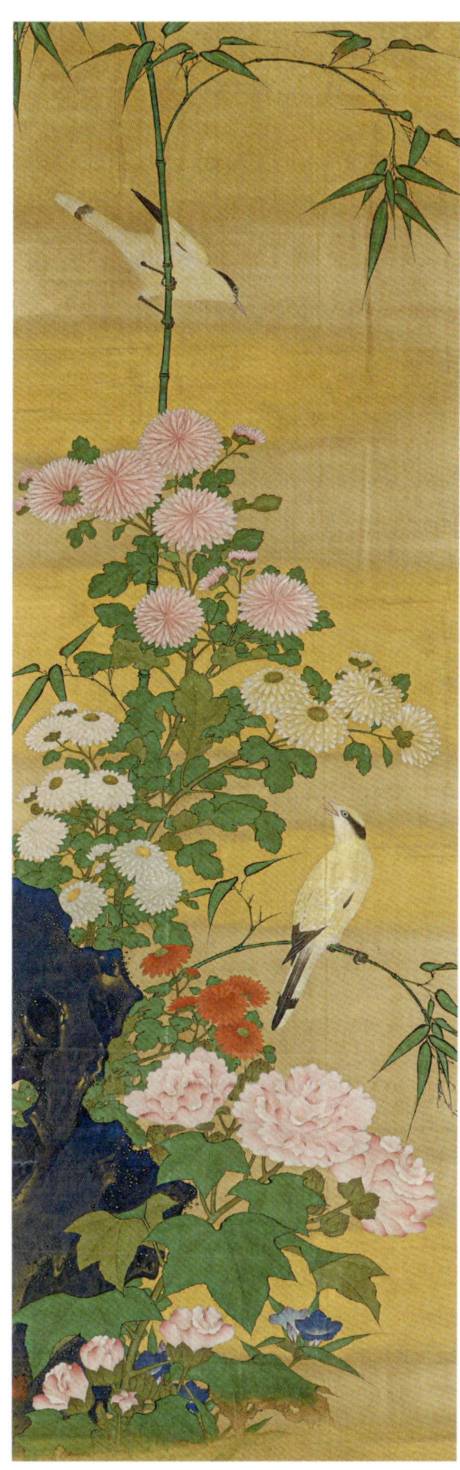
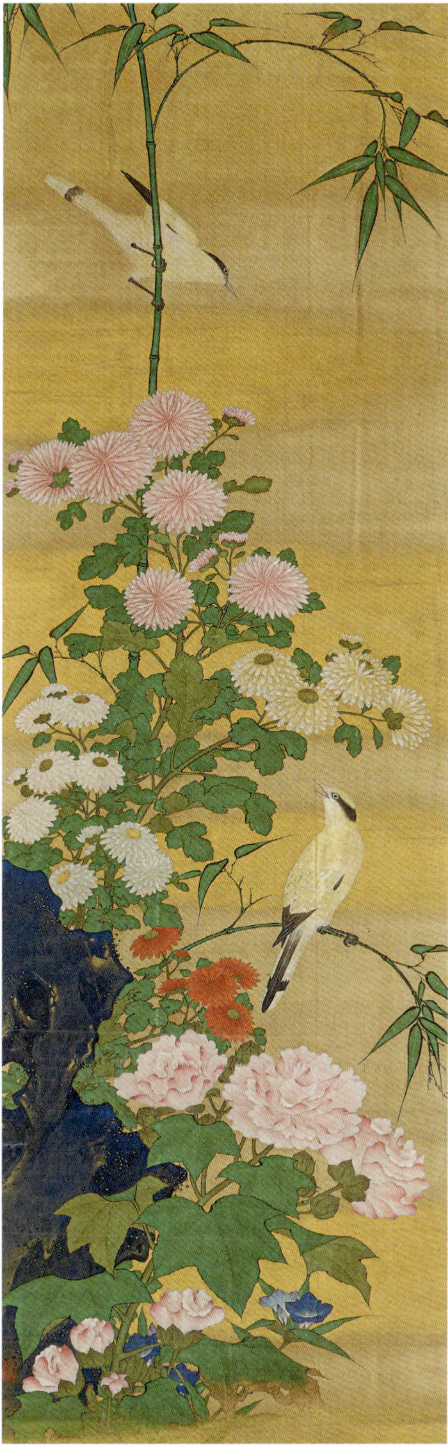

**3.6**
Maruyama Ōkyo, *Birds and Flowers of the Four Seasons*, 1764–72. Pair of hanging scrolls, ink, colour and gold on silk. 101.5 × 33.8 cm (each). British Museum, London, 1913,0501,0.513-514. Gift of Sir William Gwynne-Evans, Bt. Ex-coll.: Arthur Morrison.

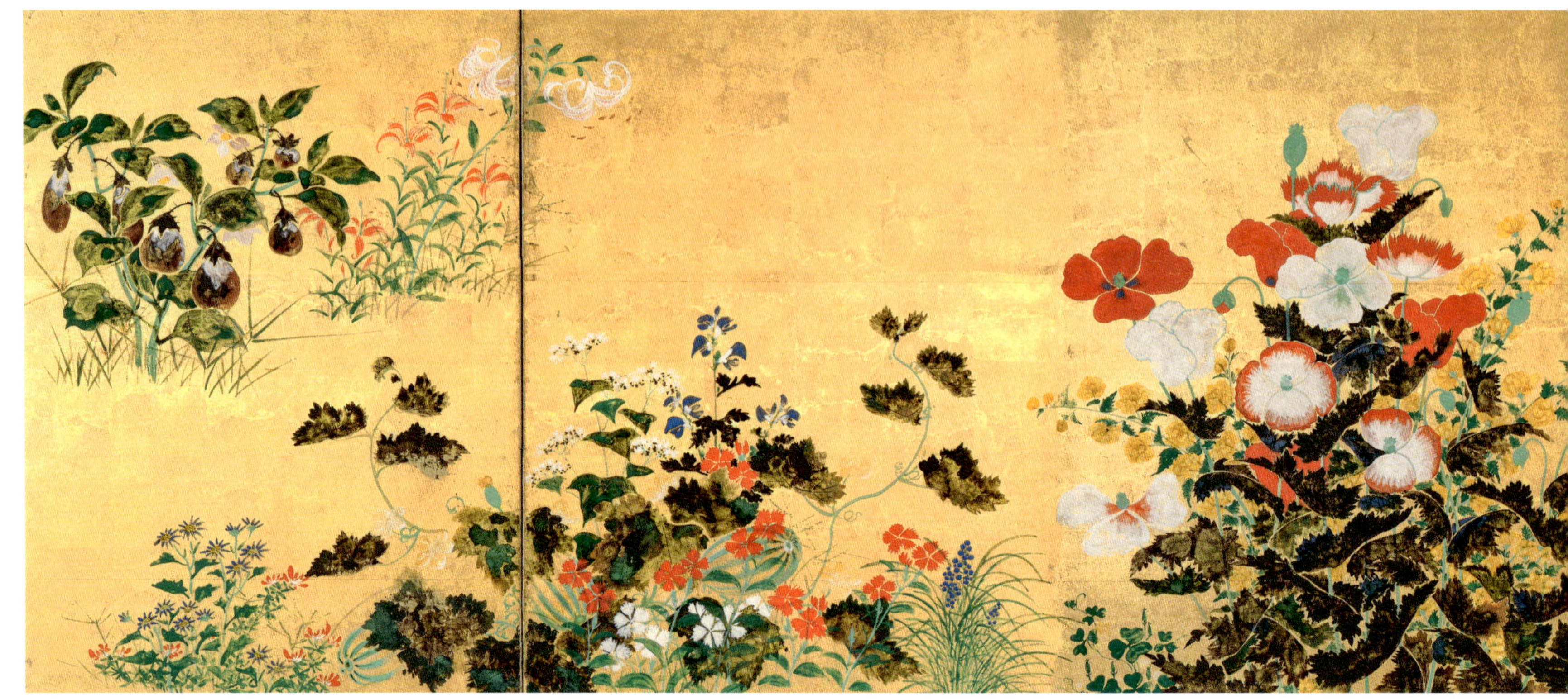

A beguiling yellow, a fragrant purple,

Growing thick and full along a cliffside path,

The king of the flowers has riches and honours,

And heirs who will flourish for generations.[17]

Dokuan's poem celebrates the auspicious associations – wealth, rank, numerous descendants – of the tree peony, known in Chinese culture as the 'king of the flowers'. Image and text suit one another, just as Kakurin's modern technique calls attention to the blossoms and reinforces their symbolic 'secondary nature'.

Two hanging scrolls by Mashiyama Sessai similarly show how cultural priorities could dominate nature painting. Sessai was the daimyō of the Nagashima domain in Ise province (in present-day Mie prefecture). He succeeded as the fifth-generation head of the domain in 1776, and two years later, the Tokugawa government appointed him as one of the four adjunct guardians (*kaban*) in Osaka Castle, positions reserved for daimyō.

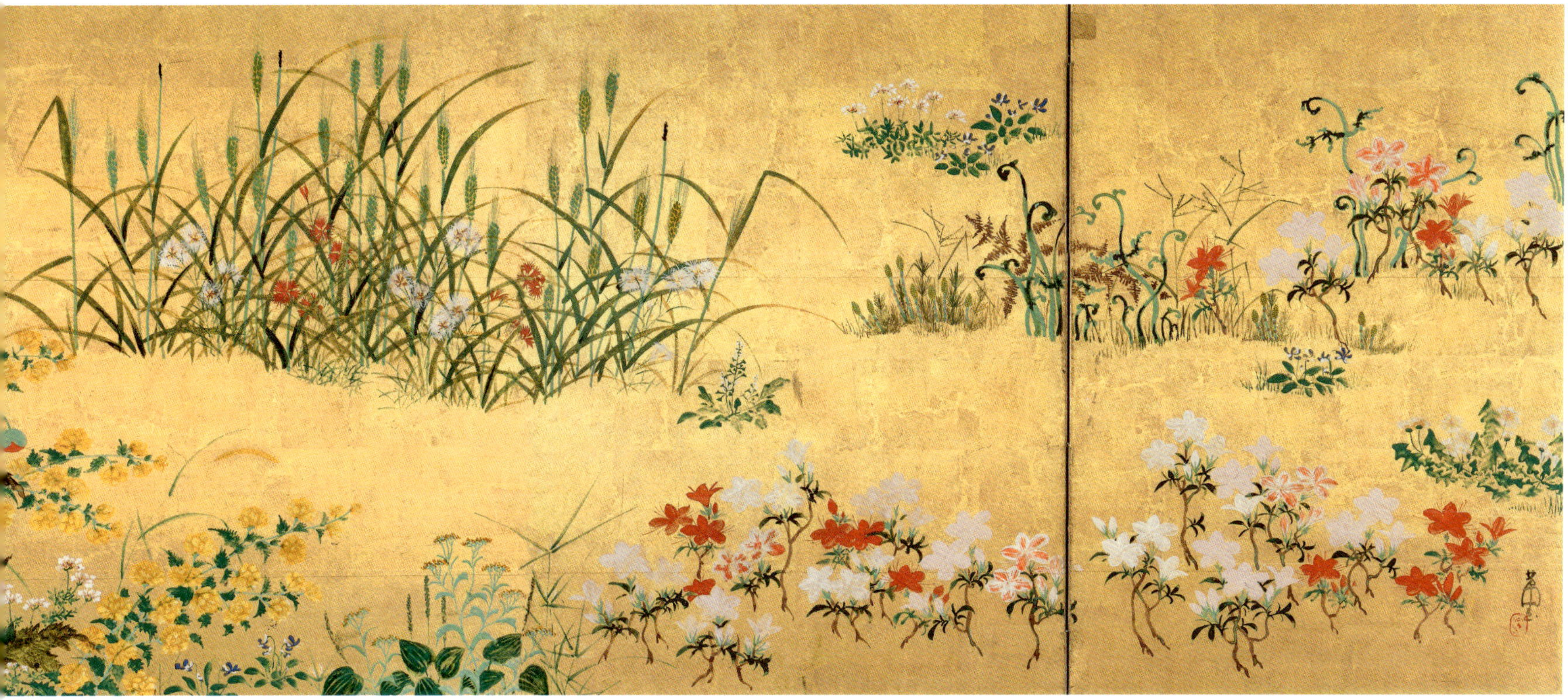

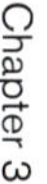



**3.7**
Nakamura Hōchū, *Flowers of the Four Seasons*, 1800–18. Right half of a pair of six-panel screens, ink, colours and gold leaf on paper. 90.5 × 353.2 cm (each). British Museum, London, 1078,0306,0.4.1-2. Purchase funded by the Brooke Sewell Bequest.

Sessai, however, took a greater interest in cultural pursuits. During his stay in Osaka, he became friendly with Kenkadō, and when in 1790 the Tokugawa shogunate prosecuted Kenkadō for contravening official limits on sake production, Sessai sheltered the brewer within his domain. Sessai was also an amateur artist who made the unorthodox choice to specialise in literati painting (bunjin-ga) and the Shen Quan style (see pp. 165–7), attracted perhaps partly to their exoticism and partly, in the latter case, to the connection with the natural world that it offered.[18] His skill is evident in a painting of a white cockatoo and an exotic bird with blue and black feathers perched on the branches of a flowering tree, with perhaps camellias flowering at the base (fig. 3.9). Sessai might have seen a live white cockatoo in a sideshow, or even kept one himself.[19] At the same time, he may have paired the two birds for the purposes of visual contrast: light and dark, large and small. As though reaching back to the Ming origins of this style of painting, he also gave prominence to the richly pigmented birds by rendering the tree and rocks in light monochrome ink. His painting balances realism and artifice. Sessai achieved something similar

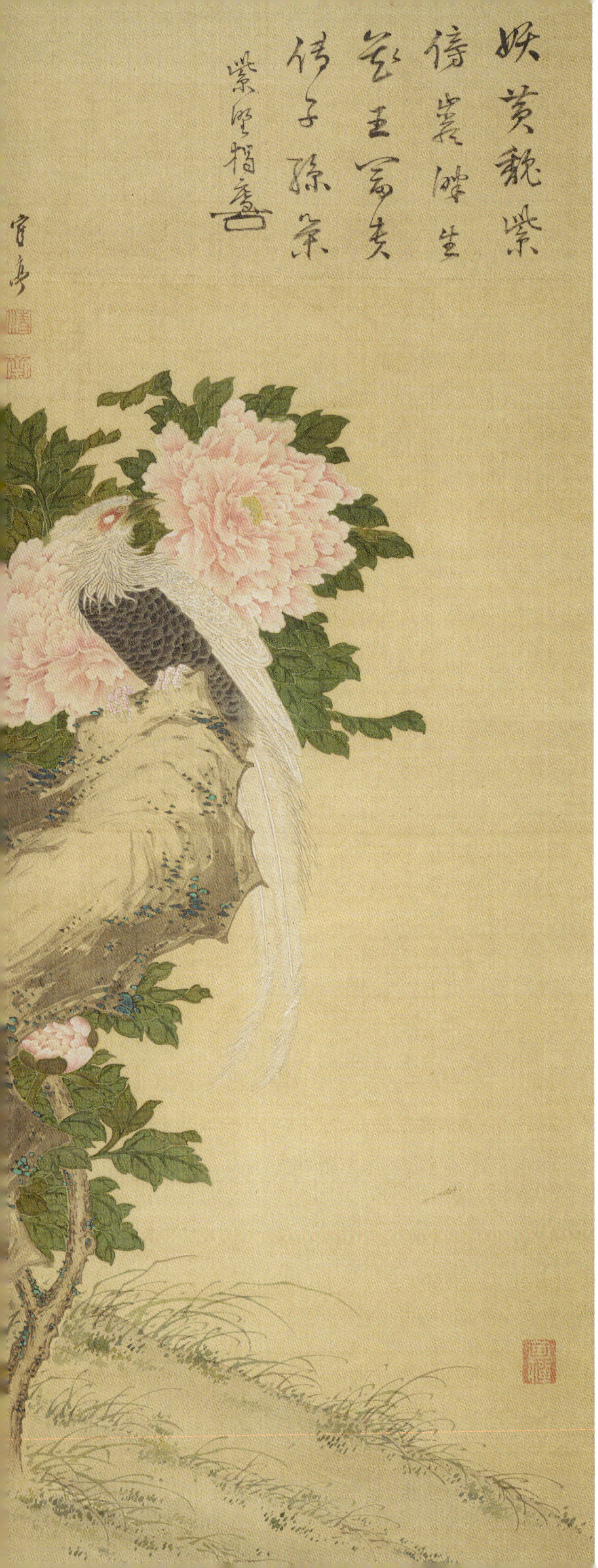

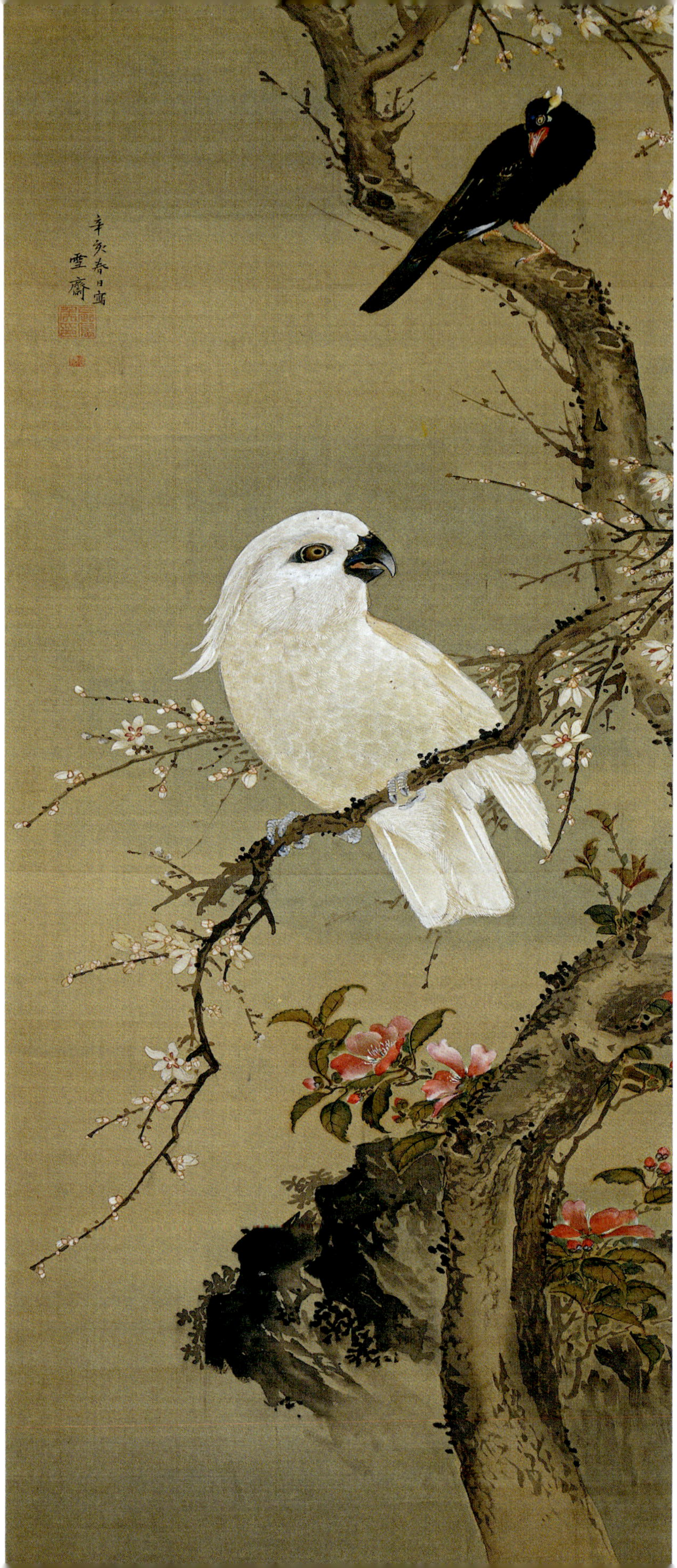

妖黄魏紫
傍崖叢生
笔王富貴
倣子孫榮
紫雲賴齋

辛亥春日寫
雪齋

in an atmospheric view of pond life known as a 'duckweed-and-fish picture' (C: *zao yu tu*; J: *sōgyo zu*) (fig. 3.10). Combining shades of monochrome ink with touches of colour, Sessai adhered to the logic of his Chinese models by placing fringed water lilies at the top, as though floating on the pond's surface, followed by shallow-water minnows, and finally a carp exploring the watery depths at the bottom of the scroll.[20] If displayed in salon contexts, both paintings might have encouraged discussion less about the natural subjects they depict than about the artist's perfected technique and style.

Adept brushwork might appear to be the only way to achieve subtle tonal gradations, as seen in the preceding works, but by the late eighteenth century, colour woodblock printing in Japan had advanced so far that the medium became accepted for collaborative salon projects, such as surimono (see p. 31) and privately issued books aiming to match the ideals of nature painting. One example is the illustrated poetry anthology *Selection of Insects at My Elbow* (*Chūka senzen*, 1820), in which text and image share equal importance (fig. 3.11). Illustrated here in its rare complete first edition, the book carries a preface, and may have been organised by Shinozaki Shōchiku (1781–1851), an Osaka-born Confucian scholar and calligrapher who earned renown after bringing orthodox neo-Confucian teachings from Edo back to his home city. At some point in his travels, he met the artist Mori Shunkei (active 1815–41), a master of observed nature studies who trained in Osaka under Mori Sosen. In *Selection of Insects at My Elbow*, classical Chinese poems, written in elegant Chinese-style calligraphy by Shōchiku and other scholars whom he probably recruited, alternate with Shunkei's depictions of insects in their natural surroundings. Shunkei's pictures seem to balance a direct knowledge of nature with an understanding of Chinese pictorial conventions. They are vividly realistic but complement the character of the calligraphy and poems. Intellectuals such as Shōchiku are usually linked solely with the literati painting movement, yet the book shows that Osaka supported a more dynamic range of cultural interactions.

Monochrome ink landscapes and views of nature, by contrast, often have a more impressionistic quality associated with Chinese literati painting. Japanese people explored this style through Chinese paintings and painting manuals which began being imported around the 1720s (see p. 186). Whereas Nagasaki-school artists generally subordinated their brushwork to the overall effect of a painting, literati artists emphasised brushwork as a tool of self-expression. A spirited example is a hanging scroll by Nakabayashi Chikutō (1776–1853) (fig. 3.12). Born in Nagoya, Chikutō moved to Kyoto in 1803 and became the leading theorist of the literati school. In his painting, an egret

**3.8**
Kakurin (Kakutei II), *Silver Pheasant and Peonies*, 1770–1800. Hanging scroll, ink and colour on silk. 97.9 × 38.3 cm. British Museum, London, 1881,1210,0.653. Ex-coll.: William Anderson.

**3.9**
Mashiyama Sessai, *Black Bird and Cockatoo*, 1791. Hanging scroll, ink and colour on silk. 111.9 × 43.1 cm. British Museum, London, 1979,1112,0.1.

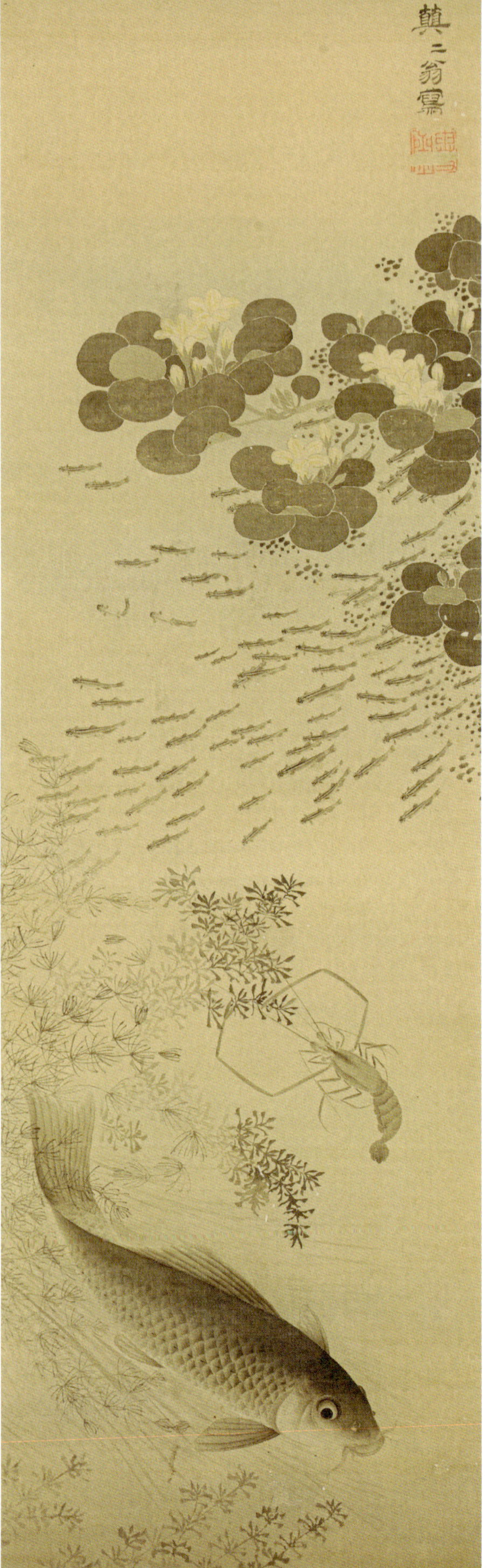

**3.10**
Mashiyama Sessai, *Duckweed and Fish*, 1780–1819. Hanging scroll, ink and light colour on silk. 87.2 × 27.2 cm. British Museum, London, 1881,1210,0.2331. Ex-coll.: William Anderson.

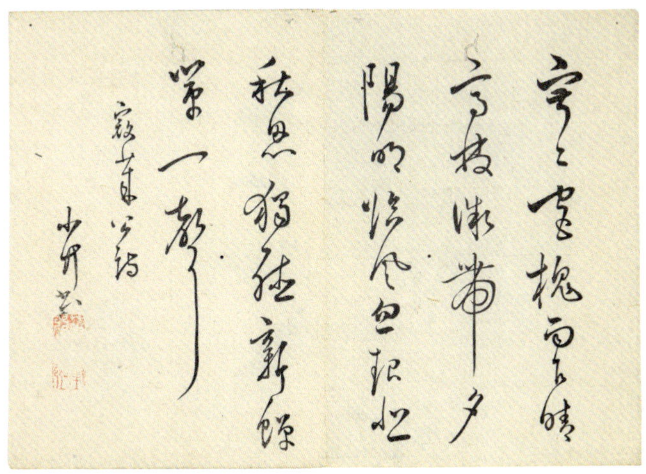 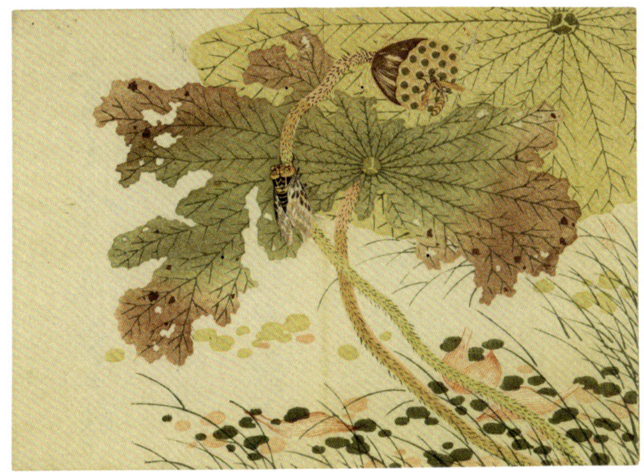

**3.11**
Mori Shunkei (artist) and
four calligraphers including
Shinozaki Shōchiku and
Morikawa Chikusō, *Selection
of Insects at My Elbow* (*Chūka
senzen*), 1 vol., 1820. Album,
colour woodblock. 21 × 14.4 cm
(cover). British Museum,
London, 2022,3013.1. Purchase
made possible by the JTI
Japanese Acquisition Fund.

The opening here is 'Cicada
and bee on a lotus seedpod',
with a corresponding Chinese
poem calligraphed by Shinozaki
Shōchiku.

hunts for fish along the edge of a stream, with the branch of a snow-covered plum tree arching overhead. This appears to be a study of avian behaviour in winter, but an egret, fallen snow and plum blossoms together comprise the set painting theme of the 'Three Forms of White' (*sanpaku*). Chikutō solved the challenge of working in monochrome ink by filling the background with brushstrokes that suggest a rippling stream and leaving areas of the white paper ground untouched to represent his three subjects. The eccentric arc of the plum tree is characteristic of monochrome 'ink-plum' (*bokubai*) paintings, a theme favoured in Japan since around the 1300s for its associations with scholarly reclusion, following Chinese models. Late in his career the haiku poet and painter Ki Baitei (1774–1810) produced a relatively subdued ink-plum painting (fig. 3.13). Bold brush marks in the rocks contrast with the delicate strokes defining the branches and flowers. Baitei trained under the influential haiku poet and literati painter Yosa Buson. He passed his early career in Kyoto, but when a fire consumed the city in 1788, he moved east across the mountains to Ōtsu, a major post station on the shore of Lake Biwa. Few of his early paintings survive, and this one dates to his fruitful Ōtsu period.

A monochrome ink hanging scroll by Suminoe Buzen gives a different perspective on older Chinese modes of depicting nature. Here three Chinese herders drive a pack of mules down a mountain road, presumably to market (fig. 3.14). The scene is luminous, with juxtaposed areas of light and dark ink wash and an almost decorative patterning in the mist. The subject may reflect an Osaka patron's dual interest in commerce and Chinese culture, but in regard to technique, here Buzen offers his personal interpretation of Ming-period variations on Song-period-type landscapes. Buzen had worked

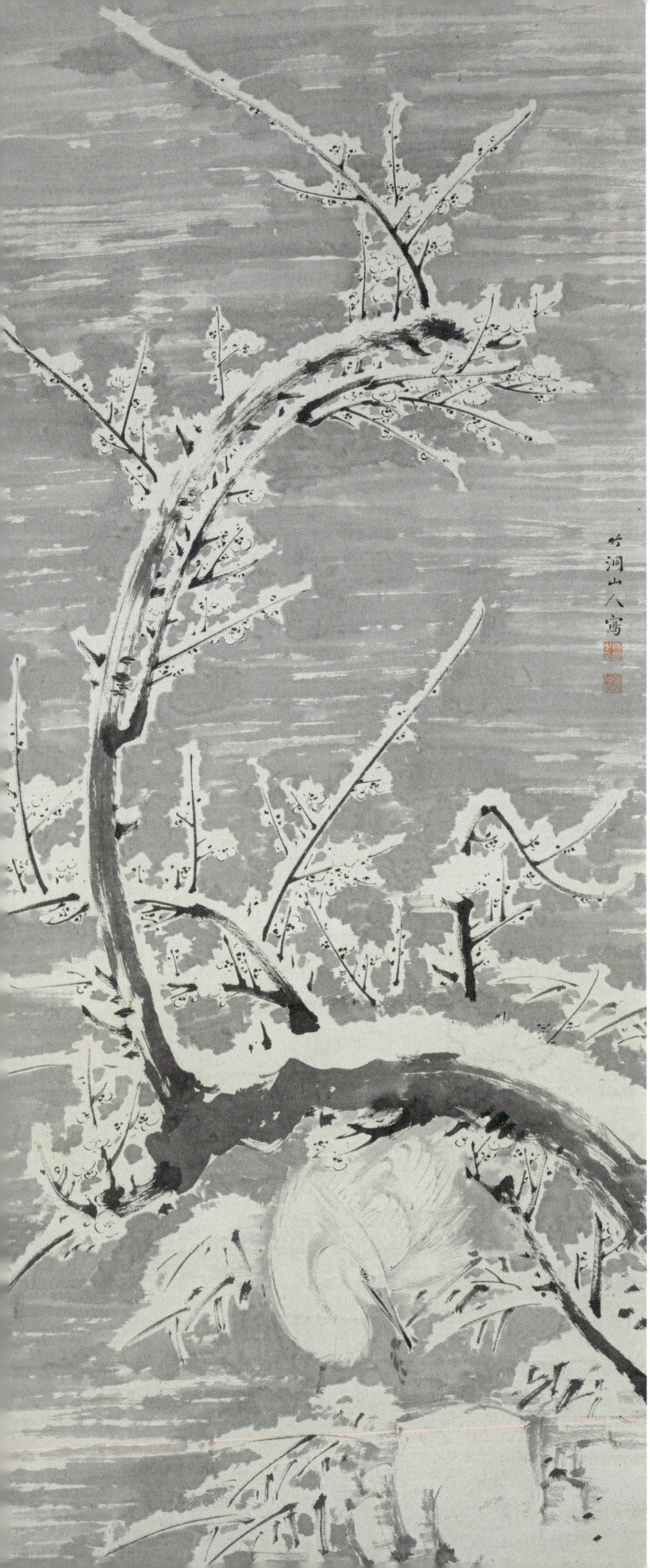

**3.12**
Nakabayashi Chikutō, *Three Forms of White*, c. 1800s.
Hanging scroll, ink on paper.
131.7 × 55.8 cm. British Museum,
London, 2003,0819,0.2.
Purchase funded by the
Brooke Sewell Bequest.

**3.13**
Ki Baitei, *Flowering Plum Branch and Rocks*, 1808.
Hanging scroll, ink on silk.
127.2 × 26.2 cm. British Museum,
London, 1986,0513,0.1.

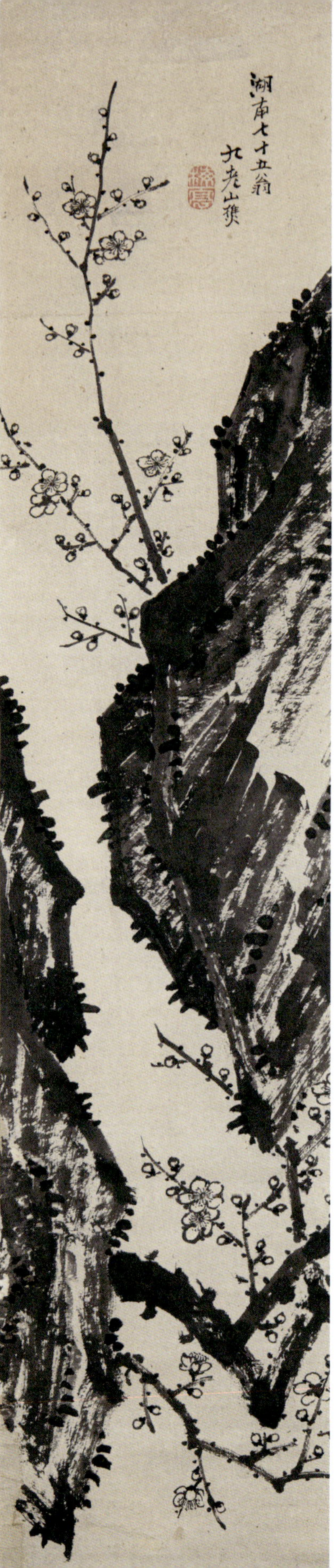

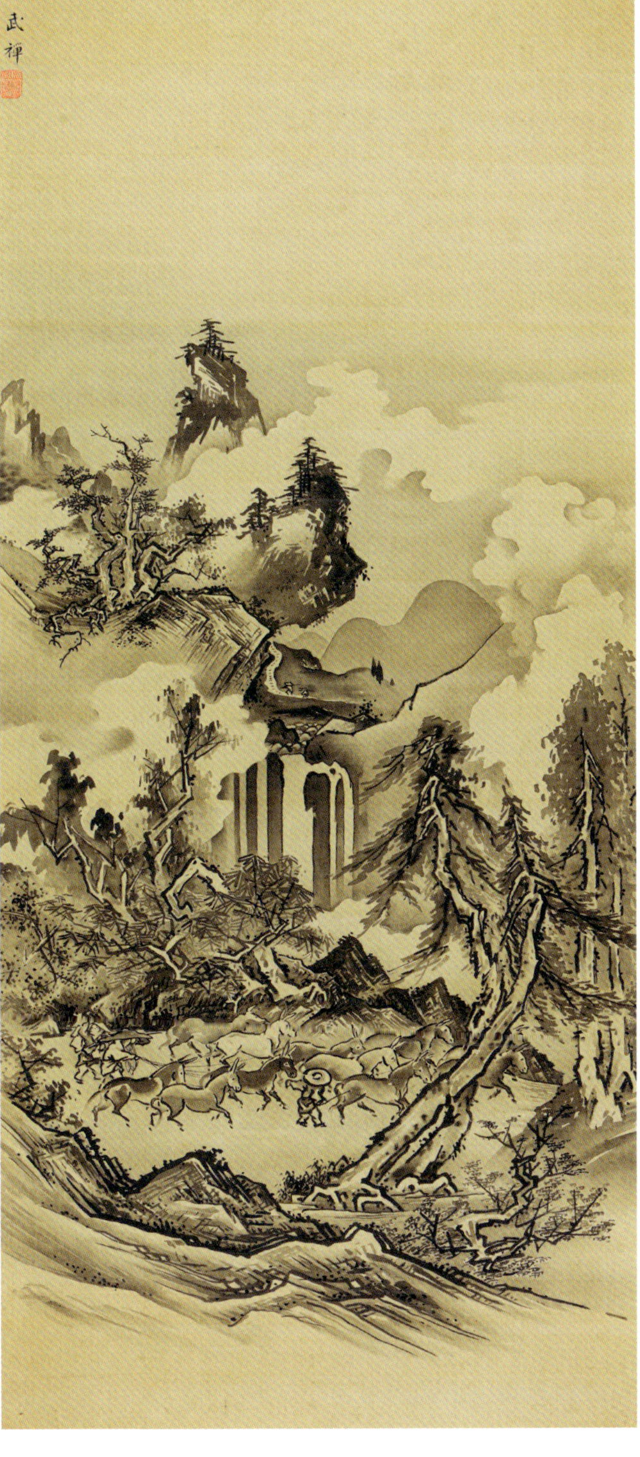

for a time as a ship's captain, one of the many who supported Osaka's bustling port economy. At some point, he, like Shitomi Kangetsu, entered the studio of Tsukioka Settei (1726–1787). By the 1770s Buzen had established himself as a painter and an accomplished carver of designs on metal objects. In later years he earned a name arranging bowls and trays with miniature Chinese landscapes (senkeiban) (see fig. 0.21). Buzen's success exemplifies the way Osaka during this period encouraged the artistic ambitions of multitalented individuals from diverse walks of life.

**3.14**
Suminoe Buzen, *Chinese Landscape with Mule Drivers*, c. 1760–1806. Hanging scroll, ink on silk. 98 × 44 cm. British Museum, London, 1881,1210,0.814. Ex-coll.: William Anderson.

## Nature as an artistic resource

In a sense Ōkyo and his students rescued nature from culture. Where Kanō artists generally treated nature as an artefact of ancient times and faraway places, Maruyama-Shijō artists reclaimed it for the here and now. This way of seeing appealed to the constituents of salon culture in Kyoto and Osaka and attracted similar audiences across Japan. The Maruyama-Shijō artists reconnected with primary nature through observation and sketching, a practice then called 'direct transcription' (*iki-utsushi* or *shō-utsushi*). The modern Japanese language usually renders 'sketching' as shasei, but for Ōkyo, that term more profoundly required the artist to endow a subject with both recognisable features and a living presence.[21] Shasei in the sense of 'capturing life' is the higher goal that Ōkyo set for his students and the quality in his own work that drew wonder, both from those who knew him and from those who encountered him indirectly through his paintings.[22] His nature paintings are windows onto an idyllic world thriving just beyond the limits of human society.

Ōkyo was not the first Edo-period artist to study nature directly. A century earlier, perhaps inspired by the growing fascination with natural history, Kanō Tan'yū explored the possibilities of the life-study in small brush sketches.[23] These drawings rarely made their way into finished works.[24] Instead, they were incorporated into the repertory of painting models that Kanō artists copied. For example, in 1792, Noda Tōmin (active late eighteenth century) produced a group of forty-seven sketches of water birds, forest birds and domestic fowl, whose immediacy appears to reflect a study of actual specimens. In an accompanying note, however, Tōmin explains that he had copied a Kanō artist's copies of Tan'yū sketches held by Kanō Tōshun (d. 1794 or 1796), the fourth-generation head of the Surugadai Kanō studio, founded by Tan'yū's adopted son Kanō Tōun Masanobu (1625–1694) (fig. 3.15).[25]

Although Ōkyo is now virtually synonymous with sketching from life, copying also formed part of his method and helped him to build a library of pictorial references.[26] His own model drawings circulated within and beyond his studio as teaching tools. In this way, he modified the procedures of life drawing where doing so proved useful, practical or necessary. As an independent thinker and experienced teacher who had travelled a long road himself, he recognised that young artists advance by stages through established techniques. His early patron, the Buddhist monk Yūjō, recorded him as saying, 'The student of the laws of painting must not relinquish the rules, then must not cling to the rules, and then will disregard the rules.'[27]

Ōkyo's life sketches survive in the form of first-generation works by his own hand and second-generation versions by an unknown copyist; yet, as with Tan'yū, few can be linked to extant finished paintings.[28] Drawing from life was for him but one tool among many, including those he learned from his teacher Ishida Yūtei (1721–1786).[29] An elegant two-panel folding screen with a deer stopping beneath a cryptomeria to view a flowing stream dates to the latter part of Yūtei's career (fig. 3.16). At once lifelike and decorative in connoting longevity and sacredness, the screen presents several techniques that would become familiar to artists of the Maruyama-Shijō school. Along the curved sides of the tree trunk Yūtei employed tsuketate, a 'boneless' technique (C: mogu; J: mokkotsu) in which the artist loads one side of a brush with ink graded dark to light and then applies the brush to the picture surface, giving the illusion of a rounded form without contours. Ōkyo may have acquired this

**3.15**
Noda Tōmin, *Sandpiper*, copied from a set of copies of brush-drawings by Kanō Tanyū, 1792. Album leaf, ink and colour on paper. 28.1 × 40.7 cm. British Museum, London, 1881,1210,0.2476. Ex-coll.: William Anderson.

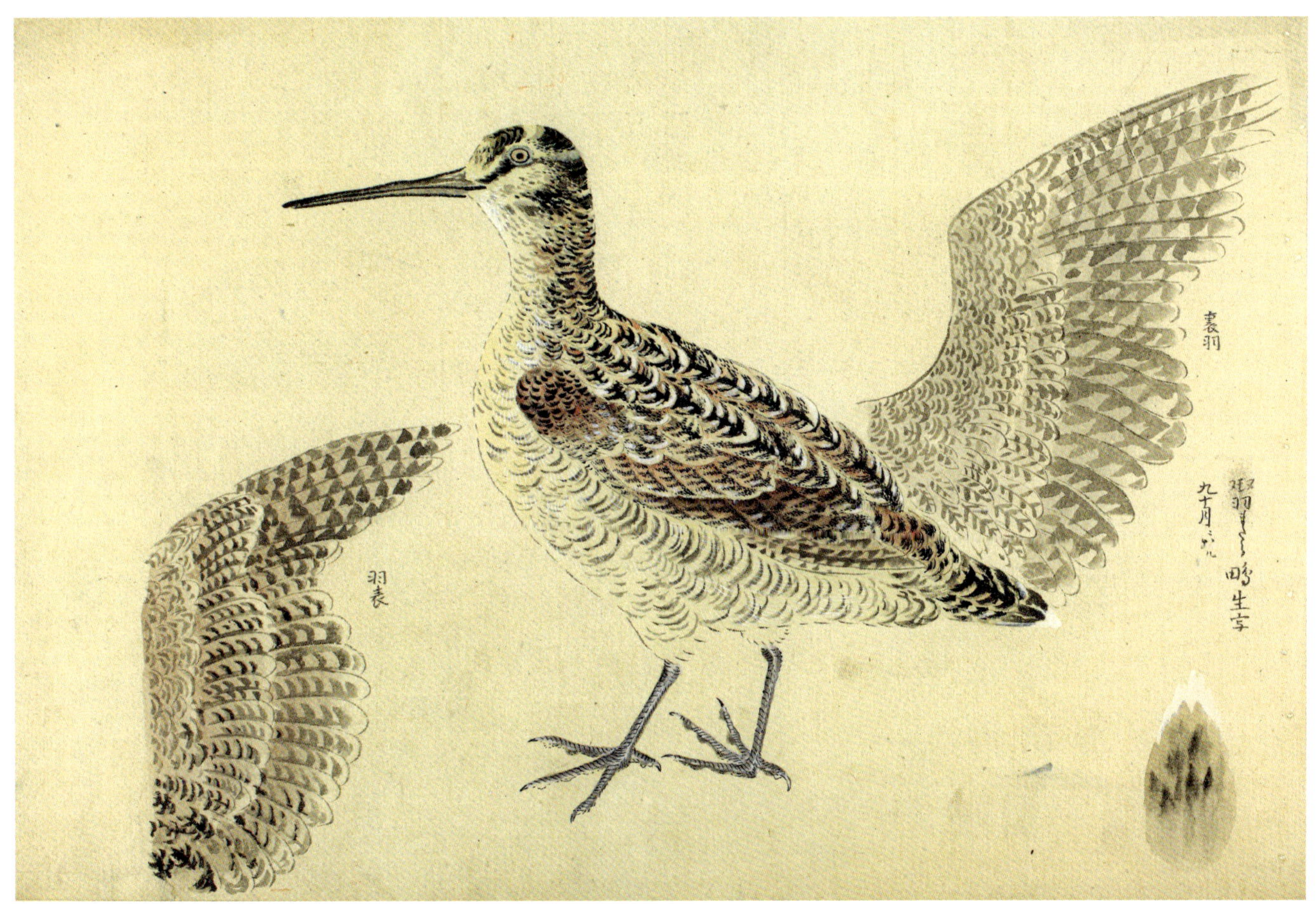

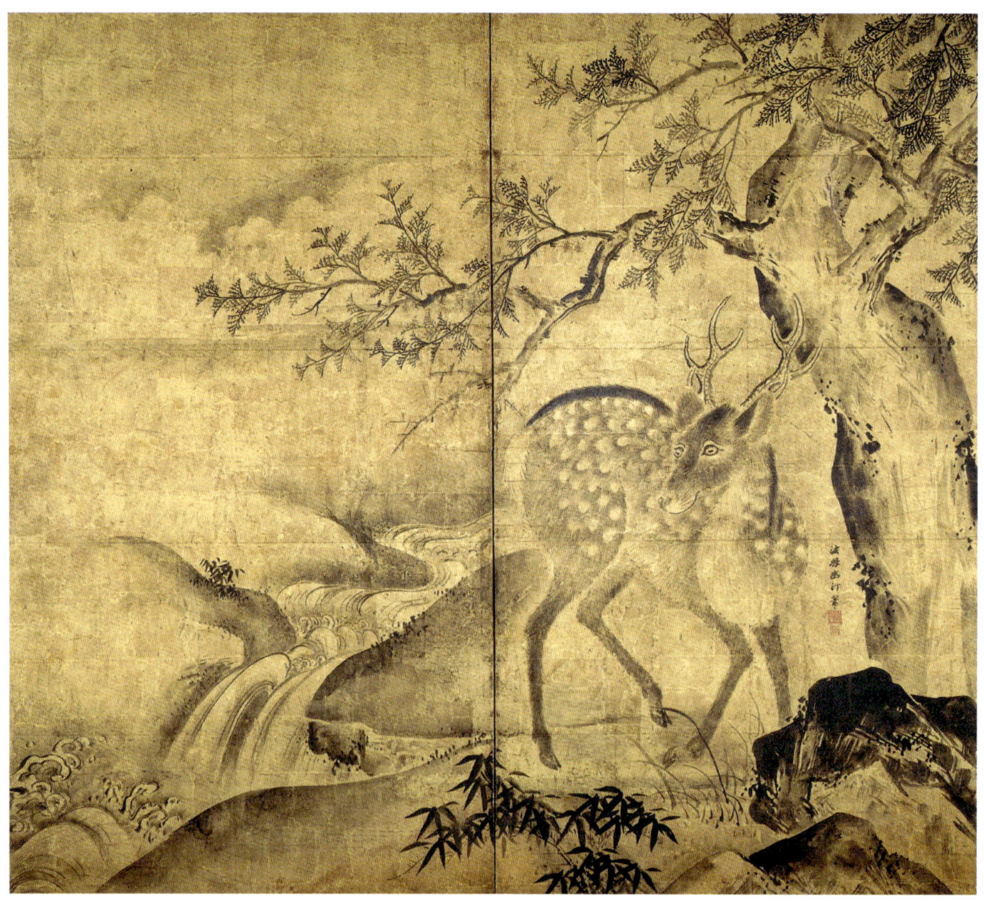

**3.16**
Ishida Yūtei, *Deer and Cryptomeria*, 1770–86. Two-panel folding screen, ink and gold leaf on paper. 164 × 176.8 cm. British Museum, London, 1998,1216,0.1.

technique in Yūtei's studio, but he went on to become its undisputed master. At bottom left, Yūtei used the 'dripping in' technique of pooled ink to introduce variety and texture. And the fine brushstrokes in the deer's fur may offer a hint as to where Ōkyo learned his extraordinary patience in rendering the fur, feathers and leaves of the many animals, birds and plants that feature in his art.

Ōkyo treated familiar nature subjects in unconventional ways and brought unfamiliar subjects into the fold of elite painting. In the first category are tigers, which became for him almost a trademark motif. Tigers are not native to Japan, and the few live imported specimens were not seen outside of Nagasaki. Instead, with reference to imported tiger skins, Chinese and Korean tiger paintings and the behaviour of domestic cats, Japanese artists formulated their own versions of the animal. For Kanō artists, tigers symbolised power and authority, and served to accessorise the living spaces of their samurai patrons. Ōkyo's seated tiger is a different kind of beast (fig. 3.17, see fig. 0.4). It addresses

**3.18** *overleaf*
Maruyama Ōkyo and pupils, *Tigers Crossing a River*, c. 1781–2. Six-panel folding screen, ink, colour and gold leaf on paper. 153.8 × 352.8 cm. British Museum, London, 2006,0424,0.1. Acquisition supported by the Brooke Sewell Bequest and the Art Fund. Ex-coll.: Yamada Shōzaemon XII; Hara Sankei.

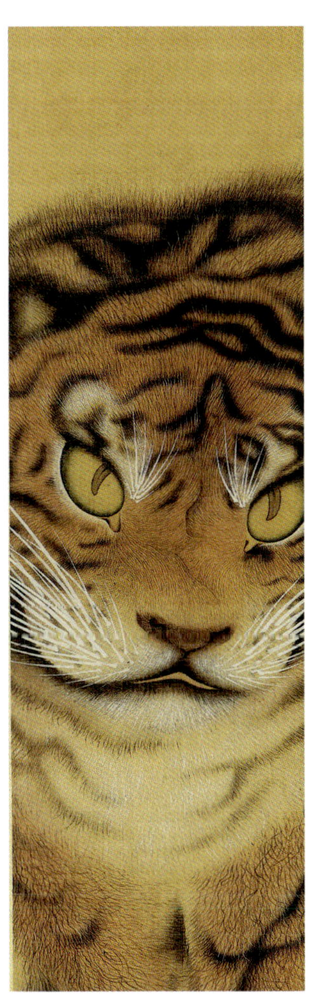

**3.17**
Maruyama Ōkyo, *Seated Tiger* (detail of fig. 0.4), 1775. Hanging scroll, ink and colour on silk. 128.7 × 14.9 cm. British Museum, London, 1977,0404,0.2. Ex-coll.: Nakamura (Kariganeya) Hanbei.

the viewer with a quizzical expression, as though we have intruded on its territory. Instead of the round, bulging eyes of a mythical Kanō tiger, it has the sleek, almond-shaped eyes of a feline, painted in gold rimmed with green, again recalling a cat's eyes. The technically 'unrealistic' crescent-shaped pupils may have in fact heightened the feeling of uncanny realism that the animal conveys, because the artist's contemporaries probably would not have known that a tiger's pupils are round and would have connected these with the experience of seeing a living cat. Ōkyo's brushwork differentiates between the hairs across the back, chest and tail and the spiky whiskers – every stroke conforming to the implied musculature and helping to create the impression of a three-dimensional figure. The inventive cropped format makes the animal appear even larger and more powerful than if depicted in full. Produced in 1775, this superb painting helps to explain why, the same year, *Record of People in Heian [Kyoto]* (*Heian jinbutsu-shi*; see fig. 1.24) listed Ōkyo for the first time at the head of its painting division, an indication that he was generally considered the best artist in Kyoto. For here, instead of deploying his subject in the way an academic Kanō painter might, Ōkyo has invoked it. No longer a symbol to be manipulated by others, this tiger is living life on its own terms. The artist has in effect placed the viewer at nature's command, a radically different way of thinking about the natural world.

With his students Ōkyo also painted a richly decorated six-panel folding screen in which a streak of tigers (mother and cubs) enacts a thirteenth-century Chinese puzzle (fig. 3.18). According to ancient East Asian lore, if a tigress has three cubs, one will be naughty and try to eat the others. If the family must cross a river, the mother can transport only one cub at a time, but the naughty one cannot remain alone with its siblings. How can they all cross safely?[30] The screen shows the story nearing a happy conclusion, as the tigress carries across her second cub, and an aggressive young tiger at right – clearly the naughty one – waits its turn. The river, rendered in subtle tones of monochrome ink, flows from right to left down a gentle gradient, generating a sense of open space and leading the eye in the direction of travel. As in Ōkyo's hanging scroll (fig. 3.17), the hairs of the fur are delicately laid down one by one, almost to the thickness of actual hairs, in white, black, orange and gold. The elaborate gold-leaf background suggests that this screen was a special commission for a wealthy patron.[31]

Among the more surprising, and even ingenious, works that flowed from Ōkyo's brush is a two-panel folding screen depicting pond ice starting to break up in early spring (fig. 3.19). The lines of monochrome ink initially appear laid down almost at random, but then they coalesce into a three-dimensional view

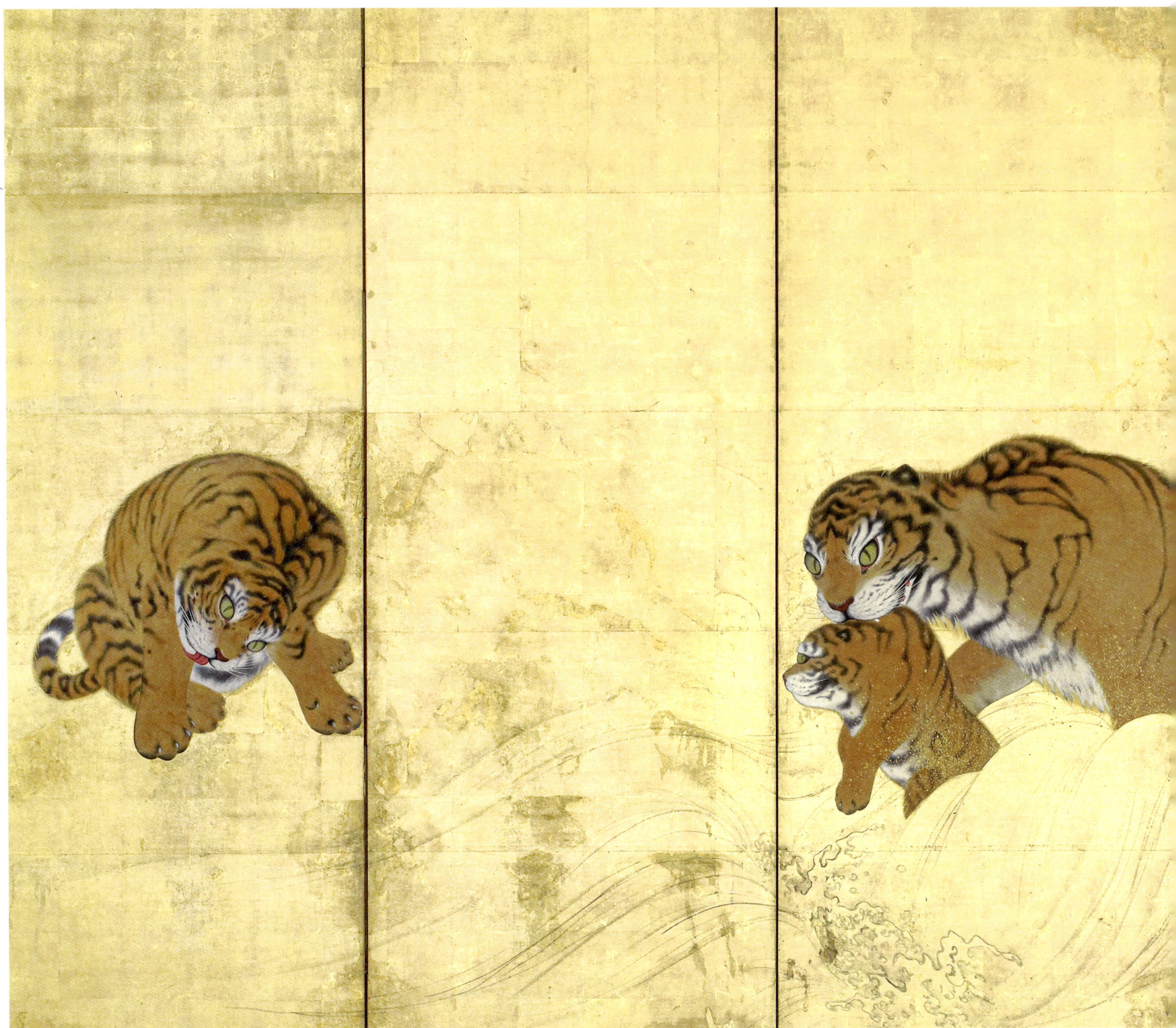

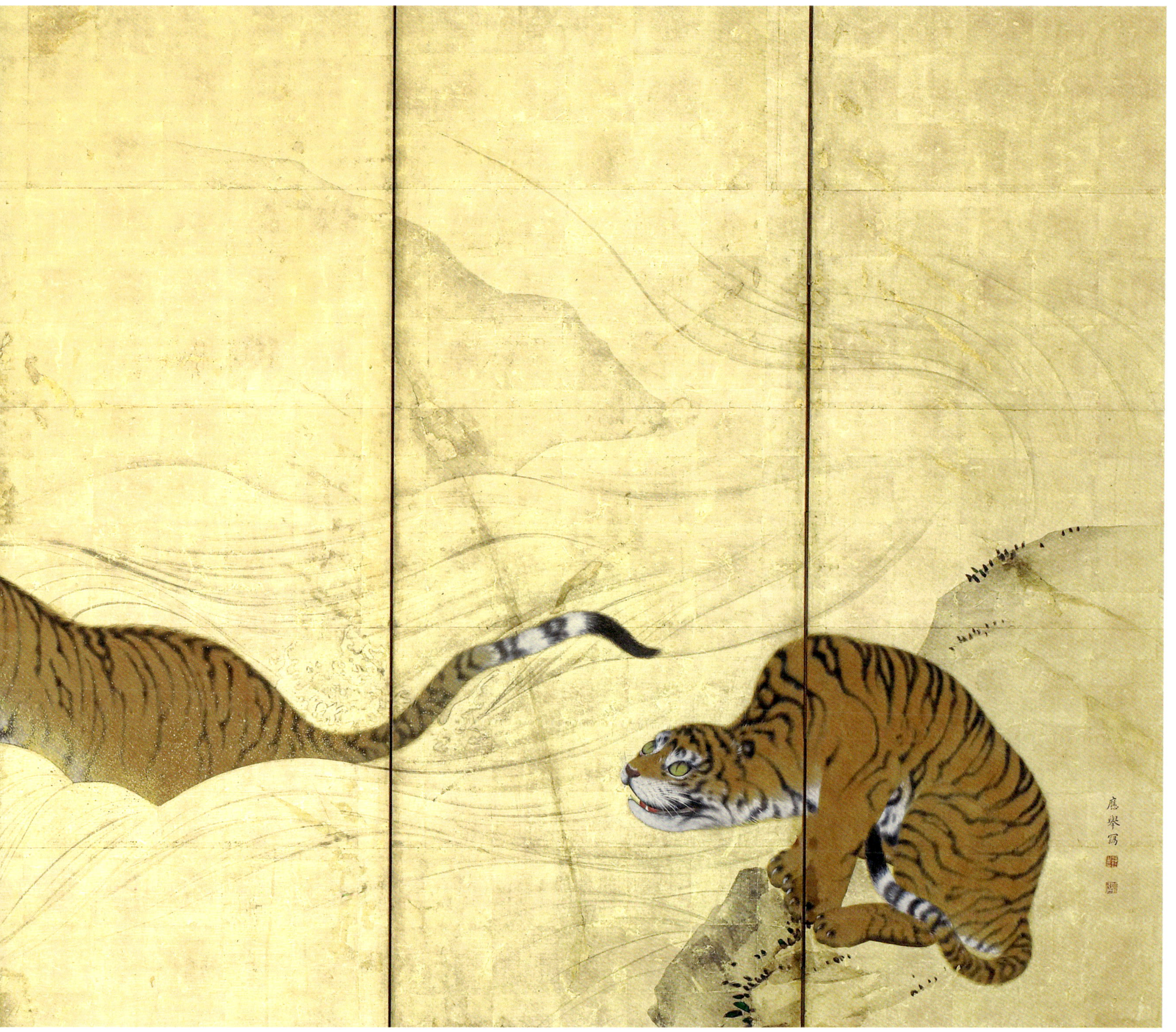

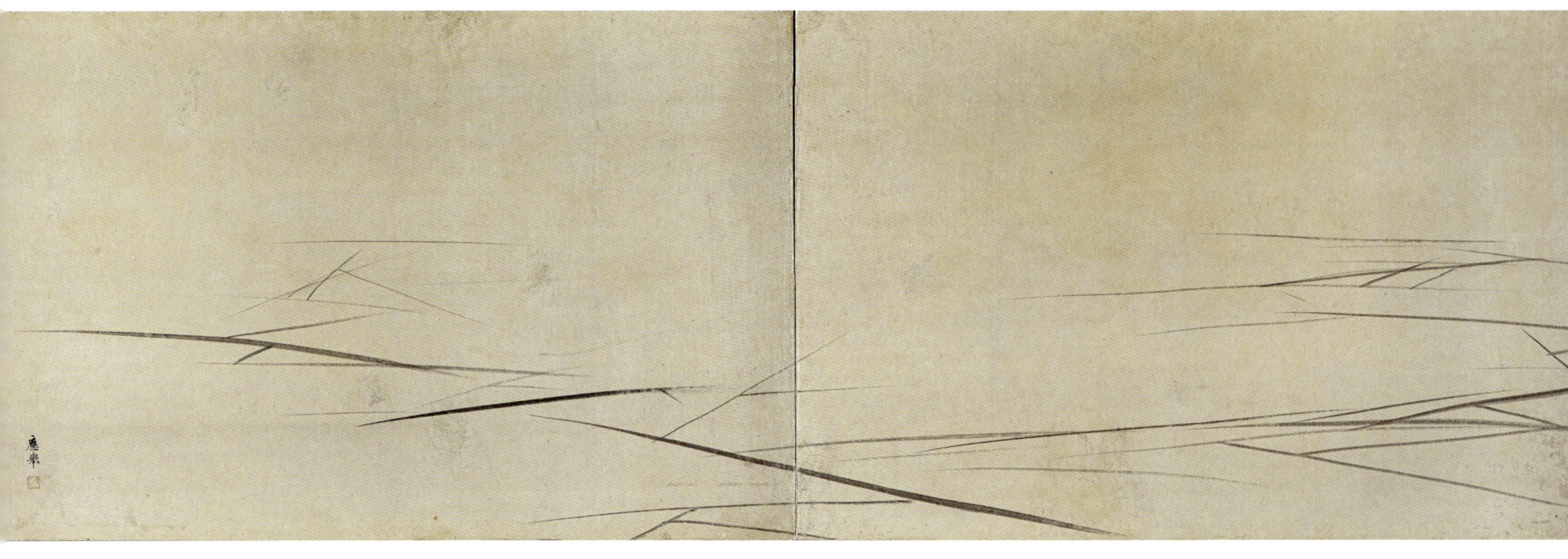

of a frozen pond. This is conceived in accordance with the rules of integrated spatial recession, which Ōkyo had learned while producing European-style scenes of Japan for a Kyoto toy merchant. With effortless precision and the simplest of means, Ōkyo sets before us a quiet, peaceful world. The low and wide two-panel format identifies this as a *furosaki byōbu*, a type of screen placed behind the brazier and other utensils used during the tea ceremony. 'Spring ice' was a familiar seasonal theme but probably had never been treated as an independent subject in painting. Ōkyo's screen might have been displayed during an indoor tea ceremony at the New Year or as cooling décor placed behind a portable brazier during an outdoor summer tea ceremony. In either context, it would have prompted refreshing thoughts of the natural world passing from winter into a season of growth.

**3.19**
Maruyama Ōkyo, *Cracked Ice*, *c.* 1775. Two-panel folding screen, ink on paper with sprinkled mica. 60.5 × 182.1 cm. British Museum, London, 1982,1012,0.1.

## Nature in the Maruyama-Shijō school

Ōkyo's school branched in several directions under the leadership of his admirers Gan Ku and Go Shun (Matsumura Gekkei), and his direct pupils – the so-called 'Ten Great Disciples' – who included Rosetsu and Yamaguchi Soken.[32] A parallel line of nature painting arose in Osaka, founded by Mori Sosen, but the Kyoto and Osaka lines soon crossed through training, marriage and perhaps also patronage. Ōkyo's disciples, Go Shun's students and the Mori school continued to distance nature subjects from the constraints of culture and shepherded Ōkyo's gentle manner of depicting nature into the modern period. Their work explored two main themes: living beings (animals and plants) and landscapes.

## Animals and plants

Unlike other artists of the Maruyama-Shijō school, Gan Ku (1749/56–1838) portrayed the unruly side of nature. He may have learned the basics of brush technique in Kanazawa, a castle-town in the Kaga domain.[33] He settled in Kyoto around 1780, and his style, previously reliant on a study of the Kanō and Nagasaki schools, underwent a change that reveals Ōkyo's impact. Imperial princes soon requested commissions, as did leading samurai families across Japan. He forged a popular style but always adapted to circumstance and the patron's requirements – as he advised his students, 'Be like the fisherman who can improvise a net.'[34] Among his other skills, he also knew how to make an indelible personal impression. In 1809, to complete a commission, he travelled back to Kanazawa like a triumphant daimyō, with an entourage numbering more than thirty, including students, a samurai official and palanquin (covered litter) bearers. Instead of causing offence, his manner brought him lordly attention and status in the form of the title Governor of Echizen, an honorary administrative position bestowed by the imperial household. He played a key role in extending the range of social circles that the Maruyama-Shijō style touched, and his style lived on through his followers, known as the Kishi school (using a different pronunciation for the character *gan*).

Two well-known hanging scroll paintings demonstrate Gan Ku's style and interests. The first, produced in 1782 towards the beginning of his career, depicts a cat sinking its teeth and claws into a blackbird (fig. 3.20). The cat wears the ecstatic expression of a successful hunter eager for more. The colouration, the brushwork in the rock and the detailing of the cat's fur recall the painting style practised in Nagasaki (see p. 165). Artists of that lineage showed cats in garden settings, and this painting may represent Gan Ku's version of the Nagasaki-school manner, strengthened by his eye for telling realism.[35] Note, for example, how the cat's flicking tail claims the red poppy as another victim of the hunt. The torn banana leaves contribute to the sense of nature as a condition of conflict, but the graded ink tones recall Ōkyo's technical elegance, as though Gan Ku were attempting to reconcile the savagery and the beauty of nature.

The second painting features Gan Ku's trademark subject: a Bengal tiger in the wild (fig. 3.21). While Ōkyo's tigers often look like stocky house cats, Gan Ku conceives of them as conquering beasts, perhaps responding to the interests of his warrior patrons, who were the apex predators of Edo society. He usually depicted a single massive animal in an untamed setting, often featuring a stream, rock and pine tree – the latter symbolising strength and endurance. Here the animal prowls along an outcropping and snarls as waves from a torrent break against the stone, producing an atmosphere of danger and violence. Gan Ku probably never saw a live tiger and, like Ōkyo, studied cats as a substitute.[36] Generations of his descendants handed down a preserved tiger's head, two forepaws and two hind paws, along with outline sketches of these body parts.[37] He and his studio were clearly committed to realism, but note that whereas Bengal tigers have amber-coloured eyes, the tiger in this scroll fixes a green-eyed gaze on prey just outside the frame of the painting. The similarities between a cat and a tiger do not quite explain why (again like Ōkyo) Gan Ku rendered tigers' eyes amber on some occasions and green on others. A preliminary survey suggests that Maruyama-Shijō artists gave tigers amber or yellow eyes when the animal appears to be in a relatively calm mood, and green eyes to communicate a state of agitation. This difference and the inclusion of symbolic motifs, such as the pine tree and the rock, illustrate how Maruyama-Shijō artists periodically introduced into their pictures rhetorical effects that stretched the limits of 'realism', although they may have served the higher goal of shasei.

In depicting certain animals, the Osaka artist Mori Sosen outdid even the astonishing Ōkyo in his ability to conjure fine detail. By the late 1780s he was renowned for realistic paintings of macaques, although as his career advanced he produced equally accomplished paintings of deer and boar. The popularity of the subject owed to Sosen's skill and the monkey's cultural association with success. Sosen's art rested on observation and sketching, as attested by a drawing formerly in the collection of his grandson Mori Ippō (1798–1871) (fig. 3.22). Working in ink wash overlaid with fine lines, Sosen captured two adults and two or three juveniles from a variety of angles that almost recall film stills. Sosen handled the foreshortening with a just sense of proportion, differentiated between the adults' and the juveniles' fur, and appears to have achieved all this without a correction. There currently seems to be no evidence that he ever saw a European animal study. Applying his first-hand knowledge of the animal, he went on to create almost dreamlike paintings usually showing just a few macaques assembled in groups that suggest family units, such as one example in which a parent caresses its young while studying a blue berry





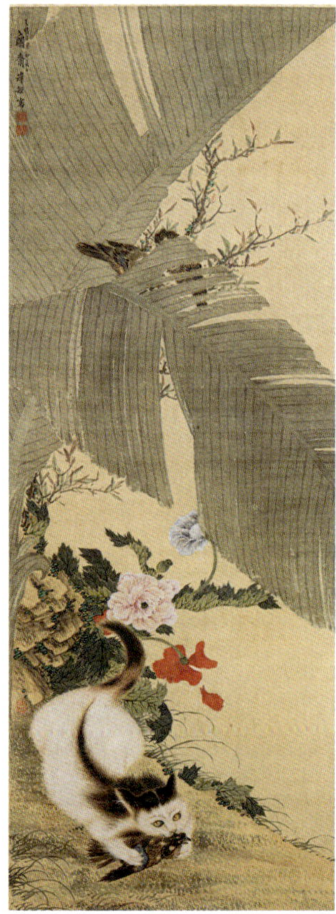

**3.20**
Gan Ku, *Cat Killing a Bird*, 1782. Hanging scroll, ink and colour on silk. 95.4 × 35 cm. British Museum, London, 1984,0301,0.1.

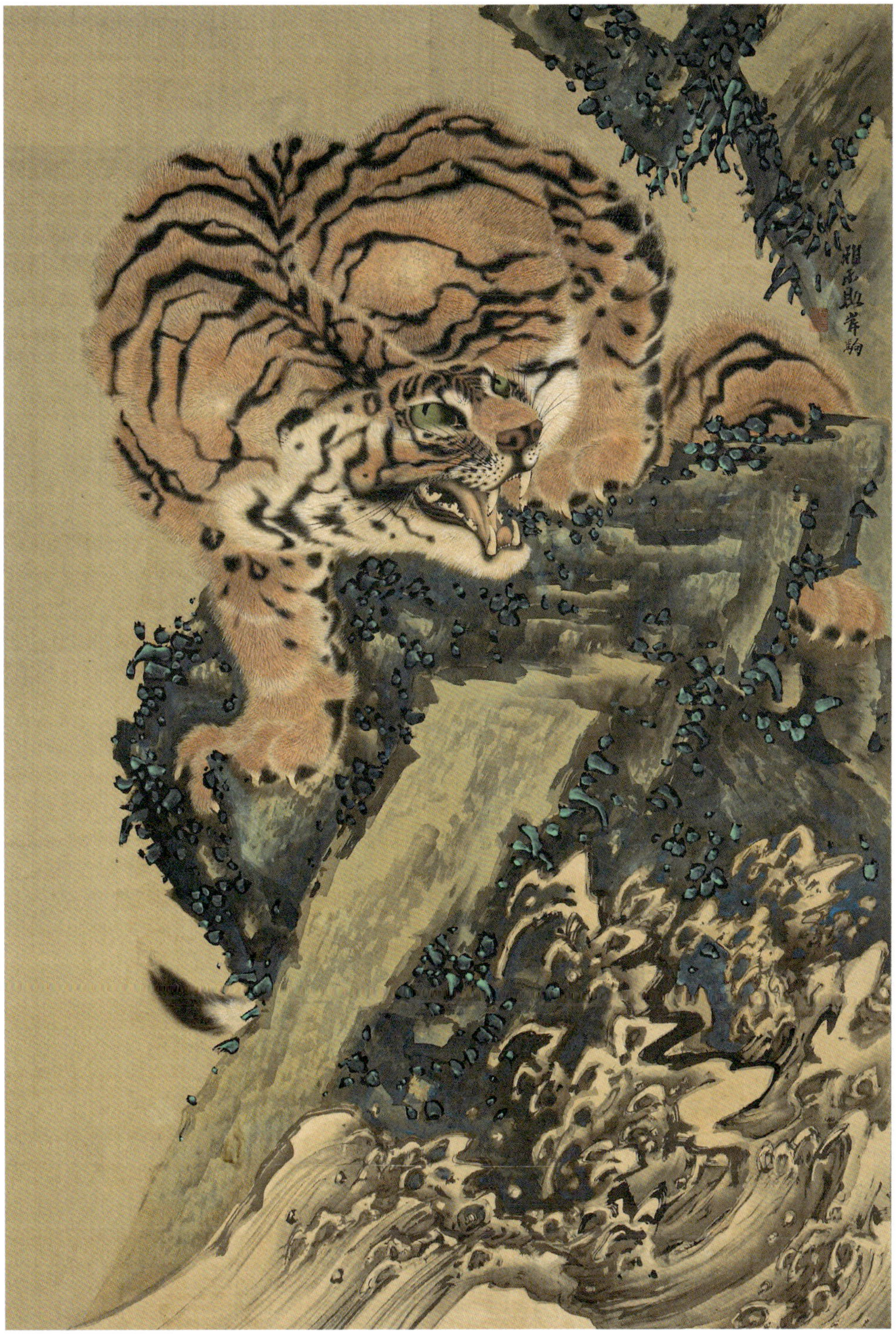

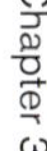



**3.21**
Gan Ku, *Tiger on a Rock*,
*c.* 1784–96. Hanging scroll,
ink and colour on silk. 169.3
× 114.6 cm. British Museum,
London, 1931,0427,0.1. Ex-coll.:
Alfred Howell.

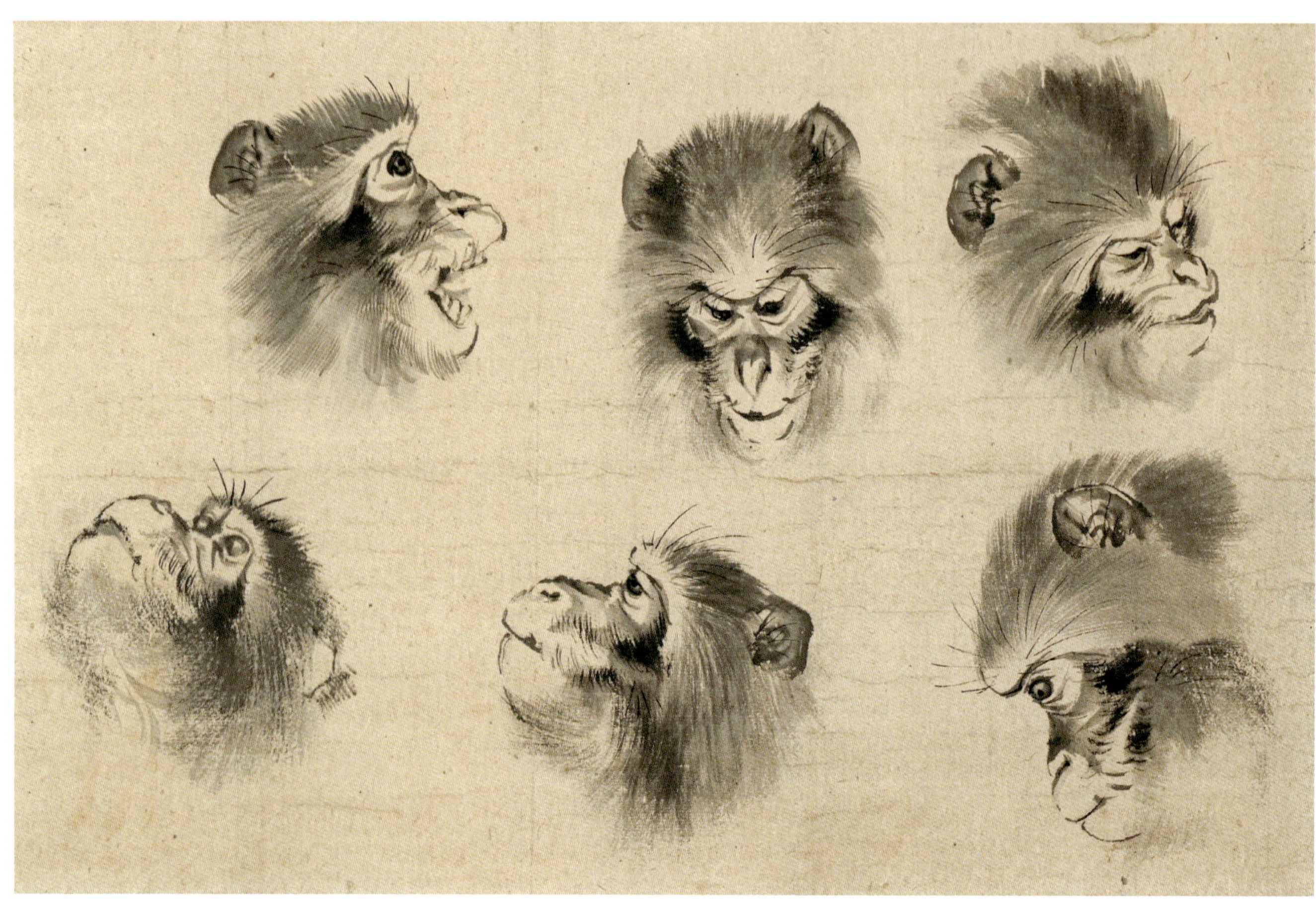

picked from a nearby plant (fig. 3.23). Thin ink washes in the rocks lend the scene a misty quality. In paintings like this, having deeply investigated his subject, Sosen returned a tender, even Buddhist, view of nature that went well beyond sketching.

Two of Sosen's major followers were Mori Tetsuzan and Mori Ippō. Tetsuzan was Sosen's nephew but trained with Ōkyo during the early 1790s and participated in one of Ōkyo's last commissions, a suite of rooms at Daijō-ji (1795). After Ōkyo's death he returned to Osaka where he introduced the Maruyama style. In 1826 he was named painter-in-attendance to the Kumamoto domain located in Kyushu (with a mansion in Osaka). His career reveals the cultural ties between Kyoto and Osaka, and the way Ōkyo's style spread beyond the Kyoto-Osaka region. Family relations also kept Tetsuzan in close contact with the Maruyama studio, since his wife's elder sister married Ōkyo's eldest son Ōzui (1766–1829). In fact, through Tetsuzan's efforts, artists



**3.22**
Mori Sosen, *Facial Studies of Macaques* (detail), *c.* 1775–1820. Hanging scroll, ink on paper. 140 × 68 cm. British Museum, London, 2004,0623,0.1. Purchase funded by the Brooke Sewell Bequest. Ex-coll.: Mori Ippō.

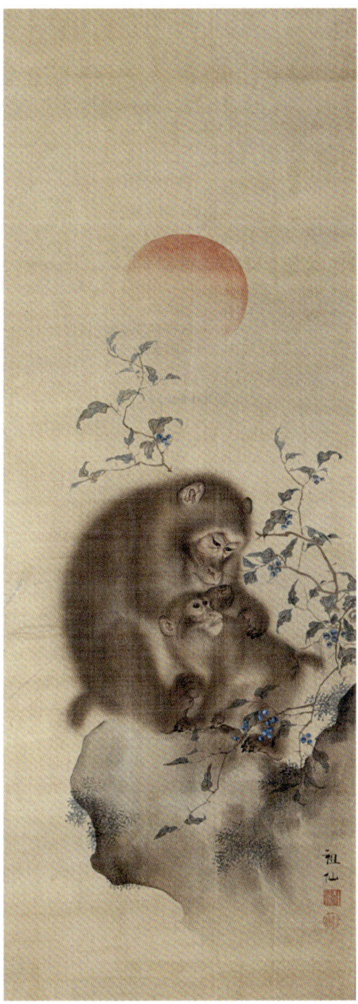

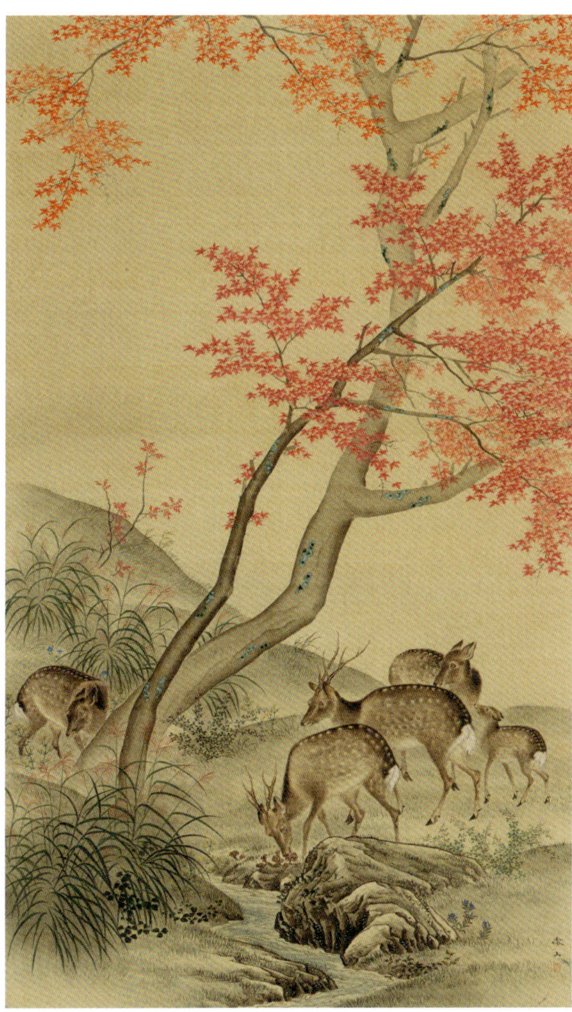

of the Mori school became the later bearers of Ōkyo's style (see fig. 4.4). Tetsuzan's painting of five deer under autumn maples demonstrates how compatible the Maruyama and Mori styles were (fig. 3.24). The herd includes two bucks, two does and one fawn, suggesting a family group. One male nibbles on *reishi* fungus, a Chinese symbol of longevity, but Tetsuzan underplays symbolism in favour of a quiet autumn scene that elaborates on a subject already associated with the Mori studio.[38] His painting might have reminded contemporary viewers of the casual beauty that sometimes occurs in nature.

Born in a village in what is now Hyōgo prefecture, Mori Ippō trained under Tetsuzan, married Tetsuzan's daughter and succeeded as the third head of the Mori school in Osaka, while his fellow pupil Mori Kansai (1814–1894) headed a branch of the Mori school in Kyoto. Ippō also inherited Tetsuzan's connections with the Kumamoto domain. He won the favour of Osaka's merchants with pictures of seaweed gatherers (*mo-(o)-karu*) because through a pun this subject was associated with 'making a profit' (*mōkaru*). Ippō's depiction of a pair of male and female ducks paddling beside a snow-covered pine tree allows the viewer to observe nature from a respectful distance (fig. 3.25). In East Asia, paired ducks suggest marital harmony, and a snow-covered pine symbolises endurance and longevity, but Ippō enlivened the conventions with a feeling of naturalness that might have delighted those attending a New Year's gathering in Osaka. This painting recalls Ōkyo's work in the graded ink tones defining the underside of the tree trunk, which find parallels in the famous pair of gold screens by Ōkyo called *Pine Tree in the Snow*, among other examples (see fig. 2.8).

Animals remained a core theme for Go Shun's successors, who included his younger Kyoto-born half-brother Matsumura Keibun. Keibun inherited Go Shun's lyrical late style and with his fellow pupil Okamoto Toyohiko steered the Shijō school through the closing years of the Edo period. Keibun's style took root in Osaka, partly through the efforts of Nishiyama Hōen (see fig. 2.11) and other students, but it was also widely received and imitated, to the extent that five of his leading students signed a pledge not to produce forgeries (see p. 26). Keibun is known for his evocative portrayals of birds in various settings, such as his hanging scroll of a cuckoo flying past a waterfall (fig. 3.26). Like a haiku, the work is pared down to essential elements: a bird, a curved rock face and falling water visible at upper right. Even in the absence of outlines, Keibun's bold forms have definition and substance due to his skilful handling of tsuketate.

Plants, too, regularly occur as independent subjects in Shijō-school painting. For example, Keibun's student Yagi Kihō absorbed the now-classic Shijō techniques and fashioned them into a stronger and crisper manner. In his painting of summer deutzia bending over five sweetfish swimming upstream (fig. 3.27), he depicted the fish and leaves in tsuketate but the petals with defined outlines, while adding delicate gradations of blue to suggest the varying depth of the water. The branch crossing the stream creates a structured composition. Kihō seems to have enjoyed a long and well-connected career, as he participated in the exhibition of calligraphy and painting commemorating the fiftieth anniversary of Ōkyo's death (1844 by traditional East Asian count) and appeared in the 1852 and 1867 editions of *Record of People in Heian* [*Kyoto*].

Yamaguchi Soken was one of the great promoters of the Maruyama studio style, certainly in his skilful paintings, but especially in dozens of illustrated

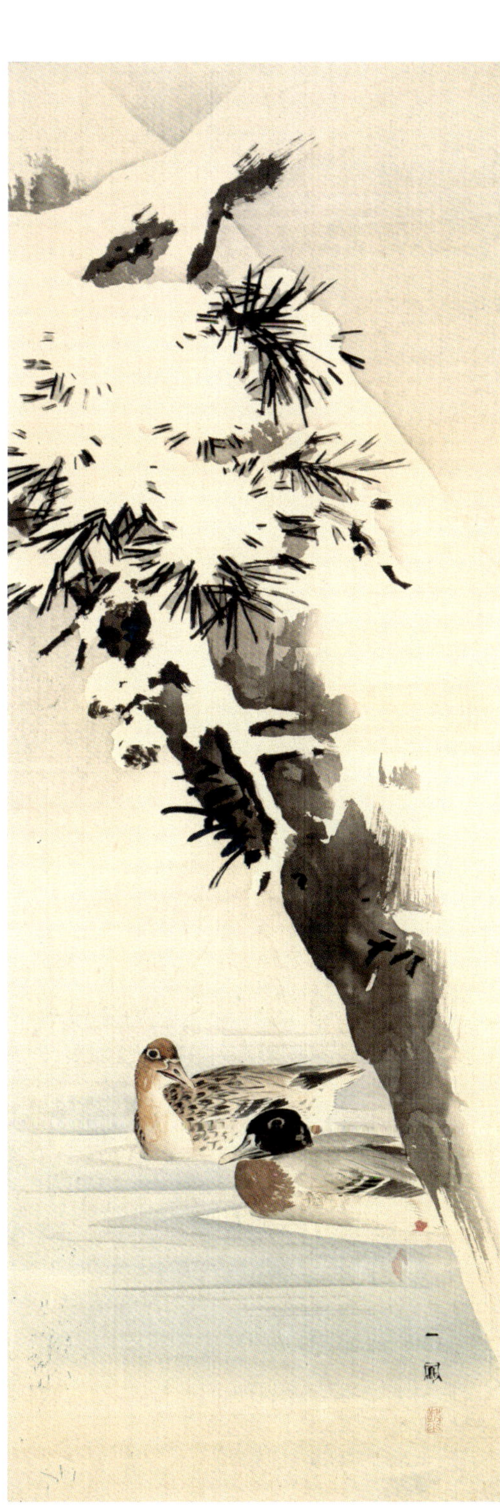

**3.25**
Mori Ippō, *Pair of Mandarin Ducks and Winter Pine*, 1830–71. Hanging scroll, ink and colour on silk. 102.4 × 35.8 cm. British Museum, London, 1881,1210,0.2274. Ex-coll.: William Anderson.

**3.26**
Matsumura Keibun, *Cuckoo Flying past a Waterfall*, c. 1825. Hanging scroll, ink and colour on paper. 136.5 × 36.3 cm. British Museum, London, 1881,1210,0.2266. Ex-coll.: William Anderson.

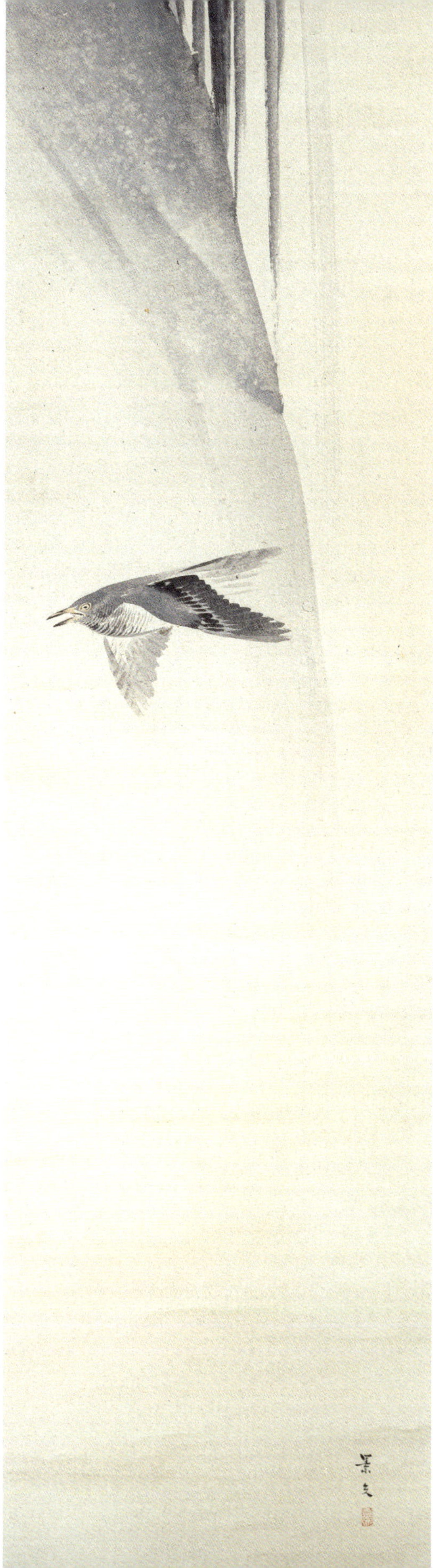

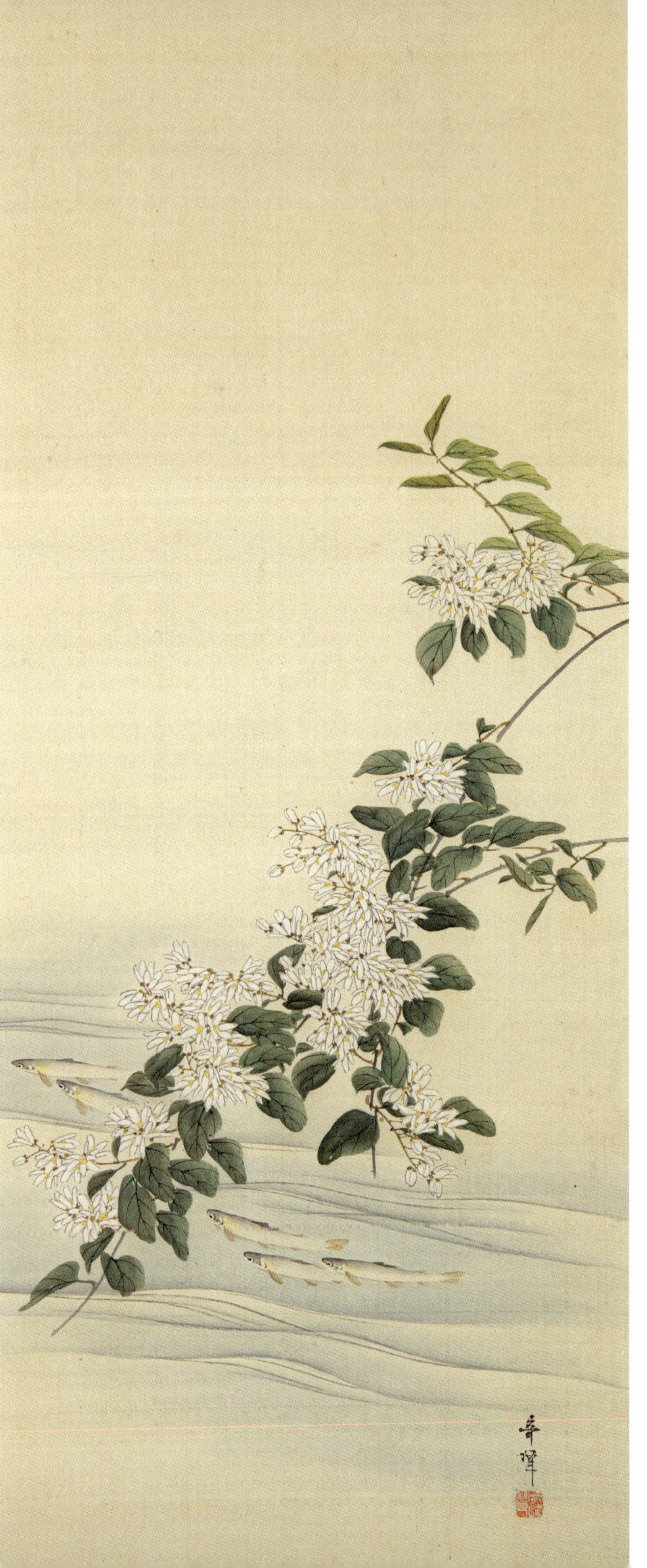

**3.27**
Yagi Kihō, *Deutzia Bending over a Stream with Sweetfish*, mid–late 1800s. Hanging scroll, ink and colour on silk. 112 × 42.5 cm. British Museum, London, 1881,1210,0.2359. Ex-coll.: William Anderson.

books that even through the medium of woodblock printing still convey the movement of the brush and the freshness of painted ink. Early publishing successes led to other book projects, including *Soken's Painting Album: Plants and Flowers Section* (*Soken gafu: sōka no bu*, 3 vols, 1806) (fig. 3.28). This illustration shows a section of clematis (*tessen-ka*; literally 'iron-wire flower'). Each composition serves to highlight the plant's individual character and in some cases an impression of setting, even without background detail. Tonal gradations demonstrate the use of tsuketate, while variations in the shapes of petals and other flower parts highlight the importance of direct observation. The book may be considered a beautiful example of shasei in published form.

## Landscape

Go Shun captured scenery as poetically as he did individual natural motifs. He came from a family of officials employed by the currency mint in Kyoto, but around the mid-1780s he became interested in the pictorial qualities of

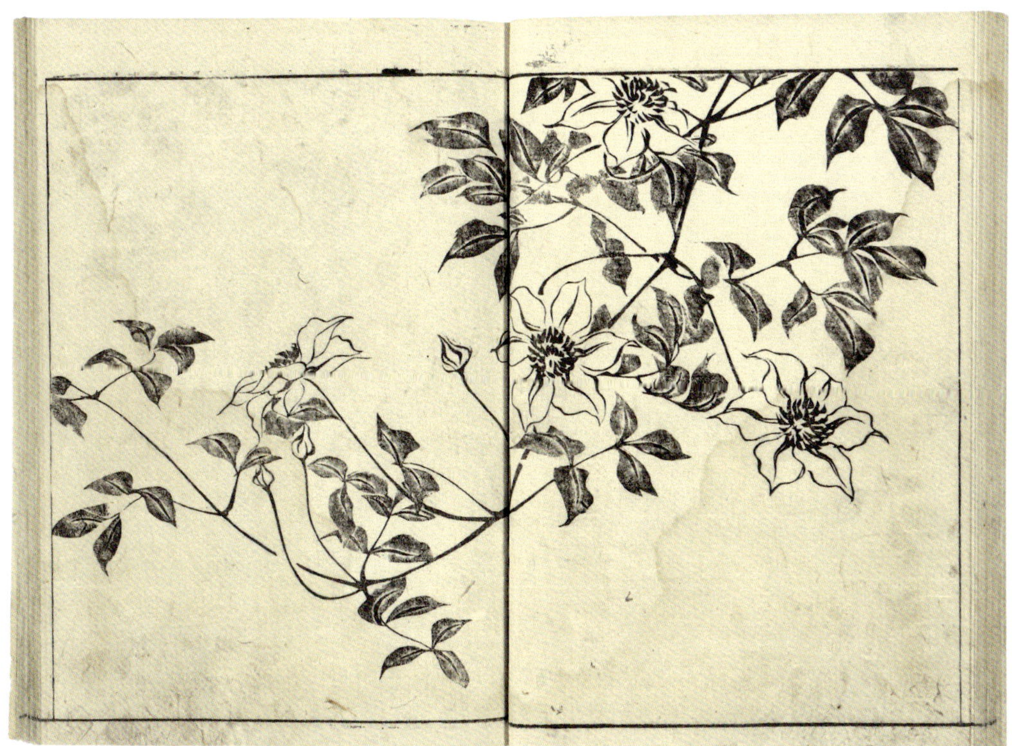

**3.28**
Yamaguchi Soken, *Soken's Painting Album: Plants and Flowers Section* (*Soken gafu: sōka no bu*), 3 vols bound in one, 1806. Illustrated book, woodblock. 25 × 16.9 cm (cover). British Museum, London, 1915,0823,0.195. Ex-coll.: William Anderson.

Ōkyo's work. The master declined to accept him as a student but included him in several studio commissions and connected him with Shinnin (1768–1805), a Tendai monk, imperial prince and patron of the arts. By the 1790s Go Shun had adopted Ōkyo's style, and after the master's death he effectively took charge of the studio and became a central figure in Kyoto art circles. The modern term 'Maruyama-Shijō' combines Ōkyo's family name with the location of Go Shun's studio in the Shijō area of Kyoto.

Go Shun's contribution to the 1795 illustrated travel book *Journey to the East: Colourful Tales from Various Provinces* (fig. 3.29) depicts the heavy sea mists that, according to the author Tachibana Nankei, typify Japan's northern coasts. Nankei mentions that the mists cause problems for shipping, but Go Shun interprets the phenomenon differently. His illustration is captioned 'Exhaling Breath', or *Kosa-fuki*, *kosa* being a local northern word for the condensation that accompanies human exhalation in cold weather. Go Shun poetically suggests that the mist is the breath of the northern sea.



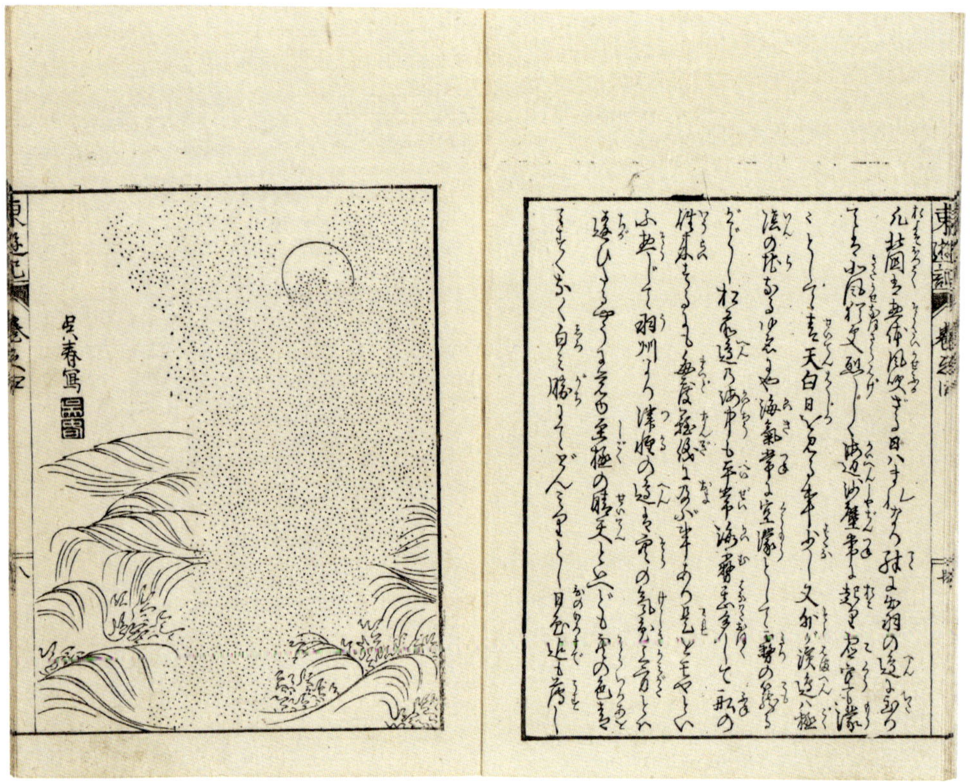

**3.29**
Go Shun (artist), *Exhaling Breath* (*Kosa-fuki*), from vol. 4 of Tachibana Nankei (author) and 12 artists, *Journey to the East: Colourful Tales from Various Provinces* ([*Shokoku kidan*] *Tōyūki*), 6 vols, 1795. Illustrated book, woodblock. 24 × 16 cm (cover). British Museum, London, 1979,0305,0.175.1–6. Ex-coll.: Jack Hillier.

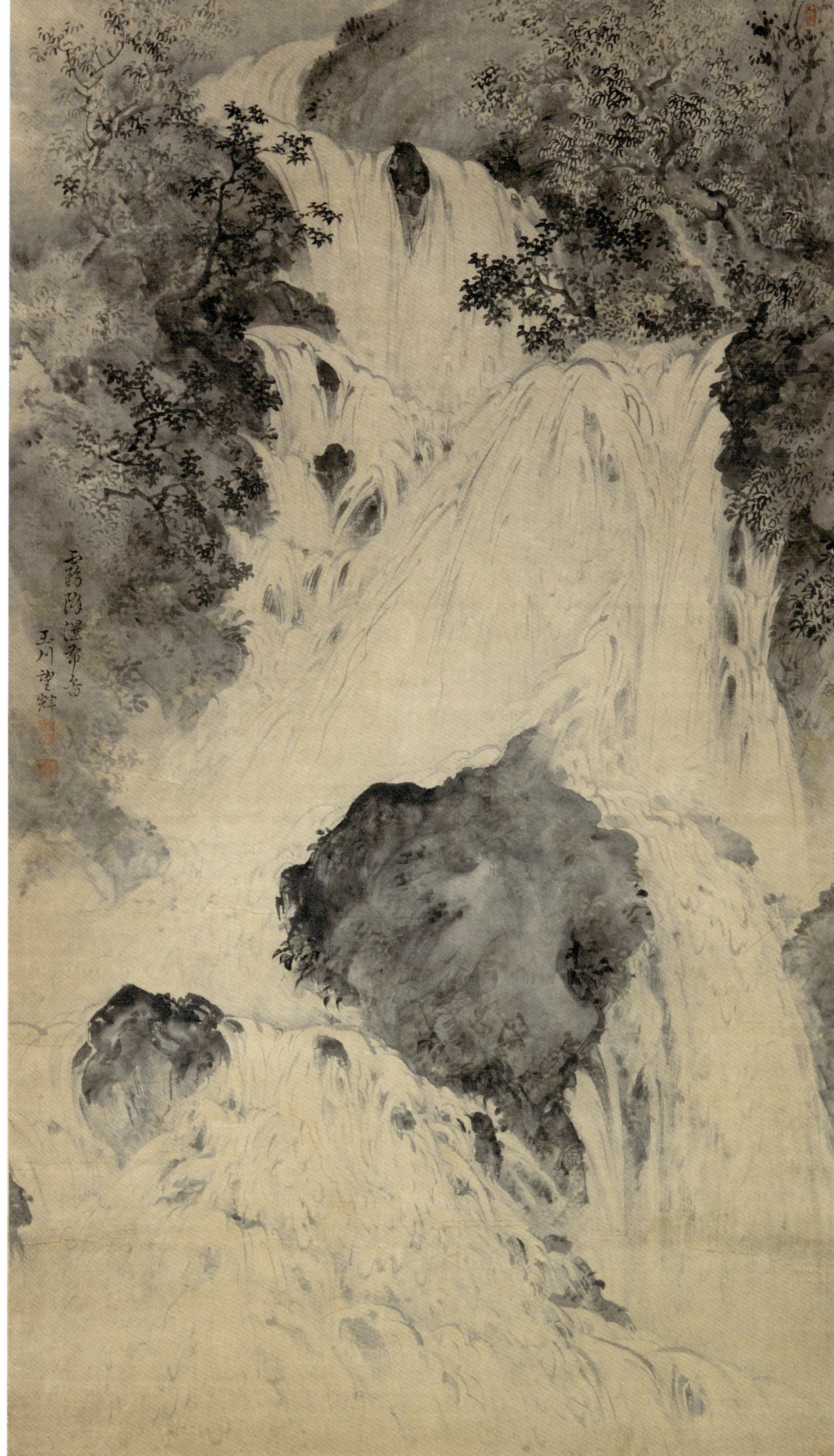

**3.30**
Mochizuki Gyokusen III, *Kirifuri Waterfall*, c. 1800s. Hanging scroll, ink and light colour on paper. 171.7 × 95.5 cm. British Museum, London, 1981,0701,0.1.

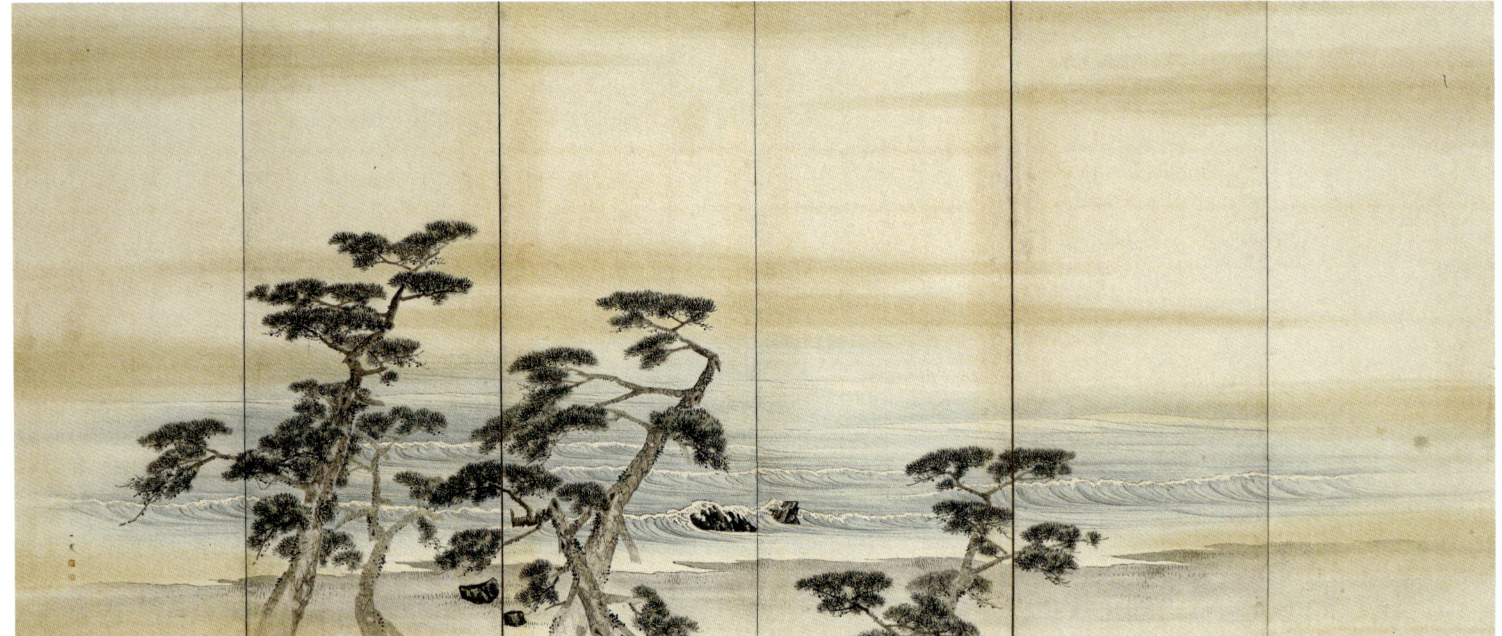

The Kyoto-born artist Mochizuki Gyokusen III (1794–1852) trained under Gan Ku, although he admired and studied other styles, including Go Shun's. In 1809 Gyokusen accompanied Gan Ku to Kanazawa. He also travelled to Nagasaki and spent time in Edo, where he studied with Tani Bunchō. As he and other late Edo artists pursued a course of independent study, they helped to reshape the boundaries of style and school affiliation. For example, his hanging scroll of Kirifuri Waterfall (fig. 3.30) at first recalls a life-sized waterfall that Ōkyo painted for Yūjō in 1772 (collection of Shōkoku-ji, Kyoto). Ōkyo's 3.6-metre-high work was designed to hang in a display alcove (*tokonoma*) and unroll across the floor, simulating the course of an actual fall.[39] Gyokusen's painting is considerably more modest in scale, and differs from its predecessor in two other respects. First, where Ōkyo combined the three types of traditional East Asian landscape perspective – high distance (looking up), deep distance (looking ahead), and level distance (looking over) – Gyokusen placed the viewer mid-stream at the base of the fall and via a European-style one-point perspective induced a compelling sense of the downward rush of water. Second, he showed a specific place, Kirifuri being one of three famous waterfalls at Nikkō, the site of a shrine dedicated to the founder of the Tokugawa government, Tokugawa Ieyasu. The central boulder and the shape of the fall identify the location. Ōkyo's painting combines aspects of several falls, while



**3.31**
Mori Ippō, *Maiko-ga-hama Beach*, 1847. Left half of a pair of six-panel folding screens, ink and colour on paper. 175 × 366.5 cm (each). British Museum, London, 1984,0601,0.1–2.

Gyokusen's painting presents a single location and could have derived from an experience of seeing Kirifuri itself. Reflecting contemporary enthusiasm for travel, the work seems well designed to introduce the power of a natural marvel into a salon setting.

Ippō developed a somewhat more lyrical style than his teacher Tetsuzan, as seen in his pair of screens capturing Maiko-ga-hama, a stretch of shore along the Inland Sea west of Osaka (fig. 3.31). Ippō positioned the beach and rolling sea low in the composition, perhaps to give a seated viewer the pleasant feeling of being at Maiko-ga-hama on a tranquil day. The screens offer a sense of continuity between human beings and nature and could have provided a welcoming setting for a salon gathering. The placement of rocks and the arrangement of tree branches suggest that in designing these screens Ippō may have consulted works by Ōkyo.

In addition to paintings of birds, Matsumura Keibun is also known for beautifully executed landscapes. A well-regarded example is a six-panel screen depicting Arashiyama in misty rain, with cherry petals drifting in the breeze (fig. 3.32). Arashiyama is a mountainous area west of Kyoto famous for spring cherry blossoms. Keibun created a highly poetic image by veiling most of the landscape in thin ink washes, with touches of gold ink wash to lend the scene urban refinement. Where his hanging scroll of a cuckoo (see fig. 3.26) follows Ōkyo in theme and technique, this screen may be closer to Go Shun, demonstrating how artists might select a painting mode to suit a given subject. Both works propose a direct, intuitive connection with the natural world.

Kyoto-born Shiokawa Bunrin (1808–1877) learned the methods of the Shijō school from Okamoto Toyohiko, but he also studied literati brushwork. His synthesis of these two approaches to painting prepared the way for modern artists in Kyoto. As a community leader, he helped to organise Jounsha, an art society that supported Kyoto's artists during the turbulent transition from the Edo to Meiji periods. In his own work, he took on the challenge of representing darkness broken by flashes of light, a recurring subject being fireflies. He may have been the first Japanese artist to treat the firefly as the main theme of a painting. One work in gold and ink assembles a host of fireflies (probably Genji fireflies) lighting a bamboo grove beside a clear-running stream, perhaps on the outskirts of Kyoto (fig. 3.33). Male fireflies dance in the air, while females shelter in the bamboo, their presence revealed only by their beckoning lights, which silhouette the leaves – a striking visual effect. Bright ripples in the water may indicate reflected moonlight.[40] The upper part of the painting describes a landscape receding into night mist, with the humid atmosphere magnifying the golden firefly lights into miniature suns.

**3.32**
Matsumura Keibun, *Arashiyama*,
*c.* 1825. Six-panel screen, ink
and colour on paper. 139.4
× 298.1 cm. British Museum,
London, 1972,0724,0.1.
Ex-coll.: Jack Hillier.

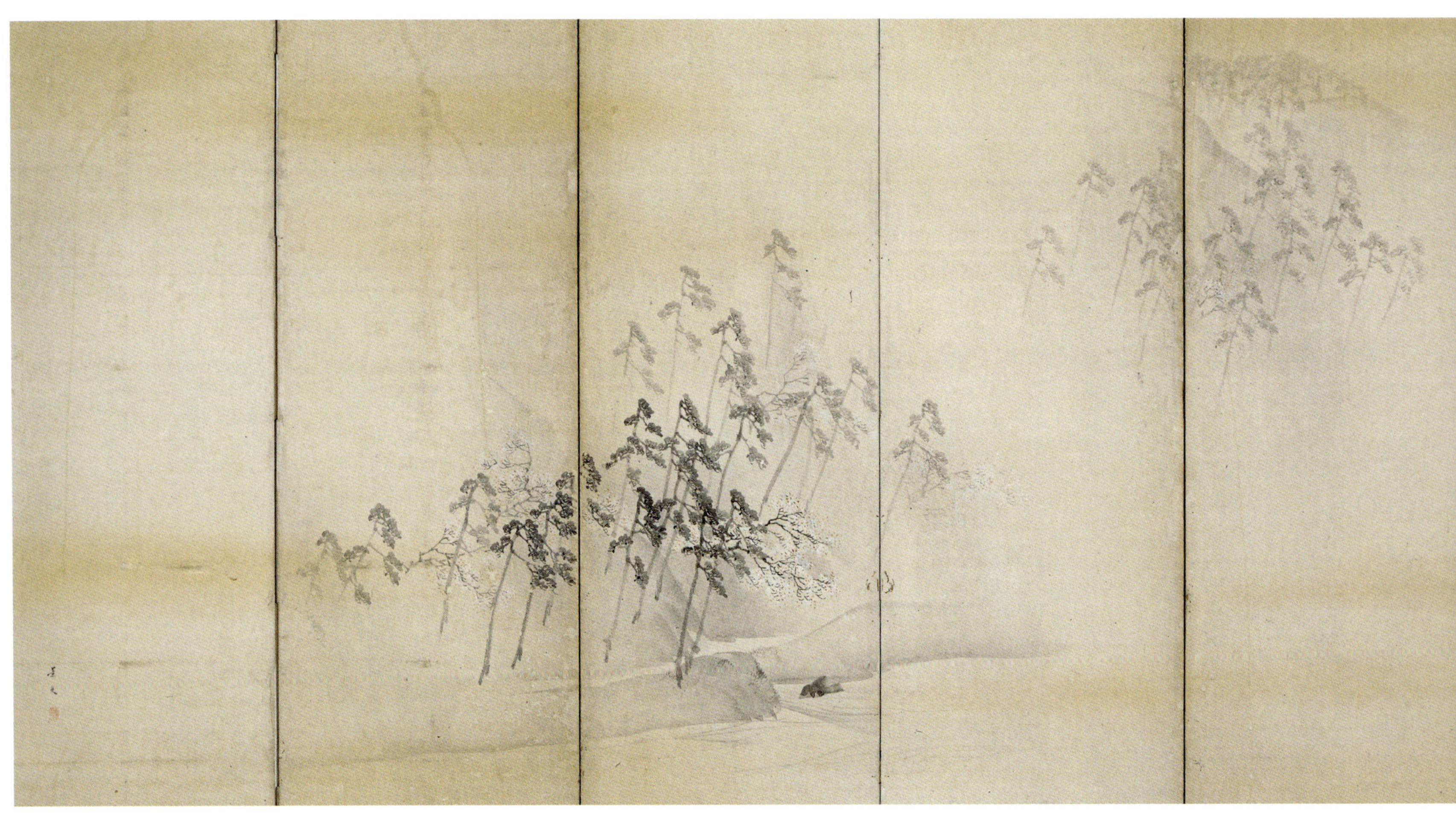

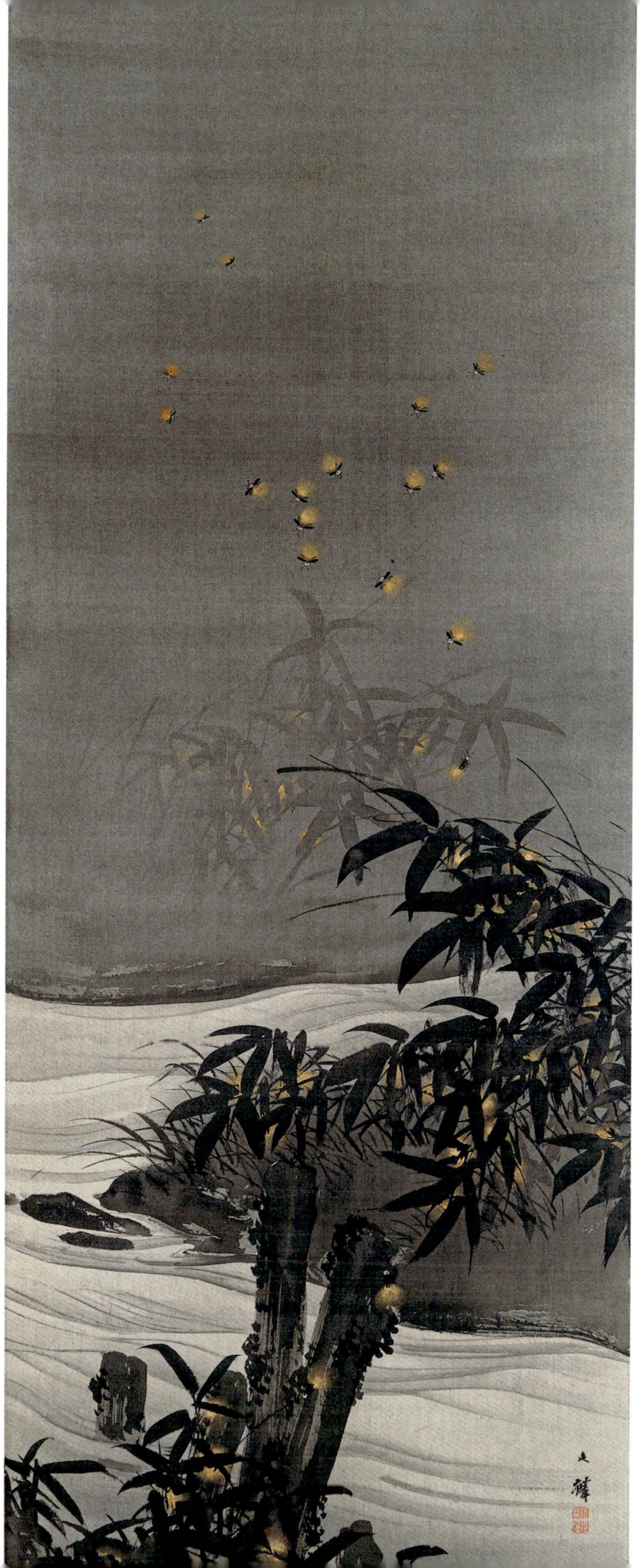

**3.33**
Shiokawa Bunrin, *Fireflies and Bamboo*, *c.* 1800s. Hanging scroll, ink and gold paint on silk. 130.6 × 50.6 cm. British Museum, London, 1980,0728,0.4.

In the foreground, the decaying stumps of a weir guide the eye into the composition, but also suggest a place formerly occupied by people and now returning to a state of nature. Here realism and poetry work together. Fireflies are associated with summer, and the painting could have been displayed during a seasonal salon gathering. It invites us to see the bright spark of courtship in relation to the darker uncertainty of transience in the natural and human worlds.

### Ōkyo's legacy

Ōkyo faced criticism in his lifetime but his detractors largely misperceived his work. Although he certainly engaged with the scientific interests of his day, he did not parrot them, nor was he mechanically tied to realism. The goals of his art did not end with observation and sketching. Rather he used these and other tools to begin disentangling nature from the idea of property or possession, and to reacquaint his patrons and the members of salon culture with a sense of nature as a pristine world apart, one unconditioned by human strife and striving. This sense may have seemed on the verge of succumbing to the programmatic demands of academic painting, the contemporary trend for describing, cataloguing and inventorying nature, and the struggle for economic survival in a commercial system tied to the control of natural resources. As though deriving fresh inspiration from a syncretic blend of Confucian and Buddhist ideas touched by the lyricism of haiku, Ōkyo and his followers found in their art a way to capture nature, and then to set it free.

# The Nagasaki school of painting
## *Hirai Yoshinobu*

The Chinese painter Shen Quan (b. 1682; in Japan known as Shin Nanpin) arrived in Nagasaki in 1731. He would leave just under two years later, but his impact on painters, not only in Nagasaki but later across Japan, was significant. This influence coincided with two major developments: an increased interest in natural history and the opening up of foreign studies in Japan. At this time, scientific methods related to the study of nature and animal life based on Positivism, the philosophy that only scientifically or logically verifiable facts are valid, became popular. In the 1720s the ban on Western books was eased under the eighth Tokugawa shogun, Yoshimune (1684–1751), who was deeply interested in foreign artefacts and information. This led to the further advancement of Dutch studies in Japan.

It was against this backdrop that Shen's Chinese court painting style reached Japan. His work, depicting mainly animal and flower subjects with auspicious connotations, and characterised by carefully detailed decorative and realistic portrayals, became widely appreciated. The artists following his style are today generally called the Nagasaki school. In Kyoto and Osaka, the monk-painter Kakutei disseminated Shen's style.[41] The painting *Silver Pheasant and Peonies* (see fig. 3.8) bears the signature 'Kakutei' but is now thought to be by his pupil Kakurin (Kakutei II, active 1770s–90s), who succeeded to his teacher's art name.[42] The inscription at the top, signed 'Murasakino Dokuan' ('Murasakino' connoting the area around the Kyoto temple Daitoku-ji), was brushed by Dokuan Sōjō, the sixth abbot of Seigen-an, a sub-temple at Daitoku-ji.[43]

As with artists of other lineages, Nagasaki-school painters studied both earlier painted examples and printed painting manuals or copybooks (gafu) (see p. 122) created by their predecessors. Several extant works have similar compositions to Shen Quan's *Autumn Stream and Horses* (The Museum Yamato Bunkakan, Nara) and *Peony in the Wind* (Kobe City Museum) (fig. 3.34), painted by his Chinese pupil Zheng Pei (active mid-eighteenth century). Similarly, the composition of *Cat Killing a Bird* (see fig. 3.20) by Gan Ku (1749/56–1838), founder of the Kishi school, resembles one that appears in a gafu by Ogura Tōkei (1748–1816), another painter who practised the Shen Quan style (fig. 3.35). The cat and butterfly motif was disseminated as a Nanpin-style subject.

The pair of hanging scrolls *Birds and Flowers* by the Kyoto painter Maruyama Ōkyo (see fig. 3.6) is considered to be one of his exemplary Nanpin-style works. Expanding on what he had learned from this mode, Ōkyo created multiple 'peony and peacock' paintings in vivid colours. Peacocks became one representative motif of the Maruyama school, not only among Ōkyo's pupils but also with Gan Ku, who painted peacocks in a style analogous to Ōkyo. At that time, live peacocks were put on show along the banks of the Kamo River around Fourth Avenue (Shijō-gawara), a locale in Kyoto famous for its popular entertainments.[44] Similar displays were held at Dōtonbori in Osaka.[45] Painters were therefore able to see peacocks at first hand in tented enclosures and probably sketched them in real life (see p. 128). Although the delicate rendering of peacock feathers and peonies was most likely based on the Shen Quan style, it was Ōkyo's exceptional ability to portray peacocks realistically and elegantly that made him a leading artist in this area.

Tigers were also a common motif for painters working in the Nagasaki-school style. Although live tigers were occasionally brought to Nagasaki, it was in fact impossible to observe them in other parts of Japan. It is well known that Ōkyo illustrated tigers modelled on domestic cats, as is evident in his *Tiger* hanging scroll (see fig. 0.4). Yet he also studied real tiger fur closely to capture its texture. Gan Ku was even more determined in his realistic representation of tigers, inspired by his collection of tiger heads and preserved paws. By observing and sketching these, Gan Ku was able to create dynamic tiger paintings that became a hallmark of the Kishi school. His tigers are painted with more vigorous and rougher brushstrokes than Ōkyo's and are often placed in a rocky landscape, as seen in his *Tiger on a Rock* (see fig. 3.21).

Coinciding with the development of studies in natural history were the increasingly popular entertainment sideshows (*misemono*) exhibiting exotic animals, together with imported rare goods. Artists were able to acquire new modes of expression due to their exposure to such things. Mashiyama Sessai, the daimyō of the Nagashima domain in Ise province (in present-day Mie prefecture), was an influential cultural figure who excelled in various literati arts,

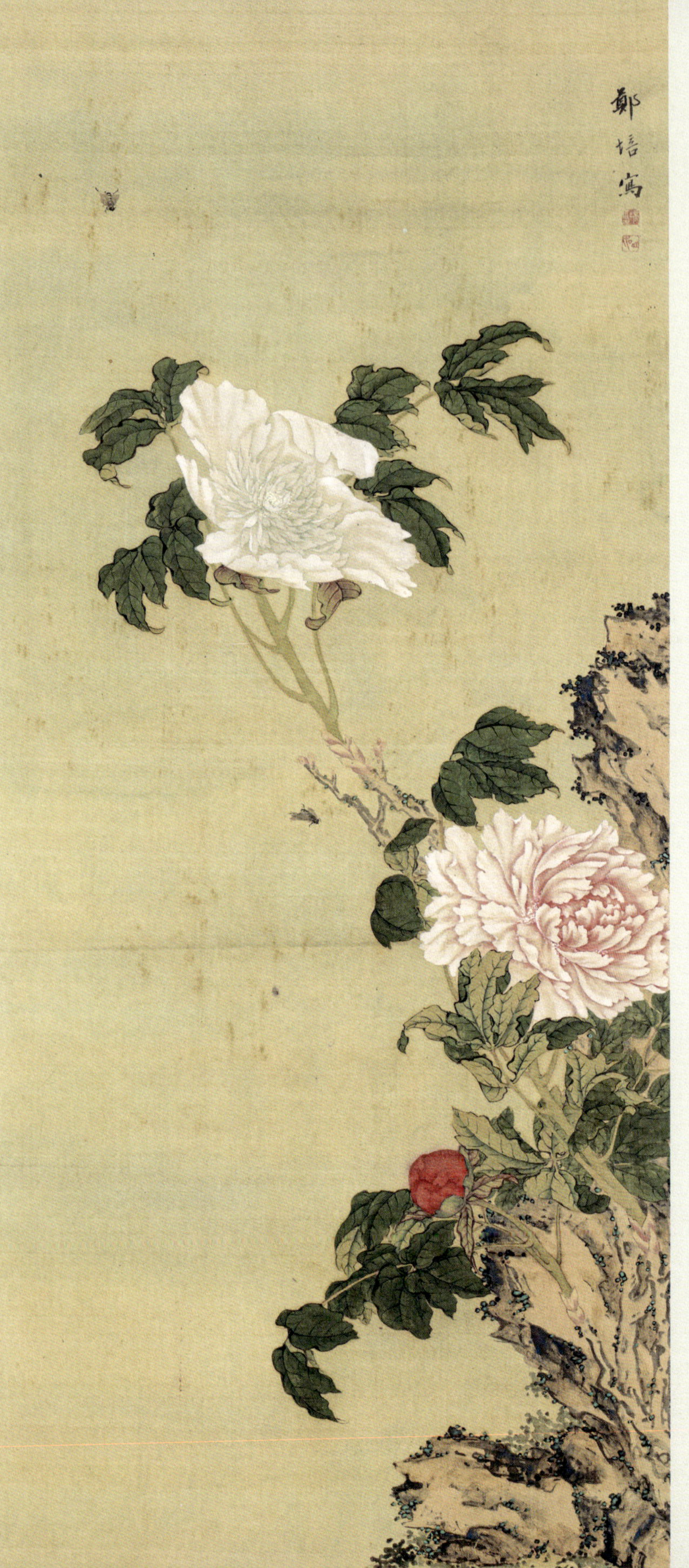



**3.34**
Zheng Pei, *Peonies in the Wind*,
c. 1700s. Hanging scroll, ink and
colour on silk. 99.5 × 41.8 cm.
Kobe City Museum, Kobe.

including calligraphy, painting, poetry, the board game go
and sencha (infused tea). Sessai is reputed to have deeply
respected the insects he sacrificed for his sketches and
had hoped to build a commemorative mound for them. He
died before this could be achieved, however, and his close
friends honoured his wishes by building a mound that still
exists at the temple Kan'ei-ji in Tokyo.[46] His *Insect Album*
(*Chūchi-jō*, 1807–12) of sketches, now in the collection
of the Tokyo National Museum, exemplifies his delicate
brushwork and his talents in drawing. The attention to
minute detail is also manifest in Sessai's finished Nagasaki-
style bird-and-flower paintings such as *Black Bird and
Cockatoo* (see fig. 3.9). Studies in natural history had a
sustained impact on the painstaking depiction and fine
colouring seen in Nagasaki-school paintings.

By absorbing influences from Shen Quan, as well as
Dutch and natural history studies, Maruyama Ōkyo became
celebrated for his close examination of nature and for
sketching it directly. This brought about a revolution in the
Edo-period art world where Kanō-school artists were the
official government painters. His painting style, characterised
by delicate, intricate brushstrokes, had immediate appeal,
not requiring the viewer to reference (or to have knowledge
of) Chinese or Japanese traditions. This, too, was epoch
making. Through the like-minded artists who followed in
Ōkyo's footsteps, the Nagasaki school developed into
diverse styles, leaving a distinctive mark on the history
of Japanese art.

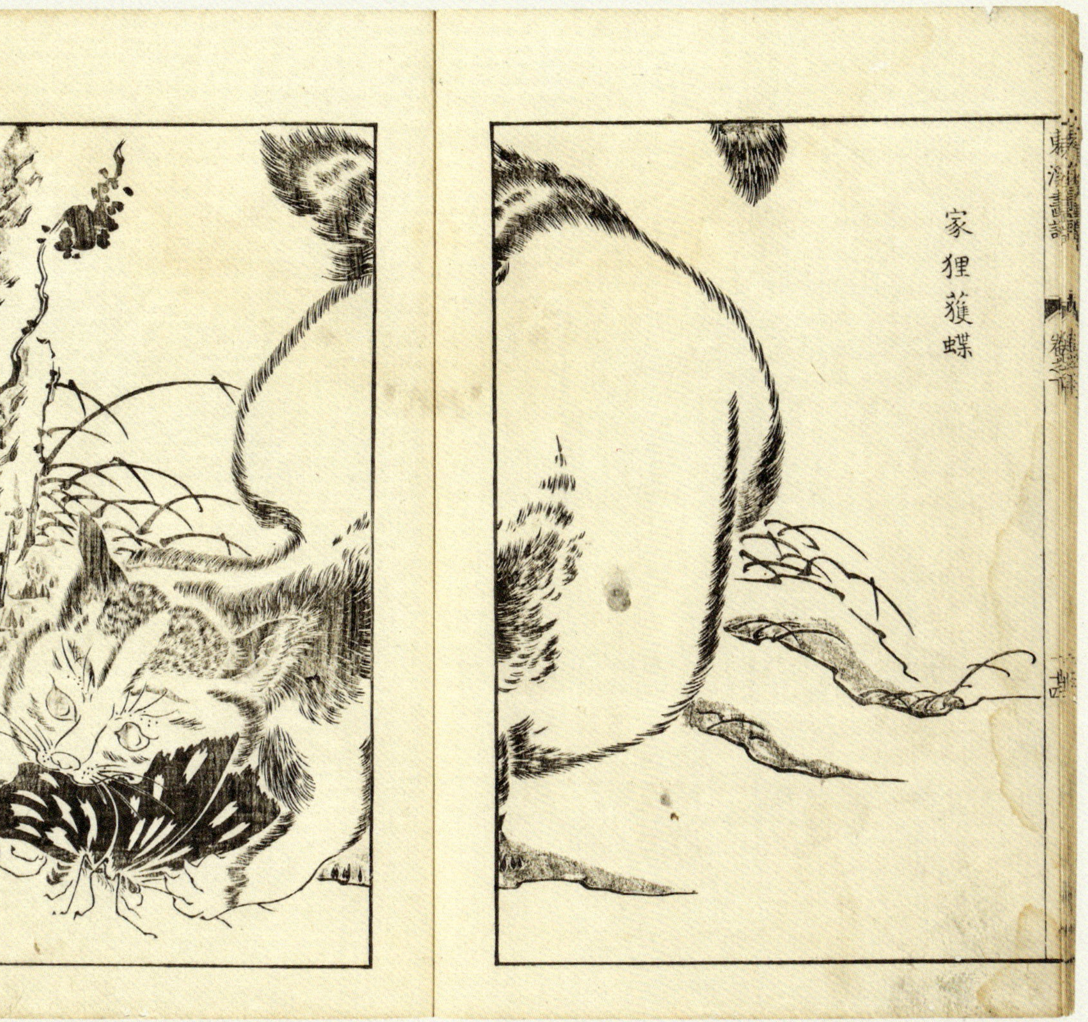


**3.35**
'House cat catching a butterfly
[*Ka-ri kaku-chō*]' from vol.
2 of Ogura Tōkei, *Tōkei's
Picture Album* (*Tōkei gafu*),
2 vols, 1787. Illustrated book,
woodblock. 27 × 18 cm (cover).
British Museum, London,
1979,0305,0.149.1–2. Ex-coll.:
Jack Hillier.

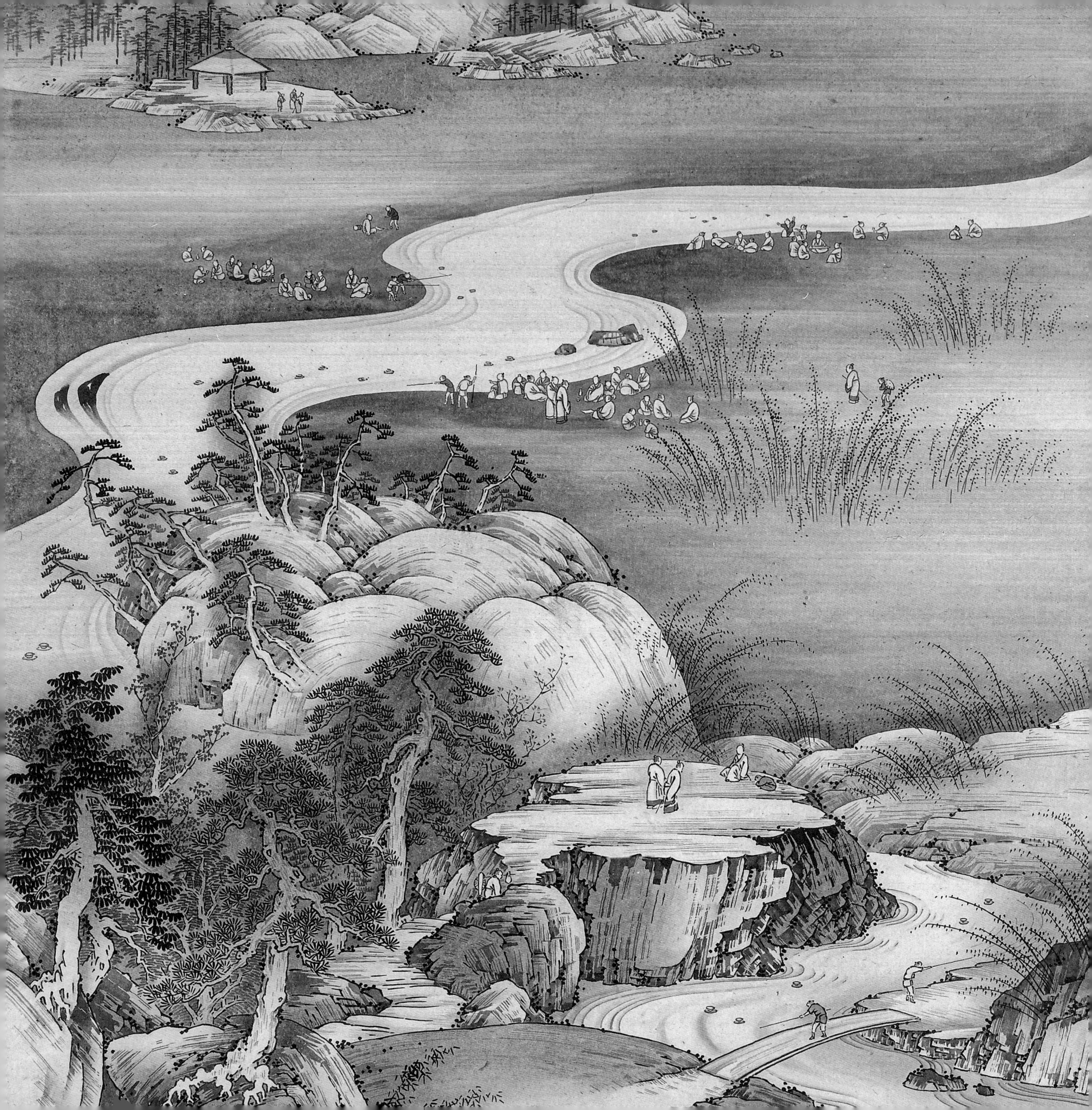

*Rosina Buckland*

# 4    China in Japan

Today, as in the past, all cultures are a blend of multiple elements, transferred across land and sea by means of traders, diplomats, travellers and objects. Japan, as a chain of islands lying to the east of the great Asian continent, was the destination over the centuries for successive waves of people moving eastwards. Throughout Japan's history, people there had looked to the civilisation of China as a source of inspiration and a model in statecraft, law, philosophy, learning, literature and the visual arts, among other areas. The ban on overseas travel imposed by the Tokugawa shogunate in the 1630s made 'China' a purely theoretical concept, limited to information transmitted in educational contexts and derived from books, which stimulated even greater demand for materials from the continent. The physical remove, however, meant that the China consumed was rarely the contemporary version but rather one drawn from history, legend and literature.

The idea of 'China' and its systems played a significant political role in Japan. The Tokugawa regime used the teachings of neo-Confucianism to justify their rule and modelled the rigid social hierarchy on that of China, crucially replacing the scholar class at the top with samurai. Successive shoguns and regional lords (daimyō) had their artists-in-service employ didactic imagery drawn from Chinese philosophy, history and legend that proclaimed the legitimacy of their rule. But these august continental sources also held the potential to express opposition to the status quo. Themes of rebellion and resistance from Chinese history could be deployed as coded rebukes to the existing regime and a rallying cry for reform.

The study of works of Chinese classical literature was an essential part of education for young Japanese men (and some women) of the social elite. They learned to read Chinese prose and poetry, using texts often glossed with Japanese explanations for better comprehension, and they could compose in the language, which was regarded as suitable for scholarly or more highbrow subjects and comparable to the role of Latin within early modern European learned society. This widely shared knowledge base created a demand for annotated editions of Chinese poetry, and there were precise fashions, such as the shift in interest from poetry of the late Tang (*c.* 827–907) to that of high Tang (*c.* 713–66) in the early nineteenth century, with their respective merits

**Previous page**
Detail of fig. 4.5

hotly debated. On the more popular level, people enjoyed reading nativised versions of Chinese novels and historical romances, illustrated by celebrated artists of the day; Katsushika Hokusai was prolific in this field. He produced bird's-eye-view maps of China with indications of all the renowned places, which were marketed as aiding understanding when reading poetry or warrior tales, thereby permitting a form of armchair travel.

The values of the literatus (bunjin) promoted reclusion and retreat from the sullying nature of worldly concerns, such as government office and financial gain. They privileged the cultivation of the integrated arts of the brush: calligraphy, painting and poetry. Although the ideal was disinterested practice as an amateur, in reality the possession of technique and essential knowledge was commercialised and made available to anyone with funds. This pragmatic transformation had already taken place in China and the same played out in Japan.

Literati values offered a means of escape from the rigidities and restrictions of Tokugawa society, a space where one could transcend social barriers and participate as equals. The world of Chinese-style, or 'sinophile', arts was well developed, active and diverse, stretching across Japan and encompassing men and women of varying social status, the samurai elite, religious representatives and the scholarly ranks of physicians, teachers, authors, scholars, artists and wealthy merchants. Sinophile arts were practised primarily through social interactions, allowing for the convivial enjoyment of a range of forms, including painting, calligraphy, music, flowers, incense, sencha (infused tea) and seal carving, alongside the appreciation of antiques.

## Chinese themes

The vast corpus of Chinese mythology and history provided a rich and enduring source of subject matter for literature and imagery. Within painting, Chinese themes constituted a repository of moral guidance, auspicious symbolism and dramatic stories. Particular incidents, settings, combinations of figures or attributes indicated which legendary, mythical or semi-historical character was being portrayed. Although both painters and viewers would have become familiar with the cast of characters from their early education, they also turned to encyclopaedias, biographical dictionaries and anthologies to assist them. Illustrated books by artists, for example *Bunpō's Chinese Pictures* (*Bunpō kanga*) by Kawamura Bunpō (fig. 4.1), served as a visual index. At top left of the opening shown here, the hero Han Xin agrees to crawl through

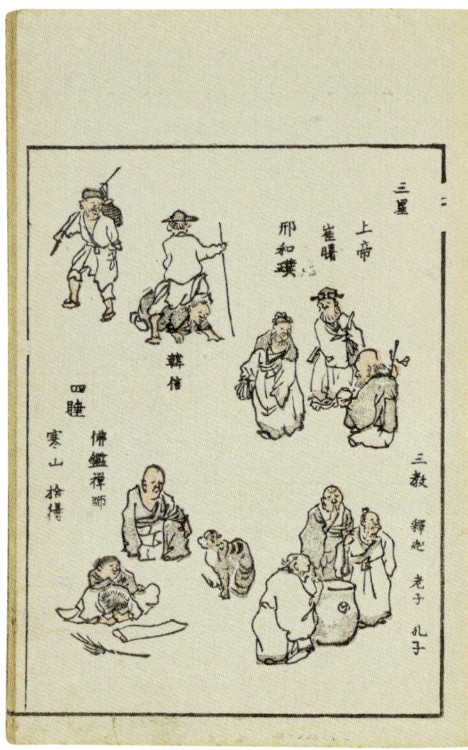
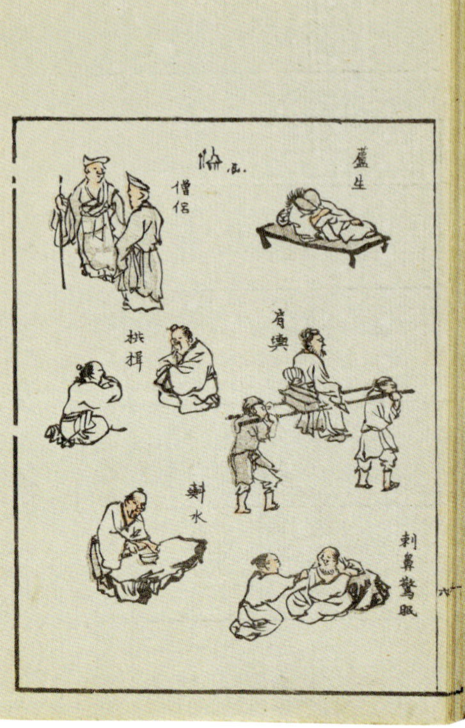



**4.1**
Kawamura Bunpō, *Bunpō's Chinese Pictures* (*Bunpō kanga*), 1 vol., 1803. Illustrated book, colour woodblock. 22.3 × 15.3 cm (cover). British Museum, London, 1956,0604,0.3.

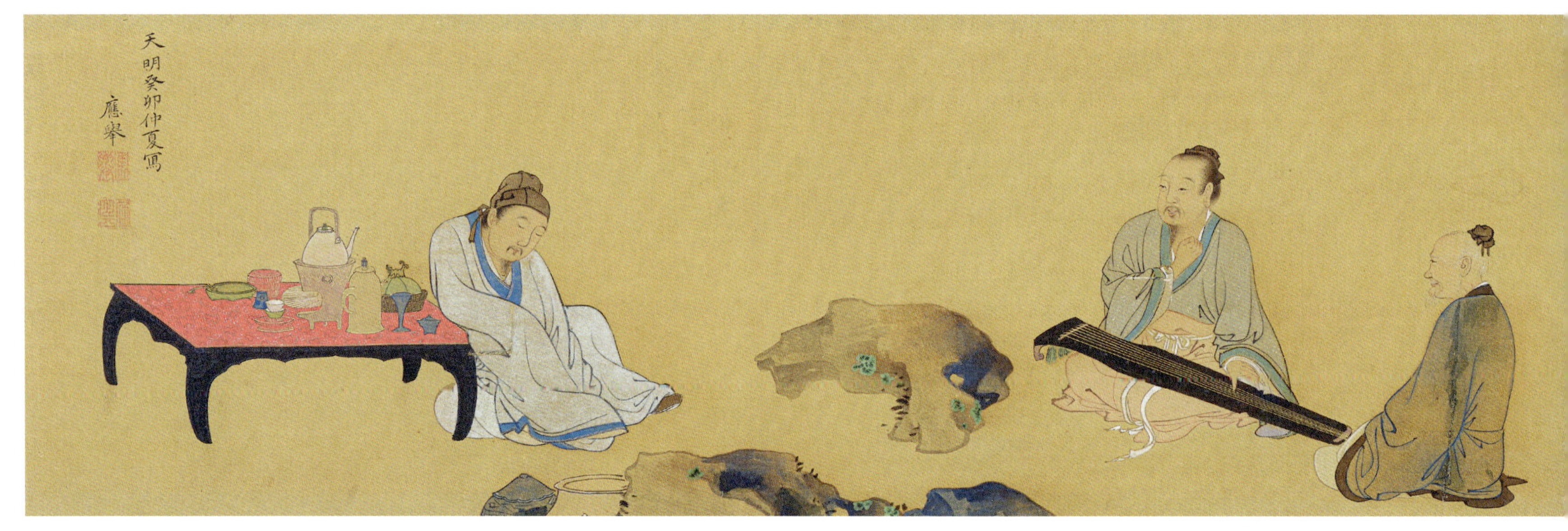

172

the legs of the braggart who has insulted him, demonstrating his wise understanding that sometimes victory must be deferred. Beside this, the 'Three Stars' confer; beneath them are the 'Four Sleepers' (the Buddhist monk Feng Gan and his pet tiger, together with the acolytes Han Shan and Shi De); and at bottom right are representatives of the 'Three Creeds' (Confucius, Shakyamuni and Lao Zi). In a lesser-known theme, at top right on the right page, Lu Sheng is identifiable lying on a bench with a Chinese fan in his hand, seeing his whole life pass before his eyes in the famous tale of the 'Millet Dream'. Other pages present a host of warriors, poets, philosophers and moral exemplars, male and female Daoist immortals, renowned beauties and *femmes fatales* as well as groupings such as the 'Twenty-Four Paragons of Filial Piety', the 'Elegant Gathering in the Western Garden' and the 'Eight Immortals of the Wine Cup', all of which remained popular subjects until the end of the nineteenth century.

The founding figure of Kyoto's distinctive mode of naturalistic painting, Maruyama Ōkyo, initially studied Kanō-school painting and drew extensively on the repertory of Chinese themes that he had acquired during his training. A low, two-panel tea screen, *Nine Old Men Gathered at Xiangshan*, is dated in the inscription equivalent to 1783 (fig. 4.2). Xiangshan, a mountain to the south-east of the ancient capital Luoyang, was the site of the retreat of the revered Tang-period poet Bai Juyi (772–846). He is seen seated at right with his companions in a garden, passing time by brushing calligraphy, viewing

**4.2**
Maruyama Ōkyo, *Nine Old Men Gathered at Xiangshan*, 1783. Two-panel tea screen, ink, colour and gold on silk. 34 × 153 cm. British Museum, London, 1989,0424,0.1. Ex-coll.: Baron Kawasaki Shōzō.

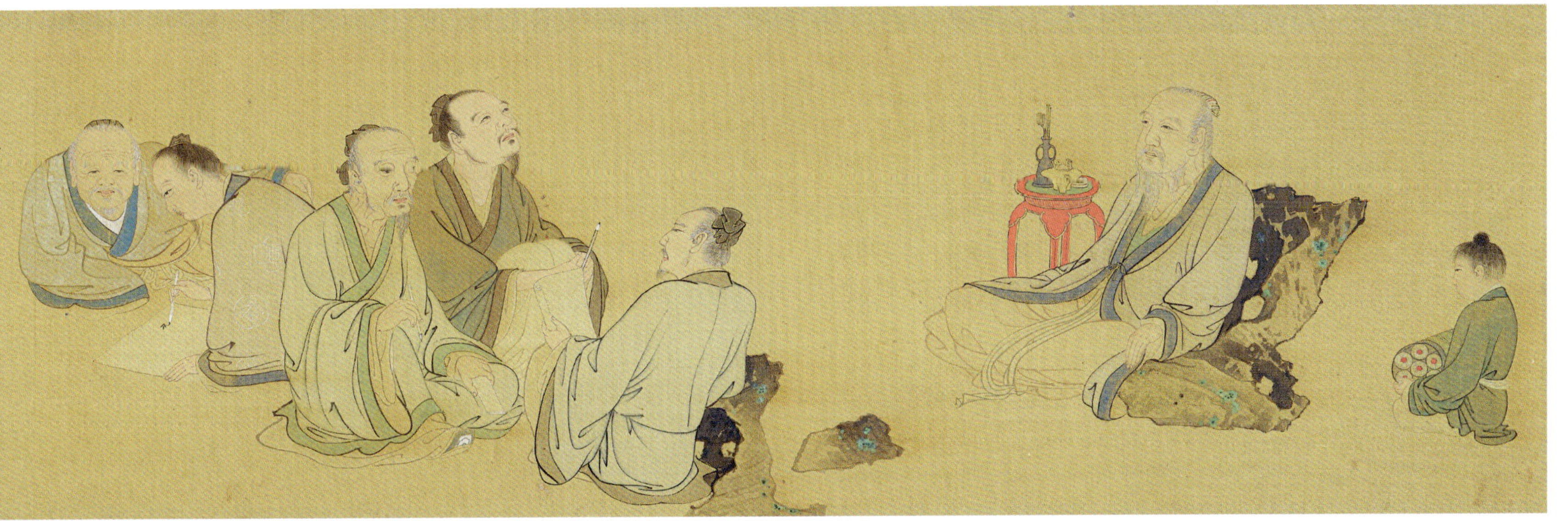

painting scrolls being brought by the servant boy and playing the stringed *qin*. At far left, a man naps as he leans on a table laden with tea utensils. The screen is suitable for placing around the tea preparation area and the scene expressed the aspiration of the Japanese literatus to a life of such reclusion and elegance. The group of nine old men was considered auspicious, conveying respect for the elderly, and the painting may have been commissioned to commemorate a man's significant birthday. It was formerly owned by the industrialist and art collector Kawasaki Shōzō (1836–1912).[1]

Elegant episodes from China's distant past were decoupled from any precise historical associations and could be endlessly repurposed to represent the eremitic (hermit-like) yearnings of viewers in contemporary Japan. A popular theme was the night-time boating excursion by the revered poet Su Shi (1037–1101) to Chibi (literally 'Red Cliff') (see fig. 2.21) just outside Huangzhou in autumn 1082. The poet, recalling a fierce battle at that location more than eight centuries earlier in 208 CE, composed a poem meditating on the rise and fall of great men of history and the brevity of life; a subsequent visit inspired a second poem. Painters typically depicted the scene on a large scale, providing a commanding vista of the riverine gorge, within which the poet drifts in a covered boat, together with companions, and the equipment for preparing infused tea. By contrast, in the rendition by Go Shun, the event is observed from close up, with only a small portion of the massive cliffs visible above, allowing the viewer to feel present. Su Shi is seated at the back, listening to his companion playing the flute. The grey surface of the cliffs and their heightened contours suggest the sharp, silvery light of the moon, while small red accoutrements in the boat add accents of colour. The painter also used the art name 'Gekkei', and



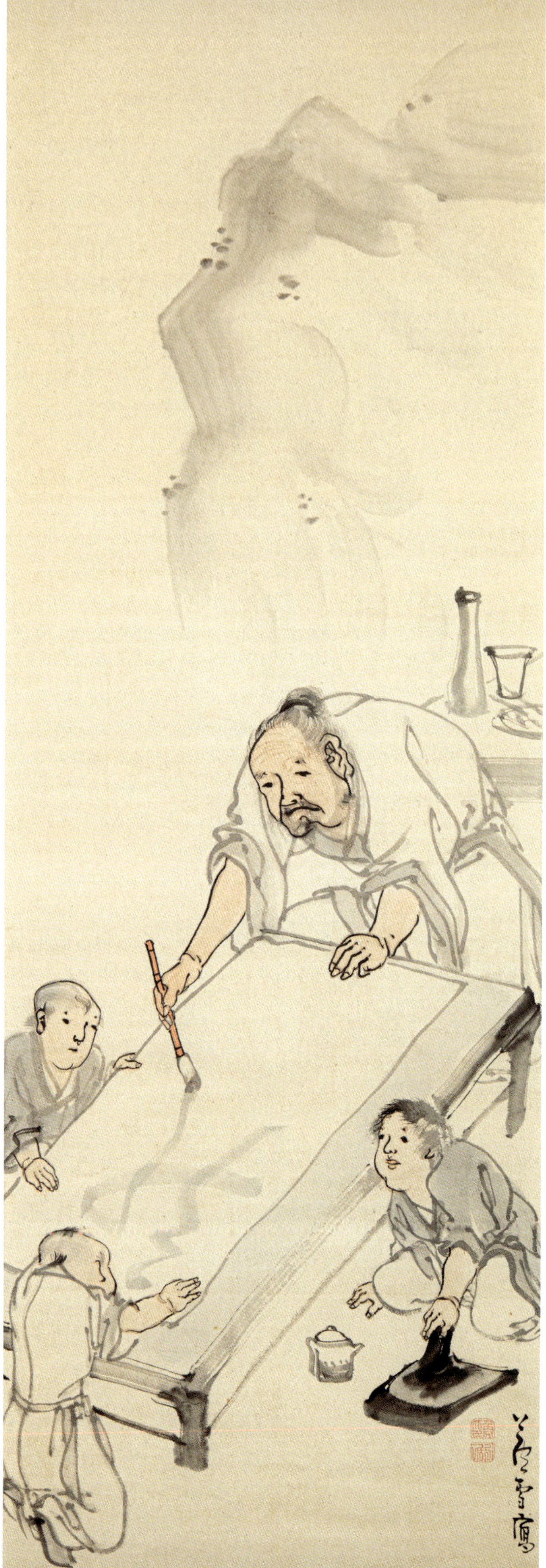

'Go Shun' was a deliberately Chinese-style two-character name, the first (read as 'Wu' in Chinese) being the name of a renowned ancient kingdom in southeast China (see p. 87). Go Shun had incorporated elements of Ōkyo's style and established his own studio by the broad avenue called Shijō, by which name his followers and lineage were known.

Another major figure in the Kyoto painting world, Nagasawa Rosetsu, frequently depicted Chinese figures, such as this painting of the poet Tao Yuanming (365–427) writing calligraphy (fig. 4.3). Tao was a revered poet of the Six Dynasties period (220–589); he was taken as a model by literati, because after more than ten years of serving in government, he retired to a rural retreat, where he engaged in farming, reading, composing poetry and hosting guests. Rosetsu takes a high viewpoint, showing Tao outdoors, as suggested by the cliff face above him, drawing the brush towards him; three boy attendants hold the paper in place or prepare ink. Rosetsu painted Tao's robes, head and arms in diluted ink first, then added dark contour lines on the body to provide definition. Despite its abbreviation, the elderly man's face is painted with great sensitivity, with multiple creases in varying tones to imbue it with emotion. The poet appears to be writing the character for 'dragon', which may indicate the work was produced for the New Year of 1796, which was a 'dragon year'.

The premier Chinese female figure was the Queen Mother of the West (fig. 4.4), as painted in 1804 by Mori Tetsuzan, who had studied with Ōkyo in his youth. This Daoist figure was believed to rule over the Western Paradise, where peach trees grew that every 10,000 years yielded fruit granting immortality. Her garb is Chinese, a voluminous outer robe decorated with scrolling gold foliage delineated in bold calligraphic contours, over which a green sash with flowers is set in a geometric frame, and on her head rests a gold diadem with peonies and a phoenix. Yet her face exhibits the gentle features and soft expression characteristic of beauties painted by artists of the Maruyama and Shijō lineages. This subject was suitable for display when celebrating an occasion in the life of a woman of the household, particularly birthdays.

Certain events in Chinese literary history were widely recognised and provided ideals of elegant sociality. Perhaps the most famous was the 'Gathering at the Orchid Pavilion', illustrated here by Yokoyama Kazan (1781–1837) (fig. 4.5). In the third month of 353 CE the statesman and calligrapher Wang Xizhi (303–361) hosted a party at Lanting ('Orchid Pavilion', in present-day Shaoxing, Zhejiang province), where the guests engaged in the 'winding stream' game. They sat along the banks of a stream on which cups of wine were set to float, and when a cup stopped in front of a guest, he had to either



**4.3**
Nagasawa Rosetsu, *Tao Yuanming Writing Calligraphy and Three Boy Attendants*, c. 1790s. Hanging scroll, ink and light colour on paper. 135.2 × 43.8 cm. British Museum, London, 2003,0106,0.1. Purchase funded by the Brooke Sewell Bequest.

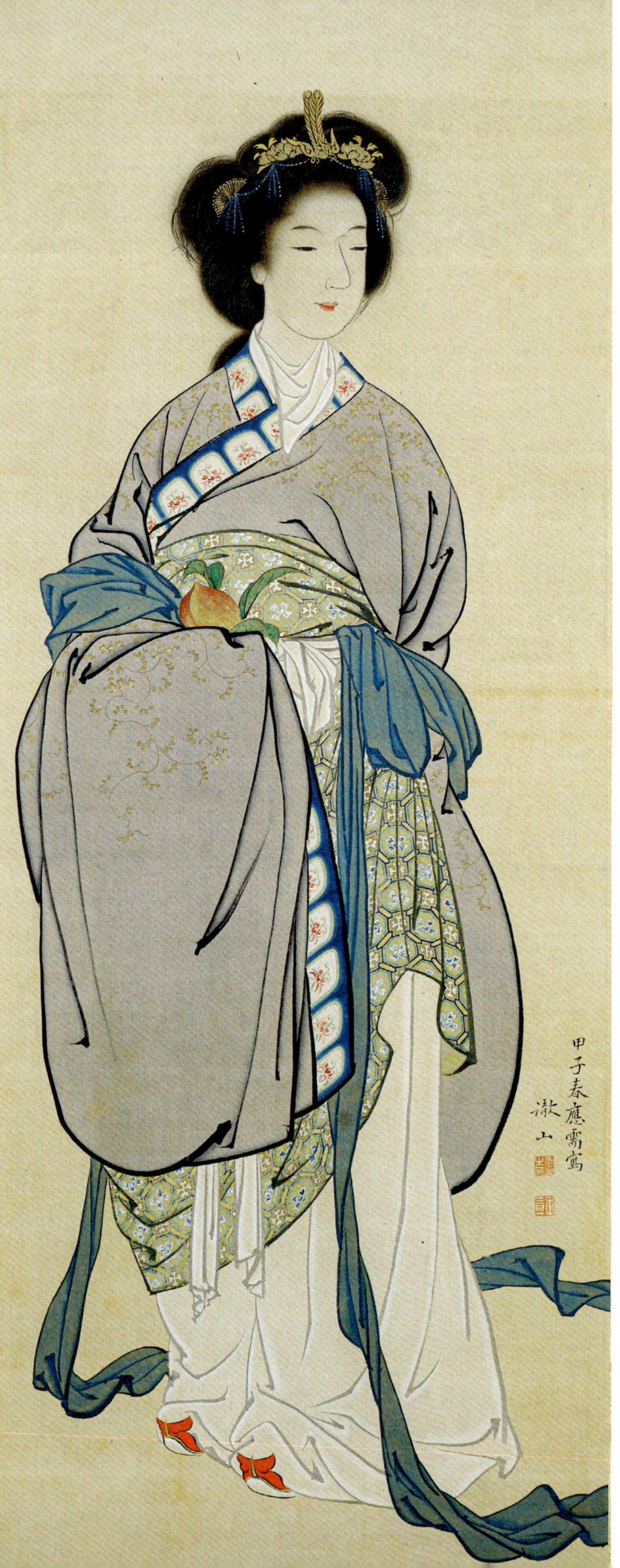

**4.4**
Mori Tetsuzan, *Queen Mother of the West*, 1804. Hanging scroll, ink and colour on silk. 116.3 × 45.1 cm. British Museum, London, 1950,1111,0.12. Gift of James Martin White.

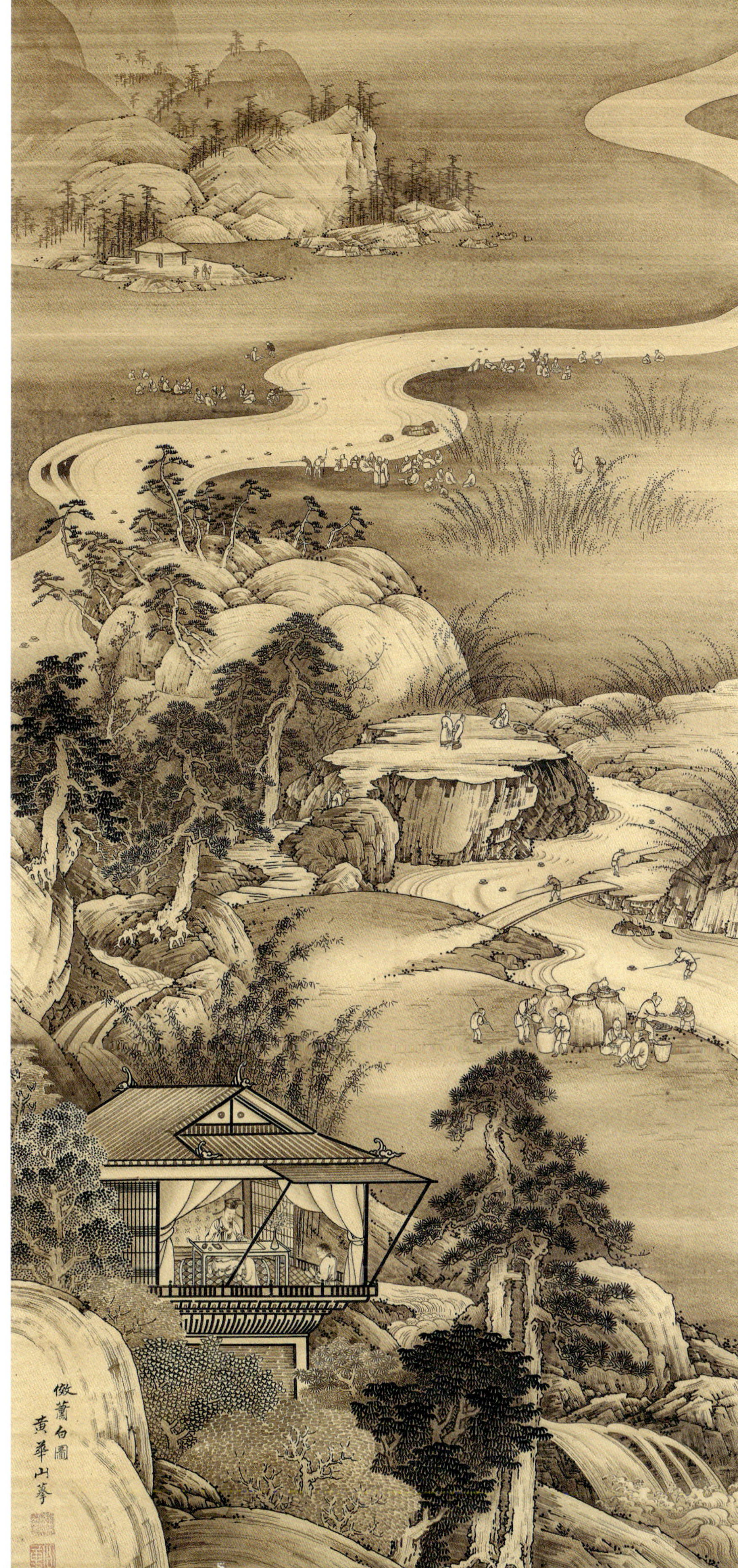

**4.5**
Yokoyama Kazan, *The Orchid Pavilion*, c. 1805–37. Hanging scroll, ink on paper. 135 × 61 cm. British Museum, London, 1998,1110,0.1.

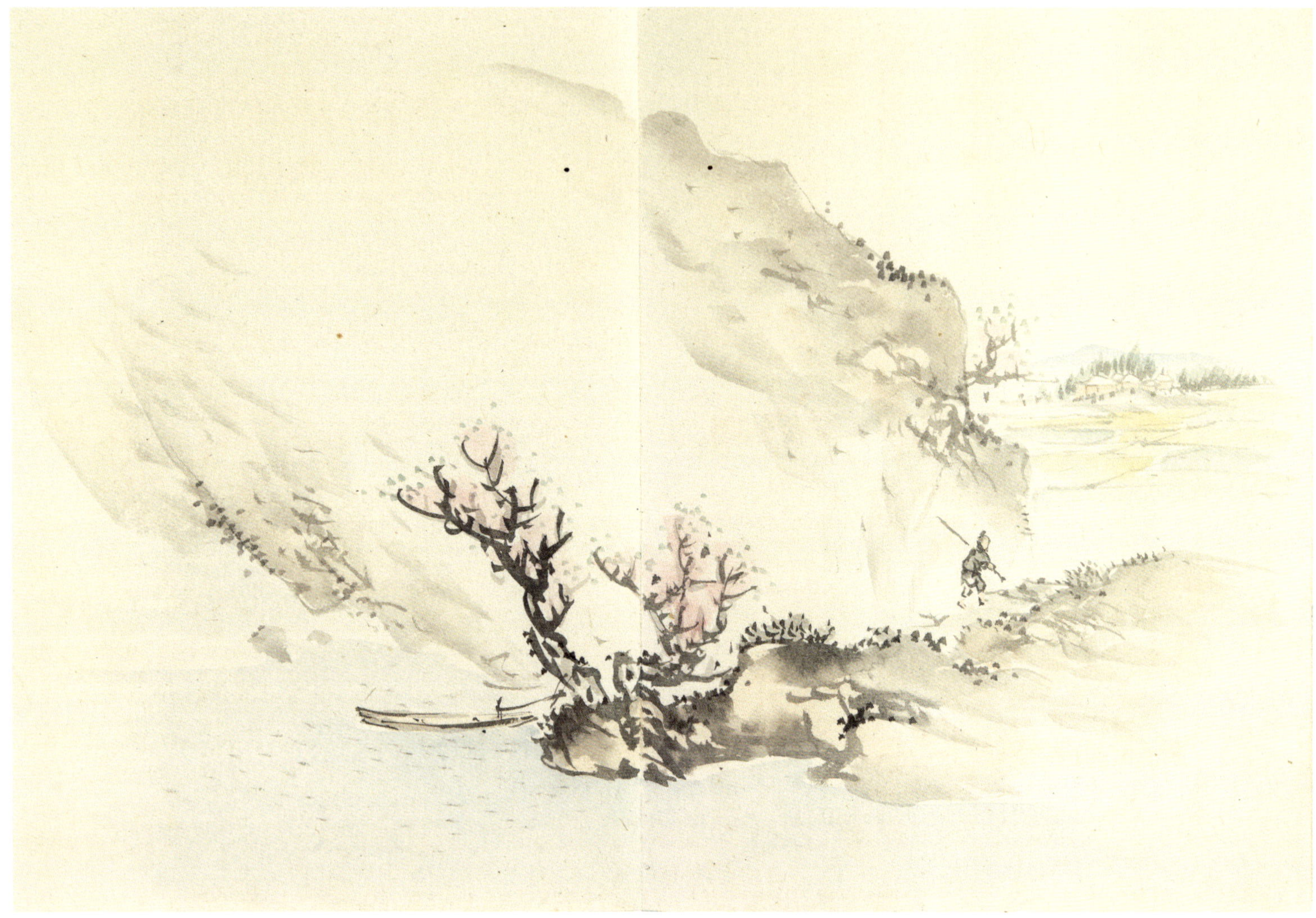



compose a poem or drink the wine. The thirty-seven resulting poems were collected together with a preface by Wang, which became a famed calligraphy model. There are varying accounts of Kazan's training – with possible periods of study with Go Shun or Gan Ku – but he seems to have frequently produced copies of the works of the 'eccentric' painter Soga Shōhaku, known for distorted topography and exaggerated facial expressions, as recorded in the inscription on this piece. The composition inverts the standard approach, wherein the pavilion is seen in the middle distance, as the stream flows towards the viewer and mountains tower above. Here, the pavilion where Wang sits is placed in the foreground, in the middle ground are the servants dispensing the

**4.6**

Gan Tai, *Peach Grove Utopia*, *c.* 1800–65. Album painting, ink and light colour on paper. 28.5 × 21 cm (cover). Jeffrey Pollard and Ooi Thye Chong Collection, Edinburgh.

wine from barrels and the participating poets are tiny figures in the distance. This arrangement creates the sense of a vast, receding landscape.

The ideal of escape into a landscape of the imagination, so central to literati painting, found perfect expression in the 'Peach Blossom Spring' (C: *Taohua yuan ji*; J: *Tōka genki*), a story by Tao Yuanming. A fisherman out in his boat sails up a river channel lined with peach trees in bloom. On disembarking at its head, he passes between cliffs and discovers a hidden village. Its inhabitants welcome him hospitably and relate that their forebears had fled from political turmoil to enjoy life in seclusion here. After a week, the fisherman departs but is warned that it would be futile to tell anyone on the outside of this place. Sure enough, even though he tries to track his route, others subsequently fail to locate this utopia. The theme was a popular one for representations of an idyllic landscape in summer. In a pair of large albums, Gan Tai, the eldest son and successor of Gan Ku (see p. 149), depicts the moment as the protagonist ascends the path. The painter renders the massive form of the cliff towering above with minimal, loose brushstrokes, and adorns three trees with clouds of pink blossoms (fig. 4.6). The viewer can see what is yet to be revealed to the fisherman: the quiet village nestling among trees, lying on the far side of fields delicately painted in yellow and green.

A popular theme expressive of bibulous conviviality was *The Eight Immortals of the Wine Cup*, derived from a poem by the Tang-period poet Du Fu (712–770) describing eight poets who were fond of wine and its effects on them. There was no tradition of illustrating the poem in China, so Japanese artists developed their own conventions.[2] Ōnishi Chinnen renders the subject in his characteristically free and humorous style; it has a looseness that suggests that the artist himself may have been inebriated (fig. 4.7). The varied palette of colours for the figures' robes and the accoutrements imparts a fresh and lively atmosphere to the painting. Despite the apparent speed of execution, there are sensitively brushed passages, such as the horse in the foreground of the right scroll, with soft modelling of the limbs in ink and the delicate strands of the mane. The poem was celebrated, having been included in the widely circulated *Tang Poetry Anthology, Illustrated* (*Tōshisen ehon*), published between 1788 and 1836, but unusually Chinnen chose to include the text, written in a quirky, angular manner, across the top of the paired scrolls.

Bird-and-flower painting (*kachō-ga*) constituted a major area within sinophile visual culture. Though its practice had been associated initially in China with academic court painters, its enthusiastic uptake in Japan demonstrated the catholicity of stylistic approaches. Its themes and compositions had been transmitted over centuries since the Song period, and various publications

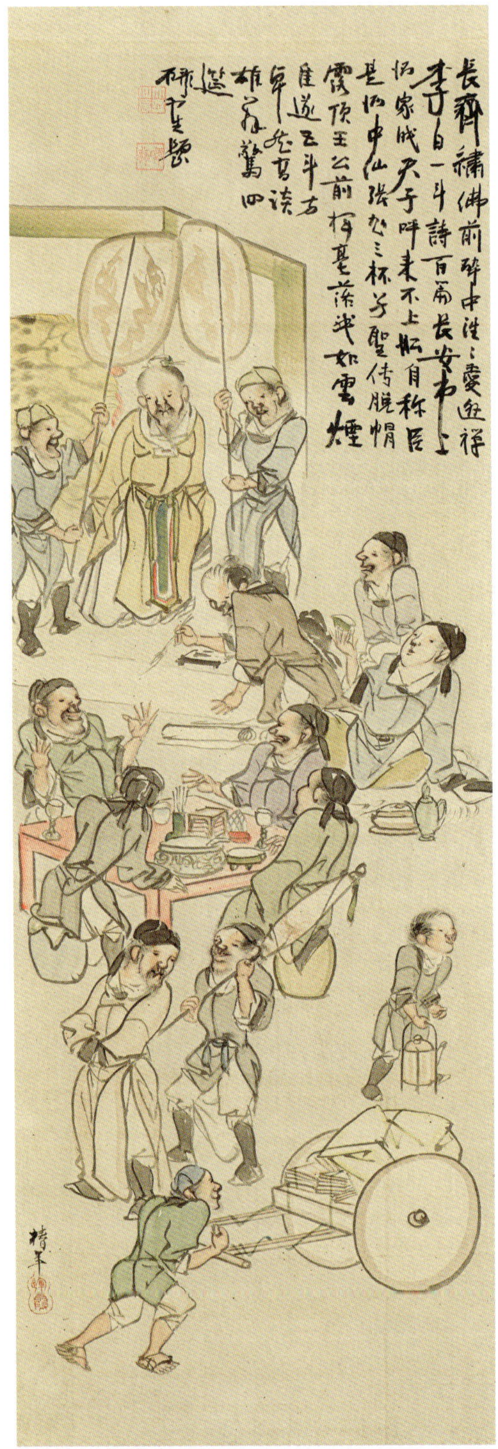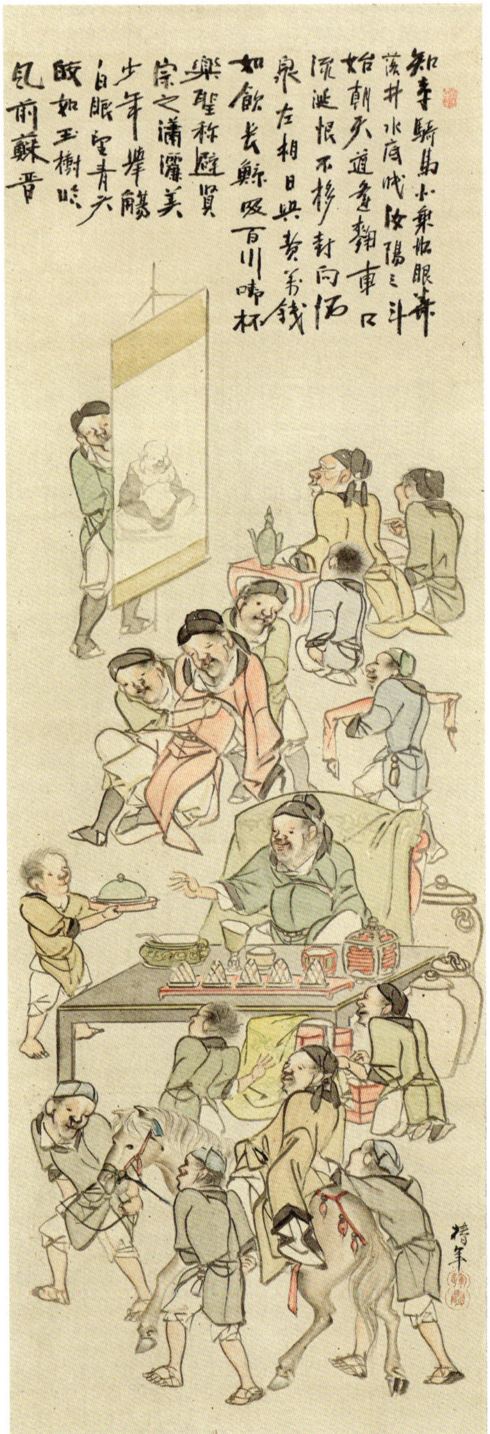

**4.7**
Ōnishi Chinnen, *Eight Immortals of the Wine Cup* (*Inchū hassen*), *c.* 1825. Pair of hanging scrolls, ink and light colour on silk. 109.5 × 37 cm. British Museum, London, 2011,3025.1.1–2. Purchase funded by Edward and Anne Studzinski.

were available as reference works for painters. The genre possessed a complex language of symbolism, such as peonies standing for a wish for wealth, or cranes for longevity, alongside topics that complemented the calendar of domestic events throughout the year.

Mori Ransai (1740–1801) was an important artist in this genre. He grew up in Echigo province, on Japan's north coast in present-day Niigata prefecture, and travelled to Nagasaki to study medicine. While there, Ransai mastered the style and manner of painting images of auspicious figures and nature themes of the Chinese artist Shen Quan, via direct transmission by his pupil, Kumashiro Yūhi (1712–1772) (fig. 4.8), and Ransai married his teacher's daughter. After Yūhi's death, Ransai moved to Osaka and lived in the Shima district, close to Kita-Horie, where the central intellectual figure Kimura Kenkadō resided (see pp. 42, 76, 204–6). The latter's diary records seven visits by Ransai between 1779 and 1787, and there were undoubtedly more, indicating that

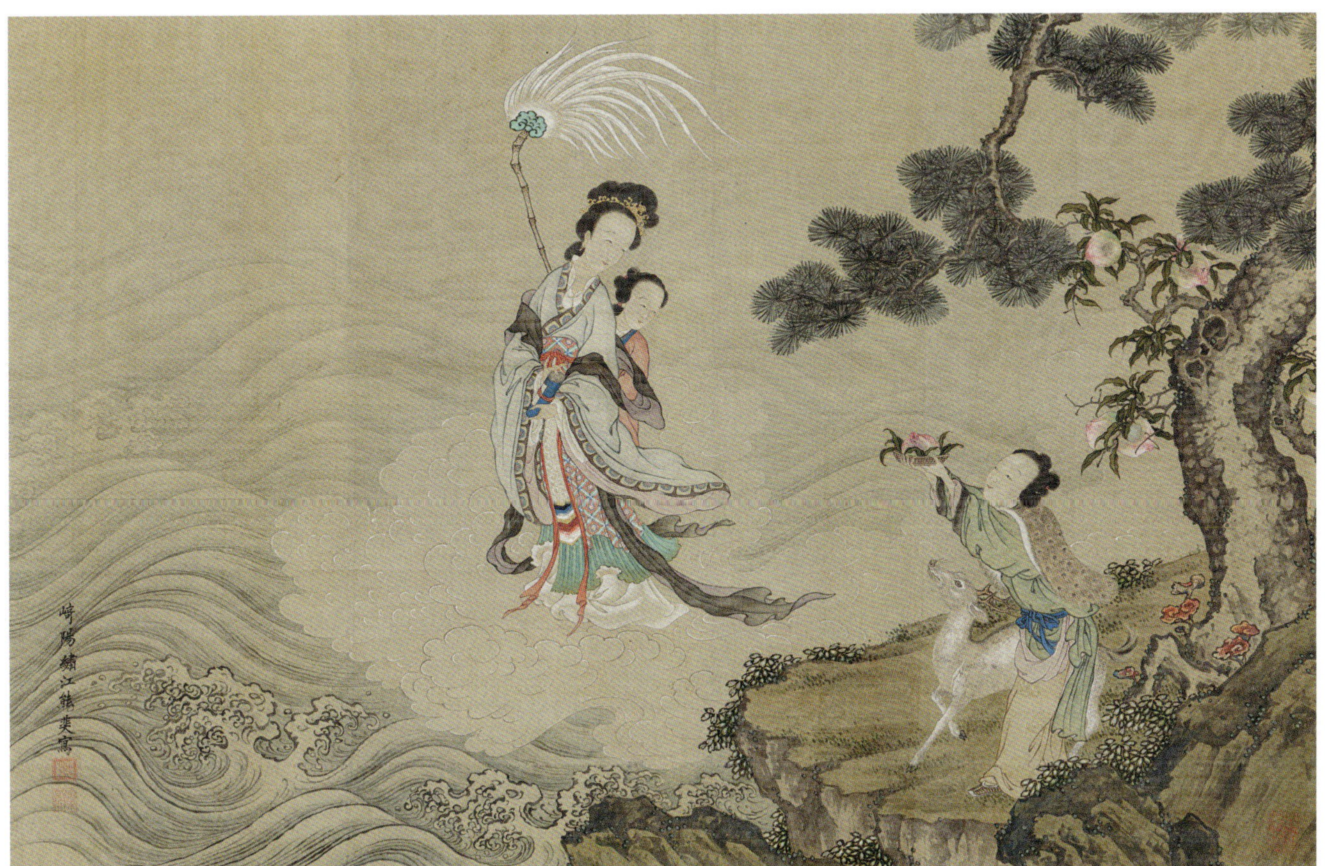


Kumashiro Yūhi, *Queen Mother of the West, Her Attendant and a Court Lady with a Deer*, 1732–72. Hanging scroll, ink and colour on silk. 64.7 × 99.3 cm. British Museum, London, 1881,1210,0.778. Ex-coll.: William Anderson.

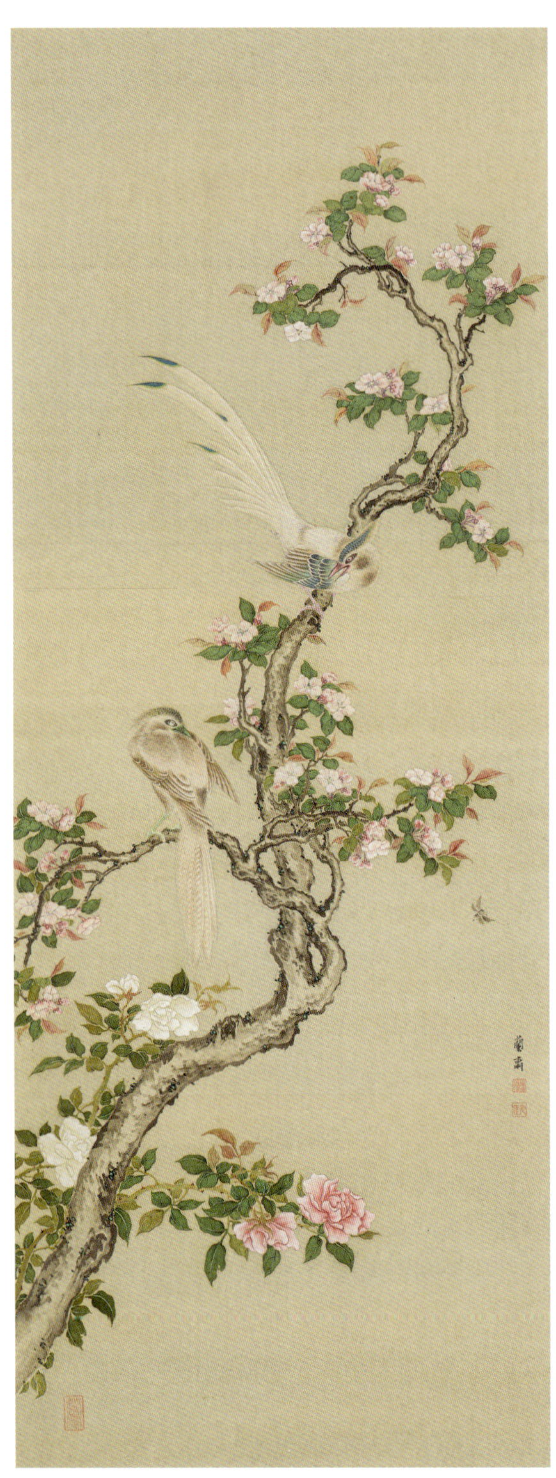



**4.9**
Mori Ransai, *Aronia and Long-Tailed Birds*, 1770–1801. Hanging scroll, ink and colour on silk. 131.6 × 49.7 cm. British Museum, London, 1979,0129,0.1. Purchase funded by the Brooke Sewell Bequest.

**4.10**
Mori Ransai, *Ransai's Picture Album: Orchid Section* (*Ransai gafu ran-bu*), 4 vols, preface dated 1778. Illustrated book, colour woodblock. 28.5 × 18.3 cm (cover). British Museum, London, 1979,0305,0.134.1–4. Ex-coll.: Jack Hillier.

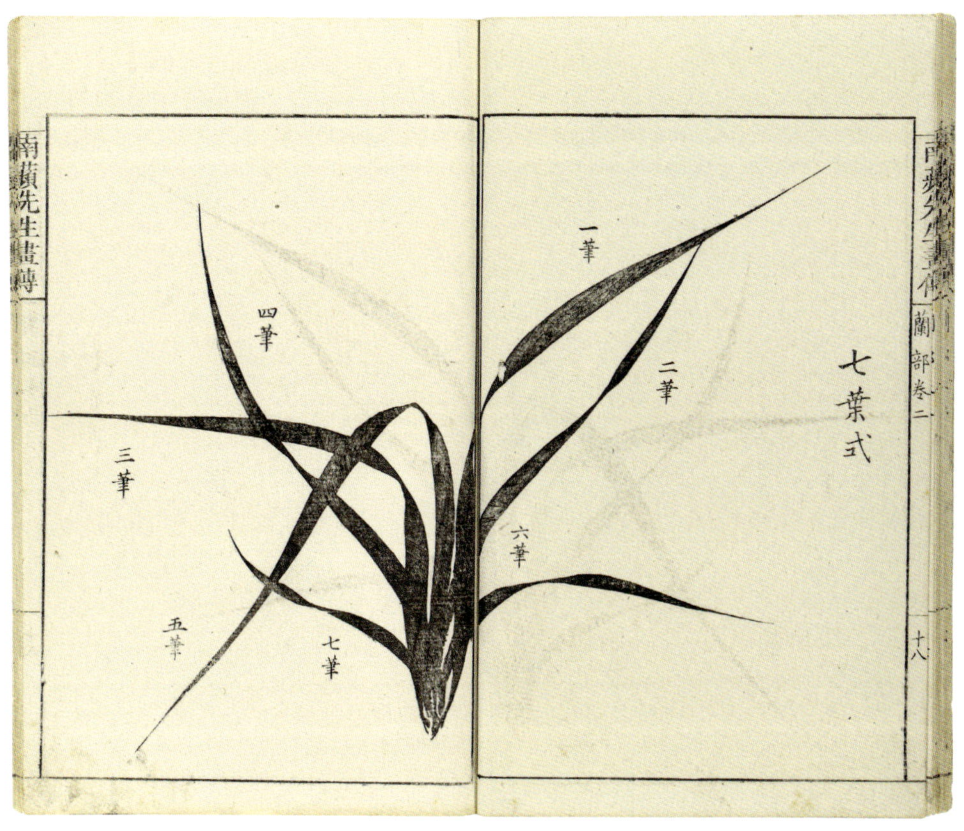

the two men enjoyed a close friendship.[3] In his painting of a pair of long-tailed fowl perched in an aronia tree, set against branches of blossoming roses at the base (fig. 4.9), the composition stretches up the vertical space of the hanging scroll format, leading the eye through the work, establishing a careful balance between the contrasting poses of the two birds. A sense of three-dimensionality and spatial recession is achieved by placing elements behind one another. In 1782 he published a comprehensive painting manual covering flowers (plum, chrysanthemum, orchid), grasses, trees, birds and rocks. Ransai employed innovative geometric diagrams to show how to paint the various plants, for example, the sequence for a seven-leafed orchid (fig. 4.10). Prefaces to the manual were provided by the neo-Confucian scholars Hayashi Jussai (1768–1841) and Itō Tōsho (1730–1804), and the daimyō-artist Toda Tadanaka (1761–1823).[4] In the 1790s Ransai moved to Edo and became painter-in-service to the Kaga domain.

Osaka had a lively painting world that has received little attention from art historians, largely due to a bias towards activities in Edo and factional

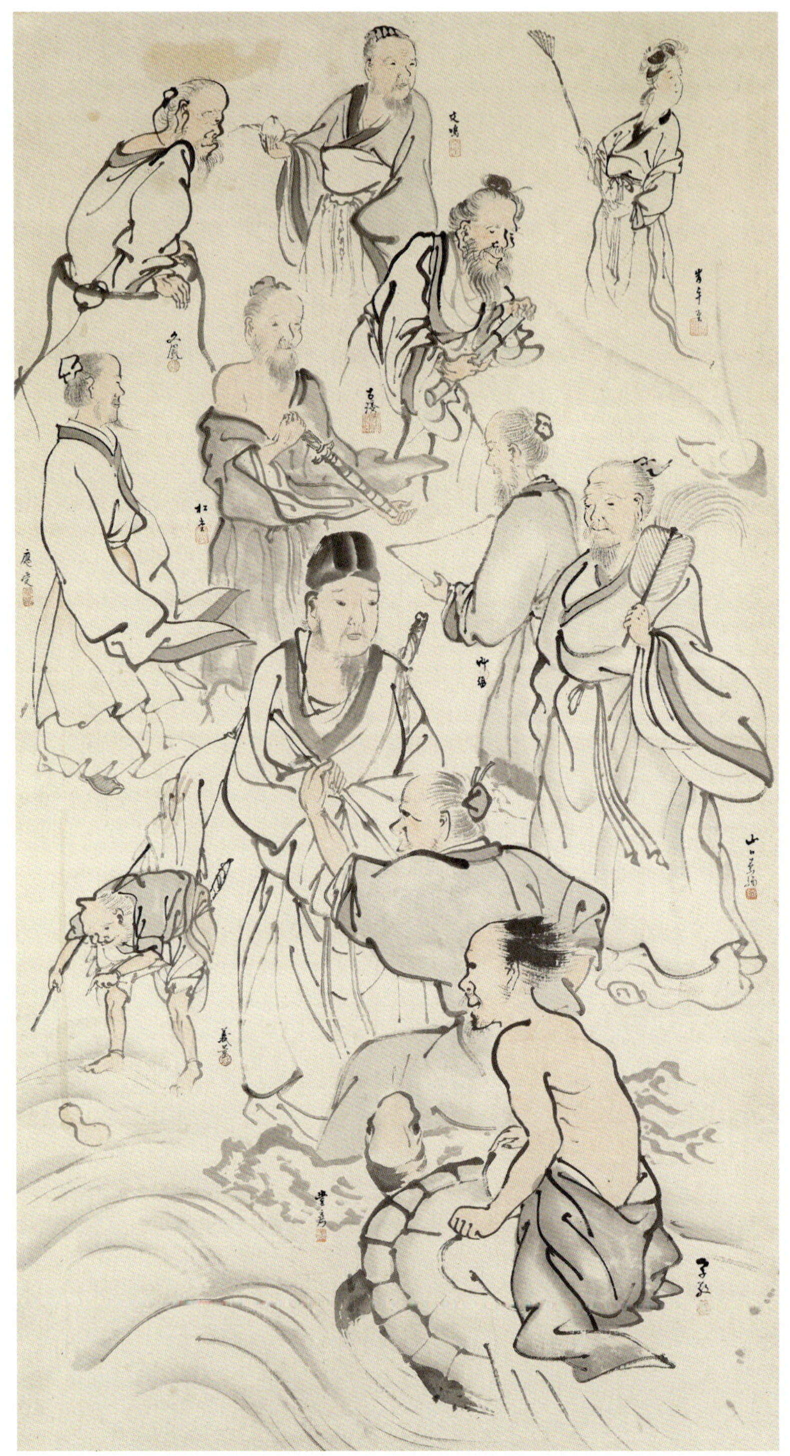

**4.11**
Chikuyū, Gan Tai, Hatta Koshū, Kawamura Bunpō, Kinoshita Ōju, Murakami Shōdō, Okamoto Toyohiko, Oku Bunmei, Shibata Gitō, Yamaguchi Soken and Yoshimura Kōkei, *Chinese Immortals*, *c.* 1805–13. Hanging scroll, ink and light colour on paper. 169.5 × 90.2 cm. British Museum, London, 2002,0906,0.2. Purchase funded by the Brooke Sewell Bequest. Ex-coll.: Dr Ellis Tinios.

rivalries.[5] Fine examples can be found in the William Anderson collection, which numbers more than two thousand items and forms the core of the extensive holdings of Japanese paintings at the British Museum (see p. 15). Anderson was a British naval surgeon, resident in Japan for seven years, and he consciously assembled a collection that encompassed all the schools of painting, represented by finished paintings, preparatory drawings and sketchbooks. Many lesser-known painters are included, such as Kakurin (Kakutei II), who studied with Kakutei in Osaka and ultimately succeeded to his master's name (see p. 132). His *Silver Pheasant and Peonies* (see fig. 3.8) employs the approach of Shen Quan, contrasting ink work for the rock with thick, opaque pigments for the flowers and birds. Kakurin achieves a convincing sense of recession in space by the skilful layering of elements, such as the bird's tail falling behind the rock and the peony bud just visible behind the rock lower down the image, as well as delicate gaps between the leaves. The Chinese poem above was inscribed by Dokuan Sōjō, the sixth abbot of the Daitoku-ji sub-temple, Seigen-an, in Kyoto. Only eight other works by Kakurin are known.[6]

Scrolls with compositions by numerous artists were a distinctive feature of Japanese visual art. Known as a 'combined work' (gassaku) or 'collective painting' (yoriai-gaki) (see pp. 16, 207), they were especially popular as a collaborative and sociable practice among the community of sinophile artists, although not limited to this group. Many gassaku were made on a single occasion, as a memento of the meeting, but they were sometimes assembled consecutively. Of these types, the spontaneous creations made at a social gathering were more challenging, requiring close coordination among the participating artists, often after considerable consumption of alcohol. Group themes lent themselves well to these multi-artist paintings, such as a gathering of Daoist immortals (fig. 4.11). Oku Bunmei was a regular participant in these collaborative scrolls, as were Okamoto Toyohiko and Kawamura Bunpō.[7]

## Literati painting

In Chinese painting practice, a conceptual distinction emerged in the eleventh century between professional and amateur. As opposed to the meticulous approach of court painting, which relied on opaque mineral pigments, the painting of the literati scholar-amateurs (bunjin-ga), prioritised the tonalities of ink: spontaneous, expressive of character and held to be closely related to both poetry and calligraphy practice. Rather than privileging originality, connoisseurs appreciated the deep links across the centuries to past masters and

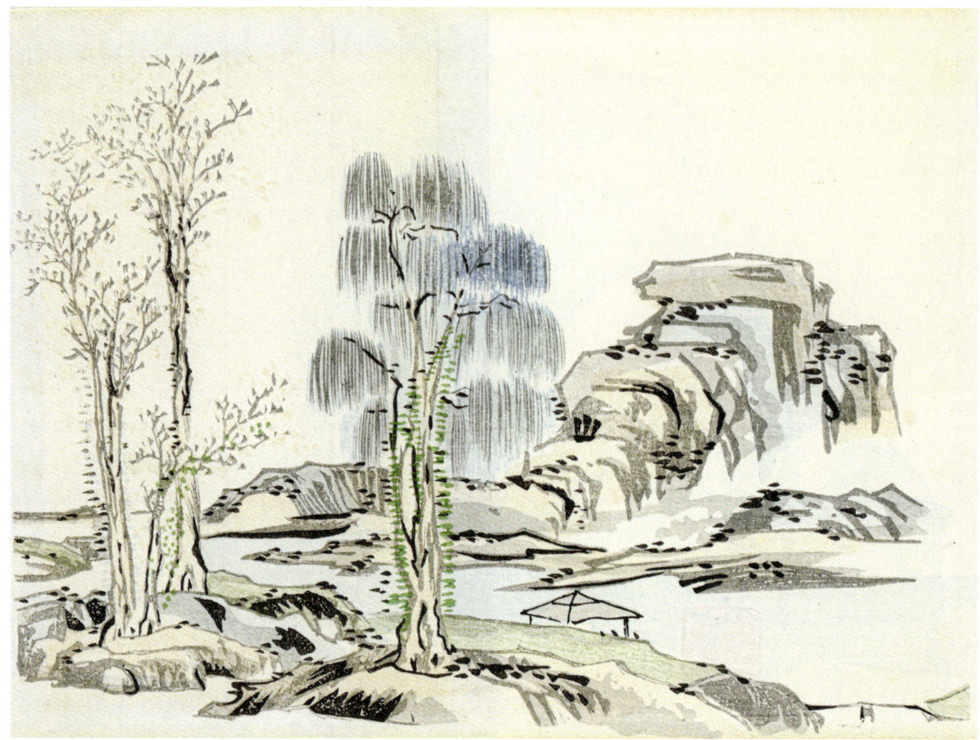

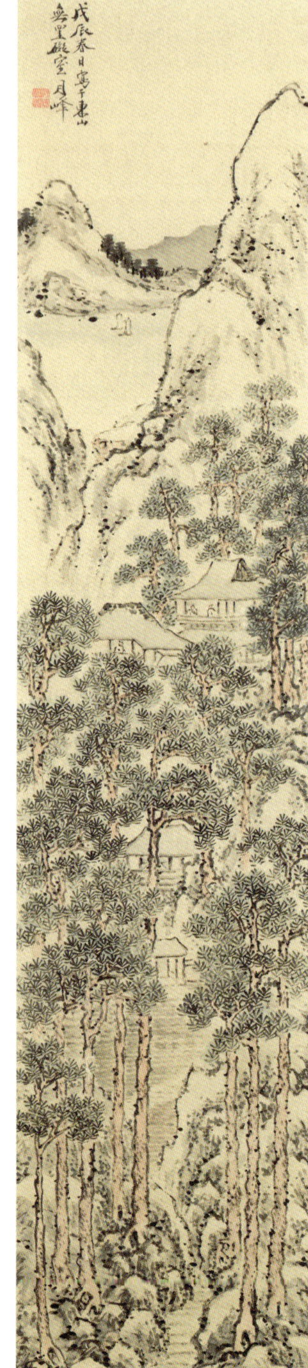

their modes of visualising the world. Even in China, too much stress may have been laid on the division between professional and amateur, but this was certainly not maintained in Japan, where literati painting was a style that could be employed in remunerated work as one of many parallel styles suited to varying occasions.

Imported material culture played a major role in transmitting the styles and principles of literati painting. While actual paintings were limited in number – and there were many of questionable authenticity – woodblock-printed painting manuals (gafu) were a compact, affordable means of dissemination (see p. 122). Books were also a source of Chinese iconography. As mentioned above, studying and honouring respected forebears was a key part of artistic practice. The earliest producers of literati painting in Japan achieved revered status and their techniques were transmitted to later generations by means of commercially published manuals. For example, *Taiga's Painting Manual* (*Taigadō gafu*) (fig. 4.12), published in 1804, was compiled by Geppō (1760–1839), the most important pupil of Ike no Taiga, who became a monk at the temple Sōrin-ji in Kyoto's Higashiyama district; the scholar and poet Minagawa Kien wrote the preface.

*Landscape with Pavilions* by Geppō (fig. 4.13) employs a classic literati composition that begins at the bottom, with a path between tall trees winding up ahead, inviting the viewer to enter the scene imaginatively. The path proceeds up the image towards a clear space where a gate gives access to a small complex of buildings. Beyond the trees are figures seated in two-storey pavilions, enjoying the peace and seclusion of the wooded locale. A sheltering mountain towers above them, and beyond it, to the left, the composition opens out onto a lake, where two sailboats can be seen on the water. The inscription at the top records that Geppō painted the work in Higashiyama in the spring of 1808.

Mori Kinseki (1843–1921) was another pivotal figure in sinophile circles of the late nineteenth century; he studied directly with Chinese painters visiting the Kansai region in the 1870s and 1880s. In 1880 he published his *Painting Manual of Ink Fragrance* (*Bokkō gafu*) (fig. 4.14) in four volumes. The first volume contains multiple literati-style landscape compositions demonstrating different approaches to brushwork, in both monochrome and colour, and examples of renowned painting themes such as 'Gathering at the Orchid Pavilion' and 'Elegant Gathering in the Western Garden'. As with so many manuals before it, the images in subsequent volumes are simple compositions – orchids,

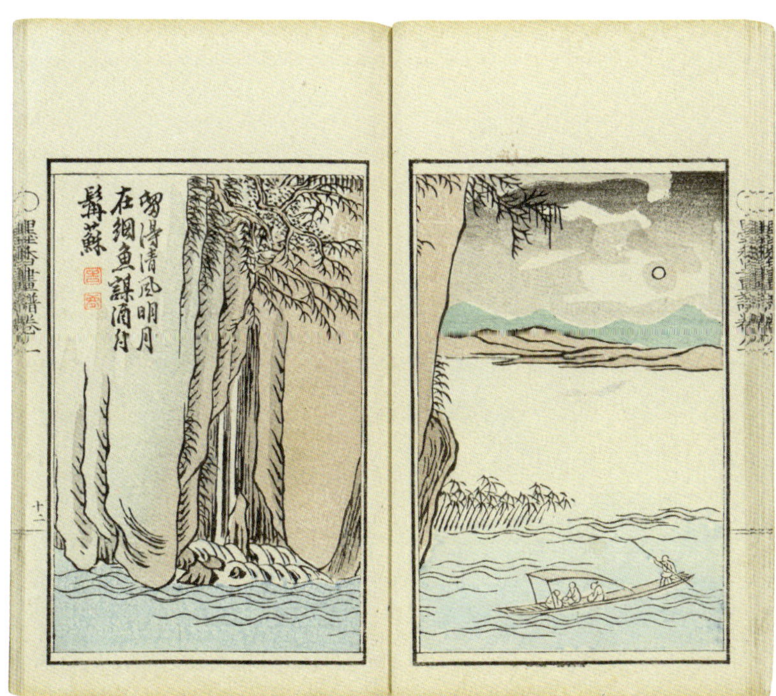

bamboo, plum blossom and chrysanthemums, to name a few – in a variety of techniques and configurations that provide guidance for the amateur painter. These manuals made the medium accessible to a wide audience and publicised the artist's own interpretation and 'brand'.

## The support of patrons

The pursuit of literati painting relied on an extensive network of patrons, who were typically wealthy merchants in the cities and landowners in the country-side. These individuals wished to participate in the sinophile cultural world, benefiting from its rich range of arts and egalitarian principles. Thanks to introductions gained at urban hubs such as Kyoto, Osaka, Edo and Nagasaki, artists could travel around the provinces of Japan, living for a period as an artist-in-residence, participating in a cultural salon or even a large-scale semi-commercial 'calligraphy and painting party' (shoga-kai). The painter Watanabe Kazan (1793–1841) recorded in his diary how he was beset with requests when he joined a shoga-kai in the town of Kiryū in 1831.[8]



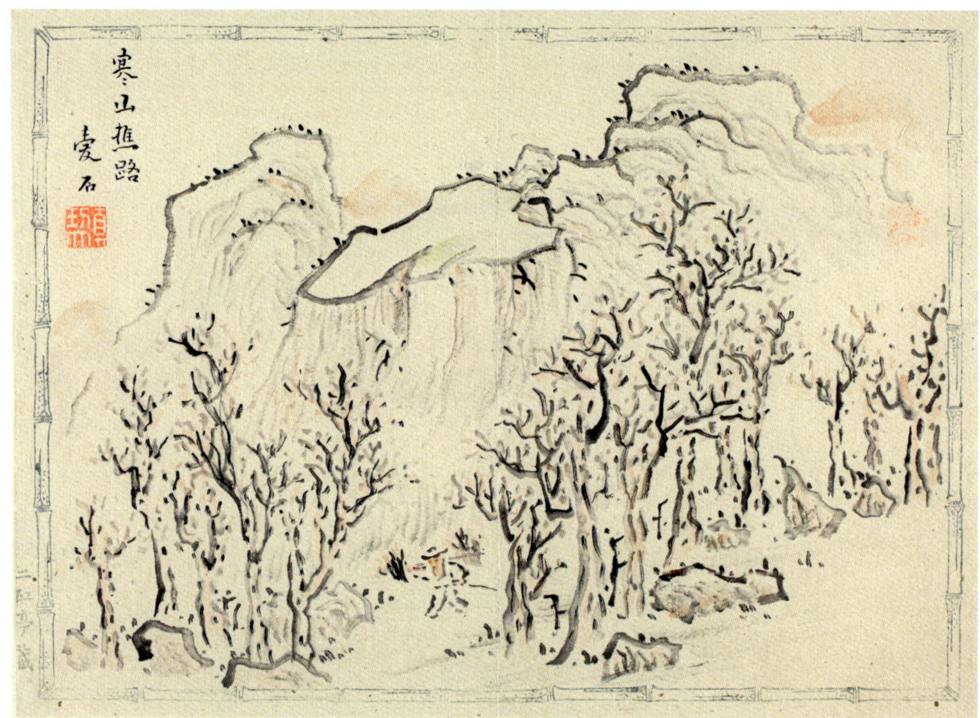

**4.15**
Aiseki, *Woodcutters' Path in the Cold Mountains* (*Kanzan shōro*), *c.* 1825. Album leaf, ink and colour on paper. 19.2 × 25.6 cm. British Museum, London, 1973,0226,0.21. Purchase funded by the Brooke Sewell Bequest. Ex-coll.: Jack Hillier.

Such patrons needed large painting collections to be used as decoration in the tokonoma alcove of a reception room at the appropriate season and occasion throughout the year. Assembling examples by an array of famous painters and calligraphers was a popular pastime, and these figures did not necessarily have to visit in person. Patrons could dispatch prepared paper to artists where they lived, together with an appropriate fee, and then have the piece sent to them. There was a well-developed overland postal network, on which couriers (hikyaku) took sections of the route in turns, carrying knapsacks of items to be delivered. *Woodcutters' Path in the Cold Mountains* (*Kanzan shōro*, 1825) by Aiseki (1768–1827) is one of four openings from a dismantled album, where the paper has a pre-printed frame of bamboo and the bottom left corner records 'Collection of Sankōtei' (fig. 4.15). The image encompasses a broad area of landscape in its compact composition and efficiently conveys Aiseki's angular, idiosyncratic style, which owed much to Ike no Taiga. Aiseki served as a monk at the temple Manpuku-ji in Uji to the south of Kyoto. Manpuku-ji had been founded in 1661 by emigré Chinese monks of the Ōbaku (C: Huangbo) sect of Zen Buddhism and retains to this day markedly Chinese architectural styles. The establishment of this newer, heavily Chinese-inflected form of worship provided a larger context for the appreciation of sinophile cultural forms in the following centuries.

*Mountain Landscape in Winter* by Yamamoto Baiitsu (1783–1856) again is structured to lead the eye up vertically through the space (fig. 4.16) that opens at the bottom where a figure riding on a mule crosses a bridge, followed by a servant; this man serves as proxy for the viewer. His destination is apparently a scholar's retreat in the middle distance, where a figure is seated inside. At left, a path winds up the side of the mountain, which fills half the painting and creates a sense of the mass towering over the lake beneath. The snow-covered landscape is conveyed by unpainted silk left in reserve against the grey sky, and ink work delineates the vegetation and contours of the mountains. The clothing of the figures offers the only accents of colour in this white-out world.

In his painting of 1815, Yokoi Kinkoku (1761–1832) employs a more conventional composition for the *Gathering at the Orchid Pavilion* (fig. 4.17). Here the space is similarly opened up by the stream that flows out towards the viewer. The eye is led to the men assembled on its banks, some holding the cups they have managed to capture. In the middle ground are buildings, with Wang Xizhi seated at a red lacquer table inside the upper one, brushing a verse on the paper before him. Outside, several plum trees are in bloom, and above this, a tall mountain looms over the whole scene. Kinkoku studied authentic paintings by Yosa Buson and in this work adopts the master's impressionistic

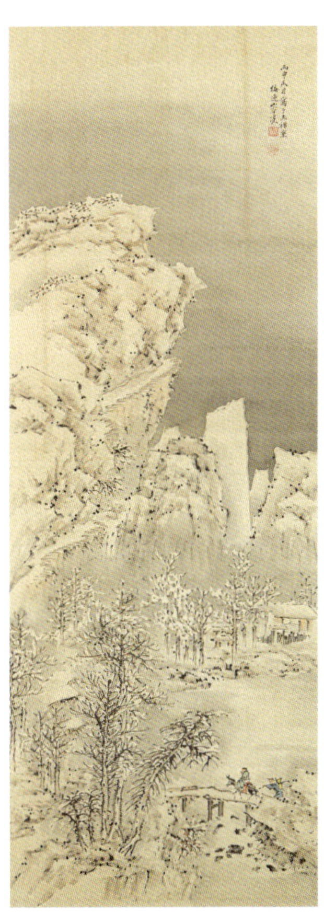

**4.16**
Yamamoto Baiitsu, *Mountain Landscape in Winter*, 1836. Hanging scroll, ink and colour on silk. 124 × 41 cm. British Museum, London, 1981,1007,0.1. Purchase funded by the Brooke Sewell Bequest.

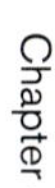

approach, employing loose contour lines to articulate the mountain and broad areas of hastily
applied colour to give volume to the ground,
mountain, trees and bamboo. Variations of green
and pink dominate the work, producing a light,
fresh feeling suited to the convivial mood of the
poetry gathering.

## China as real/imagined place

For Japanese of the early modern era, the Asian
continent was a remote place, inaccessible owing
to the ban on overseas travel. This had been
implemented since 1639, intended to evade the
threat of incursion by European colonial powers.
In this way, China was a place conjured in the
imagination, stimulated by stories, paintings and
books. Just as gazetteers of places (*meisho zue*) in
Japan were popular, so too was there a demand
for information about the topography and appearance of China. *Illustrated Guide to Famous Places in
China (Morokoshi meishō zue)* (fig. 4.18) was published
in six volumes in 1806, edited by Okada Gyokuzan
(1737–1812), with illustrations by Oka Yūgaku
(1762–1833) and Ōhara Tōya (1771–1840). The
locations depicted are in and around Beijing and
in the northern regions of China, which were less
frequent painting subjects than places from southern China around the ancient capitals. As well as
images, the book contains descriptions of cities,
temples, famous historical sites, scenic spots and
legendary incidents, and it presents information on
the legal system, clothing, utensils, contemporary
life, rituals and ceremonies, musical instruments
and festivals, among other topics. The book served
as a practical reference and allowed the reader
to travel in his or her imagination to the famous
locales of the continent, celebrated in historical





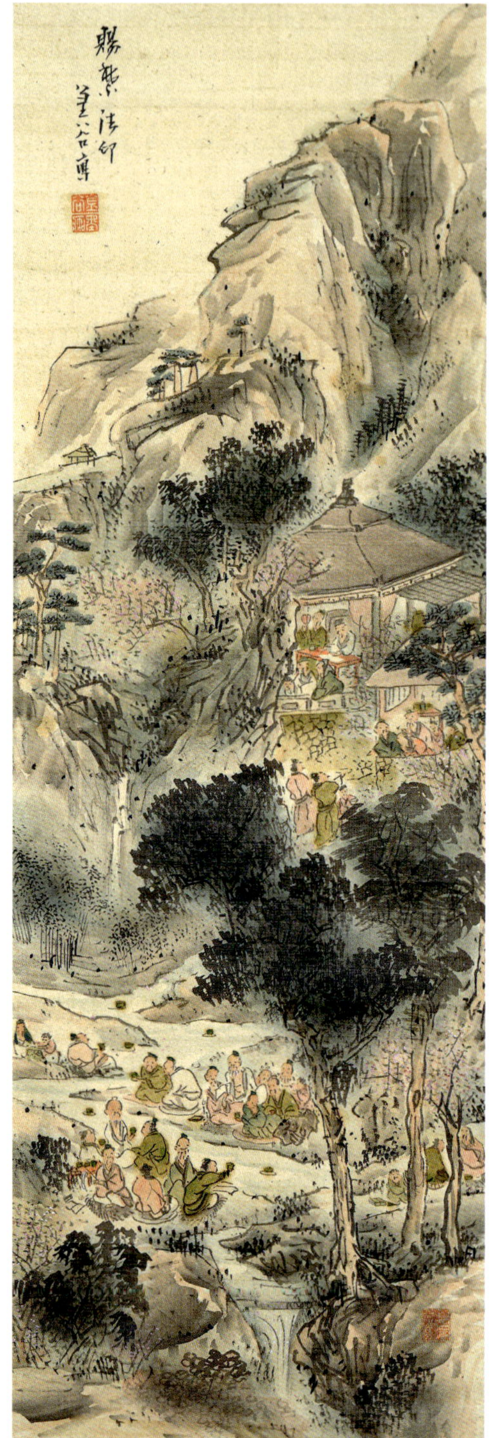

works, stories and poetry. The list of source materials runs to fifty-one items, indicating the thorough research that went into the project, and the broad access that scholars had to Chinese books, despite the restrictions. A further five parts were planned but never realised. The content of such books could even provide inspiration for makers of three-dimensional objects. Volume 4 of *Illustrated Guide to Famous Places in China* was the basis for a netsuke carved by Matsumoto Masayoshi (active mid-nineteenth century) (fig. 4.19) bearing a miniaturised but panoramic view of the landscape of Kunming Lake. The inscription on the reverse names the site and states that the piece was carved after a picture by Gyokuzan.

The one place in Japan where the genuine atmosphere of China could be experienced was the international port of Nagasaki, situated in a deep and wide bay on the western coast of the south-western island of Kyushu (see pp. 10, 55). Outnumbering the small body of about twenty Dutch traders on the artificial island of Dejima – the only Europeans permitted owing to their non-proselytising stance on Christianity – was the community of Chinese traders, numbering around 2,000 and living in a walled compound known as the 'Chinese people's residence' (*Tōjin yashiki*) in the east of the town (fig. 4.20).[9] The Chinese trade involved about 200 ships a year, exchanging silk and other goods for silver. Among the Chinese merchants stationed in Nagasaki were many amateur and professional painters whose output was dominated by the ink monochrome landscapes that were central to literati-style painting. One such was Hua Kuntian (active 1840s), who did a simple

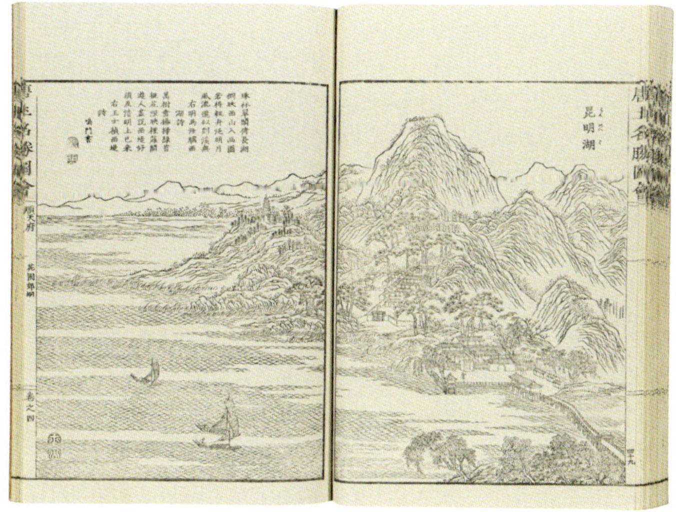

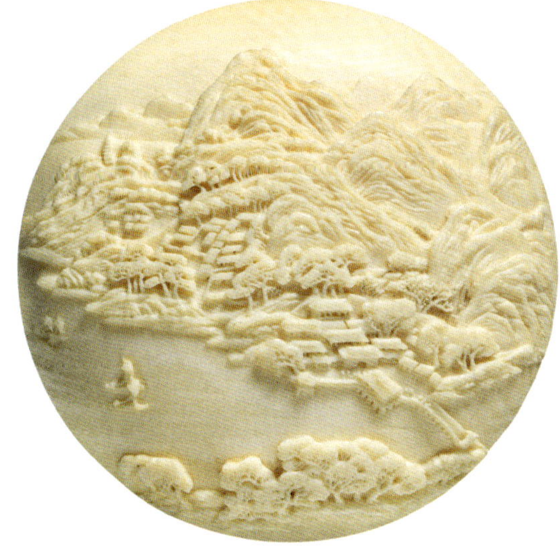

painting of orchids on specially shaped paper, dated to 1849, which was then mounted as a folding fan (fig. 4.21). These Chinese men were unable to leave Nagasaki for other parts of Japan, but they struck up friendships with men visiting the town, who spread their reputations by taking their paintings to distant cities. Kuntian is known to have become friendly with Taki Katei (1830–1901), a painter from Edo who spent six months in Nagasaki in 1851.

If a visit to China was impossible, an enthusiast could recreate its atmosphere by playful transposition. This was a common approach in Japanese visual culture, but usually reconceived from 'high' to 'low', or 'elegant' to 'vulgar', typically by replacing figures in a classical theme with alluring beauties from the pleasure quarters. By contrast, Bunpō upgraded local activities to the height of elegance found in China. *Enjoying the Evening Cool on the Riverbed* (fig. 4.22) demonstrates his 'sinification of Kyoto', depicting the platforms erected over the Kamo River in summertime; the participants are literally cast in Chinese garb, with Chinese-style lanterns and railings.[10] Their pursuits are not 'elegant': at the rear, a couple relaxes with their young son, in the middle is a party of two men being entertained by two richly attired female escorts, and in the foreground two men relax with wine. This is an archetypal Kyoto scene that has no parallel in China, and Bunpō creates an imagined precedent, making the city a sinitic urban space fit for the literati.

Similarly, in *Bunpō's Painting Manual* (*Bunpō gafu*), the artist dresses up the participants in a public art exhibition in Chinese robes (fig. 4.23). These were popular events in the Kyoto calendar, showing a wide range of recent paintings and calligraphies. In a sequence of four charming scenes, attendants unpack a crate of scrolls, the organisers unroll and assess the submissions, the works are hung in the display room, and finally visitors gather to enjoy the exhibition.

As seen in Bunpō's imagery, the China idealised by literati in Japan was that of the Ming period. They considered that 'authentic' Chinese civilisation had been lost through conquest by the Manchu people, who had established the Qing period in the mid-seventeenth century. Therefore the robes, hair and headgear of the Chinese figures depicted are always those of Ming period: the loose, scholarly garb that had been replaced by Manchu-style flaring skirts and horseshoe-shaped cuffs, together with the long queue of hair.

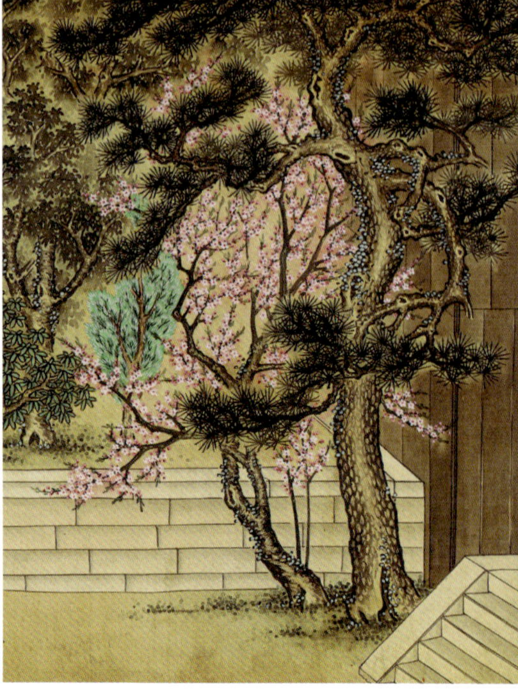

**4.20**
After Watanabe Shūseki,
*Scenes of Life in the Chinese
Settlement in Nagasaki* (detail),
late 1700s. Handscroll, ink and
colour on silk. 33 × 463 cm.
1944,1014,0.23. Purchase funded
by the Marjorie Coldwell Fund.

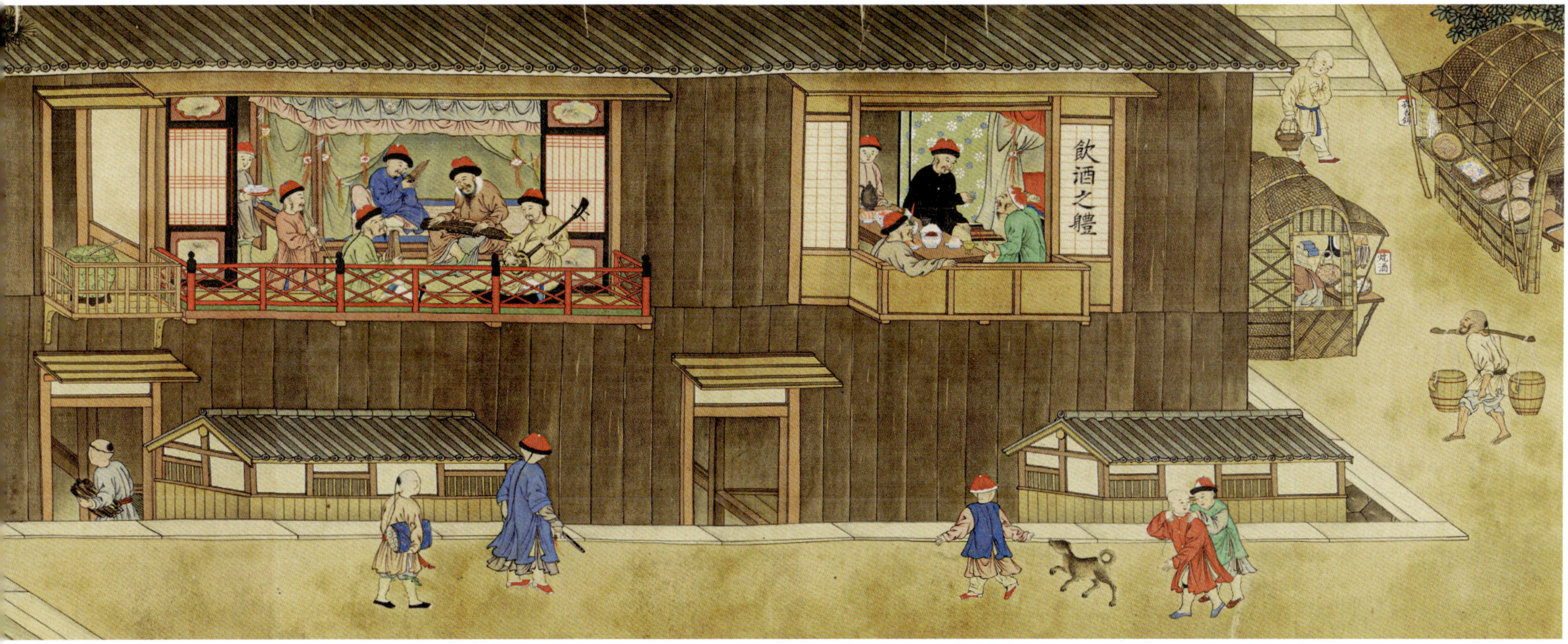

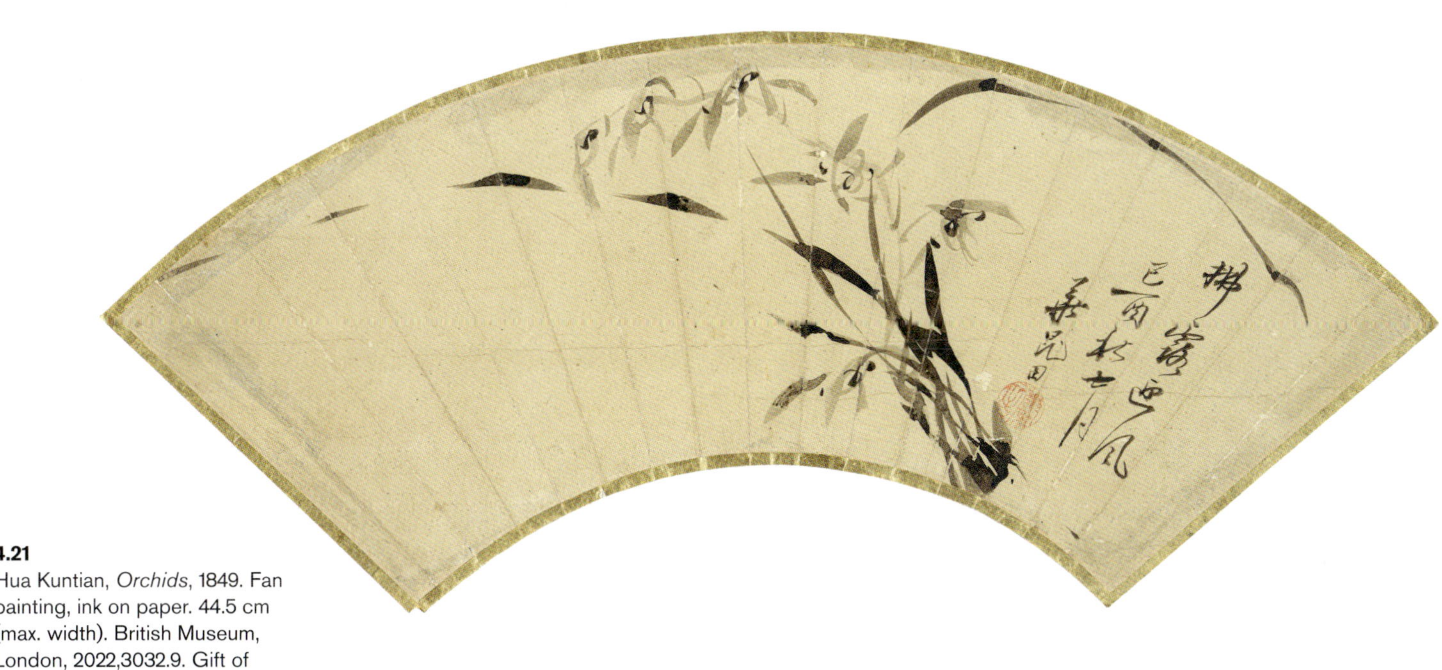

**4.21**
Hua Kuntian, *Orchids*, 1849. Fan
painting, ink on paper. 44.5 cm
(max. width). British Museum,
London, 2022,3032.9. Gift of
Dr Ellis Tinios.

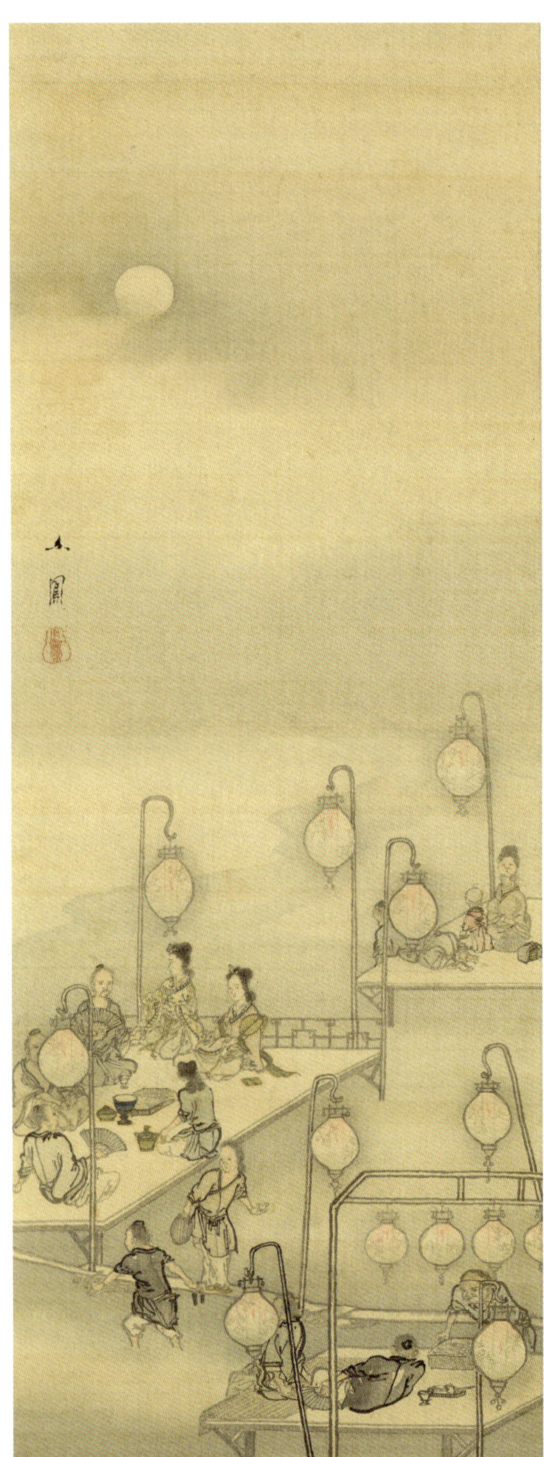

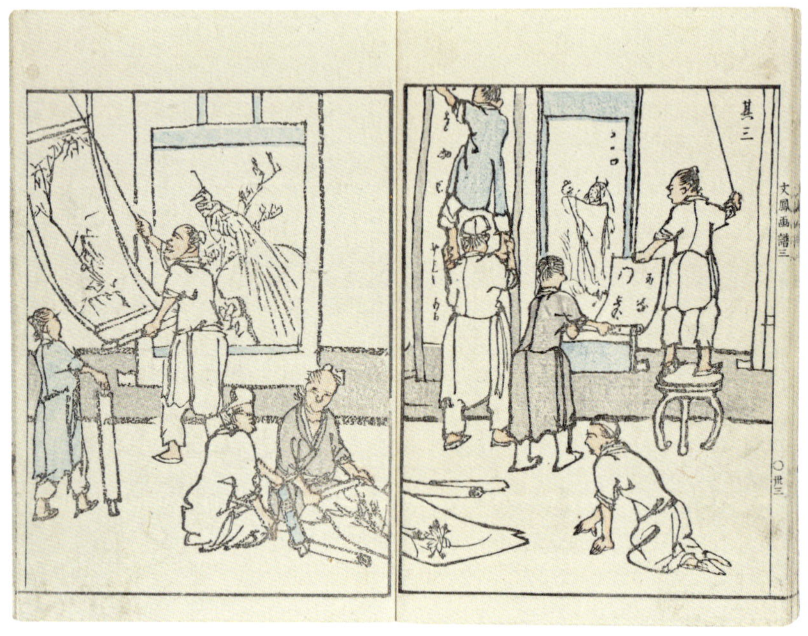

**4.23**
'Exhibition of calligraphies
and paintings, No. 3', from
Kawamura Bunpō, *Bunpō's
Painting Manual, Part III*
(*Bunpō gafu, sanpen*),
1 vol., 1813. Illustrated book,
colour woodblock. 26 ×
17.7 cm (cover). British Museum,
London, 1979,0305,0.215.3.
Ex-coll.: Jack Hillier.

**4.22**
Kawamura Bunpō, *Enjoying the
Evening Cool on the Riverbed*,
1800–21. Hanging scroll, ink
and light colour on silk. 97.5 ×
36.3 cm. British Museum,
London, 2006,0804,0.1.
Ex-coll.: Dr Ellis Tinios.

## Chinese books as source material

Chinese publications on a wide range of topics were imported to Japan by the large number of traders based in Nagasaki and were eagerly consumed. They also provided a rich source of inspiration and visual material for artists to create their own paintings and books. An early example is Ōoka Shunboku, who used illustrations from the 1679 publication *Mustard Seed Garden Painting Manual* (J: *Kaishien gaden*) in his *Living Garden of Ming Painting* (*Minchō shiken*, fig. 4.24), published in Osaka in 1746. Two years later, the Kyoto publisher Kananrō issued a Japanese version of the *Mustard Seed Garden* manual, which was to be a highly influential source for literati painting. It gave guide images of numerous isolated motifs, such as plants, vegetation, flowing water and rocks, as well as landscape compositions for budding painters to incorporate in their work.

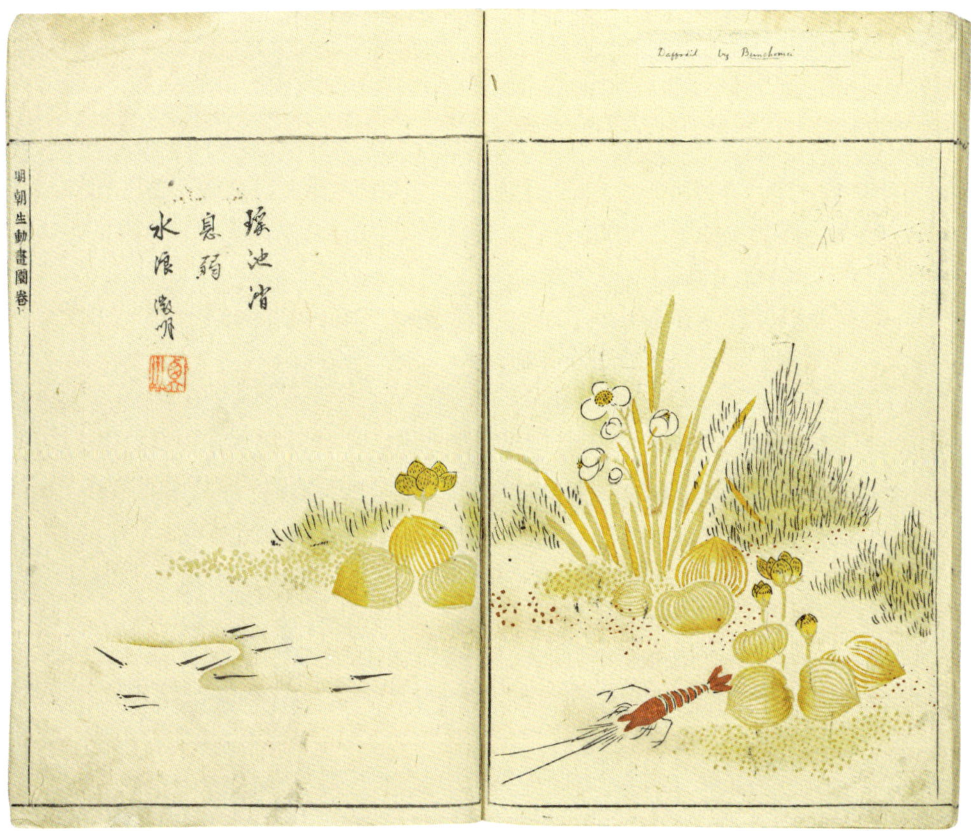

**4.24**
Ōoka Shunboku, *Living Garden of Ming Painting* (*Minchō shiken*), 2 vols, 1746. Illustrated book, colour woodblock. 26 × 17.7 cm (cover). British Museum, London, 1920,0916,0.1.1–2. Gift of Arthur Morrison.

Bunpō's primary publisher was Hishiya Magobei (Gosharō), who specialised in Japanese editions of Chinese books and books based on Chinese themes. One book, *Kinpaen's Picture Album* (*Kinpaen gafu*), was composed entirely of bird-and-flower pictures and indcbtcd to Chinese models (fig. 4.25). This was the only one of Bunpō's books to be printed in full colour, using this to full effect to sensitively reproduce the subtle gradations of pigment and the delicate 'boneless' (C: *mogu*; J: *mokkotsu*) painting technique derived from Chinese practice, wherein leaves and petals are rendered without contour lines. Planned in 1811, it was finally published in 1820 in a single volume. The book was inspired by Chinese precedents, such as the *Mustard Seed* manual, which Hishiya was issuing in a new edition just as Bunpō's book was being prepared, and the earliest impressions of the latter were even printed on expensive imported Chinese paper. The preface was lifted from *Mōkyō's Miscellany of Japanese and Chinese Paintings* (*Mōkyō wakan zatsuga*) of 1772 by Takebe Ayatari (1719–1774), with slight alterations. It has the appearance of Chinese text, being composed entirely of Chinese characters, but grammatically it is in fact Japanese. While some Chinese characters are used for their meaning, all the inflections of verbs and adjectives (*okurigana*) are written using *man'yōgana*, characters that carry solely phonetic value.[11]

Publishers were able to make a profit by issuing reprints of Chinese books. *New Copies of Famous Mountains and Splendid Landscapes* (*Shinmo meizan shōgai zu*) (fig. 4.26) was the Japanese edition of a Chinese publication of landscape compositions compiled by the painter Suzuki Fuyō (1752–1816) and published





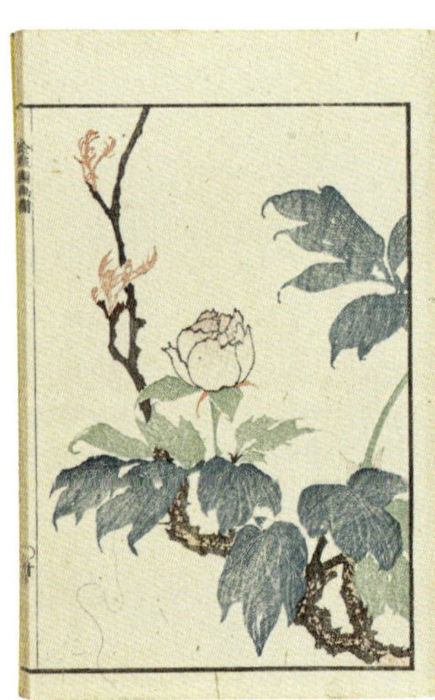
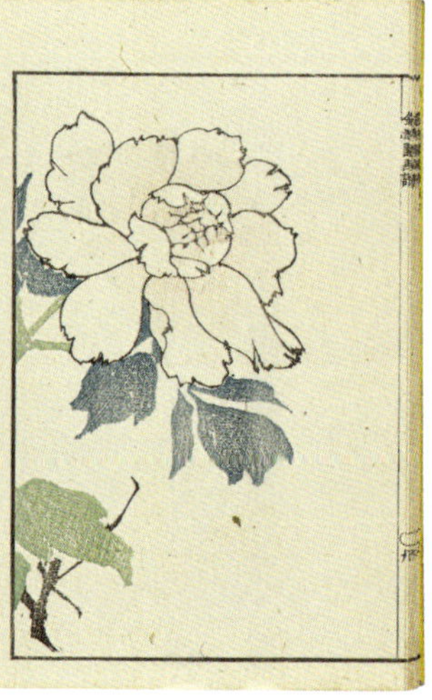
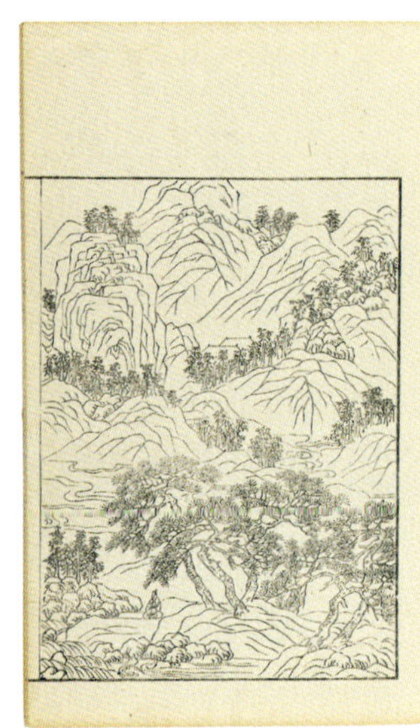
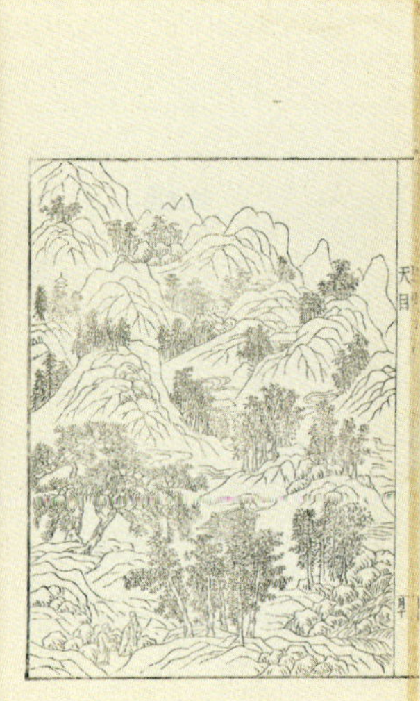

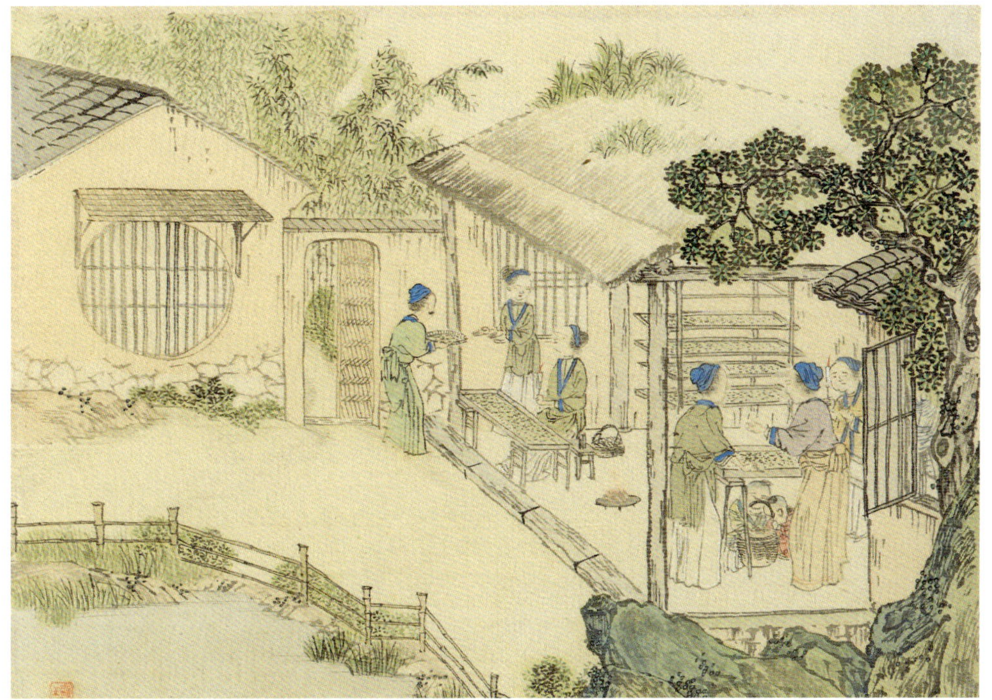

in 1801. Its three volumes presented huge, sweeping landscape views, each labelled with the place name, which allowed the reader to travel imaginatively and gain a sense of the scale of renowned Chinese locales. The scenes employed a variety of brushwork techniques, and those viewing the book could draw on these to incorporate into their own paintings. This spread shows the complex, layered topography of Mount Tianmu, situated eighty kilometres to the west of the ancient Song-period capital, Hangzhou. This site was well known in Japan as the source of 'Tenmoku' ceramic ware, which was prized for its unpredictable 'oil spot' patterning within dark glossy glazes, achieved by crystals of iron coming to the surface.

Other Chinese books attracted the attention of painters in Kyoto. Bunpō's primary pupil, Kawamura Kihō, created a set of album paintings in 1824 based on a Chinese publication concerning rice cultivation and silk production (fig. 4.27), *Illustrations of Riziculture and Sericulture* (C: *Yuzhi gengzhi tu*) by Jiao Bingzhen, which was published with imperial sponsorship in 1696. Its twenty-three images detailed the processes of planting, harvesting, threshing and storing rice, cultivating silkworms, spinning thread and weaving silk cloth. The two themes were originally transmitted to Japan in the early fifteenth century and were typically depicted on large folding screens, expressive of bucolic harmony and economic prosperity. The images in Jiao's book, combined with the accompanying texts, provided practical information but also possessed visual interest as genre scenes of life in China.

## Chinese tea culture

A central aspect of social encounters within sinophile culture was the enjoyment of sencha. This infused tea was distinct from the whipped, powdered form of green tea known as matcha. Both had originated in China, but while matcha, brought over to Japan in the late twelfth century, developed nativist cultural associations, sencha became established only in the eighteenth century and retained strong Chinese identifiers.

In painting, a typical idealised scene of male companionship showed friends in a quiet, sylvan setting, provided with the utensils necessary for preparing tea. Gan Tai painted Chang Sangjun and Bian Que, two semi-legendary figures from the sixth century BCE, seated conversing under a leafy tree in a garden while a boy attendant gathers water for tea from a stream in the foreground (fig. 4.28). The tea utensils – brazier, teapot, two cups and tea caddy – are seen at the right edge. The *Records of the Grand Historian* (C: *Tai shi gong shu*) by Sima Guang (1019–1086) recounts that the two men met when Bian gave Chang attentive service in a hostel, whereupon the latter presented him with a packet of medicine to be boiled in water. After drinking this, Bian gained supernatural powers of healing, with vision that could penetrate the body's layers and perceive ailments in the internal organs.

The enjoyment of sencha was concentrated initially in the Osaka region, and a major figure in the formalisation of the methods and settings for

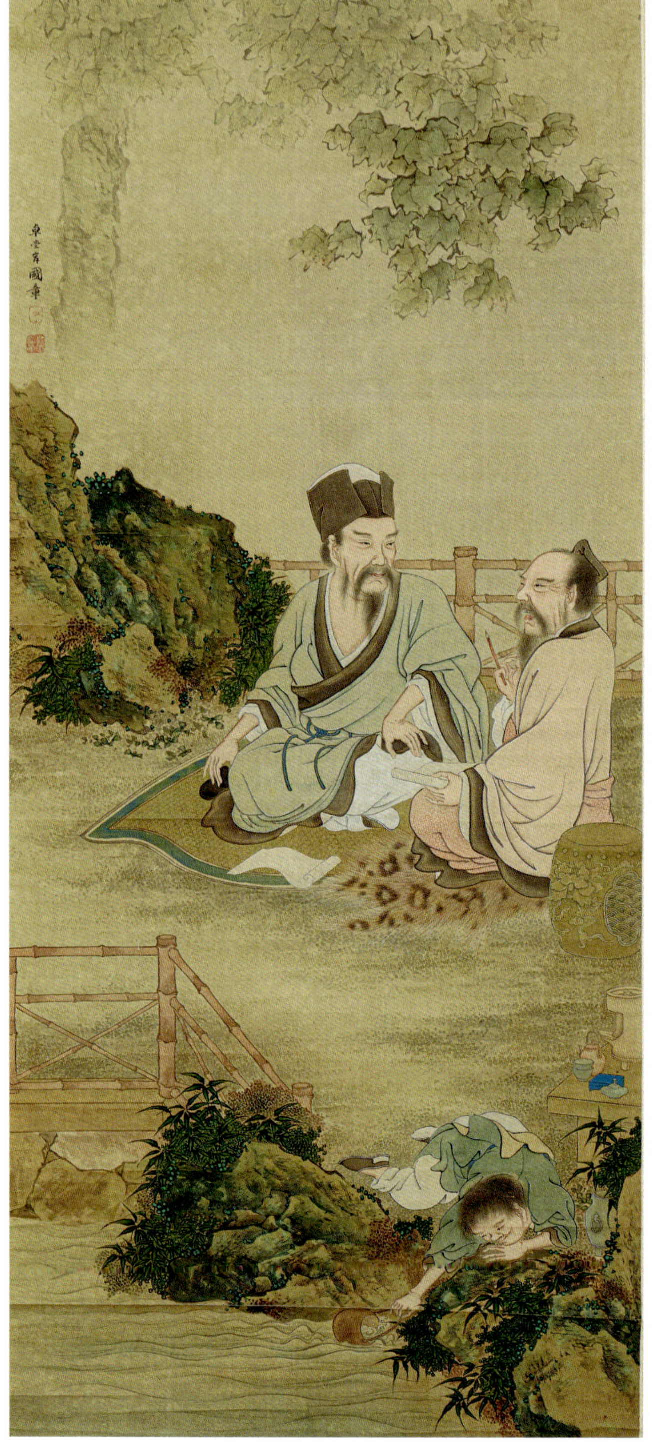

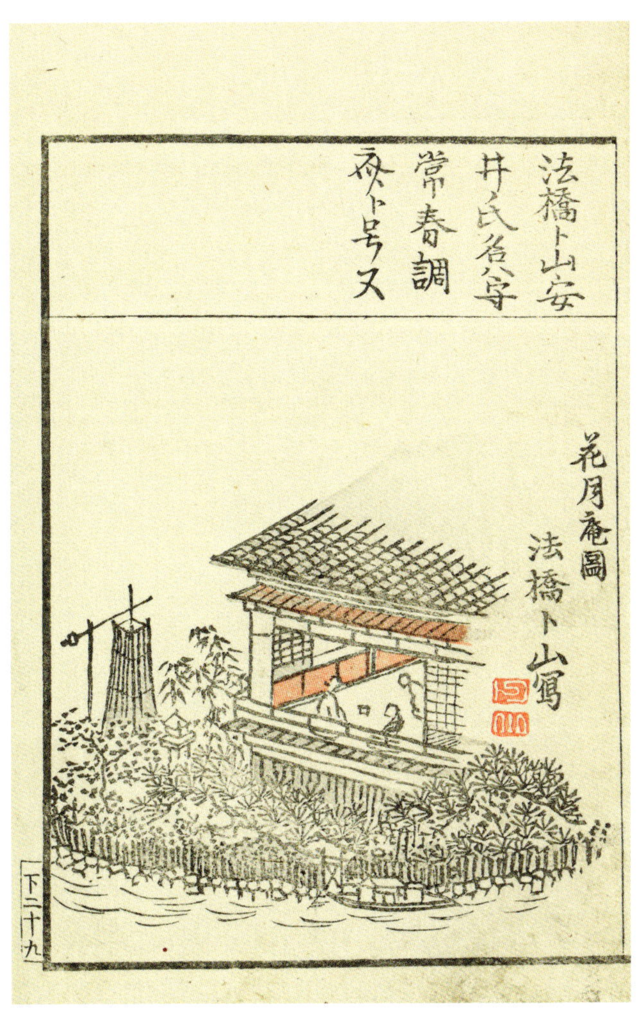


**4.28**

Gan Tai, *Bian Que* (J: *Henjaku) and Chang Sangjun* (J: *Chōsōkun*), 1820–65. Hanging scroll, ink and colour on silk. 129.2 × 56.1 cm. British Museum, London, 1913,0501,0.567. Gift of Sir William Gwynne-Evans, Bt. Ex-coll.: Arthur Morrison.

**4.29**

Yasui Bokuzan (artist), 'Picture of the Hermitage of Flowers and Moonlight (*Kagetsu-an zu*)', from Higaki Masatane (editor), *Record of Elegance and Prosperity in Osaka* (*Naniwa fūryū hanjō-ki*), 1 vol., *c.* 1833. Illustrated book, colour woodblock. 18 × 12 cm (cover). British Museum, 1979,0305,0.517. Ex-coll.: Jack Hillier.

consuming the drink was the sake brewer Tanaka Kakuō (1782–1848).[12] Kakuō had studied the precepts of the tea ceremony (chanoyu) in his youth but was drawn towards sencha through contact with the Ōbaku Zen monk Monchū (active early nineteenth century) during the 1820s. A depiction by the painter Yasui Bokuzan (active early nineteenth century) of Kakuō in a small thatched hut named Kagetsu-an ('Hermitage of Flowers and Moonlight') appears in the directory of calligraphers and painters, *Record of Elegance and Prosperity in Osaka* (*Naniwa fūryū hanjō-ki*), published around 1833 (fig. 4.29). Sencha had hitherto been consumed without formality in the studies or reception rooms of literati, but Kakuō adapted the rules of etiquette and terminology of chanoyu, codifying the spaces where it should be served and the appropriate utensils, and produced a handbook that circulated in manuscript editions. Kakuō travelled widely and was acquainted with prominent sinophile poets and painters in Osaka, Kyoto and Edo, among them Tani Bunchō, Ōkubo Shibutsu (1766–1837), Aoki Mokubei (1767–1833), Tanomura Chikuden and Yamamoto Baiitsu, and was patronised by courtiers and daimyō. He hosted gatherings and made the formal serving of sencha a key part of memorial services.

From the mid-nineteenth century, large social gatherings called *meien* aimed to create an immersive world imbued with a Chinese aura. They offered multiple displays of paintings, calligraphies, antiques, flower arrangements, tray plants (*bonsai*) and writing utensils, and they were accompanied by the serving of sencha and performances of Chinese-style music. These meetings were staged in large temple complexes or private villas as well as at open-air sites and on covered sailing vessels out on the water. Hundreds of visitors moved through the multiple 'settings' (*seki*) to admire the works on display and drink tea in what was an early form of a special exhibition. They experienced a boom during the 1870s in the large cities of Kyoto, Osaka, Nagoya and Tokyo (the name of Edo after 1868), and in numerous regional cities from Toyama to Nagasaki.[13]

In January 1874 a sencha meeting was held along the Yodo River in Amijima, Osaka, in memory of Yamanaka Kichibei II (d. 1872), proprietor of the art dealer Yamanaka Shōkai. The event boasted thirteen seki, with a total of 193 Chinese paintings and calligraphies, together with bonsai, cut-flower displays, writing equipment, bronze vessels, baskets and musical instruments. Outside, on the water, were dragon boats with performers playing Chinese music. This was one of several events organised from the 1860s onwards by Tanomura Chokunyū (1814–1907), a literati-style artist from Kyushu who had studied with the eminent painter Tanomura Chikuden

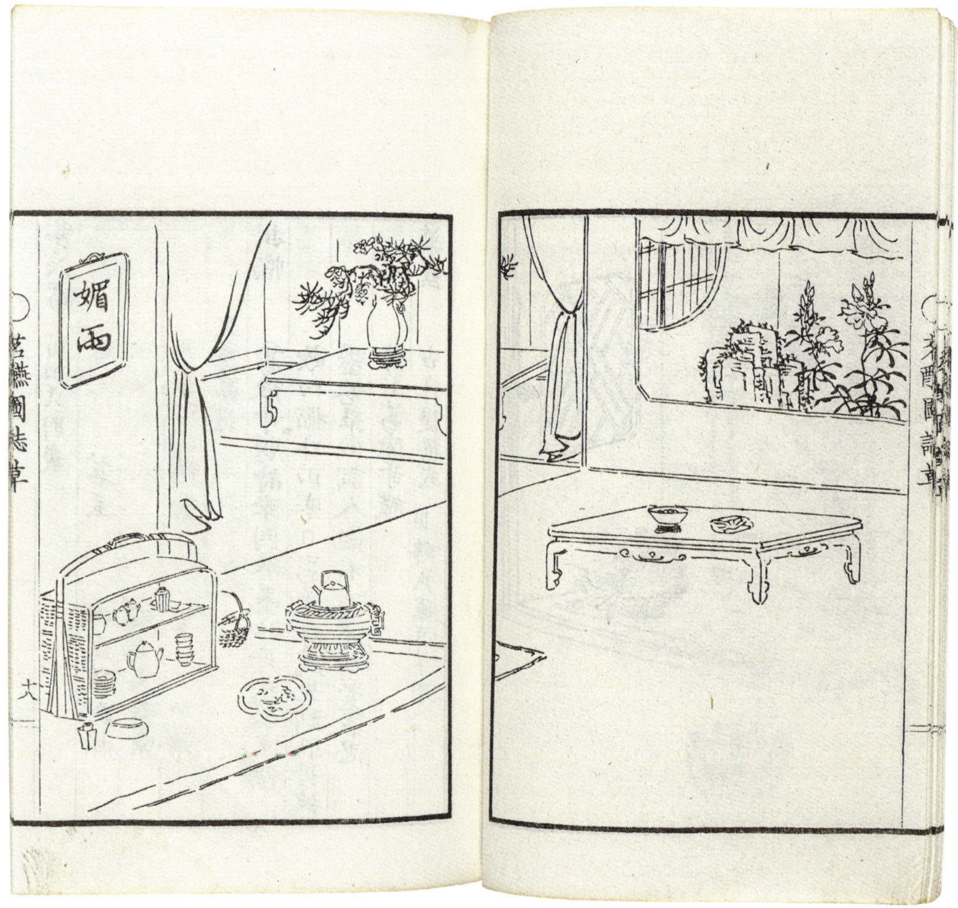

4.30
Yamanaka Kichirōbei (editor), *Pictorial Account of the Azure Bay Tea Gathering* (*Seiwan meien zushi*), 4 vols, 1876. Illustrated book, woodblock. 17.3 × 11.2 cm (cover). British Museum, London, 2023,3007.1. Purchase made possible by the JTI Japanese Acquisition Fund.

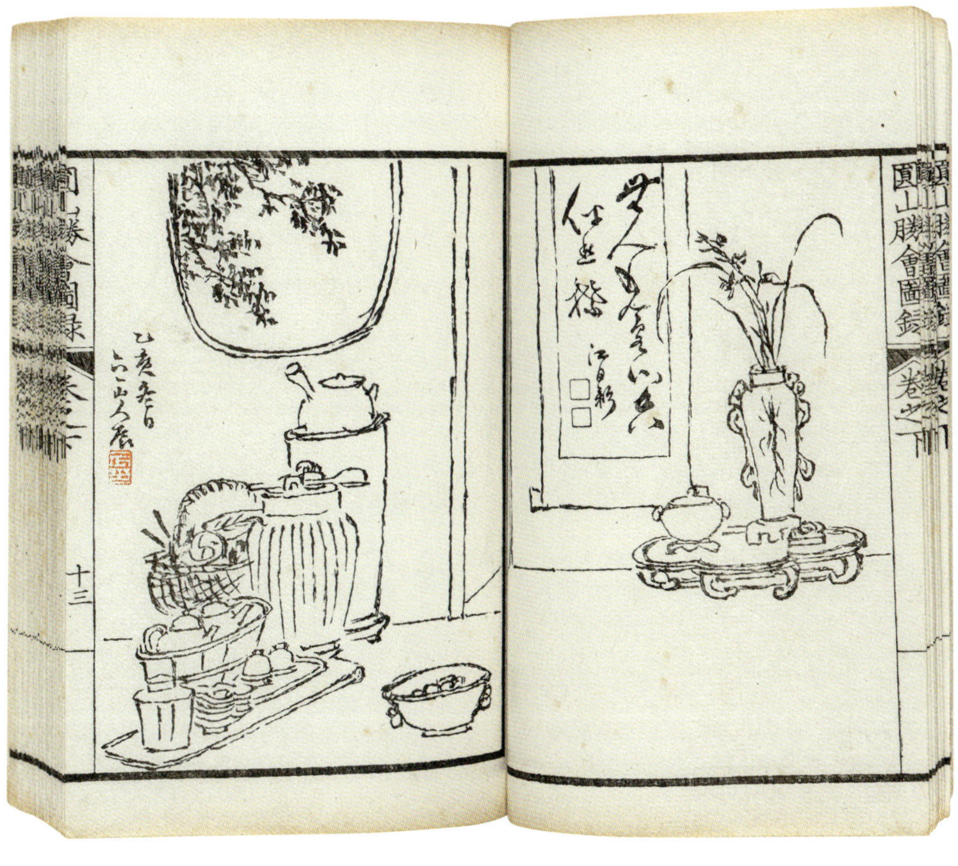

mentioned above, and he provided images for the subsequent 1876 publication, *Pictorial Account of the Azure Bay Tea Gathering* (*Seiwan meien zushi*) (fig. 4.30), which painstakingly recorded the appearance of the settings and was the first to focus on the Chinese-style objects suitable for sencha.[14]

A similar event was held in Kyoto over two days in November 1875 in memory of Kumagai Naotaka (1817–1875), an amateur artist, art collector and proprietor of the specialist stationery shop Kyūkyodō, still in business today. Named *'Enzan shōkai'*, the meeting occupied ten teahouses in the Higashiyama district and fourteen sites along the banks of the Kamo River. Within these, a grand total of 502 Chinese calligraphies, paintings and utensils from 132 lenders were on display. Again, a lavish document of the event, *Illustrated Record of an Excellent Gathering in Maruyama* (*Enzan shōkai zuroku*), was published in May 1876 (fig. 4.31).

Kyoto and Osaka were geographically separated from the new government in Tokyo, which experienced politically charged shifts in policy, and were

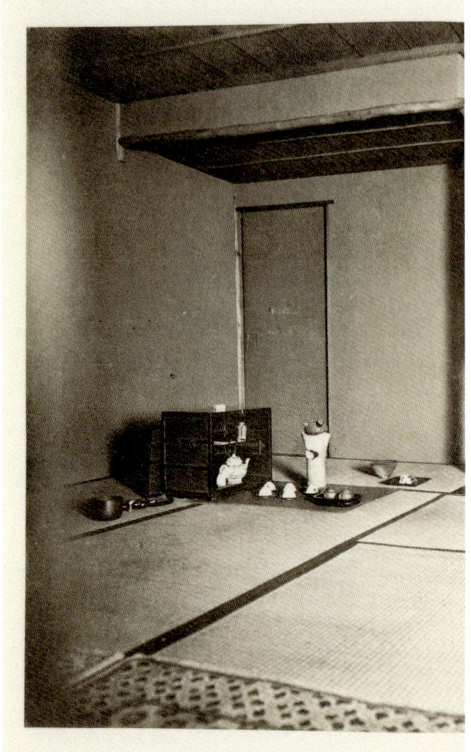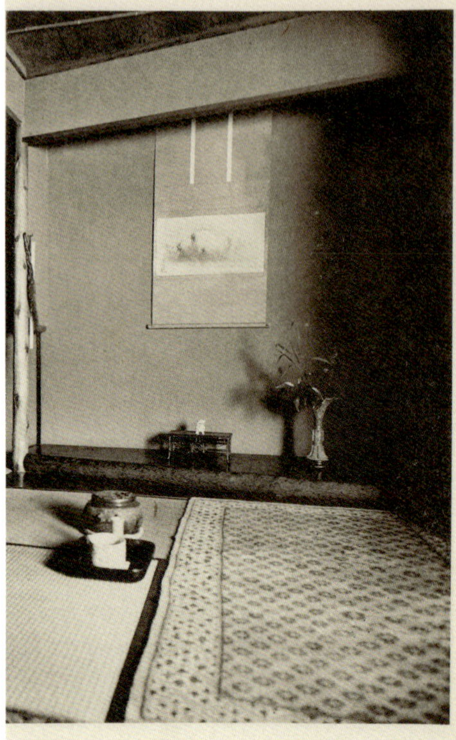



therefore less affected by changing currents of cultural practice. These centres preserved literati culture, including sencha, and in any case private tastes typically continued irrespective of official attitudes. The Shōryū-sha ('Prosperous and Noble Group') was formed in 1876 to bring together aficionados and collectors, and it lasted for half a century. Towards the end of the group's existence, a grand tea ceremony was held in 1925, comprising thirteen settings that featured an extensive collection of Chinese and Japanese artworks. The event was commemorated the following year with a two-volume catalogue, the preface of which was written by Nagao Uzan (1864–1942). This included photographs of the settings, which demonstrates how new reproductive technology was being applied to the established form of the meien illustrated record (fig. 4.32).

Another salon that continued into the twentieth century was the 'Group of Eighteen' (Jūhachi-kai) formed in 1902. It comprised eighteen connoisseurs (*sukisha*), mainly based in Osaka and Kobe, who met each month to consume tea (both sencha and matcha) and to appreciate Chinese and Japanese antiques. The group was formed by the two co-owners of the *Asahi shimbun* newspaper, Ueno Riichi (1848–1919) and Murayama Ryōhei (1850–1933; his collection is now the Kōsetsu Museum of Art, Kobe), together with the businessman Fujita Denzaburō (1841–1912). Other members included the founder of Nankai Railways and Asahi Beer, Matsumoto Jūtarō (Sōken, 1844–1913), the financier Tonomura Hei'emon (dates unknown), the brewer, railway owner and banker Kanō Jihei (1862–1951) and the head of the long-established Sumitomo enterprise, Sumitomo Kichizaemon XV (Tomo-ito, 1864–1926). The 'Group of Eighteen' is a testament to the continuing importance of the cultural salon as a social forum, encouraging these titans of industry to develop their collections, seek out rare and valuable items and support contemporary artists.

## The fate of China in Japan

In the late 1860s the shogunate lost power and was replaced in 1868 by a new government, drawn largely from lower-ranking samurai of a league of south-western clans. The new regime undertook to modernise Japan to ensure its participation as an equal on the international stage. In the opening years of the Meiji era (1868–1912), the widespread appreciation of, and participation in, Chinese-style cultural forms was largely unchanged, at least in private practice, with literati painting undergoing a boom in popularity that lasted until the mid-1880s. This form did not fit with government policy, however, which sought to promote the export of craft items in order to generate foreign revenue. From the mid-1880s a new conceptual system of 'fine art' (*bijutsu*) was established and art institutions were created that taught only Western-style forms. In addition, the defeat of China by Japan in the First Sino-Japanese War for control of the Korean peninsula in 1894–5 and the desire to promote 'uniquely Japanese' art forms expressive of a nationalist mood resulted in the decline of sinophile arts. Nevertheless, there was a renewal of interest in collecting Chinese art in the 1910s, particularly with the outflow of objects subsequent to the fall of the Qing regime, and with the academic efforts of figures such as the art historian Ōmura Seigai (1868–1927).

Given the considerable influence of China on Japanese culture, one may be tempted to ask where 'China' ends and 'Japan' begins, but the reality is complex. As Takebe Ayatari declared in his 1772 manual: 'the quality of painting consists first of loftiness of mind/heart, second of proficiency of brush and third of capturing well the sense of things. Such being the case, the character need not be [restricted] either to Yamato [Japan] or Kara [China].'[15]

# Kimura Kenkadō: scholar, painter, collector
*Nakatani Nobuo*

Celebrated as a literatus (bunjin), Osaka-based Kimura Kenkadō was a 'giant of knowledge' in the late Edo period. An influential cultural figure, Kenkadō had close relationships with intellectuals from all over Japan, as well as artists such as Ike no Taiga, cultural figures such as Baisaō (Kō Yūgai, 1675–1763) and Katayama Hokkai, and even with daimyō such as Mashiyama Sessai (see p. 134). Kenkadō studied under Ono Ranzan, a scholar of pharmacology (*honzōgaku*) in Kyoto. He collected specimens and objects related to the study of natural products (*bussangaku*), including botany. He accumulated tens of thousands of objects that were kept on display to the public at his home. Kenkadō also authored *Research on the Narwhal* (*Ikkaku sankō*, 1795) and edited the five-volume *Illustrated Guide to Notable Products of Japan's Mountains and Seas* (*Nippon sankai meisan zue*, 1799). The former is a scientific study of the narwhal that Kenkadō completed in collaboration with the Dutch studies (*rangaku*) scholar Ōtsuki Gentaku (1757–1827). Such a range of interests suggests that his vision was international in scope. This approach of 'observing and accurately recording things' was likewise in line with the spirit of Positivism (see p. 165), which was popular in the eighteenth century across East Asia.

The Chinese painter Shen Quan, who came to Nagasaki in 1731, introduced a painting style combining realistic representation with elaborate decorative elements (see p. 165). His art would have a significant impact on Japanese painters, particularly the Nagasaki school. Kenkadō began his training in painting at a young age under Kakutei (Kaigan Jōkō), a painter who worked in the Shen Quan style. Shen Quan's paintings were popular not only in Edo and Kyoto but also in Osaka; they inspired artists such as the calligrapher Itsuzan (1702–1778) and Mori Ransai (see figs 4.9–4.10), who actually studied Shen Quan's style in Nagasaki and also interacted with Kenkadō. The hanging scroll *Peach Blossoms* (fig. 4.33) was painted when Kenkadō was twenty-two; accurate observation was key to painting realistically but also characteristic of the study of natural products.

Kenkadō was active in the study of nature and of painting, but he clearly distinguished his illustrations of plants – part of his observation-based botanical studies – from his Chinese-style literati paintings. The latter were created

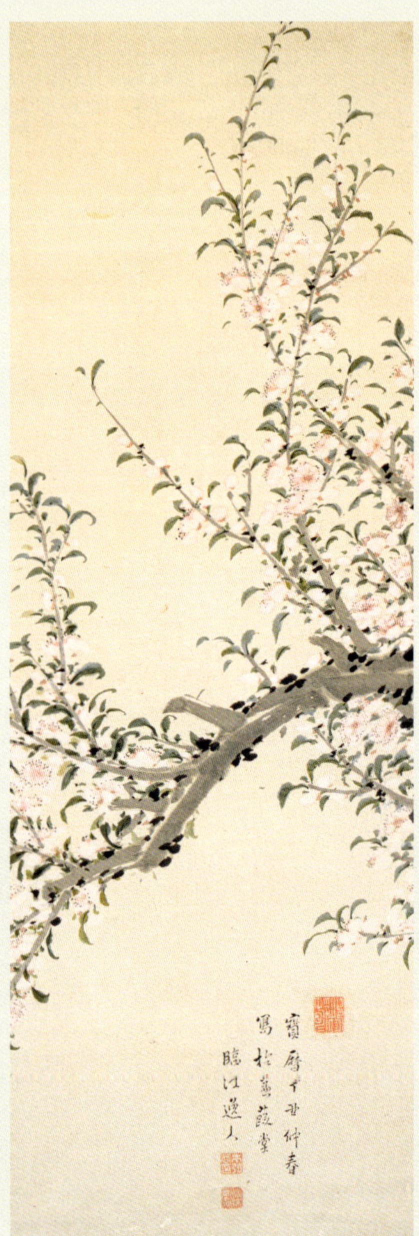

**4.33**
Kimura Kenkadō, *Peach Blossoms*, 1757. Hanging scroll, ink and light colour on paper. 110.8 × 37.2 cm. Kobe City Museum, Kobe.

**4.34**
Kimura Kenkadō, *Withered Tree, Bamboo and Rock*, 1799. Hanging scroll, ink and light colour on paper. 188 × 49.4 cm. British Museum, London, 2023,3002.1. Purchase made possible by the JTI Japanese Acquisition Fund. Ex-coll.: Inatsuka Takeshi.

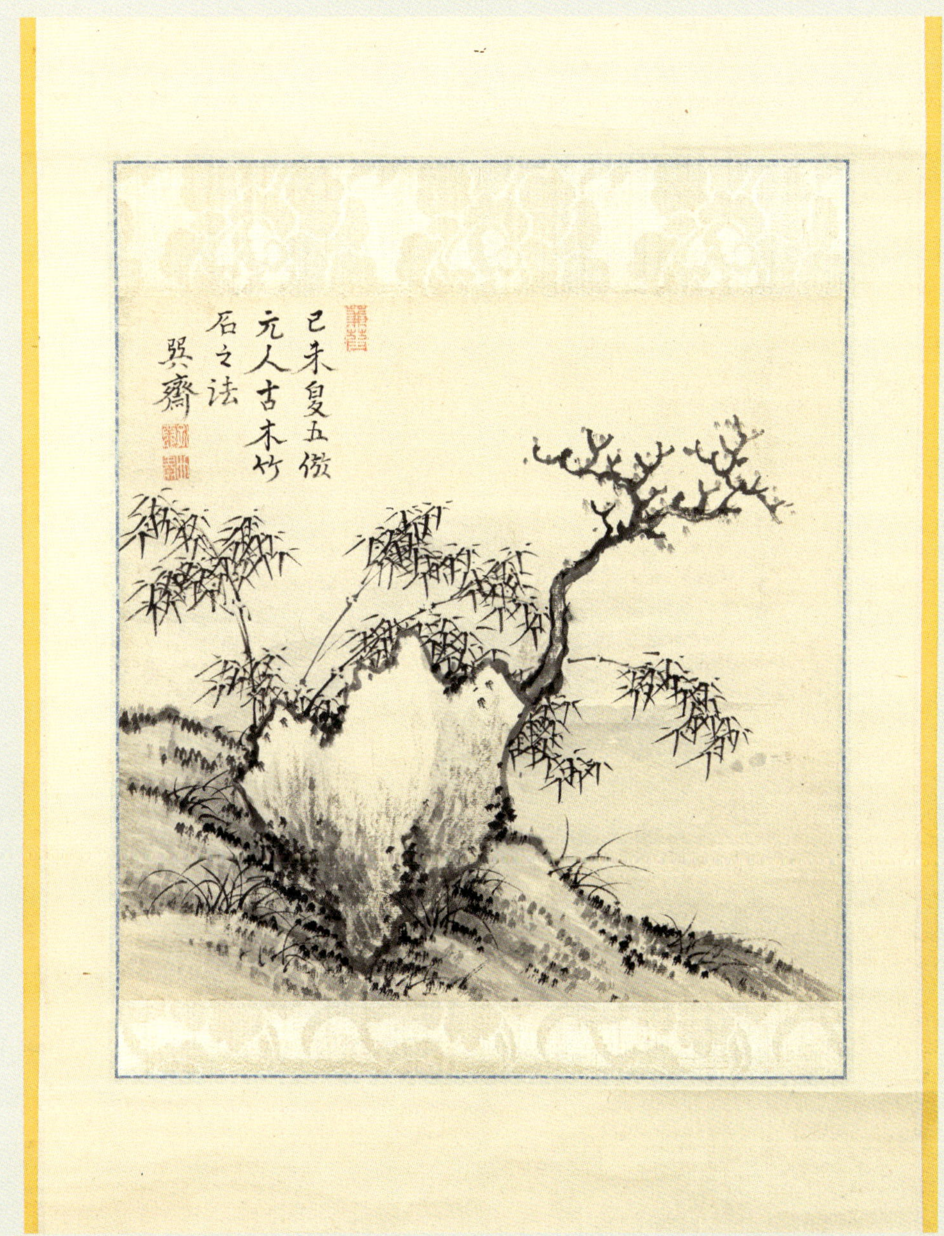

from his middle years onwards as he sought his ideal in the creative realm of 'painting'. Although sometimes criticised by modern art historians for lacking skill,[16] Kenkadō's 'gentle' literati paintings were by no means poorly executed, even though they could not compare with those by his teacher Ike no Taiga. Kenkadō demonstrated a certain level of artistic prowess in his late work; for instance, the excellent *Small Birds and a Lychee Tree* (today in a private collection) is rendered in the Nagasaki-school style.[17]

The hanging scroll *Withered Tree, Bamboo and Rock* (fig. 4.34) is likely a deliberate attempt by Kenkadō to emulate Chinese literati painting. In its more robust approach it differs from the calm – rather than expressive – compositions characterising Japanese literati paintings. The seals and inscription indicate that this painting was done in the fifth month of 1799, when Kenkadō was sixty-four. He produced pieces that were intended as gifts for his literati friends, as he was not a professional painter and therefore had no need to sell his paintings. In this sense, this work embodies the essence of literati painting and the custom of exchanging artworks within creative circles. *Withered Tree, Bamboo and Rock* is a typical example of Kenkadō's talent for smaller-scale paintings of landscapes, orchids, bamboo and rocks; it was praised by the literati painter Tanomura Chikuden.[18]

Kenkadō returned to the realistic style of the Nagasaki school, alongside his production of literati paintings, from around 1795, after turning sixty, an important life marker. This artistic approach fitted well with Osaka townspeople culture and directly connected to the botanical studies of the time. It is possible that in his late years, images of botanical pictures and detailed paintings of the Nagasaki school overlapped in Kenkadō's mind. By envisioning and creating Chinese-style literati paintings, Kenkadō probably aimed to transcend the restrictions of the Tokugawa government's ban on travel outside the country, by journeying to the imagined land of China.

In eighteenth-century Japanese society, both studies of nature, including botany, and the art of literati painting flourished. The philosopher Ishida Baigan (1685–1744) popularised the Sekimon-shingaku school of thought, which taught morals and ethics to the general populace. Osaka

in particular developed advanced education institutions for townspeople, such as Kaitokudō, a Tokugawa-chartered academy of Chinese studies established in 1724 (see pp. 62, 64). At the same time, urban popular entertainments such as jōruri chanting and kabuki evolved in works by the Osaka playwright Chikamatsu Monzaemon (1653–1724). Popular too were the inexpensive colour ukiyo-e woodblock prints that illustrated scenes from the kabuki theatre and the licensed pleasure districts. In this way the creators of 'culture' expanded from courtiers and the samurai class to ordinary townspeople. As a literatus and a figure with good connections, Kenkadō stood at the centre of this cultural milieu.

# Painting literati
*Paul Berry*

The Japanese practice of collaborating on painted works (gassaku) followed an earlier Chinese custom of artists working in concert on a painting from the Song period onwards. Artists could contribute paintings, calligraphy inscriptions and poems to gassaku in formats that included hanging scrolls, handscrolls, fans, poetry slips (*tanzaku*), folding screens and albums. Over the course of the Edo period, the popularity of gassaku continued to grow and utilised many artist lineages. In the nineteenth century, in particular, large numbers of gassaku were created by those associated with literati painting, as well as those of the Maruyama and Shijō schools. Their popularity reflected the increasing number of artists and patrons, in combination with a desire to appreciate artists as members of various traditions and aesthetic interests.

Typically, a collaborative work has the signatures and/or the seals of each participant, yet gassaku fall into three different categories depending on the circumstances and timing of the production. Works completed on the same occasion (*sekijō*) are usually spontaneous, quickly brushed with loose organisation. A smaller number had the materials prepared in advance, with outlined squares or other formatting devices into which each artist would place their work. The final, larger category consists of collaborations over a longer period of time, from days to many years, permitting more complex compositions and careful arrangements. This division encompasses many different situations, including those prompted by patrons who wished to assemble small paintings by their favoured artists in a single scroll. Sometimes dates are found on the works, allowing a clear understanding of the overall time period of the scroll and the order of creation. Paintings of the so-called 'immortal poets' (*kasen*), who wrote canonical works of Japanese literature, often had a famous poem by the relevant poet calligraphed by a court noble.

One such example is the joint creation *Pine, Bamboo, Chrysanthemum and Rock* (fig. 4.35), composed by four literati (bunjin) painters of diverse origins that were active in the Kansai area: Nakanishi Kōseki (1807–1884), Hine Taizan (1813–1869), Yamamoto Chiku'un (1819–1888) and Rai Shihō (1823–1889). This work dates to around the 1860s, as Taizan signed it Kinrinshi ('The Sage of Kinrin'), a name

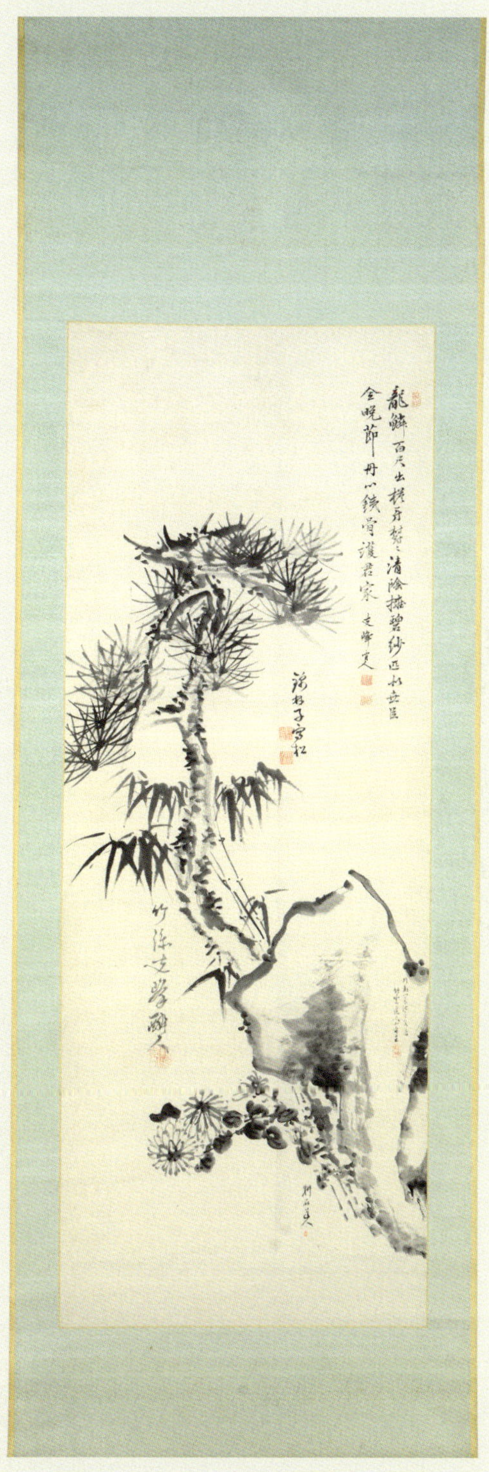

**4.35**
Hine Taizan, Nakanishi Kōseki, Rai Shihō and Yamamoto Chiku'un, *Pine, Bamboo, Chrysanthemum and Rock*, before 1869. Hanging scroll, ink on paper. 145 × 49.5 cm. British Museum, London, 2000,0725,0.1.

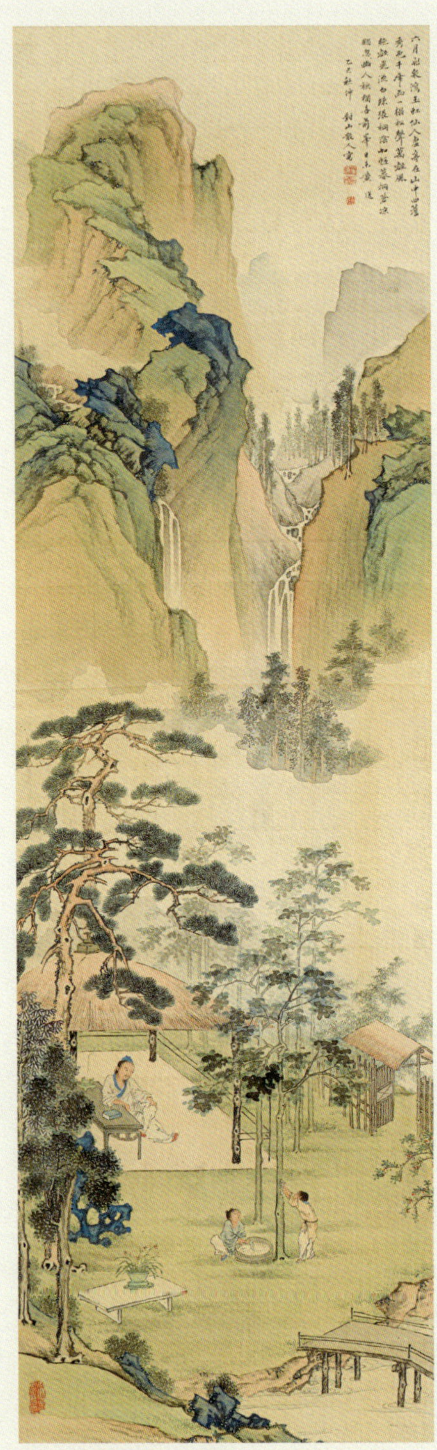

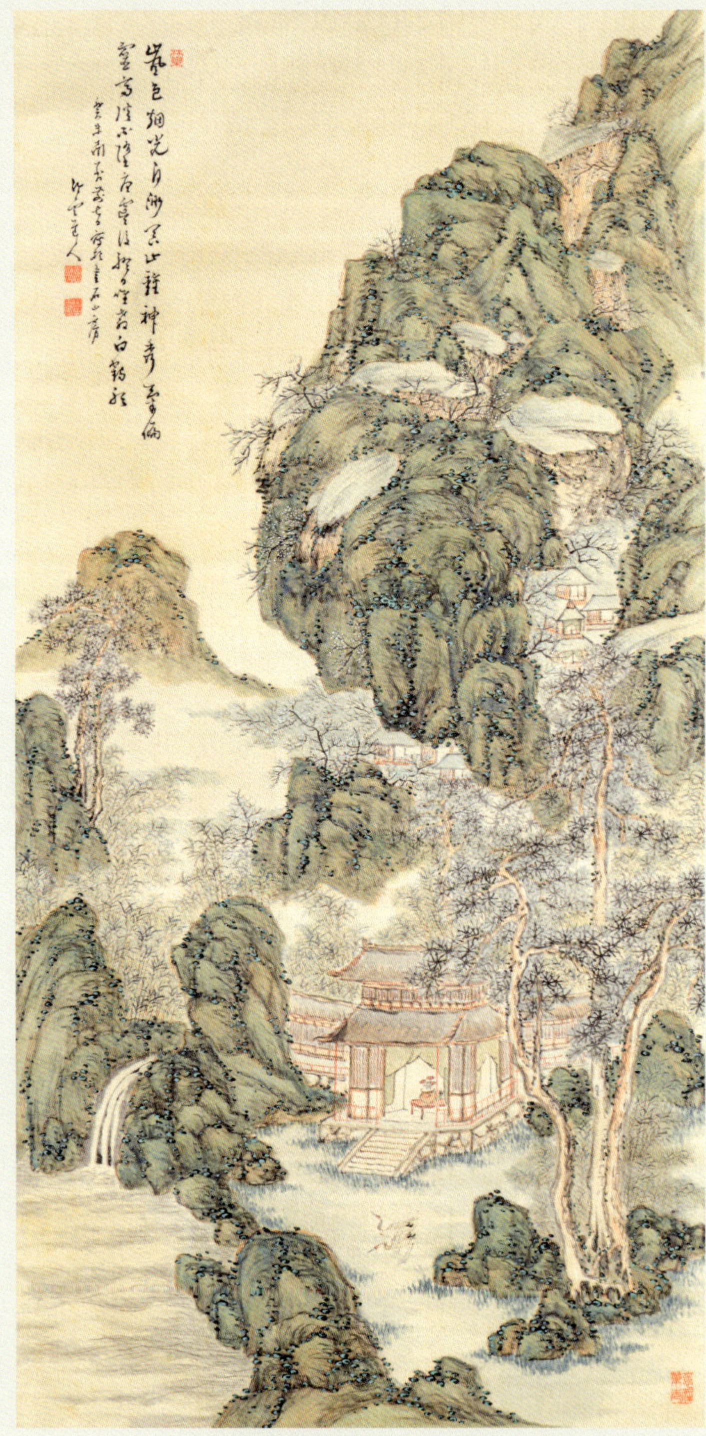

**4.36**
Hine Taizan, *Studio in the Shade of Wutong Trees*, 1845. Hanging scroll, ink and colour on silk. 139.4 × 41.1 cm. Freer Gallery of Art, National Museum of Asian Art, Washington, D.C. F2019.3.6a-e. Gift of Mary and Cheney Cowles.

**4.37**
Yamamoto Chikuun, *Three Friends of Winter*, 1883. Hanging scroll, ink and colour on satin. 133.7 × 66 cm. Mary and Cheney Cowles Collection, Seattle.

he used while living in Shōgoin village, east of Kyoto, from 1861 until his death. This name was borrowed from Kinrin, the popular name for the woods at Shōgoin. The theme of the painting and Shihō's poem in the upper right is the protective power of the pine tree eulogised in the poem, which employs the customary identification of standard compositions, wherein the foreground is painted first, followed by the middle-ground and background elements. In this case, the foreground rock by Chiku'un was likely followed by Taizan's pine tree, with the bamboo by Shihō and the chrysanthemum by Kōseki added in either order. The youngest of the group, Shihō, was the second son of the illustrious literatus and imperial loyalist Rai San'yō; he had high status owing to his father's prestige as well as his own talents in poetry, calligraphy and painting. His verse in the upper-right corner may have set the theme of the collaboration. The seven-character-line quatrain focuses on the power of the pine, using the traditional metaphysical imagery of a dragon:

> Hundred feet of dragon scales with fangs bared
> Gloomy cool shadows embracing pale greenery
> Resembling an enormous beast at the end of the world
> Sincerity of its iron bones protects the ruler's family.[19]

Owing to the closely intertwined composition of the painting, it is likely that this work was the sekijō type of gassaku, made during a meeting of these four friends. The pine tree represents longevity and the bamboo and prominent rock endurance, while chrysanthemums can refer to the imperial lineage and also have autumnal associations. As all these artists were imperial loyalists at the time of the 1868 Meiji Restoration, it is plausible that the last line is in praise of the emperor; it could equally have been conceived as an auspicious gift to a family.

Paintings such as *Pine, Bamboo, Chrysanthemum and Rock* – which demonstrate skilful brushwork with an impromptu combination of popular symbolic motifs – illustrate a signal feature of bonding among literati painters. Such works were a way for old friends to celebrate their ongoing relationship and explore their similar attitudes to art and poetry. The enjoyment of these kinds of paintings, produced in a more casual environment, was bracketed by the appreciation of the participants' more complex and polished studio creations known for the sophistication of their brushwork, colouration and compositions. Their full-blown talents can be seen in hanging scrolls made by two of the collaborators on *Pine, Bamboo, Chrysanthemum and Rock*: Hine Taizan's 1845 *Studio in the Shade of Wutong Trees* (fig. 4.36) and Yamamoto Chiku'un's monumental landscape of 1883, *Three Friends of Winter* (fig. 4.37). Rather than display the sophistication of their finest studio productions, collaborative works such as the one under discussion here focused on the relationship between the participants and the intended recipients.

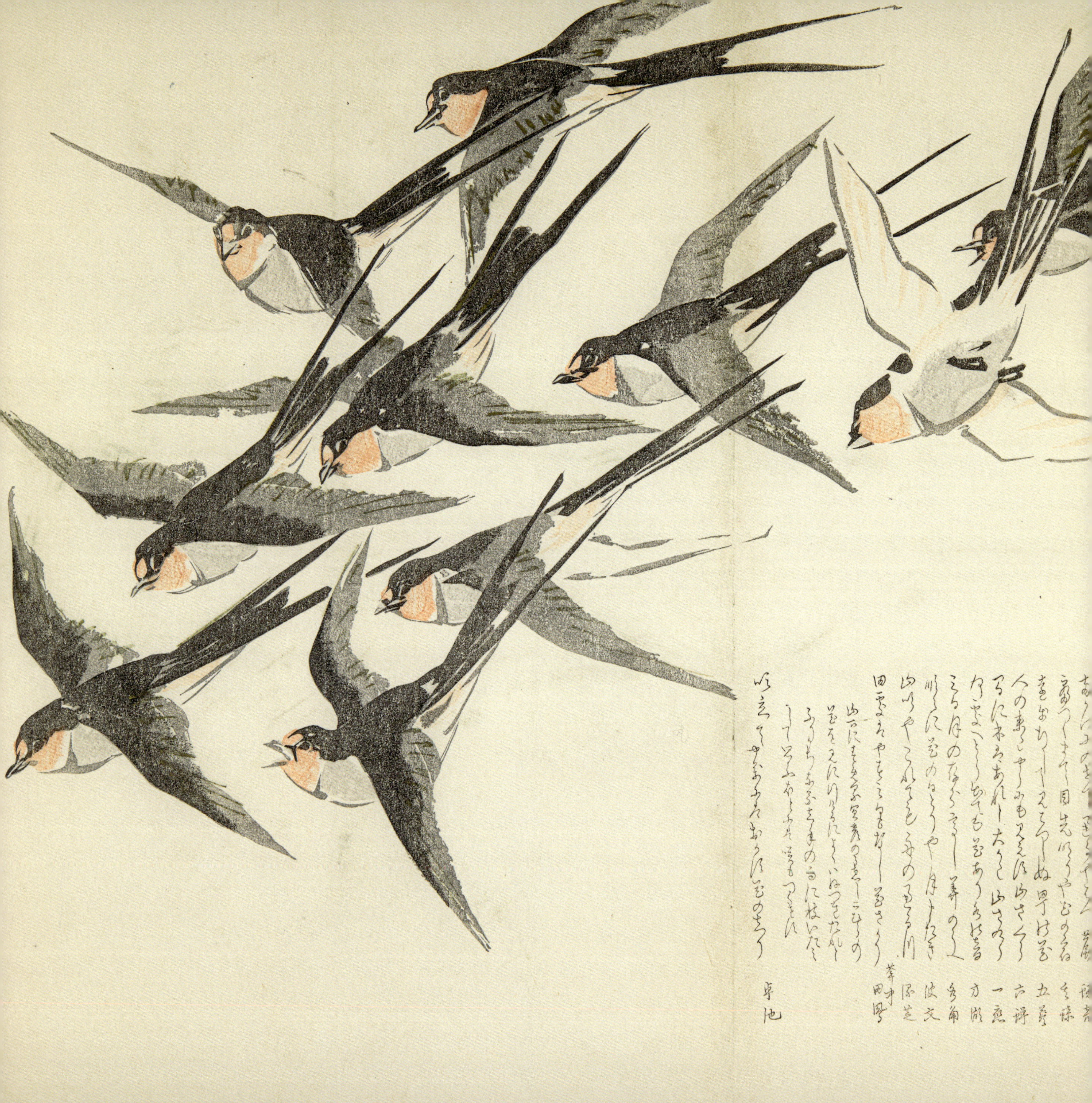

*Akiko Yano*

# 5 Poems and images

Poems and images sit together naturally in Japanese art. Each is distinct in its expression but no stranger to the other. In the tradition of East Asian art theory, poetry is often termed a 'picture with sound' and a picture 'poetry without sound'. Japan's aristocratic culture in the ninth to tenth centuries of the Heian period favoured the practice of composing poems inspired by paintings on large folding screens – frequently with seasonal themes incorporating sites famous in poetry – and conversely paintings on screens were sometimes made based on motifs from poems.

In the late Edo period of the eighteenth and nineteenth centuries, poems and images were still regularly encountered together, each enhancing the other. Although professional poets and artists are usually the focus of scholarly attention, what makes Edo-period Japan exciting – in cultural and in social

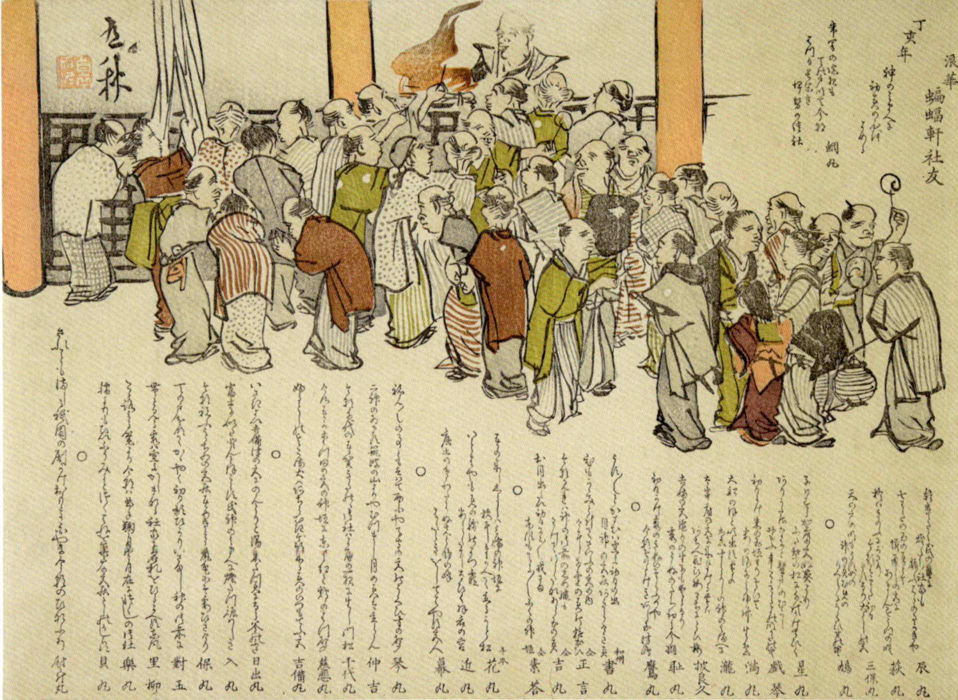

**Previous page**
Detail of fig. 5.27.

**5.1**
Ueda Kōchō (artist) and 32 poets, *Okera-matsuri Festival*, 1827. Surimono, colour woodblock. 34.7 × 47.1 cm. British Museum, London, 2021,3013.353. Purchase made possible by the JTI Japanese Acquisition Fund. Ex-coll.: Dr Scott Johnson.

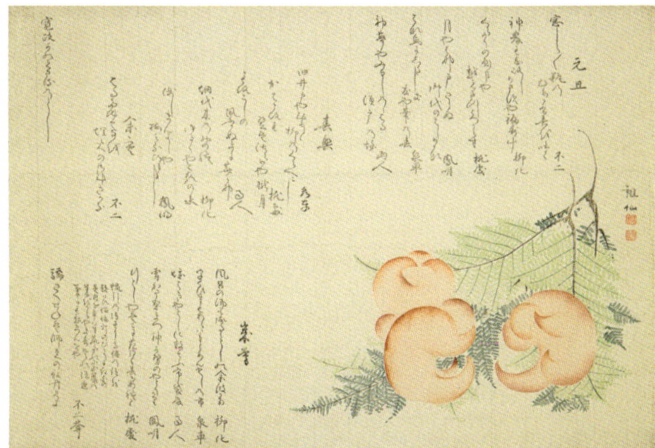

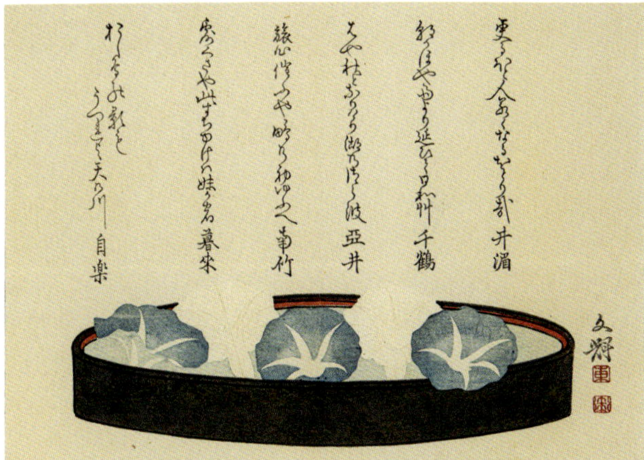

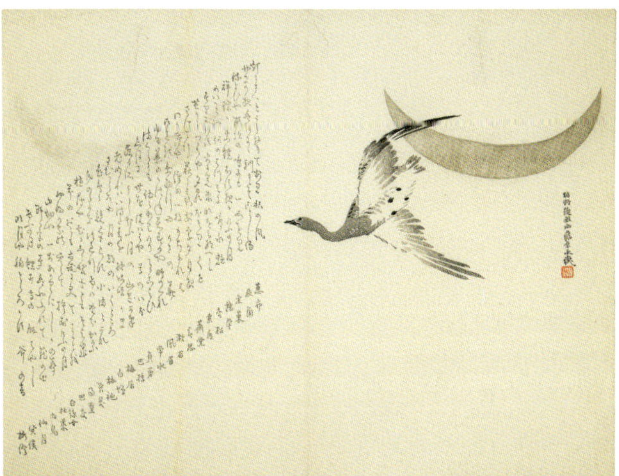

terms – is that opportunities to learn and practise arts as lifelong hobbies were open to people from all walks of life. Both poetry and painting seem to have been popular hobby subjects. Among the different types of poetry, the composition of Chinese poetry (kanshi) was demanding because it required a knowledge of classical Chinese. Poetry in Japanese, following on from a time-honoured aristocratic tradition, developed two major variations from the seventeenth century onwards. One is kyōka and the other is haiku. Kyōka, generally translated as 'crazy verse', is a 31-syllable classical-style verse with up-to-date witty twists. Well known even outside Japan, haiku (or haikai as a literary genre) is the most widely practised form, consisting of an even briefer 17 syllables, commonly incorporating words referencing a season or seasonal motifs. Thanks to its conciseness, haiku is accessible to everyone; it is inherently a communal literary art.[1] In its original form, one poem was expected to be followed by another composed

**5.2** *above*
Mori Sosen (artist) and 18 poets, *Monkey-Shaped Talismans and Fern*, 1800. Surimono, colour woodblock. 39.3 × 56.6 cm. British Museum, London, 2021,3013.177. Purchase made possible by the JTI Japanese Acquisition Fund. Ex-coll.: Dr Scott Johnson.

**5.3** *centre*
Yabuta Bunki (artist) and 6 poets, *Morning Glory Flowers in a Basin*, from an album, before 1837. Surimono, colour woodblock. 18.5 × 12.8 cm (album covers). British Museum, London, 2021,3013.1539.1–15. Purchase made possible by the JTI Japanese Acquisition Fund. Ex-coll.: Dr Scott Johnson.

**5.4** *below*
Kanō Eigaku (artist) and 25 poets, *Goose and Crescent Moon*, c. 1820. Surimono, colour woodblock. 38.2 × 49.2 cm. British Museum, London, 2021,3013.5. Purchase made possible by the JTI Japanese Acquisition Fund. Ex-coll.: Dr Scott Johnson.

in response to the imagery of the previous verse. Such a sequence of resonance among members of a group created a larger collective literary work known as *renga*, or 'linked verse'.

Poetry circles were usually centred around a 'master' poet and by the mid-eighteenth century were common throughout Japan. Regular and intermittent meetings of poets were often commemorated with privately commissioned prints recording the poems and including substantial pictures. One print, for instance, names thirty-two poets and depicts a New Year's event at Kyoto's Yasaka Shrine, during which each worshipper was given a sacred flame, a symbol to start the new year in peace (fig. 5.1). These prints, called surimono, were beautifully produced and were distributed among the members, their friends and acquaintances (see p. 31). In Kyoto and Osaka, surimono with haiku were more common than those with kyōka.

Many examples were produced for occasions such as New Year and spring, summer and autumn (figs 5.2–5.4), but surimono were not just records

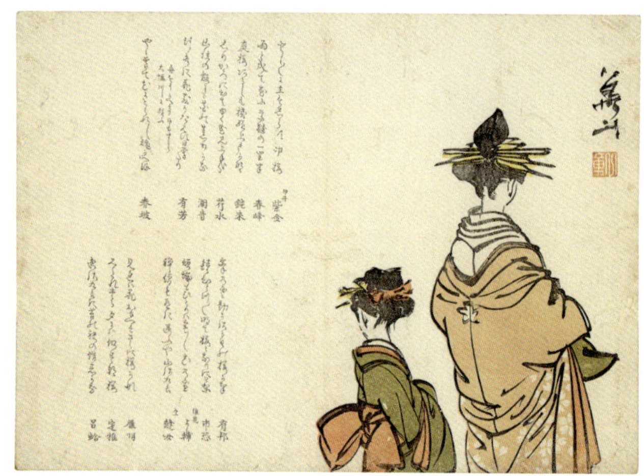

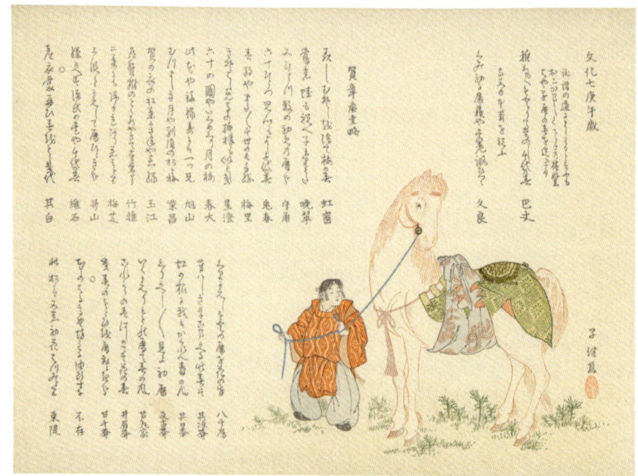

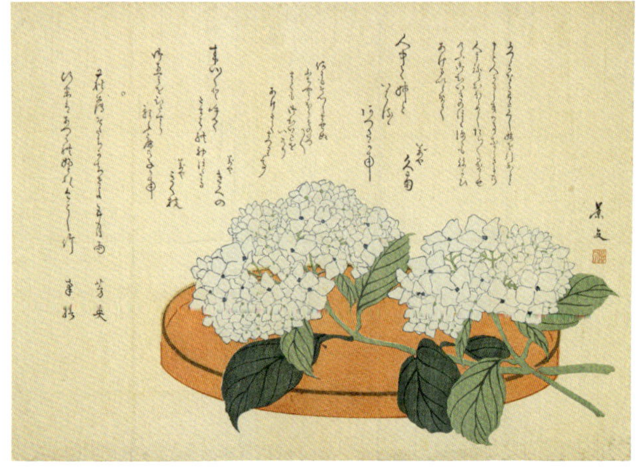

**5.5** *above*
Yokoyama Kazan (artist) and 14 poets, *Courtesan and Girl Attendant*, before 1810. Surimono, colour woodblock. 38.4 × 51.4 cm. British Museum, London, 2021,3013.654. Purchase made possible by the JTI Japanese Acquisition Fund. Ex-coll.: Dr Scott Johnson.

**5.6** *centre*
Taga Shiken (artist) and 26 poets, *Boy Attendant with White Horse*, 1810. Surimono, colour woodblock. 39.3 × 52 cm. British Museum, London, 2021,3013.637. Purchase made possible by the JTI Japanese Acquisition Fund. Ex-coll.: Dr Scott Johnson.

**5.7** *below*
Matsumura Keibun (artist) and five poets, *Hydrangeas on a Tray*, early 1800s (before 1843). Surimono, colour woodblock. 38.9 × 52.3 cm. British Museum, London, 2021,3013.517. Purchase made possible by the JTI Japanese Acquisition Fund. Ex-coll.: Dr Scott Johnson.

of poetry group meetings. Friends also gathered together for outings and wrote poems, which were then recorded on these prints (fig. 5.5). Examples here celebrate the milestone sixtieth birthday of a poet with a picture of an auspicious white horse (fig. 5.6), or a trainee dancer attaining the status of her mentor (fig. 5.7). The text on the latter expresses gratitude to patrons for their support. The stunning design of hydrangeas on a tray in this composition would have been appropriate for a surimono that was most likely distributed to patrons as a summer gift.

## Making art together: collective creativity

Even a small selection of surimono conveys a sense of the spontaneous expression of the members of a circle – pictures, poems, calligraphy and overall layout. Nevertheless, artists' work in such printed formats has not been given due attention by scholars. The artists appearing in this book are almost all painters active in Kyoto and Osaka who had a broad clientele. Many composed single-artist as well as collective paintings (gassaku; see p. 16) and designs for surimono and illustrated books. A fascinating aspect of this period is that some of the poets contributed pictures as amateur painters alongside professional artists. Sometimes poems written by artists are recorded. The roles of artists and poets in printed collaborative works that include haiku and kyōka are more fluid than in a single-author literary or visual work. The relationships among them are dynamic.

The process to reach the final design in paintings with inscriptions seems to have differed from that of printed works. One example is *Yamauba and Kintarō* by Mori Tetsuzan (fig. 5.8). The two figures – an old woman (Yamauba) and a boy (Kintarō) – are based on the popular legend of a female demon who lived in the mountains and raised a boy possessing superhuman strength. In this hanging scroll, Yamauba looks far from monstrous, however, as she walks smiling and clasping the hand of the well-fed, healthy-looking Kintarō. He holds an axe, indicating his strength to cut down trees for firewood.

The Japanese poem (*waka*, classical-style verse in 31 syllables) at top left celebrates the aged mountain cherry (*yama-zakura*),

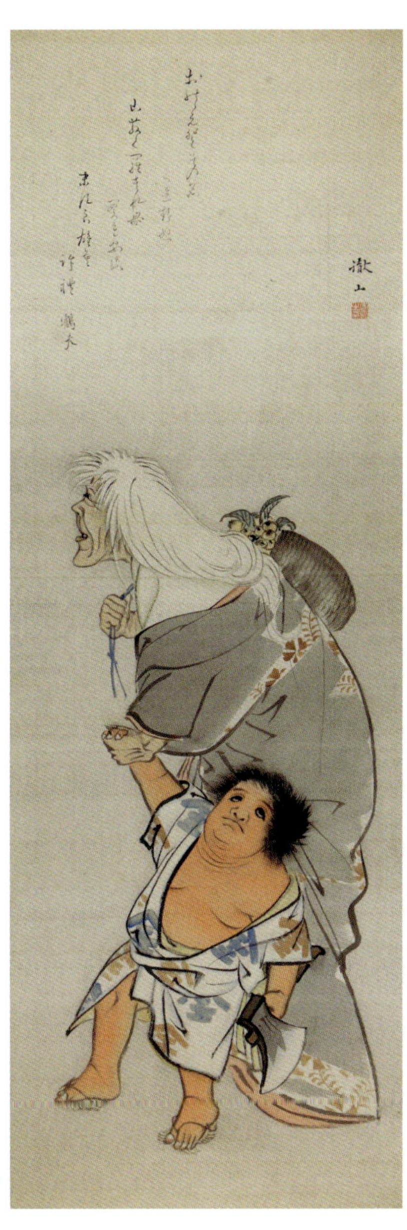

**5.8**
Mori Tetsuzan (artist) and Osada Tazuo (poet), *Yamauba and Kintarō*, c. early 1800s. Hanging scroll, ink and colour on silk. 101 × 33.1 cm. British Museum, London, 1881,1210,0.2306. Ex-coll.: William Anderson.



215

probably a reference to Yamauba, and contrasts this motif with an axe handle that will inevitably rot, a concept based on a classical Chinese tale and suggesting the passage of much time. It also praises Kintarō's strength and impressive presence:

| | |
|---|---|
| *ono no e to* | unlike axe handles |
| *sono na kuchisenu* | its reputation will never decay, |
| *yama-zakura* | the mountain cherry |
| *hana mo mi mo aru* | its flower [bravado] and fruit [substance] |
| *masurao zo kore* | his remarkable strength[2] |

The poem was composed by the wealthy Osaka businessman and poet Osada Tazuo (1783–1844). The history surrounding the creation of this work is not known: the poem may have been inscribed by Tazuo as a response to the painting. Alternatively, the entire project may have been a collaborative work by Tetsuzan and Tazuo, since both lived in Osaka. Whatever the circumstances, text and image directly interact, no doubt intended to elicit a response from the viewer.

## Interplay of text and image: poetry anthologies and illustrated books

In his preface to the printed illustrated haiku anthology, *Album of Auspicious Birds* (*Ranpō-jō*, 1806) (fig. 5.9), the Kyoto poet Emori Gekkyo (1756–1824) explains that one Tenrai from Chikugo province (in present-day Fukuoka prefecture) was fortunate enough to spend spring and summer in Kyoto and Osaka, and autumn and winter in Harima and Tajima provinces (present-day Hyōgo prefecture). This was thanks to the generosity of his friends and acquaintances from various haiku networks. To express his heart-felt gratitude for the hospitality of his fellow poets, Tenrai conceived the idea of compiling an album of the haiku assembled as a result of his interactions with professional and amateur poets in the places he had visited. The album paper, most likely commissioned by Tenrai, is printed with delicate blue dragon-patterned borders. The poets' places of origin are recorded next to their pen names (gō): they include towns and villages around Kyoto and Osaka and those along the route from Chikugo. Among the poets are a small number of women and a boy. Two poets specify that they are 'on a pilgrimage', which perhaps indicates that their encounter with Tenrai was fleeting.

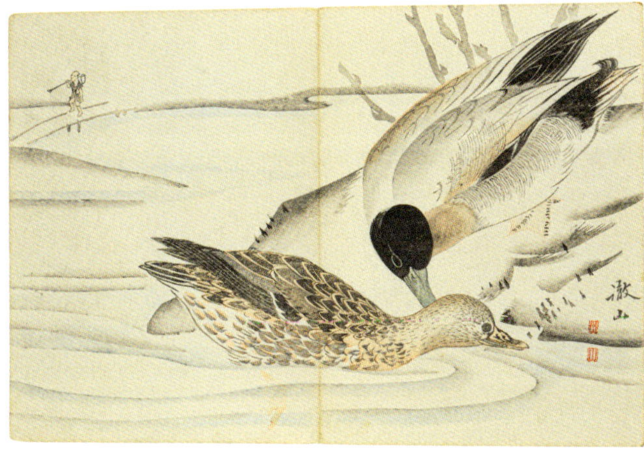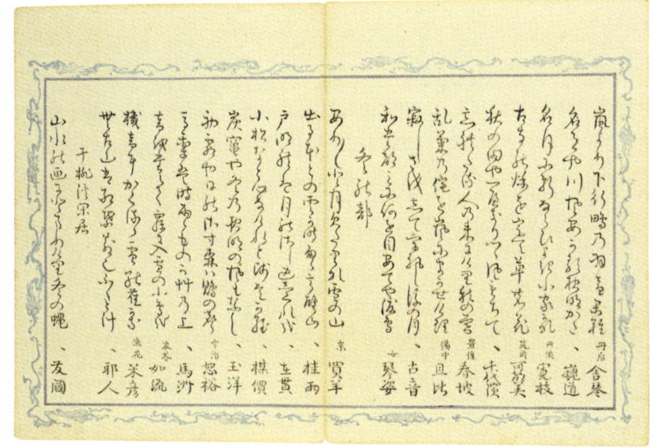



**5.9**
Hōen, Mori Tetsuzan, Nakai Rankō, Watanabe Nangaku (artists), Tei Sekijō (C: Cheng Chicheng, calligrapher) and over 270 poets, *Album of Auspicious Birds* (*Ranpō-jō*), 1 vol., 1806. Album, colour woodblock. 26.5 × 18.5 cm (cover). British Museum, London, 1979,0305,0.211. Ex-coll.: Jack Hillier.

Pictures by major artists from Kyoto and Osaka alternate between double-page spreads of poems.[3] Mori Tetsuzan's composition of a pair of ducks at a pond, captured close-up, may allude to the album's title *Ranpō-jō*. 'Ran' is a mythical bird with auspicious connotations and '*hō*' ('*pō*') means 'phoenix'. When placed together, these symbolise the harmony between two birds, and by extension between a couple or friends. In Tetsuzan's work, the human figure in the distance appears relaxed, perhaps heading home from a day's work. He looks tiny against the impressive naturalistically rendered birds, as if to playfully suggest an upside-down view of the world. The frontispiece calligraphy is by Tei Sekijō (Cheng Chicheng, also Yi Bingshou, 1754–1815), a Chinese calligrapher who frequently visited Nagasaki and whose works were much sought after by Japanese sinophiles, including daimyō lords. The colophon records the names of the block-cutters for image and text, the printers, the editor (Tenrai) and the publisher in Kyoto, Kikuya Tahei (b. 1756).

*White Silk, Ornate Silk: An Album* (*Soken-jō*, 1768) is a folding album printed in the elegant black-background technique, imitating the effect of stone-rubbings (fig. 5.10). The title, referring to two contrasting colours of sumptuous silk fabric, is an unexpected choice for a book printed in black and white. In a Confucian context, the pairing of pure white and elegant colour can be read as an analogy for the good nature with which a person was born and the polite social skills acquired later in life. The title may imply both the essence and the appearance of the plants in this album.

Each of the thirty-six double pages of *White Silk, Ornate Silk* has a Chinese poem on the right and a picture on the left. The poems are by the Zen Buddhist monk Daiten (1719–1801) and the pictures are by the artist Itō Jakuchū, both

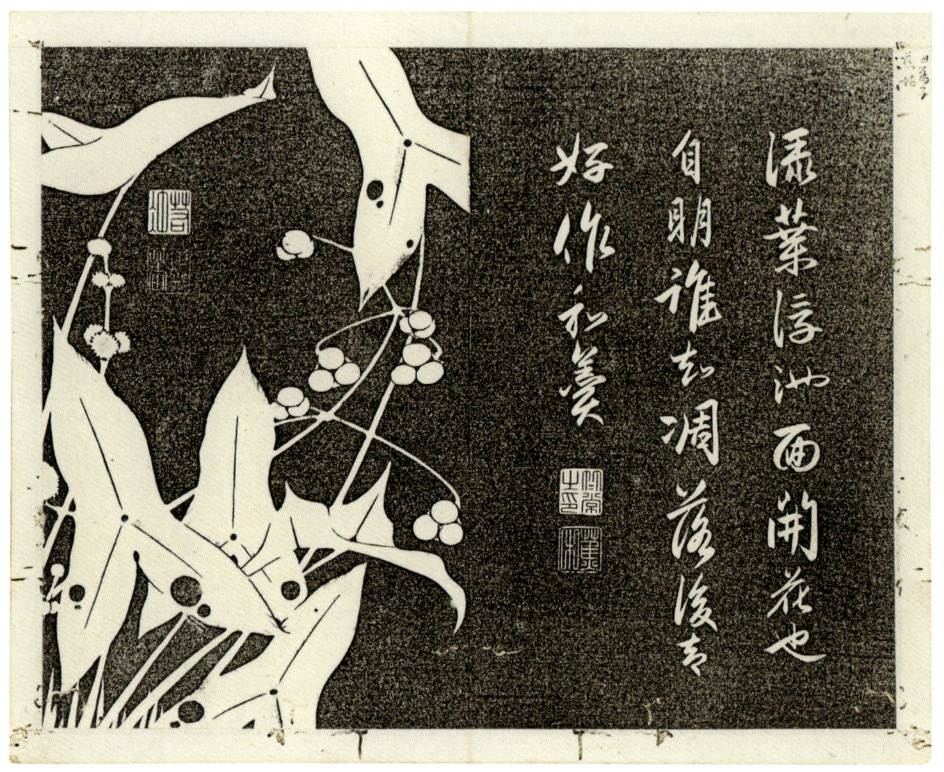

**5.10**
Itō Jakuchū (artist) and Daiten
Kenjō (poet), *White Silk, Ornate
Silk: An Album* (*Soken-jō*),
1 vol., 1767–8. Album,
woodblock. 31 × 19 cm (cover).
British Museum, London,
1979,0305,0.114. Ex-coll.:
Jack Hillier.

active in Kyoto. Daiten was said to have a gentle, intelligent character. Highly regarded by his fellow literati for his Chinese verse, he was friends with many artists and scholars, including Ike no Taiga and Kimura Kenkadō, as well as with samurai and courtiers. He was also Jakuchū's spiritual and artistic mentor, and friend.

Before devoting his life to painting, Jakuchū ran his family's vegetable wholesale business. His depictions of nature express an unmistakably unique vision. In *White Silk, Ornate Silk* the small and large black circles on the leaves of the sleek arrowhead plant convey an enigmatic and almost fantastical feel. In response to Jakuchū's picture,[4] Daiten's poem takes an unforeseen, humorously down-to-earth turn in the last line:

green leaves floating over the pond
blossoms brighten upward
after the flowers have fallen, who knows –
it might taste good in a stewed dish?[5]

The colophon in the album states that the original set of paintings (by Jakuchū) and poetry calligraphy were made into a printed album by Daiten's pupils and that the set of woodblocks was owned by the temple Junshō-ji in Kyoto. The postscript is by the Kyoto aristocrat Yotsutsuji Kinmichi (1728–1788),[6] demonstrating that a range of individuals was involved in the production of this work.

A fair number of Maruyama-Shijō artists designed pictures for surimono and poetry anthologies. In one such surimono from 1793, mounted as a handscroll, thirty-three poets each composed a haiku on the theme of spring (fig. 5.11). The compiler of this work, Nishimura Teiga (d. 1826), was a Kyoto merchant, author and poet. He states in the title description that the season of shimmering heat (*itoyū*) has arrived. It is a natural phenomenon caused by warmth in which vertical 'strands' of glistening air appear as if rising from the ground. Teiga explains that the threads are lengthening even as he collates all the spring verses for the print: 'So, I now give this scroll the title "*itoyū*" and pray that the friendship of this group may long continue like the strands of shimmering heat.'

Some of the poets have their place of origin, locations in Ōmi province (present-day Shiga prefecture) and Fushimi (an area south of Kyoto), inscribed next to their pen names. Teiga is unacknowledged, confirming the theory that all those without a named place of origin most likely hail from the site of production, in this case Kyoto. Teiga was a wholesaler of sewing needles who later in life turned his focus to the composition of haiku; he built an atelier called Haisendō ('Hall of Haiku Immortals') in Kyoto's Higashiyama district.[7] This group was probably a local Kyoto haiku circle centred around Teiga. Some in the group were professional poets, others were merchants or otherwise unknown. At least one female poet is among them, and her poem, composed under the pen name Shinjo ('Devotional Woman'), reads:

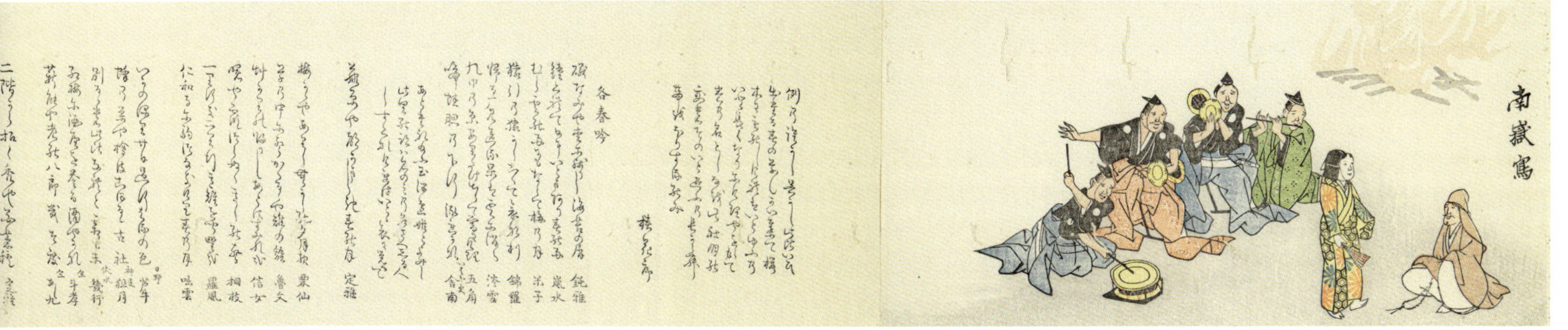

**5.11**
Watanabe Nangaku (artist) and 33 poets, *Torchlight Nō Performance* (detail), 1793. Surimono, colour woodblock, mounted as a handscroll. 19 × 138.2 cm. British Museum, London, 2021,3013.1535. Purchase made possible by the JTI Japanese Acquisition Fund. Ex-coll.: Dr Scott Johnson.

Watanabe Nangaku, celebrated for his surimono and work in poetry anthologies, contributed a picture of a 'torchlight nō' performance (*takigi-nō*) to this surimono. The to-date unidentified play shows the masked main character in a female role, the actor's raised toes an indication that he is performing a dance. Nangaku, however, imbues it with his typically warm and subtly comical note: four musicians play drums and flute, vigorously accompanying the two performers. At least one among the thirty-plus poems refers to a 'torchlight nō', which indicates the season of spring. The poems and pictures are loosely connected and appear to provide two different dimensions.

The relationship between the artist Nangaku and the Teiga surimono group has yet to be clarified, but this design is in fact Nangaku's earliest known documented work, done when he was 26. He would subsequently produce images for a number of surimono, as well as for haiku and kyōka anthologies. An example is *Roots of the Heart* (*Kokoro no nezashi*, 1793) (fig. 5.12),[8] which contains several names of the same poets found on the Teiga surimono. It is

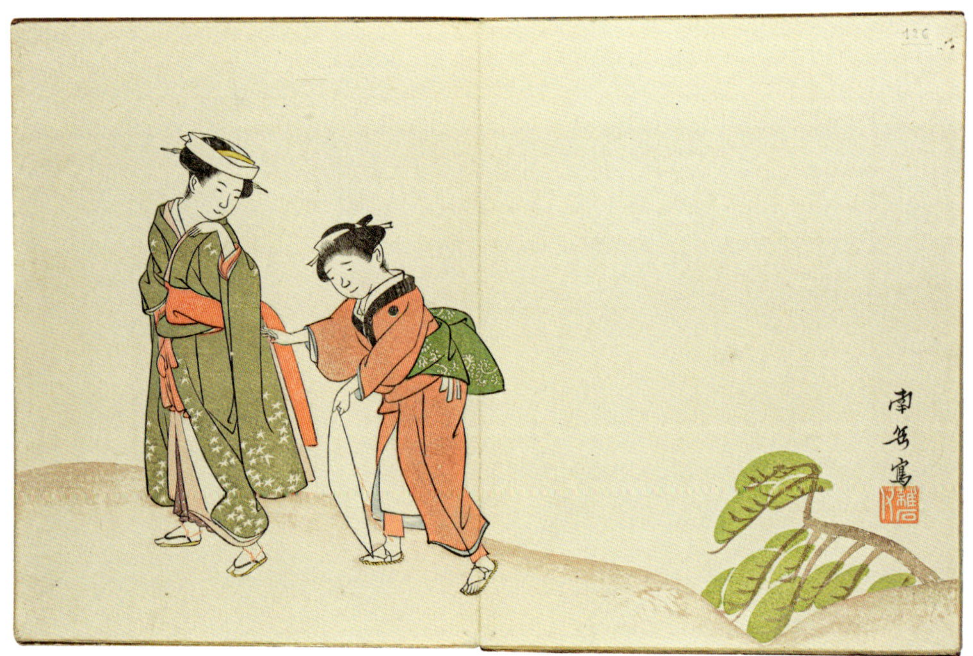

**5.12**
Gen Ki, Go Shun, Kazaore Yūjō, Mikuma Katen, Watanabe Nangaku (artists) and over 120 poets, *Roots of the Heart* (*Kokoro no nezashi*; original title missing, attributed title)*, 1 vol., 1793. Album, colour woodblock. 27.8 × 21.1 cm (cover). British Museum, London, 1979,0305,0.169. Ex-coll.: Jack Hillier.

therefore likely that artists and certain groups of poets formed personal ties, not just as professional surimono illustrators but as active members within a particular coterie.

Artists regularly collaborated to produce pictures that resonated with the poems included. *Coast Road Kyōka Contest* (*Kaidō kyōka awase*, 1811) is a kyōka poetry anthology jointly issued by Osaka and Kyoto publishers (fig. 5.13). The poems are all by the author Ueda Akinari, who was multitalented and well known for his sharp temper and trenchant character. The preface, which was written by Akinari's good friend the artist Kawamura Bunpō, notes that he was always able to visit Akinari at his eastern Kyoto studio, despite the author's refusal to see anyone else. Akinari wrote the preface for Bunpō's picture handscroll of Kyoto's local festivals (see fig. 2.35a–b). Bunpō recounts how one day Akinari showed him a roll of paper with his poems that captured the lively scenes along the country's roads and post stations. The poems were divided into 'left' and 'right' as if composed for a courtly poetry competition. Akinari asked Bunpō to create pictures to accompany the poems on the right and Nangaku to do those on the left. In the fifth match, Akinari incorporates 'teahouse' and 'barber' in the paired poems:[9]

Teahouse: fifth match, left

| | |
|---|---|
| *yasurawan* | let's take a break |
| *kemuri kuyurasu* | smoking |
| *asaka no ka* | in the fragrance of morning flowers |
| *dare kurushichō* | who would be uncomfortable |
| *Abe-gawa no yado* | at the inn along the Abe River |

Nangaku's corresponding teahouse scene is animated (fig. 5.13, left) – travellers rest on a bench, their bags on the ground, as they smoke and order drinks. The teahouse server, with a bemused but somewhat annoyed expression, brings out cups. Above her, banners advertising various sake brands flutter in the wind.

Bunpō's tranquil barber scene offers a striking counterpoint (fig. 5.13, right). A man sits in a streamside hut, his head tilted backwards as a barber gives him a shave. The sign at the window reads 'your hair dressed and pate shaved for 16 *mon*' (about £3). A solitary gecko scuttles up the shop wall. A plant in a shallow basin at the rear window seems to suggest the barber's tender care and sensitivity. Akinari's poem reads:

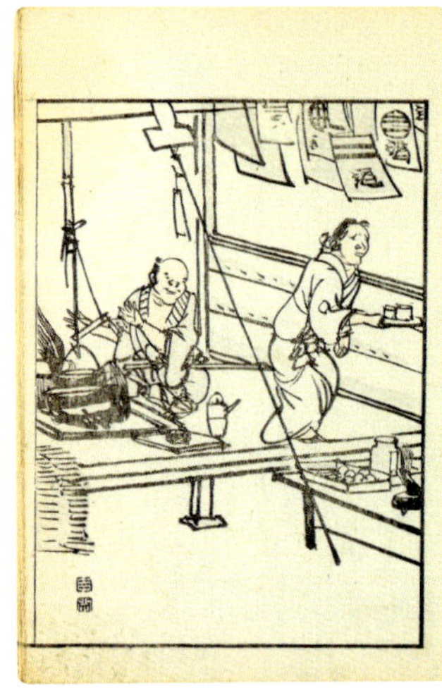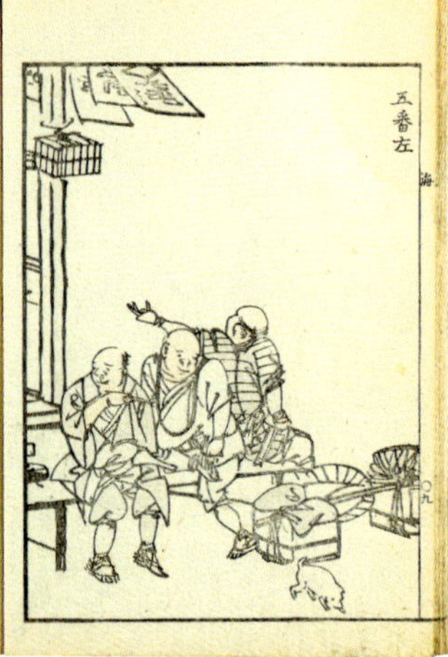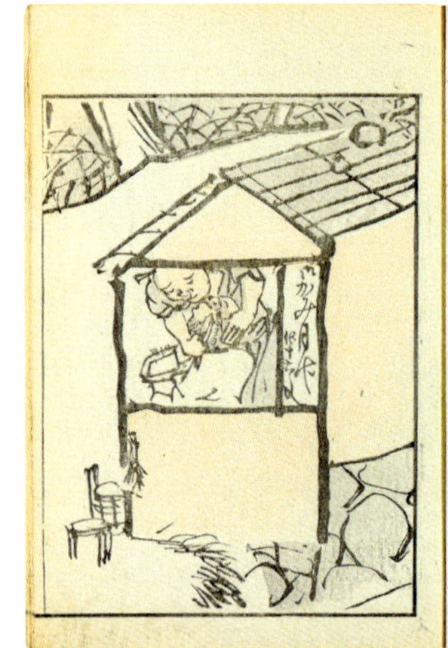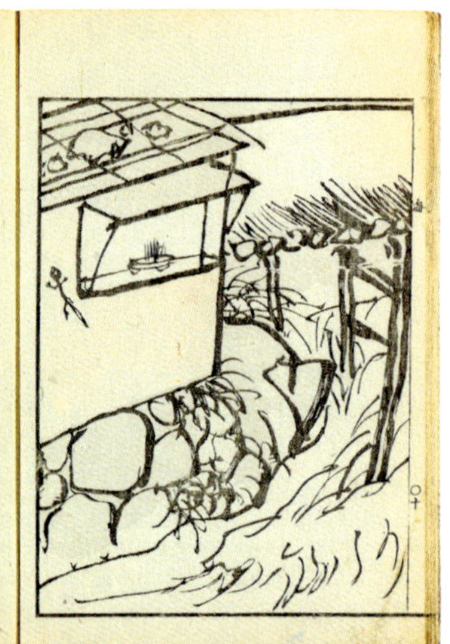

Barber shop: fifth match, right

| *kakinadeshi* | barely managed to contain |
| *hina no nagaji no* | messy hair after the long journey |
| *odoro-gami* | from the countryside |
| *akete iranan* | I'll enter the capital tomorrow |
| *asu no miyako ni* | my hair nicely tied back |



Bunpō was a prolific artist, best known for his paintings of Chinese figures (see fig 4.11), urban scenes (see figs 2.34, 2.35a–b, 4.22–4.23) and publications of picture albums (see figs 4.23, 4.25). At first glance, his brushwork appears bold, but a closer examination reveals that he intricately depicts the human figure by applying layers of various brushstroke types.

Bunpō is not generally known for his surimono, but fortunately some rare examples by him exist, such as *Begonia and Kinglet* from before 1821 (fig. 5.14), in which the greens of the leaves and pinkish red flowers provide a refreshing contrast. While the plant is captured naturalistically, the two white round spots on the bottom right leaf – probably dew – are graphically stylised. The poets who contribute to this surimono are from central Kyoto, northern Kyoto and Ōmi. Each of their poems incorporate autumnal scenes and motifs, including a lingering moon at dusk. The choice of subject for the accompanying picture was likely left to Bunpō.

Poetry anthologies with poets and artists from a broad spectrum of society spawned vigorous creative interaction between text and image. For example,

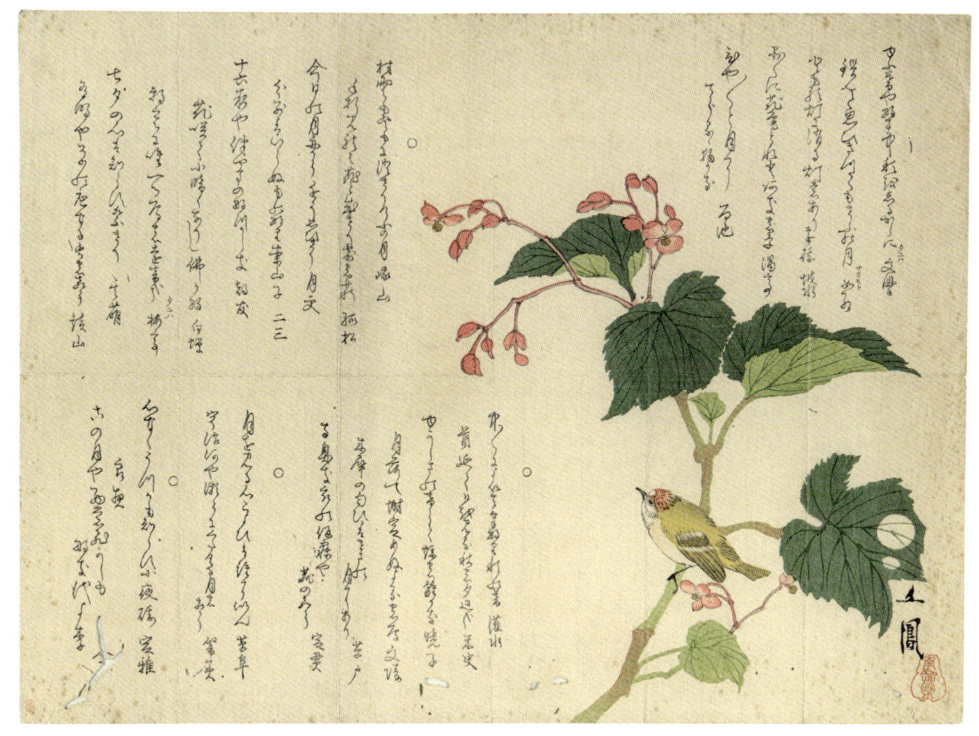



**5.14**
Kawamura Bunpō and 23 poets, *Begonia and Kinglet*, before 1821. Surimono, colour woodblock. 38.4 × 51.3 cm. British Museum, London, 2016,3029.1. Gift of Dr Ellis Tinios.

in a two-page spread from *Spring Picture-Contest* (*Haru no e-awase*, 1796) (fig. 5.15), the right side has a picture of a rapeseed plant about to bloom by the Kyoto artist and monk Geppō (see figs 4.12–4.13) and a poem by Yūjō, who states he is from Osaka. The verse reads:

| | |
|---|---|
| *haru no mizu* | spring water warming |
| *miya mo watarase* | a prince would have |
| *tamai keri* | crossed over [to see his dear lady][10] |

The plant's spindly stalks extend energetically upwards as if they are competing with the poem in the shared space of this vertical composition. On the left page, the poem and picture have a horizontal orientation. Rendered using rich, dark ink tones, the sturdy leaves of mooli (*daikon*) are spread out and appear to be firmly rooted in the ground. The poem reads:

| | |
|---|---|
| *tsumikusa no* | out picking spring greens |
| *ame ni narubeki* | surely it will rain |
| *yūbe kana* | this evening |

The poet is a certain 'Richō from Fushimi', and the artist, who signs as Shishin, is the young Matsumura Keibun (see figs 2.22, 3.26, 3.32, 5.7).[11] The diverse calligraphic styles suggests that each poet is likely to have brushed his or her own verse and signature; the artists would have then drawn the pictures and added their signatures. Each page has one poem and one picture from two individuals: each resonates with the other, yet they remain independent in their portrayals of an aspect of spring. It is intriguing to imagine how the poets and artists (or artists and poets) took turns to complete a one-page design before it was block-cut and printed.

The haiku anthology *Shell-Matching* (*Kai-awase*, 1820) again marries verse and imagery (fig. 5.16) to celebrate the sixtieth anniversary of the Osaka haiku poet Suganuma Kien (1765–1834). While artists composing pictures for a poetry anthology are usually from the same area as the compiler, the poets could be from across Japan, and here the range of poets is especially great. How exactly the participants knew one another, or whether they had ever met in person, invites further investigation, but Edo-period Japan did have highly developed mail and courier systems. Poems composed in regions far from where they were published could be sent considerable distances. Kyoto and

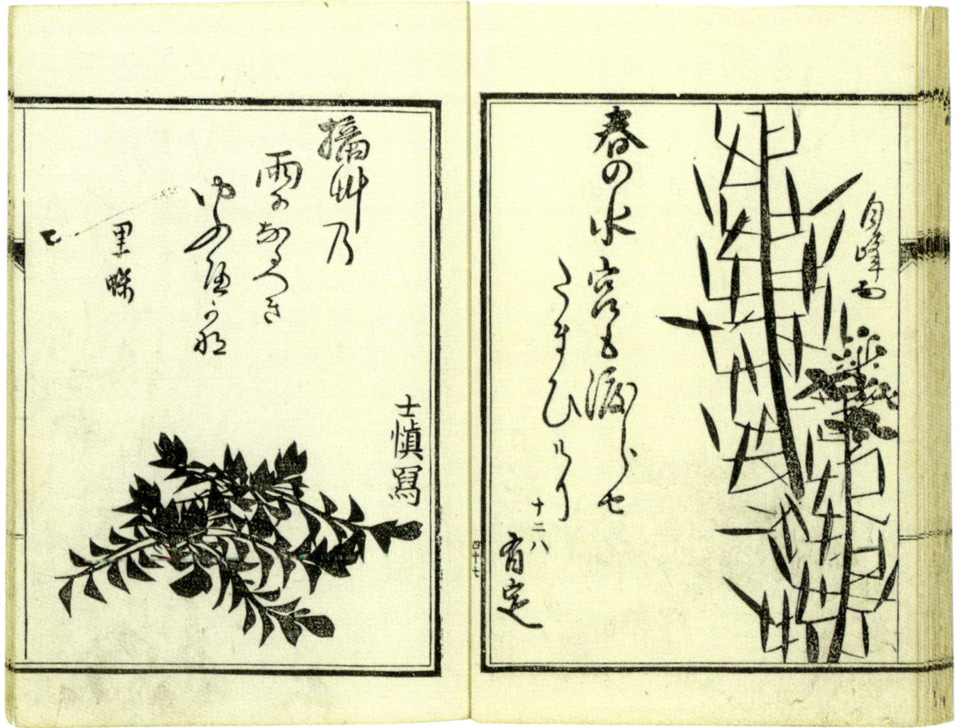

5.15
36 artists, including Kawamura Bunpō, Ki Baitei, Matsumura Keibun, Okamoto Toyohiko and Watanabe Nangaku, and over 70 poets, *Spring Picture-Contest* (*Haru no e-awase*), 1 vol., 1796. Illustrated book, woodblock. 23.5 × 16.5 cm (cover). British Museum, London, 1991,1112,0.113. Ex-coll.: Dr Scott Johnson.

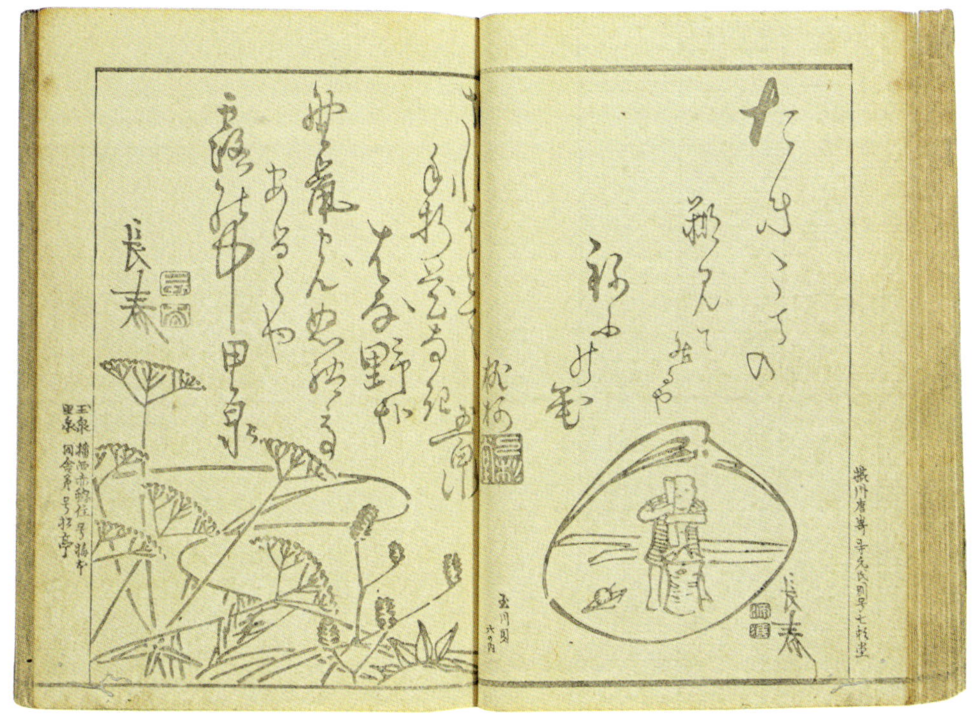

Osaka poetry publications, for example, include individuals from towns and cities from Matsumae on the northern island of Hokkaido to Kyushu in the far south-west (see map, p. 8).

*Shell-Matching* even has a poet from Korea, who uses the pen name Taihei-ō ('Old Man of Peace'), and the brief biography in the page margin records that he is a Korean official. He composes prose in Chinese instead of producing a Japanese haiku. His piece is paired with a contribution on the opposite page from a samurai of the Tsushima domain, on Tsushima island between Japan and Korea, which functioned during the Edo period as the diplomatic gateway between the two countries.

Probably owing to the celebratory nature of this anthology, some of the haiku are light-hearted. One monk from Suō province (in present-day Yamaguchi prefecture), with the pen name Kindō ('Hibiscus Hall'), has the following poem:

| | |
|---|---|
| *Shaka wa Shaka* | Shakyamuni does his job |
| *Kōshi wa Kōshi* | Confucius as well – |
| *yo wa hanami* | I enjoy cherry-blossom viewing |

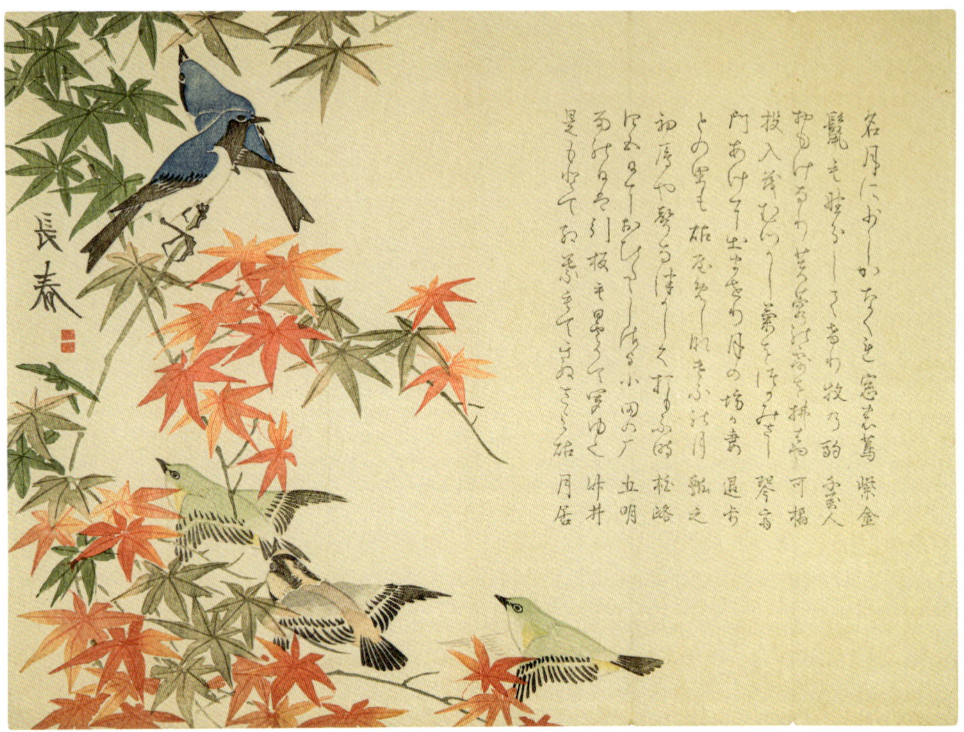

**5.17**
Nakamura Chōshun (Nagaharu; artist) and ten poets, *Birds and Autumn Foliage*, *c*. early 1800s (before 1824). Surimono, colour woodblock. 38.4 × 51 cm. British Museum, London, 2021,3013.128. Purchase made possible by the JTI Japanese Acquisition Fund. Ex-coll.: Hayashida Ryōhei; Dr Scott Johnson.

The nine artists who participated in this anthology are from Osaka.[12] Nakamura Chōshun (also read Nagaharu, active early nineteenth century) is the most prominent. His sense of graphic design and colour is extraordinary, as seen in a gorgeous surimono depicting birds and autumn foliage (fig. 5.17). Little is known about Chōshun's life, except that almost all his known works today are in printed form and he actively collaborated with poets.[13] Artists contributed not only pictures but occasionally poems as well in surimono and anthologies.

## From painting to print: the art of surimono

Surimono and illustrated poetry anthologies have rarely been integrated into the study of an artist's body of work.[14] This is particularly the case for Kyoto and Osaka artists, who were mainly painters, but for whom printed designs were no less important – cross-genre approaches are essential to understanding the collective art and artistic interactions of the late Edo period. The delicate quality of the artist's work in surimono is instantly noticeable. For example, Go Shun's charming design of a rabbit holding a pestle (fig. 5.18) is based on a popular East Asian image of a beautiful full moon in autumn, in which people perceive a rabbit pounding rice cakes.[15]

A scene of a local festival by the Kyoto artist Hatta Koshū (1760–1822) captures his typically lively brushwork in a surimono made by a local haiku group in Ōmi called Seiko-sha ('West Lake Group') (fig. 5.19). West Lake in China was a famous beauty spot and a well-known literary and artistic trope in Japan. Since classical times, Lake Biwa in Ōmi was treated as Japan's 'West Lake'. There are two lion dancers under the costume, musicians, a man with a fan wearing a contented smile, and two men towards the front who are probably the bearers of the portable festival shrine. One wipes away sweat with a cloth, while the other relaxes, lighting his tobacco pipe. Two children romp around them. Koshū's style of figures is at once spontaneous and playful.

Flowers and plants are another common surimono subject. *Millet Plant* by Murakami Tōshū (d. 1820) (fig. 5.20) is a relatively early example of a surimono in a large format with a dominating, painterly image. It is possible to date the work to 1788–9 based on the death date of the last poet, Takai Kitō

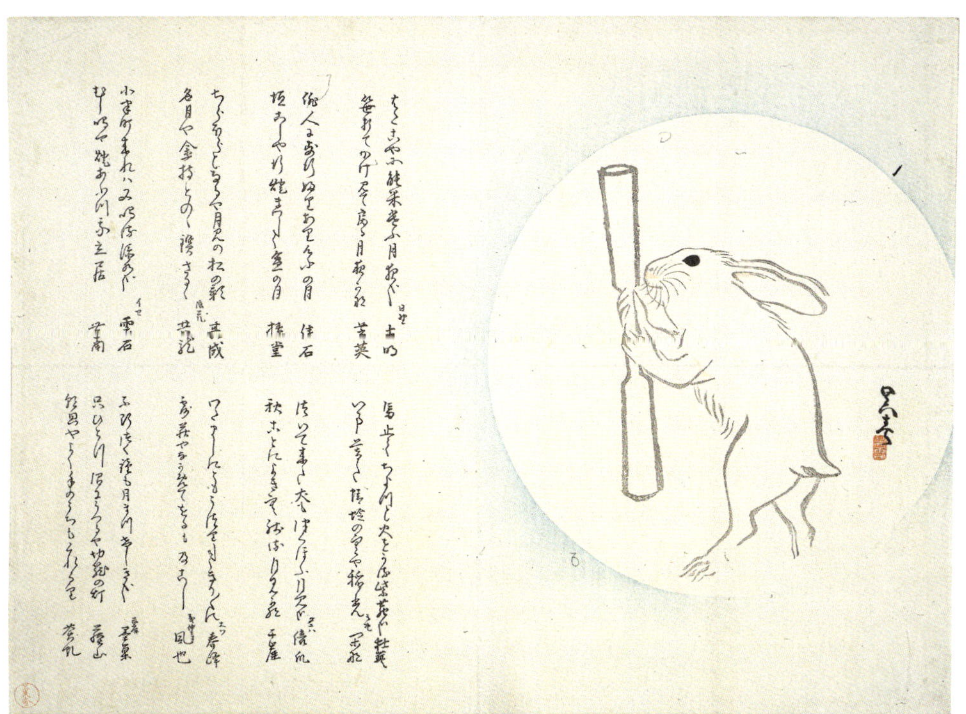

**5.18**
Go Shun (artist) and 17 poets, *Moon Rabbit, c.* 1800–11. Surimono, colour woodblock. 38.4 × 52.4 cm. British Museum, London, 1993,0405,0.1. Purchase funded by the Brooke Sewell Bequest. Ex-coll.: Theodor Scheiwe.

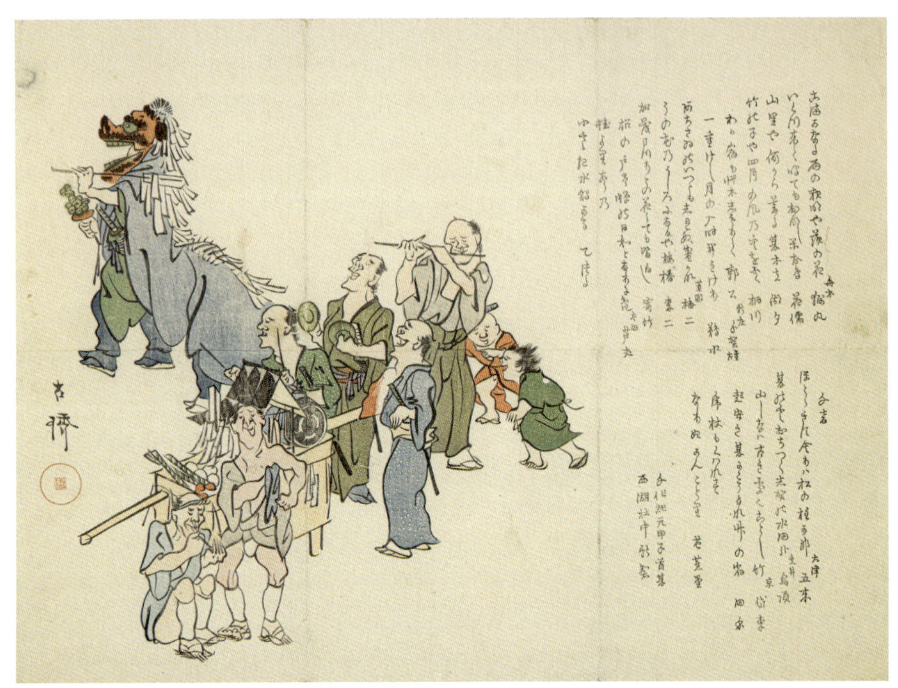

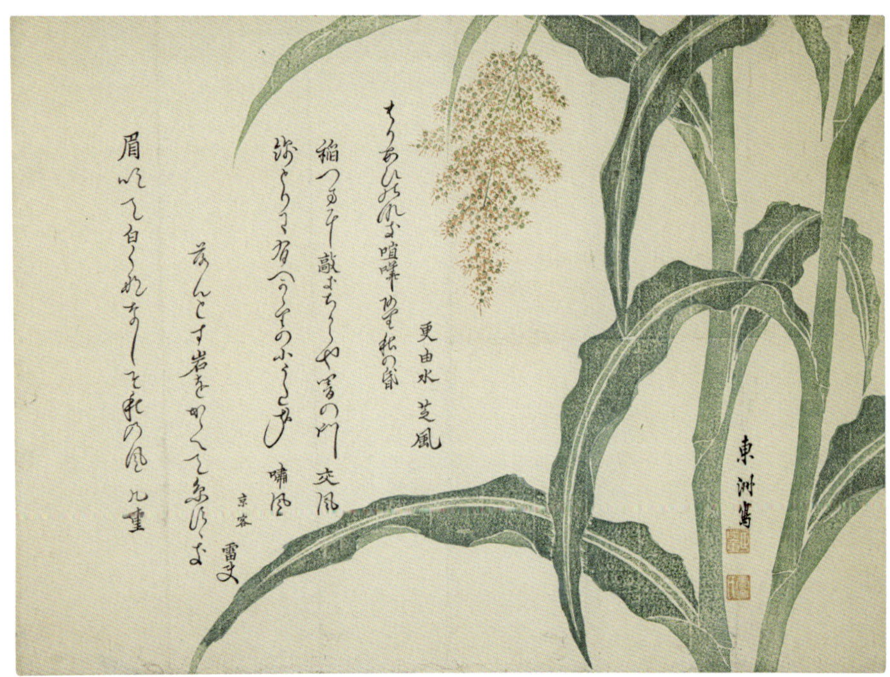

**5.19**
Hatta Koshū (artist) and 16
poets, *Local Festival*, 1804.
Surimono, colour woodblock.
43.6 × 57.4 cm. British Museum,
London, 2021,3013.265.
Purchase made possible by the
JTI Japanese Acquisition Fund.
Ex-coll.: Dr Scott Johnson.

**5.20**
Murakami Tōshū (artist) and five
poets, *Millet Plant*, *c.* 1788–9.
Surimono, colour woodblock.
38.8 × 51.9 cm. British Museum,
London, 2021,3013.182. Purchase
made possible by the JTI
Japanese Acquisition Fund.
Ex-coll.: Dr Scott Johnson.

(1741–1789), who was one of the most trusted pupils of the celebrated haiku poet and artist Yosa Buson, and the first poet's inscription, which states that he had just changed his pen name.[16]

One of the most exceptional designs in surimono is Matsumura Keibun's elegant and naturalistic composition of hibiscus and begonia that accompanies a set of twelve poems on late summer and early autumn (fig. 5.21).[17] Neither the calligraphy nor the picture is visually subordinate. Each poem refers to seasonal motifs – the sound of insects, the beautiful moon, bush clover flowers, mushroom hunting and evening dew, among them. The poet Emori Gekkyo appears with other poets, some well known, others not. His verse reads:

| | |
|---|---|
| *samishisa o* | this feeling |
| *kari mo tsukusanu* | of sadness lingers |
| *susuki kana* | even after the pampas grass is cut away |

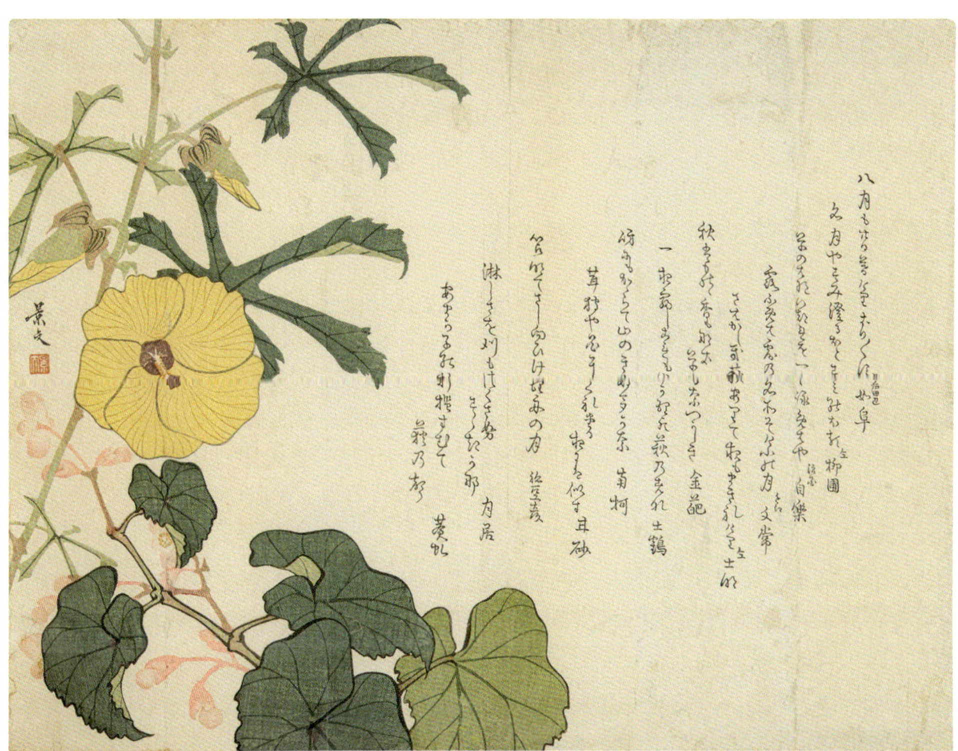

**5.21**
Matsumura Keibun (artist) and 12 poets, *Sunset Hibiscus and Begonia*, before 1824. Surimono, colour woodblock. 44.6 × 57.3 cm. British Museum, London, 2021,3013.262. Purchase made possible by the JTI Japanese Acquisition Fund. Ex-coll.: Dr Scott Johnson.

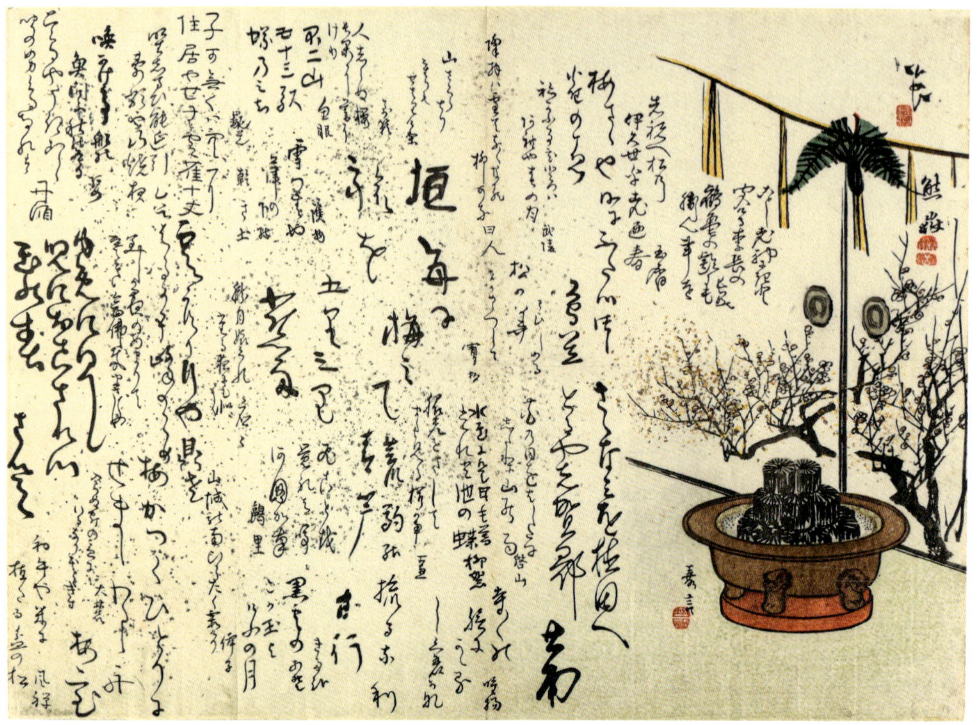

**5.22**
Murata Kagen, Oka Yūgaku, Ueda Kōchō (artists) and 80 poets, *New Year Celebration* (right sheet), 1826. Diptych surimono, colour woodblock. 37.8 × 51.8 cm. British Museum, London, 1993,0405,0.20.1–2. Purchase funded by the Brooke Sewell Bequest. Ex-coll.: Karel Reisz.

Paired with Keibun's picture of early autumn flowers, it adds a tinge of melancholy that enhances our full engagement with the surimono.

One extravagant production is a diptych commemorating a celebration (fig. 5.22). Its compiler is unknown – his large circular red seal at the end reads Gobatei ('Atelier of Five Horses'). The images are a collaborative work by three artists: Murata Kagen, Oka Yūgaku and Ueda Kōchō. Judging from the imagery – a fern and straw hanging decoration, white plum blossoms on the sliding-door panel and charcoal in a metal basin – the occasion was most likely the New Year. Each poem on the right sheet has a different calligraphic style, an indication that each poet brushed their own poem in one composition. They might have contributed them at a gathering, or perhaps the original sheet of paper was circulated among them. This surimono might well appear busy, but that sense of busyness conveys the energy of producing such a work with a large group of people, both professionals and amateurs. The artists, all from Osaka, are established figures.

At times an even greater number of artists collaborated to make a surimono. In this example (fig. 5.23), the haiku poems refer to autumn motifs. Nine artists – evident in the nine sets of signatures and seals – designed pictures of



230

autumn flowers with insects to accompany them. The result is a congenial and elegant bouquet. Some of the artists, including Oda Kaisen (1785–1862), Nakabayashi Chikutō (see fig. 3.12) and Higashiyama Giryō (active 1830s, son of Geppō), are better known as literati painters who depicted classical Chinese figures and landscapes. Providing pictures for surimono was not a genre limited to any particular school of artists.

A subgenre of surimono was created by performing artists such as kabuki or bunraku players (see pp. 73–4). The poets on a surimono with a picture of two empty cages for birds and insects by the Kyoto artist Yokoyama Kazan include kabuki actors from Osaka, a courtier, a wealthy merchant and several women whose occupations are unknown (fig. 5.24). It is unclear what brought this group together – possibly a celebration, a kabuki actor's name change or their retirement, all moments when celebratory surimono were issued and circulated among patrons.[18] One poem has a title 'On the occasion of mingling with a small group of people at a "House of Sparrows"', which makes it almost certain that they met in person. It could, however, be a later assemblage of poems by the last poet, the Kyoto merchant Shunpa, since he states in his long title inscription before his own poem that he is '(re)reading letters sent to me

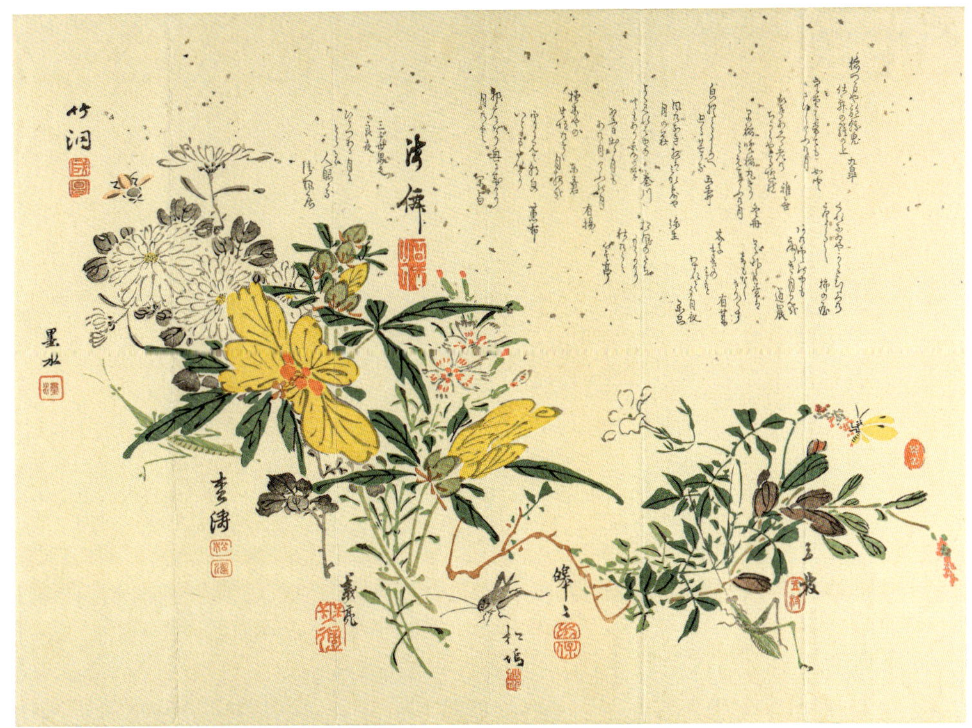

**5.23**
Bokusui, Gyokushi, Higashiyama Giryō, Kizan, Shirakami Kōkō, Nakabayashi Chikutō, Oda Kaisen, Shōtō, Shōu (artists) and 17 poets, *Autumn Flowers and Insects*, *c.* 1831. Surimono, colour woodblock. 35.4 × 47.5 cm. British Museum, London, 1993,0405,0.15. Purchase funded by the Brooke Sewell Bequest. Ex-coll.: Karel Reisz.

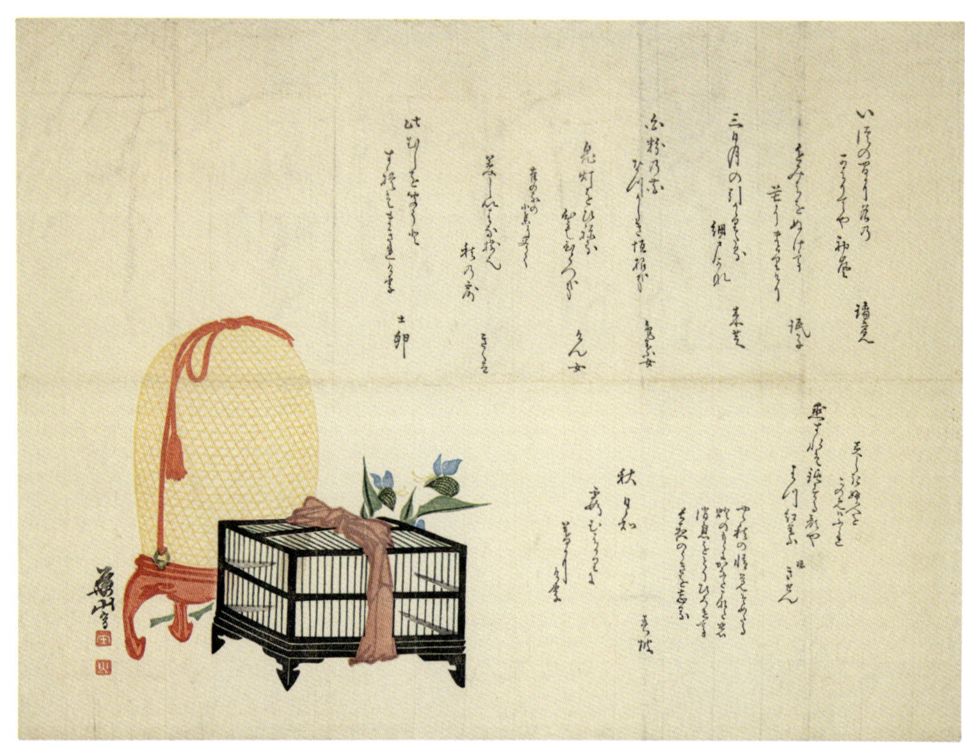

**5.24**
Yokoyama Kazan (artist) and
nine poets, *Insect and Bird
Cages*, *c.* 1800–10. Surimono,
colour woodblock. 43.8 ×
57.8 cm. British Museum,
London, 2021,3013.547.
Purchase made possible by the
JTI Japanese Acquisition Fund.
Ex-coll.: Dr Scott Johnson.

**5.25**
Yokoyama Kazan, *Three
Monkeys* (fragment), *c.* 1800–37.
Surimono, colour woodblock.
22.1 × 57.4 cm. British Museum,
London, 1993,0405,0.10.
Purchase funded by the
Brooke Sewell Bequest.

**5.26**
Yokoyama Kazan (artist) and
Daikō Sōgen (poet), *Puppies
and Lantern Plants*, early 1800s
(before 1837). Hanging scroll,
ink on paper. 101.2 × 27.8 cm.
British Museum, London,
2000,0724,0.6. Purchase funded
by Japanese Purchase Fund.
Ex-coll.: Dr Scott Johnson.

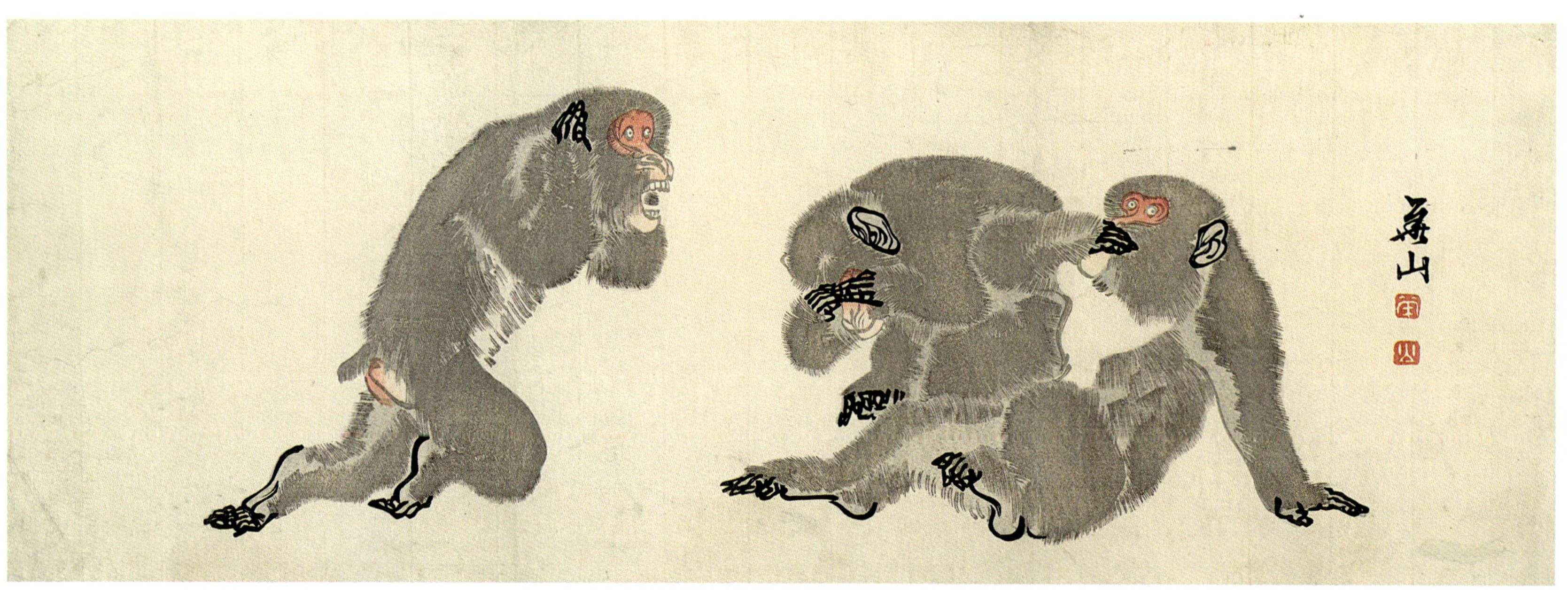

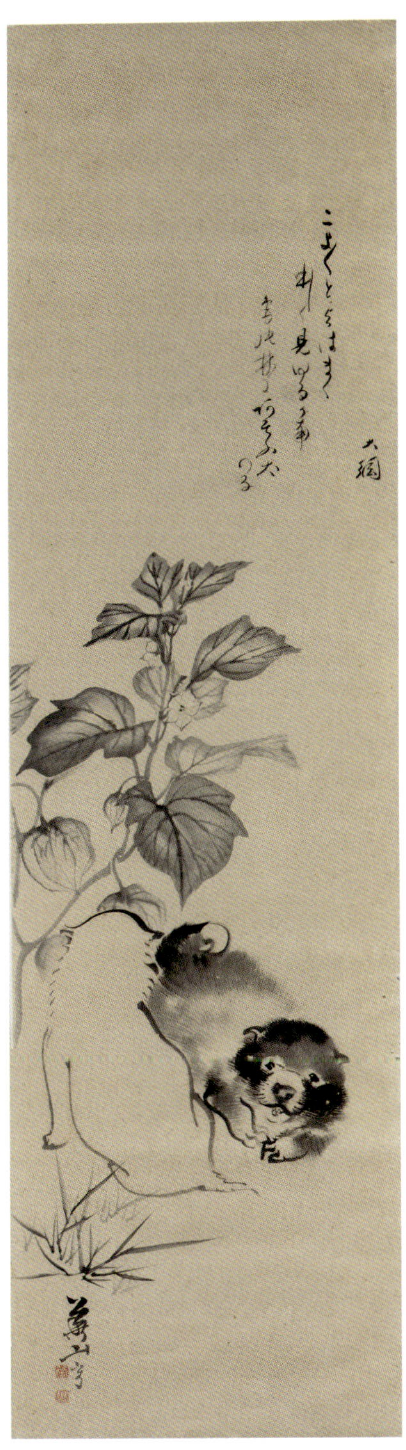

from near and afar on an autumn evening to forget about the sadness of a long, lonely evening'. The empty cages may subtly allude to such feelings. In essence, a close reading of text and images in surimono can give us glimpses into how much informal, congenial meetings such as this one might have meant to the participants.

Kazan contributed images to a number of surimono (fig. 5.25, see fig. 5.5). He was born into a family of physicians serving the lord of the Fukui domain (in present-day Fukui prefecture) and at an early age was adopted by a family who ran a silk-weaving business in the Nishijin textile district of Kyoto.[19] Through his prodigious artistic talent and the relationships formed owing to the family business, he established a wide range of connections around Kyoto.[20] Kazan's adorable puppies and lantern plants painting (fig. 5.26), rendered simply but skilfully in ink, bears an inscribed poem by the Zen monk Daikō Sōgen (1772–1860) of the temple Daitoku-ji in Kyoto.

The production of surimono flourished throughout the nineteenth century and continued well into the Meiji era, weathering the enormous social and political changes of the period. The popularity of forming circles in the various traditional arts continued at this time, and the *esprit* of salon culture retained its independent ethos despite the impact of Western culture. As the custom of making surimono spread, by the mid-nineteenth century examples with an impressive number of poets – sometimes 200 or more – became increasingly common. Surimono in multi-sheet formats with bold and striking designs also began to appear, such as a triptych by one artist, Harada Keigaku (1803–1885), and 159 poets (fig. 5.27). Cities all around Japan developed their own skills to create surimono. Interestingly, while most designs adhered to more traditional seasonal



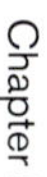

233

motifs, there were exceptions that reflected the shifts in customs influenced by Western culture, ranging from dining scenes to new clothing (figs 5.28–5.29). The tradition remained buoyant into the Taishō (1912–26) and early Shōwa (1926–89) eras. The most recent surimono in the British Museum collection in fact date to the 1940s, with one in 1941 to celebrate the occasion of a name change of a bunraku puppet theatre chanter (see fig. 1.21) and another in 1942 to commemorate the name change of a shamisen player. Such works are evidence of the enduring legacy of surimono from the earliest known example dated 1752 (fig. 5.30), spanning a history of almost two centuries.

The distinctive culture of surimono in Kyoto and Osaka, which allocated poetry and pictures equal weight, make this expressive form, together with paintings and illustrated books, an invaluable record of collaborative efforts among professionals and amateurs in the creation of poetry and visual art. But most importantly, these forms were driven by the inventiveness of a broad spectrum of individuals. The level of participation in artistic circles is therefore impressive: salon culture enriched life and communication in Japanese society, both locally and nationally, on a level that we today are just beginning to understand and appreciate. And the examples from the British Museum's rich collection offer us a taste of this intricate and diverse cultural world.

**5.27**
Harada Keigaku (artist) and 159 poets, *Swallows*, mid-1800s. Triptych surimono, colour woodblock. 30 × 148.9 cm. British Museum, London, 2021,3013.293–5. Purchase made possible by the JTI Japanese Acquisition Fund. Ex-coll.: Dr Scott Johnson.

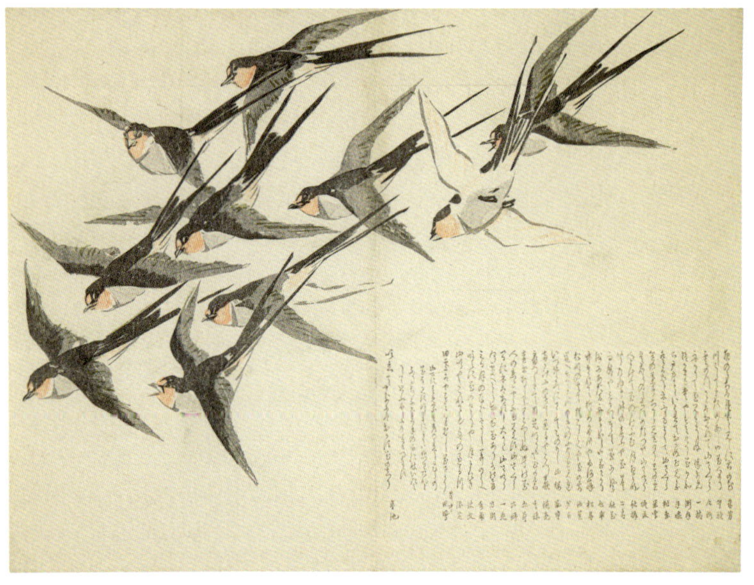
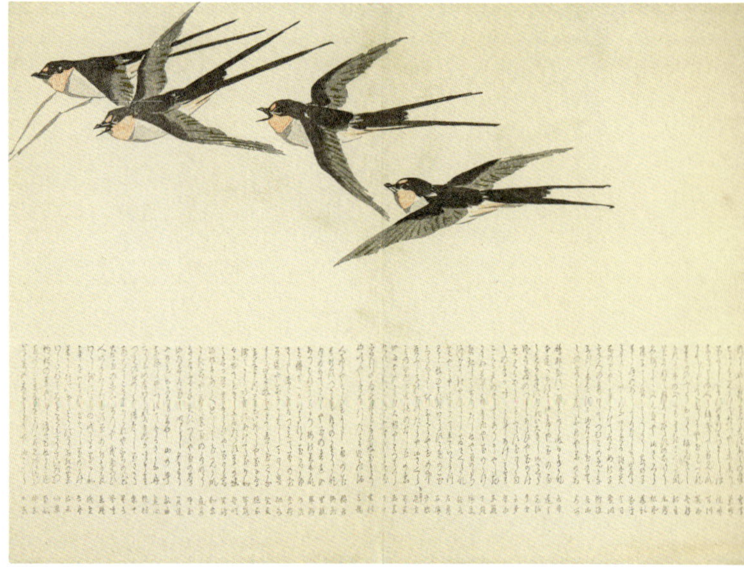

**5.28**
Imao Keinen (artist) and 109 poets, *Western-Style Dining Scene*, 1872. Surimono, colour woodblock. 38.4 × 51.1 cm. British Museum, London, 2021,3013.212. Purchase made possible by the JTI Japanese Acquisition Fund. Ex-coll.: Dr Scott Johnson.

**5.29**
Satō Gyodai II (artist) and seven poets, *Workman in Western-Style Uniform Weighing Silkworm Cocoons*, *c.* 1875. Surimono, colour woodblock. 18.6 × 25.4 cm. British Museum, London, 2021,3013.938. Purchase made possible by the JTI Japanese Acquisition Fund. Ex-coll.: Dr Scott Johnson.

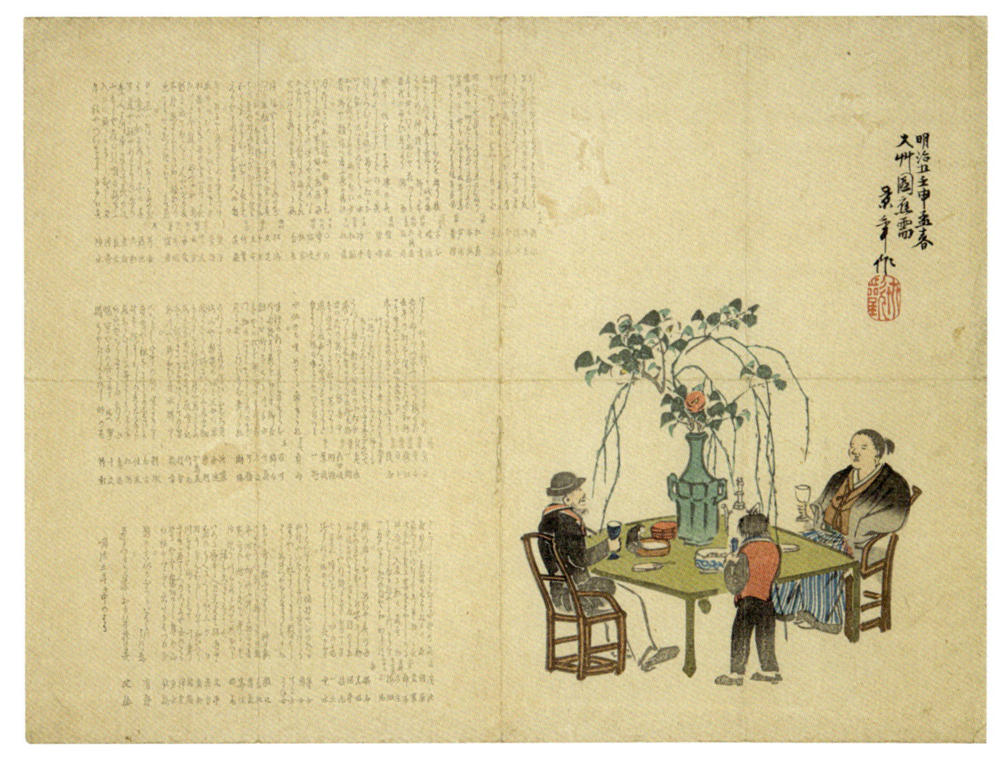

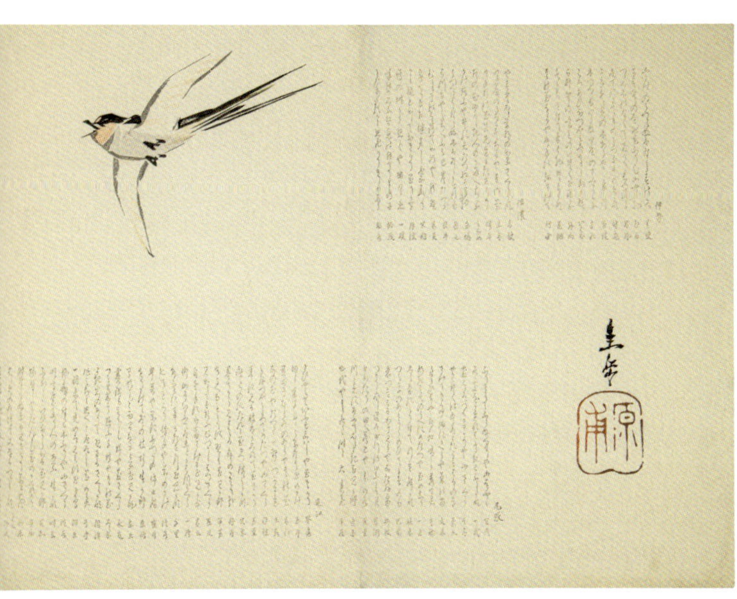

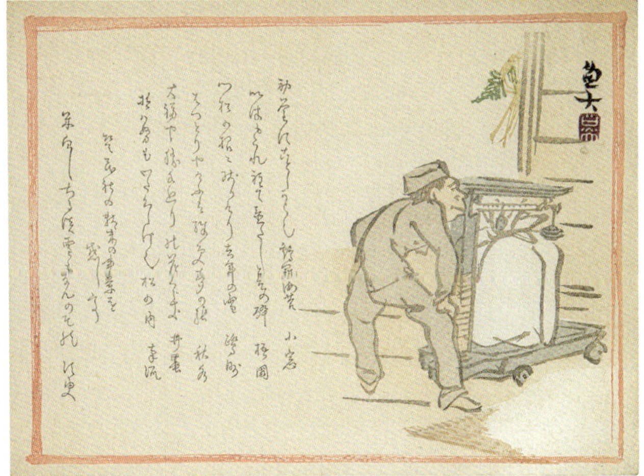

235

# Surimono in Kyoto and Osaka
*Scott Johnson*

The Japanese characters for the word 'surimono' mean 'printed thing', but in the Edo period it meant a privately printed paper with text, especially kyōka and haiku poems. In nineteenth-century France, as Japanese prints became commercially popular, surimono came to mean small, squarish and lavishly produced ukiyo-e prints, illustrated by artists such as Katsushika Hokusai, with kyōka poems. These Western ukiyo-e enthusiasts minimised the other type of Japanese poetry print with haiku poems.[21] These haiku poetry prints are often called Shijō surimono (after the Shijō school). Maruyama-Shijō art became popularised in Japan's Kamigata region, the Kansai area that today includes Osaka and Kyoto.[22] Such surimono frequently have seasonal references, with pictures by artists from many non-ukiyo-e styles, and with text set apart from pictures. From 1750 to

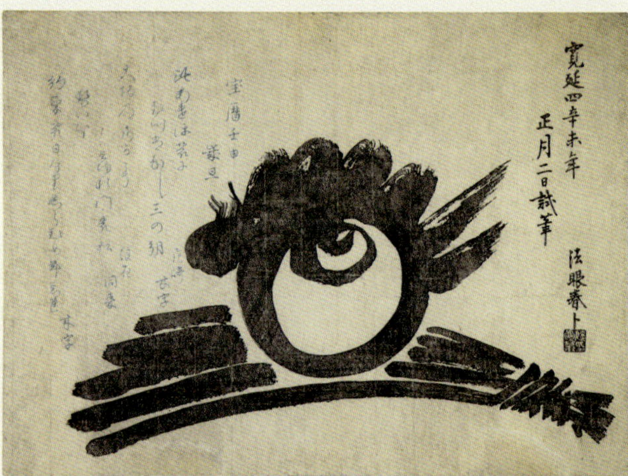

**5.30**
Ōoka Shunboku (artist) and three poets, *Flaming Jewel*, 1751/2. Surimono, colour woodblock. 39.5 × 53.5 cm. British Museum, London, 2021,3013.176. Purchase made possible by the JTI Japanese Acquisition Fund. Ex-coll.: Dr Scott Johnson.

1850, the number of artists in Kyoto and Osaka increased dramatically, and the major Maruyama, Shijō, Rinpa and Literati (bunjin-ga) schools fostered numerous sub-schools. This led to great variety in Kamigata surimono subject matter and style over roughly a 200-year history.

Kamigata surimono were made by haiku groups for exchange with like-minded friends. Their exact beginning is unknown, but one striking early example is by the Osaka artist Ōoka Shunboku (fig. 5.30). The block-cutters of this work have faithfully followed Shunboku's powerful brushstrokes, a recurring feature of Kamigata surimono, to produce a flaming, wish-fulfilling jewel that rests on bundles of rice straw, a potent hope that 1752 (see p. 234) would be a bounteous new year.[23] The poets are unidentified, but one is from the Osaka suburb of Amagasaki, where Shunboku had created folding screens in 1750 for a prominent local temple.[24]

There was no standard format for Kamigata surimono. Many were quite small, such as the colour-printed cucumbers of the early 1790s by the Kyoto artist Watanabe Nangaku (fig. 5.31) or the possibly unique surimono made into a small woodcut handscroll (see fig. 5.11). The latter was compiled in 1793 by the wealthy merchant Nishimura Teiga, a haiku student of the famous poet-painter Yosa Buson. The handscroll begins with a depiction of a 'torchlight nō' performance, again by Nangaku,[25] and it includes haiku by thirty-three poets.

From around 1802 Nangaku travelled to Edo to introduce the Maruyama-Shijō style of painting there. This was shortly after Osaka artist Nakamura Hōchū arrived in Edo with the aim of introducing his Osaka Rinpa style of painting. Both artists were already familiar with the Kamigata surimono style, as seen in a small surimono by Hōchū, compiled in 1801 by the Edo-based haiku poet Inoue Shungi (d. 1813) (fig. 5.32). Interestingly, Hōchū shows Kyoto courtiers gathering new year pine seedlings for this surimono made in Edo – perhaps an allusion to him bringing Kamigata culture to Edo.

The most famous haiku poet – even today – is Matsuo Bashō. There were many activities acknowledging the centennial of his death, which encouraged increasing numbers of poets in the late eighteenth century to improve their haiku skills. By the early nineteenth century, it became

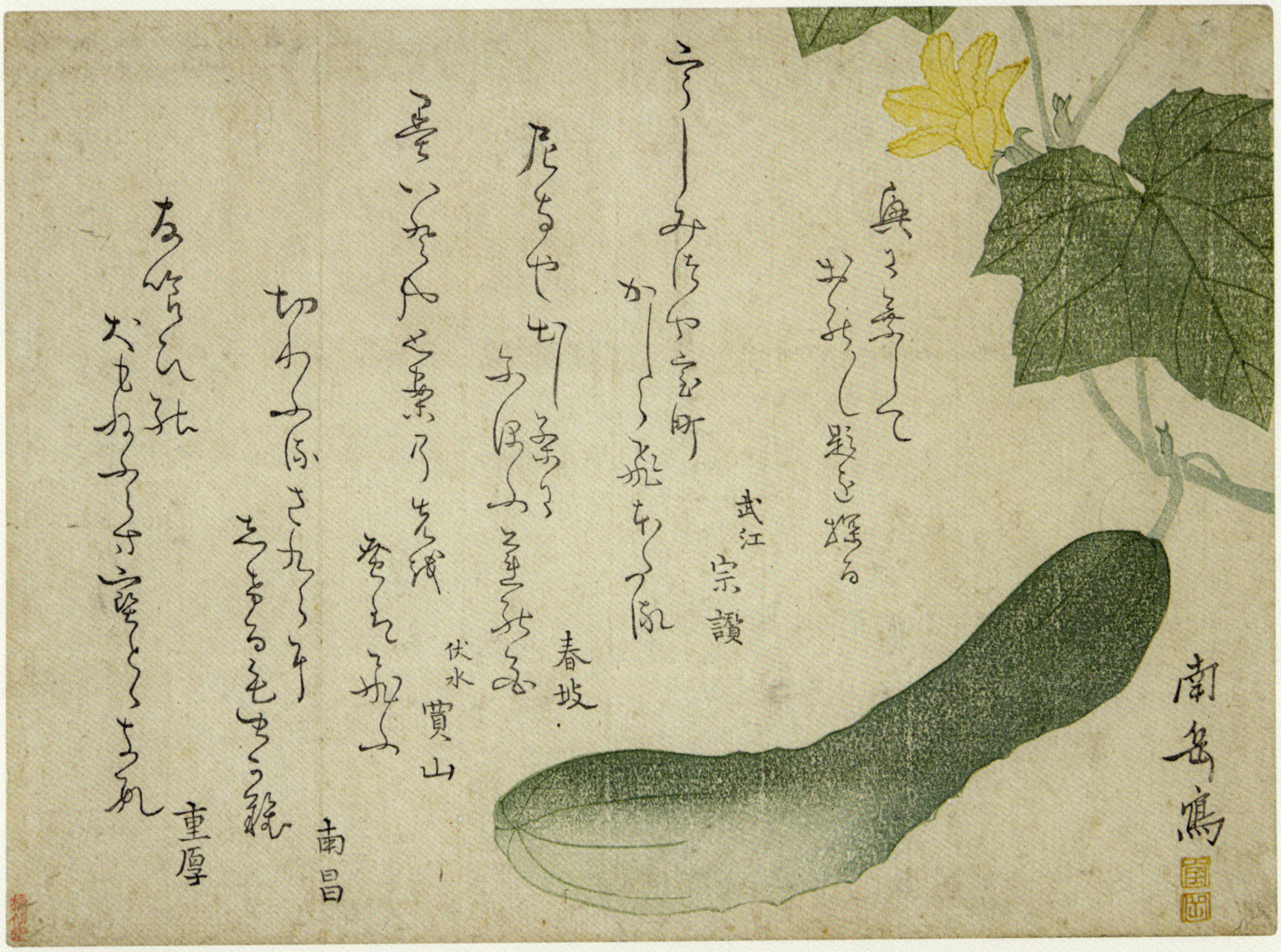

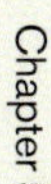

**5.31**
Watanabe Nangaku (artist)
and six poets, *Cucumber*,
early 1790s. Surimono, colour
woodblock. 19.50 × 26.3 cm.
British Museum, London,
2021,3013.1040. Purchase made
possible by the JTI Japanese
Acquisition Fund. Ex-coll.:
Dr Scott Johnson.

possible for accomplished haiku poets with good business sense to make a living compiling haiku books and surimono.

One such compiler, Oka Seibi (1760–1837), took advantage of the growing network of bonded couriers to advertise his terms, indicating deadlines for haiku and fees for surimono, with contributing poets to receive five large or ten small completed prints.[26] The long surimono with two pictures by Satō Suiseki (Gyodai), here signed with his early art name, Masuyuki, may have been the lower half of a large surimono (fig. 5.33). Seibi worked in Osaka, but the ten poets include one from Edo, one from Ōmi, near Kyoto, and two from Dewa and Yonezawa in the far north of the main island of Honshu. These distant contributors imply the need for couriers to collect brushed poems and fees, and later, to distribute printed surimono. The specifics of Seibi's business

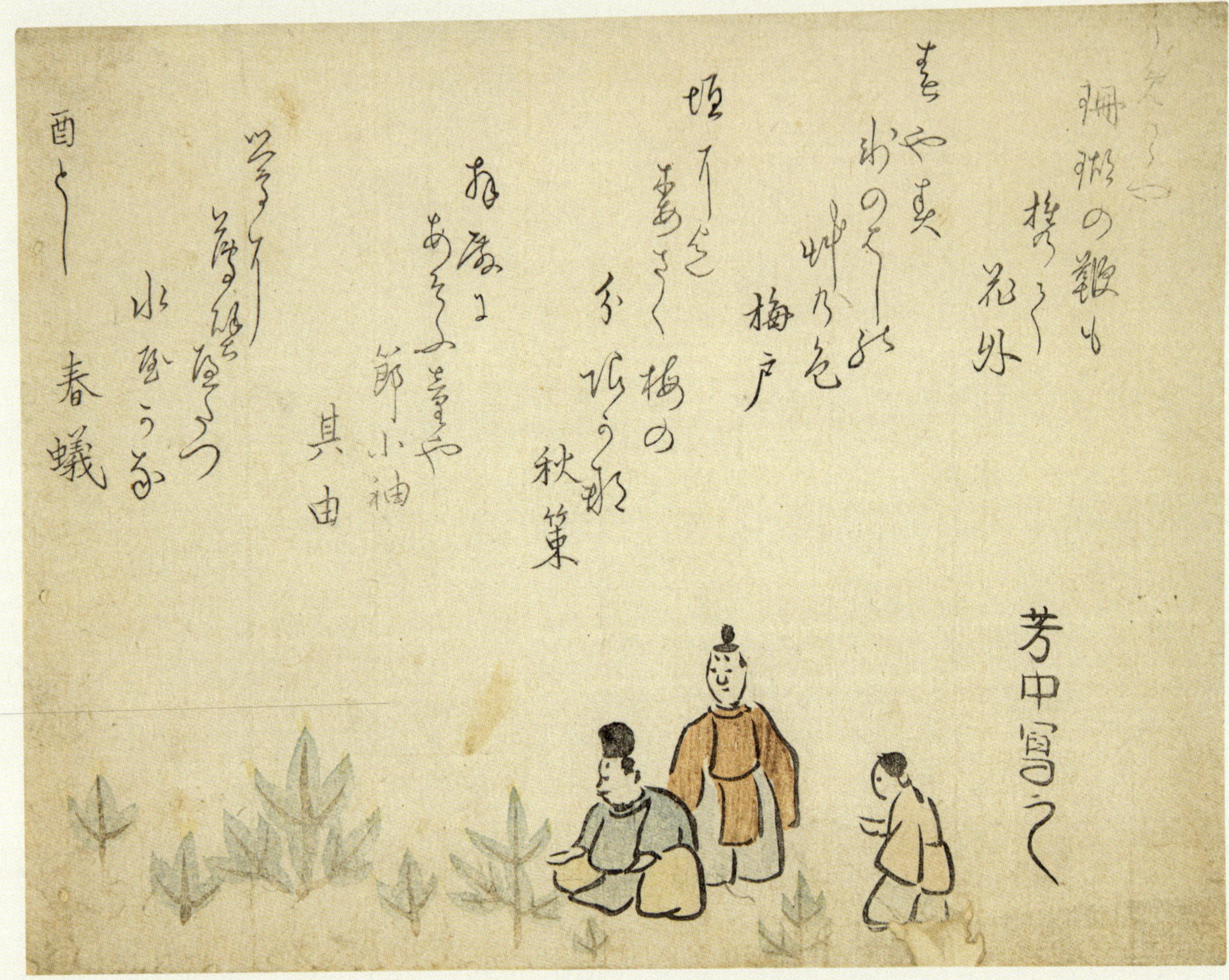



**5.32**
Nakamura Hōchū (artist) and
five poets, *Courtiers Selecting
Pine Seedlings* (*Wakamatsu*),
c. 1801. Surimono, colour
woodblock. 18.5 × 23.6 cm.
British Museum, London,
2021,3013.1041. Purchase made
possible by the JTI Japanese
Acquisition Fund. Ex-coll.:
Dr Scott Johnson.

practices may not have been universal, but contributions from distant poets are a major feature of Kamigata surimono.

In 1844, as the 150th anniversary of Matsuo Bashō's death approached, greater numbers of amateurs wanted to see their haiku printed in surimono. Specialists in tiny but precise calligraphy made it possible to incorporate increasing numbers of haiku onto surimono, which soon became common practice. Each poet received multiple impressions, leading to more surimono exchanges, and such late Edo to early Meiji Kamigata surimono are the most common to survive.

Kamigata-style surimono also came to flourish – in Edo and then Tokyo, as Edo was known after 1868 – with the best-known artist being Shibata Zeshin (1807–1891). The style also spread to Nagoya and the Tōkai region (towns between Nagoya and Edo), sometimes with spectacular results, such as the three-sheet surimono featuring swallows by Harada Keigaku (1803–1885) (see fig. 5.27).[27] In spite of the modernisation of Japan during and after the Meiji era, the conservative haiku world continued to produce small, seasonal Kamigata surimono into the 1920s. There was also a resurgence of large Kamigata surimono from the 1890s, financed by the twin brothers Shirai Matsujirō and Ōtani Takejirō, the founders of the entertainment company Shōchiku in 1895 (see p. 74). The occasions for these works included name changes of kabuki actors in Tokyo and bunraku performers in Osaka. Surimono issued by Shōchiku were illustrated by a new generation of artists, such as the 1923 *Shrine Monkey* by Tsuji Kakō (1871–1931).[28] The last known publishing date for a Kamigata surimono was in late 1942,[29] 190 years after Ōoka Shunboku's 1752 surimono (see fig. 5.30).

Luxury publications were forbidden during the Asia-Pacific War (1941–5) and further prevented by the privations of the immediate post-war years. The Kamigata surimono tradition never revived, but the surviving prints of its eighteenth- and nineteenth- century heyday demonstrate a superb marriage of text and image, created by successive generations of major artists, skilled artisans and compilers, and paid for by thousands of dedicated amateur haiku poets from all walks of life.

**5.33**
Satō Masuyuki (Suiseki, Gyodai, artist) and ten poets, *Houses, Flower and Poems*, early 1800s. Surimono, colour woodblock. 18.5 × 12.8 cm (album covers). British Museum, London, 2021,3013.1539.1-15. Purchase made possible by the JTI Japanese Acquisition Fund. Ex-coll.: Dr Scott Johnson.

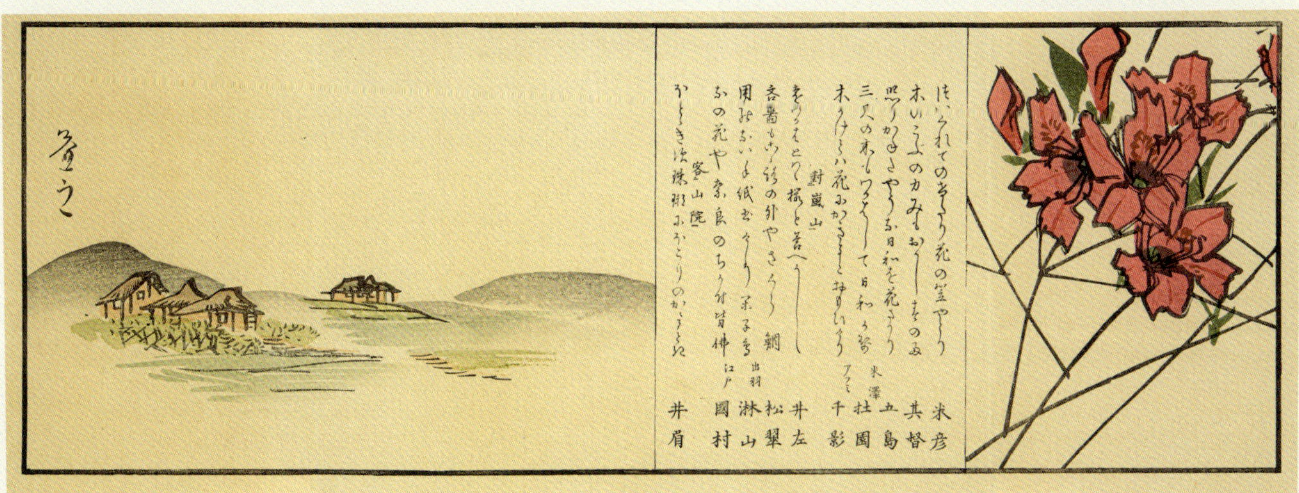

# Notes



### Introduction

1   The Kyoto painter Go Shun (see figs 0.5, 2.6, 2.21, 3.29, 5.18) was a well-known gourmet. During his time in Osaka, he held twice-a-month meetings with the name Issaikai ('One Dish Gathering') to taste and discuss *tōfu* (soybean curd). Sugimoto Yoshihisa, 'Shijō-ha no so Go Shun', in *Shijō-ha e no michi: Go Shun o chūshin to shite*, ed. Edamatsu Ako, Nishinomiya: Nishinomiyashi Ōtani Kinen Bijutsukan, 2019, p. 122.

2   Iwasa Shin'ichi, 'Maruyama-ha to Shijō-ha ni yoru yoriai-gaki "Aki nana-kusa zu" ni tsuite', *Ōsaka Rekishi Hakubutsukan kenkyū kiyō*, no. 10 (March 2012), pp. 105–12.

3   Iwasa Shin'ichi, 'Ōsaka ni okeru shoga-kai to tenran-kai ni tsuite ichi', *Ōsaka Rekishi Hakubutsukan kenkyū kiyō*, no. 2 (October 2005), pp. 25–39.

4   Tetsuo Najita, *Visions of Virtue in Tokugawa Japan: The Kaitokudō Merchant Academy of Osaka*, Chicago, IL: University of Chicago Press, 1987.

5   The 'Various Master Artisans' (*shoshiki meishō*) section in the same volume includes many fields, from applied arts, to medicine, to long-distance express couriers; the subject entries total about 260.

6   Moriya Takeshi, 'Yūgei and Chōnin Society in the Edo Period', *Acta Asiatica*, no. 33 (1977), pp. 32–54.

7   Chikamatsu Monzaemon (author), Torigoe Bunzō et al. (eds), *Chikamatsu Monzaemon shū*, Tokyo: Shōgakkan, 1997, p. 109. For an English translation, see Donald Keene, *Major Plays of Chikamatsu*, New York: Columbia University Press, 1961, p. 162.

8   Among the many exhibitions curated by Lawrence Smith at the British Museum, *The Maruyama/Shijō School* (1976) and *The Schools of Ganku and Bunchō* (1977) are directly related to the themes of the current book. The former was inspired to a great extent by Jack Hillier's monumental 1974 publication *The Uninhibited Brush: Japanese Art in the Shijō Style*, London: Hugh M. Moss (Publishing) Ltd. Timothy T. Clark has also curated numerous exhibitions at the Museum, including his 1997 exhibition *Images of Kyoto and Osaka in 19th-century Japanese prints, paintings and illustrated books*.

9   Little is known about Murata Gesshō's life. He appears in a sumo-style ranking bill of Osaka artists published in 1807. I would like to thank Scott Johnson for sharing the information about the inclusion of the artist in this material. See Ōsaka Shiritsu Bijutsukan (ed.), *Kinsei Ōsaka gadan*, Kyoto: Dōhōsha, 1983, p. 182.

10   Rinpa, known for its distinctive decorative style, originated in the artwork of Tawaraya Sōtatsu (late sixteenth–early seventeenth centuries) and was further refined by Ogata Kōrin (1658–1716), whose example remained inspirational for future generations of artists in Kyoto and Edo.

11   The artists are Hishida Nittō (1817–1873), Suzuki Hyakunen (1828–1891), Suzuki Shōnen (1848–1918), Imao Keinen (1845–1924), Kubota Beisen (1852–1906), and the following artists of unknown dates: Chikusen, Ōyabu Kodō, Sakurai Hyakurei, Izawa Kyūkō, Suzuki Hyakusui, Mokusen and Rankei.

12   The artists, from top to bottom, are Masuda Kyūboku (1782–1848), Hōdai (dates unknown), Kawamura Bunpō (1779–1821), Bunshō (dates unknown), Kawamura Kihō (d. 1852), Akamatsu Kakunen (active early nineteenth century) and Gan Tai (1785–1865).

13   The artists are Murata Kōkoku (1831–1912), Himejima Chikugai (1840–1928), Kawasaki Bokkei (b. 1874), Mori Kinseki (1843–1921), Niwayama Kōen (1869–1942), Nakagawa Wadō (b. 1880), Sakata Kōsetsu (1871–1935), Koyama Unsen (1855–1911), Shōzan (dates unknown), Wakabayashi Shōkei (1858–1938), Nobuchika Shunjō (1885–1938), Fukada Chokujō (1861–1947), Ueda Tōrei (dates unknown), Kawabe Seiran (1868–1931) and Nagamatsu Shun'yō (1850–1931).

14   The artists are Tosa Mitsuzane (1780–1852); Kanō Eigaku (1790–1867); Gan Tai (1785–1865) and Kishi Renzan (1805–1859) from the Kishi school; and Takemura Bunmin (active mid-nineteenth century), Mori Gishō (1802–1873), Yagi Kihō (1806–1876), Shūsui and Tomita Kōei (both active mid-nineteenth century), Yokoyama Seiki (1793–1865), Nakajima Raishō (1796–1871) and Isono Kadō (active mid-nineteenth century) from the Shijō school.

15   Yokoya Ken'ichirō, 'Shūzōhin shōkai 28: Matsumura Keibun nana-kai-ki tuizen yoriai jūnikagetsu zu', *Ōtsu Rekihaku-dayori*, no. 30 (August 1997), unpaginated.

16   Nakamura Denzaburō, 'Shijō-ha shiryō: "Matsumura-ke ryakkei" to Go Shun Keibun den', *Bijutsu kenkyū*, no. 216 (January 1962), pp. 33–40.

17   An account of the event from the princes' perspectives is given in Prince Albert Victor, Prince George of Wales with additions by John N. Dalton, *The Cruise of Her Majesty's Ship 'Bacchante' 1879–1882*, 2 vols, London: Macmillan, 1886, vol. 2, p. 84.

18   Takeda Yōjirō, 'Kansei-do kinri gosho zōei ni okeru eshi no sentei ni tsuite', in *Kinsei goyō-eshi no shiteki kenkyū*, ed. Takeda Yōjirō, Eguchi Tsuneaki and Kamata Junko, Kyoto: Shibunkaku, 2008, pp. 78–129.

19   Itō Shiori, 'Shōshunpō-jō to Iwagaki Ryūkei shusai Shōrakan shisha', in Suzuki Jun and Asano Shūgo (eds.), *Edo no ehon*, Tokyo: Yagi Shoten, 2010, pp. 355–78.

20   Taiga was deceased by the time of publication. His design was

copied by Iwatani Sūdai (active 1760s) as a contribution to this anthology.

21 Itō, 'Shōshunpō-jō', 2010.

22 The artists include Nagayama Kōin (figs 0.8, 2.39) and his son Nagayama Kōchoku (1800/3–1862), Mori Yūsen (fig. 0.7), Shitomi Kangyū (active early nineteenth century), a Chinese studies scholar and poet Shinozaki Shōchiku (1781–1851) (fig. 3.11) and a haiku poet and rice merchant in Dōjima, Osaka, Tanabe Hyakudō (active early nineteenth century).

23 The illustrators are Tosa-school, Kanō-school and Kanō-related artists, Maruyama Ōkyo's son and pupils, Hara Zaisei (d. 1810) of the Hara school, who was knowledgeable about traditional court rituals and customs, Go Shun, some local artists whose names are unidentifiable today and the popular Edo ukiyo-e artist Kitao Masayoshi (1764–1824).

24 The illustrators of this publication include major Maruyama-Shijō artists: Maruyama Ōzui, Yamaguchi Soken (figs 2.18–2.19, 2.43–2.44, 3.28), Nagasawa Rosetsu (figs 0.23, 3.4, 4.3), Yoshimura Ranshū, Go Shun, Kinoshita Ōju, Yoshimura Kōkei (fig. 4.11), Azuma Tōyō, Murakami Tōshū (fig. 5.20) and others.

25 Ban Kōkei, annotated by Mori Senzō, Kinsei kijin den, Tokyo: Iwanami Shoten, 1971, pp. 157–60.

26 Ibid., pp. 155–7.

27 Ibid., p. 13, also see p. 3. Translation by the author.

28 Sugimoto Yoshihisa, Maruyama Ōkyo no monjin tachi, Nishinomiya: Kurokawa Kobunka Kenkyūjo, 2014, p. 102.

29 Katō Sadahiko, 'Ōtomo Ōemaru no kenkyū', Kokubungaku Kenkyū Shiryōkan kiyō, no. 2 (March 1976), pp. 47–113.

30 Justin Jesty, Art and Engagement in Early Postwar Japan, Ithaca, NY: Cornell University Press, 2018.

31 Richard Bowring, In Search of the Way: Thought and Religion in Early-Modern Japan, 1582–1860, Oxford: Oxford University Press, 2017, pp. 52–3.

32 For instance, Asao Naohiro (ed.), Nihon no kinsei: mibun to kakushiki, Tokyo: Chūō Kōronsha, 1992; Kurushima Hiroshi et al. (eds), Mibun o toinaosu, Tokyo: Yoshikawa Kōbunkan, 2000.

33 David Howe, Geographies of Identity in Nineteenth-Century Japan, Berkeley, CA: University of California Press, 2005.

34 Maeda Isutomu, Edo kyōiku shisōshi kenkyū, Kyoto: Shibunkaku Shuppan, 2016.

35 Moriya (1977), pp. 32–54.

36 Owaki Hidekazu, Kinsei shakai to ichinin ryōmei: mibun, shihai, chitsujo no tokushitsu to kōzō, Tokyo: Yoshikawa Kōbunkan, 2020, pp. 3–4.

## Chapter 1

1 I wish to thank Professor Iwata Hideyuki for his help in deciphering and interpreting the texts from Edo-period sources. All translations are by the author, unless otherwise indicated.

2 Nishiyama Matsunosuke et al. (eds), Kinsei geidōron, Tokyo: Iwanami Shoten, 1972, p. 511. Translation in Katherine Saltzman-Li, Creating Kabuki Plays: Context for Kezairoku, 'Valuable Notes on Playwriting', Leiden: Brill, 2010, p. 201.

3 Kyūkei sōdō zuihitsu (private publication), 1970, p. 140. The preface is dated 1857, and the original passage appears in vol. 7. Translation by the author.

4 Tetsuo Najita, Visions of Virtue in Tokugawa Japan: The Kaitokudō Merchant Academy of Osaka, Chicago, IL: University of Chicago Press, 1987.

5 Patricia J. Graham, Tea of the Sages: The Art of Sencha, Honolulu, HI: University of Hawai'i Press, 1998, pp. 100–35.

6 C. Andrew Gerstle, 'Takemoto Gidayū and the Individualistic Spirit of Osaka Theater', in Osaka: The Merchants' Capital of Early Modern Japan, ed. James L. McClain and Wakita Osamu, Ithaca, NY: Cornell University Press, 1999, pp. 104–24.

7 Moriya Takeshi, 'Yūgei and Chōnin Society in the Edo Period', Acta Asiatica, no. 33 (1977), pp. 32–54.

8 Beatrice B. Shoemaker, 'Ōoka Shunboku: Osaka between China and Japan', Andon, vol. 114 (December 2022), pp. 5–34.

9 Cited in Tsunoda Ichirō and Yokoyama Tadashi (eds), Nihon shomin bunka shiryō shūsei, vol. 7, Ningyō jōruri, Tokyo: San'ichi Shobō, 1975, p. 493. Translation by the author.

10 Ibid., p. 232.

11 Ibid., pp. 274–8.

12 'Playful Map of Amateur Jōruri Performers in the Capital, Ranked and with Addresses Listed' (Kyō shirōto jōruri kurai wake jūsho mitate no zu, 1818).

13 The National Institute of Japanese Literature (NIJL) in Tokyo has a copy.

14 The Kansai University Library in Osaka has a copy.

15 Nose-chō Kyōiku Iinkai (ed.), Nose no jōruri-shi: mukei minzoku bunkazai chiiki denshō, Nose: Nose-chō Kyōiku Iinkai, 1996.

16 Tsunoda and Yokoyama, Ningyō jōruri, pp. 618–37.

17 Matsudaira Susumu, 'Hiiki Renchū (Theatre Fan Clubs) in Osaka in the Early Nineteenth Century', in A Kabuki Reader, ed. Samuel L. Leiter, Armonk, NY: M.E. Sharp, 2002, pp. 112–22; Kaguraoka Yōko, 'Osaka Kabuki Fan Clubs and their Obsessions', in C. Andrew Gerstle, with Timothy Clark and Akiko Yano, Kabuki Heroes on the Osaka Stage 1780–1830, London: The British Museum Press, pp. 30–5.

18 He was active in haiku circles and his commonly known name was Maeda Heijirō, according to the book One Hundred Haiku by One Hundred Poets (Haikai hyakunin isshu, 1810, British Museum, 1991,1112,0.103). He is listed as a koto master in Record of Fellow Osakans, Continued (Zoku naniwa kyōyū roku, 1823); see Mori Senzō and Nakajima Masatoshi, Kinsei jinmeiroku shūsei, Tokyo: Benseisha, 1976–8, vol. 1. He lived in Amagasaki-chō 1 chōme, Osaka.

19 Matsudaira Susumu cites a source attesting to Hokushū being an amateur and possibly in the lumber business. See Matsudaira Susumu, Kamigata ukiyo-e no saihakken, Tokyo: Kōdansha, 1999, pp. 128–9.

20 Elegant Words of Praise: Rikan Album (Shōsan gagen Rikan-jō, 1815).

21 Takemoto Tsudayū, *Bunraku sandai: Takemoto Tsudayū kikigaki*, Osaka: Ōsaka Shoseki, 1984.

22 Converting a historical monetary value to present-day prices is not straightforward. The figure of 50,000 *kan* might be equivalent to the price of approximately 830,000 *koku* of rice in late seventeenth-century Japan. *Koku* is a unit used before the modern era to measure the volume of rice; 1 *koku* is usually said to be enough to feed one adult person for one year. Although literary exaggeration must be taken into account, sales in the Osaka rice trade were certainly extremely profitable.

23 Abridged extract from Saikaku's *Japanese Family Storehouse* (*Nippon eitai-gura*, 1688). Translation by the British Museum team. For a full translation of this work, see G.W. Sargent (trans.), *The Japanese Family Storehouse, or, the Millionaire's Gospel Modernized*, Cambridge: Cambridge University Press, 1959.

24 His given name (*na*) was Kōkyō and his other names adopted as an adult (*azana*) included Seshuku, Kenkadō and Sonsai. Tsuboiya Kichiemon was his common name (*tsūshō*) as a merchant.

25 Mizuta Norihisa, Noguchi Takashi and Arisaka Michiko (eds), *Kanpon Kenkadō nikki*, Hiroshima: Geika Shoin, 2009.

26 *Memories of My Days in Settsu* [*Osaka*] (*Zaishin kiji*), 1828. Translation by the British Museum team.

27 These statements are found on the opening title page and in the general note for the reader of the book. Translation by the British Museum team.

**Chapter 2**

1 Jack Hillier, *The Uninhibited Brush: Japanese Art in the Shijō Style*, London: Hugh M. Moss (Publishing) Ltd, 1974. The Ōkyo and Constable comparison appears on pp. 30–1, pls 14–15.

2 See a post by the Nezu Museum on the subject: www.facebook.com/NezuMuseum/posts/1172252849505518.

3 The painting is described in detail on the British Museum's YouTube channel: Timothy Clark, 'Why Japanese Tigers have Flat Heads: Screen Painting by Maruyama Okyo | Curator's Corner S6 Ep4', 5 January 2021, www.youtube.com/watch?v=Q-c8yQKglgw&t=4s.

4 Gennifer S. Weisenfeld, *Imaging Disaster: Tokyo and the Visual Culture of Japan's Great Earthquake of 1923*, Berkeley, CA: University of California Press, 2012, pp. 19–33, addresses imagery generated by the Ansei earthquake of 1855, but does not discuss any earlier disaster pictures of the Edo period, apart from the Ōkyo *Seven Disasters and Seven Happinesses* referenced in the following note.

5 Weisenfeld, *Imaging Disaster*, pp. 17–19, discusses Ōkyo's *Seven Disasters and Seven Happinesses* as a key precedent for disaster imagery in the modern era.

6 Quoted in Timon Screech, *The Shogun's Painted Culture: Fear and Creativity in the Japanese States, 1760–1829*, London: Reaktion Books, 2000, p. 198; a transcription of the original Japanese text can be found in Yamakawa Takeshi, *Nihon bijutsu kaiga zenshū*, vol. 22, *Ōkyo, Go Shun*, Tokyo, Shūeisha, 1977, p. 119.

7 Screech, *The Shogun's Painted Culture*, pp. 144–8.

8 Following the interpretation given by Yamamoto Yoshitaka in his presentation 'Poetic Inscriptions as Contemporary Art Criticism: "[Female Performer Playing the *Shamisen*]" by Yamaguchi Soken and Minagawa Kien', at the workshop 'Creative Collaboration: Kyoto-Osaka Pictorial Arts and Salon Culture, 1750–1900', SOAS University of London, 10 April 2019.

9 Hillier, *The Uninhibited Brush*.

10 Joan O'Mara, 'Bashō and the Haiga', in *Matsuo Bashō's Poetic Spaces: Exploring Haikai Intersections*, ed. H. Eleanor Kerkham, New York: Palgrave Macmillan, 2006, pp. 201–15.

11 Translation by Cheryl A. Crowley. From *Five Cartloads of Wastepaper* (*Gosha hōgu*), 1783, cited in Cheryl A. Crowley, *Haikai Poet Yosa Buson and the Bashō Revival*, Leiden: Brill, 2007, p. 127.

12 Which might be translated using the apparent oxymoron 'living dead nature'.

13 Simon Schama, *The Embarrassment of Riches: An Interpretation of Dutch Culture in the Golden Age*, London: Collins, 1987.

**Chapter 3**

1 *Catalogue Assessing the Quality of Recent Japanese Paintings* (*Honchō kinsei gahin roku*, 1850s–60s) placed Ōkyo, Tani Bunchō and Watanabe Kazan in its top category of artists, 'highest among the miraculous' (*myōhin no jō*). According to *New Catalogue of Calligraphy and Painting Prices* (*Shin shoga kakaku roku*, 1861), Ōkyo's work sold for 10 gold *ryō*, while Tan'yū's sold for 5. See Segi Shinichi, *Meiga no nedan*, Tokyo: Shinchōsha, 1998, p. 92.

2 Cited in Mabuchi Miho, 'Ōkyo ga o kangaeru: sono Nihon kaiga-shi ni okeru "atarashisa" to wa', in *Maruyama Ōkyo ten*, ed. Aichi-ken Bijutsukan and Chūnichi Shinbunsha, Nagoya: Maruyama Ōkyo Iinkai, 2013, p. 15.

3 Cited ibid., p. 16.

4 For example, for the farmer, hunter or fisherman, nature meant a livelihood, while for a daimyō it could hold untapped sources of revenue.

5 During the Edo period the Japanese language had no equivalent for the English term 'nature'. Strings of Chinese characters instead referred to 'heaven-and-earth', 'flowers-and-birds', 'fundamental herbs', 'plants-trees-birds-beasts-insects-fish-metals-jewels-earths-stones' or, without a defining perspective, 'everything' (*banmotsu/banbutsu*). See Federico Marcon, *The Knowledge of Nature and the Nature of Knowledge in Early Modern Japan*, Chicago, IL: University of Chicago Press, 2015, pp. 16–22.

6 According to neo-Confucian teaching, all existence is a manifestation of the ordering ethic called 'principle'. Studying nature and the Confucian classics represented a two-fold way of discovering the workings of 'principle'. From the late 1600s onwards teams of professional scholars conducted surveys of medicinal herbs and many other types of natural resources. East

Asian encyclopaedias and similar reference books supplied the vocabulary needed to perceive the ethical framework of 'principle' within the endless diversity generated by 'material force' (C: *qi*; J: *ki*). A complementary idea in Buddhism taught the sanctity of life, leading to the popular practice of freeing trapped animals ('life release' or *hōjō-e*). Throughout the Edo period, visitors to temples could, for a small donation, accrue good karma by releasing sparrows from cages, or terrapins and fish into a nearby pond. For a study of early Japanese botanical encyclopaedias, see Matthias Hayek, 'On the Reception and Uses of Li Shizhen's *Classified Materia Medica* (*Bencao gangmu*) in Seventeenth-Century Japan: Text, Categories, Pictures', *Studies in Japanese Literature and Culture*, vol. 4 (March 2021), pp. 95–122.

7   Ōkyo's Buddhist patrons included the Tendai priest Yūjō (1723–1773) (see pp. 95–7), the Tendai monk Shinnin (1768–1805) and the Shingon temple Daijō-ji in present-day Hyōgo prefecture, for which he and his students produced a suite of wall paintings in 1787, 1789 and 1791.

8   Edo-period documents on coastal shipping suggest that sake, lamp oil, soy sauce, cotton cloth and ginned cotton dominated trade between Osaka and Edo. See Louis M. Cullen, 'Statistics of Tokugawa Coastal Trade and Bakumatsu and Early Meiji Foreign Trade', pt. I, *Japan Review*, 21 (2009): pp. 204 and 206.

9   Watanabe Nobuo, 'Fune ni yoru kōtsū no hatten', in *Nihon no kinsei*, vol. 6, *Jōhō to kōtsū*, ed. Maruyama Yasunari, Tokyo: Chūō Kōronsha, 1992, p. 299.

10  The remaining four volumes name products of every kind, including mushrooms, honey, wax, vines and hunting equipment (vol. 2); the seafoods of western Japan (vols 3 and 4); and jellyfish, seaweed, ceramics and finished cloth (vol. 5). The final volume also reports on trade with the Dutch and Chinese, who would have carried a certain proportion of the region's notable products overseas.

11  Kenkadō's main aim in collecting seems to have been delight in the wonders of nature, although he must have known that natural history could be a topic for serious research. See Marcon, *The Knowledge of Nature*, pp. 186–7.

12  Hirai Yoshinobu, discussion of fig. 192, in *Salon Culture and the Pictorial Arts of Kyoto and Osaka/Saron! Kyō no taika to shirarezaru Osaka gadan: ga to zoku*, Kyoto: Kyōto Kokuritsu Kindai Bijutsukan, 2022, p. 217.

13  References to morning glories occur in classical Japanese poetry and literature, notably in the *Tale of Genji* (*Genji monogatari*, c. 1100). The flower reportedly reached Japan as early as the late ninth century and was promoted for medicinal use, but did not attract garden designers and never gained prominence in traditional or elite painting. By the late eighteenth century, however, morning-glory vendors were a familiar sight on city streets, and potted samples of the flower featured in commercial prints. See Sadakane Hideyuki, *Shōhi wa yūwaku suru: yūkaku, hakumai, henka asagao*, Tokyo: Seidosha, 2015, pp. 10–15.

14  Haruo Shirane, *Japan and the Culture of the Four Seasons*, New York: Columbia University Press, 2012, pp. 18ff.

15  Ōkyo could have seen Chinese paintings in the collections of his patrons, many of whom were linked to the imperial family in Kyoto, such as Yūjō. The realism of the Chinese precedents may have encouraged his interest in the study of actual plants. See Sasaki Jōhei and Sasaki Masako, discussion to figs 42–43, in *Hizō Nihon bijutsu taikan*, vol. 3, *Daiei Hakubutsukan III*, ed. Hirayama Ikuo and Kobayashi Tadashi, Tokyo: Kōdansha, 1993, p. 229.

16  Hōchū gives prominence to humble garden vegetables that would be left behind when the Rinpa style migrated to samurai-dominated Edo. See Kōno Motoaki, discussion to figs 28–29, in *Hizō Nihon bijutsu taikan*, vol. 1, *Daiei Hakubutsukan I*, ed. Hirayama Ikuo and Kobayashi Tadashi, Tokyo: Kōdansha, 1992, p. 239.

17  Hirai Yoshinobu identified the author. My thanks to Sophie Gong for advice on reading and interpreting the poem.

18  For a survey of Sessai's art and career, see Yamaguchi Yasuhiro (ed.), *Edo no fūryū saishi: Mashiyama Sessai ten*, Tsu: Mie Kenritsu Bijutsukan, 1993, pp. 4–11. The scholar-amateur painting tradition gathered momentum in China during the fifteenth century, the middle decades of the Ming period, led by such innovators as Shen Zhou (1427–1509), Wen Zhengming (1470–1559) and Dong Qichang (1555–1636).

19  Kōno Motoaki, discussion of fig. 71, in *Hizō Nihon bijutsu taikan*, vol. 3, *Daiei Hakubutsukan III*, ed. Hirayama Ikuo and Kobayashi Tadashi, Tokyo: Kōdansha, 1993, p. 245.

20  Ibid., p. 246.

21  For a discussion of Edo-period usage of the term 'shasei' and related terms, see Kōno Motoaki, 'Edo jidai "shasei" kō', in *Nihon kaiga shi no kenkyū*, ed. Yamane Yūzō-sensei Koki Kinen-kai, Tokyo: Yoshikawa Kōbunkan, 1989, pp. 387–427.

22  The quality applied not exclusively to nature subjects. In 1831 the hallucinatory experience of viewing a set of Buddhist Hell paintings by Ōkyo left Anzai Un'en (1807–1852) wondering whether the artist had not personally travelled to the underworld and back. In his judgement, 'Ōkyo achieved the marvellous in *shasei*'. Anzai Un'en, 'Ōkyo shasei ni myō o eshi koto', in Anzai Un'en, *Kinsei meika shoga dan*, pt. 2, vol. 2, 1844, quoted in Kōno, 'Edo jidai "shasei" kō', p. 392.

23  Nishimoto Shūko, discussion of fig. 44, in *Hizō Nihon bijutsu taikan*, vol. 2, *Daiei Hakubutsukan II*, ed. Hirayama Ikuo and Kobayashi Tadashi, Tokyo: Kōdansha, 1992, p. 279.

24  Discussion of fig. 7, in Fukuoka Kenritsu Bijutsukan, *Goyō eshi: Kanō Tan'yū to kinsei no akademizumu*, Fukuoka: Fukuoka Kenritsu Bijutsukan, 1987, p. 17.

25  Eleven of Tōmin's drawings are identical to bird studies that Ogata Kōrin was previously thought to have produced from life, and another thirty-one Kōrin drawings are copies of Kanō-school plant and animal studies.

26  The birds in his *Pictures of Birds and Insects* (also called the *Shasei Album*, 1776) are detailed in ways that suggest sketches from life, but he copied the majority from a handscroll of life drawings that the artist Watanabe Shikō (1683–1755) produced from 1718 to 1742.

27  According to Yūjō, he also recommended sketching human hands

and feet when reflected in a mirror, rather than viewed directly, and devised shorthand formulas for depicting some animals: deer should be drawn like goats, not horses; monkeys should be drawn like dogs, not humans (otherwise the ears will appear too close to the neck). Aichi-ken Bijutsukan and Chūnichi Shinbunsha (eds), *Maruyama Ōkyo ten*, pp. 180–2, references transcribed in discussion of fig. 18.

28 Noguchi Takeshi, 'Maruyama Ōkyo: "Shasei" o koete', ibid., p. 13.

29 Yūtei trained under Tsurusawa Tangei (1688–1769), head of the Tsurusawa school, a branch of the Kyoto Kanō school patronised by the imperial household. Yūtei similarly produced commissions for the imperial household, which awarded him the honorary title Bridge of the Law (*hokkyō*) in 1757, and Eye of the Law (*hōgen*) in 1777.

30 The mother must make seven crossings, starting with the naughty cub. Tsuji Nobuo advised the subject of this screen in 2006.

31 The screen is illustrated with a discussion in *Nihon bijutsu gahō*, vol. 2, no. 5 (October 1895), unpaginated; my thanks to Rosina Buckland for sharing this reference. It reportedly had a companion screen showing a Chinese lion (*shishi*) by Tsurusawa Tansaku (1729–1797), Tangei's son and Yūtei's younger contemporary in the Tsurusawa school. Since Tsurusawa-school artists painted for the imperial family, and Ōkyo himself is known to have produced numerous imperial commissions, it seems likely that the commission for this screen originated in an imperial connection.

32 The other eight were Gessen (1741–1809), Komai Genki (1747–1797), Mori Tetsuzan (1775–1841), Nishimura Nantei (1755–1834), Oku Bunmei (1773–1813), Watanabe Nangaku (1767–1813), Yama'ato Kakurei (active 1804–17) and Yoshimura Kōkei (1769–1836).

33 Extant documents list him as an affiliate of Ōkyo's studio, suggesting that he benefited from the master's tutelage. A year later he painted a pair of screens for the occasion of Emperor Kōkaku's accession to the throne, a commission that probably reached him upon the recommendation of Ōkyo, who since the mid-1770s had been producing screens and other work for Kōkaku's mother and grandfather. Gan Ku must have advanced quickly because the 1782 edition of *Record of People in Heian* [*Kyoto*] lists him as an established artist. His work then caught the attention of Prince Arisugawa VI (1753–1820), from whom he received numerous painting commissions. Other biographical information from Sasaki Jōhei, 'Gan Ku no shōgai to geijutsu', in *Gan Ku to sono keifu,* ed. Rittō Rekishi Minzoku Hakubutsukan, Rittō, Shiga prefecture: Rittō Rekishi Minzoku Hakubutsukan, 1996, pp. 5–8.

34 Quoted in Araki Tadasu, *Dai Nippon shoga meika taikan, denki jōhen*, Tokyo: Daiichi Shobō, 1975; originally published 1934, p. 1164.

35 For examples by Shen Quan and his Japanese student Kumashiro Yūhi (1693–1773), see *Jūhasseiki no Nihon bijutsu*, Kyoto: Kyōto Kokuritsu Hakubutsukan, 1990, cats 84 and 91. During the 1820s–40s, Katsushika Hokusai (1760–1849) produced a variation on the theme; see British Museum, 2020,3015.10.

36 In 1799 he reportedly produced a picture of Mount Fuji for a Chinese man named Tang Qihui (dates unknown) and for his fee requested not cash but the body of a tiger, which he duly received and most likely then arranged in various poses for the purpose of sketching. That year he also adopted the art name Kotōkan ('Tiger's Head Hall'). Anecdote cited in Araki, *Dai Nippon shoga meika taikan*, p. 1165; date given in Sasaki, 'Gan Ku no shōgai to geijutsu', p. 8.

37 A note on one drawing identifies the group of sketches as 'genuine transcriptions' (*shinsha*). The head in profile view has a flattened cranium not unlike that of the tiger in this painting, The legs and sketches still survive, but the location of the head is unknown. Rittō Rekishi Minzoku Hakubutsukan (ed.), *Gan Ku to sono keifu*, Rittō, Shiga prefecture: Rittō Rekishi Minzoku Hakubutsukan, 1996, cat. 21, pp. 34–5.

38 He preserved a feeling of balance across this impressively large composition, and integrated the deer smoothly into the landscape, two technical skills that he may have acquired under Ōkyo. Tanabe Masako, discussion of fig. 62, in *Hizō Nihon bijutsu taikan*, vol. 3, *Daiei Hakubutsukan III*, ed. Hirayama Ikuo and Kobayashi Tadashi, Tokyo: Kōdansha, 1993, p. 239.

39 Discussion of fig. 11, *Maruyama Ōkyo to Shijō-ha*, ed. Toyama-ken Suiboku Bijutsukan, Toyama: Toyama-ken Suiboku Bijutsukan, 2014, p. 17.

40 Hoshino Suzu, discussion of figs 54–55, in *Hizō Nihon bijutsu taikan*, vol. 3, *Daiei Hakubutsukan III*, ed. Hirayama Ikuo and Kobayashi Tadashi, Tokyo: Kōdansha, 1993, p. 235.

41 Ueda Akinari, *Words about the Young Reed* (*Ashikabi no kotoba*), in *Ueda Akinari zenshū*, vol. 1, Tokyo: Kokusho Kankōkai, 1917, pp. 185–90.

42 Kakurin appears in the 1775 edition of the Osaka who's who, *Record of Fellow Osakans* (*Naniwa kyōyū roku*), where he is recorded as Kakutei's pupil using another art name, Kyō Seisai. The British Museum painting also bears the seal 'Gazen', which Kakutei had previously used, and two further seals 'Sei' and 'Sai' indicate that it is Kakurin's work.

43 The author of the inscription has recently been identified following the examination of the painting by Hirai Yoshinobu at the British Museum in 2019.

44 Motojima Tomotatsu (Getsudō, active 1690s–1730s) left a record of what he had seen and heard in Osaka, Kyoto and Edo. In the entry for the 16th day, 7th month of 1717 in *Collection of What Getsudō Saw and Heard* (*Getsudō kenmonshū*), he wrote, 'there was a show at Shijō-gawara of rare birds such as peacocks, cockatoos, golden pheasants, parrots, and so forth'. See Mori Senzō and Kitagawa Hirokuni (eds), *Zoku Nihon zuihitsu taisei*, vol. 3, Tokyo: Yoshikawa Kōbunkan, 1982, p. 62.

45 Hamamatsu Utakuni, *Curious Records of Settsu Province* (*Setsuyō kikan*), in *Naniwa sōsho*, vols 1–6, ed. Funakoshi Sei'ichirō, Osaka: Naniwa Sōsho Kankōkai, 1926–30, p. 23.

46 Murakami Kei, Tanaka Yoshiaki and Michida Miki (eds), *Mashiyama Sessai ten: botsugo 200-nen kinen*, Tsu: Mie Prefectural Art Museum, 2019, p. 10.

**Chapter 4**

1   Reproduced in Ōsaka Bijutsu Kurabu (ed.), *Kōbe Kawasaki danshaku-ke zōhin nyūsatsu mokuroku*, no. 149 (1928).

2   The British Museum holds versions by Suzuki Nanrei (1913,0501,0.510) and Chō Gesshō (2004,0504,0.2). A collaborative work on the theme is in National Museums Scotland (V.2014.29).

3   I am grateful to Nakatani Nobuo for providing this information.

4   For the British Museum's copies, see 1979,0305,0.134.1–4 and 1979,0305,0.192.1–4.

5   For discussion of how and why the Osaka painting world was elided from the modern art historical account, see Nakatani Nobuo, 'Okakura Kakuzō and the Osaka Painting Schools of the Tokugawa Era', in *The Tokugawa World*, ed. Gary P. Leupp and De-min Tao, London: Routledge, 2022, pp. 764–80.

6   See Kōbe Shiritsu Hakubutsukan, Nagasaki Rekishi Bunka Hakubutsukan, and Mainichi Shimbunsha (eds), *Waga na wa Kakutei*, Tokyo: Mainichi Shimbunsha, 2016.

7   The other eight painters contributing are Yoshimura Kōkei (1769–1836), Shibata Gitō (1780–1819), Kinoshita Ōju (1777–1815), Murakami Shōdō (1776–1841), Chikuyū (dates unknown), Yamaguchi Soken (1759–1818), Hatta Koshū (1760–1822) and Gan Tai (1785–1865).

8   For an example of a literati painter who spent a decade travelling around northern Japan from the 1850s to the 1860s, see Rosina Buckland, *Painting Nature for the Nation: Taki Katei and the Challenges to Sinophile Culture in Meiji Japan*, Leiden: Brill, 2013. The information on Kazan is taken from Ueno Kenji, 'Shoga-kai annai shū', *Tochigi Kenritsu Bijutsukan kiyō*, no. 6 (1978), p. 56.

9   The Edo-period appearance is recorded in a handscroll painting in the British Museum, 1944,1014,0.23. The district is still physically identifiable, today called Kannai.

10  For further discussion of this sinifying transposition, see Ellis Tinios, *Kawamura Bunpō: Artist of Two Worlds*, Leeds: The University Gallery Leeds, 2004, p. 29.

11  For further discussion, see ibid., pp. 50–2.

12  The following information is from Patricia J. Graham, *Tea of the Sages: The Art of Sencha*, Honolulu, HI: University of Hawai'i Press, 1998, pp. 148–55.

13  For further discussion of these events and publications, see ibid., pp. 170–8.

14  Graham, *Tea of the Sages*, pp. 176–7.

15  Lawrence Marceau, *Takebe Ayatari: A Bunjin Bohemian in Early Modern Japan*, Ann Arbor, MI: Center for Japanese Studies, University of Michigan, 2004, pp. 150–1.

16  See, for example, Fujioka Sakutarō, *Kinsei kaiga-shi*, Tokyo: Kinkōdō Shoseki, 1926.

17  Ōsaka Rekishi Hakubutsukan (ed.), *Kimura Kenkadō: Naniwa chi no kyojin: tokubetsuten botsugo 200-nen kinen*, Kyoto: Shibunkaku Shuppan, 2003, pl. 70.

18  From his critical essay on Japanese paintings, *Chatter of a Mountain Hermit* (*Sanchūjin jōzetsu*, 1835). Chikuden was from Bungo province in present-day Ōita prefecture.

19  Translation by the author.

**Chapter 5**

1   Ogata Tsutomu, *Za no bungaku*, Tokyo: Kadokawa Shoten, 1973.

2   Translation by the author.

3   The contributing artists are Hōen (active early 1800s), Nakai Rankō (1766–1830), Watanabe Nangaku (1767–1813), and Mori Tetsuzan (1775–1841).

4   The poems by Daiten in this book are recorded in his poetry anthology, in which the group has a title clearly defining it as a set of thirty-six poems for the picture album by Jakuchū. Tokuriki Tomikichirō, Maekawa Fumio and Yamanouchi Chōzō (eds), *Jakuchū no takuhanga*, Tokyo: Ruri Shobō, 1981, p. 38.

5   The interpretation of the poem is based on ibid., p. 42.

6   Aimi Kōu, 'Jakuchū no takuhanga', *Geijutsu shinchō*, vol. 6, no. 9 (1955), p. 77.

7   Mizuochi Roseki, *Chōkeitei zappitsu*, Osaka: Mizuochi Kyōji, 1921, p. 101.

8   The British Museum copy is missing its title slip. The title here was tentatively given by the Japanese literature scholar Nakano Mitsutoshi (1935–2019) based on a phrase found in the preface.

9   *Kaidō kyoka awase* was apparently a popular book, especially the illustrations. Many later copies contain only the pictures and bear the variant title *Picture Album of Hand [Skill] Matches* (*Tekurabe gafu*) or *Double Pictures along a Highway* (*Kaidō sōga*).

10  I would like to thank Shibuya Kazukuni for his generous assistance in interpreting this and the following poems.

11  For the identification of Shishin as the young Keibun, see Sugimoto Yoshihisa, 'Shijō-ha no so Go Shun', in *Shijō-ha e no michi: Go Shun o chūshin to shite*, ed. Edamatsu Ako, Nishinomiya: Nishinomiya-shi Ōtani Kinen Bijutsukan, 2019.

12  The contributing artists are Nagayama Kōin (1765–1849), Nakamura Chōshun (active early nineteenth century), Murata Kagen (or Yoshikoto, d. 1849), Yamanaka Shōnen (d. *c*. 1819), Tōkyo (active *c*. early nineteenth century), Tamate Tōshū (1795–1871), Mokushō (Hakutōsai, active 1820s), Ichidō (Keika, active *c*. early nineteenth century) and Satō Suiseki (Gyodai, active 1806–40). Some poets provided their own drawing to accompany the poem.

13  Jack Hillier, 'Sato Suiseki', in *The Fascinating World of the Japanese Artist: A Collection of Essays on Japanese Art by Members of the Society for Japanese Arts and Crafts*, ed. H.M. Kaempfer and W.O.G. Sickinghe, The Hague: Society for Japanese Arts and Crafts, 1971, pp. 49–62.

14  Hillier discussed both painted and printed works of the Maruyama-Shijō school artists to understand the full range of their oeuvre. Jack Hillier, *The Uninhibited Brush: Japanese Art in the Shijō Style*, London: Hugh M. Moss (Publishing) Ltd, 1974.

15  A hanging scroll painting by Go Shun is known with a very similar design. See Edamatsu, *Shijō-ha e no michi*, nos 1–54.

16  I would like to thank Shibuya Kazukuni for sharing his insights into the surimono discussed here.

17  The same design is known to have been reused for another set of poems at a later date. See Hillier, *The Uninhibited Brush*, 1974, pl. 89. For a discussion about surimono designs, see

Scott Johnson, 'Tōtaru dezain (total design) o reishō suru haikai surimono', *Edo Bungaku*, no. 25 (2002), pp. 159–65.

18 Examples can be found in C. Andrew Gerstle, with Timothy Clark and Akiko Yano, *Kabuki Heroes on the Osaka Stage, 1780–1830*, London: The British Museum Press, 2005, nos 50, 167 and 231.

19 Nagata Seiji and Hattan Yūtarō, *Yokoyama Kazan: A Superb Imagination at Work*, Tokyo: Nihon Keizai Shimbun, 2018.

20 Kazan's artworks were apparently distributed widely even outside Kyoto. His folding screens depicting the production of *beni* (a dye using safflower red) in Yamagata are known to have been created for a merchant involved in this trade. Beni was one of the most important colourants for textiles and cosmetics. See Nagata and Hattan, *Yokoyama Kazan*, pl. 88.

21 Daniel J. McKee compares the history of haiku and kyōka surimono as follows: 'haikai *surimono* in fact precede, outlast and surround kyōka *surimono* like an ocean around an island'. Daniel J. McKee, 'Leaves of Words: The Art of Surimono as a Poetic Practice', PhD dissertation, Cornell University, 2008, p. 49, n. 61.

22 In his book *The Uninhibited Brush*: *Japanese Art in the Shijō style*, London, Hugh M. Moss (Publishing) Ltd, 1974, Jack Hillier conflates the Maruyama, Shijō and Kishi schools of art as simply 'Shijō'. He contrasts ukiyo-e surimono with 'Shijō surimono'; the expression subsequently caught on among dealers, collectors and museums.

23 There are two dates on this surimono (1751/52), which is unusual. The explanation is simple, however; at the beginning of 1751 Shunboku created this image, labelling it the first work of his brush for that year. When asked to contribute an image for a 1752 surimono, he submitted this auspicious work, and it was copied faithfully, including the original date.

24 Beatrice B. Shoemaker, 'Ōoka Shunboku: Osaka between China and Japan', *Andon*, no. 114 (December 2022), pp. 5–34. The reference to the 1750 folding screens for the temple Honkō-ji in Amagasaki is on p. 11.

25 Ogata Tsutomu et al. (eds), *Hai-bungaku daijiten*, Tokyo: Kadokawa Shoten, 1995, pp. 587–8. Teiga developed a popular embroidery needle, which led to family wealth. He invested part of that wealth in his literary hobbies, but his descendants credit him as the founder of the business that a century later became the Daimaru Department Store in Kyoto. Nishimura Teiga was a key member of Yosa Buson's inner circle of haikai students.

26 Katō Sadahiko, 'Haikai "*surimono*" jijō', *Edo bungaku*, no. 16 (1996), pp. 64–82. Details of fees for surimono are on p. 66. 'Large' meant an uncut sheet, standardised as 42 × 57 cm; 'small' meant such a sheet cut into nine pieces, approx. 19 × 25.5 cm.

27 The compiler is Tsuruta Takuchi (1768–1846), who travelled from his home in Mikawa along a circuit of Tōkai haiku groups. There were some particularly rich haiku poets in Hamamatsu, who may have paid for this triptych. The artist, Harada Keigaku (1803–1885), was also born in Mikawa but moved to Edo to study under Suzuki Nanrei (1775–1844), one of Nangaku's first students in Edo. The surimono was probably produced in Edo for Takuchi's group.

28 This work is in the British Museum collection, 2021,3013.571.1. The surimono announces the name-taking of the shamisen player Nozawa Enshi (1878–1957). The 'en' in 'Enshi' is the character for monkey so the artist Tsuji Kakō created this shrine monkey in celebration.

29 The last two known Kamigata surimono (British Museum, 2021,3013.566 and 2021,3013.568) are undated, but both celebrate the name-change of the shamisen player Nozawa Katsuhei to Nozawa Kizaemon II in November 1942.

# Select bibliography

**English-language publications**

Beerens, Anna, *Friends, Acquaintances, Pupils and Patrons: Japanese Intellectual Life in the Late Eighteenth Century: A Prosopographical Approach*, Leiden: Leiden University Press, 2006.

Bowring, Richard, *In Search of the Way: Thought and Religion in Early-Modern Japan, 1582–1860*, Oxford: Oxford University Press, 2017.

Cahill, James, *Scholar Painters of Japan: The Nanga School*, New York: Asia Society, 1972.

Carpenter, John T. (ed.), *Reading Surimono: The Interplay of Text and Image in Japanese Prints: With a Catalogue of the Marino Lusy Collection*, Zurich and Leiden: Museum Rietberg/Hotei Publishing, 2008.

Chen, Xiangming, 'Curators of China Knowledge: *Morokoshi meishō zue* and Osaka–Kyoto Cultural Networks in Late Tokugawa Japan', *Journal of Art Historiography*, no. 29, December 2023, pp. 1–32.

Clark, Timothy, 'Utagawa Hiroshige and the Maruyama-Shijō School', in *The Commercial and Cultural Climate of Japanese Printmaking*, ed. Amy Reigle Newland, Amsterdam: Hotei Publishing, 2004, pp. 143–64.

— 'The Jakuchū Memorial Exhibition of 1885', in *The Artist in Edo*, ed. Yukio Lippit, Washington D.C.: National Gallery of Art, 2018, pp. 247–82.

Forrer, Matthi (ed.), *Essays on Japanese Art Presented to Jack Hillier*, London: R.G. Sawers Publishing, 1982.

Gerstle, C. Andrew (ed.), *18th Century Japan: Culture and Society,* Richmond: Curzon, 2000.

— with Timothy Clark and Akiko Yano, *Kabuki Heroes on the Osaka Stage, 1780–1830*, London: The British Museum Press, 2005.

Graham, Patricia J., *Tea of the Sages: The Art of Sencha*, Honolulu, HI: University of Hawai'i Press, 1998.

Guth, Christine, *Japanese Art of the Edo Period*, London: Weidenfeld & Nicolson, 1996.

Hanaoka, Kiyoko and Clare Pollard, *Plum Blossom and Green Willow: Japanese Surimono Poetry Prints from the Ashmolean Museum*, Oxford: Ashmolean Museum, 2018.

Hillier, Jack, *The Harari Collection of Japanese Paintings and Drawings: An Exhibition Organized by the Arts Council at the Victoria and Albert Museum*, London: Arts Council of Great Britain, 1970.

— *The Uninhibited Brush: Japanese Art in the Shijō Style*, London: Hugh M. Moss (Publishing) Ltd, 1974.

— 'Shijō Surimono of Large Size from the Mitchell Collection', *Minneapolis Institute of Arts Bulletin*, vol. 64 (1978–80), pp. 24–41.

— and Lawrence Smith, *Japanese Prints: 300 Years of Albums and Books*, London: The British Museum Press, 1980.

Ikegami Eiko, *Bonds of Civility Aesthetic Networks and the Political Origins of Japanese Culture*, Cambridge: Cambridge University Press, 2005.

Keyes, Roger, *The Art of Surimono: Privately Published Japanese Woodblock Prints and Books in the Chester Beatty Library, Dublin*, London: Philip Wilson Publishers Ltd/Sotheby Publications, 1985.

Lachaud, François, 'The Scholar and the Unicorn: Antiquarians, Eccentrics, and Connoisseurs in Eighteenth-Century Japan', in *World Antiquarianism: Comparative Perspectives*, ed. Alain Schnapp, Los Angeles, CA: Getty Publications, 2014, pp. 343–71.

Leupp, Gary P. and De-min Tao (eds), *The Tokugawa World*, London: Routledge, 2022.

Lippit, Yukio with Ōta Aya, Oka Yasuhiro and Hayakawa Yasuhiro, *Colorful Realm: Japanese Bird-and-Flower Paintings by Itō Jakuchū*, Washington, D.C. and Chicago, IL: National Gallery of Art/University of Chicago Press, 2012.

Marceau, Lawrence, *Takebe Ayatari: A Bunjin Bohemian in Early Modern Japan*, Ann Arbor, MI: Center for Japanese Studies, University of Michigan, 2004.

McKee, Daniel, *Colored in the Year's New Light: Japanese Surimono from the Becker Collection*, Ithaca, NY: Herbert F. Johnson Museum of Art, Cornell University, 2008.

McKelway, Matthew et al., *Traditions Unbound: Groundbreaking Painters of Eighteenth-Century Kyoto,* San Francisco, CA: Asian Art Museum of San Francisco, 2005.

— and Khanh Trinh, *Rosetsu: Ferocious Brush,* Munich: Prestel, 2018.

Mitoholl, C.H. and Osamu Ueda, *The Illustrated Books of the Nanga, Maruyama, Shijo and Other Related Schools of Japan: A Biobibliography*, Los Angeles, CA: Dawson's Book Shop, 1972.

Moriya, Takeshi, 'Yūgei and Chōnin Society in the Edo Period', *Acta Asiatica*, no. 33 (1977), pp. 32–54.

Najita, Tetsuo, *Visions of Virtue in Tokugawa Japan: The Kaitokudō Merchant Academy of Osaka*, Chicago, IL: University of Chicago Press, 1987.

Nishiyama Matsunosuke, *Edo Culture: Daily Life and Diversions in Urban Japan, 1600–1868*, trans. and ed. Gerald Groemer, Honolulu, HI: University of Hawai'i Press, 1997.

Ohki, Sadako and Adam Haliburton, *The Private World of Surimono: Japanese Prints from the Virginia Shawan Drosten and Patrick Kenadjian Collection*, New Haven, CT: Yale University Press, 2020.

Redfern, Mary, *The Art of Friendship: Japanese Surimono Prints,* Dublin: Chester Beatty Library, 2017.

Rosenfield, John M., *Mynah Birds and Flying Rocks: Word and Image in the Art of Yosa Buson,* Lawrence, KS: Spencer Museum of Art, University of Kansas, 2003.

Saint Louis Art Museum, *Ōkyo and the Maruyama-Shijō School of Japanese Painting*, Saint Louis, MI: Saint Louis Art Museum, 1980.

Saunders, Rachel (ed.), *Catalogue of the Feinberg Collection of Japanese Art*, Cambridge, MA: Harvard Art Museums, 2021.

Screech, Timon, *The Western Scientific Gaze and Popular Imagery in Later Edo Japan: the Lens within the Heart*, Cambridge: Cambridge University Press, 1996.

— *The Shogun's Painted Culture: Fear and Creativity in the Japanese States, 1760–1829*, London: Reaktion Books, 2000.

Smith, Lawrence, 'The Early Influence of Maruyama Ōkyo's New Style: A Handscroll by Komai Genki in the British Museum', in *Artistic Personality and Decorative Style in Japanese Art*, ed. William Watson, London: Percival David Foundation of Chinese Art, University of London, 1977, pp. 86–100.

Suzuki Jun and Ellis Tinios, *Understanding Japanese Woodblock-Printed Illustrated Books: A Short Introduction to Their History Bibliography and Format,* Leiden: Brill, 2013.

Tinios, Ellis, *Kawamura Bunpō: Artist of Two Worlds*, Leeds: The University Gallery Leeds, 2004.

Tsuji Nobuo, *Lineage of Eccentrics: Matabei to Kuniyoshi*, trans. Aaron M. Rio, Tokyo: Kaikai Kiki, 2012.

— *History of Art in Japan*, trans. Nicole Coolidge Rousmaniere, New York: Columbia University Press, 2019.

**Japanese-language publications**

*The names of Japanese institutions (and publishers) are given in original Japanese with established English translations, when known.*

Chiba-shi Bijutsukan (Chiba City Museum of Art), *Edo no surimono: suijin-tachi no okurimono*, Chiba: Chiba-shi Bijutsukan, 1997.

Edamatsu Ako (ed.), *Shijō-ha e no michi: Go Shun o chūshin to shite*, Nishinomiya: Nishinomiya-shi Ōtani Kinen Bijutsukan (Otani Memorial Art Museum, Nishinomiya City), 2019.

Geinō-shi Kenkyūkai (ed.), *Nihon geinōshi*, vol. 6, *Kinsei-Kindai*, Tokyo: Hōsei Daigaku Shuppankyoku (Hosei University Press), 1988.

Hirai Yoshinobu (ed.), *Salon Culture and the Pictorial Arts of Kyoto and Osaka / Saron! Kyō no taika to shirarezaru Osaka gadan: ga to zoku*, Kyoto: Kyōto Kokuritsu Kindai Bijutsukan (The National Museum of Modern Art, Kyoto), 2022.

— and Furuta Ryō (eds), *Maruyama Ōkyo kara kindai Kyōto gadan e*, Tokyo: Kyūryūdō (Kyuryudo Art Publishing Co.), 2019.

Iwasa Shin'ichi, Itō Shiori and Matsuoka Marie (eds), *Karaemon: Buzen ni Rōen, Jakuchū mo*, Osaka, Chiba and Tokyo: Ōsaka Rekishi Hakubutsukan (Osaka Museum of History)/Chiba-shi Bijutsukan (Chiba City Museum of Art)/Sankei Shimbun, 2015.

Kakimori Bunko, *Haikai ichimai-zuri*, Itami: Kakimori Bunko, 1991.

Kimura Shigekazu, Ito Shiori, Nakamura Mariko and Fukui Masumi, *Kōrin o shitau: Nakamura Hōchū*, Tokyo and Kyoto: Unsōdō, 2014.

Kira Sueo, *Haisho no sekai*, Tokyo: Seishōdō Shoten, 1999.

Kitagawa Hiroko et al., *Kamigata no ukiyo-e: Ōsaka Kyōto no sui to waza*, Tokyo: NHK Puranetto, 2014.

Kōbe Shiritsu Hakubutsukan (Kobe City Museum), Nagasaki Rekishi Bunka Hakubutsukan (Nagasaki Museum of History and Culture) and Mainichi Shimbunsha (eds), *Waga na wa Kakutei*, Tokyo: Mainichi Shimbunsha, 2016.

Kōno Motoaki, *Bunjin-ga: ōkansuru bi*, Kyoto: Shibunkaku, 2018.

Kōsetsu Bijutsukan (Kōsetsu Museum of Art), *Kamigata kaiwai, eshi saisai*, Kobe: Kōsetsu Bijutsukan, 2019.

— *Kamigata kaiwai, eshi saisai 2,* Kobe: Kōsetsu Bijutsukan, 2021.

Kyōto Bunka Hakubutsukan (The Museum of Kyoto) (ed.), *Miyako no eshi wa hyakka ryōran: 'Heian jinbutsu-shi' ni miru Edo jidai no Kyōto gadan*, Kyoto: Kyōto Bunka Hakubutsukan, 1998.

Mori Senzō and Nakajima Masatoshi, *Kinsei jinmeiroku shūsei*, 5 vols, Tokyo: Benseisha, 1976–78.

Nagata Seiji and Hattan Yūtarō, *Yokoyama Kazan: A Superb Imagination at Work*, Tokyo: Nihon Keizai Shimbun, 2018.

Nakamura Shin'ichirō, *Kimura Kenkadō no saron*, Tokyo: Shinchōsha, 2000.

Nakatani Nobuo, *Ōsaka gadan wa naze wasurerareta noka – Okakura Tenshin kara Higashi Ajia bijutsushi no kōsō e*, Kyoto: Daigo Shobō, 2010.

Nezu Bijutsukan (Nezu Museum), *Maruyama Ōkyo: shasei o koete*, Tokyo: Nezu Bijutsukan, 2016.

Nihon Keizai Shimbun Ōsaka Honsha (ed.), *Kamigata ukiyo-e 200-nen ten*, Osaka: Nihon Keizai Shimbunsha, 1975.

Nishiyama Matsunosuke et al. (eds), *Kinsei geidōron*, Tokyo: Iwanami Shoten, 1972.

Ōsaka Nakanoshima Bijutsukan (Osaka Nakanoshima Museum of Art) and Tōkyō Sutēshon Gyararī (Tokyo Station Gallery), *Ōsaka no Nihonga*, Osaka: Ōsaka Nakanoshima Bijutsukan/Mainichi Shimbunsha, 2023.

Ōsaka Rekishi Hakubutsukan (Osaka Museum of History), *Kimura Kenkadō: Naniwa chi no kyojin: tokubetsuten botsugo 200-nen kinen*, Kyoto: Shibunkaku, 2003.

— et al., *Saru-kaki Sosen sankyōdai*, Osaka and Kumamoto: Ōsaka Rekishi Hakubutsukan/Kumamoto Kenritsu Bijutsukan (Kumamoto Prefectural Museum of Art), 2020.

Ōsaka Shiritsu Bijutsukan (Osaka City Museum of Fine Arts) (ed.), *Kinsei Ōsaka gadan*, Kyoto: Dōhōsha, 1983.

Sasaki Jōhei and Sasaki Masako, *Maruyama Ōkyo kenkyū,* Tokyo: Chūō Kōron Bijutsu Shuppan, 1996.

Sugimoto Yoshihisa, *Maruyama Ōkyo no monjin tachi*, Nishinomiya: Kurokawa Kobunka Kenkyūjo (Kurokawa Institute of Ancient Cultures), 2014.

# Glossary
*Sophie Gong*

**bijin-ga** *see also* **ukiyo-e**
'Pictures of beautiful people', primarily women, but also attractive young men. From the mid-seventeenth century a popular subject in paintings and prints by artists specialising in 'pictures of the floating world' (*ukiyo-e*). Artists from other schools followed suit, creating works in their own style.

**bunjin** *see also* **bunjin-ga**
A 'literatus' or educated individual who practised cultivated arts such as poetry, calligraphy, painting, music and other elegant practices in the pursuit of sophistication and self-expression. A Chinese ideal (C: *wenren*) initially adopted by Japanese intellectuals of Chinese studies in the eighteenth century, and thereafter shared widely.

**bunjin-ga** *see also* **bunjin**
Paintings by professional and amateur artists following the ideal of the bunjin, which drew heavily on Chinese literati paintings, especially from the Ming period (1368–1644). Often landscapes with figures. Also called Nanga (Southern painting), a term deriving from the 'Southern school' Ming literati paintings, which many Japanese artists emulated.

**bunraku** *see also* **jōruri**
Modern term for puppet theatre accompanied by narrative chanting (*jōruri*) and shamisen music, which was named as *bunraku-za* in 1872. Together with kabuki, a leading form of popular theatre in the Edo period. Osaka and Edo were two major centres. Plays on contemporary and historical themes were frequently produced and are still performed to this day. The term derives from the name of a particular troupe. *Ningyō jōruri* (puppets and chanting) is a broader term.

**bussangaku** *see also* **honzōgaku**
The study of raw materials and how to make them useful for human life. Grounded in field observation. A mid-Edo period outgrowth of *honzōgaku*. The basis for many illustrated books describing local products across Japan.

**Confucianism**
A school of philosophical, ethical, political and religious thought originating in the teachings of Kong Zi (Confucius, 551/552–479 BCE). Significantly revised by the Southern-Song scholar Zhu Xi (1130–1200), whose teachings comprise the eponymous school (C: *Zhuzi xue*; J: *shushigaku*), also known as neo-Confucianism. The official school of thought under the Tokugawa shogunate, especially neo-Confucianism by the end of eighteenth century.

**daimyō** *see also* **Tokugawa shogunate**
Japanese samurai feudal lords who ruled regional domains under the authority of the shogun. While maintaining a degree of autonomy in their territories, their power was counterbalanced by loyalty and service to the shogun. Around 260 daimyō held power at any given time under the Tokugawa regime.

**Edo** *see also* **Tokugawa period**
Historical name for present-day Tokyo, located along Edo Bay in southeastern Honshu, Japan's main island. First became the political capital in 1603 when Tokugawa Ieyasu (1543–1616) was appointed shogun by the imperial court, and he established his government there. Often contrasted with Kyoto, then the seat of the emperor and the official capital of Japan. Taking the name of the city, the period of Tokugawa rule is also called the Edo period. Edo was renamed Tokyo after the Meiji restoration of 1868.

**gafu**
Albums and books containing an assortment of pictures by one or several artists. The term appears in the title of many late eighteenth and nineteenth-century woodblock-printed art books intended to showcase a particular brush style. They could be viewed for pleasure, but many had a pedagogical aim and served as a reference for those learning how to paint.

**gassaku**
'Combined work', a single work of art or literature produced collaboratively by more than one artist. Also applied to such works of plural authorship. Synonymous with *yoriai-gaki* ('collective painting'), a term used particularly in the context of painting and calligraphy.

**gō**
Art or pen name. During the Edo period, professional and amateur practitioners of the arts commonly adopted an art name or pen name different from their real name. *Azana* was also another name taken by educated men, particularly *bunjin,* following the Chinese precedent of choosing a name upon reaching adulthood. *Haimyō* (or *haimei*) refers to a haiku pen name and *kyōmei* to a name used by kyōka poets.

**ha/-school**
Most painters in Edo-period Japan trained under a master. The master and pupils formed a 'school' (*ha*), which in some cases lasted for many generations, such as the Maruyama and Shijō schools. Japanese art history tends to focus on schools and their styles.

### *haikai*/haiku

A type of Japanese verse consisting of 17 syllables arranged in a 5-7-5 pattern. Recognised today as an independent form, but originally a segment in a longer, linked-verse sequence (*renga*). Characterised by seasonal references and concision. Matsuo Bashō (1644–1694) was the most revered haiku poet of the Edo period.

### Heian

Historical term for the city of Kyoto, where Japan's emperors resided from 794 to 1868. Literally, 'peace and tranquillity'.

### *honzōgaku*

A branch of natural history concerned mainly with plants, but also some animals and minerals, for medicinal use. Introduced to Japan from China as early as the eighth century. Japanese interest in the discipline surged in the eighteenth century.

### *jōruri* see also bunraku

Narrative chanting accompanied by music. Origins date back to the Muromachi period (1333–1573). The playwright Chikamatsu Monzaemon (1653–1724) and the chanter Takemoto Gidayū (1651–1714) together created the narrative and chanting style that continues today.

### kabuki

Initially a style of theatre performed by female performers in early seventeenth-century Kyoto, but an edict in 1629 banning women from the stage on the grounds that they disturbed public order led to performances including young men, and then solely being performed by male adults after 1652. Actors appear in both male and female roles. Kyoto, Osaka and Edo developed major permanent theatres dedicated to kabuki, which became an important form of popular entertainment.

### *kaidō*

Major roads connecting important cities and towns. In the Edo period, five main 'highways' (the *gokaidō*) starting from Nihonbashi in Edo came under the direct control of the Tokugawa government for political and taxation reasons. The most famous among them is the Eastern Sea Road (Tōkaidō) connecting Nihonbashi and the Sanjō-bashi in Kyoto, with fifty-three post stations.

### Kamigata see also Kansai

The direction of the imperial palace from anywhere outside Kyoto – *kami* (upper) *gata* (or *kata*, direction) – hence in the Edo period an alternative term for Kyoto. It also referred to surrounding areas, including Osaka, and was used to indicate the culture of the Kyoto-Osaka region in contrast to that of Edo.

### Kanō school (Kanō-*ha*)

The most successful artistic school in the history of Japanese art before the modern period, founded by Kanō Masanobu (1434–1530), who served as an official painter to the shogun. Kanō artists worked for samurai clients throughout the Edo period until the fall of the Tokugawa government. Their Chinese-influenced style carried enormous prestige, but was deemed conventional and uninspiring by the mid-eighteenth century.

### Kansai see also Kamigata

Originally a geographic term referring to the region west of a yet undetermined official checkpoint located in central Japan. The region to the east is called Kantō. Today used to contrast western Japan (centring on Osaka, Kyoto and Kobe) with eastern Japan (centring on Tokyo). Many cultural differences, both real and perceived, are formulated around the term.

### *kanshi*

Poems in Chinese composed by Japanese authors, popular from the Muromachi period onwards among the elite and the erudite. In the Edo period, Confucian scholars and literati (bunjin) studied classical Chinese poetry and composed their own verses.

### *kasen*

A classical poet of great renown; literally, 'immortal poet'. It first appeared in the pivotal anthology *Collection of Japanese Poetry from Ancient and Modern Times* (*Kokin wakashū*) in the 910s, denoting a group of outstanding Japanese poets of the Heian period (794–1185). This term later spurred the formation of new groups of esteemed poets in sets over time.

### *kyōka*

A type of Japanese verse consisting of 31 syllables arranged in a 5-7-5-7-7 pattern. Commonly translated as 'crazy verse'. Characterised by humour and satire with references to classical Japanese poems. Popular especially from the late eighteenth century.

### *kyō/miyako* see also Heian

Original meaning was 'the land of the imperial palace'; both terms refer to Kyoto when it was the capital of Japan (794–1868). Kyoto historically was also referred to as Heian, Raku and Keishi.

### *meisho*

'Famous places' known for beautiful scenery, historical events, ancient temples and shrines and contemporary attractions. From the late eighteenth century, often discussed in 'illustrated guides to famous places' (*meisho zue*), which covered not only the principal cities of Kyoto (miyako), Osaka (Settsu) and Edo, but many other areas renowned for a variety of features.



Salon culture in Japan

**Naniwa**
Historical name for present-day Osaka city and the surrounding
area. Osaka and Naniwa were used almost interchangeably during
the Edo period.

**neo-Confucianism** *see* Confucianism

**nō**
The foundations for this form of Japanese theatre were laid by the
playwrights Kan'ami (1333–84) and Zeami (1363/4–1443). In almost
all plays, the protagonists are wearing masks and accompanied by
chanting and music. In the Edo period, nō was performed mainly for
the ruling samurai, but chanting excerpts from famous plays became
a popular pastime (*utai*).

**rangaku**
'Dutch studies', a branch of learning focusing on Western science,
technology and medicine, and derived from books written in
Dutch and imported through trade with the Dutch United East
India Company in Nagasaki. Emerged in the 1720s with the official
endorsement of the Tokugawa shogun Yoshimune (1684–1751).
Attracted many capable scholars, medical doctors, authors and
artists, and profoundly influenced the development of early modern
Japanese science and art.

**shasei**
An artistic approach emphasising the importance of sketching
from life for authentic representation of the subject in its natural
environment. Artists such as Kano Tan'yū (1602–1674) and Watanabe
Shikō (1683–1755) produced many sketches of plants and birds, but
perhaps the best-known advocate of the practice is Maruyama Ōkyo
(1733–1795).

**shoga-kai**
'Calligraphy and painting gatherings'. An organised event at which
artists, calligraphers and poets produced work impromptu before an
audience. Also a public exhibition of contemporary calligraphy and
painting, as well as displays of work by deceased famous artists.
Frequently held at a restaurant, with a charge for entry, they were
usually lively social occasions where artists could gather, and where
the public could meet artists.

**sencha** *see also* **bunjin**
'Infused tea'. A method of preparing tea by steeping green tea leaves
in hot water, distinct from the use of powdered tea (*matcha*). The
custom was introduced from China as early as the ninth century, but
developed as a practice in the early Edo period by late Ming-dynasty
Chinese and Japanese monks of the Ōbaku Zen lineage. Favoured by
literati among the nobility, monks, samurai and wealthy merchants.

**surimono**
'Printed things', privately commissioned woodblock prints that feature
poems composed during a poetry gathering, often accompanied
by a picture from a well-known artist. Often produced to celebrate
a special occasion, such as the New Year. Produced in a variety of
formats from the mid-eighteenth century onwards. Due to limited print
runs and circulation, few examples of individual designs survive today;
some examples are now unique.

**Tokugawa shogunate**
The military government of Japan established in Edo by Tokugawa
Ieyasu in 1603 and administrated by the shogun of the Tokugawa
family. The shogun had absolute power in governing Japan while the
authority of the emperor and imperial court was nominal. The last
Tokugawa shogun, Yoshinobu (1837–1913), resigned in 1867 to return
the status as head of the country to the emperor.

**Tokugawa period** *see also* **Edo**
Another appellation for the Edo period taken from the name of the
ruling Tokugawa shogunate. The period is typically dated 1603–1868
or, depending on interpretation, beginning in 1600, when Tokugawa
Ieyasu enjoyed a decisive victory at the Battle of Sekigahara, or in 1615
when the previous ruling family, the Toyotomi clan, was destroyed by
the Tokugawa in the Siege of Osaka (1614–15).

**Tosa school (Tosa-*ha*)**
A prestigious Japanese artistic lineage that continued from the
fifteenth century to the end of the Edo period. Served mainly the
imperial court and aristocrats, with delicate paintings of classical
Japanese subjects. Heads of this school led the imperial painting
bureau for generations.

**ukiyo-e**
'Pictures of the floating world' (*ukiyo*). A genre emerging in the
seventeenth century treating popular subjects such as famous actors
and courtesans, seasonal pleasures enjoyed by commoners and
iconic landscapes. The term applies to both paintings and prints.

**yūgei**
Arts practised by amateurs for pleasure, such as the tea ceremony,
poetry, painting and calligraphy, music, chanting, dance and many
others. Enthusiasts took lessons with an instructor for self-cultivation
and often pursued said art throughout their lives. In the early Edo
period, such hobbies were perceived as a pretentious indulgence by
wealthy commoners, but by the late Edo period they were popular
among a wide range of people. *Yūgei* provided a setting for social
interaction regardless differences in social status.

# Acknowledgements

This book accompanies a special display in the British Museum's Mitsubishi Corporation Japanese Galleries, *City life and salon culture in Kyoto and Osaka, 1770–1900*. I would like to express my gratitude to the Mitsubishi Corporation for their long-standing sponsorship of the Galleries. A significant number of objects in this book and display were acquired with the generous support of the JTI Japanese Acquisition Fund.

The publication is one outcome of a three-year research project, 'Creative Collaborations: Salons and Networks in Kyoto and Osaka 1780–1880', funded by UK Research and Innovation through the Economic and Social Research Council and the Japan Society for the Promotion of Science (2022–5). This international collaboration, principally between the British Museum, London, and Ritsumeikan University, Kyoto, was supported by scholars across Japan, Europe and North America. The British Museum encouraged the project and I would particularly like to thank JD Hill and Jane Portal for their advice.

Special thanks are extended to the authors of this book, who are also members of the research project: Akama Ryō, Akeo Keizō, Paul Berry, Rosina Buckland, Timothy T. Clark, C. Andrew Gerstle, Sophie Gong, Alfred Haft, Hirai Yoshinobu, Scott Johnson, Nakatani Nobuo and Ellis Tinios.

Our work was made possible through the collection-building and research of several individuals, past and present: William Anderson, Jack Hillier, Scott Johnson, Roger Keyes, Arthur Morrison, Lawrence Smith and Ellis Tinios. Many colleagues unstintingly shared their expertise with the authors: thank you to Anna Beerens, John Carpenter, Bettina Gramlich-Oka, Ida Tarō, Iwasa Shin'ichi, Iwata Hideyuki, Michael Kinski, Shibuya Kazukuni, Sugimoto Yoshihisa, Tsukuda Ikki, Tsukuda Shiō, Yamamoto Yoshitaka, Yamamoto Yukari and Yokoya Ken'ichirō.

I am grateful to those who edited, produced and promoted the book. Particularly heartfelt thanks go to Senior Development Editor, Lydia Cooper, and copyeditor, Amy Newland, whose tireless work sharpened up the text. In the Publishing team, I would like to thank Head of Publishing, Claudia Bloch, Project Editor, Yvonne Thouroude, Sales and Marketing Manager, Toni Allum, Production Manager, Beata Kibil, Editorial Assistant, Laura Meachem, and Publishing Assistant, Nathaniel Balch. Thank you to designer, James Alexander, proofreader, Phoebe Colley, and indexer, Amanda Speake, as well as to Marina Asenjo for her work on the colour reprographics with Jules Bettinson at Altaimage. I would also like to thank the authors who granted us permission to quote their translations – Cheryl A. Crowley, Lawrence Marceau, Katherine Saltzman-Li and Timon Screech – as well as Hayashino Masato and the Kurayoshi Museum, who shared information about Suga Tatehiko.

Many objects from the Museum's collection are published here for the first time, so organising photography was a major task. I am grateful to Matsuba Ryōko and the Sainsbury Institute for the Study of Japanese Arts and Cultures, Norwich, for their research partnership with the Museum to help digitise the collections, and to photographers Marco Borsato, Stephen Dodd, Isabel Marshall, Saul Peckham and Bradley Timms. I would also like to thank Gavin Bell, Paul Chirnside, Tamara Irish and Simon Prentice for making arrangements for photography, and conservators Joanna Kosek, Kyōko Kusunoki and Matthias Sotiras for ensuring the sound condition of the objects. Thank you to Natalie Buy, Amelia Evans and Stuart Frost for their interpretation work.

Fifty years have passed since Jack Hillier's landmark book *The Uninhibited Brush* (1974) opened readers' eyes to the beguiling world of the Shijō style. Taking inspiration from Hillier's work, we have set the artists and their works within the ambitious framework of 'salon culture', thereby helping us to better understand and appreciate the art and the society that created it. Creative minds from the past continue to inspire us.

# List of contributors

**Akama Ryō** is Professor in the College of Letters at Ritsumeikan University, Kyoto.

**Akeo Keizō** is Professor in the Department of Public Affairs at Osaka University of Commerce, Higashi-Osaka.

**Paul Berry** is an independent scholar of Japanese art history and cinema. He has published catalogues and articles on Japanese painting. He has taught at the University of Michigan, University of Washington and Kansai Gaidai University and has lectured internationally at a variety of universities, museums and conferences.

**Rosina Buckland** is Curator of the Japanese Collections at the British Museum.

**Timothy T. Clark** is Honorary Research Fellow in the Department of Asia at the British Museum. He was Head of the Japanese Section at the Museum until 2019.

**C. Andrew Gerstle** is Emeritus Professor of Japanese Studies at SOAS University of London.

**Sophie Gong** is Research Assistant: Creative Collaborations in the Department of Asia at the British Museum.

**Alfred Haft** is JTI Curator for the Japanese Collections, Department of Asia at the British Museum.

**Hirai Yoshinobu** is Curator at the National Museum of Modern Art, Kyoto.

**Scott Johnson** is Emeritus Professor in the Faculty of Foreign Language Studies at Kansai University and a scholar and collector of Japanese art.

**Nakatani Nobuo** is Emeritus Professor at Kansai University, Suita, Osaka.

**Ellis Tinios** is an independent scholar who has long been engaged in the study of book and print production in early modern Japan.

**Akiko Yano** is Mitsubishi Corporation Curator for the Japanese Collections, Department of Asia at the British Museum.

# Credits

The publisher would like to thank the copyright holders for granting permission to reproduce the images illustrated. Every attempt has been made to trace accurate ownership of copyrighted images in this book. Any errors or omissions will be corrected in subsequent editions provided notification is sent to the publisher.

Further information about the Museum and its collection can be found at britishmuseum.org. Registration numbers for British Museum objects are included in the image captions. Unless otherwise stated, copyright in photographs belongs to the institution mentioned in the caption. All images of British Museum objects are © 2024 The Trustees of the British Museum, courtesy the Department of Photography and Imaging.

1.4 Cortazzi Collection, on loan to the Lisa Sainsbury Library, Sainsbury Institute for the Study of Japanese Arts and Cultures
1.6–1.8 Courtesy of Japanese Maps of the Tokugawa Era, Rare Books and Special Collections, University of British Columbia Library, G7964 K98 E635 1864 T2, G7964 .O8 1854 M6, G7964 .E3 1848 O5
1.13 National Institute of Japanese Literature / CC by 4.0 SA

1.24 Courtesy of the C. V. Starr East Asian Library, University of California, Berkeley
2.8 Image: TNM Image Archives
2.9 © Victoria and Albert Museum, London
2.12 Maekawa Gorei, *Civil War in Kyoto (Koshi heisen zu)* Vol. 1, Harvard Art Museums/Arthur M. Sackler Museum, Bequest of the Hofer Collection of the Arts of Asia, Photo © President and Fellows of Harvard College, 1985.758
2.13 Osaka Museum of History
3.34 City of Kobe, Kobe City Museum
4.6 Reproduced by kind permission of the Jeffrey Pollard and Ooi Thye Chong Collection
4.33 City of Kobe, Kobe City Museum
4.36 Hine Taizan / National Museum of Asian Art, Smithsonian Institution, Freer Collection, Mary and Cheney Cowles Collection, Gift of Mary and Cheney Cowles, F2019.3.6a–e
4.37 Reproduced by kind permission of the Mary and Cheney Cowles Collection
5.13 Ebi Collection, UK. Photo: Art Research Center, Ritsumeikan University

# Index

References to illustrations are in *italic*.

Kumashiro Yūhi, 181–3, *181*
Kyoto, 28, 78, 91, 104, 106
    collaborative painting, 15–16,
      18, 23–6, *29*
    cultural life, 13–14, 59, 145
    cultural network of Kyoto–
      Osaka–Edo, 45, 53–64,
      79–81
    depictions of, *53, 58,* 66, 67,
      *67,* 79, *81,* 92–4, *94,*
      106–11, *106–15*
    pleasure districts, 80, 99,
      *103,* 104

**L**
landscape painting, 99–100,
    140–1, 157–64, 174–5
literati (*bunjin*)
    figure styles, 99–102, 120
    nature paintings/studies,
      137–9, 204, 206
    paint ideas (*sha'i*) ethos,
      16–18, 40–2, 64, 88, 171,
      175, 178
    sinophile arts, 16, 40, 175,
      185–8

**M**
Maekawa Gorei, 93, *93*
Maki Sadanaka, *10*
Maruyama Ōkyo, 15, 16, *16,* 28,
    *34,* 35, 37, 45, *53,* 90–2,
    *90, 91,* 95, *96,* 106, 126, 129,
    130–2, *133,* 142–7, *146–7,*
    150, 152, 153, 154, 158, 160–1,
    164, 165, 166, *172–3,* 173–4
Maruyama Ōzui, 32
Maruyama-Shijō school, 16–18,
    33, 37, 45, 87–8, 106, 132,
    142, 147–8, 158, 236
Mashiyama Sessai, 78, 134–7,
    *136, 138,* 165–6, 204
Masuda Kyūboku, *26*
Matsukawa Hanzan, *81*
Matsumoto Masayoshi, 191
Matsumura Keibun, 26, 31, *31,*
    32, 100, *100,* 154, *155,* 161,
    *162,* 214, *224,* 229–30,
    *229*
Matsuo Bashō, 32, 79, 85, 116,
    236, 238
medical schools, 80–1
Mihata Jōryū, 104, *105*

Mikuma Katen, *220*
Minagawa Kien, 79–80, 81, 104
Miyamoto Kunzan, 38, *39*
Mochizuki Gyokusen III, *159,*
    160, 160–1
Mokusen, *24–5*
Mori Gishō, 26, *29*
Mori Ippō, 150, 152, 153–4, *155,*
    *160,* 161
Mori Kansai, 12, *12, 13*
Mori Kinseki, 28, 187–8, *187*
Mori Ransai, 179–81, *182,* 183,
    *183,* 204
Mori school, 18, 153–4
Mori Shūhō, 18, *20,* 28
Mori Shunkei, 137, *139*
Mori Sosen, *124,* 137, 148, 150–2,
    *152,* 153, *153, 176, 213*
Mori Tetsuzan, 18, *20,* 152–4, 161,
    175, *176,* 215–16, *215,* 217, *217*
Morikawa Hōbyakudō, *58*
Morrison, Arthur, 15
Murakami Shōdō, *184*
Murakami Tōshū, *34,* 227–9, *228*
Murase Kōtei, 80
Murata Gesshō, *20,* 21
Murata Kagen, 32, 72–73, *73,*
    *225,* 230, *230*
Murata Kōkoku, *28*

**N**
Nagai Seppō, 11
Nagamatsu Shun'yō, *28*
Nagasaki, 10, 55, *55, 56–7,* 191,
    *192–3,* 195
Nagasaki school, 149, 165–7,
    204–6
Nagasawa Rosetsu, 37, 38, 130,
    131, 148, *174,* 175
Nagayama Kōin, *20,* 21, *21,* 117,
    *117*
Naitō Tōho, *86*
Nakabayashi Chikutō, 137–9, *140*
Nakagawa Wadō, *28*
Nakai Chikuzan, 48
Nakai Rankō, *20,* 21, *22,* 217
Nakajima Raishō, *29*
Nakamura Chōshun, *100,* 101,
    *225, 226*
Nakamura Hōchū, *20,* 21, 134–5,
    236, *238*
Nakanishi Kōseki, 207–9, *207*
Nanmei, *26*

nature
    animals and plants, 128–30,
      132–9, 149–57, 165–6
    as an artistic resource, 142–8
    Chinese influences in, 130–2,
      137, 165
    as a cultural resource,
      130–41
    Edo-era concept of, 126
    landscape painting, 99–100,
      140–1, 157–64, 174–5
    as a tangible resource,
      127–130
    tiger paintings, 16, *16,* 144–5,
      *146–7,* 150, *151,* 165
Netherlands, 10, 53, 55, *56–7,*
    80, 165, 204
Nichōsai, 65, *65*
Nishida Chikusen, *24–5*
Nishimura Nantei, 32, 123
Nishimura Teiga, 219–20, 236
Nishiyama Hōen, 92, *93,* 129, 154
Nishiyama Kan'ei, *84,* 129, *129*
Niwa Matasaburō, *10*
Niwa Tōkei, *60, 77,* 119, *119,* 128,
    *129,* 130, *131*
Niwayama Kōen, 28
nō drama, 15, 64, 220
Nobuchika Shunjō, *28*
Noda Tōmin, 142, *143*
Nukina Kaioku, 16, *18–19*

**O**
Oda Kaisen, 32
Ogata Kōan, 80
Ogata Kōrin, 88, 132
Ogura Tōkei, *167*
Ōhara Donshū, 73–4, *74,*
    119–20, *121*
Ōhara Tōya, 190
Ōishi Matora, *14,* 15
Oka Seibi, 237–8
Oka Yūgaku, 190, 230, *230*
Okada Gyokuzan, 190
Okamoto Toyohiko, 31, *31,* 32,
    109, *110, 184,* 185, 224
Oku Bunmei, *184,* 185
Ōkubo Shibutsu, 199
Ōnishi Chinnen, 45, *46,* 101–2,
    *102,* 123, 179, *180*
Ono Ranzan, 128, 204
Ōoka Shunboku, 64, 195, *195,*
    236, *236,* 239

Osaka, *14,* 15–16, 18, *52,* 53–64,
    *58,* 66, 69–70, *69,* 76–8, *77,*
    79–81, 127–8, *127,* 154
Ōshima Raikin, *34,* 35
Ōshio Heihachirō, 93
Ōyabu Kodō, *24–5*

**P**
patronage, 64, 72–3, 79, 95, 139,
    150, 188–90, 207
pen names (pseudonyms), 7,
    10–11, 31, 49, 54, 72–3, *73,*
    74, *75*
performing arts *see jōruri*
    chanting; kabuki theatre;
    puppet theatre
picture albums (*gafu*), 37, 38–9,
    *39,* 40, *41,* 97, *98,* 109, 118,
    122–3, *123,* 157, 165, *172, 183,*
    186, *186, 187, 194, 196*
pictures of the floating world
    (*ukiyo-e*), 57, 85, 98–9
poetry *see also* haiku (*haikai*)
    poetry; *surimono*
    in anthologies and printed
      books, 130, 137, 215–26
    Chinese-style, 33, 79–80,
      170–1, 213
    collaborative works, 31, *213,*
      214–16
    *kyōka,* 21, 213, 215, 221, 236
    poems and images, 212–13
    in *surimono,* 31, 219–20,
      226–35
publications, 35–6, 57–9, 65–6
    *see also* gazetteers; picture
    albums (*gafu*)
puppet theatre, 64–7, *67, 68,*
    234

**R**
Rai San'yō, 79, 80
Rai Shihō, 207–9, *207*
Rai Shunsui, 78, 80
Rankei, *24–5*
Rinpa school, 21, 87, 132, 236
Rōkanshi, 80
Ryū Sōro, 79

**S**
Saitō Shūho, *86*
Sakata Kōsetsu, 28
sake brewing, 119, *119,* 127–8, *127*